10-29-02

STANDARDS AND SCHOOLING IN THE UNITED STATES

An Encyclopedia

STANDARDS AND SCHOOLING IN THE UNITED STATES

An Encyclopedia

VOLUME TWO

Edited by

Joe L. Kincheloe and Danny Weil

A B C 🞄 C L I O

Santa Barbara, California • Denver, Colorado • Oxford, England

Library of Congress Cataloging-in-Publication Data
Standards and schooling in the United States : an encyclopedia / edited by Joe
L. Kincheloe and Danny Weil.
    p.   cm.
Includes bibliographical references and index.
   ISBN 1-57607-255-X (hardcover : alk. paper); 1-57607-704-7 (e-book)
   1. Education—Standards—United States.   2. School improvement
programs—United States.   3. Education—Aims and objectives—United
States.   I. Kincheloe, Joe L.   II. Weil, Danny K., 1953–
   LB2822.82 .S82   2001
   379.1′58′0973—dc21   2001005683

06   05   04   03   02   01   10   9   8   7   6   5   4   3   2   1

This book is also available on the World Wide Web as an e-book. Visit abc-clio.com for details.
ABC-CLIO, Inc.
130 Cremona Drive, P.O. Box 1911
Santa Barbara, California 93116-1911

This book is printed on acid-free paper.
Manufactured in the United States of America

CONTENTS

VOLUME ONE

Epistemology

Evaluation

Florida State Standards

Functionalism

Goals of Standards

History

Interpretation

Politics of Education

Purposes of Education

VOLUME THREE

Queer Sexuality

Reductionism

Regulating Teachers

School Accreditation

Science

Urban Education

Vocational and Work Education

Working with Knowledge

STANDARDS AND SCHOOLING IN THE UNITED STATES

An Encyclopedia

STANDARDS, NOT STANDARDIZATION

Student Learning in a Democratic Classroom

David Hursh and Aggie Seneway

One morning, second graders John, Lee, and Marcia burst into my (David's) classroom excited about sharing their shoeboxes filled with rocks and shells. After sharing their treasures with me, they sat on the floor exuberantly displaying them to anyone who showed interest. For me, as their teacher, the immediate question became: Should I incorporate the students' interest in rocks and shells into the life, and therefore the curriculum, of the classroom, and if so, how? The incident also raised less immediate and larger questions: How do we achieve standards without subjecting students to standardized tests and standardization in learning? How should curriculum decisions be made in the classroom? What is the role of the teacher as the more experienced person? How do we ensure that students are learning what they need to know in order to live in and with the world?

In this chapter we use examples from our own elementary teaching to demonstrate our Deweyan approach to teaching as a passionate, moral, and intellectual enterprise. We begin by asserting that even though we do not follow the prevalent approach of using prepackaged curriculums and standardized tests, we hold our students to high standards. We object to linking standards to high-stakes standardized tests that are used, not as they might be, to improve instruction, but instead to rank and hold "accountable" students, teachers, and schools. We then turn to describing the principles that guide us in our teaching practices. Our principles reflect Dewey's ideas that the school should be democratically organized so that students cultivate the ways of being democratic citizens, that teachers should base their authority on their greater experience, and that the curriculum should connect the experience of the student with the "achievements of the past and the issues of the present" (Dewey, 1963, p. 23).

Our vision contrasts sharply with the current emphasis on linking curriculum standards to high-stakes standardized tests. National curriculum organizations such as the National Council of Teachers of Mathematics and nationally commissioned organizations such as the one that created the National History Standards led initial efforts to create subject area standards. While we find the curriculum standards useful as teaching guides, we object to more recent efforts to connect standards or curriculum frameworks to standardized tests that are used to assess not only students but also individual teachers and schools. Linking standards to standardized tests, tests that are increasingly used to determine whether students should be promoted from one grade to another or from high school, has resulted in mandated state control of what knowledge is of most worth (Kornhaber, Orfield, & Kurlaendar, in press; McNeil, 2000). "Although states . . . deny that these frameworks amount to 'curriculum,' their practical effects are the equivalent, particularly when frameworks, standardized tests, and textbooks are aligned" (Ross, 2000, p. 208). Rather than promoting teachers as thoughtful and knowing practitioners capable of thinking about their teaching, "standards and related efforts [such as standardized tests] undercut teachers' abilities to make professional judgments about what to teach" (Ross, 2000, p. 219).

For both of us, a central educational goal is cultivating in students the "ways of being" required of democratic citizens. Like Dewey, we believe students learn to be democratic citizens through making decisions within the democratically organized institution of school. Dewey argued that for students to become participatory members of a democratic community, they must have the "power of self-direction and power of directing others, powers of administration," and the "ability to assume positions of responsibility" as citizens and workers. Moreover, students must have "a command of the fundamental methods of inquiry and the fundamental tools of intercourse and communication" (Dewey, 1902, p. 93). Therefore, we aim to provide students with opportunities for decision making and responsibility.

However, by stating that students should be involved in making decisions regarding their own learning, we are not implying, as have some "progressive" educators in both Dewey's time and in the 1960s and 1970s (e.g., Neill, 1960; Holt, 1970, 1972), that students should entirely direct their own learning or that all learning is of equal significance. For example, we disagree with Holt, who stated: "I think children would like to divide their lives between children's activities, things thought up and done by children for their own purposes; and adults' activities, things thought up and done by adults for their own purposes, with children taking part. But I am more and more troubled by the thought of adults thinking up things for children to do, no matter how creative" (Holt, personal communication, 1979).

Holt (1972) further stated that schools should model themselves after a Swedish school he visited where the adults and children do what they want, and the teachers never suggest, however subtly or gently, that children do any activity.

In contrast, we agree with Graubard, who in *Free the Children* (1972) wrote one of the clearest and most thoughtful analyses of the misconceptions of those promoting traditional curriculum and teaching and those promoting laissez-faire reforms in the 1960s and '70s. He criticizes Holt for arguing that there is no sense in choosing any subject matter over any other. "Holt assumes," writes Graubard, "that the criterion to be used is future usefulness of the knowledge, and that we cannot do a good job of predicting this, because knowledge and the world are changing so fast" (1972, p. 217).

Graubard rebuts that we do have some idea of what knowledge is worthwhile. Certainly, he suggests, learning multiplication and tic-tac-toe are not of equal value. Further, what students should learn can be determined without relying on what Dewey described as either a "subject-matter centered" or "child-centered focus" (1915, pp. 6–7). While we may rightly reject the idea that the curriculum should come entirely from the teacher, wrote Dewey, the task then becomes not to see "the child as the starting point, the center, and the end" (1915, p. 7) but to respond to the "problem of discovering the connection which exists within the experience between the achievements of the past and the issues of the present" (1963, p. 23). We need to avoid rejecting the experience of either the adult or child. Dewey stated: "Because the older [traditional] education imposed the knowledge, methods, and the rules of conduct of the mature person on the young, it does not follow, except on the basis of the extreme Either-Or philosophy, that the knowledge and skill of the mature person has no directive value for the experience of the immature" (Dewey, 1963, pp. 21–22).

Dewey described the former approach, in which adults imposed their views on the young, as constituting arbitrary authority. Instead, argued Dewey, we need to develop an approach that makes use of the adult's natural authority. Dewey again:

> The greater maturity of experience which should belong to the adult as educator puts him in a position to evaluate each experience of the young in a way in which the one having the less mature experience cannot do. It is then the business of the educator to see in what direction an experience is heading. There is no point in his being more mature if, instead of using his greater insight to help organize the conditions of the experience of the immature, he throws away his insight. . . . The mature person, to put it in moral terms, has no right to withhold from the young on given occasions whatever capacity for sympathetic understanding

his own experience has given him. (Dewey, 1963, p. 38)

The following example from the elementary teaching of one of the authors (David) in the 1970s in Kansas highlights the necessity for teachers, as adults, to use their greater experience to guide the students.

The dialogical relation between the experience of teachers and students: Kindergartners learn geology.

In my classroom I usually team-taught with another teacher. Each day we posted activities for which students could sign up, some of which were led by one or both of the teachers, some led by students, and some students could do on their own. As children entered the classroom one morning, a five-year-old boy asked me to read the book about the Grand Canyon that his father had brought back from hiking the canyon. I agreed and posted listening to the book as one of the possible activities for which children could sign up.

Later, when sitting with students to read the book, I began by asking if they knew how the canyon was formed. The students responded by suggesting earthquakes and tornadoes as the likely causes, to which I responded that the river eroded the soil, forming the canyon. After the students exclaimed that I couldn't possibly be correct—they described my explanation as crazy—I offered to teach a unit over the next month

that would demonstrate sedimentation, erosion, and the formation of canyons. If they would agree to participate in the lessons over the next month, I would plan the unit and begin teaching it within a few days. They agreed, and for a month we explored erosion through a variety of projects. For example, we studied the effects of rainwater on our playground and the erosion and layers of sedimentary shale and limestone in a streambed. We constructed and used a "stream table" to explore how erosion varied depending on the amount and force of water, the slope of the land, and the kinds of soil.

In this example the curriculum grew out of the students' interest in canyons. However, they did not initially express an interest in geology; indeed, they did not know that such a scientific discipline existed. Rather, I took their nascent interest in canyons and expanded it to include the field of geology. Further, I agreed to teach the unit only when they agreed that it was something they wanted. After all, since geology is not typically included in the kindergarten curriculum, there would be no harm in not teaching it and moving on to something else.

My questioning the students regarding their knowledge of geological processes and offering to teach geology depict how I differ from Holt's view and agree with Dewey's. While Holt would wait for the students to ask, Dewey would argue that the adult has a "natural authority" based on greater experience that needs to be brought to the situation. I was not, I would argue, imposing my authority arbitrarily but offered my greater experience and knowledge as an organizing force and resource.

In the preceding example, with kindergarten students, the adult was primarily responsible for organizing the curriculum. But it is also possible for teachers and students to share the organizing experience. The process of organizing students' learning experiencing is key. Dewey wrote that "finding the material for learning within experience is only the first step. The next step is the progressive development of what is already experienced into a fuller and richer and also more organized form, a form that gradually approximates that in which subject-matter is presented to the skilled, mature person" (Dewey, 1963, pp. 73–74).

In the following example, from David's classroom teaching of primarily older elementary students in the early 1970s in Omaha, Nebraska, the teachers and students collaborated in developing the curriculum. Further, because collaboratively determining curriculum is not without its problems, progress ebbed and flowed, with at one point all the participants temporarily resigning from the project.

Learning Together: Developing a Television Program on City Planning

While my (David's) interests have included architecture and city planning, I had not thought about developing a curriculum around these two interests until students began to express interest in them. I regularly arranged for my students, ages five to thirteen, to present at conferences. One fall, several students and I participated in a conference at which we attended a session on designing and building playgrounds. Consequently, we began designing our own.

The following year we moved to a different building that consisted of only two large rooms. Under the leadership of another teacher, Ken, we began building lofts and partitions in order to create new spaces in the school. The children became excited by the new spaces and worked with teachers to create spaces for different activities. As we moved around shelves, lofts, tables, sofas, and chairs, we talked about how different arrangements affected our movement and feelings of spaciousness and privacy.

Later in the year, several children asked if we could visit an architectural office. I arranged a visit, and the children were impressed with the architects' planning, drawings, and models. After that experience I built a drafting table, and the children began designing buildings, drawing elevations and floor plans, and building models from their plans.

In the meantime we had been asked by the local public television affiliate to do a program on some aspect of government; they suggested "how a bill becomes a law." Because of our developing interest in design and the environment, Ken and I decided to propose to the older elementary students that we create a program on city planning by focusing on Omaha's regional planning agency: The Metropolitan Area Planning Association (MAPA).

The students initially responded enthusiastically, in part because of the prospect of "being on television." However, developing a half-hour show required more than enthusiasm. My own thinking inclined toward the political and theoretical, which proved, not surprisingly, too difficult for the students and too difficult to portray. Ken had some ideas for the actual presentation, promoting the idea of explaining MAPA by "filming a tour" of the agency with the students portraying agency employees.

Unsure of what we would actually do (of course, none of us had ever written a television program), we first tried to learn about MAPA by reading MAPA's publications, interviewing staff, and sitting in on a board meeting. Besides becoming bored, we didn't understand what MAPA really did, in part because the agency's role in area planning was unclear. None of the students came up with feasible ideas, and Ken and I began to pressure the students to develop the promised program. I realized that my ideas were inappropriate. The students rejected the idea of a "tour" as "sophomoric," but they had no ideas of their own.

After several months we gave up on the project. The students and teachers were frustrated and tired. But after letting the project remain dormant for a few weeks, we started to explore new ways of learning about MAPA. We toured some of their projects, met with a staff member, looked at their maps, and videotaped some "person-on-the-street" interviews. We began to get a better understanding of issues regarding urban renewal and suburban sprawl. We set deadlines and actually began to believe that we had something to say. From then on, the students knew what they could do, and completing the project was easier and more enjoyable.

The final half-hour program was composed of two dozen short vignettes that only children could have conceived. We herded fifty-five students off to the studio where the students took responsibility for all the aspects of creating a program: setting up the scenery, manning the cameras, creating special effects, and, of course, acting. A few vignettes should suffice to convey the students' spirit.

We had learned that some areas near streams and rivers were designated as "hundred-year flood plains," meaning that the area would flood on average once a century. Two building uses were permitted in such areas: drive-in theaters and the misleadingly named "mobile homes." Therefore, in one vignette an owner of a mobile home stands outside his front door just as it begins, through special effects, to rain. Then, as water, through more special effects, begins to rise around the homeowner, a MAPA employee comes up to query the homeowner about whether he knew that he lived in a flood plain, patiently showing him a regional planning map. As he does so, the mobile home floats off.

Other vignettes included can-can dancers singing a song praising city planning and a student narrating students' photographs portraying downtown urban renewal and the environmental effects of suburban sprawl. In the end we included every one of the fifty-five students in some aspect of the production. The program, which we titled *MAPA Who?* was shown on public television and later used by MAPA to introduce regional planning to area citizens.

Throughout the project, teachers and students frequently exchanged leadership roles, and on one occasion everyone quit, giving everyone time to gain perspective and to come back with better ideas. The teachers were clearly in charge of the overall planning, but the students owned the creative process of writing and acting. In fact, the kinds of vignettes the students wrote were more creative than any the adults could have written. I, for one, would not teach about regional planning through can-can dancers!

In these two examples from David's classroom, teachers used their greater experience to organize and direct the curriculum. In the first example, the impetus for the unit came from a student's interest in the Grand Canyon, and the teacher organized the unit. In the second example, the interest came from both teachers and students, with students taking the primary responsibility for the creative aspects of the project. In the following example, we turn to Aggie's classroom, where students democratically decide many as-

pects of the school day and entirely direct their own learning on one day each week.

The Classroom as a Democratic Community: Classroom Practices and Committee Day

In teaching and organizing my (Aggie) classroom, I am guided by five principles. First, what occurs in my classroom should be about students and not about the teacher. In planning activities and responding to students, I try to remember that what is important is what the students are learning, not whether they are trying to satisfy some arbitrary demands. For example, when we begin an activity I monitor myself so I will not tell them that they need to do it in a particular way. Instead I ask: What information are you interested in? Where do you think you will find it? What will you do when you find it?

As I ask them questions, I remind myself that while it may take more time for the students to figure things out for themselves, it is crucial that they do so. I am reminded of the parent who told me that she, rather than her daughter, cleans the guinea pig cage at home. When I remarked that her daughter did an excellent job of caring for the class guinea pig, she replied that she cleaned the cage because it was easier for her to do so. It has been said that a classroom teacher makes over three thousand decisions a day. Are we, as teachers, too quick to make decisions for students because it is easier than engaging students to figure out what to do and what and how to learn?

Second, students need to drive the agenda. The students need to be able to make decisions about what occurs during the day. In our classroom, the students are responsible for many of the daily routines or rituals, such as lunch count, attendance, morning meeting, and class meeting. Although I have done the actual schedule for the day and week, they will identify a need on a particular day and will adjust the schedule to fit the need. For example, if books are needed for independent reading and research, the students will schedule library time. The student in charge of morning meeting also acknowledges transition time. As each activity draws to a close, the student announces that it is time to transition to the next activity.

Third, in a classroom we are all learners and teachers. While it is clear that I know more than the students, I am continually learning about and with them. They teach one another and me. I am always struck by the student who asks me, "Did you know that?" and I did not. I have become comfortable saying, "I never heard of that" or "I didn't know that"; if necessary, we will research together to find more information. By responding honestly, I don't look or act like the adult who has all the answers; I become a learner alongside the students.

Fourth, children need to be physically and verbally active in order to be engaged. Students learn through language and need to be provided opportunities to use language in meaningful ways. Talking among themselves enables students to review and think through what they are learning.

Fifth, teachers need to know their own belief system about learning. Our practices are driven by the belief system we hold. Once we can articulate our beliefs, we can then reflect on whether our practices match our beliefs.

These principles have led to students' becoming central to creating curriculum, as well as teaching and learning from one another. In the fall of 1995 several students asked me if they could use class time to demonstrate some science experiments they had tried at home. Since I was concerned that by setting aside only a few hours for this we would not give their experiments adequate attention, I suggested that we set aside an afternoon, which worked well. Soon after, we became involved in a time-consuming project with two other classes. I suggested that from then on we set aside a whole day for projects. For the past three years my students have been using one day per week to carry out projects by committee.

At the beginning of the year students choose which day of the week will be committee day and assign it a name. Over the past years committee day has been called Project Day, Terrific Tuesday, and Wacky Wednesday. Once the day is established, students are asked to think of a subject area or topic that interests them. After determining their research question and naming their committee, they are encouraged to recruit other students.

After forming the committee membership and refining the research goal, the goal is shared with the whole class so students can help clarify the committee's goal. Next, each committee, to guide their research, charts what they know and want to know. Committees then turn to undertaking their research. Students work on the computer, read encyclopedias, go to the library, discuss with their committee members, and talk with adults about what they have discovered. Students accomplish more on committee day than during the rest of the week.

Near the end of the day, all the committees share with the class the activities they did in working toward their goal. When they have completed all their work, including reports and demonstrations, they present what they have learned to the class. When committees present, they ask for comments and feedback from the whole class. I am continually amazed at the seriousness with which students question and respond to presenters.

After the year has begun, committees form whenever students express an interest that they can entice others to join. After enlisting other members, they develop a goal and describe what they will learn. On committee days each committee's goals are reviewed at the beginning and middle ("halftime") of the school day. Students ask each other to clarify what they are researching and what they think they will learn.

This day remains sacred through the year. Students will add and subtract activities from other days, but committee day remains the same. They express resentment of any activities that interfere with the day. When asked why they value committee day, they consistently answer: "We get to choose what we want to learn about and how we want to share our learning."

Over the last two years, students have investigated a variety of topics, including tsunamis, deserts, bears, parrots, World War I, Germany, newspapers, caterpillars, and butterflies. One summer, two students started a committee to learn about Anne Frank's life, an interest originating with an older sister. The students continued the committee in the fall because they wanted to teach their classmates. "Maybe," they stated, "other kids don't know who she was. We want to tell them." Students often engage in projects not only for their own learning but because they are taking responsibility for one another's learning.

Part of the process of committee days includes assessing the students' learning. For me, assessment is a continuous process of determining where children are in their learning. I've asked my students: "How do you demonstrate to Ms. Seneway what you have learned?" One student wrote: "Look at a project, think about how people would talk about it, like if they did a good job or needed to do better; kids evaluate other kids not in the committee; you evaluate yourself and go back and think [about] what I did, how did I do it, and did I like it or not?"

I've also asked the students how they might assess their other activities. They've responded: "Tests; stuff like cursive papers, one when started and one now; keep a portfolio; tell what happened; math think-alouds [students report on how they think through a problem]; writing letters; projects for science, do problems; make a book or resources about grasslands; retells." Students actively determine how they will be assessed.

In order to carry out a project successfully, the students engage in setting standards to be reached and assessing whether they met them. They use skills from all the disciplines: reading, writing, speaking, social studies, math, science, and the arts. The students and I are, therefore, actively engaged in a democratically organized classroom that achieves the standards without focusing on students' scores on standardized tests.

Committee day is just one feature of my democratic classroom. Students as a group decide how long we will work on an activity and what counts as satisfactory work. Further, we make many decisions by consensus, so students have a real voice in the life of the classroom. We often vote on issues, but rather than a simple yes-or-no vote, I ask students to show "fist, three fingers, or five fingers." A fist means you strongly disagree with the proposal and cannot live with it, three fingers means you are in agreement, and five fingers means you strongly agree. Recently, all the students in our school building began raising money for a playground. In my classroom students

had been collecting money for several months to save the rain forest. A student suggested that we donate the money already collected for the rain forest to the playground. Using the consensus method, the class president (an office that rotates weekly) asked for "fist, three, or five." Many fists were raised, and those students had to explain why they could not live with the idea. Debate ensued, and the class officers sought a middle ground. Finally one of the students said, "Even if we don't give money to the playground, it will be built, and the rain forest is more important than what we need." With that comment, those who agreed with the original proposal changed their minds, and all agreed to keep the money for the rain forest.

Reaching High Standards without Standardization

In our own elementary teaching we have aimed, like Dewey, to develop classrooms in which students participate in deciding what and how they will learn within a community that continually asks: "What is worth learning? How will we assess what we learned? How will we teach others?" In this way we collaborate in developing meaningful standards and assessment methods.

Further, we have *not* divided the curriculum into what Dewey described as "formal and artificial" subject areas that are contrary to "the way a child [and, we would add, adults outside of educational institutions] would see them" and that "obfuscate rather than enhance their relationship to human purpose" (Dewey, 1896, pp. 64–65). Instead, we desired that our students become engaged in asking and answering essential questions that are central to making sense of the world as a whole. For example, David's students, in researching, writing, and producing *MAPA Who?* were engaged in answering questions regarding the goals and issues involved in regional planning. In answering those questions and then presenting them to others, the students learned, at minimum, history, geology, politics, writing, and acting.

Our assessment has focused *not* on how well students perform on centrally created standardized tests but on how well students demonstrate their learning to other students and the teachers. The real test, we feel, of whether students have achieved high standards is in the complexity and sophistication of the students' learning. That kindergartners become excited about geology and fourth graders about Anne Frank and the holocaust demonstrates that high standards can be achieved by developing an environment in which teachers and students engage in the dialogical process of introducing one another to the wider world.

Acknowledgments

We would like to thank doctoral students Donald Furiuso and Camille Martina for their assistance in writing this chapter.

Bibliography

Dewey, J. (1898). The primary-education fetish. *The Forum 25*, 315–328.

Dewey, J. (1902). The school as a social centre. *Middle works of John Dewey, 1899-1924.* Carbondale: Southern Illinois University Press, 1981-1991, vol. 2, p. 93.

Dewey, J. (1915). *The child and the curriculum and the school and society.* Chicago: University of Chicago Press.

Dewey, J. (1963). *Experience and education.* New York: Macmillan/Collier. (Original work published 1938).

Graubard, A. (1972). *Free the children: Radical reform and the free school movement.* New York: Pantheon.

Holt, J. (1970). *How children fail.* New York: Dell.

Holt, J. (1972). *Freedom and beyond.* New York: Dell.

Kliebard, H. (1986). *The struggle for the American curriculum: 1893–1958.* New York: Routledge.

Kornhaber, M., Orfield, G., & Kurlaendar, M. (in press). *Raising standards or raising barriers?* Boston: Harvard Civil Rights Project.

McNeil, L. (2000). *Contradictions of school reform: Educational costs of standardized testing.* New York: Routledge.

Neill, A.S. (1960). *Summerhill: A radical approach to child rearing.* New York: Hart Publishing Co.

Ross, E. W. (2000). Diverting democracy: The curriculum standards movement and social studies education. In D. W. Hursh & E. W. Ross (Eds.), *Democratic social studies: Social studies for social change* (pp. 203–228). New York: Falmer.

FROM POSITIVISM TO AN EPISTEMOLOGY OF COMPLEXITY

Grounding Rigorous Teaching

Joe L. Kincheloe

From Barbara Thayer-Bacon's three blind men and the elephant, we come to understand the meaning of epistemology. Building on her essay, I will examine the reductionistic epistemology or positivism that grounds technical standards. Then I will develop an epistemology of complexity that moves us to a far more intricate and sophisticated understanding of the ways our view of knowledge profoundly shapes the nature of the education we embrace. For readers who do not have a background in philosophy, please do not be frightened by the term *epistemology*. The word signifies a very simple concept—the study of knowledge. The word and the concepts it represents are too important to waste only on philosophy majors. Epistemology is important because it invisibly shapes not only the form school takes but also the way we think, our consciousness, the way we see the world, our images of ourselves, even our identities.

Indeed, epistemology matters as it shapes us and the world around us. Epistemological questions might include: How do we know? Is that true? Is this an objective test? Why do you believe that? Is history based on fact or interpretation? Are the answers on the standards exit test based on truth, or are they opinion? What we refer to as knowledge is problematic. Human knowledge—knowledge about humans, groups of humans, human institutions, human interaction, and knowledge derived by research conducted by humans—is constructed by a variety of forces. In this portion of the encyclopedia, we will analyze the complex notion of epistemology in light of its effect on educational standards and the purpose of education in general. Any knowledge, any curriculum, any method of teaching, any standard assumes—whether consciously or not—an epistemological stance. Standards of complexity maintain that anyone involved with devising standards or with teaching or learning should be keenly aware of these epistemological dynamics.

One task of epistemology is to provide theories of the nature of knowledge, of its genesis and its justification. Traditionally, many scholars have assumed that once we were conversant with theories of knowledge, we would be better prepared to proceed with our research and teaching. These diverse theories of knowledge, of course, conflict with one another over the definition of "true knowledge"; indeed, some epistemologies deny even the possibility of true knowledge. Nevertheless, different epistemologies promote different forms of knowledge along with different methodologies, ways of knowing, and ways of learning. Thus, we accept religious knowledge and ways of knowing, ethical knowledge and ways of knowing, linguistic knowledge and ways of knowing, intuitive knowledge and ways of knowing, and emotional knowledge and ways of knowing. "How do you know you're in love?" "I just know; I feel it very strongly."

In the social and physical sciences and in educational and psychological fields, scholars in the past three decades have been confronted with an epistemological crisis. The crisis has produced some difficult questions for researchers and educators. What is the proper method of pursuing social, physical, and educational knowledge?

What constitutes knowledge in these domains? How do we teach such forms of knowledge and knowledge production? How do we—or even should we—teach about the epistemological disagreements among various scholars in classrooms? There is great dissatisfaction among social and physical scientists and educational and psychological researchers with the positivistic definitions of knowledge—though the discomfort is not by any means universal. Among the uncomfortable, no consensus has been reached on a new definition of knowledge. The debate over technical standards and standards of complexity represents its extension into the realm of educational policy. The debate over epistemology and the way the epistemological crisis is resolved will exert a profound impact on humanity—it will shape the nature of what we deem knowledge. And to a significant extent, we are what we know—it shapes us.

No matter what scholarly, social, cultural, educational, or even vocational domain, epistemology is always lurking in the shadows, shaping what is going on. The following is an excerpt from my book *Toil and Trouble: Good Work, Smart Workers, and the Integration of Academic and Vocational Education*. In this section of the book I am exploring the forces that shape our view of workers:

Contrary to mainstream depictions of it, schooling is always a struggle over particular ways of life and particular epistemologies. Epistemology refers to the nature of knowledge, what constitutes it and how we produce it. The debate over how America deals with work education is an epistemological debate over what knowledge is of most worth. Two worlds have developed within schools: one, a world that values academic knowledge and prepares students for college; the other, an "antimatter world" that values the knowledge of work and prepares students for jobs. Because mainstream society refuses to value the knowledge of job preparation, the status of work-related knowledge is very low. Thus, society treats vocational high school students as if they are deficient and incapable of thoughtful behavior. These epistemological assumptions structure not only work education but also the nature of work itself. For example, if the knowledge of particular jobs is not valued then low incomes and dehumanized work places are justified. The phrase, "he's just a maintenance worker" reveals so much. Since he works in an unvalued, low-skill job, why should we care if he has input into how the job is performed, or if he makes a livable wage, or if he and his family have health care coverage? These epistemological assumptions also determine what jobs are appropriate for particular demographic groups to perform, e.g., jobs suitable for women, racial minorities, or youths. Struggle after struggle arises as individuals from these groups attempt to obtain "inappropriate jobs." (1995, 32)

It is important to note that any notion of epistemology has been erased from the discussion and debate over educational standards. Such an omission is deeply troubling because educational standards are by nature an epistemological issue. In the following pages, I will delineate two important epistemological stances. In no way do I mean to imply by such a categorization that there are no other epistemological positions possible—of course there are. The reason I chose the epistemology of modernism—positivism—and an epistemology of complexity is because technical standards consistently seem to be influenced by positivism and an epistemology of complexity grounds our standards of complexity. Drawing upon Thayer-Bacon's insights into epistemology and this description of positivism and complexity, readers should enter the standards conversation with an expanded perspective. A key to making sense of many of the entries in this encyclopedia revolves around the epistemological distinctions in this chapter.

The Epistemology of Modernism: Positivism

The epistemological position of Cartesian modernism is known as positivism. Few philosophical orientations have been so influential on the way we live our lives and construct education as modernist positivism. Yet, concurrently, few philosophical orientations have been so little understood. From a technical perspective, the term *positivism* began to be used widely in the nineteenth century. French philosopher Auguste Comte popularized the concept, maintaining that human thought had evolved through three states: the theological stage, where truth rested on God's revelation; the metaphysical stage, where truth derived from abstract reasoning and argument; and the positivistic stage, where truth arises from scientifically produced knowledge. Comte sought to discredit the legitimacy of nonscientific thinking that failed to take "sense knowledge" (knowledge obtained through the senses and empirically verifiable) into account (Kneller, 1984; J. Smith, 1983). He saw no difference between the ways knowledge should be produced in the physical sciences and in the human sciences, and he believed one should study sociology just like biology. This had a dramatic impact on the way we would approach the educational act. Social knowledge and information about humans would be subjected to the same decontextualizing forces as the study of rocks. Social, educational, and psychological scientists would pull people out of their cultural setting and study them in laboratory-like conditions.

Society, like nature, Comte argued, is nothing more than a body of neutral facts governed by immutable laws. Therefore, social actions should proceed with lawlike predictability (Held, 1980). In a context such as Comte's, education would also be governed by unchanging laws; the role of the educator is to uncover these laws and then act in accordance with them. For example, educational laws would include universal statements regarding how students learn and how and what they should be taught. The positivist educator, in other words, sees only one correct way to teach, one correct body of knowledge to transmit to students, and he or she has unwavering faith that scientific study can reveal these methods and knowledge if we search for them diligently.

The following ten characteristics of positivism help us understand the impact of epistemology on our consciousness, the larger society, and technical educational standards.

1. *All knowledge is scientific knowledge.* First, positivism insists that only scientifically produced information should be regarded as authentic human knowledge. Scientific knowledge can be verified and proven. It is knowledge about which we are positive—hence the name *positivism.* When Newton formulated the theory of gravity, he told us that the apple *always* falls to the ground and that what goes up must come down. No exceptions to these scientific generalizations exist. Scientific knowledge is not merely one form of knowledge, the positivists maintain, for knowledge can be produced *only* by science. Positivists hold nonscience in disdain, and they dismiss ways of knowing through religion, interpretation, metaphysics, intuition, and emotion as unverifiable nonsense. This might help us to understand why indigenous and native people were thought by modernist European colonizers to be ignorant savages.

The positivist view of the world exerts a dramatic impact on all of us, teachers in particular. If expert-produced scientific knowledge constitutes the only valuable information about education, then schooling should be organized so that experts and administrators simply tell teachers how to perform their jobs. And this is exactly what devisors of technical standards have done. In this situation, experts do all of the thinking, and teachers merely execute plans. Any thoughts about the purposes of education and the daily work of the complex classroom remain separate. The positivistic context denies teachers their skills, and the teaching act and classroom practice are torn apart. Once deskilled, teachers are provided with teacher-proof materials and must simply implement lessons prepared in advance by textbook companies, computer programs, or state and district supervisors—all of these knowledge providers are tied to the standards provided. The teacher then functions as a proctor in an ACT, SAT, or standards-test session by reading instructions, distributing materials, regulating time, monitoring for cheating, and answering questions.

Teacher-proof curriculum materials assume that teachers are incapable of making instructional decisions and must be guided through their daily work. Examples of teacher-proof materials include "scripted" lessons that teachers actually read to their classes.

The teacher says, "OK class, take out your books and turn to page 23. Do not proceed until all books are on desk and open to the appropriate page." Then the teacher says to a selected student: "Read the first sentence on flax production in Brazil, Karen."

Unfortunately, this positivism-inspired school scenario is becoming all too familiar. Standards of complexity fight such positivism and continue the effort to secure or restore teacher empowerment in democratic workplaces where they are viewed as self-directed and reflective professionals rather than monitors. The political implications of teacher-proof materials and the logic behind them alarm those of us who value democracy; thus, standards of complexity challenge this first premise of the epistemology of positivism: that all true knowledge is scientific.

2. All scientific knowledge is empirically verifiable. Positivism assumes that when we use the phrase *scientific knowledge*, we are referring to knowledge that can be verified empirically (through the senses). What the eye sees, what the ear hears, what we can count, what we can express mathematically—these things constitute empirical knowledge. But the complexity principle contends that many aspects of education resist empirical validation. These invisible factors might include ways of seeing or sets of assumptions. They might include a student's feelings of hurt or humiliation, the self-esteem of an abused child, or the value positions that move people to join a political revolution—such human dynamics do not lend themselves to quantification or empirical verification. Indeed, the existence of positivism itself as a force that shapes what we "see" cannot be empirically verified. In other words, positivism cannot study its own assumptions because they are not empirically verifiable.

When we encounter educational knowledge and content standards that use such an epistemological base exclusively, we find it limited in what it can tell us about schooling and the learning process. Indeed, when students learn from materials produced by such a positivist science, they tend to find that the most important aspects of education are left out or distorted. To become the best possible teacher, one should understand the epistemological dynamics of knowledge production. Knowledge about the world and about the educational cosmos in particular is never neutral. It is always based on a set of values and assumptions about the nature of the world and the people who live in it. These epistemological dynamics shape beliefs about the purposes of education, the knowledge it deems valuable, and the way it is taught.

3. *One must use the same methods to study the physical world as one uses to study the social and educational worlds.* Serious problems result when one applies positivistic physical-science methods to the study of the social world, education, or, after Einstein, the physical world itself. A key aspect of positivistic research in the physical sciences involves the attempt to predict and control natural phenomena. When applied in psychology and education, physical-science methods then apply such knowledge as a tool to control human beings. Thus, students come to be viewed, understood, used, and controlled just like any other *thing*. Positivism loses sight of the idea that the objects of social, psychological, and educational research—humans—possess a special *complexity* that sets them apart from other objects of study.

Positivist social, psychological, and educational scientists fail to understand that the physical scientists they emulate impose their observations on the objects under observation. Physical scientists do not have to consider the consciousness of their objects of study or their history and sociocultural contexts. Neither need they consider their own consciousness and assumptions, many argue—though I don't agree. This makes research on humans different from the study of, say, sulfuric acid or field mice. If we fail to understand this difference, then we miss the very elements that make us human, that shape us or restrict our freedom.

Here rests one of the key points in our discussion of epistemology in general and positivism in particular: modernism and its positivist epistemology lead to a devaluation of human beings and a depersonalization of our institutions. People become merely more variables in a larger social equation; our sacredness as spiritual beings disappears. Think of how degraded we feel when we are being processed by large institutions—insurance companies, welfare agencies, university business offices, the court system—that see us as a social security number or Case 5 on the docket. Impersonal positivism promotes this kind of treatment. If for no other reason, anything that exerts this much impact on the social world deserves attention in the analysis of standards and educational purpose.

4. *If knowledge exists, it exists in some definite, measurable quantity.* Positivism teaches that we can express knowledge in mathematical terms. If something exists, positivists argue, we can measure how much of it exists. Indeed, we can express the generalizations, principles, and theories derived from positivistic data in mathematical language (Beed, 1991; Garrison, 1989). Positivists define systematic observation that produces valid knowledge in terms of mathematical experiments. In this context, researchers look for mathematical relations between variables. If such mathematical relations emerge, then they generalize the relationships to produce a universal law.

Many of us who call for standards of complexity and a democratic system of meaning find ourselves uncomfortable with the positivist assumptions that "to be is to be measurable" and that human endeavor can be expressed in mathematical terms. Much of what education researchers have to study does not lend itself to measurability or even direct observation. To address this problem, positivists developed what they call "reduction sentences," which are characteristics that summarize statements in a way that makes them easier to observe and measure. A hard-to-measure concept such as hunger in a positivist epistemology becomes "20 percent loss of original body weight" for a mature man or

woman. Since weight is a measurable concept, hunger can be expressed in terms of weight. Behavioral psychologists who operate within a positivistic context label such reduction sentences "operational or working definitions." Thus, we develop operational definitions for concepts such as intelligence (what one scores on an IQ test), productivity (output by workers per hour), and quality education (a 10 percent increase in exit-test scores). Indeed, positivists argue, even concepts such as love or creativity can be operationally defined and measured.

These operational definitions may or may not help us understand the phenomena under investigation. But such an orientation often focuses our attention on merely the symptoms of larger issues or ideas—that is, on the consequences rather than the causes. Thus, a belief in the measurability of everything actually distorts our understanding of reality, because it hides the assumptions often made in the production of knowledge. For example, what mental characteristics do questions on a standardized standards test really address? Short-term memory? The ability to store and call up a wide range of factual data? Certainly, standards tests cannot measure an ability to see connections between ostensibly unrelated concepts or the skill to apply such understandings to the identification and solution of problems. Such tests de-emphasize such difficult-to-measure but important abilities, whereas easy-to-measure but trivial abilities gain center stage. Education is thus undermined, reduced to memorization, computation, and busywork with little purpose or connection to the passions and complexities of human beings. Examine the way standardized-test scores in Texas were increased in the late 1990s and the early twenty-first century: state educational officials merely eliminated the lowest 20 percent of test takers. In these positivistic testing situations, learning becomes a mindless game, the trivial pursuit of abstract and inert information.

5. *Nature is uniform and whatever is studied remains consistent in its existence and behavior.* Positivists assume that the objects they study will remain constant. They believe in an underlying natural order in the way both the physical and the social worlds behave. These regularities, or social laws, positivists argue, are best expressed through quantitative analysis using propositional language and mathematics. The goal for educational research within this tradition, therefore, is to develop theories that regularize human expression and make it predictable.

An epistemology of complexity posits, by contrast, that human beings are much less regular and predictable than the positivists portray them. As humans exhibit their irregularities and unpredictabilities—their diversity— agents of complexity make the case that men and women defy positivist attempts to reduce their behavior to measurable quantities. Teachers and students, for example, are hardly uniform, predictable, and consistent in their personalities, actions, psycholo-

gies, and responses. Contrary to positivist opinions, humans are not machines whose behavior can be easily broken down into separate parts. Thank goodness researchers cannot yet provide full and final explanations of the human dynamic. These should be central issues in the standards debate because we are talking about how the social and human world is studied, taught, and learned. When we find a statistical correlation between social dynamics, we still have not asked what exactly the correlation means. Different observers may *interpret* (a key act in an epistemology of complexity) the correlations very differently. What criteria do we use to determine the validity of different interpretations? And since human beings are constantly changing and evolving entities, is the interpretation we offered last week of the correlation between particular social features still valid this week? At the very least, we recognize a complexity in these matters that modernist positivists often miss. This would seem to lay a firm foundation for a more rigorous form of scholarship, teaching, and learning.

6. *The factors that cause things to happen are limited and knowable, and in empirical studies these factors can be controlled.* Positivists believe that variables can be isolated and studied independently to determine specific causes for individual events. Following Newton's laws of the physical universe, they believe that for every action there is an opposite and equal reaction, and that these actions and reactions can be identified and measured. Positivists

refuse to acknowledge the complexity of the world, especially the world of human beings. The world, they believe, is neat and tidy, and the noise and confusion foisted on it by the "humanness of human beings" makes positivists edgy. Research would be so much easier if researchers and the researched could only avoid this untidy world and the imprecise medium of verbal language.

Positivists dream of a spick-and-span science in which all researchers are identical, unbiased, infallible measuring instruments. Modernist positivism accepts a cause-and-effect linearity that works like a machine. For example, when the human body breaks down, doctors may reliably identify one certain factor immediately contributing to the illness. But in reality, the causes are always multiple. Some are environmental, some psychological, and some physical. Diet, stress, chemicals, exercise, emotions, heredity, and viruses all affect the health of the human body, and these multiple causes rarely function in a simple, easily traced manner. Life processes, like social and psychological processes, are rarely neat and tidy; we must view them in the context that shapes them if we want to make sense of the way they operate.

As we think about the positivistic assumption that causative factors are limited and knowable, imagine the way we study classroom management or, as some call it, discipline. Hundreds of researchers have studied classroom discipline in the past thirty years. In addition to problems of sample size and the relationship between what gets defined as good discipline and desirable educational achievements, the control of variables in discipline research presents several other special difficulties. Literally thousands of unmentioned factors can significantly influence what happens in any classroom (D. Fiske and R. Schweder, 1986; Barrow, 1984). One student may respond to a specific teacher's discipline one way—not because of the discipline itself but because he or she is accustomed to a certain type of discipline at home. For example, a student raised in a permissive home may interpret a subtle, mildly coercive, noncorporal disciplinary act quite differently from a student raised in a strict home where punishment is physical. To the student from the strict home, subtle discipline reveals the teacher's weakness. Another student reacts differently to the subtle, mildly coercive discipline because of the nature of his or her relationship with the teacher. One student, whose parents are long-time acquaintances of the teacher, may know the teacher as a trusted friend. When confronted with corrective action of any kind, this student may feel uncomfortable because he or she is unaccustomed to conflict in his or her relationship with the teacher. What appears to the observer to be a mild admonishment provides a great deal of embarrassment to the student. Another student is affected by the presence of an outside observer and reacts in a way that is inconsistent with prior behavior. Still another student's behavior may be triggered by Tourette's syndrome or some other physical condition that may or may not be diagnosed or known to the teacher. A researcher can hardly account for all the possible variables that may affect what is being observed (Barrow, 1984). Veteran teachers recognize this. When a supervisor or observer enters the classroom, the atmosphere changes dramatically. Students who are usually well behaved and participate actively may suddenly become disrespectful or inattentive.

So the various facets of a student's or a teacher's nature, of every individual's background, of every context, and of all the interrelationships and combinations of factors may be each or in conjunction the key elements in explaining what happens in a classroom. This reflects what is sometimes called *chaos theory*, or *complexity theory*. These crucial elements elude positivist researchers. In this context, a professional education that provides a teacher with five scientifically validated "surefire methods" to discipline students no matter who they are is probably worthless. Unless the methods are contextualized by attention to the teacher's philosophical assumptions; the purposes of education he or she embraces; and the ethnic, class, socioeconomic, religious, cultural, racial, and gender backgrounds of the students, such methods generally will lead one astray. In fact, they often can keep a teacher from connecting with students in a way that motivates, validates, and inspires them. This is ex-

actly what classrooms structured by technical standards often do.

7. *Certainty is possible, and when we produce enough research we will understand reality well enough to forgo further research*. The goal of positivist research involves the quest for answers to specific questions, and such a quest implies a definite end point. But because we cannot control all variables, as we just saw—because the factors that cause various behaviors are unlimited—the quest for positivist certainty is futile and quixotic. If we learn anything definite from positivist science, it is that our ideas about the world change with new revelations and that they will continue to change, probably for all time. The chance of arriving at some juncture in human history where research becomes unnecessary because we all understand the nature of reality is slight.

Better, then, to abandon the quest for certainties that focus our attention on the trivial—on only those things we can easily measure. One of the reasons history tests often emphasize dates, people, places, and battles is that teachers find it easy to measure whether students have "learned" this kind of information. They find it much harder to evaluate an essay test, with its potential ambiguity and complexity. In fact, the quest for absolute certainty in testing and evaluation encourages the lowest form of thinking (rote memorization) and dismisses higher-level thinking (analysis, interpretation, contextualization, and application).

For these and many other reasons, democratic educators often view with skepticism the certainty with which positivists make "valid" arguments. Advocates of standards of complexity are generally inclined to have a more humble and limited perspective. Indeed, it seems safe to predict that educational researchers will never determine the five best ways to teach economics, the five steps to teaching excellence, or the eight steps to teacher popularity. There are as many good ways to teach as there are good teachers, and some of them conflict. I am always humbled when I watch great teachers teach and find that they are brilliant at what they do. Though I disagree with their conclusions and many of the decisions they make, I still would argue that they are great teachers who inspire many of the students who may find me boring and even offensive. Indeed, what we do successfully in one context may fail in another. The best teachers adjust lessons and adapt to changing classroom environments. This relatively simple concept is exactly what technical standards don't understand. All teachers, technical advocates argue, must teach alike. Standards of complexity reject this "Stepford teaching."

Discuss this concept with an experienced teacher in a departmentalized school who teaches five periods of math every day, and he or she will tell you that even though the lesson plans may be identical, each period proceeds differently. The teacher may gain an insight in the first period that is applicable in the next four periods. A student in the second period may ask a question that alters the structure of the lesson. Students in each class ask different questions, have different personalities, have unique learning styles and learning needs, and respond differently because of the time of day, weather conditions, events in the school schedule, and so forth. A uniform lesson plan for all five sections of the class may be possible, but because of the complexity teachers cannot control, uniform lessons are not. In fact, even if teachers could control every lesson, such control would hinder learning. The best teachers are comfortable with the variety of interpretations, paradigmatic insights, experiential understandings, political perspectives, and historical analyses their students bring to class.

8. *Facts and values can be kept separate, and objectivity is always possible.* Unlike positivists, I do not consider scientific research a value-free activity. The popular image of science reflects the belief that the only parameters that limit a scientist's activities are intellect and curiosity. This belief is misleading because values and power dynamics continually shape research. If educational researchers operate in a college of education dominated, for example, by positivist assumptions about the nature of research, then they might lose such career benefits as tenure if they attempt to conduct research that deviates from the rules of positivist methods. More important, because financial grants from govern-

ment and private foundations often determine the type of research that takes place, funded inquiries typically reflect the values and interests of funding agencies. A brief survey of accepted and rejected grants will illuminate the political values that drive knowledge production in education and elsewhere.

Nevertheless, positivist educators continue to insist that researchers suppress their personal value judgments, convictions, beliefs, and opinions (Beed, 1991). They insist that empirical inquiry should remain value free and objective and that values are tainted because they are subjective. Thus, the proclamations issued from the positivist pulpit project the illusion of political and moral neutrality. Accordingly, the wizard may be exposed, and the epistemological rules that dictate exactly what we can and cannot count as facts must be uncovered (Garrison, 1989).

The implicit rules that actually guide our generation of data almost always reflect specific worldviews, values, religious and political perspectives, and definitions of intelligence. Research can never really be nonpartisan, for we have to choose the rules that guide our research. Inquiry, teaching, or standards development can never really be nonpartisan, for we have to choose the rules that guide our research, our methods, and our choices. Particular rules focus our attention on certain aspects of education and deflect it from others. Positivism, for example, focuses our attention on education as a technical act. When we

measure certain aspects of education to determine how well school systems or particular schools or teachers are doing, we cannot separate this question from the political issue of what schools *should* be doing. Therefore, if positivist research can establish the criteria by way of research instruments that measure how well we are doing, it has also established what we should be doing. If I believe the role of schools is to develop critical, democratic citizens who seek to do away with social injustice, I will develop different educational standards than someone who does not hold these beliefs. Positivism becomes a political instrument of social control, even while its adherents proclaim their neutrality, their disinterestedness, and their disdain for mixing politics and education (Bowers, 1982).

For example, if researchers describe students' readiness for work as the ability to follow orders, respect authority, and function as team players, the schools with good evaluations teach these skills. The "objective" process of defining work readiness conceals some very specific values: From a variety of ways to define *work readiness*, the researchers choose the definition closest to their political and economic beliefs. They want to prepare a society of compliant workers who obey orders without raising questions or challenging authority. Having made a value-driven choice, the researchers, contrary to their protestations, are no longer political innocents.

The same holds true for the teacher who gives a multiple-choice test. The test appears to be an objective, value-free instrument of evaluation, but closer examination reveals a set of hidden value assumptions. In constructing the test, the teacher had already chosen the textbook on which the test material was based, a value choice that prioritized one book over several others. The teacher also considered particular material from the book to be more important than other material, a value choice of some "facts" over others. The teacher chose a multiple-choice format over other evaluation formats, a value choice that advanced certain forms of learning (fact memorization) over others (for example, analysis, interpretation, and application in an essay or a series of short written answers). Such value choices are inherent in teaching and living. Although we can hardly avoid them, we should understand that we are making them. This awareness is a key goal of a democratic education and the type of rigorous standards it demands. With this understanding, we can change the world of education. Such recognitions ground a democratic form of education and constitute a cardinal aspect of higher-order thinking.

9. *There is one true reality, and the purpose of education is to convey that reality to students.* Positivists generally contend that one best way to accomplish a task exists somewhere. For example, given one undisputed best way (best method) to teach, the purpose of the positivist teacher educator is to pass that method along to students; the purpose of the positivist biology teacher is to pass along the "truth" about biology. Advocates of complexity know that the truth about biology is not simple. At the very least, it depends upon whom you ask. Educational science grounded in positivist research assumes that the laws of society and the knowledge of human existence are verified and immutable and ought to be inserted directly into the minds of children. Operating on this assumption, educational "engineers" devise curricula and organizational strategies for schools as if no ambiguities or uncertainties in the social, physical, and educational worlds exist. Nothing is problematic: "Columbus discovered America." "The Indians were an impediment to westward expansion, but by the turn of the century this hindrance had been removed." "After the Mexican War ended and land disputes had been resolved, the size of the United States increased." All of these "facts" express points of view that many scholars don't accept. Pass the facts along to students; don't ask too many questions about the values and assumptions embedded within them. In standards of complexity, an understanding of these embedded values and assumptions in a variety of fields is important to becoming an educated person.

Contemporary culture teaches us to revere science and the scientific method and, interestingly enough, to accept its primacy on faith, which is to say, unscientifically. The authoritarian voice of positivist science silences our languages of intuition, aesthetics, spirituality, and insight. The view of science that regards the aesthetic and subjective as soft, effeminate, impressionistic, and nonscientific devalues such articulations. Cowed by the authority of positivist science, we accede to its demands and allow it to define teachers as mere practitioners (Aronowitz, 1983; Koller, 1981; Eisner, 1984; Hinchey, 1998; Hicks, 1999; Britzman, 1991).

In his studies of the street-corner culture in Toronto's Jane-Finch Corridor, Peter McLaren found students from lower socioeconomic classes questioning the school's view of themselves as passive recipients of sacred and official facts. The teachers less frequently questioned their own passive position in relation to the expert producers of knowledge (McLaren, 1989). When positivists control knowledge and student-teacher evaluations, we find the range of behaviors considered to be good teaching considerably narrowed. Many positivistic educational supervisors find it easy to label creative lessons that fail to follow the "one best method" unsatisfactory. Thus, teachers earn rewards less for their sophisticated notions of competence and creativity and more for their adherence to a prescribed format. Like workers on a factory assembly line, teachers in positivist school systems become rule followers with little influence over how the rules are made. They become the executors of managerial strategies for keeping students on the task of rote memorization. Even among the best teachers, the passion for creativity and engagement slowly erodes as positivistic science

becomes ever more deeply entrenched in our schools and society. Blind faith in positivism may be one of the great tragedies of our era. But along with many researchers and scholars who are aware of epistemological complexity, we are trying to reverse its philosophical dominance.

10. *Teachers become "information deliverers," not knowledge-producing professionals or empowered cultural workers.* In such a positivist context, we wonder why society should bother with teacher-education programs or even with educating teachers past the eighth grade—and among many right-wing advocates of technical standards, there are calls to end the type of teacher education advocated here. If teachers are merely information deliverers, we need hire only those with the abilities to read the scripted teacher-proof material and intimidate and control students. In the technical standards–driven schools emerging in the early twenty-first century, managers are calling for exactly these types of teachers. In such a context, the idea of a scholarly teacher with interpretive, analytical, or research abilities becomes irrelevant. School is simply a memory game in which the more creative teachers make memorization palatable by creating contests and mnemonic devices designed to ease rote learning. Only a desire to compete or to please their teachers or parents can motivate students in such an educational purgatory. Education has no intrinsic value, no connection to the lived world of human beings.

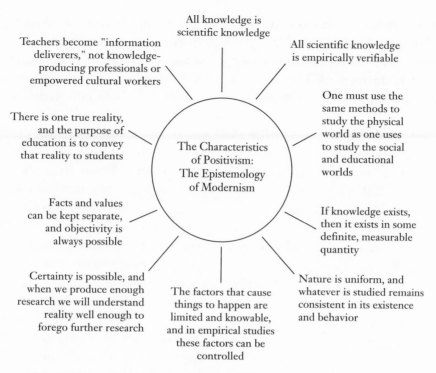

All knowledge is scientific knowledge

Teachers become "information deliverers," not knowledge-producing professionals or empowered cultural workers

All scientific knowledge is empirically verifiable

There is one true reality, and the purpose of education is to convey that reality to students

The Characteristics of Positivism: The Epistemology of Modernism

One must use the same methods to study the physical world as one uses to study the social and educational worlds

Facts and values can be kept separate, and objectivity is always possible

If knowledge exists, then it exists in some definite, measurable quantity

Certainty is possible, and when we produce enough research we will understand reality well enough to forego further research

The factors that cause things to happen are limited and knowable, and in empirical studies these factors can be controlled

Nature is uniform, and whatever is studied remains consistent in its existence and behavior

The Epistemological Assumptions behind Technical Standards

Indeed, knowledge-producing, scholarly teachers who understand the tenets of positivism can be viewed as dangerous undesirables in unreflective, technical standards–driven schools. In my own teaching experience, I have been viewed by administrators as a subversive who exerted a negative influence on my students. When I was teaching geography and history in high school, my principal told me after observing a geography class: "Why don't you get rid of all that interpretation and analysis crap and just give the students the facts they need to know? They'll be happier and I'll be happier." I couldn't do it. I had to get behind the epistemological curtain and find out why these facts and not others. My view of teaching transcended mindless, positivistic information delivery. If I had wanted to be a deliverer, I could have gone to work for Domino's. In a positivist, technical standards–driven system, I will probably be better off there. Certainly, my administrators and supervisors will be happier with my career decision. Indeed, technical standards–driven, positivistic schools will drive the best and brightest teachers away from the profession. Such teachers will find it increasingly difficult to deal with the black-and-white authoritarian orders given to them. They will find a new vocation where they can exercise their own professional judgment and retain a degree of creative control. Epistemology matters.

Understanding Epistemology—
We Appreciate the Need to
Respect Our Teachers and Raise
Our Expectations of Them:
Complex Teachers as Scholars

After all the technically rational studies of "what works" are completed, all
the practical methods are dissemi-
nated, and all the standards are written, teaching will still primarily be a
scholarly activity. What does this
mean? It implies that educational
leaders and teachers must be capable
of creating an environment in which
scholarship can thrive and analytical
thinking can develop. To accomplish
such difficult tasks, teachers must be
capable of analysis and synthesis
themselves. A complex teacher education must do its part to contribute to
such abilities. Teacher educators must
be aware of the ways in which positivist epistemology structures the
school in a way that subverts such
abilities. Teachers must be prepared
for the assault on their psyches that
they will face in schools marked by
prespecified objectives, top-down
standards, and strict accountability
based on standardized posttests.

Analysis, synthesis, interpretation,
research skills, and epistemological
awareness are the martial arts for the
twenty-first-century teacher. Given
the threat against teacher conceptualization and teacher control presented
by the positivist structure of many
technical standards–driven schools,
educators need black belts. Teachers
so equipped will be able to take data,
concepts, methods of knowledge pro-

duction, and social and pedagogical
theories and adjust them to the demands of diverse learning situations.
Such teachers by necessity must be
committed to independent democratic
thinking rather than to an unanalyzed
allegiance to positivistic, prespecified
practices. Teacher education that promotes such professionalism emphasizes the type of contextual studies
that aids teachers in their quest to formulate questions of purpose. When
they are able to formulate and con-
template such questions, teachers are
ready to assume a larger role in redefining the nature and spirit of what
an educator does. Empowered by such
abilities, they are now ready to help
change the conditions under which
they work. These intellectually capable, self-directed, empowered teachers
will create a workplace in which scholarly work is nurtured and teacher control of the conceptualization of their
own teaching is jealously guarded. Incompetent and authoritarian administrators will not survive very long as
leaders of such a competent and self-
confident teaching force that understands the dangers of positivistic technical standards.

Teachers armed with historical and
epistemological understandings will
ask good questions of education. They
will be seekers of patterns, revealers of
hidden agendas and ideologies, and
agents of educational progress. Such
educators will demand modes of
teacher evaluation that go beyond assessment of classroom cleanliness, order, and student test scores. First, the
new evaluation will demand evaluators

who themselves possess the aforementioned analytical skills; second, it will respect and appreciate the potential diversity of individual teacher goals, while it facilitates the attempts of teachers to work out the relationship between curricular conception and execution; and third, it will patiently observe and aid the efforts of educators to glean meaning from the plethora of elements that continually shapes and reshapes a learning environment (Mathison, 2000).

Teachers who are good question generators and question askers will hold subject-matter knowledge up to creative critical inquiry. Teachers in higher education, though often possessing superior command of a body of information, sometimes fail their students as they fail to question the significance of certain knowledge in the overall education of an individual. The study of education promoted in an epistemology of complexity concerns itself with questions about the meaning of the knowledge of a discipline, its connection with the lived world, its role in education, its proper place in a course of study, and its contextual relationship to the lives of the students (Cadenhead, 1985).

As standards of complexity view teaching as a critical scholarly activity, educators automatically begin to think of such questions. Teacher education operating in the epistemological zone of complexity may choose to examine the great teachers of the past, focusing on the relationship between educational purpose and pedagogical methods. As individuals note the diversity of methods and purposes utilized by successful teachers throughout history, they begin to recognize the positivistic attempt to foist on teachers rationalized, predetermined, standardized methods applicable in all circumstances as an unfortunate expression of a rationalized bureaucracy. Such standardization serves the ideology of deskilling and reductionism as it attempts to control teachers by specifying instructional behaviors and rendering them measurable. Thus, accountability is facilitated and quality is undermined.

Teachers who are empowered by their ability to analyze and synthesize are free to choose pedagogical methods that are based on their own knowledge production, consistent with their own epistemological beliefs, compatible with their own temperaments, and contextually sensitive to their students' needs. They are not obliged to follow a manual written by someone else; they are capable of determining their own guidelines. There is no finite quality of good methods; there are as many methods as there are imaginative teachers to think of creative ways of approaching, producing, and delivering information. An understanding of an epistemology of complexity alerts teachers to their limitless options. It frees them to consider possibilities congruent with informed notions about ideal classrooms. An epistemology of complexity provides teachers the metaperspective that enables them to talk about the language, discursive location, and ideological assumptions of a body of knowledge. In this way, it takes teachers and students to a social and cognitive place where few educational experiences can go. Standards of complexity push the frontiers of learning and human possibility.

A rigorous, complex teacher education takes these epistemological understandings to rethink the nature of the knowledge acquired in the classroom, how it was presented, and the ways it was learned. Was it presented unproblematically as truth? Were alternate interpretations provided? Were the values implicit in the information exposed? What were the epistemological assumptions of the teacher? What were the student's epistemological assumptions now that you understand what epistemology is? With these understandings, teachers become scholars who move to a new level of consciousness. They see pedagogical and ideological features of schooling that were previously invisible. With this new knowledge and set of conceptual understandings, they are prepared to turn the rigor and value of their teachings up a couple of notches. They now have the ability to connect their lessons to the lived worlds of their students and to engage them in a rigorous exploration of themselves, the world, and their relation to it. This is no simple task.

Constructing an Epistemology of Complexity

To escape from the TV-dinner pedagogies and the covert ideological distortions of technical standards while at the same time pushing for new under-standings and life-changing modes of teaching, it is important to understand an epistemology of complexity. In this context, we can construct our own democratic system of education and imprint our creative stamp on professional practice. In that spirit, the following is a delineation of a democratic transformative epistemology that recognizes the complexity of the lived world and the teaching act. To be a scholarly researcher and knowledge worker who is capable of creating rigorous schools that offer quality education for everyone regardless of race, ethnicity, or economic background, this epistemological understanding is basic.

Knowledge Is Socially Constructed

What we designate as knowledge is complex and always problematic. Social knowledge, knowledge about humans, and knowledge produced about education are all shaped by a variety of forces—they are always constructed by human beings. The angle from which an entity is seen, the values of the researcher that shape the questions he or she asks about it, and what the researcher considers important are all factors in the *construction* of knowledge about the phenomenon in question. Any knowledge presumes an epistemological stance. Most of the time, knowledge producers don't even know their own epistemological stance. Such a lack of consciousness exerts a dramatic effect not only on the nature of knowledge production but also on how the social, physical, and educational spheres operate. Positivist educators do not understand the epistemological assumptions they are making. As democratic educators, it is our charge to understand our own and other people's epistemological stance, to understand how the knowledge we come into contact with has been constructed. Such an understanding changes the way we see the world around us, as we begin to understand the problems and limitations of what is known.

Thus, if knowledge is socially constructed, then democratic educators are interested in the nature and effects of that construction. If knowledge about the world does not just exist "out there," waiting to be discovered, but is more of a construction of human minds, then democratic educators want to understand that process. This constructivist epistemological view holds profound implications for knowledge production and teaching in that democratic teachers seek no final perspective on a topic—they know different constructions of events will continue to be produced as times and thus perspectives change. Knowledge is always in process, always subject to new perspectives molded by social and historical change. Thus, constructivist teachers, for example, are very suspicious of those who would offer the "final truth" or the "last word" on the Mexican War or the role of African Americans in U.S. history. In this same context, science teachers understand that after Albert Einstein our view of the nature of gravity was dramatically different.

The epistemological crisis I referenced earlier in this essay is real. Many researchers and educators are horrified by the constructivist contention that findings in the sciences depend on the research methods employed. The uniqueness of the information obtained from different approaches to research has led to the existence of separate bodies of knowledge. When the same event or phenomenon is studied by a variety of methods, the information produced has little covariation. This means that researchers using different methods share so little common ground that they have no way to relate their diverse findings.

Understanding that knowledge is a social construction, democratic teachers come to realize that their job is much more complex than once perceived. Whose knowledge do we teach? Positivistic knowledge? Socially constructed knowledge? Neither? Both? Why or on what basis do we write our educational standards and choose our curriculum? These are not simple questions, but if educators are to rise above a deskilled status, then they must deal with them. In the domain of educational psychology, for example, consider how this dynamic plays out. When a specific intelligence test is examined by a complexity-grounded sociologist and a psychometrician (a psychologist who statistically measures different aspects of cognitive functions), divergent constructions of the test's use and meaning emerge. To the sociologist who assumes the value of an epistemology of complexity, the test reflects an unexamined set of socioeconomic and cultural assumptions about the nature of intelligence. To the psychometrician, the test may suffer from internal inconsistency—that is, its rank ordering of individuals relative to their intelligence differs significantly from other intelligence tests. Thus, from the psychometrician's perspective, it is a flawed instrument. The point, of course, is that depending upon the paradigm (the model used for making sense of a body of knowledge), our views of this test may vary widely. A rigorous education must understand these epistemological dynamics.

Consciousness Is a Social Construction

This constructivist theme runs throughout our epistemology of complexity. As with knowledge, human consciousness is not something that exists independently of the world. Our consciousness, identity, self-concept, and view of our relationship to the world and other people are shaped by the culture in which we live, our historical era, our family, our peer group, and the information with which we come into contact. In part, we are what we know. For example, if, as Tom Puk (1994) argues, students are taught a false history, a view of the past that never existed, then our understanding of knowledge as a social construction assumes even more importance. Our study of epistemology and knowledge production takes on (in the language of philosophy) ontological dimensions

(ontology is the branch of philosophy that studies the nature of being, what it means to be human). If we are what we know, then our very being is shaped by these epistemological issues. In my opinion, that makes them more than worthy of study.

Although we appear to one another as single, bounded identities, an epistemology of complexity maintains that we humans are socially superabsorbent—like humanoid Husky paper towels. This simply means that our consciousness is shaped by that with which we come into contact. Again, we are more complex social beings than the Cartesians imagined. In hyperreality, we are all part TV game-show host, evangelist, interviewee in a breakfast cereal commercial, cop or criminal, and local news anchor. All personalities are latent and, given the right stimuli, are ready to come alive. Thus, the boundaries of individualism begin to fade like the chalk lines of a late inning batter's box. As they do, we become more aware of a critical constructivism's (the term is used here to denote a consciousness of the effects of power) notion of the social construction of the individual. Indeed, we even begin to recognize the limitations of middle-class notions of individualism. In the name of individualism, we are taught a "me-first" perspective on self-gratification that renders us vulnerable to appeals such as "I believe in equality; everyone gets a tax cut—rich or poor!" This emphasis on self-gratification trivializes critical conceptions of citizenship, friendship, and sexual relationships, as each becomes something designed to get what we want. Of course, technical standards use testing not only as a sound way of assessing the value of education, but also as a means of motivating our individualistic students. As we gain an awareness of the construction of our consciousness, maybe it becomes possible to critically reconstruct our understanding of the nature of individualism and interdependence.

Always concerned with power, this epistemology of complexity studies the exaggerated role it plays in the social construction of consciousness. Teachers employing the democratic system of meaning analyze their own and help students analyze their consciousness constructions, especially around the ways race, class, gender, and religious dimensions of power contribute to the process. Novices in this context would explore the historical purposes of schooling and how these purposes were manifested in their own school lives and their own consciousness constructions. In other words, an epistemology of complexity would transform teacher education into an intense sociopsychological and cultural analysis of the effects of schooling. The ways that women and men construct their consciousnesses and the role that education plays in that process would become a guiding concern of college and university teacher education and school and community consortiums—an innovation that would necessitate interdisciplinary connections and research alliances across universities, school districts, and local communities.

Democratic teachers use this epistemological understanding of consciousness construction to shape the purposes of their teaching and self-explorations. In this context, such teachers seek a variety of methods to heighten individual awareness. Edmund Husserl, the great phenomenologist (phenomenology is concerned with the study of consciousness, as it attempts to grasp the ways individuals make meaning among themselves and other people), delineated research methods designed to facilitate understanding of the structure of consciousness and its relation to the world. One aspect of this method, bracketing, involves consciously setting aside everyday, accepted assumptions about one's immediate perceptions (Chamberlin, 1974; Schwandt, 2000). Once this bracketing of assumptions takes place, the individual examines and makes explicit all the meanings that were hidden in initial perceptions. In this way, individual awareness is heightened as previously hidden assumptions are revealed. The individual thus finds himself or herself more in touch with the values, political forces, fears, and associations that unconsciously direct his or her actions. Continued analysis of such factors may uncover their origins, thus contributing to greater self-understanding and self-knowledge. The foundations of the phenomenological method must rest on a self-knowledge that, once gained, allows teachers and students to turn their focus outward to more textured understandings of the interior experiences of others. Thus, we become more sensitive to the ways consciousness is socially constructed. We begin to understand the impact certain forms of education make on individuals and groups of students. In this way, the scholarly rigor of the educational enterprise is intensified.

Power Plays an Exaggerated Role in Shaping the Production of "Truth," of Constructing Our Consciousness

An epistemology of complexity understands that there is simply no such thing as neutral or unpoliticized knowledge, no matter what advocates of technical standards may argue. In its social construction, knowledge is shaped by the dynamics of power. Who's producing it and for what purposes? In the construction of our consciousness, power plays an exaggerated role in the process as one must hold power to produce certified public knowledge. Epistemologically aware educators reject the reductionistic notion of politically neutral research into social phenomena, arguing that such a stance constitutes a form of ideological mystification—that is, an attempt to hide the political interests of educational practice and the research about it. For example, when Lynne Cheney as the head of the National Endowment of the Humanities fought against the history standards developed by professional historical associations, she charged them with a politicization of history education. How could they produce such a biased curriculum, she asserted, mentioning, for example, Harriet Tubman more than

Nathan Hale? As with most advocates of technical standards, she put forth her content standards as politically neutral. If researchers fail to keep the normative, political, or value dimension of educational research in mind, the research they produce and the ends to which it is applied will simply serve to reproduce hegemonic social relations—in Cheney's case the exclusion of African Americans from the curriculum. Thus, from a complex epistemological perspective, an awareness of the value orientation of research is essential, as it brings to consciousness the fundamental embodiments of power that move social and educational events (Soltis, 1984; Kincheloe and Steinberg, 1997).

Beloved emancipatory educator Myles Horton put this power-related concept so simply in his conversation with Paulo Freire in 1990:

> When I first started thinking about the relationship of learning and social change, it had nothing to do with Highlander [the Highlander education center in Tennessee]. It was years earlier when I was debating with myself this whole idea of neutrality. Academicians, politicians, all the people that are supposed to be guiding this country say you've got to be neutral. As soon as I started looking at that word *neutral* and what it meant, it became very obvious to me there can be no such thing as neutrality. It's a code word for the existing system. It has nothing to do with anything but agreeing to what is and will always be—that's what neutrality is. *Neutrality is just following the crowd.*

Neutrality is just being what the system asks us to be. Neutrality, in other words, was an immoral act. I was thinking in religious terms then. It was to me a refusal to oppose injustice or to take sides that are unpopular. It's an excuse, in other words. So I discarded the word neutrality before I even started thinking much about educational ideas. Of course, when I got more into thinking about educational ideas and about changing society, it became more and more obvious that you've got to take sides. You need to know why you take sides; you should be able to justify it. (Horton and Freire, 1990, 171)

Thomas Popkewitz (1981) maintains that educational research expresses the researcher's interests in at least two important ways:

1. The research we undertake reflects our view of sociopolitical values. Our research allows us to reconcile what we see as social contradiction and to ponder the consequences of the actions of institutions. For example, we may see a class-stratified society beset by problems resulting from the existence of a so-called permanent underclass. We want to know how the arrangement of educational institutions affects this situation. Our research questions and the manner in which we approach our study have been shaped by our value orientations.
2. Since scientific research (especially quantitative research) holds such a high status in the society,

many individuals promote the belief that educational problems can be solved only through the application of rigorous science. Thus, solutions that emerge from community participation and democratic negotiation are dismissed—society has come to rely on the cult of the expert, those social scientists with precise, dispassionate answers to technical problems.

When researchers fail to note the existence of this omnipresent value dimension, Kenneth Howe (1985) contends, unpleasant outcomes typically result:

1. The research will be useless as information that informs practical action. Value judgments are inseparable from educational descriptions because of the relationship between educational research and educational practice. If researchers do not allow values to serve as a link between research and practice, educational inquiry will be irrelevant to what teachers and administrators actually do. In other words, the relationship between what we know and how we act upon the knowledge is problematic. Values inform not only what we claim to know but the actions that we take as a result of the knowledge as well.
2. Value-free research will be insufficient. If research in the field is not grounded upon explicitly

stated values that are open to evaluation, little benefit will ever be derived from such research. Thus, energy and resources will have been wasted.

3. Value-free research holds the potential to produce harmful results. When research purports to be value free but covertly promotes specific values, various groups and individuals are rendered quite vulnerable. Students who are culturally different may be labeled emotionally disturbed, young girls and boys who attempt to transcend gender restrictions may be seen as maladjusted, or thoughtful young people with intelligent questions about social convention may be labeled as troublemakers. Power's ability to dominate hides in the shadows of knowledge producers' claim to neutrality and objectivity.

Obviously, values in social knowledge production affect human beings in very concrete ways. If the values of research are typically hidden, then the justifications for the educational politics that are based on them are also concealed. When such restrictions are out of sight, teachers have only a restricted view of why they do the things that they do. An analysis of the historical forces that have structured values is an integral part of a democratic education. As we know, research is never a neutral means to a particular end. Research and its methodology grow out of the values of a particular worldview.

This particular worldview, this paradigm, determines what constitutes legitimate research or an acceptable way of thinking. Even though positivistic, instrumentally rational research models have been challenged in some academic settings, they still dominate the mind-sets of many elementary and secondary schools. Emerging from business and military sources, contemporary manifestations of positivistic research inject the values of business management and the military into the life of the school. Here is where phenomenological, semiotic, and ethnographic forms of research become so important to the democratic teacher. They provide the tools with which we reveal the forces that make schools what they are, that tacitly construct the goals of education (Orteza, 1988; Cherryholmes, 1988).

Why do social and educational researchers use particular words, metaphors, and models when they design their inquiry, interpret it, and suggest policies based on it? Their research language reflects the effects of the influence of power in the larger society. Power, as Michel Foucault has argued, has served to censor, exclude, block, and repress like a great superego; but, he continues, it also serves to produce knowledge, creating effects at the level of consciousness construction. As a censor in educational research, power serves to limit what constitutes a legitimate question, excluding "dangerous" investigations such as explorations of how class factors affect student performances in school. As a producer in social and educational research, power serves to reward particular ways of seeing and particular activities. For example, educational researchers who desire success in the field learn and follow particular research norms that allow them the rewards of funded grants and promotions based on scholarly productivity. The way different research orientations draw boundaries between what is acceptable and what is not constitutes the ideological dimension of the act of inquiry (Cherryholmes, 1988). Here, power is at work, promoting particular views of educational excellence and educational failure—often around race and class demarcations.

As democratic teachers, we make a mistake when we assume that this power is always consciously exercised by a cabal of conspirators seeking to control the educational world. Much of the time, the ideological construction of consciousness emanating from sources of power does not take place at the level of conscious intention. For example, positivistic educational researchers most of the time do not seek to design research that results in the perpetuation of business and military values in school practices. School administrators do not typically seek to use educational research that represses ethical considerations and questions of justice in their efforts to run their schools. And teachers most of the time certainly do not consciously attempt to suppress their students' ability to think at a more critical level, nor do they try to punish the underprivileged or reward the privileged. But all of these unfortunate things happen, and

most of the time we have no clue why. We don't catch on because we don't understand the subtle dimensions of power reproduction, that is, how codes, symbols, and signs subtly construct our worldviews. As teachers who are researchers, we begin to see how educational research produced by such subtle forces legitimizes particular values and delegitimizes others, and we begin to expose the false neutrality of technical standards and the ways particular students are hurt by this erasure of power interests.

Emphasis on Consciousness Even Though It Is Hard to Measure Empirically: William Pinar's Currere

This point in our delineation of an epistemology of complexity is an extension of the above subsection "Consciousness Is a Social Construction." We begin with this assumption and extend it by arguing that even though consciousness does not lend itself to positivistic quantitative measurement, it still is the most important domain in the educational process. The behaviorist psychologist B.F. Skinner was so disturbed by the positivistic immeasurability of consciousness that he simply proclaimed that it didn't exist. Skinner was the perfect example of a modernist positivist, and his pronouncement about consciousness is quite revealing for democratic teachers guided by standards of complexity: even though consciousness is the domain that may best express our humanness, if it didn't lend itself to positivist methods then it was nonexistent. Skinner's pronouncement once again illustrates the way the world is socially constructed by the hidden power of our epistemological assumptions. The existence of consciousness was not as important in Skinner's formulation as the framework he used to understand reality.

Consciousness is obviously an essential part of what it means to be human, many analysts, including the phenomenolgists, have argued, and should be studied if we are ever to gain significant insight into the affairs of human beings. However, the study of consciousness, phenomenologists warn, is limited by two important factors: (1) consciousness is not an object that is similar to the other objects of nature; and (2) there are aspects of consciousness that cannot be studied via traditional quantitative methods of science. Ever fascinated with the content of elusive consciousness, therefore, phenomenologists cannot be concerned with the empirical question of what is or is not real. They simply begin with the nature of consciousness—whatever that nature might be—as significant data to be studied. At the very least, the study of human consciousness is different from the study of nature in that humans—unlike rocks, acids, and atoms—are meaning-making entities. This meaning-making or thinking process will shape humans' behavior in ways that differentiate people from rocks. If you kick a rock, for example, you know pretty well how it will react. Kicking a human, however, will elicit a wide variety of actions depending on the human kicked and the context in which

he or she is kicked. Such a human response does not lend itself to precise measurement and predictability.

Phenomenology attempts to render problematic all presuppositions about the nature of its own activity, the object being investigated, and the method appropriate to this kind of inquiry (Husserl, 1970). The attempt to rid oneself of as many presuppositions as possible grants phenomenology the prospect of unmasking hidden assumptions about the nature of reality. Phenomenologists also attempt to view consciousness as intentional, meaning that it is directed toward a specific object. Another way of expressing this thought is that consciousness is consciousness of something. Thus, phenomenologists think that it is absurd to divide reality (or the research process) into subjects and objects. The two cannot be separated, and the attempt to do so distorts reality (Steward and Mickunas, 1974; Schwandt, 2000).

Thus, an important concept about knowledge production that holds profound implications for the scholarly insights of complex educators emerges in this context. As these educators attempt to evaluate, produce, and teach information, they begin to differentiate between research that does and does not understand the special status of human consciousness and the epistemological insights it necessitates. Democratic teachers operating in the zone of complexity are suspicious of data that are produced by experts who don't grasp the difference between human beings and sedimentary rocks.

They are also suspicious of the content standards grounded in such information. Phenomenology may provide one of the best methodological pathways for educators to grasp the specifics of this epistemological problem. It is obsessed with the effort to discern the meaning individuals ascribe to their lived worlds. Phenomenological understanding involves putting oneself in place of another person and attempting to re-create his or her feelings in oneself. Using this empathetic function, phenomenology provides a much thicker, deeper, and useful form of social knowledge than the Cartesian attempt to record the frequency of particular behaviors.

It is easy to see the impact of phenomenology on modes of research such as ethnography. When researchers ask not about the absolute meaning of a work of art but instead of its meaning for a certain individual or a group, they move research in new directions. The qualitative knowledge that emerges when researchers ask about and attempt to interpret the meanings that particular persons give to particular phenomena allows us new understandings and unique perspectives on social events and the human beings who participate in them. The human realm of intersubjective meaning becomes accessible in a way never imagined by positivistic researchers, as scholars interrogate the conventions, forms, and codes of everyday life (J. Smith, 1983; Donmoyer, 1985; Soltis, 1984; Denzin and Lincoln, 2000; Kincheloe and McLaren, 2000).

Phenomenologically produced understanding of the way individuals construe their world and their place in it is one way in which intersubjective knowledge leads us to new dimensions of seeing social experience. In educational inquiry, such ways of seeing allow educators to understand how teachers and students give meaning to their lived worlds in light of social and cultural forms that they reflect and help produce. Indeed, such forms of inquiry facilitate our understanding of the often hidden and always ambiguous process by which education initiates us into our culture (Carspecken, 1996, 1999). Positivism and the technical content standards it justifies are totally uninterested in these dynamics. "Why should we bother with phenome-what-ya-may-call-it? All we need to do is teach students the truth."

Phenomenology is a qualitative alternative to the epistemology of positivism. It presents in a sense a starting point for a democratic teacher in standards of complexity to move beyond the positivistic, reductionistic mindset that too often runs the schools, perpetuates teacher deskilling, and makes schools bad workplaces. Using our democratic system of meaning and its concern with understanding and acting justly in the sociopolitical world, we embrace a phenomenology of complexity that helps us abandon the role of teacher as a deskilled implementer of administrative policy; no longer do we see research as a part of a process of explaining, controlling, and predicting. Phenomenology teaches us that we cannot understand an educational act without understanding the framework, the context within which teachers, students, and administrators give meaning to their thoughts, feelings, and actions. Our *critical* phenomenology takes us one step *beyond* traditional conceptions of phenomenology by adding our concern with power to the mix. We must question the power relations, the ideological forces that shape that framework, the context that helps construct our thoughts, feelings, and actions (Fowler, 1984; Wilson, 1977; Kincheloe and McLaren, 2000). We are comfortable on this difficult terrain because ours is an epistemology that understands and seeks to deal with the complexity of the world.

Phenomenology teaches scholarly teachers to abandon positivistic, deductive devices such as prior hypothesis formation that restricts researchers by directing their attention to often irrelevant variables. As with qualitative forms of research in general, the focus of our study in phenomenology emerges as the inquiry progresses. We focus on the perceptions of individuals, seeking the insider's perspective. Of course, at the critical level, we search for the various ways this perspective is constructed by larger social forces. To the critical phenomenologist, the most influential reality of the many realities with which humans must deal is human perception. This reality is more important than any so-called objective reality because people act on what they perceive—perceptions have consequences, they move events, they shape lives. Consider how these ideas affect teaching and knowl-

edge work, for example. While the positivist seeks objective, factual, verifiable portrayals of reality, phenomenologists will seek to understand the participants' comprehension of what is happening and how such perceptions affect their lives. Because they hold such different goals, research data derived via the two approaches will present quite different perspectives on the world, the school (Fetterman, 1988). They will construct profoundly different curricula. Which one will you teach? I don't think a teacher can stay neutral here.

Certainly, one of the most important thinkers of the late twentieth and early twenty-first centuries about these issues is educator William Pinar. His work in this epistemological domain is essential knowledge for democratic teachers. In his attempt to develop a practical method of analyzing the educational experience of the individual, Pinar takes this phenomenological orientation and fuses it with psychoanalysis and aesthetics. He calls his analytical form *currere* (the Latin root of the word *curriculum*, meaning the investigation of the nature of the individual experience of the public). We are returned once again to the inner psychological world (the *Lebenswelt*) and to its relationship to the educational experience. A traditional criticism of much of the theoretical work in education is that it is not connected with the everyday experiences of teachers and students. Pinar's use of the concept of *currere* helps bring about the synthesis of theorizing and *Lebenswelt* with all the benefits that are to be accrued from such a fusion (Pinar, 1975, 1994, 1999).

Pinar claims that in *currere*-based research and teaching, meaning is typically derived from the analysis of the relationship between signs and experience. Taking his cue from Maxine Greene (1975), Pinar contends that the quest for an understanding of experience impels researchers to tap their own subjectivity so that common sense may be transcended—that is, we must go beyond what we take for granted. As knowledge workers in schools, we must ask questions such as: What is involved in moving beyond the commonsense world? How does one initiate the process? What possible benefits are to be derived? Are there examples of other individuals who have accomplished such a complex move, and what did they gain? How do such attempts affect what we know in education? It is through such questions that we approach the *Lebenswelt*, or, in Pinar's words, "that realm of the *Lebenswelt* associated with *currere*" (Pinar, 1975, 396).

As we engage in this phenomenological bracketing of experience in our own lives, Pinar argues that we are better prepared as researchers and teachers to apprehend the contents of consciousness as they appear to us in educational contexts. The liberation that results involves a freedom from modes of perception that reflect cultural conditioning and result in inauthentic and counterdemocratic behavior. We must loosen our identification with the contents of consciousness so that we gain some critical distance from them—a metaperspective. From our new vantage point, we may be able to see those psychic realms that are formed by conditioning and unconscious adherence to repressive social convention. Using *currere*, teachers in the complexity zone demystify the ideological construction of their own and their students' consciousnesses. Empowered with this ability, teachers in schools shaped by standards of complexity are able to move beyond pseudoneutrality and help students examine and participate in the great issues of our time.

Once we have embarked on our quest to understand *currere*, Pinar tells us, we will uncover a great diversity of formats and sources. Teachers will gain great insight into the consciousnesses of themselves and their students. The educational *Lebenswelt* comes in a variety of packages—one package may contain historical information, another the insights of free association, another the contemplations of specific literary passages, and still another ostensibly insignificant slices of school life. Both cognitive and intuitive insights (or a creative synthesis of the two) will inform our perception of *currere*.

At first, Pinar concludes, the information derived from our attempt to examine *currere* may be idiosyncratic. Eventually, however, our examinations will uncover aspects of a collective or transpersonal realm of educational experience. In other words, once we transcend the unique details of an individual's biography, we may unlock the doors to a secret room where fundamental structures of human experience have been hidden from view. Such structures may, as phenomenologists have anticipated (Merleau-Ponty, 1962), appear very different when viewed at the stratum of individual personality but may be very similar when analyzed at the level of their roots. The understanding of these basic structures and their relationship to the sociopolitical world and thus their impact on education may be one of the most important outcomes of phenomenological research applied to the educational *Lebenswelt* (Pinar, 1975, 1994; Pinar et al., 1995). Instead of just throwing out fragments of data and hoping students commit them to memory, teachers using *currere* in standards of complexity help students make meanings that are connected to their individual lives. Education can never be the same.

Concern with Logic and Emotion and Feeling in the Process of Knowing: The Importance of Empathy

With a little reflection, we realize that in our everyday life we often speak of different epistemologies, different ways of knowing, without even thinking about it. We all have some idea of a positivist epistemology when we say that science proves that nicotine causes cancer in lab rats. But most of us make counter-Cartesian epistemological knowledge claims as well. Consider for instance: "I knew when I met him that he couldn't be trusted"—intuitive knowing; "My heart told me I loved her"—emotional knowing; "My

'gay-dar' went off the screen when she walked in the room"—empathetic knowing; "I know there is more to life than meets the eye. I plan to enjoy the afterlife immensely"—spiritual knowing; "Don't tell me there's no God. I know Jesus is my personal savior"—divine knowing; "If I have to explain rap music to you, you'll never understand it"—cultural knowing. An epistemology of complexity recognizes that there are many ways of knowing, some more appropriate in particular situations than others. For example, I did not use a positivistic way of knowing to discern whether or not to marry my wife, Shirley. I relied much more on an emotional form of knowledge, a feeling. If I ever have to have my appendix removed, I hope my surgeon uses a different epistemological perspective as she decides where to make her incision—you get the idea. The epistemological concept I want to get across here is that both logical and emotional ways of knowing are important in schools shaped by standards of complexity. I will lay out how educators can use both epistemological orientations, sometimes together, sometimes separately, for emancipatory effect.

Feminist educator Madeline Grumet (1988) extends our understanding of the epistemologically complex attempt to transcend sole reliance of logic (logocentrism) by connecting with an epistemology of the body, of feeling. Science, she argues, has been emeshed in a male-dominated snare of logical abstraction. Grumet has sought new methods of inquiry that are capable of drawing the body and feeling into the public conversation about education. Making use of qualitative research methodologies such as history, theater, autobiography, and phenomenology, she confronts androcentric abstraction with the uncertainty, specificity, and contradiction of the private, the corporeal, the feminine. From the perspective of the guardians of the positivistic tradition, such epistemological confrontations constitute overt subversion. After exposure to such concepts, inquiry can no longer be viewed as a cold, rational process. As feeling, empathy, and the body are injected into the research and teaching process, as the distinction between knower and known is blurred, as truth is viewed as a *process* of construction in which knowers play an active role, passion is injected into inquiry. Democratic teachers see themselves as passionate scholars who connect themselves emotionally to that which they are seeking to know, understand, and teach.

Several decades ago, Michael Polanyi wrote about personal knowledge—that is, a way of knowing that involves the passionate participation of the knower in the act of knowing. Guided by such notions, complex educators embrace a passionate scholarship, a reconceptualized science that is grounded upon and motivated by our values and solidarities (Belecky et al., 1986). Passionate knowers use the self as an instrument of understanding, searching, as Madeline Grumet has, for new methods to sophisticate the way the self is used in research. Søren

Kierkegaard anticipated this notion of feminist passion, arguing in the first half of the nineteenth century that there *is* an intimate connection between commitment and knowing. Subjectivity, he maintained, is not simply arbitrary; instead, it reflects the most profound connection between an individual thinker and the world.

As inquirers grow passionate about what they know, they develop a deeper relationship with themselves. Such a relationship produces a self-knowledge that initiates a synergistic cycle—a cycle that grants them more insight into the issue being investigated. Soon, Kierkegaard argued, a form of personal knowledge is developed that orients the mind to see social life as more than a set of fixed laws. Social life is better characterized as a process of being, a dialectic where the knower's personal participation in events and the emotional insight gained from such participation move us to a new dimension of knowing. Not only did Kierkegaard anticipate the concept of passionate knowing and Polanyi's personal knowledge, but he also foreshadowed a post-Piagetian, postformal mode of thinking; produced knowledge; and developed curricula that ground our notion of a rigorous education (Reinharz, 1979; Kincheloe, Steinberg, and Villaverde, 1999).

Another precursor of the notion of passionate scholarship that shapes our rigorous education (and should serve to humble Eurocentric academicians) concerns the ways that indigenous peoples have defined knowing. Note the similarities of Afrocentric and

American Indian ways of knowing with the counterpositivistic perspectives of Kierkegaard, Polanyi, and advocates of an epistemology of complexity. To such peoples, reality has never been dichotomized into spiritual and material segments. Self-knowledge lays the foundation for all knowledge in the African and Native American epistemologies. Great importance has traditionally been placed on interpersonal relationships (solidarity), and a connected logic has moved these traditions to appreciate the continuum of spirit and matter, individual and world.

Indeed, indigenous ways of knowing and the European positivistic tradition come into direct conflict over the epistemological issues of mind and body, individuals and nature, self and other, spirit and matter, and knower and known—a conflict that has generated serious historical consequences. It is only in the past thirty years that some Eurocentric people have come to recognize the epistemological sophistication of indigenous ways of seeing that discern a unity in all things and a connected spiritual energy embedded in both human and natural elements. Thus, that deemed primitive by traditional Western scholars becomes, from the perspective of democratic teachers, a valuable source of insight into our attempt to extend an emancipatory education (Myers, 1987; Nyang and Vandi, 1980; Semali and Kincheloe, 1999).

The ability to create a new form of thinking that brings together logic and emotion and the human capacity for empathy is dependent on our understanding of the forces that shape the self—a theme that emerges time and again in our quest for a democratic pedagogy and rigorous education. Knowledge of self allows researchers to understand how social forces and research conventions shape their definitions of knowledge, of inquiry, of effective educational practice. Knowledge of the self allows them the consciousness to choose between epistemologies that depersonalize the process of knowing in hopes of gaining certainty and producing pure objective knowledge and research orientations that assert that since the mind of the observer is always involved, it should be utilized as a valuable tool. Humans possess a tacit knowledge that can be drawn upon to make sense of social and educational situations. Such tacit, intuitive knowledge guides researchers as they conduct interviews, make observations, document analyses, and so on. A primary purpose of the democratic form of knowledge work is to connect teachers to the nature and formation of such tacit knowing and, in turn, to help them learn how to employ it for maximum benefit.

Can't Separate Knower from Known—Thus, the Questions the Knower Asks Shape What Can Be Known

Throughout this discussion of an epistemology of complexity and what it means for democratic teachers, I have alluded to the inseparability of the knower and the known. This point is a brief extension of this basic epistemological understanding and its highlighting of the profound importance of question formulation in shaping the knowledge we produce. Simply put, there is no knowledge without a knower. As a living being, a perceiving instrument, the *perspective* of the knowledge producer must be granted the same seriousness of attention as is typically accorded the design of research, the research methods in traditional forms of inquiry (Lowe, 1982; Gordon, Miller, and Rollock, 1990). This understanding should be a central feature of every rigorous classroom.

Like knowledge, the knower also belongs to a particular, ever changing historical world. The human being as a part of history is a reflective subject, meaning, an entity who is conscious of the constant interaction between humans and their world. Such a critically conscious knowledge worker–teacher recognizes that all knowledge is a fusion of subject and object. In other words, the knower personally participates in all acts of understanding. Moreover, the world in general, the educational world in particular, is not an objective structure, but a constructed, dynamic interaction of men and women organized and shaped by their race, class, gender, and countless other features. Thus, it is impossible from the perspective of an epistemology of complexity to conceive knowledge without thinking of the knower (Reinharz, 1979; Lowe, 1982).

This separation of the knower and the known is a cardinal tenet of the positivist epistemology and the educational standards it supports. The impact of this "way of seeing" on the theory and practice of Western science and education has been profound. As discussed elsewhere in the encyclopedia, René Descartes's analytical method of reasoning, often termed *reductionism*, has formed the foundation of modern scientific research. Cartesian reductionism asserts that all aspects of complex phenomena can be best appreciated by reducing them to their constituent parts and then piecing these elements together according to causal laws (Mahoney and Lyddon, 1988). This is the opposite of an epistemology of complexity.

The educational implications of this epistemological understanding are compelling. In particular, such an epistemological awareness highlights the importance of the questions an educator might ask. What knowledge is produced in the teaching domains depends on the questions asked about the topics at hand. Democratic educators engage themselves and their students in the process of revealing the questions and the values that generate them that stand in the shadows of all data. This ability is necessary to the formulation of a complex, rigorous, and democratic education as it helps unlock the secrets to why a curriculum contains this information and not other types of knowledge.

Such an epistemological analysis forces us to move beyond positivism's concern with simply answering unanalyzed questions or solving prearranged, structured problems. This question-formulating, problem-posing stage, Albert Einstein argued, is more important than the answer to the question or the solution to the problem. Critical democratic teachers are question analysts and problem posers. When epistemologically naive teachers set up a problem, they select and name those things they will notice. Thus, questioning is a form of world making—how we select the problems and construct our worlds is based on the values we employ. Without an epistemological consciousness, teachers and administrators learn how to construct schools but not how to determine what types of schools to construct. In other words, teachers, school leaders, and teacher educators need to realize that school and classroom problems are not generic or innate. They are constructed and uncovered by insightful educators who possess the ability to ask questions never before asked, questions that lead to innovations that promote student insight, sophisticated thinking, and social justice (Schon, 1987; Ponzio, 1985).

If the genius of, say, an Einstein revolved around his ability to see problems in the physical universe that no one else had ever seen, then the genius of a teacher in standards of complexity revolves around his or her ability to see physical, psychological, social, and educational problems that no one else has ever seen (Kincheloe, Steinberg, and Tippins, 1999). The application of such skills moves education to a level unimagined by teachers trapped within the positivistic tradition. Not only is such an educational orientation grounded in a democratic conception of teacher empowerment, but it also serves to expose previously hidden forces that shape the consequences of the educational process. It is a testimony to what can happen, what can be revealed, when teachers transcend the limitations of positivistic definitions of research and explore the relationships between the knower and the known.

With these understandings in mind, the very source of the knowledge found in classroom texts and curriculum guides involves the asking of value-laden questions. Julie Ellis (1998) writes that in her classroom, she assigns interpretive exercises where students attempt to make sense of the texts they have encountered in class. In this context, she asks students to identify the questions that drive their interpretations and the origins of such inquiries. In this way, students can understand that questions produce knowledge, values produce questions, and that one's location in the web of reality produces the values we hold. Such recognitions provide students and teachers a far more sophisticated view of why individuals (themselves included) believe what they do, why the world operates the way it does, and what they might do to bring about democratic and egalitarian change. This is one example of a rigorous classroom in schools shaped by standards of complexity. Such activities can be adapted for use even in early elementary education.

Starting with questions such as: Why does this exist? Or more specifically, why does homelessness exist? Or what can be done to improve the situation? teachers engage students in a reflective awareness of their own questioning processes. Being exposed to that which is different from our common experiences—different cultural understandings and epistemologies, for example—may be central to our attempt to raise new questions, to become the Einsteins of education. Paulo Freire helps us in this context not only as he teaches how to expose the questions hidden in all knowledge forms but also as he demonstrates his ability to formulate critical democratic questions concerning information with which we are confronted. When we are aware of our values and how they help shape our questions, we are much better equipped to make sense of an incoherent body of data. We become in this context interpreters of the social world who understand the roots of our own and other people's explanations of human affairs (Freire and Faundez, 1989). What dramatic cognitive leaps such understandings catalyze.

Our View of the World Is Grounded on the Perspectives of Those Who Have Suffered as the Result of Existing Arrangements

Often those who produce knowledge about the world come from the dominant culture—academics infrequently base their views of reality on the viewpoints of marginalized and excluded individuals. Because of this tendency, scholars who validate the views of the marginalized have in essence encountered "difference." And as we have contended, our consciousness is raised when we take difference seriously. Valuing the productive power of difference, democratic teachers take a cue from liberation theologians in Latin America and begin their analyses of social and educational institutions by listening to those who have suffered most as a result of their existence. This understanding constructs a key distinction between technical standards and standards of complexity.

Derived from dangerous memories of history that have been suppressed and information that has been disqualified by educational gatekeepers, the perspectives of those who have suffered or "subjugated knowledge" play a central role in an epistemology of complexity. Through the conscious cultivation of these low-ranking forms of knowledge, alternative democratic and emancipatory visions of society, politics, education, and cognition are possible. In a democratic curriculum, subjugated knowledge is not passed along as a new canon but becomes a living body of knowledge open to different interpretations. Viewed in its relationship to the traditional curriculum, subjugated knowledge is employed as a constellation of concepts that challenges the invisible social and cultural assumptions embedded in all aspects of schooling and knowledge production. The subjugated knowledge of African Americans, Native Americans, working-class people, women, and many other groups has contested the dominant culture's view of reality.

Confronted with subjugated knowledge, individuals from white mainstream culture begin to appreciate the fact that there are multiple perspectives on all issues. Indeed, they begin to realize that textbooks discard data about unpopular viewpoints and information produced by marginalized groups. Curricula that include subjugated perspectives teach a lesson on the complexities of knowledge production and how this process shapes our view of ourselves and the world around us. The curriculum cannot stay the same if we take the knowledge of working-class men and women seriously; if we get beyond the rosy, romanticized picture of immigration to the United States and document the traumatic stories of the immigrants; if we seek out women's perspectives on the evolution of Western culture; or if we study the culture that enslaved Africans brought to the New World.

The white cultural power blocs that dominate North America in the first decade of the twenty-first century seem oblivious to the need to listen to marginalized people and take their knowledge seriously. Western power wielders are not good at listening to information that does not seem to contribute to hegemony—their ability to win the consent of the subjugated to their governance. Knowledge that emerges from and serves the purposes of the subjugated is often erased by making it appear dangerous and pathological to other citizens. Draw-

ing up work within the discipline of cultural studies that seeks to reverse conditions of oppression, subjugated knowledge seeks new ways of validating the importance and relevance of divergent voices. Technical standards, it must be pointed out, want not an inclusive curriculum of multiple perspectives but information to be accepted as truth with no dissenting voices—an authoritarian curriculum. Subjugated viewpoints are excluded not merely from schoolrooms and curriculum guides, but from other sites of knowledge production, such as popular culture, as well. Having become a major pedagogical force in Western societies over the past few decades, the popular culture "curriculum" is monitored for emancipatory expressions of subjugated knowledge. Though not always successful, power wielders attempt to neutralize the subjugated forms of knowledge that find their way into TV, the movies, popular music, the Internet, and other popular cultural sites (Dion-Buffalo and Mohawk, 1992; J. Fiske, 1993; Mullin, 1994; Nieto, 1996; McLaren and Morris, 1997).

Thus, teachers devoted to the value of subjugated knowledge uncover those dangerous memories that are involved in reconstructing the process through which the consciousness of various groups and individuals has come to be constructed. Such an awareness frees teachers, students, and other individuals to claim an identity apart from the one forced upon them. Indeed, identity is constructed when submerged memories are aroused—in other words, confrontation with dangerous memory changes our perceptions of the forces that shape us, which in turn moves us to redefine our worldviews, our way of seeing. The oppressive forces that shape us have formed the identities of both the powerful and the exploited. Without an analysis of this process, we will never understand why students succeed or fail in school; we will be forever blind to the tacit ideological forces that construct student perceptions of school and the impact such perceptions have on their school experiences. Such blindness restricts our view of our own and other people's perception of their place in history, in the web of reality. When history is erased and decontextualized, teachers, students, workers, and other citizens are rendered vulnerable to the myths employed to perpetuate social domination.

When we study social domination along with subjugated histories and cultures such as those of women and non-Western societies, we are able to expose the socially constructed nature of Western science, the logic implicit within it, and the curriculum derived from it that often accepts ecological destruction and the exploitation of nature. Science is not the only area where an epistemology of complexity searches for alternative subjugated knowledge, for such information exists around each axis of domination. In the domain of gender, for example, critical analysts value ways of knowing that have traditionally been viewed as feminine. Such forms of knowledge expose the hidden gender assumptions

as male centered, as they provide alternative ways of looking at the sociocultural world. Ways of understanding and functioning in the world employed by disabled people, such as the use of sign language, are forms of subjugated knowledge that can be taught in a multidimensional, complex curriculum. Also important in this context is gay and lesbian subjugated knowledge that provides significant insight into the construction of sexual preference, sexual desire, and the cultural dynamics of gender-role production. Both homosexually oriented and heterosexually oriented individuals can gain insight into the production of their identities from a confrontation with such subjugated knowledge.

Because of their race, class, and gender positions, many educators are insulated from the benefits of the double consciousness of the marginalized and are estranged from a visceral appreciation of suffering. Until I was placed in a lower-track set of courses as a high school student—I was not viewed as a good student—I never understood what it felt like to be viewed as "slow." Such an experience alerted me to the pain of my fellow slow students and provided me with a deeper, lived understanding of students in such a position. Such empathy has, in my opinion, served as one of the most important insights I have brought to my career as an educator. Such awareness is a subjugated knowledge, a way of seeing that has been ignored in too many educational situations, technical standards in particular.

Contemporary social organization

and its sanctioning of the suffering of various individuals and groups such as low-track students are often viewed as acceptable in the curriculum of technical standards. Educational leaders who often come from dominant groups don't typically challenge the ways of seeing that justify the prevailing social and educational system. What lived experiences would create a cognitive dissonance within the minds of such leaders that would make them uncomfortable with the status quo? The oppressed—though often induced by the mechanisms of power to accept injustice and to deny their own oppression—often use their pain as a motivation to find out what is not right and to discover alternate ways of constructing social and educational reality. Standards of complexity draw upon this epistemological dynamic and make it a central aspect of their efforts to develop curriculum. The benefits of such an educational orientation are dramatic as students gain the cognitive benefits of seeing the world from different angles.

There Are Multiple Realities— Realities Constructed by Our Location in the Web of Reality

An epistemology of complexity teaches us that the reality we construct depends on our location (or placement) in the web of reality. Cartesian reductionism privileges a single, scientifically validated vantage point from which we can perceive "the one true reality." With different locations in the web of reality come different perspectives on the world around us (Lincoln and Guba, 1985; Denzin and Lincoln, 2000; Briggs and Peat, 1989; Slaughter, 1989). Educators who understand an epistemology of complexity understand that reality, schools, and texts of all types hold more within them to be discovered than first impressions sometimes reveal. In this sense, different frames of reference produce multiple interpretations and multiple realities. Contrary to the problem solving of positivism, an epistemology of complexity sees the mundane as multiplex and continuously unfolding (Greene, 1988, 1995; Haggerson, 2000).

An epistemology of complexity constructs a distancing from reality that allows an observer diverse frames of reference. The distancing may range from the vastly distant astronauts looking at Earth from the Moon, to the very close, as in Georgia O'Keeffe viewing a flower. At the same time, this complex epistemological perspective values the emotional intimacy of feminist connectedness that allows empathetic passion to draw knower and known together. In the multiplex vision of reality, linearity often gives way to simultaneity, as texts become a kaleidoscope of images filled with signs and signifiers to be examined. William Carlos Williams illustrated such complex qualities in the early twentieth century as he depicted multiple, simultaneous images and frames of reference in a verbal manner. Williams attempted to poetically interpret Marcel Duchamp's *Nude Descending a Staircase* with its simultaneity serving as a model for what might be labeled *cognitive cubism*. Democratic teachers in standards of complexity use such ideas to extend the holographic nature of their own and their students' memories, as they create situations where students come to view reality from as many frames of reference as possible. The single angle of the traditional photograph is replaced by the multiple angles of the holographic photograph (Dobrin, 1987; Mandell, 1987; Talbot, 1986, 1991).

Armed with their cognitive cubism, democratic teachers come to understand that the models of teaching they have been taught, the definitions of inquiry with which they have been supplied, the angle from which they have been instructed to view intelligence, and the modes of learning that shape what they perceive to be sophisticated thinking all represent a particular vantage point in the web of reality. Like reality itself, schools and classrooms are complex matrices of interactions, codes, and signifiers in which both students and teachers are interlaced. Just as epistemological complexity asserts that there is no single, privileged way to see the world, there is no one way of seeing the classroom, intelligence, the purpose of education, or teacher or pupil success. Once teachers escape the entrapment of the Cartesian-Newtonian way of seeing, they come to value and thus pursue new frames of reference in regard to their students, classrooms, and workplaces.

In this context of complexity with its multiple frames of reference, the Cartesian-Newtonian quest for a final certainty about the knowledge we produce and consume seems limited and parochial. If we have learned anything in recent years, it is that our ideas about the world change and that they will continue to change in the coming years. The chance of arriving at some juncture in human history where further research will become unnecessary because we will understand the nature of reality—as many social scientists and psychologists predicted rather recently—is slim. There is unlikely to be any single research strategy or theoretical view that will allow us to grasp the whole of reality. In this context, the multiple perspectives of an epistemology of complexity expose the tyranny of technical standards' one-dimensional, authoritarian view of the world.

Given such prospects, an epistemology of complexity tells us that knowledge workers should welcome a proliferation of research paradigms and take advantage of the new angles they provide for viewing the world. This epistemological pluralism or eclecticism will take our understanding of the world to previously unexplored dimensions. Those who accept pluralism will recognize that divergent theoretical systems and research paradigms designate different phenomena as data and that what we consider reality cannot be separated from the methodological procedures employed to produce those conclusions (Eisner, 1984). The path to such eclecticism, however, is beset with obstacles. Indeed, philosophers of science speak of a crisis in inquiry. It is a crisis with roots in two attempts: (1) the fight to free science from the positivistic quest for certainty; and (2) the struggle by those freed from the first quest to figure out what to do with their freedom—in other words, how to cope with the choices presented by accepting multiple frames of reference.

Evidence of the crisis is manifested by an inability to agree upon standard criteria for judging the progress of a field of study. With so many frames of reference available, many scientists find it increasingly difficult to make evaluations across the wide range of activities undertaken in the name of their disciplines. Maybe even more disconcerting is the inability of knowledge producers to understand the assumptions, aims, and languages of one another. Yet, what is the alternative? The attempt to bond our studies in a common language with shared assumptions takes us back to a positivistic quest for a universally understood language of research—an Esperanto of inquiry.

Shared aims in knowledge production, advocates of an epistemology of complexity maintain, stifle our creativity and interpretive possibility. Much of the great physical and social scientific research of the past seemed irrelevant to the patriarchs of the disciplines when it was first encountered. In the most healthy scientific situation, there is generally little consensus about what the next step should involve, which method should be utilized to pursue the next step, or how exactly success should be measured.

The price of our abandonment of the quest for certainty is untidy diversity, but the world itself (especially the educational world) is not all that neat (J. Smith, 1983; Eisner, 1984).

Thus, We Come to Understand Where We Are Located in the Web of Reality: Becoming Humble Knowledge Workers

From the previous point, we can appreciate that individuals cannot separate what they perceive from where they stand in the web of reality. By understanding an epistemology of complexity, educators can become more aware of where they stand in the web and how it shapes their views of world and self. These epistemological concepts lay the foundation for the concept of positionality. Positionality involves the notion that since our understanding of the world and ourselves is socially constructed, we must devote special attention to the differing ways individuals from diverse social backgrounds construct knowledge and make meaning.

Thus, depending on our location in the web with its diverse axes of power, we will designate what constitutes the most important information in the curriculum very differently. For example, when I read E.D. Hirsch's construction of what essential knowledge citizens should know, I never cease to be amazed at how his location as a white, upper-middle-class, American male shaped his choice of knowledge—it is predominantly made up of data about white, upper- and upper-middle-class males from a Western heritage. I want Hirsch (and myself) to understand the ways his (and my) location in the web of reality shapes his (my) perspectives about such content standards.

An epistemology of complexity teaches us about the world's complicated weblike configuration of interacting forces. Knowledge producers, like all of us, are entangled in, not disengaged from, the web. As previously asserted, knower and known are inseparable—both a part of the web of reality. No one in this weblike configuration of the universe can achieve a godlike perspective—no one can totally escape the web and look back at it from afar. We all must confess our subjectivity; we must recognize our limited vantage point. To recognize how our particular view of the web shapes our conception of educational reality, we need to understand our historicity—our position in time and space. Positivist epistemology and the knowledge production it supports tend to ignore the way our historicity shapes our consciousness; as a result, our concept of the world is stripped of its complexity and reduced to a static, one-dimensional frame. Thus, the positivistic knowledge producer feels confident that he or she can make precise predictions, settle controversial questions once and for all, and ignore the complex, interactive process within which all social activity is grounded. From this positivistic perspective, linear mathematics controls the variables, eliminates extraneous influences, and paints a "realistic" Norman Rockwell

portrait of education (Doll, 1989; Slaughter, 1989). In this context, advocates of technical standards confuse the painting with reality.

Because democratic teachers understand their limited view of the world from their locations in the web of reality, they embrace a new humility in their knowledge work. They claim new perspectives, not truth, when producing information about the social world. For example, democratic teachers avoid particular forms of patriarchal, positivistic knowledge production that promote a particular view of the world as simply right or wrong. Drawing upon feminist research methods, democratic teachers understand that our location in the web of reality undermines the possibility of an absolute pronouncement about physical scientific, mathematical, historical, social, or political "truth."

Thus, democratic teachers operating in standards of complexity always pause before announcing an interpretation. In a patriarchal culture, such a pause may not be viewed as a bow to complexity as much as it is perceived as a sign of weakness, an inability to "shoot from the hip" like John Wayne as researcher. Feminist analysts thus tend to avoid the either-or thinking that can serve as an obstacle to the complex epistemological ability to conceptualize multiple frames of reference, to imagine a variety of solutions to perplexing situations. Positivistic either-or thinking promotes less investigation of the "whys" in a physical scientific or sociopolitical situation; an epistemology of complexity, always digging deeper, places great value on the asking of "why" questions. "Why" questions lead to ambiguity, uncertainty, and, one hopes, humility that shakes up the dominant epistemological terrain of certainty (Greene, 1988, 1995; Anderson, 1987).

As we confront the new electronic world with its globalization, exploding imagery, and cultural interchange, our epistemology of complexity with its self-reflection based on an awareness of where we are situated in the web of reality becomes extremely valuable. No longer are we comfortable with macho proclamations of our ability to totally comprehend reality. We begin to speak in terms of constructions of reality. With our awareness of the various information filters that are employed by the media and other power groups, we begin to understand the process by which things get constructed. As democratic teachers reject positivism's universal reason as the supreme form of knowing the sociopolitical world, they seek alternate forms of thinking and epistemological approaches that are historically and socially contingent, that are grounded in an awareness of what can be seen from particular locations in the web of reality. The view one gets of Manhattan standing in the canyons of Wall Street is very different from what one sees of the same island in an airplane making a low approach into JFK Airport. Both views are partial—just like all other perspectives on the city. There is no one correct point in the web from which we can see everything large and small about Manhattan. What is a "true" picture of Manhattan? Concurrently, what is a true picture of chemistry?

Understanding Where We Are Located in the Web of Reality, We Are Better Equipped to Produce Our Own Knowledge

As complex democratic teachers learn their location in the web of reality, understand the ways it affects them and other producers of knowledge, and appreciate the contingency of social information, they begin to grasp the need to become producers of their own knowledge. In positivist teacher-education programs, and the technical standards they support, teachers don't produce knowledge. James Garrison (1988) finds such a situation strange and remarkable. No wonder teachers are disempowered, Garrison argues; they are not even viewed as professionals. The knowledge they convey to students is on loan from the experts; it is not the property of the teachers and their students. Teachers as researchers audaciously claim the right to participate in the production of knowledge, while at the same time retaining their humility concerning the tentative, provisional nature of the knowledge. Standards of complexity cannot operate without scholarly teachers capable of conducting research and teaching such abilities to their students.

The production of new knowledge gleaned from the lived world of the students and the members of the community surrounding the school is very much a part of a critical, democratic effort to reconceive the role of education around a democratic system of meaning and an epistemology of complexity. As long as officially certified experts retain the power to determine what counts as knowledge, little educational reform is possible. Education will continue to be pushed and pulled every few years by fads moving schools in one direction or another. If we hold the power to produce our own knowledge, then we are empowered to reconstruct our own consciousness. The tyranny of expert-produced interpretations of traditions can be subverted and our futures can be reinvented along the lines of a critical epistemology of complexity.

This issue of knowledge control moves us into a direct confrontation with teacher power. We cannot maintain a view of students as democratic participants and teachers as disempowered technicians. More than sixty years ago, John Dewey argued that teachers must assume the power to assert their perspectives on matters of educational importance with the assurance that this judgment will affect what happens in schools. Present technicist models of teacher education do not accept this argument, often teaching novices not to seek empowerment, not to think in an independent manner. Indeed, the hidden curriculum of technicist teacher education and technical standards promotes a passive view of teachers; they are seen as rule followers who are rendered more "supervisable" with their

standardized lesson-plan formats and their adaptation to technical evaluation plans. Such a reality teaches a hidden curriculum of disempowerment to students. Complex, democratic teachers, for their students' sake, must rebel against such totalitarianism, encourage their students to be uncomfortable with authoritarian pronouncements of truth in texts, and help them become researchers of multiple perspectives on any data confronted. Both teachers and students in standards of complexity become knowledge producers.

This ethic of teacher and student as researchers is central to the notion of rigorous educational reform promoted here. Our epistemology of complexity pushes this ethic even further, asserting that if we are serious about our work as agents of democracy, then we must help *all citizens* become researchers—the future of democracy depends on it. Dewey argued that in a truly democratic society where all parties have a voice in the formulation of policy, parents and community members must be participants in the public conversation about education. These citizens need the empowerment that an understanding of primary and secondary research can provide. One of the most democratic roles a public educator might play involves sharing research skills with the public, especially the disempowered public. This is a radical action on a number of levels. First, it negates the cult of the expert. It helps destroy the myth that men and women should seek guidance from those blessed with society's credentials to direct them. In this way, it celebrates human self-direction. Second, it expands the role of the teacher. The teacher moves from classroom technician to active political agent, as he or she views education as a vehicle to build an egalitarian community. And third, it positions the school as an agent of democracy that is dedicated to an ethic of inclusion and negotiation. Operating as a democratic agent, the school seeks to uncover those forces that thwart participation as its teachers carefully map the web of reality that supports such powers.

Research, of course, involves the production of new knowledge. Paulo Freire and Ira Shor (1987) write of a complex concept of knowing, arguing that there are two moments of knowing: (1) the production of new knowledge; and (2) when one knows the existing knowledge. What typically happens is that we separate these two moments. Rigorous research in standards of complexity insists that they be brought together. Knowledge in technicist classrooms is produced far from the teacher and the students. Knowing is thus reduced to taking existing knowledge and transferring it. The teacher is not an inquirer who researches existing knowledge; he or she is merely a specialist in *knowledge transference*.

Teachers in this situation lose the indispensable qualities that are mandated by scholarly knowledge production: critical reflection, a desire to act, discomfort, uncertainty, restless inquiry, and the like. When such qualities disappear in teachers, schools become places where knowledge that supports dominant interests is stored and delivered. Knowledge is produced by official researchers, scholars, textbook writers, and sanctioned curriculum committees—it is not created and re-created by teachers and their students in the daily life of the school. Teaching and researching, the official story goes, are separate entities. Rigorous teaching is not viewed as a form of inquiry. The symbiotic ties between teaching and research are not seen.

In this context, we begin to get a more specific perspective on the nature of a complex and rigorous form of knowledge production in U.S. classrooms. We are attempting to create not objective knowledge for storage in a warehouse, but a useful form of knowledge that can be applied to teaching and social problems, that is connected to the lived world and the complex web of reality. If educators don't possess an understanding of the purpose of knowledge production and its relationship to their teaching, then studying research methods and epistemology is irrelevant. In my next point, I will explore this dynamic in more detail, focusing on a form of knowledge production that produces practical knowledge for social and democratic action.

Producing Practical Knowledge for Social Action

Knowledge based on connections, John Dewey (1916) argued, is concerned not only with the immediacy of the knowledge itself but also with the vantage point it creates from which to consider a new experience. To Dewey, the *content* of knowledge is what has happened, that is, what is considered finished and settled. But the *reference* of knowledge, he argued, is the future. Knowledge in the Deweyan sense provides the means of understanding what is happening in the present and what is to be done about it. In a typical pragmatist context, Dewey was concerned with the consequences of ideas—in the lexicon of this section, the practical value of knowing something. It is this pragmatic aspect of Dewey's theory of knowledge that informs the *critical* intent of education itself. As Aronowitz and Giroux (1985) put it: "the ability to connect contemporary experience to the received information that others have gained through their generalized experience" (9). Here rests a central feature of an epistemology of complexity and standards of complexity: knowledge in complex epistemology does not simply rest after it is produced and learned. It goes to work, it has use value, it is worth the process engaged in learning it.

Positivist educators have never understood the notion of practical knowledge, of knowledge based on connections. This lack of understanding has profoundly shaped the history of U.S. education and the type of knowledge that has been included in its curriculum across the decades. The notion of epistemological complexity is lost in this positivistic context, as curriculum developers failed to comprehend the inexact and ever changing

nature of practical knowledge. Technicist educators, Dewey maintained, regard knowledge as an entity complete in itself. Dewey's Hegelian background, with its emphasis on the dialectic, helped move his view of knowledge beyond the "knowledge in isolation" format. The dialectical notion of process grounded his view of the nature of knowledge. Knowledge from this perspective could never be viewed outside the context of its origins and its relationship to other information. We have to call to mind, Dewey wrote, only what passes in our schools as acquisition of knowledge to understand how it lacks any meaningful connection with the experience of students. A person, he concluded, is reasonable in the degree to which he or she sees an event not as something isolated "but in its connection with the common experience of mankind" (342–43). Of course, positivists do not possess the evaluative ability to measure such a practical, connected form of knowledge. Thus, they assume that it doesn't exist.

As we know, positivists seek to produce a form of knowledge—sometimes referred to as a *formal* knowledge—that is a timeless body of truth. Such a formal knowledge is removed from connection with the world, from consideration of its consequences. Privileged in the schools, formal knowledge is viewed as separate from issues of commitment, emotion, or ethical action. Indeed, such a formal knowledge often privileges social adaptation rather than social action. The objectivity inscribed in formal knowledge often becomes a signifier for political passivity and an elevation to an elite sociopolitical and economic location. Thus, in its "esteemed position," formalism refuses to analyze the relationship between knowledge production and democratic and professional and vocational practice. Teachers obtain formal knowledge and then are expected to directly insert it in their classes.

Such application of formal knowledge involves, for example, pronouncements such as: "The research tells us to teach language and literacy in this way." The problem here involves formalism's failure to study the complex relationship between professional knowledge about education and educational practice. Formalism fails to discern the phenomenological complexity of teaching—that is, the complicated ways knowledge, consciousness, everyday life, and professional practice intersect. Without this critical recognition, knowledge production is irrelevant to school teachers. Formal knowledge production too often fails to question the relationship between professional knowledge and indeterminant zones of practice characterized by complexity, conflict, ambiguity, and uniqueness. Such a practical zone exists outside the boundaries of positivism and the formal knowledge it produces. Epistemological formalism can't cope with everyday life's and the classroom's ill-formed problems.

With this type of understanding, complex, democratic teachers can develop new epistemologies of practice that employ multiple frames of reference. Such different views allow us to observe professional practice from the perspectives of different stakeholders in the educational process. We begin to understand that knowledge about practice is not universal but contingent on the particular context in which it is applied. Viewing from the perspective and needs of marginalized groups, we may see that practices that might work with students from privileged backgrounds may serve to further oppress students facing the forces of class bias and racism. Teachers with this epistemological understanding begin to understand in a very practical way that there is not one answer to any question, one accurate representation of an event, or one right way to teach macroeconomics or biology.

Educators guided by their epistemology of complexity seek to produce a *dialogical* form of knowledge. Such knowledge is many times expressed as a series of questions and tentative answers rather than an arrogant factual knowledge. In this complex context, educators produce knowledge that is less linear and procedural (for example, the four steps to teaching the way a bill becomes law) and more circular and recursive (for instance, how do we help a group of low-achieving students to perceive research abilities as important in helping them achieve personal goals?). In this way, teachers as knowledge producers are emancipated from formalistic, decontextualized, and universal rules for conducting research and teaching their students.

Such positivistic rules often allow

teachers and educational leaders to see only "what is there." That which is readily apparent often involves the least significant aspects of a situation. As they are emancipated from the formalistic, teachers as knowledge producers decenter their perception in ways that allow them to see previously occluded relationships among entities—not just discrete features. Informed by these insights, researchers produce a practical knowledge characterized by three features: an integrative dimension, an applicative dimension, and a hermeneutic (interpretive) dimension.

The integrative dimension constructs meaning for isolated facts in the process, placing data into a larger perspective, connecting it to understandings emerging from a variety of disciplines, and questioning its moral and political inscriptions. The applicative dimension questions how knowledge can be applied to important problems. The hermeneutic dimension searches for the variety of ways knowledge can be interpreted and the various horizons (contexts) within which it can be viewed. In all of these dimensions, emphasis is placed on the process of knowing rather than the production of a final, positive knowledge.

The practical knowledge championed here cannot even be produced by positivist researchers—positivist formal knowledge and complex practical knowledge are incommensurable, an epistemological mismatch. Complex practical knowledge must be produced by a process informed by and contin-

gent on context. It is an embodied form of knowledge that cannot be separated from specific contexts. Like indigenous knowledge, practical knowledge is less informed by abstract rules of research procedures than by an intimate understanding of a specific situation. In line with the various features of an epistemology of complexity, practical knowledge is produced by a form of research that uses the human self as an instrument of inquiry and emotional and logical insight. Democratic teachers in standards of complexity feel they have contributed to the production of practical knowledge when they are able to describe the living context in which the knowledge is based. Human interactions and experiences that take place in these breathing contexts are not events to be simply described but complex circumstances to be interpreted.

In their awareness of these living contexts, democratic educators expose the values and contradictions in values that shape the contexts themselves and their own questions about them. Thus, the level of awareness of social and physical complexity is raised. The practical benefits of such a heightened awareness of complexity help us escape the simplistic, reductionistic data of more traditional epistemologies. Awareness of such omnipresent values helps us explain the meaning of the context and the uses to which such meaning can be applied. In this context, the knowledge producer comes to understand that these values are not absolute qualities but perpetually subject to questioning, interpretation, clarification, and transformation. Appreciating the complex relationship connecting knowledge, values, and context, critical analysts can cope with random occurrences via their self-reflective, self-evaluating, and self-adjusting orientation. Thus, they are attuned to and undaunted by the messy aspects of everyday life.

The move from explanatory knowledge to practical knowledge demands a profound sociocognitive and epistemological leap. Such a move constitutes a criterion for a reconceptualized notion of rigor. Such a criterion falls outside the boundaries of formal research with its prearranged, operational definition of rigor as fidelity to an objectivist methodological procedure. It is important to delineate this new notion of rigor in relation to the language of educational excellence and calls for high standards. Our reconceptualized notion of rigor and the epistemology of complexity that grounds it can help teachers reshape the public conversation about high-quality, rigorous education. This new notion of rigor is also important as democratic teachers and students produce practical knowledge for inclusion in the curriculum.

How do we exercise courageous and smart citizenship in diverse communities? How do we reconceptualize our social values in light of the epistemological concept of difference? Where do we begin the process of helping the public rethink its notion of intelligence as more than high scores on standardized tests? How do we help students and other teachers understand the ways poverty and racism inscribe themselves on the consciousness of the oppressed and undermine their relationship with learning? All of these questions form the basis for the production of practical forms of knowledge that sets up the possibility for individual self-direction and community-building action. With such questions in mind and an understanding of an epistemology of synthesis, integration, and application, we can begin to produce knowledge and engage consciousness in a way that leads to progressive social and educational change. As epistemological horizons are expanded, human possibility is enhanced. We can all become people who push the moral, civic, cognitive, and democratic envelope. Standards of complexity can help us get on with this task.

Appreciating the Nature of Complexity: Overcoming Reductionism

In this context, a brief review of the nature of complexity may be in order. The web of reality is composed of too many variables (or, as Nobel Prize winner Ilya Prigogene puts it, "extraneous perturbations") to be taken into account and controlled. One extraneous variable, for example, in an educational or any other experiment can produce an expanding, exponential effect. Inconsequential entities can have a profound effect in a complex, nonlinear universe. The shape of the physical and social world depends on the smallest part. The part in a sense is the whole, for via the action of any particular part the whole in the form of transformative change may be seen. To exclude such considerations is to miss the nature of the interactions that constitutes reality. The development of a counter-Cartesian reconceptualization of education and educational knowledge production does not mean that we simplistically reject all empirical science—obviously, there are questions in education that involve counting, figuring percentages and averages, and so on. It does mean, however, that we conceive of such empirical questions as one part of the web, that is, the interactive configuration.

A complex epistemological reconceptualization of education means recognizing, as Dewey did, as feminist epistemology does, that the knower and the known are intimately connected, that a science that separates fact from value, purpose, belief, and complexity is a pseudoscience divorced from the *Lebenswelt*, the lived world of human consciousness. Such a reconceptualization reminds us as knowledge producers that we can display our findings and argue for their value, but always with a hesitation, a stutter, a tentativeness—never as the simple truth (Besag, 1986b; Doll, 1989; Briggs and Peat, 1989).

The complexity of reality may be illustrated by medical and mechanical examples. When the human body breaks down, doctors may identify a certain factor, but the "cause" of the illness is always multiple. Living entities are always composed of a multitude of feedback loops—a cardinal

concept in chaos theory. A home furnace is one of the most familiar forms of a simple feedback loop. We all know that when the room cools down below the temperature set on the thermostat, the thermostat responds by switching on the furnace. As the furnace heats up the room to a point above the second temperature set on the thermostat, the furnace automatically shuts off. The ear-splitting screeches produced when a microphone is placed close to a speaker, feedback, is another example of a feedback loop. Output from the amplifier is detected by the microphone and looped back into the amplifier. The chaotic sounds that result are the consequence of a feedback loop where the output of one stage turns into the input of another. Because human beings are composed of so many feedback loops—for example, the transformation of food into energy, the increase in heart rate in the presence of danger, and so on—the attempt to study them takes on far more complexity than traditional conceptions of cause-effect linearity could imagine (Lincoln and Guba, 1985; Briggs and Peat, 1989; Capra, 1996; O'Sullivan, 1999).

In order to study such complex systems, educators have to move from hierarchic to heterarchic conceptions of order. Positivism saw an inherent order in the physical and social world: for example, the divine right of kings to govern or Carl Brigham's (the founder of the Educational Testing Service) hierarchy of the intelligence of ethnic groups. Researchers operating in an epistemology of complexity maintain that if orders exist, then they exist side by side; if one order dominates, it is merely temporary and is subject to a variety of rapidly shifting forces. Because of this heterarchic conception of order, any simplistic notion of determinism is destroyed. In a hierarchic universe, positivists have maintained that if a knowledge producer knows the location and velocity of all the bits and pieces of the world, then the future can be predicted and controlled. But change is complex, and qualitative researchers informed by a complex epistemological understanding have to accept the notion that change occurs dramatically and unpredictably (Lincoln and Guba, 1985; Denzin and Lincoln, 2000; Briggs and Peat, 1989).

Operating in a closed system where variables are controlled, positivists have often promoted an orderly and predictable view of change. When the variables were controlled and protected from outside contamination, equations could be formulated and exact predictions about the physical, social, and educational worlds could be devised. But even ostensibly very minor variables could have dramatic effects, sometimes not exhibiting themselves for long periods of time. When they did manifest themselves, their effect seemed to the positivistic researcher as an aberration, probably a mistake in the construction of an equation. Not only does the critical analyst in the counter-Cartesian context lose the possibility of certainty, but he or she is also faced with a need to find

methods of exploring these complex, multiple constructions of reality.

In this context marked by complexity, think of an everyday classroom. A wide variety of kids with different backgrounds, special needs, different home experiences, diverse strengths and weaknesses, and changing moods and dispositions inhabit those desks in our rooms. As we survey our classrooms, we come to realize that there is more to teaching than meets the modernist eye, more than is included in technicist teacher-education programs. The purpose of an epistemologically complex teacher education is not to learn the right answers, the hand-me-down knowledge of the research experts; on the contrary, a complex, democratic teacher education consists of making the most of the unanticipated complications of the classroom. Technicist methods courses and student teaching do not address the innate and complex uncertainty of teaching—they attempt to deny it. Thus, complex teacher educators refuse to promise the provision of a generic form of teaching applicable to all students in all contexts. Neither does it promise to reduce the uncertainty of the profession by the application of quick technical fixes. The counterreductionist turn implies an admission that teacher educators also agonize over the confusing uncertainties of everyday practice. To do otherwise would be to revert to the dishonesty of modernism's veil of simplicity and certainty (Clark, 1987).

An epistemology of complexity

adopts a progressive view of knowledge that even as information is being gathered by researchers, it is being analyzed and interpreted. A more positivistic view of knowledge assumes that only after one knows the facts is he or she ready to analyze. Such a view misses the important point that what we designate as the facts is an act of interpretation—in the case of positivistic research, it is an unconscious act of interpretation. Privileged knowledge producers often assume that knowledge is a static or inert entity—writers of elementary and high school textbooks and content standards often take this viewpoint. Knowledge production operating with an understanding of an epistemology of complexity proceeds tentatively, ever mindful of ambiguity and uncertainty. When we know for certain, little need exists to pursue alternative ways of knowing. "Deviant ways of seeing" are dismissed as irrelevant; they are not viewed as an important source of new insight and socioeducational innovation (Romanish, 1986; Schon, 1987).

This view of knowledge production and teaching within an epistemology of complexity revolutionizes the way we conceptualize education. The negative consequences of the quest for certainty are avoided, as teacher-researchers and teacher educators begin to imagine and construct new ways of thinking about teaching and teacher education. If the act of teaching was known and constant, teachers could act on empirical generalizations and teacher educators would know exactly what teachers needed to know to perform successfully. But teaching is not constant and predictable; it always takes place in a microcosm of uncertainty. Thus, what we call valuable practitioner knowledge is elusive. How to teach teachers what to do in conditions of uncertainty is even more elusive.

The positivism of professional schools of education in the early twentieth century used Cartesian science to eliminate the uncertainty of professional practice and replace it with empirical knowledge about the teaching act. The cult of the expert in the educational sphere precluded an admission of uncertainty. The uniqueness of particular teaching situations was ignored by educational researchers or experts whose clients demanded official knowledge—knowledge that specified the scientifically sanctioned "right way" to proceed (Schon, 1987). In a culture that relies on the expert for guidance, uncertainty doesn't play well; indeed, denial of the useless complications of complexity with the attendant certainty that can be asserted signifies strength and positive, affirmative leadership in a macho, patriarchal culture. The higher our levels of epistemological understanding, the weaker our perspectives often appear to a culture that has been conditioned to buy into a quest for certainty. This cruel irony tends to impede the attempt to teach complex, sophisticated, critical thinking and to retard the movement to put teachers into positions of control over their

workplaces. Teachers with an epistemological consciousness of complexity
must resist asking experts to tell them
what to do when they experience difficulty. This does not mean they can't
ask experienced educators for advice;
they must also adeptly resist frustrated
students' calls to "just tell us what you
want us to memorize and we'll do it."
Teaching with an understanding of
epistemological complexity is a subtle
task that takes practice and patience.

One of the major problems of U.S.
schooling involves its inability to understand this epistemology of complexity, its inability to deal with ambiguity, to perceive ambiguity as a
valuable characteristic. Without such
an understanding, educational leaders
have continually sought naïve and
simplistic answers to the complex social and cognitive questions that confront education—a reflection of the
epistemological predisposition of
modernism to seek certainty in its inquiries about human and educational
affairs. Rigorous education operating
in standards of complexity attempts to
overcome our socially engrained discomfort with the enigmatic, our desire
to have something we can all subscribe
to together, and our need for a shared
certainty.

Critical, democratic teachers who
embrace an epistemology of complexity deal with a realm so complex that
they must accustom themselves to the
mistakes they will make in their attempt to make sense of it all. We will
never have enough data to be assured
that we "have it right." In this complex context, our goal for teachers is

not that they parlay the truth to their
students, but that they turn out students who are aware of both the complexity of the process and their own
and other individuals' fallibility in
their quest to understand the world
and themselves. What an amazing
scholarly insight this would be.

All Knowledge Is in Process, a Part of a Larger Process

An epistemology of complexity is inseparable from an epistemology and
pedagogy of process. Positivism and
the educational standards it supports
see the fundamental nature of reality
as "separate things." Reality and consciousness itself in a process-oriented
epistemology are seen as fundamentally a collection of processes, always
interacting with other things and
processes, and thus always changing.
Process, thus, is the fundamental state
of the physical and social worlds.
Processes are more fundamental to reality, therefore, than separate entities—a notion that flies in the face of
Cartesianism (Mashalidis, 1997).
Knowledge in this epistemological
context has a past and a future; we always see it in a particular stage of its
development. When knowledge is removed from its process(es), it is no
longer capable of *being* known—it has
become known, resulting in its life force
being stripped away (Postman, 1995;
Krievis, 1998). When teachers witness
such a move in the top-down techni-
cal-content standards they are provided, they witness an epistemological
murder.

Aware of a complex epistemology of process, democratic teachers understand that the knowledge of today changes tomorrow. It is not stable, immobile, or static. Albert Einstein clearly understood this dynamic and used it to change the way we understand the world around us. Using his understanding of nineteenth-century German philosopher George W.F. Hegel's concept of process, Einstein walked through a conceptual window unimaginable to most individuals trapped in a Cartesian-Newtonian house. Writing in the nineteenth century, Hegel was conceptually uncomfortable with Isaac Newton's absolutist explanation of gravity and the way things work. Most important for our educational, social, and cognitive concerns, Hegel was unimpressed with the manner in which Newton reached his conclusions about the physical universe. From Hegel's perspective, every entity's existence could be understood only in relation to other things. In his philosophical view, the concept of relationship took on an importance not valued by Newton and his scientific descendants.

Relationship was so significant to Hegel that he described the interaction between entities as a living process. In such a process all things in the world are affected and shaped by all other things—just as in Einstein's relativity theory, mass works on space and space works on mass ("Einstein on spacetime," 1998). Operating without the benefit of this lesson, educators fall into the *irrationality of the fragmentation of conventional reason*. We see the importance of the world in things in themselves, in isolation from their contexts, removed from the larger processes that provide their meaning. Informed by Einstein's lesson, the curriculum becomes more than fragments of data. In the call for educational standards over the past few years, we have seen the effects of this failure to learn Einstein (and Hegel's) lesson: We judge educational quality by the quantity of data accumulated (Woods and Grant, 1998; Madison, 1988).

An epistemology of process was so important to Einstein that he could not have developed the general theory of relativity without it. A quick look at the relationship between process and the genesis of the theory is instructive to all teachers. Picking up where we left off in the introduction to the encyclopedia, Einstein often used the notion of a rubber sheet stretched over a baking dish to explain the complex notion of space. When a bowling ball or a BB is placed on it, the sheet is bent or warped around the objects. This distortion exemplifies what massive objects such as the sun or the moon do to the fabric of space. This is one of the basic concepts of Einstein's general theory of relativity. The rubber sheet is flat when no objects are placed upon it; Einstein referred to this as the absence of gravity. When the bowling ball depresses the sheet, the curvature around the depression represents a gravitational field. A BB rolled along the sheet will fall into the trough, just as an asteroid will fall to Earth if it gets too close to its gravitational field. The more massive the object, the greater the bending of space. The bowling ball will distort the sheet more than the BB.

So, according to Einstein, mass causes a depression in space. If a comet, for example, moves too close to a star, then it is drawn into its gravitational well and seized. Thus, entities in space follow the shape of the universe when they fall to Earth. They are not pulled by some gravitational force! Whereas the rubber sheet is merely a metaphor and reduces the complexity of Einstein's relativity, it does help us appreciate the structural unity of space, matter, and motion— the *process* of space. (A tricky part is that we have to add time to that unity as well.) Gravity, therefore, is simply a part of the structure of the universe— and, amazingly, Einstein figured that out. Objects fall into the valley in space-time produced by the bowling ball or sun. In this context, the orbits of the sun's planets can be better conceptualized; Mercury and Venus as well as Neptune and Pluto "roll" around the indention in space caused by the sun's gravity trough.

The general theory of relativity even asserted that if a massive object in space is disturbed, then it will cause ripples in space like ripples from a rock splashing in a pond. In space, these "gravity waves" are illustrated again by the rubber sheet, as we imagine dropping a ball bearing on it. BBs and bowling balls placed on other portions of the sheet will be affected by the dropping of the ball bearing. Einstein asked us to use our rubber sheet

to imagine a massive object that revolves. In this situation, the "gravity well" it produces in space is not just a depression in the rubber sheet but a spinning indentation that twists space. Such twisting induces other objects around it to move in particular ways. Although the general theory of relativity is, undoubtedly, very complex and mysterious, the point I am making about it is quite easy to understand. This point holds revolutionary significance for our analysis of epistemology and educational reform.

As Einstein sought to understand the force of gravity, he discovered that there is no such thing as "nothingness" in the structure of the universe. Space, like everything else, *is something*—it is an intrinsic part of the fabric of the cosmos. Space is neither empty nor separable from matter. The *relationship* between space and matter is central to making the universe what it is. In light of Einstein's assertion, the old Newtonian notion of gravity was destroyed; but most important to our point, the Newtonian universe and the Cartesian-Newtonian *way of looking at the universe* (epistemology) were overturned. When Newton developed his universal theory of gravitation in the 1600s, he focused on gravity as a thing-in-itself. If gravity, as he believed, was simply a force, why would one look at it in any other way? Thus, he and especially those who came after him, followed the emerging scientific method and removed gravity from its larger process so it could be efficiently analyzed. And this was exactly their mistake ("Astronomical instruments," 1999; "Gravitational radiation," 1998; "Still right. ...," 1998; Evans, 1997; Woods and Grant, 1998; Peoria Astronomical Society, 1998).

Einstein operating in the first decades of the twentieth century was able to escape the Newtonian mistake that had misled physicists for a quarter of a millennium by one conceptual move. Instead of searching for gravity as a *thing*, he saw it as a *relationship*, a part of a grander process. Einstein saw gravity *in relation* to other aspects of the universe. Indeed, he understood that the relationship between matter and space—illustrated by the rubber sheet, bowling balls, and BBs—is exactly what makes the world what it is. What we experience as gravity is not a force made up of tiny gravitons but a reflection of the structure of the universe moving us along a path existing in curved, multidimensional space. Space, he figured, is not the package in which the universe is stored—it is a key aspect of the process of creation. For those who understood the basic idea of Einstein's theory, the physical world could never be viewed the same way again (Woods and Grant, 1998).

The focus on process connecting space, time, and matter that eventuated in Einstein's revolutionary theories can also change our social consciousness, cognition, and education. As we pursue modes of thinking that account for changes and interactions in the physical, social, and psychological domains, we begin to gain dramatically different and more *complex* perspectives on that which surrounds us.

In this concept of interactive processes, the etymology of Shirley Steinberg and my concept of postformalism or postformal thinking is revealed. At this point, however, it is important to explain Einstein's role in leading us to new ways of making meaning, to new appreciations of the process of both being and becoming (Kovel, 1998).

Using Einstein's example of thinking in physics and Hegel's dialectical insights, we are led to post–Cartesian-Newtonian forms of analysis. In this context, we begin to appreciate the hidden processes that place the physical, social, psychological, and educational worlds in a sea of constant change. Newtonian and Cartesian ways of seeing often provide a metaphorical photograph of an entity. This photograph is an isolated moment in time, a still life that may miss the significance of the larger dynamic of which it is but a part. When we see—as postformalism labels it—facts as a part of a larger process, we begin to understand how things move beyond what they are but still retain their identity. For example, though gravity no doubt exists, it moves far beyond its existence as an entity involved merely with the attraction of one object to another when conceived as a part of an inclusive whole—the structure of the universe. Imagine the difference between a science lesson taught to middle school students about gravity that takes this processual feature into account and one that doesn't.

The process-based thinking delineated here is a form of holistic analysis that insists on the inseparability of mind and body, politics and economics, math and science, consciousness and cultural context, facts and values, the biological and the social, and gravity and matter. What education in its disciplinary organization or in its fragmentation of information treats as separate, an epistemology of complexity considers parts of larger processes. There is nothing wrong, process analysts maintain, with separating entities for the purpose of labeling and analysis as long as this step is followed by the act of putting them back together. Step 1: gravity is defined as the attraction of one object to another; step 2: this attraction is viewed as a result of the interrelationship among space, mass, time, and motion. Thus, this mode of analysis can be described as examining an entity from differing vantage points: (1) gravity as experienced by an earthling throwing a baseball into the air and watching it return to Earth; and (2) gravity from the perspective of one who views (or, like Einstein, is capable of imagining) the universe as a whole and frames it in such a perspective. Understanding both modes and their relationship is important in the complex effort to make sense of gravity (Bookchin, 1995; Kovel, 1998; Levins, 1998).

Thus, informed by these ways of seeing, an epistemology of process and complexity assumes that little in the universe is as it appears to be. In this context, democratic teachers argue that considering an entity only as a thing-in-itself can be viciously misleading. The reason for this examination of Einstein's general theory of relativity in an educational context involves his phenomenal ability to avoid this Cartesian-Newtonian quicksand and to model a rigorous form of process-oriented cognition that can lead us out of the cognitive and educational briar patch in which we are presently ensnared. The implications of such a critique of Cartesian-Newtonian logic (conventional reason) are sobering and are not offered frivolously. Based on Einstein's mode of thinking and numerous analyses of the limitations of mainstream Western epistemology, complex, democratic teachers come to understand that there are important flaws in accepted forms of logic, research, and knowledge production.

Do not misread this assertion. I am not arguing that we throw out the Cartesian-Newtonian baby with the bathwater—that is, that mainstream science is of no benefit. Of course, it is; its contributions are significant and well documented. An epistemology of complexity maintains, however, that we can do better, go further, and address the limitations inherent in the Cartesian-Newtonian system—in particular, the limitations Einstein had to overcome to develop his frame-shattering theories. An epistemology of complexity demands a new rigor in cognition and education. Such an epistemological approach helps teachers develop ways of transcending conceptually impoverished definitions of high educational standards grounded in recall of fragmented bits of knowledge—long on memorization and recitation, short on an understanding of larger processes, interpretation, applicability and transferability, and connectedness. When students and teachers move into the processual realm, they gain the ability not only to explain the dynamics that move events but also, like Einstein, to develop the capacity to transform them in progressive ways (Kovel, 1998; Woods and Grant, 1998; Lawler, 1975).

With these Einsteinian insights into an epistemology of process, we begin to notice the processual nature of other aspects of the lived work. Consciousness, for example, can be understood as a process-oriented dynamic. Consciousness and knowledge acquisition in this context are not separate entities, things-in-themselves, but parts of a mutually constructive process. As with the process connecting the knower and the known, consciousness cannot be understood separate from the world. With this understanding, we can reconceptualize education not only as an epistemological dynamic but also as an ontological force as it shapes who we are as human beings (Mashaldis, 1997). In such a processual context, disciplines of knowledge cannot be arbitrarily separated from one another but must be viewed as parts of larger multidisciplinary contexts.

Teachers who attempt to act on their understanding of this epistemology of process, of course, have to continually battle the forces of positivism within the schools—especially in technical standards. Instead of exploring and constructing new insights into mathematical, physical, linguistic, so-cial, cultural, and political processes, teachers and students in the grips of Cartesianism are fed a diet of isolated, unproblematized data. Such a pedagogy works not to promote analytical thinking and stimulate the social imagination but rather to adjust one uncritically to the status quo. Contrary to such Cartesian teaching, a complex epistemology of process alerts teachers and students to the realization that meanings are never closed but remain forever open in light of the appreciation of another process in which they can be understood. Positive knowledge doesn't age well; it often turns to vinegar. New facts come to light, and fresh interpretations uncover new processes that render traditional accounts passé. Albert Einstein the student is viewed as a failure, the scientist as a genius. Yesterday's certainties are tomorrow's superstitions (Slaughter, 1989; Rineharz, 1979; Lincoln and Guba, 1985; Denzin and Lincoln, 2000).

The Importance of Interpretation: Hermeneutics

Ever since positivists applied physical science methods to social science research, there has been a struggle to address those aspects of the human condition that need not just counting but understanding. The information that social analysts collect may include observed behavior, documents, and artifacts, but these source materials cannot be separated from the meanings granted them by past, present, and future human agents. The hermeneutic dimension of research attempts to appreciate this question of meaning by focusing on the interpretive aspects of the act of knowledge production. In positivism, this hermeneutic dimension is typically dismissed. Understanding that all knowledge is an interpretation, teaching based on an epistemology of complexity places great emphasis on the hermeneutic dimension.

An epistemology of complexity appreciates that in knowledge production—no matter how much Cartesian experts may argue that the facts speak for themselves—interpretation is always at work. Sometimes it is a conscious process (as in education based on standards of complexity); many times it is unconscious (as in positivistic education and research). Nevertheless, it is always there (Grondin, 1994; Gross and Keith, 1997; Rosen, 1987; Vattimo, 1994). The hermeneutic act of interpretation involves, in its most elemental articulation, making sense of what has been observed in a way that communicates understanding. Not only is all knowledge production merely an act of interpretation, but, hermeneutics contends, perception itself is an act of interpretation as well. Thus, the quest for understanding is a fundamental feature of human existence, as encounters with the unfamiliar always demand the attempt to make meaning, to make sense. The same, however, is also the case with the familiar. Indeed, as in the study of commonly known texts, we come to find that sometimes the familiar may be

seen as the most strange. Thus, it should not be surprising that even the so-called objective writings about both the physical and the social domains are interpretations, not value-free descriptions (Denzin, 1994; Gallagher, 1992; Jardine, 1998; D. Smith, 1999).

Learning from the hermeneutic tradition and an epistemology of complexity, educators have begun to reexamine textual claims to authority. No pristine interpretation exists; indeed, no methodology, social or educational theory, or discursive form can claim a privileged position that enables the production of authoritative, unquestionable knowledge. Knowledge producers must always speak and write about the world in terms of something else in the world, "in relation to. . . ." As creatures of the world, we are oriented to it in a way that prevents us from grounding our theories and perspectives outside of it. Thus, whether we like it or not, we are all destined as interpreters to analyze from within its boundaries and blinders. Within these limitations, however, the interpretations emerging from the hermeneutic process can still move us to new levels of understanding, appreciations that allow us to "live our way" into an experience described to us.

Despite the impediments of context, hermeneutically informed teachers can transcend the inadequacies of thin descriptions of decontextualized facts and produce thick descriptions of social texts characterized by the contexts of their production, the intentions of their producers, and the meanings mobilized in the processes of their construction. The production of such thick descriptions and interpretations follows no step-by-step blueprint or mechanical formula. As with any art form, hermeneutical analysis can be learned only in the Deweyan sense—by doing it. Researchers in this context practice the art by grappling with the text to be understood, telling its story in relation to its contextual dynamics and other texts first to themselves and then to a public audience (Carson and Sumara, 1997; Denzin, 1994; Gallagher, 1992; Jardine, 1998; Madison, 1988; Ellis, 1998).

These concerns with the nature of hermeneutical interpretation come under the category of philosophical hermeneutics. Working this domain, hermeneutical scholars attempt to think through and clarify the conditions under which interpretation and understanding take place. The hermeneutics that grounds complex knowledge production moves more in the direction of normative hermeneutics in that it raises questions about the purposes and procedures of interpretation. In its critical context, the purpose of hermeneutical analysis is to develop a form of cultural criticism revealing power dynamics within social and cultural texts. Teachers familiar with critical hermeneutics build bridges between reader and text, text and its producer, historical context and present, and one particular social circumstance and another. Accomplishing such interpretive tasks is difficult, and researchers situated in normative

hermeneutics push ethnographers, historians, semioticians, literary critics, and content analysts to trace the bridge-building processes employed by successful interpretations of knowledge production and culture (Gallagher, 1992; Kellner, 1995; Kogler, 1996; Rapko, 1998).

Grounded by the hermeneutical bridge building, educators in a hermeneutical circle (a process of analysis in which interpreters seek the historical and social dynamics that shape textual interpretation) engage in the back-and-forth of studying parts in relation to the whole and the whole in relation to its parts. No final interpretation is sought in this context, as the activity of the circle proceeds with no need for closure (Gallagher, 1992; Peters and Lankshear, 1994; Pinar et al., 1995). This movement of whole to parts is combined with an analytic flow between abstract and concrete. Such dynamics often tie interpretation to the interplay of larger social forces (the general) to the everyday lives of individuals (the particular). A critical hermeneutics brings the concrete, the parts, and the particular into focus, but in a manner that grounds them contextually in a larger understanding of the social forces, the whole, and the abstract (the general). Focus on the parts is the dynamic that brings the particular into focus, sharpening our understanding of the individual in light of the social and psychological forces that shape him or her. The parts and the unique places they occupy ground hermeneutical ways of seeing by providing the contextualiza-tion of the particular—a perspective often erased in positivism's search for abstract generalizations (Gallagher, 1992; Kellner, 1995; Miller and Hodge, 1998; Peters and Lankshear, 1994).

When these aspects of the interpre-tation process are taken into account, analysts begin to understand Hans-Georg Gadamer's (1975) contention that social frames of reference influ-ence researchers' questions, which, in turn, shape the nature of interpreta-tion itself. In light of this situating process, the positivist notion that a text has one valid interpretation evap-orates into thin air. Researchers, whether they admit it or not, always have points of view, disciplinary orien-tations, and social or political groups with which they identify (Kincheloe, 1991; Lugg, 1996). Thus, the point is not that knowledge producers and teachers should shed all worldly affili-ations but that they should identify those affiliations and understand their impacts on the ways a researcher, a teacher, or a standards writer ap-proaches educational issues. Gadamer labels these world affiliations of re-searchers their "horizons" and deems the hermeneutic act of interpretation the "fusion of horizons." When re-searchers and teachers participate in the fusion of horizons, they enter into the tradition of the text. Here they study the conditions of its production and the circle of previous interpreta-tions. In this manner, they begin to uncover the ways the text has at-

tempted to represent truth (Berger, 1995; Ellis, 1998; Jardine, 1998; Miller and Hodge, 1998; Slattery, 1995). Is it not obvious that such a process moves the quality of educa-tion, the rigor of teaching and learn-ing, to a new level?

The hermeneutic tradition puts the politics of interpretation at center stage in education and knowledge pro-duction. Like ordinary human beings, complex knowledge workers make history and live their lives within structures of meaning they have not necessarily chosen for themselves. Un-derstanding this, students of herme-neutics realize that a central aspect of their sociocultural analysis involves dissecting the ways people connect their everyday experiences to the cul-tural representations of such experi-ences. Such work involves the unrav-eling of the ideological codings embedded in these cultural represen-tations. This unraveling is compli-cated by the taken-for-grantedness of the meanings promoted in schools and other social institutions and the typi-cally undetected ways these meanings are circulated into everyday life (Den-zin, 1992; Kogler, 1996). The better the analyst, the better he or she can ex-pose these meanings in the domain of "what goes without saying," that activ-ity previously deemed "noise" unwor-thy of comment. Schools need a healthy dose of this analysis of what goes without saying. The interpretive rigor of the hermeneutic tradition is an essential ingredient in our recipe for rigorous educational reform.

Locating the Frontier of Classroom Knowledge at the Points Where One's Personal Experience Intersects with Academic Information

In an epistemology of complexity, teachers are hermeneutical scholars who engage in rigorous thinking, extensive reading, ongoing dialogue, thorough analysis, and synthetic reflection. Technical standards and the teaching they support are grounded in the positivist epistemological assumption that knowledge is an external body of information independent of human beings. The teacher's role in this context is to *insert* this knowledge into the minds of students. Frequently, this "knowledge" is a body of isolated facts (factoids) to be committed to memory by uninterested students. Evaluation procedures that emphasize the retention of isolated bits and pieces of data strengthen this view of knowledge.

Conceptual thinking vanishes as technical standards–driven classes trivialize learning. Students are evaluated on the lowest level of human thinking—their ability to memorize. This "stupidification" process is directly related to the unstated, tacit positivist epistemology lurking in the hallways of the school. Thinking skills involving the ability to ask unique questions, to see connections among concepts, or to apply conceptual understandings lose importance. Empowered teachers aware of this epistemology of complexity focus on using these thinking skills to guide the in-

teraction between them and their students and the content and learning processes that they all want to engage. In this situation, both students and teachers reinterpret their own lives and in the process uncover new insights and talents. Unless students and teachers can incorporate academic information into their lives to produce new knowledge, their schooling will remain an ideological rite of passage into an existentially unconscious adulthood.

If teachers cannot engage their students in the development of an epistemological consciousness where they can produce knowledge, then my effort to educate thoughtful, emancipated, knowledgeable teachers is quite irrelevant. Why bother requiring a college degree if teachers simply deliver factoids? Why struggle to interest teacher-education students in the task of knowledge production, the quest for an epistemological consciousness, the effort to expose the values hiding in particular kinds of information and modes of teaching, or the formulation of questions about the effects of social context or power? The genius of great thinkers lies much less in their ability to retain the information they encounter than in their ability to produce new knowledge. When teachers gain an epistemological consciousness and come to understand that the collision of student experience with the information of the humanities, social sciences, and physical sciences produces new knowledge, then traditional information is not simply discarded. Complex, democratic teachers indeed reexamine what constitutes traditional knowledge, the traditional canon, but at the same time recognize value in the knowledge that others have produced.

The important epistemological point here is that we interrogate this knowledge and consider it in light of new contexts and questions. As we develop this point, the new contexts and questions on which we are focusing here involve our personal experiences and consciousnesses. How does this academic information, we ask, help us rethink, reinterpret, our prior experiences? How does it affect our political beliefs, our view of citizenship, our view of the way the physical world operates? How does it help (or hinder) us from becoming the people we want to become? What does it mean to us, given where and how we have lived our lives? These questions and others like them are important steps in the creation of emancipatory knowledge because they preclude the epistemologically reductionistic, concrete-level "mastery" of secondary (secondhand) data and the disempowerment they leave in their wake. There has to be more to education than this. Brilliant teachers are always working on new ways to help their students connect their lives to secondary academic data in ways that create new syntheses of knowledge, new ways of being.

Appreciating the epistemology of complexity, teachers understand that there is nothing simple about setting up this synthesis of secondary or academic information and personal experience. Such teachers grow comfortable with the uncertain, tentative syntheses that they and their students develop. They are keenly aware of the presence of contradiction and treasure the effort to integrate ostensibly dissimilar phenomena into new revealing combinations. Teachers conscious of these epistemological dynamics escape the confines of Cartesianism and set foot into new pedagogical, ontological, and even cosmological (used here to mean the nature of the universe and the inseparability of the nature of life and human consciousness from this larger whole) realms.

Only an individual with a consciousness of epistemological complexity who understands self in its critical, cosmological (interconnected) context is ready to jump into this new realm. Whereas the formal, operational orientation of Cartesianism functions on the basis of isolation of parts, linear causality, and determinism, the epistemology of complexity assumes a holism based on a complex, nonlinear interconnection of events. In particular in the context of my previous point, this holism involves the continuum of cosmos and self. Where does the cosmos end and the self begin? The frontier that connects (not separates) world and self is a living part of both (O'Sullivan, 1999; Van Hesteran, 1986; Kramer, 1983).

As democratic teachers grow accustomed to this self-world connectedness, they are reminded once again of the epistemology of complexity's rejection of universal, *correct* ways of viewing the social, physical, and educational worlds. Such teachers not only will see multiple interpretations of social phenomena but also will be able to identify the contexts from which they emanate and the ways they intersect with the life experiences of themselves and their students. They appreciate what systems of meaning various knowledge producers have employed to shape the data they disseminate—from whose perspective their stories are told.

With these understandings, educators emancipate themselves from Cartesianism and the structural forces that limit human ability to see the world from outside our restricted place in the web of reality. In logic-centered modernism, this monitoring of self-perception was subverted in positivism's discounting of the centrality of the terrain of private, inner reality. In line with the modernist impulse, what purpose did the realm of consciousness serve in the process of industrialization, the quest for material progress, or the manly conquest of nature? As epistemological complexity rediscovers the sensuous and erotic dimensions of humanness, it incorporates such notions into new ways of exploring and perceiving the social, physical, educational, and even intrapersonal domains (Gordon, Miller, and Rollock, 1990; Kramer, 1983; Slaughter, 1989).

Such new modes of thinking, producing knowledge, and teaching incorporate sensual and self-knowledge in interesting and rigorous ways. Teachers, researchers, and teacher-researchers who do not understand the way information interacts with their own experiences and shapes their own consciousnesses tend to misconstrue the pronouncements, actions, and feelings of others. The multiple readings characteristic of a complex epistemology are remote to modernist, formal teachers and knowledge producers, as they seek comfort in the prescribed methods, the objectivity, and especially the depersonalization of traditional positivistic social and educational science. Such positivistic teachers and knowledge producers are nervous purveyors of the *correct answers* of traditional positivistic science (Van Hesteran, 1986; Steinberg and Kincheloe, 1998).

In a sense, the positivist, objectivist tradition provides a shelter in which the self can hide from the deeply personal issues that permeate all social and educational phenomena. Such personal issues, if it were not for the depersonalization of Cartesian knowledge production, would force an uncomfortable element of researcher self-disclosure. Epistemologically conscious teachers, of course, move beyond this positivist veil of secrecy, exploring and revealing how their own perspectives and values came to be constructed—how the information they encounter shapes their pedagogies and worldviews. They transcend Cartesian formalism's concern with problem solving by seeking the genesis of the problems they discern. In this way, they develop a form of intrapersonal intelligence, as they learn to contextually examine the origins and nature of their own thinking—a key aspect of becoming an educated person.

Reflective Ontology: Searching for New Forms of Human Being

One of the most important ways that a complex education moves us to new levels of consciousness and being involves gaining awareness of ourselves as social and historical beings. Individuals who gain such an awareness understand how and why their political opinions, religious beliefs, gender roles, or racial perspectives have been shaped by dominant perspectives. Our epistemology of complexity plays such an important role in this attempt to gain new understandings and insights as to who we could become. As it exposes the particular ways knowledge is produced and the impact it exerts on the shaping of self, we all begin to understand that our present state of being (our ontological selves) is in part a social and historical construction. Just as it has been shaped by social action, it can be rethought and reshaped by social action. This subsection, our last feature of an epistemology of complexity, blurs the lines of knowledge production and being (ontology), as we focus on how we move from the gaining of epistemological consciousness to new ways of being human. In this context, teachers and their students move into a realm where they pursue what might be labeled a "reflective ontology."

A critical epistemology of complexity promotes self-reflection that results in attitudinal changes. The basis of these changes rests on insights into the scars and traumas of the past. Teachers thus help their students begin the process of understanding themselves by bringing to consciousness the process by which their identities were formed. Action that is to be taken by students to address social pathologies such as racism, sexism, or class bias that shape individual consciousness can begin to be negotiated once self-reflection has taken place. Prudent ontological action that involves asking questions of ethics, morality, politics, emotion, and gut feeling does not take the form of rules and precise regulations. Our understanding of a democratic system of meaning vis-à-vis an epistemology of complexity provides a framework of principles around which can be discussed action rather than a set of procedures. Teachers who engage in the quest for new, expanded, more just, and interconnected ways of being human—a democratic, reflective ontology—are never certain of the exact path of action they will take in such a pursuit. An awareness of contextual factors will always complicate the effort.

A part of the democratic, reflective action we might take involves questioning accepted definitions of particular social entities such as intelligence, school success, a good society, popularity, or competence. As active interpreters with a social and ontological imagination, we can redefine such notions in more just and conceptually expanded ways. In such a context, we can involve ourselves and others in a process of social reconstruction, educational reconceptualization, and self-improvement. According to an epistemology of complexity, we hold the power to reconstruct our consciousness. If this is the case, then in a reflective ontological context, we possess the ability to reshape ourselves—a process that given our location in the social web of reality concurrently demands that we reinterpret our traditions and reinvent our futures together in solidarity with other self-directed human agents.

The thinking of teachers and students is intimately connected to these ontological features. As epistemologically conscious teachers and students get behind the curtain of the lived world, they come to understand both the complexity and the limitations of history. Teachers ask not only how do we know but also why does knowing matter to us in this particular place and time? How does this knowledge shape me? What does it demand of me now that I know it? Such questions are central to the reconceptualization of the civic self and to the future of democracy in a world where power squashes democratic impulses (Pang, Gay, and Stanley, 1995). Given such hostile sociopolitical circumstances, democratic educators seek catalysts for ontological evaluation. How do we use our epistemological consciousness to push the boundaries of humanness?

A key step involves freeing ourselves from the machine metaphors of positivism. An epistemology of complexity recognizes the reductionism of viewing the universe as a well-oiled machine and the human mind as a computer. Such ways of seeing subvert an appreciation of the amazing life force that inhabits both the universe and human beings. This machine cosmology positioned human beings as living in a dead world, a lifeless universe. Ontologically, this positivism separated individuals from their lifeless surroundings, undermining any organic interconnection of the person to the cosmos. The life-giving complexity of the inseparability of human and world was lost, and the study of people was *abstracted*—removed from context. Such a removal has had disastrous ontological, psychological, and social effects. Human beings in a sense lost their belongingness to the world and people around them (O'Sullivan, 1999).

Again, Ladi Semali and my (1999) concept of the importance of indigenous knowledge in the twenty-first century emerges. With the birth of modernism and the scientific revolution, many premodern, indigenous epistemologies, cosmologies, and ontologies were lost—ridiculed by European modernists as primitive. Although there is great diversity among premodern worldviews, there do seem to be some discernible patterns that distinguish them from modernist European perspectives. In addition to developing meaning systems that were connected to cosmological perspectives on the nature of creation, most premodern viewpoints saw nature and the world-at-large as living systems. Western, often Christian, observers condescendingly labeled such perspectives as *pantheism* or *nature worship* and positioned them as an enemy of the notion of monotheism. As such, they needed to be stamped out and replaced with a belief in the one true God. Not understanding the subtlety and nuance of such indigenous views of the world, Europeans subverted the sense of belonging that accompanied these enchanted views of nature. European Christomodernism transformed the individual from a connected participant in the drama of nature to a detached, objective, depersonalized observer.

The modernist individual emerged from the process alienated and disenchanted. As Edmund O'Sullivan (1999) puts it, Cartesianism tore apart "the relationship between the microcosmos and the macrocosmos" (82). Such a fragmentation resulted in the loss of cosmological significance and the beginning of a snowballing pattern of ontological imbalance. A reflective ontology involves the process of reconnecting human beings on a variety of levels and in numerous ways to a living social and physical web of reality, to a living cosmos. Teachers in this context help students connect to the civic web of the political domain, the biotic web of the natural world, the social web of human life, and the epistemological web of knowledge production. In this manner, we all move to the realm of reflective ontology where new ways of being and new ways of being connected reshape all people.

Philip Wexler (2000) picks up on these ontological issues, arguing that an intuitive disenchantment with positivist fragmentation and its severing of the self-environment relationship are fueling a diffuse social revaluation. He employs the term *revitalization* for this mass decentered movement taking place throughout Western societies. It constitutes an attempt, he contends, to resacralize our culture and ourselves. Such an effort exposes the impact of Eurocentrism and positivism on what human beings have become, as at the same time it produces an ontological "change from within." Understanding the problems with positivism's lack of self-awareness or concern with consciousness and interconnectedness, Wexler's resacralization picks up on wisdom traditions to construct an ontology of complexity. In this context, the Cartesian bifurcation of the mind and body is repaired, and new relationships and comfort with the body, mind, and spirit are pursued. In the transcendence of modernist notions of bodily ego-greed, a new understanding of the body's role in meaning making is obtained.

Resacralization positions the body in relation to cognition and the process of life itself. The body is a corporeal reflection of the evolutionary concept of *autopoiesis*—self-organizing or self-making of life. *Autopoiesis* involves the production of a pattern of life organization. Cognition in this ontological context involves the process of self-production. Thus, life itself is a cognitive activity that involves establishing patterns of living, patterns that become the life force through self-organization. If life is self-organized, then there are profound cognitive, epistemological, and ontological implications. By recognizing new patterns and developing new processes, humans exercise much more input into their own evolution than previously imagined.

Human evolution (and, in the context of our discussion, cognitive evolution) is not as random as previously thought. Life is self-produced in forms of escalating diversity and complexity. The interaction of different living forms can catalyze the self-production feature of living systems. In both its corporeal and its cognitive expressions, the *autopoietic* life process reaches out for difference, for novelty, to embrace its next ontological level (Wexler, 2000; Capra, 1996). Teachers who understand an epistemology of complexity can use these ontological notions to rethink their lives and their teaching. With these understandings, we can "self-organize and reorganize" education to achieve new levels of complexity where new patterns and processes allow us to rethink the nature of our being and the possibility of our being. Schooling in this complex context takes on an unprecedented importance, as it pursues ways of knowing and being that shape the evolution of the human species. Thus, standards of complexity and the epistemological complexity on which they rest not only can improve schooling but also can place education where it should have been all along—at the forefront of our journey into the future.

References

Anderson, E. 1987. Gender as a variable in teacher thinking. In *Higher order thinking: Definition, meaning, and instructional approaches*, ed. R. Thomas. Washington, DC: Home Economics Education Association.

Aronowitz, S. 1983. The relativity of theory. *Village Voice* 27: 60.

Aronowitz, S., and H. Giroux. 1985. *Education under siege*. South Hadley, MA: Bergin and Garvey.

Astronomical instruments. 1999. <http://www.scinet.org.uk/database/physics/Instruments/p00827c.html>.

Barrow, R. 1984. *Giving teaching back to teachers*. Totowa, NJ: Barnes and Noble.

Beed, C. 1991. Philosophy of science and contemporary economics: An overview. *Journal of Post-Keynesian Economics* 13(4): 459–94.

Belecky, M., B. Clinchy, N. Goldberger, and J. Tarule. 1986. *Women's ways of knowing: The development of self, voice, and mind*. New York: Basic Books.

Berger, A. 1995. *Cultural criticism: A primer of key concepts*. Thousand Oaks, CA: Sage.

Besag, F. 1986. Reality and research. *American Behavioral Scientist* 30(1): 6–14.

Bookchin, M. 1995. *The philosophy of social ecology: Essays on dialectical naturalism*. 2nd ed. Montreal: Black Rose Books.

Bowers, C. 1982. The reproduction of technological consciousness: Locating the ideological foundations of a radical pedagogy. *Teachers College Record* 83(4): 529–57.

Briggs, J., and F. Peat. 1989. *Turbulent mirror*. New York: Harper and Row.

Britzman, D. 1991. *Practice makes practice: A critical study of learning to teach*. Albany: State University of New York Press.

Cadenhead, K. 1985. Is substantive change in teacher education possible? *Journal of Teacher Education* 36: 17–21.

Capra, F. 1996. *The web of life: A new scientific understanding of living systems.* New York: Anchor Books.

Carson, T., and D. Sumara. 1997. *Action research as a living practice.* New York: Peter Lang.

Carspecken, P. 1996. *Critical ethnography in educational research: A theoretical and political guide.* New York: Routledge.

_____. 1999. *Four scenes for posing the question of meaning and other essays in critical philosophy and critical methodology.* New York: Peter Lang.

Chamberlin, G. 1974. Phenomenological methodology and understanding education. In *Existentialism and phenomenology in education,* ed. D. Denton. New York: Teachers College Press.

Cherryholmes, C. 1988. *Power and criticism: Poststructural investigations in education.* New York: Teachers College Press.

Clark, C. 1987. Asking the right questions about teacher preparation: Contributions of research on teacher thinking. Occasional paper no. 110. East Lansing: Institute for Research on Teaching, Michigan State University.

Denzin, N. 1992. *Symbolic interactionism and cultural studies: The politics of interpretation.* Cambridge, MA: Blackwell.

_____. 1994. The art and politics of interpretation. In *Handbook of qualitative research,* ed. N. Denzin and Y. Lincoln. Thousand Oaks, CA: Sage.

Denzin, N., and Y. Lincoln, eds. 2000. *Handbook of qualitative research.* 2nd ed. Thousand Oaks, CA: Sage.

Dewey, J. 1916. *Democracy and education.* New York: Free Press.

Dion-Buffalo, Y., and J. Mohawk. 1992. Thoughts from an autochthonous center: Postmodernism and cultural studies. *Akwe:kon Journal* 9(4): 16–21.

Dobrin, R. 1987. The nature of causality and reality: A reconciliation of the ideas of Einstein and Bohr in the light of Eastern thought. In *Einstein and the humanities,* ed. D. Ryan. New York: Greenwood Press.

Doll, W. 1989. Foundations for a postmodern curriculum. *Journal of Curriculum Studies* 21(3): 243–53.

Donmoyer, R. 1985. The rescue from relativism: Two failed attempts and an alternative strategy. *Educational Researcher* 14: 13–20.

Einstein on spacetime. 1998. <http://web plaza.pt.lu/public/fklaess/html/space time.html>.

Eisner, E. 1984. Can educational research inform educational practice? *Phi Delta Kappan* 65(7): 447–52.

Ellis, J. 1998. Interpretive inquiry as student research. In *Students as researchers: Creating classrooms that matter,* ed. S. Steinberg and J. Kincheloe. London: Falmer.

Evans, J. 1997. Relativity and black holes. <http://www.physics.gmu.edu/classinfo /astr228/coursenotes/In_ch19.htm>.

Fetterman, D. 1988. Qualitative approaches to evaluating education. *Educational Researcher* 17(8): 17–23.

Fiske, D., and R. Shweder. 1986. *Metatheory in social science: Pluralisms and subjectivities.* Chicago: University of Chicago Press.

Fiske, J. 1993. *Power plays, power works.* New York: Verso.

Fowler, G. 1984. Philosophical assumptions and contemporary research perspectives. Paper presented to the Speech Communication Association, Chicago.

Freire, P., and A. Faundez. 1989. *Learning to question: A pedagogy of liberation.* New York: Continuum.

Freire, P., and I. Shor. 1987. *A pedagogy for liberation: Dialogues on transforming education.* South Hadley, MA: Bergin and Garvey.

Gadamer, H-G. 1975. *Truth and method.* Ed. G. Barden and J. Cumming. New York: Seabury.

Gallagher, S. 1992. *Hermeneutics and edu-*

cation. Albany: State University of New York Press.

Garrison, J. 1988. Democracy, scientific knowledge, and teacher empowerment. *Teachers College Record* 89(4): 487–504.

———. 1989. The role of postpositivistic philosophy of science in the renewal of vocational education research. *Journal of Vocational Education* 14(3): 39–51.

Gordon, E., F. Miller, and D. Rollock, eds. 1990. Coping with communicentric bias in knowledge production in the social sciences. *Educational Researcher* 19(3): 14–19.

Gravitational radiation. 1998. <http://zebu.uoregon.edu/~imamura/122/jan12/gw.html>.

Greene, M. 1975. Curriculum and consciousness. In *Curriculum theorizing: The reconceptualists*, ed. W. Pinar. Berkeley: McCutchan.

———. 1988. *The dialectic of freedom*. New York: Teachers College Press.

———. 1995. *Releasing the imagination: Essays on education, the arts, and social change*. San Francisco: Jossey-Bass.

Grondin, J. 1994. *Introduction to philosophical hermeneutics*. New Haven: Yale University Press.

Gross, A., and W. Keith, eds. 1997. *Rhetorical hermeneutics: Invention and interpretation in the age of science*. Albany: State University of New York Press.

Grumet, M. 1988. *Bitter milk: Women and teaching*. New Haven: Yale University Press.

Haggerson, N. 2000. *Expanding curriculum research and understanding: A mythopoetic perspective*. New York: Peter Lang.

Held, D. 1980. *Introduction to critical theory: Horkheimer to Habermas*. Berkeley and Los Angeles: University of California Press.

Hicks, E. 1999. *Ninety-five languages and seven forms of intelligence*. New York: Peter Lang.

Hinchey, P. 1998. *Finding freedom in the classroom: A practical introduction to critical theory*. New York: Peter Lang.

Horton, M., and P. Freire. 1990. *We make the road by walking: Conversations on education and social change*. Philadelphia: Temple University Press.

Howe, K. 1985. Two dogmas of educational research. *Educational Researcher* 14: 10–18.

Husserl, E. 1970. *The crisis of European sciences and transcendental phenomenology: An introduction to phenomenology*. Evanston, IL: Northwestern University Press.

Jardine, D. 1998. *To dwell with a boundless heart: Essays in curriculum theory, hermeneutics, and the ecological imagination*. New York: Peter Lang.

Kellner, D. 1995. *Media culture: Cultural studies, identity, and politics between the modern and the postmodern*. New York: Routledge.

Kincheloe, J. 1991. *Teachers as researchers: Qualitative paths to empowerment*. New York: Falmer.

———. 1995. *Toil and trouble: Good work, smart workers, and the integration of academic and vocational education*. New York: Peter Lang.

Kincheloe, J., and P. McLaren. 2000. Rethinking critical theory and qualitative research. In *Handbook of qualitative research*, ed. N. Denzin and Y. Lincoln. Thousand Oaks, CA: Sage.

Kincheloe, J., and S. Steinberg. 1997. *Changing multiculturalism*. London: Open University Press.

Kincheloe, J., S. Steinberg, and D. Tippins. 1999. *The stigma of genius: Einstein consciousness and education*. New York: Peter Lang.

Kincheloe, J., S. Steinberg, and L. Villaverde. 1999. *Rethinking intelligence: Confronting psychological assumptions about teaching and learning*. New York: Routledge.

Kneller, G. 1984. *Movements of thought in modern education*. 2nd ed. New York: John Wiley and Sons.

Kogler, H. 1996. *The power of dialogue: Critical hermeneutics after Gadamer and Foucault*. Cambridge, MA: MIT Press.

Koller, A. 1981. *An unknown woman: A journey to self-discovery*. New York: Bantam Books.

Kovel, J. 1998. Dialect as praxis. *Science and Society* 62(3): 474–80.

Kramer, D. 1983. Post-formal operations? A need for further conceptualization. *Human Development* 26: 91–105.

Krievis, L. 1998. Creating north. In *Students as researchers: Creating classrooms that matter*, ed. S. Steinberg and J. Kincheloe. London: Falmer.

Lawler, J. 1975. The Marxian dialectic: Dialectic investigations by Bertell Ollman. *Monthly Review* 46(9): 48–51.

Levins, R. 1998. Dialectics and systems theory. *Science and Society* 62(3): 375–89.

Lincoln, Y., and E. Guba. 1985. *Naturalistic inquiry*. Beverly Hills, CA: Sage.

Lowe, D. 1982. *History of bourgeois perception*. Chicago: University of Chicago Press.

Lugg, C. 1996. *For God and country: Conservatism and American school policy*. New York: Peter Lang.

Madison, G. 1988. *The hermeneutics of postmodernity: Figures and themes*. Bloomington: Indiana University Press.

Mahoney, M., and W. Lyddon. 1988. Recent developments in cognitive approaches to counseling and psychotherapy. *Counseling Psychologist* 16(2): 190–234.

Mandell, S. 1987. A search for form: Einstein and the poetry of Louis Zukofsky and William Carlos Williams. In *Einstein and the humanities*, ed. D. Ryan. Westport, CN: Greenwood Press.

Mashalidis, S. 1997. Consciousness and education: A process perspective. <http://faculty.erau.edu/meshalis/consciousness.htm/s>.

Mathison, S. 2000. Promoting democracy through evaluation. In *Democratic social education: Social studies for social change*, ed. D. Hursh and E. Ross. New York: Falmer.

McLaren, P. 1989. *Life in schools*. New York: Longman.

McLaren, P., and J. Morris. 1997. Mighty Morphin Power Rangers: The aesthetics of macho-militaristic justice. In *Kinderculture: The corporate construction of childhood*, ed. J. Kincheloe and S. Steinberg. Boulder, CO: Westview.

Merleau-Ponty, M. 1962. *Phenomenology of perception*. London: Routledge and Kegan Paul.

Miller, S., and J. Hodge. 1998. Phenomenology, hermeneutics, and narrative analysis: Some unfinished methodological business. Unpublished paper.

Mullin, J. 1994. Feminist theory, feminist pedagogy: The gap between what we say and what we do. *Composition Studies/Freshman English News* 22(1): 14–24.

Myers, L. 1987. The deep structure of culture: Relevance of traditional African culture in contemporary life. *Journal of Black Studies* 18(1): 72–85.

Nieto, S. 1996. *Affirming diversity: The sociopolitical context of multicultural education*. White Plains, NY: Longman.

Nixon, J. 1981. Postscript to *A teachers' guide to action research*, ed. J. Nixon. London: Grant McIntyre.

Nyang, S., and A. Vandi. 1980. Pan Africanism in world history. In *Contemporary black thought: Alternative analyses in social and behavioral science*, ed. M. Asante and A. Vandi. Beverly Hills: Sage.

Orteza, Y. M. 1988. Broadening the focus of research in education. *Journal of Research and Development in Education* 22(1): 23–28.

O'Sullivan, E. 1999. *Transformative learning: Educational vision for the twenty-first century*. London: Zed.

Pang, V., G. Gay, and W. Stanley. 1995. Expanding conceptions of community and civic competencies for a multicultural society. *Theory and Research in Social Education* 23(4): 302–31.

Peoria Astronomical Society. 1998. Beyond the event horizon: An introduction to black holes. <http://www.astronomical.org/astbook/blkhole.html>.

Peters, M., and C. Lankshear. 1994. Education and hermeneutics: A Freiran interpretation. In *Politics of liberation: Paths from Freire*, ed. P. McLaren and C. Lankshear. New York: Routledge.

Pinar, W. 1975. *Currere:* Toward reconceptualization. In *Curriculum theorizing: The reconceptualists*, ed. W. Pinar. Berkeley: McCutchan.

_____. 1994. *Autobiography, politics, and sexuality: Essays in curriculum theory, 1972–1992.* New York: Peter Lang.

_____. 1999. *Contemporary curriculum discourses: Twenty years of JCT.* 2nd ed. New York: Peter Lang.

Pinar, W., W. Reynolds, P. Slattery, and P. Taubman. 1995. *Understanding curriculum.* New York: Peter lang.

Ponzio, R. 1985. Can we change content without changing context? *Teacher Education Quarterly* 12(3): 39–43.

Popkewitz, T. 1981. The study of schooling: Paradigms and field-based methodologies in education research and evaluation. In *The study of schooling*, ed. T. Popkewitz and B. Tabachnick. New York: Praeger.

Postman, N. 1995. *The end of education: Redefining the value of school.* New York: Knopf.

Puk, T. 1994. Epistemological implications of training social studies teachers: Just who was Christopher Columbus? *Social Studies* 85(5): 228–32.

Rapko, J. 1998. Review of the power of dialogue: Critical hermeneutics after Gadamer and Foucault. *Criticism* 4(1): 133–38.

Reinharz, S. 1979. *On becoming a social scientist.* San Francisco: Jossey-Bass.

Romanish, B. 1986. Critical thinking and the curriculum: A critique. *Educational Forum* 51(1): 45–56.

Rosen, S. 1987. *Hermeneutics as politics.* New York: Oxford University Press.

Schon, D. 1987. *Educating the reflective practitioner.* San Francisco: Jossey-Bass.

Schwandt, T. 2000. Three epistemological stances for qualitative inquiry: Interpretivism, hermeneutics, and social constructivism. In *Handbook of qualitative research*, ed. N. Denzin and Y. Lincoln. 2nd ed. Thousand Oaks, CA: Sage.

Semali, L., and J. Kincheloe. 1999. *What is indigenous knowledge? Voices from the academy.* New York: Falmer.

Shweder, R., and D. Fiske. 1986. Introduction: Uneasy social science. In *Metatheory in social science: Pluralisms and subjectivities*, ed. D. Fiske and R. Shweder. Chicago: University of Chicago Press.

Slattery, P. 1995. *Curriculum development in the postmodern era.* New York: Garland.

Slaughter, R. 1989. Cultural reconstruction in the post-modern world. *Journal of Curriculum Studies* 3: 255–70.

Smith, D. 1999. *Pedagon: Interdisciplinary essays in the human sciences, pedagogy, and culture.* New York: Peter Lang.

Smith, J. 1983. Quantitative versus qualitative research: An attempt to clarify the issue. *Educational Researcher* 12: 6–13.

Soltis, J. 1984. On the nature of educational research. *Educational Research* 13: 5–10.

Steinberg, S., and J. Kincheloe. 1998. *Students as researchers: Creating classrooms that matter.* London: Falmer.

Steward, D., and A. Mickunas. 1974. *Exploring phenomenology.* Chicago: American Library Association.

Still right after all these years. 1998. <http://news3.news.wisc.edu/052einstein/frame_drag4.html>.

Talbot, M. 1986. *Beyond the quantum.* New York: Bantam Books.

_____. 1991. *The holographic universe.* New York: HarperCollins.

Van Hesteran, F. 1986. Counseling research in a different key: The promise of human science perspective. *Canadian Journal of Counseling* 20(4): 200–234.

Vattimo, G. 1994. *Beyond interpretation: The meaning of hermeneutics for philosophy.* Stanford, CA: Stanford University Press.

Wexler, P. 2000. *The mystical society: Revitalization in culture, theory, and education.* Boulder, CO: Westview.

Wilson, S. 1977. The use of ethnographic techniques in educational research. *Review of Educational Research* 47(1): 245–65.

Woods, A., and T. Grant, 1998. Reason in revolt: Marxism and modern science. <http://easyweb.easynet.co.uk~zac/chapter7.htm>.

AN EXAMINATION AND REDESCRIPTION OF EPISTEMOLOGY

Barbara J. Thayer-Bacon

The Blind Men and the Elephant

There were six men from Industan
to learning much inclined
who went to see the elephant
though each of them was blind
so that by observation
each might satisfy his mind.[1]

Many of us are familiar with this poem, having read it in school and laughed at the silly blind men who didn't know they were feeling different parts of an elephant: One felt the tail and thought the elephant was like a rope, another felt a leg and thought the elephant was like a tree. One felt the ear and decided the elephant was like a fan, one felt the trunk and reported the elephant was like a snake, one felt the side of the elephant and suggested the elephant was like a wall, and the last man felt the elephant's tusk and announced the elephant was like a spear.

The poem serves as a metaphor for this chapter. Maybe the six blind men

from Industan are not so silly after all; maybe they represent all of us, as we struggle to make sense of the complex world in which we live. I plan to refer to the elephant poem and see if it can't help us understand the world in a new way and from a different perspective than we've been taught.

Richard Rorty describes philosophers as poets, prophets, and soothsayers. Theirs is the task of trying to envision the world in new ways, trying to redescribe the familiar through the use of imagination and metaphors (Rorty, 1989). Philosophers do not have a "God's-eye view" or an "inside line to truth." Their skills, the ability to reason and envision, are ones that are available to all, as are their tools, including logic and critical thinking. With this in mind, I plan to use the metaphor of the six blind men from Industan and their elephant to take another look at knowledge. I will look at the distinctions and categories people have created to describe knowledge and suggest that perhaps these past descriptions are in need of revision. I will suggest that defining and describing *epistemology*, a study of theories of knowledge, the way many others have described it leads to a narrow representation of the world and creates serious problems that need to be addressed. Is it possible that in defining knowledge we have excluded qualities that are essential to knowledge? Have we focused on parts of the elephant and lost sight of the larger animal? Is what we are each describing part of something much larger and more comprehensive then any of its parts? I strive to soften distinctions and encourage a more interactive perspective among categories such as epistemology, metaphysics, and psychology; the knower and the known; and belief and knowledge.

This examination and redescription of epistemology as a branch of philosophy is necessary in order for me to be able to offer my own epistemological theory, what I wish to describe as the nurturing of a *relational epistemology*.[2] This chapter is meant to motivate the development of an expanded conception of epistemology. The further development of a relational epistemology is published in another article.[3] In this chapter I look at others' contributions to epistemological theory. In doing so, I hope to bring out some important issues and concerns, as well as others' attempts to address these concerns. I intend to highlight past epistemological theories and then turn my discussion to some key theorists who

are currently working in the field of epistemology, hoping that the past theories, which have influenced the current theories, will indirectly be included in the conversation. I have chosen these people based on their extensive contributions to the discussion and my judgment that they represent different perspectives that need to be heard.[4] The second section of the chapter highlights key classical epistemological answers to the question, What is it to "know"? The third part describes current epistemological theories and uses these theories as a way to examine the questions and concerns others have raised about a traditional approach to epistemology. The fourth part concludes with the need to redescribe epistemology.

The Elephant Poem in Relation to Past Theories

Please imagine that the elephant poem is a metaphor for theories that explain what it is to know—epistemological theories. There are many examples of important theories from our past, and it is impossible for me to do any of them justice in the space allowed. But I hope that by highlighting some and comparing them to the elephant poem, I will demonstrate the need to reexamine our conceptions of epistemology.

Plato described knowledge as something that was Ideal, beyond the grasp of the world that we experience as reality (Plato, 1970a, p. 17). Even though we may each experience a different kind of elephant, we can all understand what an elephant is, because we each have an idea of "Elephant-ness" in its Ideal Form. According to Plato, our souls have all knowledge before they are born and inhabit a physical body. It is the inhabiting of a physical body that causes our souls to forget that knowledge. Learning is re-membering what we each already knew: "The soul, then, as being im-mortal and having been born again many times, and having seen all things that exist, whether in this world or in the world below, has knowledge of them all; . . . for as all nature is akin, and the soul has learned all things, there is no difficulty in a man eliciting out of a single recollection all the rest . . . ; for all inquiry and all learning is but recollection" (Plato, 1970a, p. 17).

It does not matter to Plato that each of us experiences the world in a different way; because we are souls in-habiting our bodies, we are blind to knowledge (what is true), just like the six blind men. We cannot trust our senses and be sure we really know what it is we are experiencing. We must tune in to what our souls know. Only by tuning in to the knowledge one's soul already possesses can a per-son hope eventually to realize the truth of what he experiences. Others, such as teachers, may act like mid-wives and help guide the soul on its journey, but ultimately each soul must find the answers by itself. Finding the answers, realizing the Ideals, is to have knowledge of what is true, according to Plato.

"The Myth of the Cave," in Plato's *Republic*, is a wonderful story that presents "reality" as something that is socially constructed. The people in the cave experience what they think is "reality"; but what they are really ex-periencing are shadows on the wall, as they sit, chained and unable to move or turn their heads to see there is a fire behind them; objects they thought were real are just shadows, the real ob-jects being carried by people behind them. Like the blind men from Indus-tan, their senses deceive them, and they cannot trust their experiences: "The prison-house is the world of sight, the light of the fire is the power of the sun, and you will not misappre-hend me if you interpret the journey upwards to be the ascent of the soul into the intellectual world, . . . my opinion is that in the world of knowl-edge the Idea of good appears last of all, and it is seen only with effort" (Plato, 1970b, p. 85).

Many students who read Plato's *Re-public* and "The Myth of the Cave" are struck by the profoundness of his de-scription. He has escaped the problem of our experiences of "reality" being partial and flawed by saying we should not trust our experiences anyway. What we need to do is trust our souls. Plato points out one of the key tools available to any person striving to know truth: what he calls *divine con-templation*. Divine contemplation is the tuning in to one's soul in search of answers.

Whereas our argument shows that the power and capacity of learning exists in the soul already; and that just as if it were not possible to turn the eye from darkness to light without the whole body, so too the instrument of knowledge can only by the movement of the whole soul be turned from the world of becoming to that of being, and learn by degrees to endure the sight of being, and of the brightness and best of being, or in other worlds, of the good. (Plato, 1970b, p. 86)

Aristotle argued that knowledge was obtained through tuning in to the soul, to one's ideas, and testing out those ideas through one's experiences (Aristotle, 1970). He presented the case that ideas can be deceptive and misleading, just as our experiences can be deceiving. We know that six blind men can feel different parts of an animal, develop ideas of what they are experiencing, and never realize they are each feeling the same animal. If each of these six men never have an idea of elephant, but rather have ideas of ropes, snakes, spears, fans, walls, and tree trunks, their ideas will not help them see the truth about what they are experiencing. Aristotle hoped that the use of both our ideas and our experiences would lead us to knowledge: "Reasoning on matters of conduct employs premises of two forms . . . one universal is predicated of the man himself, the other of the thing" (Aristotle, 1970, p. 117).

Stating that one's ideas and one's experiences can both be flawed, Aristotle sent the Western world philosophers off on a task that still has not been resolved. Some philosophers have developed epistemological theories that have leaned in Plato's direction and fa-

vored ideas, such as Descartes (1960); some have made suggestions that have leaned toward favoring experiences over ideas, such as Locke (1894). Descartes recommended that the blind men use a doubting method whereby everything they can doubt, they should dismiss, until they reach that which they take to be self-evident; what is beyond doubt is what they can be sure is true. This view says that what our minds believe to be self-evident we can trust to be a mirror of the world as it exists. Locke recommended that, since each of us came into this world as a blank slate (*tabula rasa*) with no knowledge prior to birth, it is our experiences we must rely on, along with our ability to reason.

Others have tried to find a balance between ideas and experience, as Aristotle recommended. Kant suggested that what we can know is not independent reality, "the thing in itself," but always reality as it appears to human beings. Our perceptions of the world are a result of our interaction with the external world and the active powers of our minds (Kant, 1966). C.S. Peirce suggested that since all of us are flawed individuals who can't trust our ideas or our experiences, what we need to do is work with others, as a community of rational inquirers, to help further our knowledge and understanding (Peirce, 1958).

Like Aristotle, Peirce approached truth from a scientific perspective. Peirce said we seek answers, new solutions, and therefore get closer to truth, as we run into problems with our current beliefs and start to have doubts about what we thought was "truth." For Peirce, the only method other than a priori speculation (Plato's Ideals) is the "self-corrective" scientific method, whose experimental results are always subject to revision on the basis of further evidence (Peirce, 1958, p. 92).

Truth, for Peirce, is absolute, but none of us will ever know absolute truth, because we are all limited beings. This is Peirce's theory of *fallibilism*. Truth is something we are emerging toward, for with each generation of inquirers we have more understanding. "The opinion which is fated to be ultimately agreed to by all who investigate is what we mean by the truth, and the object represented in this opinion is real. That is the way I would explain reality" (Peirce, 1958, p. 133). Truth is not something one person can find, all on his own; it is found through the collection of all rational inquirers' investigations; because it takes all of us, the truth in the end will be the same for all of us. "The method [for fixing beliefs] must be such that the ultimate conclusion of every man shall be the same, or would be the same if inquiry were sufficiently persisted in. Such is the method of science" (Peirce, 1958, p. 107). As Peirce described truth, it is something the last person on earth will know: "True opinion must be the one which they would ultimately come to" (Peirce, 1958, pp. 133–134).

Kant would advise the six blind men from Industan that they can never know the elephant as the-thing-in-itself, Elephant, but only the elephant as it is represented in relation to

their experiences and their minds. Peirce would advise the six blind men to start talking to each other and share the information each of them has. Only by acting as a community of inquirers can they hope to gather a more complete understanding of elephants, one they can all agree upon. But they had better be cautious and aware that because they are limited human beings, they will likely not understand all there is to know about elephants because the next generation will build on the knowledge they have gained through sharing with each other, and the next generation will reach an even better understanding of elephants than current inquirers can possibly reach.

The Elephant Poem in Relation to Current Theories

The issues and concerns about epistemology are still debated today as heatedly as they were in early Greece. If we look at the debate in the present, it can be described this way: We begin with the world as a given (there is an elephant), and then say any description of the world, the sense that is made of the world, is something people create; the meanings people give to the world derive, in part, from the descriptions people develop to explain the world, "reality." So the blind men of Industan offer descriptions of what they experience, each experiencing a different part of an elephant; this feels this way, based on their past experiences and the meanings that have been attached to those experiences.

When one man feels a snakelike shape, the trunk of the elephant, he describes the elephant as a snake, based on the meaning he has attached to an object having that particular shape. Attaching meaning to what each man describes helps each person make sense of the world he is experiencing, the part of the elephant.

Sociologists have labeled this making sense of the world the "social construction of reality" (Berger & Luckmann, 1966).[5] People give meaning to the reality they experience, through language, and then pass that meaning on to their children through conversation and education. Children internalize their parents' socially constructed "reality" through the language they learn and what they are taught. "The child does not internalize the world of [his or her] significant others as one of many possible worlds. [She or he] internalizes it as the world, the only existent and only conceivable world, the world tout court" (Berger & Luckmann, 1966, p. 134). One could imagine that each blind man from Industan had children whom he proceeded to teach that an elephant is a fan, a snake, or a spear, because that is "reality" as he knows it. He has pieced together that "reality" and then passed it on as "reality" to his children. His children do not know that this view of elephants is partial or flawed; they take it to be truth, the only way an elephant could possibly exist, for example, is in the shape of a fan. Elephants as fans (or snakes, or walls) is the only way they can conceive of "Elephantness."

If descriptions of the world are created by people, that means they are open to reexamination, criticism, and possible redescribing. For we know from the six blind men poem that people are fallible and flawed in their understandings; their experiences and insights are partial and limited, and their views are affected by their surroundings. Descriptions of the world and theories of why things are so are explanations that are socially constructed by people, who are contextual beings. People exist in relation to other people,[6] and they are "embedded and embodied" (Benhabib, 1992). People are born into a setting, a certain time and place, surrounded by a certain culture, inhabiting a body that is uniquely their own, relating to at least one other person (even in utero), their mother. All of this social context makes it necessary to assume that people have a past and have been affected by other people's views. They are not neutral, impartial, objective beings; their approach to the world is transactive (Dewey, 1965), meaning that people affect the world and each other, individually and collectively, just as the world affects people. My belief is that people are able to become reflective and critical of their context, but how that happens will need to be discussed. Improving people's skills necessary for the development of knowledge, such as reasoning and critiquing skills, imagining and intuiting skills, and communicative and relational skills, makes it possible for knowledge to continue to grow and develop, as well as be redescribed and become more beautiful.[7]

Dividing Up the Elephant

Fields of study such as philosophy, psychology, sociology, and anthropology are descriptive categories people have developed over time as a way of making sense of the world. (I am referring to the descriptive categories that have been developed by the Euro-Western world, as those are the ones of concern here.) Branches within those fields provide further descriptive categories. For philosophy these branches include metaphysics, aesthetics, ethics, politics, and epistemology. Epistemology, as it has been defined historically by philosophers, involves study of the justification of people's beliefs, not how people come to believe certain things (the province of sociologists and psychologists). Philosophy is concerned with the normative status of knowledge claims and what warrants those claims (the evidence for the claims); psychology and sociology are concerned with causal questions of how beliefs are developed.

Epistemology is a branch of philosophy that considers theories of knowledge and looks at truth as a necessary condition for knowledge. One cannot "know" something that is false; such knowledge would not be classified as knowledge, but rather as a belief. Beliefs are not necessarily true. Mere beliefs, or right opinions, are stated as "S believes that p." "S" is the subject, and "p" is the object of the proposition.

Rational beliefs are ones that are supported by compelling reasons ("S has good reason to believe that p"). "S knows that p" means that S has evidence for the truth of p, S believes that p, and that p is true.[8]

If we compare the preceding statements with our elephant poem, we recognize that the blind men take their study of elephants (the world) and divide it up into more manageable categories. When they are trying to understand how they have come to know about the elephant, they say they are studying psychology. When they are looking at themselves in relation to others studying the elephant, they say they are studying sociology. They say that with either of these kinds of studies, the kinds of claims they will be making are causal ones.

When the blind men are trying to make universal claims of truth about elephants, they are studying philosophy. They say they offer evidence to support those claims. When they are trying to make universal claims about the beauty of elephants, the blind men say they are studying aesthetics. When they are looking at the essence of elephantness, and the necessary and sufficient qualities of elephants, the blind men say they are studying metaphysics. When they are trying to make claims about what they know about elephants in a universal sense, they are studying epistemology. As the blind men define knowledge, they will only say that they know something that is true. In order for something to be true, they say, they must believe that something is true, have compelling reasons to support their belief about such-and-such being true, and such-and-such must be true.

Let us consider these categories and distinctions, as the blind men have defined them, and see if there are any problems in dividing the world (elephants) up in this way. Have we missed anything by focusing on elephants in parts? When we divide the elephant into parts in order to handle better the studying of it, have we stopped understanding the whole? Have we ever been able to understand the whole elephant? Do these categories provide the best way to consider elephants, or should we redesign our categories and redescribe our studies of elephants (the world)? In separating the study of the people who study the elephant from study of the elephant itself, have we created any problems or concerns? I will begin in the middle, with the field of epistemology, as commonly defined, then move to the distinctive studies within philosophy, then look at the field of philosophy itself, in relation to others, in hopes of teasing out some problems and concerns that dividing up the world this way may have caused or overlooked. As I do so, I plan to add some "blind women's" perspectives into the discussion.

Belief, Knowledge, and Truth

Given that I am hoping to offer an improved theory of knowledge, a relational epistemology, I begin with epistemology and the suggestion that we take a closer look at how the field has been defined. The Enlightenment conception of epistemology assumes "(1) that knowledge properly so-called is autonomous in that it is of no epistemological significance whose it is; (2) that knowledge acquisition may be of psychological interest but it is irrelevant to an epistemologist's quest for criteria of justification, validity, and verification; and (3) that knowledge is objective in the sense that discussion of the character and epistemic circumstances of subjects has nothing to contribute to the proper epistemological task of assessing the product" (Code, 1987, pp. 25–26). In other words, the blind men are trying to gather knowledge of elephants. Who these blind people are or how they derive this knowledge is not of concern; from an epistemological perspective, what's of concern is the knowledge they derive. That derived knowledge is separate from the blind men who have derived it, and if what they derive is in fact knowledge, it should be true for any of us, no matter who we are, what our perspective is, or what our situation is. From the perspective of the field of epistemology, as commonly defined, what the blind men need to be concerned with is what evidence they will have in finding knowledge.

Remember my earlier statement that the blind men would define as knowledge only something that is true. In order for something to be knowledge, the blind men (S) must believe that such-and such (p) is true, they must have compelling reasons to support their belief that p is true, and p must be true. The first requirement, that the blind men must believe that p is true, doesn't help find knowledge very much, for we know it's possible for the blind men to believe that an elephant is a fan or a spear or a rope! (Just as we know it is possible for people to believe the world is flat.)

How about the second requirement? The blind men need "compelling reasons" to support their belief, but what counts as "compelling reasons"? This has been a heatedly discussed topic since the beginning of the study of philosophy. Remember, Plato said we can't trust our experiences alone to give us good reasons, and Aristotle said we can't trust our ideas alone, either. The criteria philosophers have used to help judge reasons include clarity, consistency, coherency, cohesiveness, and comprehensiveness. Are the reasons clearly stated, do they follow logically and not contradict each other, do they make sense, do they answer all the questions we can ask, do the reasons fit together with other beliefs we consider knowledge? Isn't it possible to imagine that our blind men are very clever and can give reasons to support their beliefs about elephants that are clear, consistent, coherent, cohesive, and comprehensive, and yet not be true? (We certainly had good reasons to believe the world was flat.) And isn't it possible to imagine that each of our six blind men would have different interpretations of what they take to be clear, or consistent, or coherent? In other words, aren't the criteria themselves subject to different interpretations?

This leads us to the final criterion for knowledge, that p is true. According to Enlightenment epistemological theory, the ultimate object of knowledge is reality itself. Even though one blind man may believe that the elephant is a fan and have compelling reasons to justify his belief, that does not make the elephant a fan, unless it is true that it really is. But how is the blind man ever going to know whether what he believes is true or not? We seem to have ended up in a circular theory. Does this mean that there is nothing we can say that we know for sure? Is knowledge ultimately based on faith? Somehow such a theory of knowledge does not appear so helpful after all. What's the point of having a theory of knowledge about the world when there is nothing we can say that fits safely into that theory, for there is nothing that we can say for sure that we know?

Maybe we can find some help in understanding the value of *epistemology* as a category by turning to a current epistemologist. I will describe Harvey Siegel's position because it is clearly an absolutist one and contrast it with a qualified relativist position embraced by many "blind women" feminist philosophers such as Flax, Code, Jaggar, and myself.

Absolutism versus Qualified Relativism

Siegel has been complimented by philosophers such as Burbules for moving epistemology away from vulgar absolutism to an absolutism that is less dogmatic, one that opens the door to fallibilism and pluralism. Siegel says that "contemporary epistemologists—absolutists and relativists alike—reject certainty, dogmatism, and all the other features of vulgar absolutism" (Siegel, 1987, p. 164). The sort of absolutism he recommends is a "non-dogmatic, non-certain, corrigible, fallible, non-unique absolutism" (Siegel, 1987, p. 164).

Translated to our elephant metaphor, Siegel is saying that all of us who are currently working in the field of epistemology realize that we cannot be certain we understand all there is to know about Elephants (the world, as reality, as truth). We all understand that people are limited and make mistakes and that people have many different views and perspectives on elephants.

Although such a description of absolute may not sound very absolute, for Siegel, *absolutism is a necessary precondition of epistemological inquiry* (Siegel, 1987, p. 165; italics added). What's absolute about a "non-dogmatic, non-certain, corrigible, fallible, non-unique absolutism" is "the possibility of objective, non-question begging evaluation of putative knowledge claims, in terms of criteria which admit of criticism and improvement" (Siegel, 1987, p. 162).

In other words, Siegel believes there must be some way to evaluate our different theories on elephants and judge that some are better than others; at the same time he acknowledges that what we use as criteria for judging people's theories on elephants

could also be flawed and must be open to criticism as well.

For Siegel, a "relativist must regard epistemological debate as pointless, insofar as there is, for the relativist, no possibility of genuinely answering central epistemological questions" (Siegel, 1987, p. 165). The relativist "gives up the absolutist conception of rightness" and therefore "cannot assert that foundationalism (non-foundationalism), correspondence (coherence) theories of truth or justification, causal (reliabilist, defeasibility, etc.) theories of knowledge, or the like are non-relatively right. *But genuine epistemological debate does have as its aim the determination of the non-relatively right answers to these questions*" (Siegel, 1987, p. 166; italics added).

While Siegel goes to great length in his book, *Relativism Refuted*, to distinguish absolutism from "vulgar absolutism," he is not so gracious with *relativism*. According to Siegel, only a "vulgar absolutist" believes that it doesn't matter what one's perspective is, in relation to the elephant; one can still know the elephant in its entirety (truth). Vulgar absolutist epistemological orientations have been labeled by feminists, such as Lorraine Code, with the help of Donna Haraway's astute observation, as "the view from nowhere." But is there only one view of relativism, or is it possible that there is a "vulgar relativist" view as well as a "qualified relativist" view? "Vulgar relativism," the belief that it doesn't matter what one's perspective is, in relation to the elephant, for all perspectives are right (true), has been labeled by Code and Haraway as "the view from everywhere." "Relativism is a way of being nowhere and claiming to be everywhere" but "absolutism is a way of being everywhere while pretending to be nowhere"(Code, 1993, p. 40).

We saw from the preceding discussion concerning the way epistemology has been defined, and the guidelines that have been given for helping to find knowledge, that indeed the guidelines seem rather circular and potentially pointless. They don't seem to help us find knowledge (what is true). At most, we can hope that Peirce is right in saying that we are getting closer to truth. Believing that we cannot find the truth about elephants does not mean we have to embrace all theories about elephants as being true. What it does mean is that we must acknowledge that we don't know the Truth about Elephants. We still try to describe elephants and seek to find out more information and learn more about elephants. We continue to inquire. And we try to support our understandings about elephants with as much "evidence" as we can socially construct, qualified by the best criteria upon which we can agree. A qualified relativist, such as Jaggar, Flax, Code, or myself, grounds her claims "in experiences and practices, in the efficacy of dialogical negotiation and of action" (Code, 1993, p. 39).

While Siegel agrees with the need to reject a formal conception of rationality and to "regard rationality as a substantive epistemic notion, involving the contents of sentences ration-

ally related" (Siegel, 1992, p. 228), he says that if rationality is determined by "the actual activities, decisions, and judgments which people make, then I see a big problem: namely, there is no room on this view for actual activities, decisions, and judgments to be irrational, for there is no role for criteria to function in assessing specific activities, decisions, and judgments as rational (or not)" (Siegel, 1992, p. 229). Siegel wishes to argue that "rationality" (as a concept) is dependent on the idea of "absolutism," and "absolutism" is dependent on a criterion of "rightness" (truth) that must be objective and nonrelative, not something socially constructed. Yet he has agreed that the criteria used to judge rival claims must be subject to critical assessment and improvement. Siegel says he is not saying philosophers have a "God's-eye view of truth" or claiming that he has found an Archimedean point. If the presently accepted criteria (the absolutist's belief system) can be critically assessed, Siegel suggests the criteria can be self-correcting and corrigible.

Principles embody rationality and define and assess reasons in a tradition at a time. As the tradition evolves, so do the principles which define and assess reasons. So what may count as good reason in a tradition may change over time; today's compelling reason may be seen as less compelling tomorrow . . . Still, the principles which determine the compellingness of reasons at a time apply to all putative reasons impartially and universally. . . . [T]he principles which define reasons and determine their force may change, but rationality remains the same. (Siegel, 1987, p. 251)

But if one embraces fallibilism and pluralism, one has to admit that the criteria as presently accepted could be wrong, *right now*. A qualified relativist position, such as the one I am proposing, says that, given the presently accepted criteria, this is the best judgment I can make, but I am aware that my criteria may be limited and I could be wrong. Although this statement seems to be exactly what Siegel is saying with his definition of "absolute," as cited previously, it really is not, as Siegel believes he can say even more. Here is where I think epistemologists who embrace an Enlightenment conception of epistemology, as defined previously, overestimate their abilities. I believe fallibilism and pluralism are theories that admit to the social construction of reality. Siegel does not agree with me. While he admits that what he believes, right now, might be wrong—the possibility is there—that does not itself show that he *is* wrong, right now. If it did, then everything would in fact be wrong, since everything could possibly be wrong. If not wrong, Siegel says, then what he believes is right: *absolutely* right (right/wrong being understood as contradictories). And his reasons can also be absolute, as he has defined *absolute*.[9]

I think Siegel's point is: "As long as I believe p is true, and I have compelling reasons to believe p is true, I can claim to be right, because p is true, even though my claiming to be

right is always subject to fallibilism. My being right, absolutely, is independent of my showing that I am." This is because there is a p that is true, independent of me and whether I can show that I am right or not. There is an elephant, who is an elephant, absolutely, independent of what any of us think about elephants and how any of us have defined elephants. Siegel is saying: "I am right, absolutely, if what I believe is right." What I am saying is: "I believe I am right, qualified by a socially constructed view of knowledge, so I know I could be wrong."

Enlightenment philosophers have defined epistemology in such a way that *the concept of absolutism is built right into the definition of what epistemology is*. Siegel, who embraces this definition, helps us to understand a central concern that all epistemologists must address. The Enlightenment conception of epistemology implies that people must have something absolute that they can appeal to, theory, or they cannot claim to know what is right. Unfortunately, or fortunately (depending on one's view), in the end the criteria used to support theories are fallible themselves, and that must be admitted. I cannot offer truth claims that are absolute any more than Siegel or anyone else can. I can offer new theory to try to explain how it is we know and argue and debate with people as to why I think my description of reality is more inclusive or beneficial than others presented previously. That is all any of us can do.

Historically, epistemologists have assumed the value of absolutism in the very way they have defined the field of epistemology. Absolutist epistemologists have argued for the value of absolutism because it offers people the opportunity to judge what's right; qualified relativists, such as myself, push for the inclusion of context because it forces people to open the door toward acknowledging they could be wrong, that "right" is judged from a social perspective. We are all, as epistemologists, hoping to warrant our theories in reality and to arrive at knowledge, but qualified relativists are acknowledging how extremely difficult that is to do, given that each of us is so embedded within our own socially constructed "realities."

Philosophers who embrace the Enlightenment conception of epistemology not only overestimate their abilities; they also tend to act as gatekeepers to the field of epistemology. Absolutist epistemologists do not consider qualified relativists even to be epistemologists due to the fact that qualified relativists have not embraced the field of epistemology as absolutist epistemologists have defined it, with an assumption of absolutism. Whereas some feminists, such as Code, conclude there can be no feminist epistemology given the Enlightenment conception of epistemology, I choose to try to broaden the definition of epistemology.

I would also like to present the case that the way the branch of philosophy called epistemology has been defined, in terms of distinguishing it from other branches, limits the possible questions and concerns an epistemol-ogist can address to a dangerously thin level. Let me elaborate further.

Ontology and Epistemology

Philosophers have distinguished ontology as a branch of philosophy, separate from epistemology, since the days of the early Greeks. By making such a distinction, philosophers have assumed that being can be separated from knowing, for ontology is the study of being (what is, the essence of things) and epistemology is the study of knowing (what is truth). These categorical distinctions separate knowers from knowledge/ideas. The distinctions treat knowledge as if it has a life of its own. This seems to me to be another central problem for philosophers.

As I have established, philosophers have created categories, distinguished fields of study, and branches within those fields, which are based on certain values and, therefore, biases. I explained in the discussion on belief, knowledge, and truth that those categories are based on an assumption of absolutism. Separating knowledge from being assumes philosophers are able to be neutral, objective seekers of truth. It assumes that it doesn't matter which blind man is studying elephants, from which perspective, or that the blind man is from Industan. The character and circumstances of the knowers is not important; it is the assessing of the product, knowledge, that is important. And yet we know from the work of feminist scholars as well as scholars in the area of cultural diversity that people's values and biases can be found in how they have defined what questions are worth considering, what methods for addressing those questions are considered valid, and what ideas and solutions are sound (Jaggar, 1989). I agree with this statement by Flax: "I assume here that knowledge is the product of human beings. Thinking is a form of human activity which cannot be treated in isolation from other forms of human activity including the forms of human activity which in turn shape the humans who think. Consequently, philosophies will inevitably bear the imprint of the social relations out of which they and their creators arose" (Flax, 1983, p. 248).

Gregory Bateson, a naturalist, effectively described the problem this way:

> In the natural history of living human being, ontology and epistemology cannot be separated. [One's] (commonly unconscious) beliefs about what sort of world it is will determine how [one] sees it and acts within it, and [one's] ways of perceiving and acting will determine [one's] beliefs about its nature. The living [human] is thus bound within a net of epistemological and ontological premises which—regardless of ultimate truth or falsity—become partially self-validating for [him/her]. (Bateson, 1972, p. 314)

Let me give an example of this "net of epistemological and ontological premises," and how the premises become self-validating, that can be re-lated to the elephant poem. Historically, many epistemological theories have described knowers as autonomous, rather than describing individual knowers as being developed out of a community of other knowers, certainly affected by their environment and the people that surround them. Peirce is an example of an exception to this autonomous approach to knowers, as he recognized the influence we have on each other's opinions. But even Peirce argued that we each have "a critical self" within us, which helps us persuade others and makes it possible for us to distinguish between absolute truth and what we do not doubt (Peirce, 1958, p. 191). That "critical self" within us is what separates us from others and helps us be able to think on our own. Peirce also favored a "scientific method" for approaching knowledge, one based on reason and logic, rather than one that might acknowledge the value of imagination and intuition, for example.

If one assumes a person can discover truth by himself, then one will approach the study of elephants on an individual basis. Each of the six blind men from Industan will not worry about trying to discuss his individual theories with the others who are also examining the elephant, in hopes of gaining a better understanding. Instead, each blind man may even avoid contact with the others for fear they might bias his own inquiry or distract him. A person who believes knowers are autonomous will trust that he can critique, from his own individual perspective, and find fault with what others have proposed. Yet we can understand, with our example of the blind men, how faulty one individual's perspective can be. On his own, a person can decide that the elephant is like a snake or a spear! If a man believes that knowers are autonomous, he is capable of believing he is right without necessarily testing his theory against those of others. Even when he goes to test his theory against other theories, if he believes he has the ability to critique others' theories against his own, he will confidently dismiss others' theories (that the elephant is like a wall or a rope) as faulty.

If the blind men favor the "scientific method," as Peirce and many other philosophers have throughout time, then each will try to collect data, likely based on their senses and their ability to reason. Yet we can predict that with such an approach to knowledge, the men may never arrive at an understanding of the whole elephant, as it exists. They will need to be able to imagine a whole that is greater than the sum of its parts. They will need to be creative and use their intuitive skills, and they will find that if they rely on their feelings and emotions as well as their mind, they will be more successful in their efforts to be creative and intuitive.

I want to question the assumption that knowers are autonomous, given the view that our "reality" is something that is socially constructed. I also want to consider whether or not it is even valuable to view each of us as autonomous knowers. Accepting Peirce's view that we are all fallible beings and

that truth is something we continue to get closer to as we work together and share our perspectives with each other, why would we want to embrace a view of epistemology that encourages us to look at people as separate knowers? Why not embrace a description of epistemology that encourages us to see how interrelated and interconnected the world is, including the people within it? If Peirce is right, then our only hope of understanding the world, even partially, comes from our willingness to work together and welcome each other's contributions in an effort to understand them, before we critique them and dismiss them.

I also want to question the assumption that the best approach to knowledge is through the use of one's reasoning ability, to the exclusion of other potential tools. It is not that I want to dismiss reasoning as a valuable tool, for certainly it is one I am relying on considerably in the writing of this chapter. But I am also using the metaphor of six blind men from Industan and their study of the elephant to encourage a better understanding of what knowledge is. The metaphor helps us to imagine and intuitively make connections, and to understand how ideas are related. The metaphor, if successful, improves understanding. I did not think of this metaphor by methodically reviewing research articles and epistemological theories. It came to me as a flash of insight, after struggling to find a helpful image. It did not come to me when I was using my logical reasoning skills, but rather when I was not "working" at all, but instead was getting ready for bed. I suspect most of us make connections and understand the world in new ways, often "by accident," when we are *not* trying to figure things out. Acknowledging and valuing the "other" tools available to us in knowing the world we live in is something I hope to accomplish with a relational epistemological approach.

Philosophy and Psychology

I have demonstrated that the categories and distinctions concerning epistemology as a branch of philosophy are based on assumptions of absolutism and autonomy, and favor methods for understanding that emphasize reason and the mind. What about the distinction that has been made between psychology and philosophy? Philosophers have described the epistemological task of assessing the quality of reasons as being quite separate from any discussion of the character and epistemic circumstances of subjects. Historically, epistemological theorists have argued that criteria for warranting knowledge claims can be found without having to consider the way human beings know. This view of knowledge treats it as a product quite separate from human beings, some "thing" that is "out there" or "in here." Depending on one's perspective, therefore, any of the six blind men should be able to discover the truth about elephants, either by using their experiences and exploring elephants "out there" or by tuning into

their soul's awareness of elephants "inside" themselves.

If one views knowledge as something people contribute to, as something that people weave together, then the distinctions between knowers and knowledge are no longer so clear. In fact, they become intertwined and interrelated. When one begins to understand the interactive connection between social beings and ideas, one realizes it is necessary to look at the kinds of relationships people experience and which ones enhance the development of ideas and the weaving of knowledge. Ethical and political issues need to be addressed in an epistemological theory that looks at knowledge as created by *people*, not just knowledge per se, for the quality of the social relationships people have will affect the ideas being constructed or created, especially in terms of whether or not the ideas have the opportunity even to be expressed.

With such a view of knowledge, it becomes important to ask questions like these: Why are these six people who are studying the elephant all men? Why are they all blind, and what effect does their blindness have on their theories about elephants? Where did these men come from, and what is the context of their social situations? How is it they have no prior experience of elephants, yet they are adults and live in a land where elephants are central to their social system?

I wish to argue that any attempt to look at knowledge claims separate from an examination of how those claims were derived is to make a serious mistake. "A theory of knowledge that lacks a reasonable understanding of how human beings can and do acquire and add to knowledge must be of dubious relevance. Sound psychological insights form an invaluable, sine qua non basis for any theory of knowledge that purports to explicate the way human beings know" (Code, 1987, p. 32). The historical distinctions epistemologists have made effectively remove epistemology as a field of study from the practical-political issues a feminist epistemology must address. As I am redescribing epistemology, any theory of knowledge is clearly affected by knowers and their circumstances. Like Lorraine Code, I argue that "theories that transcend the specificity's of gendered and otherwise situated subjectivists are impotent to come to terms with the politics of knowledge" (Code, 1991, p. 315).

The writing of a relational epistemology is motivated by the desire to expand what epistemology means to include the qualities of knowing that have historically been viewed as detrimental or distracting to the obtaining of knowledge, qualities such as feelings, emotions, and intuitions, which are usually linked to women rather than men. I choose to attempt to redescribe knowledge, and the only tools I have available to me are the same ones that are available to anyone else: my ability to reason and think critically, my intuition, my relational skills and communication skills, my emotions and feelings, and the fact

that these are questions I care enough about to pursue. Like any other philosopher, all I can ever hope to do is "attempt to describe how understanding is possible in particular contexts; [philosophy] cannot create a universalizing theory of knowledge that can ground and account for all knowledge or test all truth claims because these are necessarily context dependent" (Flax, 1990, p. 38).

Am I not trying to offer a universalizing theory of knowledge myself? I argue for the need to redescribe knowledge, and I present the case that what I am doing I consider to be epistemology. I cite evidence to support my claim that the field of epistemology has been too narrowly defined and has been based on assumptions such as that absolutism, autonomy, and knowledge are products separate from human beings as knowers. I do think it is possible to justify claims concerning reality, but I am also aware that it is hard to know if what one considers "evidence" is real, rather than socially constructed.

The relational epistemological theory I plan to describe is one I will offer up for discussion. I do not claim to have the best theory, the truest theory, for I know many other theories will follow mine and that others currently are being developed, based on understanding I do not have. Although it is not the truest, the best, the most complete, or the final explanation of knowledge, I do think it has important advantages to offer over other epistemological theories. One of the advantages is that it is a more encompassing description of knowledge, because a relational epistemology includes vital aspects of knowledge that other theories tend to overlook or exclude from the discussion. My attention to and valuing of such qualities as relationality and caring in an intersubjective world should make a relational epistemological theory one that is more inclusive and less open to ideological abuse. Both women and men should find this theory applies to them, including people from different ethnic backgrounds and ways of life. This must be the case if I am right at all in my claim that the theory I am developing is an improved description of how people know. I also hope that a relational epistemology opens the possibilities for valuing contributions from all people. We need each other to nurture the constructing/quilting of knowledge and help make it sound, comprehensive, coherent, and cohesive, as well as beneficial and beautiful. Whether this theory meets these criteria or not (or other criteria deemed valuable and important) must be tested by all of us as contributors to knowledge.

A Redescription of Epistemology

In the process of gaining a voice, growing and developing as human beings, people learn from others. Through others we learn language and our culture, how to communicate with each other, and ways of relating with each other. Because of this necessary social beginning that all human beings have, which helps form who we are, we can never claim to know solely based on our own individual perspective. Who we are as individuals and how we think depend greatly on the social relationships we have with others and the time, place, culture, and social setting we are born into. Qualities such as our language and our gendered customs all affect the constructing of knowledge. *A relational epistemology views knowledge as something that is socially constructed by embedded, embodied people who are in relation with each other.*

Given that we are social beings contingently placed in this world, affecting each other from the beginning, it is easy to understand that we need each other in order to be better thinkers. The idea that one person, all by himself, could claim to find Truths, Facts, or know the Answers begins to sound absurd. Nobody enters this world without a history, which has already begun before birth. Nobody is able to develop thoughts or a language to express one's thoughts without having contact with others. And nobody can come into contact with others without being affected by them. How can we think we find solutions all by ourselves? Such an idea begins to sound arrogant, to say the least. Solutions to problems and truths are things that emerge and evolve, just as we do, for we participate in their development. No one of us can ever hope to find Truth, because of the sure fallibility of individual human knowledge, due to its contingency; but all of us together, as communities of knowers, can work together, share with each other what each of us understands individually, and collectively help to create theories of knowledge for the next generation of knowers to contribute to. With such a model, knowledge takes on a fluid image, always being redescribed as it changes and develops; the quality of the theories is dependent on the ability of people to relate to each other and share their insights.

With a relational epistemological theory, it is important to discuss how a sense of self is evolved and the importance of that development to the constructing of knowledge. I assume knowledge is constructed by human beings who are in relation with each other. These human beings were once young children, and when they were born they were not born with a sense of self. Historically, epistemologists have tended to treat people, when they come into the discussion, as if they were adults who never went through the process of being formed through relations with others. I assume that people begin their lives in a relationship (even in utero), that they are already interacting with someone else and affecting that other person (mother) as well as being affected by that other person, before they are physically born. People are not isolated beings who are born fully developed. I assume people develop a sense of self through their relationships with others, which are internalized and interact with their own innate constitutions. I take early infantile experiences and child rearing to be vital to the constructing of knowledge.[10] I assume

relationships, first with one's mother, then with others, develop prior to as well as simultaneous with the development of language, thoughts, and ideas. It is because we are social beings in caring relations with each other that we develop a sense of self, our own voice. Without the opportunity to develop a healthy sense of self, one cannot become a knower/thinker able to contribute to the construction of knowledge.

By this account, we develop our thinking skills as we develop our communication skills and our social skills, by being in relationships with others. We test out our ideas with other people, and we come across problems we must solve while relating to other people. What we come to believe is an answer or a solution—our most trustworthy knowledge—is derived through the use of conversation with others. What implications this relational theory of knowledge has for education (in particular, formal schooling) must also be addressed.

Acknowledgments

I wish to thank the following individuals who commented helpfully on earlier drafts of this chapter: Andrea Boyea, Richard Brosio, Nicholas Burbules, Sophie Haroutunian-Gordon, James Garrison, Stephen P. Norris, Conrad Pritscher, Harvey Siegel, and Barbara Walton. There is some overlap in this chapter with a paper I gave at the 1995 Philosophy of Education Society conference titled "Navigating Epistemological Territories." I am grateful to my institution for the basic grant I was awarded, which afforded me the opportunity to perform the research on this topic. This chapter was first presented as a conference paper, "An Examination and Redescription of Epistemology," at the enGendering Rationalities conference, April 18–20, 1997, University of Oregon, Eugene, Oregon. It was first published with *The ERIC Clearinghouse on Teaching and Teacher Education*, ED 401 279, under the same title in 1997, and it was then included as part of Chapter 2 in Barbara Thayer-Bacon with Charles S. Bacon, 1998, *Philosophy Applied to Education: Nurturing a Democratic Community in the Classroom*, Upper Saddle River, NJ: Prentice-Hall. I am currently writing a book on this topic, with the working title *Relational (e)pistemologies*.

Notes

1. "The Blind Men and the Elephant" is an old tale from India. A children's book version is retold by Lillian Quigley (*The Blind Men and the Elephant*, New York: Charles Scribner's Sons, 1959). I will use the term *men* in describing past epistemological theories because they were written by men, and that is one of the underlying points of my feminist perspective.

2. I cannot identify the exact source for this term; it occurred to me as I was reading a long list of works by feminist writers. This relational epistemology could also be labeled a social feminist epistemology. Three works by philosophers who helped me see the need for a relational epistemology were as follows:

> Grimshaw, Jean. (1986). *Philosophy and Feminist Thinking*. Minneapolis, MN: University of Minnesota Press.
> Noddings, Nel. (1984). *Caring: A Feminine Approach to Ethics and Moral Education*. Berkeley, CA: University of California Press.
> Ruddick, Sara. (1989). *Maternal Think-*

ing: Toward a Politics of Peace. Boston: Beacon Press.

3. Barbara Thayer-Bacon. (1997, Spring). "The nurturing of a relational epistemology." *Educational Theory, 47*(2), 239–260.

4. I do not wish to imply, by my choice of authors, that there are not many important contributions being made by others, whom I have had to simply reference or leave out of this discussion. Please see, for example, the works of Robert Ennis, Richard Paul, and John McPeck, as well as those of Judith Butler, Nancy Fraser, Linda Nicholson, Nancy Harstock, and Iris Young.

5. Berger and Luckmann begin their treatise by noting they are not claiming to answer the philosophical question, how is one to know? The sociologist is forced to use quotation marks around "reality" and "knowledge." Sociologists can't differentiate between valid and invalid assertions about the world, whereas a philosopher "is driven to decide" (Berger & Luckmann, 1966, p. 2).

6. My original sources for this idea are:

> Mead, George Herbert. (1934). *Mind, Self, and Society: From the Standpoint of a Social Behaviorist*. Charles W. Morris (Ed.). Chicago: University of Chicago Press.
> Dewey, John. (1944). *Democracy and Education*. New York: Macmillan. (Originally published 1916).

For more on "social epistemology," see the works of Steve Fuller, Alvin Goldman, and John Hardwig. I am indebted to Steve Norris and Harvey Siegel for these references.

7. I am suggesting that other than the typical criteria used by philosophers to justify theories as based on compelling reasons—criteria such as clarity, coherence, and consistency—there are other criteria that should be considered as well, such as beauty, elegance, harmony, inclu-

siveness, and beneficiality. I will say more on this later.

8. Harvey Siegel points out that this way of discussing knowledge is found in the introduction to any epistemology text. My sources for this description were John Hardwig, 1985, "Epistemic Dependence," *Journal of Philosophy*, *82*(7): 335–349, and Siegel's direct correspondence to me. Burbules labels this description of epistemology the "Enlightenment conception" (Burbules, 1992).

9. Siegel, personal correspondence, August 1994 and May 1995.

10. I am not alone in drawing attention to the infant in discussions of epistemology. See the works of Seyla Benhabib, Jane Flax, Nel Noddings, and Sara Ruddick.

References

Aristotle. (1970). "Nichomachaen Ethics." In *The Philosophical Foundations of Education*. Steven M. Cahn (Ed). New York: Harper & Row.

Bateson, Gregory. (1972). *Steps to an Ecology of Mind*. New York: Ballantine.

Benhabib, Seyla. (1992). *Situating the Self: Gender, Community and Postmodernism*. New York: Routledge.

Berger, Peter L., & Luckmann, Thomas. (1966). *The Social Construction of Reality: A Treatise in the Sociology of Knowledge*. Garden City, NY: Anchor Books.

Burbules, Nicholas C. (1991, Spring). "Rationality and Reasonableness: A Discussion of Harvey Siegel's Relativism Refuted and Educating Reason." *Educational Theory*, *41*(2):235–252.

Code, Lorraine. (1987). *Epistemic Responsibility*. Hanover, NH: University Press of New England.

Code, Lorraine. (1991). *What Can She Know? Feminist Theory and the Construction of Knowledge*. Ithaca, NY: Cornell University Press.

Code, Lorraine. (1993). "Taking Subjec-

tivity into Account." In *Feminist Epistemologies*. Linda Alcoff, Elizabeth Potter (Eds.). New York: Routledge.

Descartes, Rene. (1960). *Meditations on First Philosophy*. Lawrence J. Lafleur (trans.). Indianapolis, IN: Bobbs-Merrill. (Originally published 1641)

Dewey, John. (1965). *Experience and Education*. New York: Macmillan. (Originally published 1938)

Flax, Jane. (1983). "Political Philosophy and the Patriarchal Unconscious: A Psychoanalytic Perspective on Epistemology and Metaphysics." In *Discovering Reality*. Sandra Harding, Merrill B. Hintikka (Eds.). Dordrecht, The Netherlands: D. Reidel.

Flax, Jane. (1990). *Thinking Fragments: Psychoanalysis, Feminism, and Postmodernism in Contemporary West*. Berkeley: University of California Press.

Jaggar, Alison M. (1989, 1992). "Love and Knowledge: Emotion in Feminist Epistemology." In *Women, Knowledge, and Reality: Explorations in Feminist Philosophy*. Ann Garry, Marilyn Pearsall (Eds.). New York: Routledge.

Kant, Immanuel. (1966). *Critique of Pure Reason*. F. Max Müller (trans.). Garden City, NJ: Doubleday. (Originally published 1781)

Locke, John. (1894). *An Essay Concerning Human Understanding*. Alexander Campbell Fraser (Ed.). Oxford, England: Clarendon Press. (Originally published 1690)

Peirce, Charles Sanders. (1958). *Values in a Universe of Chance: Selected Writings of Charles Sanders Peirce (1839–1914)*. Philip P. Wiener (Ed.). Garden City, NJ: Doubleday.

Plato. (1970a). "The Meno." In *The Philosophical Foundations of Education*. Steven M. Cahn (Ed.). New York: Harper & Row.

Plato. (1970b). "The Myth of the Cave," Book VII of *The Republic*. In *The Philosophical Foundations of Education*. Steven

M. Cahn (Ed.). New York: Harper & Row.

Rorty, Richard. (1989). *Contingency, Irony, and Solidarity*. Cambridge, England: Cambridge University Press.

Siegel, Harvey. (1987). *Relativism Refuted: A Critique of Contemporary Epistemological Relativism*. Dordrecht, The Netherlands: D. Reidel.

Siegel, Harvey. (1992). "Two Perspectives on Reason as an Educational Aim: The Rationality of Reasonableness." *Philosophy of Education 1991*. Proceedings of the 47th Annual Meeting of the Philosophy of Education Society. Margret Buchmann, Robert E. Floden (Eds.). Normal, IL: Philosophy of Education Society.

JOHN DEWEY AND EDUCATIONAL EVALUATION

Douglas J. Simpson and Michael J.B. Jackson

Dewey's theory of educational evaluation was significantly shaped by his opinion of what the nature, aims, and means of education are. Given this philosophical perspective, it is not surprising to find that for him educational evaluation is a comprehensive social and institutional endeavor: Each aspect of society—the family, neighborhood, school, community, and larger environment—needs to be evaluated in the light of the purpose of cultivating individuals and communities who are progressively becoming more capable of growing and sustaining that growth in a democratic setting. Educational evaluation should focus upon both means and ends, paying particular attention to the ends of personal and societal growth. The growth Dewey envisioned was a developing understanding and associated behavior that is immediately important but also enabling in the future. Whether evaluating schools and neighborhoods or teachers and stu-

dents, primary attention should be given to the quality of thought, imagination, creation, communication, and behavior exhibited by individuals. These emphases set Dewey apart from most educational thinkers in his and our day and provide a framework for critiquing educational assessment and evaluation endeavors today.

In Dewey's day, educational evaluation was not yet a specialized area of study, and its complexities, challenges, benefits, and dangers were not well known. Still, many informed people during his lifetime knew that teachers regularly made assessments of students' perceived abilities, needs, interests, and prospects in life and of those experiences and studies that would be suitable for them to pursue. Sometimes less consciously, society as a whole, school districts in general, and administrators in particular—often tracking students into allegedly appropriate careers or on the basis of assumed abilities—made similar evaluations or judgments about students. Society, including many parents, held expectations for schools and teachers, and consequently, they were subject to informal and formal evaluation. Schools, for example, were expected to teach students what was deemed apposite for the young, and teachers were held accountable for their behavior outside of schools as well as inside.

An outgrowth of Dewey's setting and thinking, then, was a rather comprehensive theory of educational evaluation that complements his wide-ranging understanding of education. Recognition of the conscious and unconscious evaluation practices of his time, combined with Dewey's belief in the value of growth in education, led him to think a great deal about ongoing or formative evaluation. He saw the relationship between formative evaluation and the important effects and potential of a child's social setting, including the family, neighborhood, community, school, and broader environment. Thus, he believed that any kind of social arrangement, including schooling, should undergo an ongoing evaluation that leads to continual improvement and transformation. What he had to say about educational evaluation and schools, sometimes in passing or apropos of other topics, was very different from the beliefs of many other thinkers, except, possibly, for the reflective common sense and practice of better classroom teachers.

In writing about schools, Dewey's ideas touched not only students, teachers, the curriculum, and teaching methods, but also the classroom and school organization, teachers' relationships with administrators and their employers, the attitudes of teachers and administrators, and the school's connection with local and larger communities. In fact, he seemed to have found it difficult to make any sharp distinction between educational and social evaluation and reform. Consequently, his theory of educational evaluation ultimately involved an analysis of how society and schools contribute to the educative learning or growth of students, educators, and other citizens. His largely implicit but comprehensive view of educational evaluation, then, was one that reviewed what social entities were doing for and with children and youth. To restate the idea, Dewey believed that educational evaluation, decontextualized from multitudes of learning variables and focused narrowly on schools, curriculums, pedagogy, teachers, and students, suffers from a myopic understanding of the nature, aims, and means of education.

Given Dewey's comprehensive theory of educational evaluation, the range of his interests, and the fact that his comments on the subject are sprinkled throughout his writings, the focus of this essay is limited to a select set of subtopics. In particular, attention is given to the evaluation of teacher preparation programs, aspiring teachers, practicing teachers, P–12 students, school environments, personal growth, curricular experiences, data interpretation, economic conditions, educational purposes, and sound pedagogy. Dewey's thinking about teachers is an interesting place to begin. He noted the importance of teachers' being masters not only of their subject matter but also of how students think. The former emphasis was a major concern for Dewey, and he stressed that teachers should "overflow" with knowledge (Boyston, 1981–1991, vol. 8). The latter expectation includes understanding what children think and talk about, the games they play, why they abandon certain activities and move to new ones, and the growth of their unplanned actions (Boyston, 1981–1991, vol. 17). Moreover, mastering how students think involves being "able to keep track of . . . mental play, to recognize the signs of its presence or absence, to know how it is initiated and maintained, how to test it by results attained, and to test *apparent* results by it" (Boyston, 1976–1983, vol. 3, p. 254). Both attained and apparent results are important for the teacher to examine, therefore, as a means of determining the thinking that led to them and, at times, the cognitive processes that will be needed to obtain different results. Dewey concluded that "the supreme mark and criterion of a teacher" is this insight into the "soul-action" of students (Boyston, 1976–1983, vol. 3, p. 254).

If Dewey is correct, prospective teachers' knowledge of their teaching fields may be a legitimate area of assessment and evaluation. Their understanding of the psychological development and learning of students in general might also be a legitimate concern of those who evaluate teacher preparation programs. But Dewey was interested in more: He wanted prospective teachers to learn how to study and come to a thorough understanding of their future students—their thinking, spontaneity, habits, and so forth. Educational evaluation from this perspective could involve coming to understand how aspiring teachers are prepared to use and how practicing teachers actually use child-study skills to aid them in teaching. Moreover, practicing teachers may be evaluated in part by determining how well they understand each student and whether they are able to lead each into an appropriate understanding of the content being taught. In turn, schools could be partially evaluated for their ability to create enabling environments or learning atmospheres where teachers pursue individual child study and use the information they learn about each child, perhaps over a period of several years.

Talk of "the supreme mark and criterion" of the good teacher shows the priority Dewey attached to this idea. The point of evaluation is to promote learning and growth, the kind of learning that gives meaning to the learner's present life and to the life of his or her community. Questions of priorities are what we might expect philosophers to bring to a discussion of evaluation. And Dewey's priorities are clear: the *quality* of the educational experience itself and its promotion of students' growth—the capacity for more, fuller, and richer experiences—are what matter. The quality that interested Dewey falls into two spheres; learning should have both an immediate and a later impact (Boyston, 1981–1991, vol. 13). Educative learning, in contrast with non- and miseducative experiences, entails growth in the present and the disposition for ongoing growth in the future. An important question for schools and teachers, then, is whether the experiences designed, the environment created, and the curriculum developed involve and create capacities for additional, broader, and deeper learning by students in the future. Or are the experiences merely noneducative or, perhaps, even miseducative? A related question is how well schools and teachers can support claims for immediate and later growth. What kinds of information, performance, and outcomes enable educators and others to assess and evaluate the quality of student growth? Are standardized tests useful? If so, in what ways? What other types of information and data are needed?

Another illustration of Dewey's interests can be seen in the way he treats the subject of the learner and the quality of her or his growth. Dewey is well known for his objections to traditional examinations as frequently employed by schools during his lifetime. He did not, however, appear opposed to the gathering of worthwhile information about individual students or educational environments. Conversely, he rejected an emphasis on external rewards and punishments—such as grades, promotion, awards, and prizes—that was at the expense of an intrinsic interest in learning (Boyston, 1976–1983, vol. 9). Many schools in his day valued norms, comparative standings, tests, promotions, and measurement of student achievement and IQs, but he insisted that good teachers should be more interested in quality, specifically the "quality of activity and consequence [means and ends] . . . than [in] any quantitative element" of learning (Boyston, 1981–1991, vol. 3, pp. 259–261). The effort to establish school norms, averages, and classification systems was particularly objectionable, he argued, because schools should be primarily interested in "individuality," and the grouping of students for "social purposes" should place a high value on "diversity of ability and experience" (Boyston, 1981–1991, vol. 3, pp. 260–261).

Dewey understood the relationship of the learner and the environment in which learning occurred, including both the school and the classroom. He believed schools should be places where the individual student is well known and cultivated, where distinct and different talents are prized and nurtured, and where the quality of one's thinking and performance is understood and refined. Schools should not be places where the aim is uniformity of standards and abilities. At this juncture, it is important to recall

Dewey's stern warning against a pedagogy that dulls one's appreciation, application, and meaning-making approach to learning and that results in the acquisition of little more than sterile information: "What avail is it to win prescribed amounts of information about geography and history, to win ability to read and write, if in the process the individual loses his own soul: loses his appreciation of things worth while, of the values to which things are relative; if he loses desire to apply what he has learned and, above all, loses the ability to extract meaning from his future experiences as they occur?" (Boyston, 1981–1991, vol. 13, p. 29). Assessment and evaluation that promote pedagogical standardization and sterility and inhibit an enthusiastic engagement with ideas and issues by students and teachers constitute a fundamental educational vice even when they are accompanied by a modest development of basic skills and valued information. Policy makers, board members, and educational administrators who unintentionally or intentionally promulgate this kind of assessment and evaluation do great harm to students, schools, and society, according to Dewey.

This emphasis of Dewey need not lead to the conclusion that only an understanding of the individual is worthwhile and that schools and classrooms are unimportant. Indeed, the opposite is the case, but the understanding of groups should provide insight into how to create more educative environments and communities for individuals learning in social groups. Dewey seemed to have little if any interest, however, in comparing one school to another, except in citing what he deemed the admirable features of the diverse and progressive schools and various educational practices he observed (Boyston, 1976–1983, vol. 8).

The fact that Dewey had little interest in comparing schools was not because he wanted students simply to enjoy the present, disregard all traditional learning outcomes, and merely learn of societal occupations, as some critics contend. Many of his proposals did involve learning about ordinary home and work activities, but these had an educational mission: understanding activities that form part of and give meaning to what people do every day. The learning experiences were not focused on training in skills that were deemed useful in raising a family, getting a job, or preparing a meal. Instead, these experiences were designed to contribute to the child's understanding of the world—beginning, in order to avoid rote learning and seemingly pointless content, with what was familiar and seemed to the child to need explanation—and were meant to lead directly to an appreciation of reading, writing, adding, and subtracting and, eventually, to a study of academic disciplines: the fields of inquiry and creativity that represent the best available understanding of the world.

The school curriculum and related learning experiences, then, should be evaluated in terms of their ability to connect the past and present in the life of each student and to promote future educative experiences for everyone. In particular, school experiences were to be evaluated in terms of their being able to take a child's "crude experiences and organize them into science, geography, arithmetic, or whatever the lesson of the hour is" (Boyston, 1976–1983, vol. 8, p. 254). Dewey believed that whatever information or funds of knowledge a child already has form part of a subject that the teacher is attempting to teach, and that the most appropriate pedagogy will use this prior knowledge and build a conscious understanding of the subject on this largely unconscious foundation (Boyston, 1976–1983, vol. 8). But assessing what each student has learned in these different disciplines is not a simple matter, for what each person brings and learns varies to a large degree by social and, especially, economic background and personal interest. Today, diverse classrooms make this practice more challenging for teachers but, perhaps, all the more important.

Teachers cannot afford to be naive about learning experiences and their outcomes, whether occurring before, outside of, or in schools. Dewey once told the story of a visit to a classroom in which students were studying the composition of the earth. Asked what the center of the earth was like, the class answered, together, "igneous fusion." When the teacher inquired further about what their answer meant, there was no reply. Rephrasing the question to ask if the center of the earth was cold or hot still produced no response from the students. Dewey's

lesson was obvious: Learning unrelated to other experiences and understandings and the mere recitation of words, facts, and formulas will not do in any school that values quality of thinking and performance. What matters is what the child understands and can do with or make of words, facts, and formulas. A similar point was made by Dewey when he discussed facts or data and their meaning for educators or anyone else: Facts or data in themselves may be dead, meaningless, or, worse, misleading (Boyston, 1981–1991, vol. 8). In understanding individuals and their multiple learning environments, it is critical that the selection and interpretation of facts or data be made and that it be recognized that neither the data nor their interpretation is final or beyond debate (Boyston, 1967–1992, vol. 3). The absence of this perspective—that data need to be carefully selected, studied, and understood as well as challenged and clarified by other pertinent data and interpretations—appears to be one of the major shortcomings of much contemporary discussion and, unfortunately, prescription and prohibition by policy makers regarding education.

Some people today seek to reduce reliance on teachers' interpretations and judgment with so-called culturally fair and objective assessment instruments. Dewey, however, observed that no one comes to a task—whether creating an examination or interpreting data or analyzing problems—with a "virgin mind" (Boyston, 1981–1991, vol. 8, p. 214). In view of this slant and his emphasis on the quality of learning experiences and growth, Dewey would probably be a great deal more comfortable with explicitly qualitative assessments and evaluations—whether portfolios, performances, discussions, or essays—that acknowledge the multiple ways in which individuals can legitimately grow and show their growth and understanding than with standardized tests and measurements. One may speculate that if standardized instruments are to be employed in a Deweyan scheme of things, they should be used as one of many efforts to understand the "soul-action" of the pupil and used as reflective psychometricians recommend.

Dewey's theory of educational evaluation diverged from the thinking of his contemporaries in other ways. Let us return to the student and learning to demonstrate his departure from the beliefs of others. If learning is to be meaningful to the learner, he argued, it must begin with what is already significant—one's immediate experience. Consequently, what is taught and learned should often look different from one community or school to another. He drove this idea home by averring: "No one would question that a child in a slum tenement has a different experience from that of a child in a cultured home; that the country lad has a different kind of experience from the city boy, or a boy on the seashore one different from the lad who is brought up on inland prairies" (Boyston, 1981–1991, vol. 13, p. 22). This being the case, it seems safe to suggest that Dewey believed that comparing the results of a school on the seashore

with another on the prairie, for example, without considering a range of other factors, would be nearly meaningless, especially with younger children. It would also seem to be evaluative nonsense if the curriculum of either locale were taken as the standard of what should be taught and studied in all locales. Would Dewey also argue that comparing the results of one teacher in an economically diverse school with the outcomes of another teacher in an economically homogeneous school, without considering a range of other factors, is both mindless and meaningless?

Educational evaluation influences schooling in other, less expected but powerful ways. Dewey saw the subtle impact that informal and unofficial evaluation can have on teaching and teachers. When teachers are viewed—informally evaluated—as being largely incapable of professional behavior and judgment, there is an effect that cannot be ignored on both practicing teachers and the appeal of the profession. The environments in which teachers work and the responsibilities and respect they are given are tacit evaluations and can have a profoundly negative impact. His stinging words were as follows:

There is not a single body of men and women in the world . . . among whom the development of professional spirit would not be hampered if they realized that no matter how much experience they got, however much wisdom they acquired, whatever experiments they tried, whatever results they obtained,

that experience was not to count beyond the limits of their immediate activity: that they have no authorized way
of transmitting or of communicating it,
and of seeing it was taken into account
by others. (Boyston, 1976–1983, vol. 7,
p. 111)

When potential educators understand this unspoken evaluation of
teachers, many turn to other opportunities. People who wish to think, be
creative, and use their imaginations are
often repelled by the kind of school
culture Dewey described, for they are
largely designed for people who will
mechanically or unthinkingly follow
prescribed aims and means. The freedom implicit in the professional judgment, autonomy, responsibility, and
ethics teachers require would probably
make largely standardized methods of
evaluating teachers, teaching, schools,
and students highly suspect for Dewey.
Furthermore, if conditions or lack of
resources make significant success unlikely, talk of holding teachers or administrators accountable for the highly
improbable result would be meaningless or, worse, morally wrong from his
perspective.

––––––––––––

In Dewey's theoretical framework, educational evaluation is chiefly a matter
of purposes: What kinds of people do
we want to cultivate for life in a reflective and dynamic democracy? What
are we assessing and trying to evaluate? Where are our activities going to

take us? What do we expect to learn
and how will the information assist us
in educating individual students? He
saw problems not so much in the
processes of evaluation as in the significance of what is being evaluated
and the uses to which evaluations will
be put: Measuring wrong or trivial
things distorts the whole activity, and
acting on the basis of largely irrelevant
or unimportant information is at least
counterproductive and often unethi-
cal. An enterprise that is directed toward promoting personal and social
growth necessarily has little use for
summative evaluation per se, just as
one that values individuality may have
little use for comparisons of individuals or groups or schools or districts or
states or nations. Where, Dewey
might ask, are our priorities, and why
do we avoid *evaluating* them and, instead, continue to identify and examine misleading but more easily measured indicators of something else? To
others, he might inquire, what do
these facts, information, and data have
to do with developing reflective and
growing individuals and communities?
We should *evaluate* the entire assessment enterprise to see how, if at all, it
relates to our educational purposes.
For still others, he may say, how do we
know that students are growing in
their understanding, appreciation, and
application of chemistry and democracy and that this growth is providing
a foundation for the future development of individuals and social groups?
When we *evaluate* our claims and the
evidence, what do we find?

Another of Dewey's interests is tied to our purposes, or where we wish to go: What can schools reasonably be expected to achieve, and for what ends can they fairly be held accountable? Considering the social setting of students, the teachers, and the school, what can we expect each to be able to achieve? While he did not excuse educators from legitimate responsibilities, he was adamant about the powerful effects of social, especially economic, conditions on students, communities, and schools: "Life . . . opportunities . . . values . . . education . . . are mainly determined by economic conditions" (Boyston, 1981–1991, vol. 4, p. 225). Even so, he stressed that educators and other citizens have a moral responsibility to advocate for changing economic conditions and material environments to better meet the needs of children (Boyston, 1981–1991, vol. 4). Believing in the power of economic influences was not an excuse to blame the external environment; it was a challenge or, better, a charge to change the external educational environment of children.

Dewey's theory of educational evaluation, therefore, is a warning against taking hastily designed, narrowly focused, easily measured, and largely quantitative approaches to understanding educational environments and their means, ends, and results. Instead, he challenges us to think carefully and frequently about our purposes and to find pertinent indicators of progress toward them. He stimulates us to cherish, look for, and evaluate the development of a number of important qualities and dispositions that are involved in pedagogically exciting teaching and learning. These include tendencies to appreciate rigorous thinking in any field, make sense of random and planned experiences, and apply the most defensible claims of knowledge to solving problems. He encourages us to examine and evaluate how educators weave together the past, present, and future in experiences that immediately influence but also open the door to future personal and social growth. He invites us to evaluate how effective educators are in leading students from their crude understandings of art, science, history, and democracy to a fairly sophisticated understanding and personal appropriation of these realms. He inspires us to prepare and nurture professional educators who are masters of their content and pedagogy and who are disposed to study their students as well as the communities where they live. He charges us with the responsibility of understanding and seeking to transform our families, neighborhoods, communities, and schools in order that they can become fully functioning and complementary educational environments. He asks us to seize the opportunity to be thoughtful inquirers, participants, and evaluators in the development of society, schools, and individuals, in part by means of an ongoing collection and application of relevant facts and data about our purposes, how we pursue them, and what standards or indicators guide us and inform us along the way.

In essence, he encourages us to be imaginative, evaluative thinkers as we plan for, engage in, and assess educational activities in any environment.

Bibliography

Boyston, J. A. (Ed.). (1967–1972). *The early works of John Dewey, 1882–1898* (Vols. 1–5). Carbondale: Southern Illinois University Press.

Boyston, J. A. (Ed.). (1976–1983). *The middle works of John Dewey, 1899–1924* (Vols. 1–15). Carbondale: Southern Illinois University Press.

Boyston, J. A. (Ed.). (1981–1991). *The later works of John Dewey, 1925–1953* (Vols. 1–17). Carbondale: Southern Illinois University Press.

FLORIDA'S ADVANCED ACADEMIC STANDARDS FOR THE ASSESSMENT OF CRITICAL AND CREATIVE THINKING

Danny Weil

A Brief History

The concept of school accountability has mushroomed into one of the most heated, controversial, and least understood issues in the current educational debate. Holding teachers, districts, schools, and students accountable to state-mandated learning standards seems to be the public policy mantra, and indeed the vogue, as we enter the twenty-first century. Yet the discussion regarding standards and assessment has focused more on *what* students need to know than on *how* they come to know it. Few citizens, other than a handful of policy makers in the current educational community, have observed, let alone entertained a discussion regarding, the necessity to teach students how to think.

In the spring of 1999, I had the unique opportunity to help revitalize the standards debate in the state of Florida. I was asked by Dr. Maria de Armas, Director of the Office of Advanced Academics for Dade County Public Schools, to devise a taxonomy of critical/creative thinking standards that teachers in the district's Academic Excellence Program might use to teach and assess students in academically enriched classes. While I believed and continue to believe that critical and creative thinking principles and strategies should be taught to all students throughout all ranges of subjects, I felt that the opportunity to work with teachers in the third largest school district in the United States was important. I have been fortunate enough to work with Dr. de Armas for the past nine years, during which her creativity and commitment to critical thinking and critical thinking instruction and assessment have been evident. Her pledge to foster critical and creative thinking, as well as her faith

429

and belief in the ability of both teachers and students, captured my interest and motivated me to develop the project. Dr. de Armas also realized the necessity of tying teaching to assessment and assessment to teaching, and concurred with the belief that the more authentic the teaching, the more authentic the assessment.

Dr. de Armas and I conceived of the project in the following manner:

1. Develop the critical and creative thinking standards.
2. Share them with teachers and professionals in the Office of Advanced Academics for feedback purposes.
3. Schedule a two-day in-service workshop for K–12 teachers using the critical and creative taxonomy of standards as the focus. This would provide an opportunity to introduce the standards to teachers and allow them to infuse them into their curriculum and develop assessment based on their understanding of the critical/creative thinking standards.
4. Allow teachers the time to use these strategies and assessment principles in their classrooms in an attempt to help them develop their own individuality when designing and assessing instruction while at the same time providing them with innovative experimentation.
5. Reunite with teachers to dialogue about what they thought was effective and ineffective, their evaluation of the critical

thinking standards, and what barriers they felt impeded their abilities to utilize this manner of instruction and assessment. (See Appendix A for a diagram depicting the themes and organization of the workshop.)

Both Dr. de Armas and I reasoned that having a healthy dialogue with teachers about critical/creative thinking and then affording them the time to utilize methods and strategies for teaching and assessing thinking would allow teachers to think about and identify their own practices. Building metacognitive opportunities into the process, we contemplated, would allow teachers to think creatively and intellectually about their own teaching processes. This would motivate them to recognize what they thought was valuable and what they thought should be changed in their curriculum and instructional methods, along with recognizing where they might be able to learn more about critical and creative thinking and instruction. The operative assumption was that by becoming more creative and critical in our own thinking, we are better able to help others think critically.

For historical purposes, it is important to mention that I have been working with Dade County Public Schools as a consultant in the area of critical thinking for close to ten years. My work with the district has included conducting workshops on how to teach critical thinking to limited English proficiency students. I have worked closely with the district and their office of bilingual education in designing workshops in legitimate assessment, including the use of portfolios, performance assessment, and other forms of authentic assessment. In conjunction with the district, I have been active in assisting in the production of critical thinking educational films and resources for teachers of all grades. I also have participated in the district's annual critical thinking conferences and have worked closely with Dr. de Armas throughout a nine-year period in furnishing powerful in-service opportunities for teachers of all grades. Many of these in-services have included modeling critical teaching in Dade County Public School classrooms through working directly with students, as well as conducting dialogues with teachers following the modeling sessions.

In the summer of 1999, at the urging of Maria de Armas, I drafted the critical and creative thinking standards using the Miami–Dade County Public Schools' *Curriculum Options for Academic Excellence Program* as a vehicle for providing examples of how strategies in critical and creative thinking might be implemented. For this reason, I have arranged the standard taxonomy and discussion that follows by introducing the principle of critical/creative thinking and then discussing the application of a given principle to aspects of classroom curriculum. The idea was also to connect theory to practice by providing examples of theory in practice as well as a formal and informal depiction of critical thinking standards and how these standards

might be conceived by a young primary student. (I have included a student's view of these standards as well as an informal depiction in Appendix A and Appendix B, respectively.)

Dr. de Armas and a group of teachers from the Office of Advanced Academics worked with me throughout 1999 as I honed and refined the standards. I was fortunate to work with these teachers and professionals, who aided me tremendously with the development of the critical/creative thinking taxonomy. Later in 1999, I returned to work with teachers from various schools in actual theoretical understanding and implementation.

All in all, the workshops held in 1999 were successful. I was able to work with about ninety teachers from throughout the district in several two-day workshops. Teachers who did attend the workshops held in 1999 were excited about the opportunity to dialogue about how to teach for thinking and creativity and were enthusiastic about the opportunities and challenges to infuse critical thinking instruction within their curriculums. They also found that the time afforded them to dialogue and think critically about their own profession and engage in critical metacognition regarding teaching, learning, and the assumptions they have developed was immensely important in allowing them to see alternative ways of looking at the teaching-learning world.

It was interesting, in working with teachers as well as staff, that all the teachers commented about the rush to adhere to state standardized tests and that this kept them from teaching creative and critical thinking. Most all agreed that these standardized tests did little to help students think more critically or creatively, failed to assess reasoning, provided no opportunities or incentives for metacognitive work or directions in curriculum redesign, and acted as an impediment to authentic learning and assessment. This was precisely because *teaching-to-the-test* took valuable time away from real instructional practices that promised to help students think. This is an important observation, as Florida is one of the more controversial states involved in academic accountability measures. Dade County Public Schools are also involved in the nation's first statewide voucher system, adopted in April of 2000, a system based on holding schools, teachers, and students accountable to state standards. Yet the majority of teachers agreed that their independence, creativity, and methods of instruction had all been compromised by the Florida Comprehensive Assessment Test (FCAT), Florida's statewide assessment instrument. If the FCAT was preventing teachers from teaching critically and creatively, these teachers wondered how the state could require such tests without input from teachers themselves. Furthermore, finding themselves held hostage to an inauthentic, state-mandated test and seeing their schools rated with an A, B, C, D, or F had left many teachers despondent, shocked, and in a state of intellectual and emotional turmoil and despair.

Dr. de Armas is an enlightened administrator committed to offering teachers powerful opportunities to develop their critical capacity to teach students how to think. None of the work we accomplished with the few teachers we were able to work with could have been done without her leadership and vision. Whether her efforts and those of her staff will be fruitful or even allowed to continue will greatly depend on the politics of education and how the controversy over learning and teaching becomes dialogically translated in the Dade County Public School District. Unfortunately, the theory and practices of the district are vitiating administrative and teacher efforts at increasing the critical and creative thinking of Dade County's children. All Florida citizens should be alarmed. At this point in time, with the school district's slavish allegiance to illegitimate state standards, the critical and creative program that Dr. de Armas and I theorized and developed has been shelved indefinitely. Our plans to have teachers experiment with the standards and then return for dialogue was sabotaged by preparation for state-mandated testing.

I was pleased to have been enlisted to develop the critical and creative assessment standards for the Office of Advanced Academics and felt privileged to work closely with teachers. I seriously believe that the time I did work with teachers allowed all of us to begin to reformulate a dialogue regarding what it means to think intelligently and creatively. We also discovered our own criticality and creativity and thought deeply about how we might reconstruct our curriculums, instructional methods, and assessment practices to help students develop their critical and creative potentials. While my frustration lies with Dade County Public School's myopic view of student achievement and their district practices in demoralizing and deskilling teachers, my optimism rests on my assumption that the creative performance art of teaching and learning will refuse to be reduced to an act of mechanical attainment and standardized evaluation. My enthusiasm is also built on my ardent belief in our citizens' ability to understand and struggle for educational opportunities that develop the critical capacities of all our nation's children.

By escalating the public's awareness of critical and creative thinking, Dr. de Armas and the teachers who participated in the critical/creative thinking project in the state of Florida, and particularly in the Dade County Public Schools, have done a tremendous service to our nation's children.

The following is a formal depiction of the critical and creative thinking standards that I developed for the Florida Dade County Public Schools Academic Excellence Program. Though these are certainly not the only critical and creative thinking skills that should be taught to students, I felt that the following thirty-five concepts were an important beginning. In presenting this taxonomy, I acknowledge the issue of multiple intelligences and do not make any

claims that these thirty-five concepts are exhaustive or exclusively significant. Rather, these principles and strategies of critical and creative thinking have been developed so that teachers, parents, and students might gain an insight into what it means to think critically and how we as educators might organize and develop critical and creative thinking curriculums that engage reasoning, self-authorship, and inventiveness. At the very least, I am hoping that they provide a subject matter and forum for continued viable and imaginative discussions regarding what students should know and how they might come to know it.

The Standards

Critical and Creative Thinking Standards for Dade County Public Schools Advanced Academic Program

Mission: Students will demonstrate growth and development in critical and creative thinking.

A Taxonomy of Critical and Creative Thinking Goals and Objectives for Students and Teachers

Rationale: Critical and creative thinkers are interested in developing

Written and prepared for Dade County Public Schools Office of Advanced Academics by Dr. Danny Weil, The Critical Thinking Institute. Edited by Holly Kathleen Anderson, MA. Copyright © Dr. Danny Weil, the Dade County Public Schools Academic Excellence Program.

their capacity to solve problems, make decisions, and continuously assess their thinking to determine its strengths, weaknesses, and limitations. They are imbued with a sense of imagination and curiosity that calls on them to seek complex answers to complex questions. They are uncomfortable with complacency and seek to find new and innovative ways of approaching life's possibilities. They are particularly interested in developing effective modes of thinking in the cognitive areas of abstract, systematic, evaluative, and collaborative thinking, and they are aware of the affective area of emotional intelligence and its relationship to creative and critical thought. Critical thinkers seek to routinely evaluate their thinking and assess their thought patterns relative to criteria. They seek to subject what they think they know to critical scrutiny in the interest of achieving the best results, the best decisions, and the best solutions to problems. Finally, critical and creative thinkers are concerned with all of the above as it affects good judgment and innovation.

The following represents a taxonomy of critical and creative thinking goals and objectives. They have been divided into categories associated with modes of thinking that have been recognized as important in the development of critical and creative thinking.

Abstract thinking is thinking that is comfortable and fluent with large ideas, a thinking that heralds ambiguity. Abstract thinking is thinking that is articulate and comfortable with abstractions and symbolic representa-

tions of information and ideas. Abstract thinkers reason deductively from general concepts to particular situations.

Systematic thinking is grounded on an understanding that we as human beings construct systems and that there is a logic to all disciplines, theories, perspectives, and positions. Systematic thinkers understand ideas and their interrelationships. Systematic thinking experiences ideas not in isolation from one another, but holistically within a complex web of interrelated ideas and principles. Systematic thinking seeks to constantly relate the parts to the whole and whole to parts and is essential to unlock logical systems of thought for purposes of analysis and evaluation.

Evaluative thinking routinely experiments with and assesses its own work and underlying thinking. It is thinking that experiences itself in a constant state of pregnancy as it continually gives birth to new ideas and creative ways to foster improvement. Evaluative thinking is a commitment to thinking that is constantly scrutinizing itself and the thinking of others in the interest of self-betterment and continuous improvement. It is motivated and achieved by inner questioning and attitudes of humility and courage.

Collaborative thinking recognizes our interdependence on the thinking of others. It is thinking that incorporates attitudes and dispositions that collaboratively confront increasingly complex problems within an atmosphere of civility and inquiry. It is founded on the notion of synergy: that if people follow a rational sequence of events and incorporate good values and attitudes of thinking amongst each other, they will perform beyond the sum of their individual resources. Collaborative thinkers understand that they do not surrender their individuality simply because they harness their efforts with others. On the contrary, much like a musician in an orchestra, collaborative thinkers understand that working with others serves to increase individual effectiveness and sense of self.

Emotional intelligence, or the affective dimension of learning, recognizes that critical and creative thinking is more than just sets of cognitive skills but also involves a compilation of attitudes or dispositions that must be cultivated and nourished. Developing emotional intelligence involves experiencing a variety of situations with others and learning to understand how others see and process the world. Critical thinking teachers know that this intelligence is learned, and they seek to offer students opportunities to develop an insight into the attitudinal aspect of thinking. They also know that these attitudes and dispositions are indispensable for open-minded critical and creative thinking and are recognized as essential for teaching creative and critical thought.

The Five Dimensions of Critical and Creative Thinking Behaviors and Attitudes

1. Problem-Solving and Decision-Making Dimension

S-1 Defining and Identifying Problems

S-2 Defining and Identifying Goals

S-3 Using Information Critically

S-4 Distinguishing Relevant from Irrelevant Information

S-5 Questioning Deeply: Learning to Think Socratically

S-6 Examining and Evaluating Assumptions and Beliefs

S-7 Generating and Assessing Effective Decisions and Solutions

S-8 Exploring Consequences and Implications

S-9 Making Plausible Inferences, Coming to Good Conclusions, Making Effective Decisions, and Learning to Interpret Critically

S-10 Giving Reasons and Evaluating Evidence and Alleged Facts

2. Analytical and Evaluative Thinking Dimension

S-11 Avoiding Overgeneralizations and Oversimplifications

S-12 Developing Criteria for Evaluation

S-13 Evaluating the Credibility of Sources of Information

S-14 Analyzing or Evaluating Arguments, Interpretations, Beliefs, or Theories

S-15 Analyzing and Evaluating Actions or Policies

S-16 Comparing and Contrasting Ideals with Actual Practice

S-17 Evaluating Perspectives, Interpretations, or Theories

3. Systematic Thinking Dimension

S-18 Comparing Analogous Situations: Transferring Educational Insights into New Contexts
S-19 Making Interdisciplinary Connections
S-20 Noting Significant Similarities and Differences

4. Collaborative Thinking Dimension

S-21 Reasoning Dialogically: Comparing Perspectives, Interpretations, and Theories
S-22 Reasoning Dialectically: Evaluating Perspectives, Interpretations, and Theories
S-23 Developing One's Perspective
S-24 Listening Critically
S-25 Practicing Questioning: Learning to Explore Beliefs, Theories, and Perspectives

5. Emotional Intelligence/
Affective Dimension

S-26 Independent Thinking: Developing an Investigative Orientation
S-27 Developing Intellectual Empathy
S-28 Developing Intellectual Humility
S-29 Developing Intellectual Imagination and Curiosity
S-30 Developing Intellectual Efficacy
S-31 Developing a Tolerance for Ambiguity

S-32 Developing Intellectual Perseverance and Discipline
S-33 Developing Intellectual Courage
S-34 Developing Intellectual Civility
S-35 Developing Intellectual Integrity

The Problem-Solving and Decision-Making Dimension

Principle S-1: Defining and Identifying Problems. Learning to clearly and precisely define problems in thinking is a substantial goal of critical thinking instruction. Fifty percent of all problem solving involves defining the problem. All good decisions and solutions to problems require a clear understanding of what the actual problem is. Helping students separate causes from solutions, symptoms from problems, and subproblems from real problems is essential for teaching students to think critically. For example, defining the wrong problem can send a student down the wrong path to, at a minimum, irrelevant solutions, and ensure that she will not understand the subject matter or concepts she is examining. Helping students define problems—to take what they are learning and phrase inquiry in the form of questions to be answered through research and collaboration—is a goal of critical instruction. We want our students to define the issues they are learning and then take intellectual responsibility for pursuing reading, writing, speaking, and listening in the interest of answering their own questions. This requires a clear understanding of exactly what problems are and how we go about identifying them. Furthermore, it involves learning how to frame problems in divergent ways, ways that call upon expansionary thinking in the interest of creativity.

Application to Classroom Instruction. The classroom application was conducted through the Miami–Dade County Public Schools Curriculum Options for Academic Excellence Program (COAEP). Using journalism, both print and broadcasting, COAEP provided students with opportunities to identify and examine problems. Teachers can ask questions like journalists do in identifying, distinguishing, and solving problems. Students can research the ways that reporters identify and examine public and private problems. They can become animated to see problems as environmentalists see them in all parts of the world and then discuss solutions to problems from various points of view. They can come to understand that how we frame issues as problems often is a result of our point of view, and they can learn to identify points of view when analyzing problem statements. This can be extremely important in environmental studies (COAEP), where points of view abound. Students can be encouraged to identify problems for journalistic purposes and then write about these problems for a real audience. In environmental studies (COAEP), students can iden-

tify and target specific environmental problems in their communities, neighborhoods, state, or country. Through an understanding of point of view gained through speech, debate, and literature (COAEP), students can discuss how people with different points of view see different problems and why. They become actively involved in critical analysis and problem solving. They can then discuss these points of view through debate or discussion. By examining problems and issues within these contexts, students can learn what happens if problems are ill-defined or if they have not been adequately examined.

Principle S-2: Defining and Identifying Goals. Whenever we think, we think for a purpose; our thinking seeks to accomplish something. All disciplines, subject mater, and in fact human endeavors in general have a purpose. Helping students see the goals and objectives in what they are studying is essential to help them understand subject matter. Many problems with students' understanding of, for example, biology or history come with the fact that they do not know why they are studying biology or history—what biologists and historians attempt to accomplish through their scholarly endeavors. By not identifying the goals contained within various disciplines, students cannot be expected to understand the discipline as a system. For example, without understanding what a biologist seeks to accomplish by studying cells, let's say, the student cannot possibly hope to identify biological problems in the area of cellular formation or development. We cannot take for granted that our students understand what historians, biologists, mathematicians, artists, or journalists do; in fact, we should assume the opposite and engage students in discussions as to the purposes behind studying one subject or another. Similarly, students too have goals, in the form of assignments, within any academic pursuit. Are they clear as to what they are attempting to accomplish and why? Have they identified their own objectives and the objectives of instruction in a given area?

Application to Classroom Instruction. Using speech and debate (COAEP), students can identify the goal of a persuasive speech or argument. The teacher can ask them to identify the objectives of a debate and then organize their thinking around accomplishing this objective. In environmental science (COAEP), students can examine and discuss environmental goals, deciding whether they are rational. They can research various environmental concerns and see how problems and goals are related in environmental studies. In art, students can see how artists' goals are enhanced by the materials they choose to use and how a clear understanding of one's goal as an artist can impact greatly on the visual representation of their work (COAEP). For example, teachers can query students regarding the goals involved in using oil-based paint as opposed to watercolors. Students can see the goals in art processes and then en-

gage in their own art activities, setting goals and trying processes designed to enhance their artistic goals. Using shared inquiry through literature, students can be animated to state clearly and precisely story characters' goals and how their objectives and purposes affected their characters (COAEP). And through simulated activities (COAEP), students can capture this understanding by setting their own goals and attempting to accomplish them in the form of simulations.

Principle S-3: Using Information Critically. Critical thinkers recognize the importance of using reliable and relevant sources of information. They constantly seek to validate sources for information, and they give less credence to sources that lack integrity or those that are biased. Critical thinkers know that they must question information critically to determine its overall validity. They pay critical attention to how information is used and marshaled for a particular purpose. They also are aware of how information is used, classified, and categorized. For example, critical thinkers know that there is more than one point of view on any given issue and that people often marshal and assemble information differently, depending on their positions, claims, and assumptions. They interpret information within the wide context of a system of thought, not in isolation. Critical thinkers understand that to use information correctly they must pay attention to how they organize the information—how they categorize it and sort it. They realize that preconceptions figure into the use of information, and they constantly seek to see information from more than one point of view. When using information, critical thinkers understand they have an obligation to verify the sources of information and seek alternative sources. Finally, they recognize that to avoid becoming roadkill on the information superhighway, they must spend time analyzing and evaluating information before they use it.

Application to Classroom Instruction. As students do research in any area of concern, whether it be art, environmental studies, literature, or drama and theater (COAEP), they will be exposed to information within the field. As teachers, we can question students as to the sources of their information, encourage them to seek out alternative sources, and then work with them to use information to gain knowledge. Through our questions and activities, we can help students see how people studying various subject matters acquire, examine, and organize information for problem-solving purposes. For example, in reporting a story in journalism, either broadcast or print, students should be encouraged to seek and examine a wide variety of information on a given issue (COAEP). Through research they can be animated to pursue information from various points of view and then compare and contrast the information to see patterns or discrepancies. In this way they can begin to see how various journalists use information and for what purposes.

In simulated learning (COAEP) involving hands-on experiences, students can assemble information, classify it, and then use it to solve problems or make plausible inferences about their subject matter. Drama and theater production (COAEP) can be used as a forum to present information to a larger audience. This can share scientific or historical information through a play or skit. And using information from various sources, students in environmental studies can make plausible inferences about world climate and then discuss problems or solutions to environmental problems (COAEP). Throughout these endeavors teachers should ask students how they assembled the information they received, what their sources were and how they determined their reliability, what patterns they saw in the information, and how they would use the information to make predictions or decisions. Students would be queried as to how they might depict this information for others, how others might react to the information they have, and what someone who disagreed with them might say. By getting students to appreciate and develop a healthy attitude regarding information acquisition and depiction, one helps them prepare for a world where information has become one of the central features of modern life.

Principle S-4: Distinguishing Relevant from Irrelevant Information. For students to think critically they must be able to tell the difference between facts that are relevant to a specific situation and those that are not. Critical thinkers focus attention only on relevant facts and seek to ferret out irrelevancy in their information bank. Since relevance is always subject to point of view, students must understand that the determination of relevancy of facts within any discipline is a matter of debate and discussion. They must become comfortable with putting forth positions and then defending why they believe facts or information are relevant or not and how this affects problem solving within a discipline. What is relevant in one context may not be relevant in another. If we want students to become good purveyors of information, they must consistently seek to categorize information within categories of relevance.

Application to Classroom Instruction. When discussing an issue or problem, when giving reasons for a position or conclusion, or when arguing for a particular solution or decision, students can become sensitive to how they use information that is relevant. Many students assume all information is relevant within a context and thus do not know how to organize their thinking around the facts needed to make plausible arguments or seek valid conclusions. By asking students how specific facts would affect their decisions, or how certain information relates to what they are studying, teachers can help students to see the necessity for relevant information. For example, in speech and debate (COAEP), students would be encouraged to organize their positions around information relevant to the topic. When students are work-

ing at putting together a speech or debate, the teacher can ask why they picked specific facts or information and how these relate to the goals of the debate or problem addressed in the speech. When sorting or evaluating groups of pictures in art instruction, for example (COAEP), students can explain why they feel the artist put certain images in her work. When viewing a picture of a spring day in an impressionistic painting, students can be queried as to why the artist included certain visualizations in her painting and why she left others out. In literature (COAEP), students can read a chapter of a text or story and note relevant details that they can then summarize in writing, offering reasons for thinking the details were relevant. They can share and discuss what they thought and thus see the necessity of relevance. Social studies in particular allows students to see how people with various positions organize information around their claims. Finally, children can develop a sensitivity to relevance by creating their own stories with irrelevant facts and then read each other's stories to pick out the irrelevancies.

Principle S-5: Questioning Deeply: Learning to Think Socratically. Critical thinkers know that to pursue issues with any depth they must put a large premium on questions. Being on the *quest* implies that we have many questions about the knowledge we seek to obtain. Helping students raise important questions about what they are studying will prepare them for the quest for knowledge within a subject area and allow them to create their own knowledge. Critical thinkers try to figure out what they do not know and thus see the importance of questioning as a source of probing their reasoning and the reasoning of others. Since each subject area has its own set of unique questions, helping students see these questions as an organizing basis for all disciplines helps them to understand the discipline as system. For example, the questions we ask in history are not the questions we ask in math; the questions we seek to answer in science are not the questions we ask when we seek to understand the English language. Helping students develop sensitivity toward and insight into the various questions that are relevant to a discipline helps them seek answers and solutions to subject-matter problems; this helps students learn to state problems about what they are learning for inquiry purposes.

Application to Classroom Instruction. Since texts fail to develop questions that delve very deeply, it is the responsibility of both the student and teacher to formulate critical thinking questions that promise to uncover the discipline in question. One idea the teacher can use is to start any activity by asking what kinds of questions students might have about what they are going to study. This allows them to begin to generate questions that can serve as the basis for classroom discussion or activity. For example, in studying global warming (COAEP), students might be asked by the teacher before inquiry begins what questions

they have about global warming or the environment. These could be listed on the board and then used as the basis for a classroom discussion as well as research and writing. In journalism (COAEP), students can be encouraged to conduct interviews using questions they have formulated beforehand. When reading texts (COAEP), students can turn the text headings into questions and then read to answer their own questions. They can then formulate questions that go beyond the text and find sources for answers that they can then judge critically.

Helping students ask and formulate questions should be a central goal of critical and creative instruction; teachers should model their own formation of questions out loud to students, letting students see them questioning themselves and the world around them. Students should be encouraged through inquiry instruction to develop an understanding of the external questions we ask others and the internal questions we ask ourselves. For example, when appreciating art (COAEP), students might wish to think about questions they would ask the artist if she were present. When organizing a speech, students might be asked what questions they need to ask themselves to assess whether they are accomplishing what they have set out to accomplish. By helping students see internal questioning as metacognition, or the art of self-assessment, students can begin to develop an outlook toward the world that seeks understanding through questioning as opposed to self-righteousness through mere statements. They can then begin not only to answer questions, but to question answers.

Finally, the variety of questions we ask students will help to model for them the types of questions that they should be thinking about.

Principle S-6: Examining and Evaluating Assumptions and Beliefs. Critical thinkers know that the starting points for all reasoning are the assumptions or beliefs we form as human beings. Whether on a personal level or within academic disciplines, assumptions make up the foundations for all knowledge and lead us to conclusions about math, science, history, environmental studies, and so on. Distinguishing between what one knows and what one merely believes is the goal of critical thinking; independent critical thinkers seek out assumptions both in their own reasoning and in the reasoning of others and subject them to the magnifying glass of scrutiny. They know that to proceed based on false assumptions will inevitably lead to false solutions and misguided decisions. Helping students question assumptions in scholarly endeavors as well as within their own personal lives must be a goal of instruction. Helping students understand the assumptions they make and the assumptions they will be studying is essential for artful critical thinking instruction. Furthermore, students should be animated to question assumptions in the interest of creativity and self- improvement. Students must first recognize assumptions and then distinguish them from

facts before they can evaluate them; it is this process that should be afforded rigorous instructional time.

Application to Classroom Instruction. Since assumptions are within everything that we hear, read, see and do, teachers should look for opportunities to encourage students to identify assumptions. Every discipline is based on assumptions about the discipline. For example, when studying dinosaurs we make assumptions about their size and diet based on bones and other paleontological evidence. We also make inferences based on these assumptions. Working with students to help them identify the underlying assumptions behind what they are studying is crucial for teaching them to make plausible assumptions. For example, within literature-based inquiry (COAEP), students can be questioned as to what assumptions characters in stories are making and how these assumptions affect their decisions, solutions, and actions. They can then be asked about their own assumptions regarding this issue or that issue. In chess (COAEP), players make assumptions and then engage in moves based on what they believe or assume is the best strategy. Engaging students in metacognitive activities that help them identify these assumptions and how they affected their game is an excellent lesson.

Asking students for their own assumptions can be part of any academic pursuit. For example, when studying the environment or reading journalistic pieces (COAEP), students can be asked what assumptions the authors might have had and what assumptions they themselves have regarding the issues. They can be encouraged to compare and contrast assumptions on one issue or another for recognition and evaluation purposes. In drama and theater (COAEP), students should be able to see the importance of understanding the assumptions of a character before that character is acted out. Understanding a character's belief structure is essential to a good dramatic enactment of that character's persona. Similarly, if students were to engage in simulation (COAEP), for example conjuring up an imaginative civilization or city, they would need to identify the assumptions that underlie how the city would be run and what rules and laws might be adopted. Finally, through questioning, teachers can ask students to examine their own assumptions within any area of academic endeavor and then discuss their reasons and evidence with other students in the form of a speech or debate (COAEP).

Principle S-7: Generating and Assessing Effective Decisions and Solutions. Generating and assessing effective decisions and solutions to problems is a goal of critical thinking. Critical thinking is required to obtain good results, and critical thinkers know that good results are the product of good reasoning. Because solutions and decisions must be generated and conjured up in thought, critical thinkers know that using information wisely, identifying problems clearly, and subjecting assumptions to the light of scrutiny go a long way toward generating solu-

tions and decisions. They also know that the process of generating effective solutions and decisions is not a product of hasty or sloppy decision making or problem solving, but is a slow methodical process whereby comparisons are employed to seek the best solution or the best decision. Because solutions and decisions affect others, critical thinkers know the importance of points of view, and they seek points of view when attempting to generate effective solutions and decisions. Because critical thinking is based on nonlinear, divergent thinking, critical thinkers know that the more expansionary their thinking becomes (that is, the more abstract and holistic), the more creative their solutions and decisions will be.

Application to Classroom Instruction. Unfortunately, what teachers and students confront in most textbooks relative to problem solving and decision making are problem-solving steps that the student is forced to accept when attempting to solve a problem. Whether it is an algorithm in mathematics or a positivistic approach to a social studies problem, the approach tends to be the same: linear, convergent thinking steps whereby students are never encouraged to generate their own solutions or, at a minimum, to understand how the solutions or steps we generate are formulated. This unnecessarily limits the divergent thinking process that seeks to expand reasoning through consideration of a host of problem-solving approaches. Students need to consider how others approach problems and come to solutions, not just study linear models that ask for blind obedience rather than for thinking. For example, when discussing environmental solutions with students (COAEP), the teacher can bring into consideration many points of view, perhaps those of Native Americans, farmers, business people, or labor organizers. Encouraging students to see how others have formulated problems and generated solutions allows them to see different reasoning and problem-solving approaches. As discussed earlier, problem solving and solution generation rely to a great degree on the problem formulation, or a clear and precise understanding of the problem. Thus, it is recommended that the teacher have the student state the problems to be solved or decisions to be made clearly.

Students should explore causes of problems, for example, causes of a problem they are looking at journalistically (COAEP); after reasoning within multiple points of view about these causes, they may seek to reformulate the problem. This encourages creative, divergent thinking and helps students see the relationship between the solutions and decisions they generate and the problems they are attempting to solve. In speech or debate (COAEP), students should seek to marshal reasons for their conclusions and solutions and explain how they came to generate these conclusions. Teachers can ask questions of students that encourage them to identify the problem, come up with solutions, examine solutions, and recognize multiple points of view surrounding issues and problems. In chess, for example

(COAEP), students should be able to see how their decision to play the game one way is a generated solution on their part; they should seek to understand their game as an attempt to solve a problem. Finally, in environmental studies (COAEP), teachers might want to provide students with opportunities to evaluate solutions tried and to propose alternative solutions based on examined assumptions and beliefs.

Principle S-8: Exploring Consequences and Implications. Critical thinkers can see the implications or consequences of statements and thinking. They reason consequentially. This allows them to develop a richer and fuller understanding of the meaning and implications of their thinking. Critical thinkers know that all thinking has implications, and they seek to understand the consequences, or what follows from thinking. When considering beliefs or decisions, critical thinkers analyze the implications of such beliefs or actions. Understanding that all thinking has consequences allows critical thinkers to plan alternative courses of action, anticipate a wide range of solutions to problems, and learn to prioritize conclusions, decisions, and solutions based on the implications and consequences of their thinking.

Application to Classroom Instruction. Teachers should ask students to state consistently the implications of the thinking they are confronting or embracing. When using literature (COAEP), teachers can ask students to state the implications of a character's actions. They can then work to change the story relative to the consequences they would like to see. In environmental studies (COAEP), students should be able to state the implications of changes in environmental policy, who is affected, problems that arise, and assumptions behind policy decisions. Through questioning they can come to evaluate the policies relative to the consequences as seen from multiple points of view. In art appreciation and instruction (COAEP), students should be able to comment on the implications of using specific colors or brush strokes when painting for one purpose or another. This will allow them to see the painting as a system that itself has a logic, that painting decisions are based on the consequences of style and stroke, not simply a product. When conducting speeches or debating issues (COAEP), students should be able to argue for points of view based on consequences that they have analyzed. This will allow them to develop a critical understanding of debate.

Principle S-9: Making Plausible Inferences, Coming to Good Conclusions, Making Effective Decisions, and Learning to Interpret Critically. An inference is a statement about the unknown based on what is known. All of us make inferences; we could not live without them. Within the body of all disciplines can be found inferences or conclusions about the world. Scientists infer the climate on Jupiter only to be confronted with evidence from the Space Telescope that tells them their inference was wrong. Social scientists advocate policy solutions to problems that they infer are correct only to discover they might have been wrong. Critical thinking seeks to reach sound conclusions, make effective decisions, and generate good solutions based on observation and information. It is thinking obsessed with good judgment. Critical thinkers know it is important to distinguish what they observe from what they conclude, and they distinguish instances when they are guessing from instances when they are coming to sound conclusions. They also know that it is important to include the reasoning of other points of view when making decisions and generating solutions. They are aware of the tendency of bias in thought and look for evidence before coming to conclusions. When interpreting situations, critical thinkers know that their perception of the world influences how they see reality or interpret life's messages, and they seek to examine the assumptions underlying their interpretations and are interested in how others interpret similar situations. Since all of our interpretations are based on what we infer, critical thinkers know that they must subject inferences to critical examination in the interest of good judgment.

Application to Classroom Instruction. Teachers can animate students to make inferences based on almost any academic pursuit. Students in primary grades can be asked to infer aspects of the world when dinosaurs roamed; students in older grades can be asked to make inferences about classmate actions or school policies; and using literature (COAEP), all students can be asked to make inferences about story titles, characters, and story actions.

Using chess as an example of inference generation, students can discuss how their inferences have consequences for the way they play the game. They can explain how they arrived at conclusions to play the game one way or another and begin to see how their reasoning develops.

In environmental science instruction (COAEP), students can propose their own inferences or predictions as to what might happen if specific environmental policies were or were not adopted. When conducting science experiments, they can learn to distinguish their observations from their inferences and learn to interpret the results of experiments critically. This will allow them to develop scientific thinking as opposed to just "doing science." In art appreciation (COAEP), students can infer situations, issues, and history from paintings and then use research to check the accuracy of their inferences. Of course, teachers should help students generate personal examples from their own lives of when they might have made good or bad inferences and what happened. Helping students gain insight into the conclusions they come to, the decisions they make, and the interpretations they engage in promotes good judgment and character development through reasoning.

Principle S-10: Giving Reasons and Evaluating Evidence and Alleged Facts. Since critical thinking is reasoning, or coming to conclusions based on reasons, critical thinkers know that their reasoning has elements or compo-

nents that they must pay attention to. They are interested in taking apart their reasoning and the reasoning of others in the interest of systematic understanding. They look to see how the dance we call reasoning is assembled and know that the dance is composed of steps. Critical thinkers know that all reasoning requires evidence for conclusions reached, and critical thinkers have a healthy appreciation for evidence and reasons. Teachers must learn to give reasons for their own actions, decisions, and directives. This modeling will allow students to see the importance of evidence in reasoning. When reasoning, critical thinkers are comfortable being asked for and giving reasons for their conclusions or decisions. They do not find a request for their evidence intimidating or threatening. In fact, they consistently look for reasons and evidence in what they are studying and in the claims they make and hear. More than that, critical thinkers look for evidence that does not agree with their conclusions, and they invite critique of evidence that does. Critical thinkers know that evidence is what we use to support claims or arguments; it's proof. They also know that not all information and facts are evidence, and they work to evaluate evidence that is collateral to assumptions or claims. Finally, critical thinkers know that evidence is not always complete, accurate, or relevant, and they evaluate evidence with a set of criteria.

Application to Classroom Instruction. Teachers should always ask students for their reasons when they come to conclusions about anything. Teachers can consistently ask questions like: *How do you know? Why do you think that is true? What evidence do you have?* When students' answers seem incomplete or not fully developed, the teacher should continue probing their reasoning. They might ask questions like these: *What other evidence do you have? How do you know the information is true? What assumptions are you making, and how do you know they are true?* When discussing interpretations of literature or art (COAEP), students should be routinely asked to show specifically where in the material they got that interpretation. The sentence, passage, or art representation can be clarified and discussed and the student's interpretation better understood and examined. Students can learn to distinguish evidence from information by instruction in the relationship between claims and evidence. For example, in environmental studies (COAEP), students should be encouraged to examine environmental claims from multiple groups with different points of view in light of the evidence and reasons being used to support the claims. They might then use speech or debate (COAEP) to discuss the evidence and comment on its veracity or validity. Some questions teachers might wish to ask would include: *Why do you think so? How do you know? Where did the evidence come from? How do we know it is true? What is the evidence supporting? Why? Is there any reason to question the evidence? What reasons? How might we find out what other evidence exists?*

Analytical and Evaluative Thinking Dimension

Principle S-11: Avoiding Overgeneralizations and Oversimplifications. Simplifying problems and experiences in an attempt to make them easier to understand and act upon is natural and normal and a necessary part of analytical and evaluative thinking. Generalizations and simplifications by themselves are not bad; however, oversimplifying and overgeneralizing (viewing issues in terms of black and white, with no sensitivity to their complexity and intricacy) can result in miscommunication, misrepresentation, and outright distortion. For example, viewing people or groups as "all bad or all good" is an example of an oversimplification leading to a stereotype. Seeing the differences between useful simplifications that serve to inform and misleading oversimplifications that seek to misrepresent and distort is an important critical thinking skill. When analyzing and evaluating situations, critical thinkers seek to scrutinize generalizations, probe for exceptions, and as a result use appropriate qualifiers in their language when discussing issues and beliefs. They are aware of the problems with overgeneralized language, such as in using the terms *everyone, all people, always* and *never.*

Application to Classroom Instruction. Using children's literature to enhance reading skills (COAEP), teachers can ask questions about literature that tends to oversimplify. For example, if a literature selection overlooks factors by stating only one cause of a problem situation, or event, the teacher can pose questions seeking students' reasoning regarding other possible contributing factors. For example, teachers can ask questions such as these: *Was it all M's fault? How or in what way? Did X help create the problem? How and why? Is this situation "just like that one"? What are some differences?* Also, through simulations of events (CO-AEP), students can play devil's-advocate roles and bring other points of view to the material they are studying. This is especially true for history or social studies, where simplistic reasons for behaviors or simplistic causes of situations are often put forth. Through such activities as speech or debate (COAEP), students can be instructed and encouraged to develop insight into the appropriate use of qualifiers in language such as *highly likely, probably, not very likely, often, usually, seldom, I doubt, most, many,* and *some.* This allows students to understand the principles of generalization.

Principle S-12: Developing Criteria for Evaluation. Since critical thinking is a search for merit, truth, and consequently good judgment, critical thinkers know that developing and using criteria for evaluation is an important thinking process. They know that their judgments are the result of the criteria they apply to their thinking. And critical thinkers know that preferential criteria (that is, the criteria we develop to make choices such as what to wear or what ice cream to buy) are different from the criteria we develop

to form reasoned judgments. Critical thinkers know that reasoned judgment involves the necessity to include multiple points of view, whereas preferential judgments are simply what we like and require no other points of view. Further, critical thinkers are aware that they have values and how those values enter into the formation of their judgments and criteria. When developing criteria, critical thinkers are aware of the purpose of their evaluation; they pay attention to what is being evaluated and the function that the evaluation is supposed to serve. Critical thinkers know that criteria can vary depending on points of view, and thus they seek to identify and take into consideration a wide variety of points of view when engaging in fair-minded evaluation.

Application to Classroom Instruction. Whether working in environmental studies, art appreciation, or literature (COAEP), the student will always be evaluating. Whenever this occurs, the teacher can ask the student the purpose of the evaluation, what they are attempting to evaluate, the criteria they are using or developing, and the consequences of the evaluation. Students need to gain insight into the difference between the preferential criteria they use, such as what movie to go to or what shoes to buy, and the criteria we develop when engaging in reasoned judgment. When evaluating a theater performance (COAEP), for example, the student should be able to explain her criteria for deciding what was good about the play and what was not. The teacher can then ask how preferential criteria might be different from the criteria we use to make judgments that require reasoning. Whenever the teacher discusses criteria in a group setting, she should elicit multiple points of view and ask students for their reasoning as to how they developed their criteria and why. The teacher might share how she evaluates students and discuss her criteria with them. Students should be encouraged through questioning to compare and contrast differing criteria and then come to conclusions as to why they are different and the consequences of using one set or another.

As much as possible, students should be encouraged to develop criteria for their own mental performance in and out of school, so that they can learn to routinely examine their own lives against criteria they have authored. These metacognitive activities can take the form of simulations (COAEP) and performance and portfolio assessment. Helping students to see that criteria are issue-specific and then having them develop and apply criteria will give them opportunities to gain insight into the purpose and objectives of a criterion. Some questions that might be useful would be: *What are we evaluating? Why do people evaluate X? What are Xs for? Can you name and describe an X that is good? One that is bad? How did you decide what is good and bad? Are there other categories of criteria we should consider when evaluating X? What are the characteristics of a good X and why?* When student responses are too vague or reveal little, the teacher can ask what the student means. This allows the student to explicate and at the same time see the importance of the criteria for choosing words when attempting to communicate.

Principle S-13: Evaluating the Credibility of Sources of Information. In a world that is characterized by information overload, learning to assess the reliability of sources of information is essential for today's consumer of information. Critical thinkers know that the information they receive is only as good as the source it comes from. They are concerned with evaluating sources of information; they know that vested interests serve often to skew information, and they seek alternative points of view when evaluating sources of information. Critical thinkers analyze not simply information that supports their position but also information that leads to disagreement. They consistently seek contradictions in information and then seek to reconcile discrepancies. They realize that misinformation and misperception influence how we think, and thus we often see what we want to see even if it is not there. Critical thinkers pay close attention to the tendency for bias when judging the credibility of informational sources.

Application to Classroom Instruction. When discussing an issue upon which people disagree, one that requires reasoned judgment, the teacher can encourage students to gather information from a variety of sources representing different points of view. We want students to research different points of view if they are to see how information is assembled by various frames of reference. They can discuss discrepancies in the information and then discuss motives behind various points of view and how these motives might influence the information provided. In speech and debate (COAEP), students should be encouraged not only to verify their sources of information but also to research sources that are not in line with their own reasoning. This is essential thinking for debate exercises, as debaters should be able to clearly and precisely set forth information and sources their opponents will rely on. When looking at art criticism (COAEP) and especially published art critiques, students could be animated to discuss the sources of the critique and how they feel these sources might influence the critique itself.

Principle S-14: Analyzing and Evaluating Arguments, Interpretations, Beliefs, or Theories. Instead of using mere preference as a tool for agreeing or disagreeing with a position or claim, critical thinkers know that they must base their judgments on reasoning. They seek to penetrate arguments and assess their merits by using their reasoning to explore assumptions, how arguments assemble and verify information, the consequences and implications of beliefs and theories, and how arguments frame issues and for what purposes. Critical thinkers are sensitive to strengths and weaknesses in arguments, and as we have discussed, they develop criteria they use

to judge claims and premises. When evaluating or judging an argument or position, critical thinkers have a healthy appreciation for evidence and attempt to justify claims and conclusions in light of the evidence set forth to substantiate them. Furthermore, critical thinkers analyze arguments and theories in opposition to one another—alongside one another, so to speak—as a way of highlighting key assumptions and differences, contrasting claims, and comparing what they might have in common.

Application to Classroom Instruction. Whether they are working on environmental studies, speech and debate, literature, or art appreciation (CO-AEP), students will be presented with arguments, interpretations, and beliefs. Their job will be to analyze them in the interest of reasoned judgment. Therefore, these moments should be capitalized on by the teacher to teach processes for analyzing arguments and theories. Instead of asking students if they disagree or agree with a position, the teacher should encourage students to analyze positions alongside one another. A teacher might use questions like these: *What do these arguments propose? How are they different? What information do they rely on? Why is it different? What sources does the information come from? Why do they use different sources? What reasons and evidence are given with these points of view in favor of their assumptions? What are their assumptions anyway?* By practicing analytic techniques such as identifying assumptions, looking for evidence, noting how arguments use information, or analyzing their own purposes and how they see problems or questions at issue, students develop the microskills of familiarizing and practicing analytic techniques. They soon become more comfortable in knowing what to look for and how to put forth a good argument. Thereafter, in speech they can plan better by knowing the components of argumentation (COAEP). In journalism, they can write a more comprehensive account of events by knowing how their information fits into theories and interpretations (COAEP). And in literature, they can better understand characters and their mental formulations (COAEP). Whenever possible, teachers should encourage students to develop their own theories, ideas, and arguments and then share them with others for purposes of analysis. This allows them to transfer these critical thinking insights into their own lives.

Principle S-15: Analyzing and Evaluating Actions and Policies. All of us are asked each and every day to evaluate actions and policies. Whether it is judging behavior, rules, procedures, actions of people, or the actions of ourselves, we are constantly analyzing and evaluating actions and policies. When evaluating actions and policies, critical thinkers pay copious attention to criteria and the consequences of actions and policies. They know that actions rest on assumptions, and critical thinkers list evaluating assumptions as an important aspect of evaluating and analyzing actions and policies.

Application to Classroom Instruction.

When reading literature, students are consistently introduced to the actions of storybook and literature characters. The teacher can encourage students to raise questions about the actions and policies they read about. The teacher can ask questions such as these: *Why did X do that? What were the consequences of his actions? What reasons did he give for his actions? Who benefited from his actions and who did not? Why? How do you decide what actions to engage in? What do you think about . . . ?* When looking at pollution in studying environmental policies (COAEP), students should examine and analyze the policies. They should look at the policies as they affect all points of view and not just the point of view of the environmentalist or polluter. They should have opportunities to discuss school policies and classroom policies and, if possible, develop their own rules for actions. This way they can learn how policies are designed, for what purpose, for whose benefit, under what conditions, and surrounding what issues. This allows them to evaluate real policies in a real context. And of course, when studying history and social studies, students can consistently analyze and evaluate the policies of governments, countries, corporations, and citizens.

Principle S-16: Comparing and Contrasting Ideals with Actual Practices. Critical thinkers attempt to contrast facts and ideals. They understand the gap between reality and possibility. This is especially true for those interested in self-improvement and social improvement. Without the ability to see ourselves accurately and clearly, we are not able to admit to our weaknesses and frailties. The tendency is to see ourselves and social reality wedded to what we would like ourselves and reality to be, not what they truly are. Critical thinkers seek to see the gaps between what currently exists and what might be, between what is and what is not. They understand that pointing out the discrepancy between ideals and actual reality is a necessary and fundamental thinking skill.

Application to Classroom Instruction. Whenever students study and discuss society and social issues, whether they are environmental, judicial, social, or ethical, they should be comparing ideals with actual practices. In literature, students could compare and contrast actions and statements by characters and narrators to show discrepancies between ideals and actual practice. When discussing issues such as generosity and honesty, for example, students can be encouraged to express their views on generosity and honesty in actual practice. They can use examples from their own lives to show relevance and understanding.

Because textbooks consistently present sanitized versions of social events, students should be afforded resources that allow them to see how what is depicted ideally compares to actual practice. For example, when studying the free market, students can see where this ideal is violated in reality. This means looking under the surface of the claim to find actual situations where this assumption does not

work. Socially idealistic claims are made in environmental studies by people of many points of view, and students need opportunities to see how actual practice compares to these claims. In assembling speeches or debates, students should be able to submit evidence from actual practice that shows idealistic claims to be false. This allows them to pay attention to details while at the same time learning to analyze generalities through specifics. The teacher might animate students to become conscious of their own actions and how their actions might or might not be supporting the ideals and behaviors the students themselves profess or want. These discussions can be used to talk about school policy, behavioral problems, and conflict resolution.

Principle S-17: Evaluating Perspectives, Interpretations, or Theories. Whenever we evaluate perspectives, interpretations, and theories, we lay them beside one another in order to test their weaknesses and strengths. We want to see how ideas stack up against one another so that we can judge them. We call this dialectical reasoning. As soon as we begin to scratch the surface of perspectives or theories, we begin to see which ideas are consistent, which clash, which are not logical, which are rational, and on and on. We do this so we might develop our own perspective, find ideas we wish to integrate with those we already accept, and reconcile conflicts that might exist. To do this, we need to feel comfortable moving in and out of conflicting theories, beliefs, and points of view. We engage in the notion of critique in the interest of synthesis or the development of new ideas.

Application to Classroom Instruction. When the student is faced with two or more points of view on any issue, she must evaluate perspectives and interpretations side by side. This dialectical reasoning can be encouraged through stories in literature (COAEP). Speech, debate, and environmental studies all engage divergent points of view (CO-AEP) and thus can be opportunities for reasoning dialectically. Real life affords countless opportunities to reason dialectically, and students should be encouraged to express their own voice alongside that of authority when evaluating perspectives. Questioning assumptions, inferences in thinking, how information is used, the consequences of thinking, and how points of view identify goals and problems would be the substance of discussion. Students should be questioned as to how people with conflicting points of view reason, and they should be able to analyze the constituent parts of a reasoned argument.

Systematic Thinking Dimension

Principle S-18: Comparing Analogous Situations: Transferring Educational Insights into New Domains. Whenever we think, our mind organizes information in such a way that we are able to use it. When we apply ideas to new situations, we look for analogies. Analogies allow us to transfer what we are learning or discovering into our own lives in new contexts. Analogies help make learning relevant and should be encouraged as a form of visualizing thinking. Critical thinkers forever look to transfer what they have learned into new contexts. They know that this transfer, or learning to reason by analogy, enhances their ability to capture an idea or system of thought. By offering teaching and learning opportunities that are personalized and relevant, students can begin to see how education affects their own lives and the issues they involve themselves in. For students to gain insight into how to analogize situations, they must have opportunities to organize course material. By organizing material and then applying insights to a multitude of analogous situations, students will be able to see repeated patterns, common situations, and varied organizing principles. Furthermore, they will increase their ability to retain information because they will learn how to develop analogous thinking as a form of reference for what they are learning.

Application to Classroom Instruction. Critical teaching asks students to become authors of their own learning. It encourages them to do this by applying what they have learned to other situations that are analogous. For example, when studying an environmental problem (COAEP) in one state or one community, the student might be encouraged to look for analogies or similar situations in their own communities or states and then study how the situation has been handled. This will allow them to transfer the insights from one situation into another, to find out what is similar and what is different. In studying literature (CO-AEP), students should be able to compare and contrast analogous situations. Conflicts in literature usually parallel something in real life, and the teacher should look for opportunities for students to transfer their insights into concrete, relevant situations they might face.

When learning a new skill or discovering a new insight or way of doing something, students should be encouraged to use it in other, analogous situations. This way they will see the shortcomings and merits of the skills they use. When learning a drama principle (COAEP), for example, the teacher could discuss with students how it might be used in analogous situations, like giving a speech or presenting an impassioned plea to a jury. And by encouraging students to come up with analogies of their own, the teacher can assess whether learning has taken place.

Principle S-19: Making Interdisciplinary Connections. Critical thinkers do not let the fragmented approach to learning control their thought patterns. They look to conceive of the parts relative to the whole and the whole relative to the parts and thus know the necessity of transferring insights across and through disciplines. They understand that all learning is interdisciplinary. By using insights from one subject matter to understand another, they are able to uncover similarities in systems, patterns, and thoughts among disci-

plines. By approaching issues from a multitude of different perspectives, critical thinkers develop a more holistic approach to learning and understanding that offers greater width and depth.

With the assembly-line or fragmented approach to knowledge that divides knowledge into disciplines or subject matters, students unfortunately often do not see the interdisciplinary connections among the subjects. They come to see mathematics as something done during math period or math time and not as something that, let's say, the author or the artist does. They learn that the arbitrary distinctions between disciplines control their thinking, and they have a difficult time discovering the logic of what they are learning.

Finally, by offering comments, questions, demonstrations, and examples of what they are learning, students will be able to see the interdisciplinary connections between their lives and what they learn in school.

Application to Classroom Instruction. Teachers can begin by viewing the interdisciplinary connections between what they teach and what they want students to learn. They can begin offering reading and writing in mathematics as well as art instruction in science. They can involve students in speeches and debates that allow them opportunities to see issues from varied points of view (COAEP) while orchestrating various disciplines. They can have students involve themselves in simulations that call upon them to harness reading, writing, and speaking in the service of a project. And, whenever possible, teachers should look for opportunities to collaborate with other teachers in weaving disciplines together. In this way learners become actively involved in extending their learning into other contexts. Students could be given opportunities to write brochures about what they are learning in environmental studies (COAEP), which would incorporate various skills and disciplines. And teachers can ensure that a good variety of resources are available that look at issues from a broad perspective involving a host of disciplines. Students can then perform research and writing using these resources. In studying journalism they can be encouraged to cover stories from more than one angle, working together to develop the story (COAEP). With the Internet, there is no shortage of interdisciplinary connections in learning, and the computer should be used to highlight the dependency of one subject on another.

Principle S-20: Noting Significant Similarities and Differences. Noting significant similarities and differences is a lifelong activity. Critical thinkers approach this process with an understanding that the way we note differences and similarities in theories, points of view, and actions influences who we are, how we choose to experience reality, and our choices and judgments. Critical thinkers understand that we look for similarities and differences in reality depending on our purpose, our reason for wanting to figure something out. Similarly, we call attention to what is similar and different about situations for a specific purpose or goal. What is important and not important in noting these differences is essential to critical thinkers, who also are sensitive to the fact that often what appear on the surface as differences are really similarities in disguise.

Application to Classroom Instruction. Students are always asked by texts and teachers to compare and contrast something or other. Whether it is an idea or a weather phenomenon, students are asked to note differences and similarities. Yet these activities are often devoid of purpose, and the student is instead immersed in trivial pursuits executing mechanical cognitive functions for no seeming purpose. For example, comparing shoe size might be important to a shoe salesperson or athlete, but it is of little importance to a first grader. Although the activity may be cute, if it is not attached to specific purposes, students fail to transfer insights into relevant contexts, and the lesson is not learned. Whenever possible, ask students to compare and contrast for specific purposes. Use relevant, real-life activities to teach this concept, because it is best learned within the context of daily life. When using academic materials, ask students what they think could be compared and contrasted and why. For example, in literature (COAEP), we might want to have students compare and contrast storybook characters or literature characters for the sake of illuminating an idea, such as friendship or love. With this goal in mind, students can then use the results of the comparing and contrasting to draw conclusions about people, develop criteria, and judge actions. Students should be actively seeking associations and learning to develop connections between ideas.

Collaborative Thinking Dimension

Principle S-21: Reasoning Dialogically: Comparing Perspectives, Interpretations, and Theories.   When we engage in dialogical thinking, we engage in dialogue and communication to reason our way through problems and issues. This thinking involves an exchange of differing points of view in an atmosphere of civility and inquiry. Critical thinkers wish to engage in fruitful dialogue aimed at uncovering truth or merit. Critical thinkers attempt to develop a dialogue that seeks to process ideas, to consider goals and purposes, to look at information and assumptions, and to generate and evaluate solutions relative to consequences. They know that much of what parades as problem-solving dialogue is really posturing and ego defensiveness. By learning to integrate critical thinking principles and strategies within dialogue, students learn to become more focused when discussing subject matter and subject matter issues; students learn a language for thinking. Students also learn to concentrate on asking questions as opposed to making statements, and they cultivate Socratic thinking when they are pursuing issues. Their dialogue becomes rich and issue specific when necessary, while they attempt to avoid unnecessary ego posturing.

Application to Classroom Instruction. By raising and entertaining open-ended questions about whatever is being studied, students are afforded ample time to engage in dialogue. By modeling questioning in front of students and consistently asking students for their input concerning ideas, teachers can encourage and engage students' dialogical thinking. Posing problems helps by affording students the questions necessary to probe through reasoning. When pursuing environmental studies (COAEP), students can be encouraged to put what they are learning in the form of a question and then, with or without teacher direction, begin to dialogue about the issue. Of course, debate is a form of dialogue (COAEP), and debate teams can be fostered to engage students in the dialogue of persuasion or argumentation. When conducting simulations (COAEP), students can write their own dialogues between people regarding issues and then act out the dialogues. It is necessary, in learning dialogical reasoning, to deal with issues that lend themselves to reasoned judgment in an atmosphere and environment that encourages students' ideas and discussion. In this environment the teacher facilitates discussion and concentrates on asking questions.

Principle S-22: Reasoning Dialectically: Evaluating Perspectives, Interpretations, and Theories.   When we reason dialectically, we are reasoning about and between different points of view. Our purpose is to test the strengths and weaknesses of ideas and opposing points of view. Placing our ideas alongside those that are different or in disagreement with our ideas lets us synthesize our understanding, rejecting some ideas and accepting others. This is a difficult process for those who have strong beliefs, and it is precisely for this reason that learning to reason dialectically is a critical thinking skill. However, to reason dialectically, we must be clear and precise when analyzing points of view. We cannot assume an understanding of competing theories and ideas, but we must strive to ensure that we actually understand them and then reason from premises not in keeping with our own. This means that we must first recognize the point of view before we can even begin to reason about or within it, and it is through questioning that we begin to excavate or uncover the point of view in question. Furthermore, reasoning dialectically involves dialogical reasoning as we discuss and debate ideas. But, more important, learning to reason dialectically translates into learning to understand points of view clearly and accurately, state them, and then examine the merits and weaknesses of the ideas before we reject or embrace them.

Application to Classroom Instruction. Whenever students are faced with competing theories, ideas, or points of view, they can practice reasoning dialectically. A debate (COAEP) or a simulated court trial (COAEP) offers

ample opportunities for students to learn the art of dialectical reasoning. Whenever they engage in mock trials or simulations (COAEP), they are scrutinizing the claims of those with competing points of view. In literature (COAEP), young children can do the same by attempting to decide who is right or wrong or who might be telling the truth or lying. Journalism and broadcasting (COAEP) should provide opportunities for students to discover multiple sides of a story and then learn to report in a dialectical manner. And in environmental studies (COAEP), there is no shortage of divergent points of view on controversial issues that promise to engage students' dialectical thinking.

Principle S-23: Developing One's Perspective. Developing our own perspective is a human process that involves and forms our identity. How we sort out our experience in the world, the ideas we are exposed to, and the beliefs we adopt to some extent define who we are as human beings. Uncritical thinkers assume that there is only one perspective that is valid—theirs. Critical thinkers understand that the notion of perspective is a result of perception and how we see and organize the world. They understand that there are many perspectives and differing perceptions about the world that have merit. While uncritical thinkers embrace their perspective as the only perspective, critical thinkers analyze differing points of view and develop their perspective through dialectical analysis and insight. They know that developing one's own perspective is an arduous task that requires reasoning within and about different points of view. Good critical thinkers look for and are sensitive to evidence that does not support their point of view. Critical thinkers understand that they must scrutinize their own claims and perspectives through questioning, and they seek to subject their reasoning and theories to rigorous examination and evaluation.

Application to Classroom Instruction. Through dialectical and dialogical reasoning, one develops perspective. Assuring that students have adequate opportunities to engage in perspective building is crucial. In debates, journalism, speech, and simulations (COAEP), students can learn to develop their perspectives in light of what others believe and then learn to defend and challenge what they believe. Because texts generally fail to engage students in thoughtful dialectical and dialogical learning, the teacher must constantly seek to bring in competing theories, ideas, and points of view. In art appreciation (COAEP), for example, students can talk about art and develop their own perspectives as to what is good art and what is not. In this manner they learn to develop artistic criteria and learn to reason artistically. Asking students to look at relevant life issues, policies, rules, laws, and arguments and then engaging them in discussions, one on one or with the teacher, allows them to develop their ideas and explore other points of view. What the teacher

wishes to do is ask students what they believe and why. This calls upon them to look at what they believe and encourages them to inquire as to how they might have come to believe what they believe and what the implications might be.

Principle S-24: Listening Critically. Many people are selective listeners rather than active listeners. This means that they selectively listen to ideas, theories, and points of view, and as a result hear what they wish to hear, not what is actually being said. Critical thinking teaches active listening or the ability to understand clearly and precisely through listening to the points of view or theories of another. Critical thinkers know that to listen critically is paramount for good reasoning, and they also know how difficult it can be to integrate auditorily the thinking of another into one's own thinking. Furthermore, critical thinkers know that good communication is a two-way street that requires not only that we broadcast our ideas, but that we listen to others. The act of critical listening is an act of accurate and precise interpretation of what one is listening to. When entertaining another point of view through auditory means, critical thinkers know it is important to place their thoughts on probation and actually enter into the point of view in an attempt to follow its train of thought.

But listening is more than artful hearing. It is a form of reasoning that requires that we engage ourselves in silent dialogue, questioning as though we might locate ourselves within the body of the thought of another. Good listeners know that they need clarification for words and concepts, and they seek examples and clarification from what they are hearing. Critical listening is a skillful process developed over time with practice. It is a highly skilled process that is absolutely essential for good learning.

Application to Classroom Instruction. Modeling good listening must be a main goal of critical thinking teachers. Using questioning to ensure that we understand what our students are saying models for students the art of critical listening. Using patience, helping students slow their thinking down, and engaging them in thoughtful conversations shows them the value of listening critically and engages them as thoughtful participants in their own educational drama. But modeling is not enough; students should consistently be learning how to listen to other students, and this is a difficult chore for both the teacher and the student. We can ask students to listen to their fellow classmates and explain their reasoning: *Shareka did you understand what Carlos just said? Juan, can you tell us what she just said?* The teacher should ask students to clarify in their own words what they have heard, whether it is another student's words or something else they are listening to. When viewing videos or educational movies, the teacher can stop the video, ask students what they heard and saw, and ask them to explain it in their own words. Having students act out, in simulations (COAEP), dis-

cussions that involve good listening can help them see the importance of listening. Debates and speeches (COAEP) provide opportunities for students to listen critically and give examples of what was said to ensure understanding.

Finally, all good dialogical and dialectical reasoning requires critical listening, and teachers can metacognitively discuss with students the consequences of poor listening. They can discuss strategies for listening and use these strategies in any thoughtful discussion.

Principle S-25: Practicing Questioning: Learning to Clarify and Explore Beliefs, Theories, and Ideas. At the heart of critical thinking lies questioning. If nothing else, good critical thinkers know the value of questions. They know that the word *quest* comes from the word *question,* and they know that to obtain knowledge one must question deeply. Furthermore, they know how to focus their questions surgically in an attempt to ask the right ones. They are aware that every discipline has its own unique set of questions, and they seek to capture an understanding of the questions asked in different disciplines. Critical thinkers not only are comfortable with asking questions, but do not feel intimidated or threatened when their thinking is questioned. They understand that questions are tools that excavate and probe thought, and they know that to figure out what they do not know they will need the power of questions. Helping students practice questioning in an environment of inquiry and civility is essential to develop their critical thinking capacities. It is not simply teacher-generated questions that we are after. Critical thinking teachers know that helping students formulate their own questions about what they are studying and learning will prepare them for continuous, lifelong learning.

Application to Classroom Instruction. Texts provide few opportunities for students to learn how to generate questions. On the contrary, they ask the questions and students answer them. We want students to ask and answer their own questions so that they might begin to learn how to probe the logic of what they are studying. For example, when introducing a new concept in environmental studies (COAEP), such as ecology, the teacher might ask students to generate a list of questions they might need answered to understand the concept better. After watching an educational video, the teacher might ask students to pair up and write down everything they remember from the film and then turn what they wrote into questions to be answered by other students. Using critical reading techniques, students can learn to turn what they are reading into questions. Turning bold subheadings into questions allows students to read to answer their own questions. Of course, when engaging the whole class in discussion, the teacher should encourage students to ask questions they would need to have answered to understand better what is being studied. These questions can be written on the board to be used as a basis for further classroom discussion or as assignments.

Because many students have little experience or negative experience with questioning, it is important to introduce the ideas slowly and gently. Students need to feel comfortable when they are questioned and when they are questioning, and this will only happen if they see questioning as an effective way to uncover the best decisions or solutions to problems and academic pursuits. They must be encouraged to discuss their own or other learner's responses and beliefs. Therefore, modeling good questioning every step of the way is essential for critical thinking teachers. Teachers should be seen thinking out loud in the form of asking questions in front of their students, probing for meaning and understanding.

In journalism and broadcasting (COAEP), students will have many opportunities to use questioning to uncover ideas and explore issues. How students put together journalistic stories could be discussed, and questioning could be highlighted as a means for storytelling.

Finally, to teach students the art of questioning, it is necessary to pose problems as part of the curriculum, that is, to present what is being studied in the form of questions to be researched and answered. This allows students to see disciplines and subject matter as little more than problems to be solved or issues to be decided and helps them learn to think in terms of questions as opposed to answers.

Emotional Intelligence/ Affective Dimension

Principle S-26: Independent Thinking: Developing an Investigative Orientation. Critical thinking at its core is independent thinking, or thinking for oneself. Critical thinkers use critical skills and insights to reveal and reject beliefs that are irrational. They try to figure things out for themselves, seek to develop their own perspectives and have a healthy orientation toward investigation and independent research. They thoughtfully form principles of thought and action and do not mindlessly accept ideas that are presented to them without investigation. They are not easily manipulated and place a high premium on discovering knowledge as opposed to mindlessly and passively accepting information and ideas. Finally, developing an investigative orientation means that critical thinkers strive to determine for themselves the relevancy of information and when and how to apply a concept or use a skill. They are self-monitoring self-starters who enjoy using their minds to uncover complex answers to complex problems.

Application to Classroom Instruction. Students should be encouraged to discover information and use their knowledge to think for themselves. Merely giving students "facts" or telling them "the right way" to do things promises that they will be trained, not educated. So, for example, in all the areas of COAEP, students should be motivated to think for themselves and investigate new ideas. In the

area of simulations, for example (CO-AEP), students would be encouraged to take an active role in their own learning, not by simply involving themselves in activities, but by making predictions and plausible inferences and generating and assessing solutions to problems within the body of those activities. Using children's literature (COAEP), students can be encouraged to formulate their own ideas and then defend them or assess them for validity. They can be encouraged to engage in environmental research and inquiries (COAEP), and within journalism and broadcasting (COAEP) to employ investigative pursuits and skills in the interest of community development. Literature lessons (COAEP) can be remodeled so that students group and discuss writings they have read, entertaining different ways to classify and organize them. Activities in speech and debate (COAEP) allow students to put forth their independent points of view and then begin the process of assembling information that provides evidence for their positions or beliefs. Similarly, engaging students in chess activities allows them to develop independent thought and action as they test and communicate complex chess ideas and investigate the results.

Principle S-27: Developing Intellectual Empathy. Intellectual empathy asks us to exercise reciprocity, or place ourselves in the shoes of others, so to speak, who may not look at the world the way we do. It is a particularly difficult skill in the face of the tendency to accommodate our own self-justifying belief systems, often adopted through habit or custom. Intellectual empathy asks us to consider points of view fairly, even if they do not agree with our experience, morals, and principles. It asks us to reason fairly by overcoming the tendency to wed ourselves to egocentric perceptions and belief systems. Often, we tend to judge other positions, thinking, issues, and theories, without accurately and precisely reconstructing them as points of view. What fair-minded critical thinking requires is that we fairly and accurately construct the reasoning of another in such a way that we reason from their premises, capture their logic, and accurately reconstruct their points of view. Developing intellectual empathy contrasts with developing what often poses for critical thinking: the ability to manipulate ideas and others for one's own purposes and agenda. Manipulation and misrepresentation also require cognitive abilities, but they are not the abilities of critical thinking. Learning to reason within points of view that are not in keeping with our own is essential for higher-order learning and character development. The opposite of empathy is narrow-mindedness, which is precisely what we do not wish to encourage in students.

Application to Classroom Instruction. Using the relevant experiences of everyday life, the teacher can encourage fair-minded thinking by approaching conflicts and disputes as teachable moments. Patience, empathy, and understanding of learners themselves must be evident in teacher practice. Helping students evaluate thinking when conflicts arise teaches them essential principles of mediation and conflict resolution as they begin to pay attention to their thinking and the thinking of others. They learn to enter into other points of view empathically and to communicate compassionately and with recognition. In simulations (COAEP), classroom or playground disputes can be reconstructed and acted out. Students can engage in setting up real-life or simulated mediation procedures for resolving disputes when they arise that require reasoning within disputed points of view.

In discussing literature (COAEP), teachers can use questioning to help students artfully reconstruct the point of view of different storybook characters for purposes of fair-minded evaluation. Debate allows for a principled exchange of ideas and points of view (COAEP). Debate and speech can be used to help students learn to state the position of others clearly and accurately, as well as learn to clarify their thinking with evidence and reasons for what they agree with and what they do not agree with. Journalistic and broadcast endeavors (COAEP) can be analyzed to help students develop criteria for fair-mindedness; students might analyze articles and broadcasts to see if the authors exercised empathy in reporting on various issues. When actually engaged in journalism and broadcasting, students can be animated to treat issues fairly, that is, from multiple points of view; as a class, students might discuss the difficulties in developing fair-minded thinking.

Principle S-28: Developing Intellectual Humility: Learning to Place Our Judgment on Probation. If critical thinking is to some extent figuring out what one does not know, then humility is a necessary component. Humility asks us to recognize and admit that we have not figured everything out, that there are limits to what we know and think we know. It asks us to substitute self-righteousness with self-questioning and is based on the assumption that one should not claim more than one knows. The opposite of intellectual humility in this context would be intellectual arrogance, or claiming more than we know. Arrogance operates to damage learning opportunities because arrogant persons fail to include and examine diverse information and points of view. "Why should I read more or listen more?" asks the arrogant person. "After all, I have it all worked out!" Humility implies that it is okay to say, "I don't know." Without humility, students cannot distinguish between what they know and what they merely believe, and thus the cognitive work required by critical thinking cannot be done.

Humility does not ask us to be submissive or indecisive but to acknowledge the limits of our knowledge and to put together plans to acquire the knowledge we need. In recognizing that we might not have enough information, or have not looked at an issue from varied points of view—or perhaps do not have the evidence we need to accept or reject an idea—we learn to suspend judgment, placing it on probation until the necessary analysis has been done. Thus, humility operates to arrest snap judgments or compulsive decision making and problem solving.

Application to Classroom Instruction. Teachers can teach humility in the way they present course material. For example, when studying any discipline, teachers can encourage students to make a list of questions that they would need to have answered in order to understand what they are studying. This can be done in pairs or individually, and the questions themselves can serve as the basis for class discussions or as questions to be researched in cooperative groups. By using questioning as a tool to help students figure out what they do not know, teachers help students to understand that learning is a *process* and not simply a *result*. They come to understand that saying *I don't know* can be translated into powerful questioning opportunities to create work plans to find out more. When researching, students can come up with questions and then exchange them with other students, thus answering each other's questions as a basis for learning.

Perhaps the most important thing a teacher can do to teach intellectual humility is to model it whenever possible in front of students. Students need to see their teacher as the embodiment of the attitudes and values of humility if they are going to gain insight into humility as a worthwhile value. Critical thinking teachers understand that it is important to think out loud in front of their students and actually muddle through thoughts at times, admitting that they do not have all the answers. They also know that humility is not a weakness but a strength, and they seek to model it whenever possible. Modeling humility would entail stating *I don't know* when confronted with questions one has not thought about or had time to answer. Then, with the class, a plan can be put together to find out what is missing and how to go about getting the answers. This contrasts with the tendency on behalf of some teachers to pretend they know the answer in order to avoid saying they do not know.

Principle S-29: Developing Intellectual Imagination and Curiosity. Developing the ability to imagine how things might be or what answers might exist to complex questions is essential for critical thinking. Having the courage to dream and think beyond the limitations of a given moment transfers into developing insight into the necessity for further exploration and discovery. Further, imagination develops an emotional intelligence that allows one to cultivate hope, creativity, and possibility. Helping students gain insight into imaginative thinking equips them with the understanding that there exist a multitude of creative solutions to complex problems and many possibilities for rational learning and living. Furthermore, creative and critical thought require a curious mind that

seeks questions and answers. Armed with curiosity, students can begin to go beyond minimalism, or reducing inquiry to what is expected from them. Instead, they can look for new and innovative ways to extend their inquiry and feedback into all areas of study they are pursuing. This curiosity and imagination has the potential to translate into lifelong living and creative problem solving as students begin to see the expansionary potential of their minds and discover inquiry as a powerful process for continuous lifelong learning.

Application to Classroom Instruction. Teachers can have students use a variety of methods to develop their creativity and imaginative minds. Simulations (COAEP) encourage students to develop themes within what they are learning and to generate questions that go beyond simple rote memorization and learning. They can use debate (COAEP) as an opportunity to do research into areas they are curious about and then learn to structure their learning for presentation purposes. Journalism and broadcasting (COAEP) can encourage students to discover new ideas and new points of view and can help them gain insight into the benefits of curiosity. By helping students formulate questions within any subject area that goes beyond the simple representation of the subject in texts, teachers help students discover that their questions will actually tell them more than the texts do. This often encourages them to do research to find out new information and ideas. Art and theater (COAEP) allow students to develop their creative qualities by using their imagination and curiosity to discover new ways to represent sets, perspective, ideas, art, and artwork. By linking art history with actual history instruction, students can learn to think holistically about art and its context in history and social reality, and they can then be encouraged to use their curiosity and imagination to find out more about a certain period in history. Whenever possible, teachers should capitalize on students' interests and motivate them to inquire and discover more about what they are learning or hope to learn.

Principle S-30: Developing Intellectual Efficacy. Critical thinkers acquire an important emotional intelligence, which involves developing confidence in the power of reason to solve problems. They realize that life is little more than problem solving and decision making, and they believe in their abilities to solve life's problems with their minds. They also realize that reasoning is an act that requires the use of reason, and they believe that developing better reason leads to better reasoning, better results, and better decisions, as well as better solutions to problems. Therefore, the development of confidence in one's reasoning ability goes hand in hand with the development of self-esteem. Self-esteem, as used here, is based on competence, and competence is accomplished through skillful and clear thinking. The development of self-esteem must involve the development of one's confidence to reason. Confidence in rea-

son is an attitude that motivates people to keep their minds open, confront irrational change through reasonable discussion, and make sense of the world with the expectation that sense can be made. Making sense of subject matter and believing one can do it are at the heart of individual accomplishment. Students who believe they can accomplish academically will translate this insight into their personal life and become lifelong learners, equipped with the confidence not only that can they learn, but that learning can help them make sense of the world and of themselves.

Application to Classroom Instruction. Every time you, as a teacher, reason in front of your students, every time you model for them that sense can be made out of academic material, rules and regulations, and daily activities, you are modeling self-efficacy, or the belief in one's ability to make sense of the world. Sharing your reasoning with students is essential for good modeling. When you question students and encourage them to question and then seek answers to their own questions, you are setting up opportunities for empowerment and the development of confidence. Students should be encouraged to question deeply within all areas of school life, including academic disciplines. They should be animated to see what they study as a system with reasonable or unreasonable constructs, and they should be encouraged to think about their roles as thinkers and learners. Many students have no confidence in reason because they are rarely asked to reason; rather, they are told what to do, when to go to bed, what grammar rules to use, what scientific principles are important, and what social studies questions will be on the test. Because they often do not see reason being used effectively in their own lives, because they have few models for reasoning, they come to see reason itself as unreasonable and do not count on their mental faculties and independent thinking to figure out problems and make decisions. As a teacher you can ask students why a person learns this skill or that skill, as opposed to mechanically introducing skills in a rote manner. When students engage in chess activities, for example (COAEP), the teacher can ask them for their reasons for executing various moves. When developing a story for journalistic purposes (COAEP), students can be animated to give their reasons for writing the report one way or another.

By asking children to consistently reason their way through subject matter, you, as a teacher, are teaching them the power of reasoning. Capitalizing on students' daily lives and interests by critically questioning them and asking them to apply what they have learned to their own lives, teachers encourage the transfer of faith in reason to daily life.

Principle S-31: Developing a Tolerance for Ambiguity. Ambiguity is a state of affairs that connotes a lack of clarity. Ambiguous situations are not quite clear or have not been figured out fully. Developing a tolerance for ambiguity or situations that are not clear,

that do not have black-and-white answers and for which information might be lacking, is essential in a world that is increasingly subject to rapid global changes. Becoming comfortable with unresolved situations, with uncertainty, and with unfamiliar situations and complex questions is an essential attitude for critical thinking. Many people have developed rigid ways of looking at the world, and when faced with uncertainty, change, and lack of clarity, they often become immobilized. Many people rummage through their past looking for answers to the future. Confronting ambiguous relationships and situations with a sense of confidence in our critical thinking is paramount if we are to sort through tremendous change and complex fluctuations. The development of tolerance for ambiguity leads to divergent thinking or expansionary thinking. Those with this tolerance have no problem with frequently changing patterns and thoughts that are hard to hold in one place. They look toward processes as opposed to results, and they learn to move comfortably in and out of situations.

Application to Classroom Instruction. Whenever possible, it is important to have students research and report on open-ended questions. Social studies, environmental studies (COAEP), and journalism and broadcasting (COAEP) allow students to tackle problems that are somewhat ambiguous or unclear. They can be encouraged to find out what information is missing, how they might find the information they need, how they should classify it and use it, and for what purposes it should be used. They can be encouraged to develop alternative scenarios in the event that circumstances do not develop as they think they should. This affords them opportunities to engage in consequential and anticipatory thinking. In simulations (COAEP), students can be encouraged to develop imaginary worlds containing mystery and enigma (COAEP).

Problem-solving opportunities in all disciplines that allow for more than one way to solve problems help students see that there are not necessarily black-and-white answers and rigid processes for problem solving. This translates into more mental ease when facing situations that are ambiguous.

Principle S-32: Developing Intellectual Perseverance and Discipline. Solving problems and making decisions can be an arduous process that takes time and effort. Critical thinkers know that to develop good thinking takes time, and they know they must discipline their minds to focus, analyze, and integrate what they learn. They recognize the need to struggle with time management, to prioritize what they feel is important, and to arrest the tendency toward impulsiveness and impatience. In a culture that tells students that they can be anything or accomplish anything with little or no effort, from reading ten books in five minutes to learning a language in thirty days, it is not difficult to understand why many students do not persevere and discipline their thinking. Patience and hard work lose their shine in a quick-fix culture of immediate gratification. Helping students gain insight into accomplishment and its relationship to hard work is essential if we are to help them develop critical thinking skills. The development of intellectual perseverance will help students develop confidence in their reasoning abilities as they see that hard work does pay off in the long run, and they learn to slow their thinking down in the interest of better mental performance.

Application to Classroom Instruction. Literature (COAEP) can provide insight into the benefits of intellectual perseverance and discipline. Students can discuss characters' actions and decisions; for example, using stories such as *The Tortoise and the Hare*, students can not only get insight into the parable, but perhaps transfer this insight into their own life. Studying great artists and their works can help students see what is involved in actual art production and the hard work that it entails (COAEP). They can be animated to engage in lengthy art projects that require them to persevere and discipline themselves for long periods of time. Chess (COAEP) provides another excellent way to develop perseverance and mental discipline as it requires time to make rational moves. Students can be encouraged to discuss what they did with their minds during a chess game and how focus or discipline helped them. Children's own experiences should be used to develop this concept and can form the basis for writing activities or classroom discussions. When looking at environmental problems, students can develop problem approaches in groups and then discuss how they came up with their thinking (COAEP).

What teachers need to do is raise deep questions that require deep thinking and design activities as much as possible that are lengthy projects that require time to complete. In this way students will come to see that how they persevere and discipline their minds has everything to do with the results they get, both academically and in real life.

Principle S-33: Developing Intellectual Courage. Having the courage to confront one's own irrationality is essential for critical thinking. Admitting to mistakes in thinking requires a great deal of intellectual courage and is an essential trait if we are to arrest our mistakes and improve our thinking. Critical thinkers know that it takes intellectual courage to admit that you might have judged someone or his or her ideas unfairly. Furthermore, to think independently requires that we develop the courage to squarely face ideas that are unpopular or viewpoints that are not fashionable. Critical thinkers do not want to get lost in the anonymity of a crowd, but seek to determine for themselves what is true, what is right, and what they should believe.

Without courage when engaging in collaborative problem solving, "group-think" can develop as cowardice replaces confrontation. To have the courage to confront ideas one does not think are rational takes a commitment to courageous thinking that is often absent from many students as they seek to belong to one social group or the next.

Application to Classroom Instruction. Simply stated, teachers promote intellectual courage as an attitude of thinking when they include students in consistent open-minded discussions. Teachers who encourage questioning and confrontation over ideas and dialectical and dialogical reasoning develop the courage to confront irrationality. They also know that controversy creates courageous moments, and they seek to raise controversial issues when discussing ideas; they work to provide a comfortable atmosphere for raising ideas. When discussing environmental issues (COAEP), for example, multiple points of view should be brought in so students can take positions and learn to defend what they believe. Debate allows for the defense of one's ideas (COAEP), and students should be encouraged to marshal evidence for what they believe in an atmosphere of civility. Bringing in unpopular beliefs through journalism or broadcasting (COAEP) allows people to take positions, discuss them, and then look at their own thinking to see if changes are necessary. Individuals and groups who exercised courage when confronting unpopular ideas—political, social, and personal—should be the object of inquiry. Students' lives should consistently be harvested for relevant opportunities to discuss peer group pressure, decision making, and problem solving.

Principle S-34: Developing Intellectual Civility. Reasonable minds may disagree, but it is the form of disagreement that remains salient. Learning how to agree to disagree in the face of a lack of consensus is paramount. It is not enough to ask students to work in groups if they do not have the ability to act and behave civilly toward those who hold ideas with which they disagree. And we cannot have dialectical and dialogical learning opportunities if students do not know how to engage in them. Helping students gain insight into how we as human beings behave civilly in light of controversy is essential if we are to learn to cooperate in a learning environment. We may not all agree, but we do not have to be disagreeable to disagree.

Application to Classroom Instruction. Any time students are engaged in debate (COAEP) or are discussing ideas related to what they are studying, they have opportunities to develop insight into the necessity for civility. As a teacher you will look for opportunities that allow for open-ended discussions that involve various points of view. This gives students opportunities to see that disagreement does not have to be disagreeable. Further, the teacher can work with students to help them develop processes for dealing with disagreement. This allows them to engage in mediation and conflict resolution through simulations (COAEP) or real-life activities. Whenever we allow students to discuss their own beliefs and worldviews with other students, we encourage this form of reasoning. Using cooperative groups as much as possible for classroom problem solving and decision making will allow students to develop civility in collaborative contexts. With the development

of intellectual civility among students, a climate of courtesy and respect becomes evident in the classroom.

Principle S-35: Developing Intellectual Integrity. Holding ourselves up to the same thinking standards that we hold others to is paramount for the development of integrity in thinking. The tendency is to have lower standards for ourselves than we do for others, which is hypocritical and antithetical to integrity and honesty in thinking. People who can honestly admit discrepancies in their thinking, who seek to raise the bar, so to speak, for themselves as well as others and who look to hold themselves up to the same rigorous standards they adopt for others, have integrity in thought. Because critical thinking requires consistent intellectual standards, it is paramount that students gain insight into the role of integrity in thinking and have opportunities to develop it.

Application to Classroom Instruction. It is important for teachers to model integrity for students. Favoritism, inconsistent application of standards and rules, and lack of modeling give the opposite message to students. Thus, the critical thinking teacher is aware of her actions and seeks to explain to students why she has done this or that. When discussing ideas in texts with students, critical thinking teachers look to see if abstract ideas are applied consistently. They lead lengthy discussions in the area of application of standards and judgment because they know that students, like many people, judge others differently than they judge themselves. Current events provide countless opportunities to discuss integrity and honesty in thinking. In literature (COAEP), students are encouraged not only to judge characters but also to talk about their own lives and how difficult it might be to act with integrity and why. Critical thinking teachers encourage inquiry into controversy and contradictions and reason with their students in open formats or individually. They also work with students in all areas to develop reasoning criteria and then reason with students about the criteria, noting their students' tendency to favor themselves.

Organization of the In-service

The appendix represents a visual representation of the proposed in-service for teachers regarding the new critical and creative thinking standards for gifted and academic excellence programs. This in-service, ideally, encompasses three days.

The first day should consist of an overview and discussion of the new standards and their relationship with teaching, learning, and classroom instruction. Participants will be able to understand critical and creative thinking and the district standards and activities that enforce and reinforce its development. They will be able to examine their own practice and develop an understanding of teaching theory and methodology. Further, there will be an overview of Socratic questioning and metacognition and how these powerful methods and tools of instruction can be used to facilitate students' thinking and learning.

Day 2 will be devoted to designing critical thinking lesson plans. Teachers will involve themselves in creating activities that infuse critical and creative thinking skills and principles as iterated by the new district standards, develop questions for instruction that fuel thinking about subject matter, and plan how instruction will take place, that is, the grouping of students and time management. Teachers will discuss graphic organizers, mindmapping, and other tactics and tools for teaching critically.

Day 3 will be devoted to the assessment of both critical and creative thinking skills as well as rudimentary skills. The appropriateness of performance assessment, portfolios, and multiple exam approaches to instruction will be examined and discussed within the context of the new standards. Participants will be able to tie effective teaching to effective assessment, completing full circle the critical-creative thinking paradigm.

This chapter is based on the proposed district standards regarding critical and creative thinking and attempts to tie practice to theory. By focusing on the standards and then offering teachers opportunities to plan lessons in accordance with these standards, their practical application and use can be assured. Finally, as teachers collaboratively practice preparing lessons based on the new district standards, they will become more comfortable with both the language of thinking and the actual implementation of critical and creative thinking lesson plans.

Appendix A

Critical and Creative Thinking Lesson Plan Design for
Dade County Public Schools Gifted and AEP

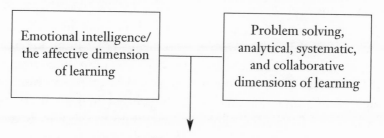

Combined to form activities that yield:

Well-reasoned lesson plans

That ask ourselves and our students:
How will we collaborate and question each other,
and how will teachers assess students and help students learn
the art of self-assessment and self-corrective thinking?

Appendix B:
Critical and Creative Thinking Standards as Might be Explained by an Unnamed, Fictional Student

Hi, I'm a sixth-grade student, and I would like to explain the critical thinking standards as they affect my ability to learn and study.

Problem Solving and Decision Making

S-1: Sometimes, I work on the wrong problem because I haven't taken the time to figure out what I am trying to solve. It really helps me to think clearly about issues and problems so I don't waste time looking for solutions to problems that don't exist or problems that I shouldn't be thinking about.

S-2: Many people pursue goals that are unrealistic or unjustifiable. When I'm studying, I want to make sure that I understand exactly what I am trying to accomplish. For example, when we studied Greek history, I had to ask the teacher why people study Greek history or I wouldn't know what was important or unimportant. Some people do things in school, and they don't even know why!

S-3: There is so much information! Especially now with the Internet. My teachers help me think about information critically, which means that I have to think about how I use information to solve problems or make decisions and how people in the fields I am studying learn to classify, sort, and use information to come to conclusions and solve problems.

S-4: With so much information, when I am studying I have to be able to find the information that I can use and discard the information that is not useful. Some people underline everything in a book with a yellow highlighter, for example. They just don't know what is important and what is not important in what they are trying to study, so they underline everything! Not me. I figure out what is important or relevant and then concentrate on that. That makes life easy!

S-5: I have learned how to question what I am studying really deeply. I try to figure out the questions that scientists, or historians, or artists ask when I am studying those things. By concentrating on the questions that people ask, I find I am more successful in figuring out subjects. This is true in my own life as well. I have learned to ask myself questions a lot and this has really helped me make decisions and solve problems.

S-6: Boy, do we take a lot for granted! I try to figure out what I believe and what I really know so I can examine what I believe. I do this with other people too! This is hard, but when I am studying, I also try to figure out the assumptions or beliefs that are behind the claims that people make. This helps me figure out where they are coming from and how they come to conclusions and make decisions.

S-7: We sure do have to make a lot of decisions and solve a lot of problems just to stay alive! I want to make good decisions and solve problems well because I know that my judgments will affect how I live. So I think about how I do these things before I do them so that I can do them right!

S-8: Sometimes people make decisions without even thinking about what might happen. I try not to do this. I want to think about what might happen so I can prioritize my thinking before I make a decision. And when I am studying, I try to think about the consequences of what I am studying and how people in history or math, for example, look at the consequences of solving a problem one way or another. This helps me understand what I am studying better.

S-9: I learned that the way I see the world is how I interpret things and come to conclusions. I try to learn to interpret the world for myself and make good decisions. By understanding what an "inference" is, I have learned how to extend my learning logically. This really helps me think better in whatever I am doing or studying.

S-10: Some people just say things, and then when you ask them why they think that way, they get mad. I think it is important for people to give reasons and evidence for what they think instead of just saying "because." I look for reasons and evidence in what I am trying to study. For example, we were studying causes of the Civil War, and there were more than two points of view. Before I would accept one or the other, I had to hear the evidence those with each point of view came up with to support their position. And when I write certain types of persuasive pieces for school, I always try to give evidence and reasons for what I believe. This helps me figure out if I am right or wrong and lets people, especially my teachers, figure out where I am coming from.

Analytical and Evaluative Thinking

S-11: My mom says that sometimes I make statements about people and things by saying "all people," "everybody," or "all of this" or "all of that." I'm like everybody else, I guess. I sometimes make vague and general statements about people and things before I have had time to really think about what I am saying. For example, we were studying about immigration in school and I was thinking that we all immigrated to the U.S. But then the teacher said that some of us did not immigrate but, like slaves, were forced to relocate here. Learning to avoid overgeneralizing about people and learning to avoid being too simple in my thinking has helped me listen and think more critically. It also allows me to present my ideas better in what I am studying because I pay attention to exceptions to the rule, not just the rule itself. Does that make sense?

S-12: We all have to make judgments. My mom makes them every day, and so do I. People who study history make them, and English, and, well, all subjects we study have people who make judgments. I learned that when we make judgments we need to

have criteria; that means a set of things we use to judge. My teachers have helped me learn to think about the criteria I use to make judgments and the criteria others use in different subjects to make judgments. My teachers make judgments about my grades and I need to know what criteria they use so I can do my best work!

S-13: Remember when we talked about information? With so much information, I know it is important to find out where the information comes from—its sources. Not all sources are good, and I am learning how to evaluate the credibility of sources of information, and this helps me think better.

S-14: It seems that every subject, in fact, every person has a point of view and argument for one thing or another. Even me! I am learning how to evaluate arguments and beliefs by developing criteria and learning how to judge. This means that I don't believe everything I hear or read, but first, I want to see how the arguments are made and what they might mean.

S-15: People do things, and it is my responsibility to analyze and evaluate what they do. This is true for myself and others, as well as whatever I am studying. We were studying Martin Luther King Jr. and trying to evaluate his actions during the Civil Rights Movement. I wouldn't have been able to understand him as a person if I couldn't understand his actions.

S-16: Sometimes things sound good but are impractical. Know what I mean? Things sound good sometimes, but how do they really work in reality? I try to think about that when I am studying. This helps me modify my thinking.

S-17: Not only do I have my own interpretations and perspectives, but not everybody agrees with me, and I need to see how other people come to their own perspectives and then evaluate them in light of what I believe. This is hard. I want people to believe what I believe, and sometimes I am not clear or precise when trying to see how others interpret the world. I guess you have to see the world from their point of view, their perspective, don't you?

Systematic Thinking

S-18: I have found that sometimes situations can be the same, even if they look different. They can also be different, even if they look the same. I like to see if I can see analogies in what I am studying and learning. Analogies help me because they are a visual way to use words, and when I find them, I can see how they fit into what I already know.

S-19: I like to see what the different subjects I am studying have to do with each other. So, for example, I like to see how word problems in math help me read better, and how what I study in art might have something to do with history. By learning to see the connections between subjects, I learn and understand more. We were studying math, and I could see how it related to what we were doing in science! Boy, did that help me!

S-20: When I study things, I like to see what they might have in common and what might make them different. When we studied how Mexican-Americans live in the United States, I looked to see what was different or the same between how they live and how African-Americans or Europeans live. By paying attention to what is the same and different in the things I do and study, I can better understand how things relate, what makes them different or the same, and how this understanding might help me. I do this at the store when I look for products my mom wants to buy. Sometimes some products are cheaper than others, but you wouldn't know it if you couldn't compare and contrast, would you?

Collaborative Thinking

S-21: When we think, it really helps if we talk about what we are thinking about. Teachers who ask me what I think and ask other people what they think are good teachers, because they know that talking about things really helps one learn. These teachers get us involved in talking about what we are studying instead of lecturing to us.

S-22: When I get two or more points of view on issues, I try to understand what each point of view means before I develop my own point of view. This is hard, though, because I have to stop thinking about what I believe and enter into all these different points of view to understand what others think. But in the end, this really helps me understand others and myself.

S-23: Developing your own perspective is really important. I want to make sure that I am thinking for my- self and not letting others tell me what to believe or what my perspective or point of view should be.

S-24: Learning to listen to people and what they say is really hard. Sometimes I think I've heard someone when really all I've done is heard what I wanted to hear. Listening critically means that I listen to what people say, not what I want them to say.

S-25: I love to ask questions! But you have to practice. When my teach- er asks us to make up questions or ask questions, I really try because I know that the questions I ask will have a lot to do with whether I understand something or whether I get the right answer. I love teachers that give me practice in questioning.

Emotional Intelligence/ Affective Dimension

S-26: Figuring things out for yourself is where it's at! I hate it when people tell me what to think or how to do things. I want to use my brain to in- vestigate and figure things out. Don't tell me how to do it until I have tried it myself!

S-27: It's hard to understand people and what they think. I try, though, and this means that I have to enter into their point of view and see the world the way they see it. Not because I agree with them, but because I want to understand them.

S-28: I don't always know things, and I think it is okay to say, "I don't know." This helps me admit to what I know so that I can learn more! But

many people don't do that. They pre- tend they know things, and I think this stops them from really learning. They need to ask more questions and stop trying to be right all the time.

S-29: Imagining and wondering are things I really like. Sometimes, I just sit around and think about why things are the way they are and how I could make them better. I am really curious about things too, and this helps me ask questions and explore things. It also helps me understand people.

S-30: Some people I know have such low self-esteem. I think that's be- cause they don't believe in themselves. Well, since I have been learning how to think better, I feel a lot more confi- dent in myself. I know I can't do everything I want, but by believing in my ability to think, I think I have re- ally increased my own feelings of self- worth. And this means that I will take risks and try things I might not have tried before!

S-31: Sometimes things aren't so black and white. Sometimes, things are downright confusing. I know when they are confusing it's easy to give up trying to understand them, but I have learned to accept the fact that not everything is clear. So I just try harder to make sense out of the world, what I am studying, my friends, and myself.

S-32: Some of my friends just give up when they can't do things. Not me. I know that trying really hard is how you get to be successful. I try to disci- pline my thinking and really hang in there when I don't understand some- thing. It usually works!

S-33: Having the courage to say that you don't agree with people, even when they all think they're right and you're wrong, is hard. I try to be courageous and disagree when I don't believe in what people are saying. This is hard. There is so much pressure to just go along. I also like to admit when I make mistakes so I don't make them again. Sometimes I don't, though, and that is when I know I am being afraid and being a coward.

S-34: When I talk with people that don't agree with me, it is easy to get mad at them. But I try to figure out what they are saying and deal with that instead of making put-downs and just making people feel bad. It's easy to put people down; it's harder to understand what they are saying and then deal with that.

S-35: I guess we all do things and say things that we shouldn't. And if I judged other people differently than myself, that wouldn't be fair. I try to judge people's thinking just like I do my own, but I know that's hard. If I didn't, though, nobody would want to work with me or play with me. It's important to treat people and their thinking the way you would want to be treated.

Appendix C:
Critical and Creative Thinking Standards Informally Depicted: Dade County, Florida

Following is an informal depiction of the critical and creative thinking strategies, in a format that allows them to be easily explained to parents, teachers, and administrators.

Problem Solving and Decision Making

S-1: Our children begin to learn it is important to be sure you clearly understand the questions you are trying to answer or problems you are trying to solve before you look for answers or solutions. This strategy teaches students to think about how they define problems and issues and how misidentifying problems can result in faulty thinking.

S-2: Our children learn to identify the goals and purpose of what they are studying or pursuing. This strategy teaches students to think critically about what they are attempting to accomplish, their goals and objectives, and the goals and objectives of others.

S-3: Our children begin to think critically about information, its sources, and how to sort, classify, and otherwise form information into patterns from which they might make plausible inferences. This strategy teaches students to think about and use information critically to solve problems.

S-4: Our children begin to think critically about information and its relevance. This strategy teaches students how to distinguish between information that is relevant to what they are pursuing and information that is not relevant.

S-5: Our children begin to think in

terms of the important questions they need to ask to find out more about what they are learning. This strategy teaches students how to formulate deep questions in given subject areas to extend their knowledge.

S-6: Our children begin to think about what they know and what they merely believe. This strategy teaches students how to critically examine and evaluate their own beliefs and the beliefs they confront in their studies.

S-7: Our children begin to think critically about how they make decisions and generate solutions to problems. This strategy teaches students how to make good decisions and arrive at good solutions as well as how to assess their thinking processes.

S-8: Our children begin to see that the solutions and decisions they and others come to have consequences, and they begin to learn to critically explore the consequences of solutions, decisions, and problems in what they are learning. This strategy teaches students how to prioritize their thinking and examine alternatives in light of their implications.

S-9: Our children begin to learn how to critically interpret situations and information and how they come to conclusions and make decisions. This strategy teaches students inferential logic: how to make statements about the unknown based on what is known.

S-10: Our children learn to give reasons and evidence for what they believe and to evaluate the reasons and evidence others offer for what they believe. This strategy teaches students how to evaluate evidence and reasons in what they are learning and in their own lives.

Analytical and Evaluative Thinking Dimension

S-11: Our children begin to see when they are thinking in overgeneralities and when they might be too simplistic in their thinking. This strategy teaches students to recognize when they and others are not being specific in their thinking and gives them an opportunity to refine their thinking.

S-12: Our children begin to understand what criteria are and how they might develop criteria for use in judging situations, themselves, and others. This strategy teaches students how criteria are developed and used.

S-13: Our children begin to develop an understanding that not all information is reliable and that the sources of information are important when evaluating information. This strategy teaches them what sources of information are, how they differ, and how they might affect what they are thinking.

S-14: Our children begin to analyze what they say and what they do and what others say and do. This strategy teaches them what arguments are, how to interpret them, and how to evaluate them.

S-15: Our children begin to learn to evaluate rules, policies, and behavior. This strategy teaches them what is involved in analyzing and how they can apply analysis to what people do, say, and think.

S-16: Our children begin to learn to distinguish what is ideal from what is actual practice. This strategy enables students to understand that often what might be stated as an ideal way of doing things, approaching problems, or making decisions varies from what actually goes on in reality.

S-17: Our children begin to understand what perspectives are, how they are interpreted, and how beliefs form points of view. This strategy teaches students that they and others have perspectives, what a perspective entails, and how they might evaluate perspectives.

Systematic Thinking Dimension

S-18: Our children begin to see how to apply what they are learning to diverse situations. This strategy teaches students what analogies are and how they might use analogies in thinking, as well as how to transfer what they are learning into new contexts so they might learn more.

S-19: Our children learn how the logic of a discipline is related to that of other disciplines and how they might connect what they are learning in one subject to insights in another. This strategy teaches our students the relationships among the subjects they are learning so they might understand them as systems.

S-20: Our children begin to look at situations, actions, people, and products and note how they might be the same and how they might be different.

This strategy teaches students what a similarity is, what a difference is, and how to use similarities and differences to make choices, analyze situations, and develop problem-solving abilities.

Collaborative Thinking Dimension

S-21: Our children begin to understand the power of dialogue as a way of learning and reasoning about diverse perspectives and ideas. This strategy teaches students how to dialogue with others about what they are thinking, whether they agree or disagree with what they are hearing or reading.

S-22: Our children begin to see how entering into points of view not in keeping with their own, reasoning from their premises to their conclusions and then stepping back to see what they believe in light of what others believe, is important for learning to understand people and situations. This strategy teaches students how to evaluate points of view by reasoning within them as well as how to reconcile what they believe with what others believe.

S-23: Our children begin to see how their own thinking and perspectives are developed. This strategy teaches students to think for themselves and learn to develop their own points of view regarding issues, people, and situations.

S-24: Our children begin to see what it means to listen critically and actively as opposed to selectively and passively. This strategy teaches them what active listening would entail, how to sum up what people say for the sake of understanding, and how to listen to points of view to understand their logic.

S-25: Our children begin to see the power of questioning as a form of learning about themselves, what they are studying, and others. This strategy teaches students how to question deeply, to go beyond questions that simply call for information and learn to question assumptions, language, points of view, and whatever they are learning.

Emotional Intelligence/ Affective Thinking Dimension

S-26: Our children begin to see the power of investigation and how to figure things out for themselves. This strategy teaches students to investigate independently what they are learning and not to depend on others for the answers to questions or life's problems.

S-27: Our children begin to see the importance of understanding others, even if they do not agree with them. This strategy teaches students to enter into diverse points of view with the object of understanding them.

S-28: Our children begin to learn that it is okay to say "I don't know." This strategy teaches students how to admit to their mistakes, realize when they don't understand something, and learn to replace self-righteousness with self-questioning.

S-29: Our children begin to see the power of curiosity and how curiosity is used to find answers to complex questions, to seek to understand, and to imagine how problems can be solved

or decisions can be made. This strategy teaches students the power of imaginative and curious thinking and helps them capture what it means to "wonder" about life and what they are learning.

S-30: Our children begin to see the power of reasoning, and as they do, they develop self-esteem and a belief that they can solve life's problems through thinking. This strategy helps students develop self-confidence in their ability to think.

S-31: Our children begin to see that often there are no black-and-white answers for situations and issues. This strategy helps students understand that life can be unclear, that what they are studying or attempting to understand may not be transparent, and that this is okay.

S-32: Our children begin to learn to arrest their impulsivity and take their time when reasoning. This strategy teaches students that there are no quick-fix solutions to complex problems and lets them know that disciplined thinking and trying as hard as they can will help them become successful.

S-33: Our children begin to see what it means to be intellectually courageous: that it is okay to admit you're wrong, to discover you have made a mistake, or to disagree with others rather than simply going along with them. This strategy teaches students that being courageous in their thinking might make them different at times, but that this is okay as long as they can defend what they believe in light of what others believe.

S-34: Our children begin to see that put-downs have no place in thinking—that you don't have to be mean or uncivil to someone just because you do not agree with him. This strategy helps students develop an understanding of how to engage in civil dialogue when they don't agree with someone or something.

S-35: Our children begin to see that it is necessary to evaluate others and their thinking the same way that they evaluate themselves and their thinking. This strategy teaches students that the rules they apply to others should be rules they are willing to accept in their own lives.

FROM FUNCTIONALISM TO NEOFUNCTIONALISM AND NEOLIBERALISM

Developing a Dialectical Understanding of the Standards Debate through Historical Awareness

Danny Weil

The politics of the current standards debate, with its recent emergence, challenges, and promises, must be understood within the sociohistorical context that spawned it. Historically, we can find a critical rethinking and reexamination of intelligence and educational standards in a multitude of educational and psychological theoretical pursuits throughout the twentieth century. These include the social functionalism of the factory school, the Dewey progressivism of the early 1900s, critical pedagogy—notably in the persona of Paulo Freire—neofunctionalism, insights into critical thinking, poststructural psychoanalysis, and Vygotskian understandings of cognition and theories.

Yet unfortunately, as educational author and reformer Herbert Kliebard has lamented, school change movements generally fail to understand the history of educational reform in the United States. According to Kliebard, "New breakthroughs are solemnly proclaimed when in fact they represent minor modifications of early proposals, and, conversely, anachronistic dogmas and doctrines maintain a currency and uncritical acceptance far beyond their present merit" (Kliebard, 1970, p. 259). Kliebard calls upon educators to examine new and popular school reform proposals from a historical perspective. For our purposes, this examination will specifically focus on the historical development of education as these developments affect the debate regarding educational standards.

Defining Educational Purpose: Why Do We Teach?

There are many perspectives on the role or purpose of schools in society—

what they should teach and how this teaching and learning should be assessed. The aspiration of this chapter is not to give a prolonged or detailed characterization of the myriad frames of reference on the subject. However, characterizing at least some of these points of view in terms of how the debate is currently constructed is essential to a truly meaningful dialogue about assessment and standards.

Currently, popular political debates regarding literacy, standards, and assessment continue to concentrate on anecdotal evidence and attention-seeking headlines that really do little or nothing to help teachers, their students, or their students' parents move toward a genuine curriculum of thinking and learning. Furthermore, many parents and community members continue to labor under old paradigms of literacy, intelligence, and assessment. These paradigms are fueled and nurtured by an ignorant and demagogic media that continues to separate assessment from learning while seeking to frame the complex issue of education in either back-to-basics or outcome-based education—for both public schools and private schools.

American Industrialism and the Twentieth-Century Development of the Factory School

The end of the Civil War and the years immediately after brought unbridled economic growth and development to America. New scientific and technological developments fueled the expansion of markets and configured a deeply changing nation. More and more Americans began to find residence in large urban centers, leading to the increased development and expansion of cities. Coupled with immigration, the increased urbanization and industrialization of the late nineteenth century and early twentieth century lent rapid growth to U.S. industry and a new concentration of economic power in the hands of emerging industrialists and corporations.

With immigration changing the political and cultural landscape of the United States in the late 1800s, not only were larger urban centers growing, but for the first time they were growing with people other than white Anglos. Along with this rapid growth came the need to assimilate these newly arriving immigrants into the melting pot of "mainstream" American life. An obvious and logical forum for this was the public school. Most work in urban centers during this time was factory work, so the emergence of the American public school began to resemble the factory. Bells were sounded to signal the beginning of classes, desks were bolted to the floor in regimented rows, and strict discipline and a rigidly imposed social order prevailed (Kincheloe, Slattery, and Steinberg, 2000, pp. 151–152).

The costs of building these new factory type schools were justified in the minds of the public by appeals to the "national interest." The argument was simple. Immigrant children were in the United States because the nation needed the labor of their parents to become rich and prosperous. This market rationale argued that educating these "immigrant children" would bring a positive return on investment, namely, a more productive workforce and a more competitive nation. One leading educational functionalist at the time, Ellwood Cubberley, wrote: "Our schools are, in a sense, factories in which the raw products (children) [his parentheses] are to be shaped and fashioned into products to meet the demands of life. The specifications for manufacturing come from the demands of twentieth century civilization, and it is the business of the school to build its pupils according to the specifications laid down" (Cubberley, 1916, p. 338).

If the public school represented the factory, the students themselves were little more than the raw material or objects of production; graduates were seen as the products to be fashioned by the public school system. In the emerging modern public schools of the United States, children, especially immigrant children, were to be trained to follow directions and routines, learn proper English, and develop rudimentary "basic skills," such as reading, mathematical, and writing skills. Schooling, in a sense, developed as a center for socialization and indoctrination as America entered the industrial age.

Post–Civil War America also saw market interests and business concerns rapidly permeate public schools. Not only was the curriculum of public schools immersed in the growth, regulation, and maintenance of urbaniza-

tion and the rise of industrialization and factory existence, but these elements of modernization were also implicated in the development of a modernist conception of knowledge and intelligence.

Between 1880 and 1920, as the factory-style public school system emerged, so too did the philosophy that specified that the reality and life of both students and teachers needs to be scientifically oriented and regulated (Kincheloe et al., 2000, p. 153). This period saw the development of standardized tests, with an emphasis on sorting and categorizing mechanisms that would place students on specific curricular tracks. Modern rationalism and specific, delineated ways of knowing emerged as the measure of intelligence, and the new standardized tests, such as the Stanford-Binet IQ test, were designed to calibrate and classify students based on emerging modernist notions of intellectual behavior. These instruments of assessment also gave specific direction to teachers, identifying specifically what they should be doing in their classrooms.

The IQ test had its origins in 1904 France, where Alfred Binet attempted to study and recommend procedures for educating mentally retarded children (Binet, 1905). The test itself was forged in the fires of actual and existent material conditions found in early-twentieth-century capitalist France and reflected the values, interests, needs, and focuses not only of Binet himself but of his cultural and socioeconomic milieu.

In 1905, Binet proposed a thirty-item scale of intelligence, a set of norms so to speak, to measure what contributes to classroom achievement. After Binet's death in 1911, his normative scale was revised, producing the Stanford-Binet IQ test. The test has been revised many times since its inception and is still generally considered the standard measure of intelligence in Western societies.

Formalist reason, Cartesian-Newtonian science, and the techno-rationalist necessities of the emerging industrial revolution, coupled with the need to develop a psychology or managerial science of the mind, all influenced and contributed to the theoretical development and practical implementation of the normative scales found in the IQ test. Similar considerations of historical reality would be necessary to understand any assessment, not simply the IQ test, as their development, use, and analysis is always historically situated and must be understood against the specific socioeconomic conditions from which they arose. Examining these conditions allows us to see why and how intelligence was defined and how this definition affects our organization of educational occasions for students and productive opportunities for teachers. Such analysis also affords us an insight into the role of standards and assessment.

The Development of Functionalist Theory

The burgeoning industrial capitalism of the late 1800s and the early 1900s needed schooling to preserve, extend, and legitimize the economic relations of production and the arrival of new forms of unprecedented consumption. Consequently, during this period we see the rise and development of an educational philosophy called "social functionalism": education organized, implemented, and controlled to meet the functional needs of business and economic interests. These needs could be equated with what was necessary in the workplace and then taught and assessed. The assessment of students would be metaphorically similar to assuring quality control, much like the quality control assurance of products.

Directly associated with the social functionalism of schools was the excessive preoccupation with the values of productivity, efficiency, and thrift (Goodman, 1995, p. 6). With the development of the assembly line, specifically the contributions of Frederick Taylor to the new science of business management, efficiency, productivity, and speed began to capture the imagination of the American public. Factory work relied on workers who could follow instructions, take simple directions, and work swiftly to increase production with maximum efficiency.

Industrial production proceeded at levels heretofore unheard of and the power and ideology of industrialized production became the national ideology during this period. It is hard not to see the parallel between this historical period and today. Although contemporary production has shifted to technological and service work as the

United States enters into the "third wave," or postindustrialism, infatuation with technological, cybernetic tycoons and the ideology of efficiency and "lean production" still dominate U.S. culture. School-to-work programs are important aspects of many public schools and have arisen, partly, in response to the demands of the new social functionalism, which is designed to prepare students for the needs of changing production in the twenty-first century.

The social functionalism prevalent in the philosophy of early-twentieth-century educational discourse along with a preoccupation for speed and efficiency was described by leading reformer Franklin Bobbitt, one of the key social functionalists for the industrial-age school restructuring movement. In 1924, Bobbitt claimed:

> It is helpful to begin with the simple assumption to be accepted literally, that education is to prepare men and women for the activities of adult life; and that nothing should be included which does not serve this purpose. . . . The first task is to discover the activities, which ought to make up the lives of men and women; and along with these, the abilities and personal qualities necessary for proper performance. These are educational objectives. When we know what men and women ought to do then we shall have before us the things for which they should be trained. (Bobbitt, 1912, pp. 259–271)

The adult activities to which Bobbitt referred were tied to economic necessities that resulted from changes in the relations of production and consumption that were exploding at the time.

Further, not only did the industrial age have an impact on the purposes and goals of education, but the social functionalism of the time also affected staffing patterns, curricular construction, and instructional design (Goodman, 1995, p. 6). What R.E. Callahan referred to as the "cult" of efficiency and productivity had an effect on every aspect of schooling (Callahan, 1962). The modern science of business management, called Taylorism after its creator, was rapidly being implemented in school production as well. Educational goals were restructured and redefined as increasing productivity in schools—in essence, increasing the quantity of what students learn. So the factory school began to predetermine outcomes and then plan backwards to restructure education so that these outcomes could be reached. As early as 1913, Bobbitt declared:

> The third grade teacher should bring her pupils up to an average of 26 correct (addition) combinations per minute. The fourth grade teacher has the task, during the year that the same pupils are under her care, of increasing their addition speed from an average of 26 combinations per minute to an average of 34 combinations per minute. If she does not bring them up to the standard 34, she has failed to perform her duty in proportion to the deficit; and there is no responsibility beyond the standard. (Bobbitt, 1913, pp. 21–22)

Specifically stated learning objectives that could be measured, controlled, and regulated became the language of educational discourse. These objectives were tied to what was needed or what was functional within the emerging industrial society. With an "objectives first" approach to education and schooling, curriculum underwent unique changes. Not only were educators concerned with efficiency and production, but they also believed strongly in the practice of differentiated staffing (Goodman, 1995, p. 10). Knowledge acquisition was fragmented into disciplines and subjects, much like the work on assembly lines in industrial factories. The most important goal for the social functionalists and efficiency educators of the day was to reduce the number of educational workers by maximizing their instructional efficiency. Thus, not much different from what Taylor advocated in the factory, no one person was to ever be responsible for too many different tasks. Scientism and the instrumentalist approaches of functionalist educators divided teaching up into distinct and differentiated tasks staffed by different individuals.

The reconfiguration of the school day and the redesign of curriculum during the industrial revolution in the early part of the twentieth century helped shape what we know now as the large, urban public school and its accompanying public school curriculum. As we shall see, Bobbitt's appeal to link school to work was not much different from positions taken by certain educational policy makers and business leaders today. And in the same way that Taylorism and the new science of business administration influenced the conception and organization of schooling during the early twentieth century, contemporary changes in production, consumption, and business management theory continue to exert a tremendous influence on the standards debate today.

Progressive Educational Responses to the Factory School

Although the factory style of education during the late nineteenth century and early twentieth century imposed a functionalist, industrial education on all American citizens—African American, Native American, newly arriving immigrants, and Anglos—and even though the prevailing wisdom at the time argued for impersonal factory schools grounded on modernist approaches to curriculum and teaching, many educators protested. They not only saw the factory school as an impersonal social arrangement, but they also saw industrial society and the factory itself as an impediment to human development. Margaret Haley, union organizer and teacher-activist at the time, expressed the following observation: "Two ideals are struggling for supremacy in American life today; one the industrial ideal, dominating through the supremacy of commercialism, which subordinates the worker to the product and the machine; the other ideal of democracy, the ideal of educators, which places humanity above all machines, and demands that all activity shall be the expression of life" (Tyack, 1974, p. 257).

Educators like Haley opposed what they viewed as the rigid and impersonal social order imposed by factory life. They felt that the rise of corporations and corporate power were far more menacing to American life than the role of government (Kincheloe et al., 2000, p. 159). These educational progressives wanted schooling to create educational experiences that expanded children's involvement in citizenship activities and civic responsibility, and they argued that public education must construct its mission and purpose to this end.

Besides W.E.B. DuBois and Haley, one of the most prominent progressive educators and philosophers during the early part of the twentieth century was John Dewey. Like Haley, Dewey argued against the reduction of schooling to mere functionalism—boring and repetitive tasks designed to prepare students for future work. Dewey's argument against social functionalism maintained that the role and purpose of education should be to prepare students to live fully in the present, not simply to prepare them for the future. Like Boyd Bode, another progressive educator of the time, Dewey argued that for schooling to become merely a preparatory institution for future market needs was dehumanizing and denied children the opportunity to find relevance and meaning in their lives. Dewey commented: "The ideal of using the present simply to get ready for the future contradicts itself. It omits, and even shuts out, the very conditions by which a person can be prepared for his future. We always live at the time we live and not at some other time, and only by extracting at each present time the full meaning of each present experience are we prepared for doing the same thing in the future. This is the only preparation, which in the long run amounts to anything" (Dewey, 1938, p. 49).

Dewey's description of the purpose and objective of education was very clear:

The problem of education in its relation to the direction of social change is all one with the problem of finding out what democracy means in the total range of concrete applications; domestic, international, religious, cultural, economic, *and* political. . . . The trouble . . . is that we have taken democracy for granted; we have thought and acted as if our forefathers had founded it once and for all. We have forgotten that it has to be enacted anew with every generation, in every year, in every day, in the living relations of person to person, in all social forms and institutions. Forgetting this . . . [w]e have been negligent in creating a school that should be the constant nurse of democracy. (Dewey, 1940, pp. 357–358)

Dewey was convinced that democracy is not a "thing" that is found, but an idea that is perpetually created. His notion of education rested upon a citizenry that wishes to develop the ability to visualize the type of society they want to live in. Dewey and his progressive contemporaries continued to argue against social functionalism and for a different conception of schooling and educational purpose. They looked to assessment to measure *how* students think, not *what* they think.

Although the debate between progressive educators like Dewey, Boyde, DuBois, and Haley on the one hand and Bobbitt and Cubberley on the other was intense and controversial, in the end it was functionalism that triumphed over progressivism. There are many reasons for the triumph of social functionalism in the U.S. educational debates in the early twentieth century, not the least being the cost of subsidizing and operating public education as an enterprise. Progressive educational ideas would have required new structural configurations of school, an emphasis on quality education as opposed to educating quantities of students, and the introduction of new assessments and more creative and innovative curricula. Social functionalist approaches to education, on the other hand, were less expensive precisely because within the factory style school, students could be "produced" on an educational assembly line in much larger numbers than with the craftsmanship required by progressive education (Wirt & Kirst, 1992). Similarly, with standardized tests, quality control could be rigidly fixed without variation.

Perhaps even more importantly, the progressive agenda for education was highly controversial and threatened the elite agenda of control and power that was taking shape in industrialized, modernist America. With the emergence of union activism and socialist movements, the creation of the former Soviet Union in 1917, and the so-called Red scare and the Sacco and Vanzetti trial of the 1920s, the last thing that U.S. policy makers in education, business, or politics wanted was an education for social liberation and individual realization. Business interests, policy makers, and politicians were worried that opening up education to such things as personal awareness, democracy, social exploration, and critical analysis might compel the public to examine the social, cultural, and economic relations that governed their lives. Such education, it was feared, could pose a considerable threat to power, authority, and control and was of little interest to the captains of a market society undergoing a huge economic expansion, technological revolution, and rising industrialization. Their notion of education for social function and control was far more pragmatic, designed to support an emerging industrial world where commercialism relied on disciplined workers and responsible consumers. Socialization and indoctrination were to be the norm for schooling, and tests and measurement instruments were developed to assist in ensuring that this indoctrination and socialization became the subject of education.

As a result of this climate, Dewey's progressive ideas had little support from administrators and other educational policy makers. And so, although the debates between progressives and social functionalists continued to dominate educational discourse during the early part of the twentieth century, schools were increasingly organized based on factory models and their curriculums wedded to organizational and intellectual endeavors that promoted education as preparation for work.

The argument between Booker T. Washington and DuBois and between the educational functionalists and educational progressives is as heated today as it was at the beginning of the twentieth century—perhaps even more so. The issues that confronted educators in the early twentieth century—curriculum construction, access to quality education, the education of minority children and newly arriving immigrants, race, gender equity, social class, market capitalism, technological innovation, work, efficiency and production, and the purpose and goals of education—represent challenges that are similar to but different from those of today.

Post–World War II Policy and the Politics of Public Education

After World War II, public education in the United States experienced some of its most dramatic challenges and changes. In the context of the Cold War, McCarthyism, economic prosperity, suburban development, technological innovations in consumer goods, the advent of television and advertis-

ing, the growth of the civil rights movement, and the rapid development of scientific innovation and discovery, controversial and rancorous debates arose over the role of education and universal access to school facilities.

Perhaps the most important event to mark post–World War II social, racial, and educational politics was the 1954 Supreme Court decision on *Brown vs. Board of Education*. Up until this time, what was referred to as the separate-but-equal doctrine, set forth as law in the famous *Plessy vs. Ferguson* case, governed relations between Blacks and Whites. The *Brown* decision swept *Plessy* away forever, declaring the separate-but-equal doctrine "inherently unequal" (*Brown v. Board of Education*. 347 U.S. 483, 74 Sup. Ct. 686. 1954). Further clarifying its position on the matter, the Court once again legally intervened in a follow-up decision by stating that public school systems that had been segregated up until that time now had to become desegregated (*Brown vs. Board II*. 349 U.S. 294, 75 Sup. Ct. 753).

The court decision also brought up the issue of "states' rights" versus federal control—an issue older than the Civil War. Many conservative southerners felt that decisions regarding local issues should be left to the bodies of state and local government, not mandated by the federal government. At the time, many conservatives saw the Supreme Court decision in *Brown vs. Board of Education* as a federal invasion of states' rights.

Another important post–World War II event that was to have a massive impact on the nation's school systems and continued influence on public debate over education was the advance of the Soviet Union into space with the 1957 launching of the *Sputnik*. American leaders reacted to the Soviet success with shock and disbelief, arguing that the Soviet Union now threatened U.S. sovereignty. Business leaders, military leaders, and educational policy makers scrambled to assign the blame to American public schools. Attacks on public education intensified, partly because it was a convenient target, easy to blame not only for the nation's lack of global and economic competitiveness but also for the new permissiveness, apparent in everything from rock and roll music to new conventions regarding sexuality and conformity (Kincheloe et al., 2000, p. 164).

With the launching of *Sputnik* and the perceived Soviet superiority in matters of technology and military development, the federal government began to become more involved in the legal and economic realities of public education. The National Defense and Education Act was passed in the late 1950s, focusing the educational emphasis primarily on science, mathematics, foreign language, guidance, career counseling, and vocational endeavors. The federal government also appropriated and spent massive sums for the construction of schools and buildings.

Worried that the Soviet Union was achieving technological and military dominance over the United States, educational policy makers saw themselves as the custodians of the public educational system. Education was now to be perceived as a vehicle for gaining skills necessary for the promotion of the "national interest," and it was directly linked to defeating communism at any cost. For the first time in its history, the U.S. government declared education a national preoccupation and a national interest. The public schools were still organized as large factories, but now they were factories that were more preoccupied with the regulation of the curriculum. In this atmosphere of political fear and educational purpose tied to military and technological preparedness, the voices of progressive education were muted and silenced.

Today's efforts to promote an educational marketplace through privatized school choice can be traced directly to the work of conservative economist Milton Friedman in 1955. Unlike those proponents of public education who sought to restructure and reform factory-style public schools, Friedman proposed that every family be given a federal "voucher" for each child attending any school. Under the proposed plan, the vouchers, all of equal worth, would be funded by public monies and would allow families to choose any school that met minimal governmental oversight. Parents could also add their own resources to the value of the voucher, and schools would operate like businesses, setting their own tuition and admission requirements (Friedman, 1955).

Friedman's proposal failed to attract public interest at the time, and the prevailing ideology argued that a simple retooling of the curriculum and the addition of advanced placement classes would remedy any problems associated with public education. Further, with the *Brown* decision, any primacy of states' rights over federal law in the form of state-imposed desegregation was now illegal. Although at the time Friedman voiced his support for integration, by asserting the primacy of freedom over equality, his proposal threatened to further segregation, directly or indirectly (Re-Thinking Schools, 1996). However, even though it was rejected by the public at the time, the Friedman proposal would return with a vengeance in the late 1980s and early 1990s.

The importance of the post–World War II era in education is significant to any understanding of the current debates regarding public schools, specifically charter schools. Issues regarding states' rights, race, market initiatives, and "failing American schools," so predominant in the educational discourse of the 1950s, now appear again in the topics and questions that the educational community faces today.

The Decade of the 1960s and the Politics of Standards

Post–World War II America experienced conformity in the 1950s, but the 1960s were anything but conventional. Changes in educational policy and the debate over educational purpose and access during the 1960s must be situated and understood within the context of political activism and resistance that characterized the decade. Anti-war demonstrations, the Civil Rights movement, boycotts, the emergence of the gay movement in 1969, multiculturalism, feminism, assassinations of political leaders, and the multiple marches on Washington all worked directly to change the conception of American identity and American consciousness. And the decade of the 1960s was to have a dramatic and far-reaching impact on educational issues and schooling as well.

Probably the most important political event of the 1960s was the passage of the Civil Rights Act of 1964. Not only did passage of the act guarantee African Americans access to all public facilities, but it empowered the U.S. government to ensure compliance with the act by bringing discrimination suits against any institution or local governmental body charged with discriminating. According to estimates, almost 99 percent of Black students in the eleven southern states remained in segregated schools in the late 1960s (Orfield, 1969, p. 45). In accordance with the Civil Rights Act, schools that segregated were now to be stripped of any federal aid.

Another consequential legislative enactment in the 1960s was the passage of the Elementary and Secondary Act of 1965. Signed into law by President Johnson as part of the War on Poverty, the act would provide another nail in the coffin for segregated schools by bringing even more African Americans into the mainstream of public schooling.

The fight over desegregation was often a violent one, and the Supreme Court once again was forced to act with its decision in *Green vs. City School Board* (391 U.S. 430. 1968). The issue involved so-called freedom-of-choice plans that had been adopted by some in the South as a way of avoiding desegregation. The *Green* decision outlawed these schemes as barriers to desegregation, further ensuring that schools would be desegregated in accordance with the *Brown* decision.

In the late 1950s and the 1960s the U.S. public school system became increasingly desegregated, and immense changes in public education occurred during this time in the South. For the first time, African Americans were allowed to attend public schools with Whites, albeit at times under protection of the National Guard. Universal access to education was won through the struggles for equality and justice on behalf of African Americans, members of labor movements, students, feminists, and other groups.

The 1960s also witnessed intense debates over school curriculum. The roots of what is currently termed the "multicultural" movement in education finds its origins in the radical challenges put forth by progressive educational forces in the 1960s and early 1970s. The movement toward a multicultural curriculum originated largely among the nation's culturally subjugated and marginalized peoples, such as African Americans, Mexican Americans, Native Americans, and women. Proponents of multiculturalism criticized traditional schools for their admission practices vis-à-vis people of color; they condemned the academic establishment for its subservience to business interests; they reprimanded schooling for its racist, sexist, and culturally biased curriculum; they chastised hiring practices for women and minorities; they exposed the pernicious practice of tracking; they lambasted the curriculum for its claim of neutrality; and they labored assiduously to ensure the establishment of beneficial entitlement programs such as bilingual education and Title VII–mandated educational programs.

Multiculturalism argued that a lack of understanding and acceptance of racial differences was a recognized problem for teachers and students alike (Stent, Hazard & Rivlin, 1973, p. 73). Among the voices of the multicultural educational community there were calls to directly address issues of prejudice and discrimination in classroom curriculum. Multicultural theorists posited that schools should not seek to melt away cultural differences within our pluralistic society but instead should celebrate these differences in an atmosphere of educational inquiry. Therefore, they pointed out, schools should be oriented toward the cultural enrichment of all students though programs aimed at the preservation and extension of cultural pluralism. They put forth the idea that cultural diversity is a valuable resource that should be recognized, preserved, and extended, and they argued that only by directly confronting racism and prejudice can society ensure an understanding and appreciation for human dignity (Weil, 1998).

The movements and educational struggles that took place during the 1960s and early 1970s produced a new language and vocabulary of educational critique. Coupled with the critiques of schooling listed above was a call for the abolition of inequality in school financing and for a commitment to federal funding for educational programs. The struggle for universal access, for changes in the curriculum, and for the passage of social legislation in the 1960s profoundly changed public education in the United States. These movements lent new currency to the progressive calls for a democratic educational purpose that had started with Dewey. Old progressive arguments and positions regarding the role and purposes of education that had been silenced by the Cold War of the 1950s began to re-emerge in the national debate. American identity itself was under reconsideration, as diversity and an understanding of difference became intense objects of controversy and debate. This was to be especially true in universities, many of which were agitated sites of militancy and resistance at the time.

Neoliberalism, Conservatism, the 1980s, and the Politics of Standards

When President Jimmy Carter received the endorsement of the National Education Association (NEA) in his bid for presidency in 1976, it was the first time that the nation's largest teachers' union had endorsed a candidate for president of the United States. Carter owed this backing to his promise to establish a cabinet-level Department of Education. The NEA had lobbied for such a national cabinet position since World War I. Finally, with the union endorsement, Carter raised education to the cabinet level in 1980.

While Carter proved to be more conservative than many observers had expected from an "education president," there is little doubt that it was Ronald Reagan, Carter's successor, who left a lasting conservative ideological stamp on American public education. Considering the Department of Education an unnecessary expense and perceiving it as an imposition to states' rights, Reagan sought to abolish the department directly after his 1980 election. Invoking free market enterprise and the logic of market forces as the panacea for American social and economic troubles, Reagan and his administration embarked on restructuring social policy, including education, to reflect the primacy of market solutions to public problems (Lugg, 1996).

Calls for the dissolution of the Department of Education met with severe resistance that made it impossible for conservatives to abolish the department. As a result, the Reagan administration sought to reconstitute the Department of Education, transforming it into a vocal mouthpiece for controversial policies like organized prayer, public and private school choice, and school vouchers. As a result, department representatives leveled blistering attacks against public education, teachers' unions, and curriculum.

It was in 1983 that the best-publicized educational achievement of the Reagan administration was issued in the form of a book-length report entitled *A Nation at Risk*. Issued by the National Commission on Excellence in Education (NCEE), the report provided a scathing critique of the public education system, arguing that American education had become a bastion of mediocrity. The report concluded that the state of American education was actually threatening the nation's future economic growth. With its dire predictions and warnings, *A Nation at Risk* once again focused public attention on the issue of education as an economic issue. As educational urgency took on market proportions, progressive educational concerns were not considered a priority (NCEE, 1983).

After the *Nation at Risk* study was released in 1983, scores of magazines and news reports jumped on the bandwagon, concentrating on the supposed "failure of public education." That year, *Newsweek* rushed to press a scathing story that asked if the schools "could be saved." The report concluded that progress from generation to generation was being "shattered" by the mediocre condition of American schools (Saving Our Schools, 1983).

Responsibility for the recessionary economic crisis that plagued America during the early 1980s was placed squarely on the back of the public educational system. Public education was now seen as an inhibitor to economic growth (Shor, 1986, p. 108). Like the *Sputnik* scare decades prior, *A Nation at Risk* was used to sound a wake-up call to educators and policy makers. This time, instead of Soviet superiority in outer space, it was the influx of quality goods from Japan that was thought to be the threat to national security. The ability of the United States to compete globally, it was argued, was jeopardized by a public educational system that simply did not work.

To build the case for the mediocrity of the school system, the NCEE had turned to an analysis of the Scholastic Aptitude Test (SAT) scores. The NCEE pointed to the long decline in SAT scores that had occurred from 1963 to 1980. It also compared U.S. education to other Western school systems, pointing out areas where the U.S. system did not measure up to its counterparts. Playing off a sense of political patriotism and economic nationalism, the *Nation at Risk* report pointed out that the United States would continue to be a preeminent country only so long as material benefits and great ideas remained part of the country's legacy. The report argued that the nation's national security was in jeopardy as long as the public schools threatened this legacy (NCEE, 1983).

In June of 1983, another report, entitled *Action for Excellence: A Comprehensive Plan to Improve Our Nation's Schools*, was published by the state governors' group, called the Education Commission of the States (ECS). Often referred to as the "Hunt Report" after Governor James B. Hunt of North Carolina, the report continued to echo the notion that American schools were failing (ECS, 1983, pp. v, 3).

The alarms did not stop with the Hunt Report. The next major statement regarding the state of public education was issued in September of 1983 with the National Science Board (NSB) report. In its dramatic study entitled *Educating Americans for the Twenty-First Century*, the NSB document warned that:

> The nation that dramatically and boldly led the world into the age of technology is failing to provide its own children with the intellectual tools needed for the 21st century. . . . Already the quality of our manufactured products, the viability of our trade, our leadership in research and development, our standard of living, are strongly challenged. Our children could be stragglers in a world of technology. We must not let this happen; America must not become an industrial dinosaur. We must not provide our children a 1960's education for the 21st century world. (NSB, 1983)

The exigencies of education were once again being linked to the nation's economic readiness, or lack of it. The 1980s built the case for a super functionalism. Instead of the rudimentary skills required by the social functionalism of industrialization, the new in-

formation and technological revolution in American society needed a different type of worker with different kinds of skills. Preparing students for the twenty-first century technological and cybernetic revolution, or the "third wave," became the mantra of reports like *A Nation at Risk*. Calls to bring education "back to basics" saw this as the antidote for the economic crisis, in a move similar to the "objectives first" clamor in the early 1900s. The NSB report defined the new cognitive-economic relationship between school and work in the following way:

> Alarming numbers of young Americans are ill equipped to work in, to contribute to, profit from and enjoy our increasingly technological society. Far too many emerge from the nation's elementary and secondary schools with an inadequate grounding in mathematics, science, and technology. This situation must not continue. . . . We must return to the basics, but the "basics" of the 21st century are not only reading, writing, and arithmetic. They include communication, and higher problem-solving skills, and scientific and technological literacy. (NSB, 1983)

Under this superfunctionalism, the new basics were now defined as "ultra-basics"—such as science, computers, higher-order reasoning, social studies, foreign language, and academic English. Schools were now to place these basics at the core of their curricula. While the "second wave" of educational restructuring had been established for the industrial age of the early 1900s, the third-wave restructuring movement of the 1980s would focus on preparing students for the information/technology age—an era of neoliberalism—the economic, historical, and philosophical posture that advocates a market primacy and domination.

Educator Larry Hutchins expressed the third-wave functionalist restructuring argument like this: "The old design worked relatively well for the society it served; it brought schooling to millions of immigrants [who] . . . were needed to stoke the engines of the industrial society. Today's society no longer requires such a work force. We need people who can think and solve problems using information and technology" (Hutchins, 1990, p. 12).

Neoliberal goals like maintaining the American empire, creating better goods and services, dominating world markets, and creating the new workforce of the future were all interwoven into the calls for a new and radical restructuring of schools. Any discussion about what type of society Americans wished to create or about the relationship between school, democracy, culture, and the emerging cybernetic society was conspicuously absent from the concerns of third-wave restructionists. Furthermore, as with the efficiency production arguments of the industrial age, teachers were encouraged to develop curricular goals based on step-by-step procedures and time schedules as their labor became more disenfranchised from creativity and

they themselves became significantly de-skilled (Goodman, 1995, p. 10).

During the 1980s, the educational reform movement increasingly found expression in a language of business efficiency, productivity, choice, and the application of management theories to the educational enterprise. More than at any other time, test scores became the products of schools. Students became the workers who create this product using instructional programs given to them by the "educational maintenance organization." Teachers were increasingly transformed into shop managers who preside over students' production through classroom management techniques that operate as technologies of power; school principals became the plant managers who manage the school personnel to ensure that the product corresponds to the standards; specialists, such as social workers or school counselors, were employed to handle students' emotional needs; and altercations became defined as educational disputes that arise between the school and parents (Goodman, 1995, p. 11). Transformed into classroom managers overseeing student-workers, teachers became further disengaged from the nature of teaching; conception was further divorced from execution as teacher-workers were galvanized to follow prescribed "teaching recipes" in the form of preformulated lesson plans. With the rise of prepackaged instructional materials, intellectual engagement with the curriculum had now become a luxury for many teachers, as they were transformed into mere technicians, quality control agents, clerks, and managers of learning.

Third-Wave Restructuring at the End of the Second Millennium: School Choice and the Politics of the Charter Movement

The development of the new educational discourse of business productivity and efficiency in the 1980s set the stage for our current educational controversies at the beginning of the third millennium. As the 1980s came to an end, unregulated capitalist markets monopolized mainstream thinking. Determined that neoliberal market solutions were the remedy for all of society's ills, economists and pundits warned the nation to concentrate on neoliberal solutions to social and individual problems in order to compete vigorously in the global arena. Unregulated markets, unrestricted globalization, and privatization were seen as an advantage for all those interested in the notion of American progress.

With the fall of the Soviet Union in 1991, this vision of America, one of unregulated markets and capitalist hegemony, became the primary vision for education as well. Not only were public schools continually perceived and cast as failing and mediocre institutions, but now people also began to suggest that these public schools would better serve American citizens if they were forced to compete with schools that were privatized. They argued that schools need to develop students the way that corporations

develop products. School choice proponents now claimed that the government should provide vouchers to pay for the schooling of students' or their parents' choice. The idea, claimed voucher adherents, was that private and public schools could then compete for the most academically able students. The schools that failed to prepare students for the emerging information/technology market in the most efficient manner would succumb to a "natural selection" (Kincheloe et al., 2000, p. 171). Friedman's proposal for privatized education was now a fait acompli.

Economic Conservatives, Neoliberalism, and the Neofunctionalist Argument

The educational foundations of American society are presently being eroded by a rising tide of mediocrity that threatens our very future as a nation and a people. . . . We have, in effect, been committing an act of unthinking, unilateral educational disarmament.

—A Nation at Risk

The prevailing point of view today, one that is embraced by both economic and neofunctionalist assertions and that resonates throughout the media, seems to be that school is merely a training ground for the necessities of market civilization—that is, preparation in school has been transformed into little more than preparation for work. With the dramatic changes in the nature of and relations among the forces of postmodern capitalist production, contemporary neofunctionalists have now refashioned and rely on neoformalist, cognitive notions of intelligence that though formal in nature, seek to expand the parameters of formal psychological theories to include such things as critical thinking skills, problem solving, and decision-making capabilities.

Part of the problem, according to neofunctionalists, is what they refer to as failing *government schools*. They go on to argue that the cybernetic economy of information and knowledge will necessitate the cultivation and harvesting of the best decision-making and problem-solving capacities among capitalist workers and managers. They talk about managers and workers as "knowledge workers" who are able to use new technology, and they advocate that students be educated to fashion large amounts of information and data into patterns from which they might make plausible inferences about business issues. They see problem-solving and decision-making skills—within the context of postcapitalist society and its political, social, and economic arrangements—as the new hemisphere of intelligence. Adaptation to change, continuous life-long learning, thinking outside of the box, flexibility, proactive thinking, open-minded thinking, intuitive thinking, and a host of other business and managerial psycho-babble are marshaled to meet the "new intelligence" needs of the postmodern capitalist global order (American Management Association, 2000).

Fundamentally, this means that students go to school for the purpose of learning how to compete in a capitalist global society; in school students learn job skills they are told are essential to get ahead. The National Skill Standards Board, containing appointees of President Bill Clinton, adopts this position in its discussion of standards: "The National Skill Standards Board [NSSB] is building a voluntary national system of skill standards, assessment and certification that will enhance the ability of the United States to compete effectively in the global economy" (NSSB, 1998).

From this point of view, education, beginning in primary school, should be designed to create producers and consumers who unquestionably accept and adapt to the business models inherent in capitalist society as well as the power relations that govern them. The new political discourse of conservative neofunctionalism discusses education only as it relates to markets, national identity, global competition, increased productivity, and unbridled consumption. Nothing is said about helping students relate to the world in critical ways that would allow them to "read their lives." For economic conservatives, schools serve national, global, and neoliberal market forces—not people.

Even among those CEOs and neofunctionalists who bemoan the current state of education as an antiquated testimony to the past and talk about the need for critical thinking, the goal is also clearly tied to the bandwagon of individual economic necessity. At President Clinton's 1992 Economic Conference, the former CEO of Apple Corporation, John Sculley, stated this quite succinctly:

We are still trapped in a K–12 public education system, which is preparing our youth for jobs that no longer exist. A highly skilled work force must begin with a world-class public education system which will turn out a world-class product. . . . It is an issue about an educational system aligned with the new economy and a broad educational opportunity for everyone. Our public education system has not successfully made the shift from teaching the memorization of facts to achieving learning of critical thinking skills. . . . It's America's choice: High skills or low wages. (Sculley, 1992)

According to the new gospel of neofunctionalism, there is a need not only for a different kind of production under post-Fordism but for a different kind of worker—the knowledge worker, the cognitive elite. This is the worker who is adaptable and amenable to multitask work environments, who has a theoretical understanding of systems and how they function, who can work in teams, who can accept new styles of managerial authority, who can form data into patterns and then interpret this data for the good of the company's profits, who can operate within wider frames of reference, who seeks out new information from multiple sources, and who can solve business problems and make business decisions. For neofunctionalists and their economic conservative counterparts, the new millennium is foisting upon us new neoliberal, market-driven cognitive demands and different and unique productive relations, and schools must

be ready to accept and meet this challenge if we want the student-worker to get ahead and the United States to be truly able to compete.

Former Labor Secretary Robert Reich makes similar arguments in his book, *The Work of Nations:* "We are living through a transformation that will rearrange the politics and economics of the coming century. There will no longer be national economies, at least as we have come to understand the concept. All that will remain rooted within national borders are the people who comprise the nation. Each nation's primary asset will be its citizens' skills and insights" (Reich, 1992, p. 3).

For neofunctionalists like Reich and Sculley, the argument is clear: Less desirable jobs will not exist in the United States but will be shipped overseas to third-world countries— the new export economies and assembly lines of global capitalism. More complex, intellectually challenging work, they argue, will become the norm in the United States, and of course, there will be winners and losers. However, this time the winners and losers will not only be individuals within nations, but will actually be entire nations themselves. This is the neoliberal message: Global economic necessities demand an educational system tied to the skills and training necessary to compete in the new millennium of cybernetic global capitalism. Critical thinking is important only as it relates to creating critical mass—designing better products, boosting productivity, fashioning better customer service, creating stronger national identity, and creating a new class of disciplined consumers and servile workers. Preparing citizen-consumers for this "new world order" seems now to have become the raison d'être of education and educational sites.

From the perspective of economic conservatives and neoliberals, educational assessment and world-class standards must be linked to what it means to be successful in the new global economy. Through their efforts they have created standard and assessment think tanks, such as Achieve Incorporated, a nonprofit organization created by a group of CEOs and the National Governors Association that was initially cochaired by IBM's chief executive officer, Louis Gerstner Jr., and Governor Tommy Thompson of Wisconsin (now secretary of Health and Human Services). Such institutions have produced reports like the National Education Goals Report, launched in 1989 as a result of the controversy over the 1983 report, *A Nation at Risk*. The Goals Report announces its mission as follows: "By the year 2000, American students will leave grades 4, 8, and 12 having demonstrated competency in challenging subject matter including English, mathematics, science, history, and geography; and every school in America will ensure that all students learn to use their minds well, so they may be prepared for responsible citizenship, further learning, and productive employment in our modern society" (National Education Goals Report, 1991, p. 9).

By adopting what they like to call "world-class standards," these corporate and business leaders are working to identify post-Fordist, neofunctionalist skills that will be necessary for the workplace of the future (Mid-continent Regional Educational Laboratory, 1997). The clamor to define world-class standards and skills has been linked to the presumed dominance of the United States in the world economy, and both economic conservatives and neoliberal policy makers have tied the development of these standards to American market competitiveness. Diane Ravitch, recognized as one of the darlings and chief architects of the modern standards movement, has stated the economic conservative and neoliberal rationale for standards: "Americans expect strict standards to govern the construction of buildings, bridges, highways, and tunnels; shoddy work would put lives at risk. They expect stringent standards to protect their drinking water, the food they eat, and the air they breathe. . . . Standards are created because they improve the activity of life" (Ravitch, 1996, pp. 8–9).

What is ironic is how this neoinstrumentalism and postfunctionalism has been redefined and refashioned to convey the appearance of progressive dialogue: the so-called new school reformers—the new corporate business and managerial elites—giving a call to arms for change. Although the functionalist rationale has changed to that of neofunctionalism, what has really changed are the historical necessities of capitalism, not a rethinking regarding the role of schools. The contemporary reformers, the neofunctionalists, still advocate and cling to an educational theory and practice allied with the needs of commercial interests and organized along business organizational theories and practices. The difference now is simply how they redefine the new functionalism and instrumentalism in face of postmodern capitalist changes in the relations and forces of production.

Neoliberalism: The Purpose of Education Is to Inculcate Basic Skills

Another argument that we hear today among contemporary conservative educational reformers is that schools must stick to the business of educating children in basic skills. This is nothing new. What is new, however, is how these basic skills are being redefined in the face of changes in the relations and forces of production in postcapitalist society. What was basic in Franklin Bobbitt's time is not so basic today, according to neofunctionalists. Where basic skills were once tied to an industrial society, they are now being recast in terms of the cybernetic-information society—the society we find ourselves in at the beginning of the twenty-first century.

And not only have basic skills been redefined and updated to meet the exigencies of postmodern capitalist development, but we now also find that terms such as *critical thinking* and *So-cratic questioning* have been hijacked from progressive educational theory and practice and are now being used to refer to the type of intelligence businesses believe worker-managers will need in the new millennium (Spitzer, 1999).

Indeed, the whole notion of examining and reexamining cognition has now become a major preoccupation of managerial programs, business educational theories, and actual educational training classes. Michael Molenda captures this well when he states: "Learning achievement is the crucial product of the educational system. Schools obviously attempt to perform many functions in American society, including socialization of youth into the community. However, the primary and unique requirement expected of schools is the attainment of the knowledge, skills, and attitudes specified by state and local boards of education. . . . It is what Reich (1991) and others insist is the vital element for economic survival" (quoted in Goodman, 1995, p. 10).

Of course what the postfunctionalists don't tell us is that the development of systematic, collaborative, evaluative, and abstract thinking, through schools modeled after effective and efficient business organizations (Reich, 1992, p. 3), is really designed to develop a cognitive elite—a postmodern managerial class that can ensure the smooth workings of global capitalism. From their point of view, the successful acquisition of capital and the velvety operation of technological control, authority, and maintenance should be the object of education—thus the postfunctionalism. The rhetoric they choose to embrace is one of citizen inclusivity and an end to the so-called digital divide—a Jeffersonian, democratic education for all. Yet as we can see by examining any number of postfunctionalist programs, their inclusivity is much like that of a private country club that admits its members in accordance with rigid, privileged, class-, gender-, and race-based criteria. It is a gated community for the privileged few—affirmative action for the affirmed.

For the first time, in a real way, the notion of public education itself is being questioned by a new generation of social functionalists. In the past, educational discussions and debates focused on how to bring the nation's public school system up to speed, but the new functionalist arguments actually question the very efficacy, existence, and necessity of public schools. Education is now being conceived of as an "educational marketplace," and a new language of "choice" has emerged to define the terms of the educational debate. Progressive educational concerns regarding the role of democracy, equity, and social justice have been purposefully marginalized and purged from educational discourse in favor, once more, of competitiveness, efficiency, and productivity needs. The new rhetoric of privatized schooling and "choice" circumscribes the language of the debate, and Americans, consciously or unconsciously, are now

embroiled in a controversy over the continued existence of public education itself.

Summary

Understanding the historical nature of American schooling and the controversies that have surrounded and continue to encompass the definition of educational purpose is crucial to understanding the current standards debate. Through meticulous, compassionate dialogue and a serious exchange of diverse points of view accomplished in an atmosphere of civility and inquiry, the standards debate in this country can become intellectually enriched. We as American citizens can profit from the controversies in education today. Through continued resistance *against* neoliberal functionalist policies and persistent resistance *for* educational equity, quality teaching, authentic assessment, and intellectual excellence, we as citizens can begin to design curricula and educational standards that meet the needs of our citizens in their quest for happy and productive lives. Without historical understanding and a critical and rigorous dialogue about educational purpose and the role of neoliberal policies, the standards debate in this country promises to hold our nation's children hostage to a neofunctionalism that prepares students only for the necessities of postmodern capitalist life. We need to ask ourselves as a nation: Is this what we really want for our nation and our children?

References

The American Management Association. (2000). *Catalogue of classes.* New York: Author.

Binet, A., & Simon, T. (1905). *Methodes nouvelles pour le diagnostique de niveau intellectuel des anormaux.* Paris: L'annee psychologique.

Bobbitt, F. (1912). The elimination of waste in education. *Elementary School Teacher, 12,* 259–271.

Bobbitt, F. (1913). Some general principles of management applied to the problems of city school systems. In S.C. Parker, *Twelfth yearbook of the National Society for the Study of Education* (pp. 21–22). Chicago: University of Chicago Press.

Callahan, R. E. (1962). *Education and the cult of efficiency.* Chicago: University of Chicago Press.

Cubberley, E. (1916). *Public school administration: A statement of the fundamental principle underlying the organization and administration of public education.* Boston: Houghton Mifflin.

Dewey, J. (1938). *Experience and education.* New York: Collier Books. (Reprint, Collier, 1976).

Dewey, J. (1940). *Education today.* New York: Greenwood Press.

The Education Commission of the States Task Force on Education for Economic Growth. (1983). *Action for excellence: A comprehensive plan to improve our nation's schools.* Washington, DC: GPO.

Friedman, M. (1955). The role of government in education. In Robert A. Solow (Ed.), *Economics and the public interest.* New Brunswick: Rutgers University Press.

Goodman, J. (1995). *Change without difference. Harvard Educational Review, 65* (no. 1), 10–12.

Hutchins, L. (1990). *A+chieving excellence.* Aurora, CO: Mid-continent Regional Laboratory.

Kincheloe, J., Slattery, P., & Steinberg, S. (2000). *Contextualizing teaching.* New York: Longman.

Kliebard, H. (1970). The Tyler rationale. *School Review, 78,* 259–262.

Lugg, C. A. (1996). *For God and country: Conservatism and American school policy.* New York: Peter Lang.

Mid-continent Regional Educational Laboratory. (1997). Aurora, CO.

The National Commission on Excellence in Education. (1983). *A nation at risk.* Washington, DC: USA Research.

The National Education Goals Report. (1991). Washington, DC: Government Printing Office.

National Science Board Commission on Pre-college Education in Mathematics, Science, and Technology. (1983). Executive summary. In *Educating Americans for the twenty-first century.* Washington, DC: Author.

The National Skills Standards Board. (1998). Washington, DC: U.S. Department of Education.

Orfield, G. (1969). *The reconstruction of Southern education: The schools and the 1964 Civil Rights Act.* New York: Wiley Interscience.

Ravitch, D. (1996). *National standards in American education.* Washington, DC: The Brookings Institute.

Reich, R. (1992). *The work of nations.* New York: Vintage Press.

ReThinking Schools. (1996). *Selling out our schools: Vouchers, markets, and the future of public education.* Milwaukee, WI: ReThinking Schools.

Saving our schools. (1983, May 9). *Newsweek,* pp. 50–58.

Sculley, J. (1992). *Critical thinking: Why it matters so much.* Speech given at 1992 Economic Conference, Arkansas.

Shor, I. (1986). *Culture wars: School and society in the conservative restoration.* Chicago: The University of Chicago Press.

Spitzer, Q. (1999). *Heads you win: How the best companies think.* New York: Mc-Graw Hill.

Stent, M., Hazard, W., & Rivlin, H. (Eds.). (1973). *Cultural pluralism in education: A mandate for change.* New York: Appleton-Century Crofts.

Tyack, D. (1974). *The one best system: A history of American urban education.* Cambridge, MA: Harvard University Press.

Weil, D. (1998). *Towards a critical multicultural literacy: Education for liberation.* New York: Peter Lang Publishing.

Wirt, F. M., & Kirst, M. W. (1992). *Schools in conflict: The politics of education* (3rd ed.). Berkeley: McCutchan.

WORLD CLASS STANDARDS?

Whose World, Which Economic Classes, and What Standards?

Danny Weil

If educational goals and core values are developed by a few educators in isolation from their communities, no matter how well thought out they may be they will not create the conditions needed for change.

—**Tony Wagner**

Several years ago, while at an in-service day with elementary and middle school teachers in the state of Washington, I heard many teachers comment that if we are going to teach for thinking we had better develop new, authentic methodologies, theories, standards, and instruments for assessment. As the teachers began to discuss, question, and attempt through dialogue to develop a clear vision of critical thinking and what it means to be an educated person in today's society, it became apparent to them that the standardized tests predominant in education today are simply not able to meet the challenge of quality assessment of student performance, much less to measure how well students un-

derstand what it means to be a human being. In fact, almost all of these primary and middle school teachers agreed that the standards debate in this country is little more than a hindrance to real educational reform, as teachers consistently complain that they must prepare their students for assessment instruments that test simply for basic skills and rote memorization. These teachers remarked that in American education, standards, or assessment, continues to be linked to a form of what I call *anorexic-bulimic learning*, whereby students starve themselves until test time only to stuff themselves with skills, facts, and details to be regurgitated without the benefit of intellectual digestion. Laced to this, they argued, is the teaching and assessment of basic skills divorced from meaningful tasks and critical inquiry.

As we sat and discussed the necessity for *authentic assessment*, as opposed to the inauthenticity of standardized tests, almost all the teachers, especially those in elementary school, commented that their students never asked them how they performed on the standardized state tests once they were completed; nor did their parents seem to use the information the scores provided to develop a clear idea of what their children were able to do as a result of the time they spend in schools or what it really means to be educated. For anyone other than political pundits, real estate agents, and bureaucrats, the test scores seemed to them to be of limited use, representing little more than a collection of anonymous numerics linked to issues of bureaucratic control and power, as opposed to wedded to critical sensibility, self-assessment, and achievements in performance.

As I listened to and participated in the dialogue with these teachers, it became clear to me that these teachers were becoming aware of the ideological nature of the current testing debate and what it implies for teaching and learning; they were beginning to see that the controversy over standards and assessment, in fact the question as to the purpose for the entire enterprise of education itself, is a *political discussion*. Realizing that the debate over education is in fact a political debate that includes issues of class, race, culture, and gender allowed these teachers to begin to move toward an understanding of what Paulo Freire so aptly characterized as "education as an act of freedom as opposed to education as the practice of domination" (Freire, 1970, p. 75). It also allowed them to connect education and its purposes to larger issues in society itself, to begin to formulate their own perspectives on the role of education, intelligence, and what it means to be an educated person.

Many, if not all of these teachers, had never been afforded an opportunity to discuss the role of education and what it means to be intelligent. Their work was defined as a "divorce from conception"—the execution of methodological techniques and practices that, for the most part, they had never even been asked to think about. As teachers, they had been told in "training" programs that learning and knowing are neutral acts separated and divorced from ideology and sociohistorical, economic, cultural, and political dimensions of life. The schools of education that "train" teachers as opposed to "educating them" (Dewey, 1997, pp. 357–358) produce teacher-technicians who have never been asked to think about the philosophical act of teaching, why they teach, for whom and what purposes knowledge and education serve, or how educational practices relate to dominant and privileged theories of learning.

As we continued our discussions and questioning, pondering our work and critically problematizing and examining the theories that guided our practice, we became aware that it is important to first broach the fundamental question rarely discussed: what is the purpose of education and why should we educate human beings? Of course, the answer to this question can vary considerably, depending on one's point of view. Yet we all concluded that before we could even think about what it means to learn or what it means to educate, let alone delve into the role of standards and assessment, the fundamental question of *what* we are trying to assess and *why* must be tied to the deeper question of why society even bothers to educate its citizens.

Linking the Discussion of Standards to Educational Purpose

REPORTER: *Mr. Ghandi, what do you think of modern civilization?*
GHANDI: *That would be a good idea.*

Perusing the newspaper or listening to television or radio, one might walk away thinking that we are all in agreement as to which educational standards should be adopted and what they should assess. The debate has been cast as a national debate, and yet as a nation, we Americans have not been involved in theorizing the debate or developing its actualities. There is no discussion about how the current standards proposals have been designed, who designed them, or for what purpose. Leaders and elites have designed the discourse, tailored the contents, and dictated the terms of debate.

Yet the current national debate regarding standards is important, for it reveals that it is not the debate we should be having. Debating standards is putting the cart before the horse. The real debate would ask us to incorporate into consideration such questions as What is good teaching? How

does one learn? What is intelligence, whose interests does it serve, and how is it achieved? It would be a debate that invited community, parents, students, and teachers to engage in discourse about what it means to be human, how to act in and with the world, and how to make sense out of one's personal life in light of historical and cultural change.

There are many points of view regarding the role or purpose of schools in society, and it is not the aspiration of this chapter to give a prolonged or detailed characterization of the myriad frames of reference on the subject. However, I think that characterizing at least some of these points of view in terms of how the debate is currently defined is essential to engaging in a truly meaningful dialogue about assessment and standards. Currently, popular political debates regarding literacy, standards, and assessment continue to concentrate on anecdotal evidence and attention-seeking headlines that really do little or nothing to help teachers, their students, or their students' parents move toward a genuine curriculum of thinking and learning. Furthermore, many parents and community members continue to labor under old paradigms of what it means to be literate, intelligent, and *assessed*, and these paradigms are fueled and nurtured by an ignorant and demagogic media that continues to separate assessment from learning while seeking to frame the complex issue of education in either *back-to-basics* or *outcome-based education*—in both public schools and private schools.

Economic Conservatives and the Neoliberal Argument

The educational foundations of our society are presently being eroded by a rising tide of mediocrity that threatens our very future as a nation and a people. . . . We have, in effect been committing an act of unthinking, unilateral educational disarmament.
—A Nation at Risk

The prevailing point of view at this juncture in history, one that is embraced by neoliberal assertions and that resonates throughout the media, seems to be that school is merely a training ground for the necessities of market civilization—that is, preparation in school is preparation for work.

Fundamentally, this means that students go to school for the purpose of learning how to compete in a capitalist global society where they are taught job skills they are told are essential to get ahead. The National Skill Standards Board, containing appointees of President Bill Clinton, adopts this position in its discussion of standards: "The National Skill Standards Board is building a voluntary national system of skill standards, assessment and certification that will enhance the ability of the United States to compete effectively in the global economy" ("President Clinton," 1999).

From this point of view, education, beginning in primary school, should be designed to create producers and consumers who accept and adapt to the business models inherent in capitalist society as well as the power relations that govern them. The new political discourse of conservative neo-liberalism discusses education only as it relates to markets, national identity, global competition, increased productivity, and unbridled consumption. Nothing is said about helping students relate to the world in critical ways. For economic conservatives, schools serve national and market forces—not people. Even for those CEOs and neoliberals who bemoan the current state of education as the antiquated testimony of the past and who talk about the need for critical thinking, the goal is also clearly tied to the bandwagon of individual economic necessity, as illustrated by a speech on education made by the former CEO of Apple Corporation, John Sculley, at Bill Clinton's 1992 Economic Conference:

> We are still trapped in a K-12 public education system, which is preparing our youth for jobs that no longer exist. A highly skilled work force must begin with a world class public education system which will turn out a world class product. . . . It is an issue about an educational system aligned with the new economy and a broad educational opportunity for everyone. Our public education system has not successfully made the shift from teaching the memorization of facts to achieving learning of critical thinking skills. . . . It's America's choice: High skills or low wages (Sculley, 1992).

According to the new gospel of neoliberalism, there is a need not only for a different kind of production under post-Fordism, beyond the dominance of the assembly line in production, but for a different kind of worker—the knowledge worker. This is the worker who is adaptable and amenable to multitask work environments, who has a theoretical understanding of systems and how they function, who can work in teams, who can accept new styles of managerial authority, who can form data into patterns and then interpret this data for the good of the company's profits, who can operate within wider frames of reference, who seeks out new information from multiple sources, and who can solve business problems and make business decisions. For neoliberals and their economic conservative counterparts, the new millennium is foisting upon us new market-driven cognitive demands and different productive relations, and schools must be ready to accept and meet this challenge if we want students to get ahead and America to be truly able to compete.

Former Labor Secretary, Robert Reich, makes similar arguments in his book, *The Work of Nations*: "We are living through a transformation that will rearrange the politics and economics of the coming century. There will no longer be national economies at least as we have come to understand the concept. All that will remain rooted within national borders are the people who comprise the nation. Each nation's primary asset will be its citizens' skills and insights" (Reich, 1992, p. 3).

For neoliberals like Reich and Sculley, the argument is clear: Less desirable jobs will not exist in the United States but will be shipped overseas to third-world countries—the new as-

sembly lines of global capitalism. More complex, intellectually challenging work, they argue, will become the norm in the United States, and of course, there will be winners and losers. However, this time the winners and losers will not only be individuals within nations, but will actually be entire nations themselves. This is the neoliberal message: Global economic necessities demand an educational system tied to the skills and training necessary to compete in the new millennium of a cybernetic global capitalism. Critical thinking is important only as it relates to creating critical mass—designing better products, boosting productivity, fashioning better customer service, creating stronger national identity, and creating a new class of disciplined consumers. Preparing citizen-consumers for this "new world order" becomes the raison d'être of education and educational sites.

Economic conservatives and neoliberals, however, go even one step further, arguing that there is now a need to eliminate what they term "frills" in education, to narrow the offerings in curriculum, to increase the number of required subjects, to standardize schools across the board so that they are barely distinguishable from community to community, and to support and promote a culture of private accumulation of wealth and individualistic choice. Silicon Valley entrepreneur Ron Unz recently made this point:

The problem isn't what schools lack but what they possess in abundance, namely half-baked educational fads produced by elite educational theorists. The list is quite long: whole language, bilingual education, inventive spelling, fuzzy math, constructivist science, endless self-esteem programs and other wrong headed pedagogical experiments. According to numerous studies, this educational machinery produces students with the highest self-esteem but the lowest academic test scores of any of their global peers. (Unz, 1999, pp. 6–7)

Unz goes on to propose that the problem be corrected not by adding to the curriculum, but by subtracting from it. He continues: "Instead of more money, more teachers, more programs or more days of schooling, we should be reducing as much of the burdensome nonsense in public schools as possible. If a straightforward academic curriculum seems to work reasonably well in nearly every other major nation, the burden of proof is on those who say that it can't possibly be tried in America's unique society" (Unz, 1999, p. 7).

Some of this "nonsense" can be found in such "frivolous pursuits" as recess in elementary schools. For many elementary school students, recess and student play has been eliminated in favor of rigid, authoritarian, and regimented learning. Joy, relationships with others in the world and with the workings of the world become educational add-ons that threaten the authoritarian structure of education. Even kid pleasures seem to be under attack as "cheap frills" (Aronowitz,

1998, p. 6). And of course the main culprits, as defined by these elite voices of industry, are public schools and public education.

From the economic conservative and neoliberal perspective, educational assessment and world class standards must be linked to what it means to be successful in the new global economy. Through their efforts, they have created standard and assessment think tanks, such as Achieve Incorporated, a nonprofit organization created by a group of CEOs and the National Governors Association that was initially cochaired by IBM's chief executive officer, Louis Gerstner Jr., and Governor Tommy Thompson of Wisconsin (now secretary of Health and Human Services). Such institutions have produced reports like the National Education Goals Report, launched in 1989 as a result of the controversy over the 1983 report, *A Nation at Risk*. The Goals Report announces its mission as follows: "By the year 2000, American students will leave grades 4, 8, and 12 having demonstrated competency in challenging subject matter including English, mathematics, science, history, and geography; and every school in America will ensure that all students learn to use their minds well, so they may be prepared for responsible citizenship, further learning, and productive employment in our modern society (National Education Goals Report, 1991, p. 44).

By adopting what they like to call "world class standards," these corporate and business leaders are working to identify the post-Fordist skills that will be necessary for the workplace of the future (Mid-continent Regional Educational Laboratory, 1997). The clamor to define world class standards and skills has been linked to the presumed dominance of the United States in the world economy, and both economic conservatives and neoliberal policy makers have tied the development of these standards to American market competitiveness. Diane Ravitch, recognized as one of the darlings and chief architects of the modern standards movement, has stated the economic conservative and neoliberal rationale for standards: "Americans expect strict standards to govern the construction of buildings, bridges, highways, and tunnels; shoddy work would put lives at risk. They expect stringent standards to protect their drinking water, the food they eat, and the air they breathe . . . Standards are created because they improve the activity of life" (Ravitch, 1996, pp. 8–9). For conservative standards advocates like Ravitch, it seems that human educational standards can be equated with "quality control" in industry, assuring that the product conforms to industry standards.

Cultural Conservatives and the Crisis in Education

The national debate on education is now focused on truly important matters: mastering the basics . . . insisting on high standards and expectations; ensuring discipline in the classroom; conveying a grasp of our moral and political principles; and nurturing the character of our young.

—William Bennett

Why should we subsidize intellectual curiosity?

—Ronald Reagan

For cultural conservatives, the role of education is far more complex than simply producing workers who can compete in the global economy. Although they agree with the notion of education for the new workplace of the future, cultural conservatives argue that the real role of schools is to transmit a common individuality, a single American identity. They understand that education is political and moral activity, and they look to schooling as a site for the transmission of Judeo-Christian values, conservative morality, and a common American heritage. Thus they place great emphasis on manipulating symbols, such as the Bible and the national flag. Arguing for back-to-basics and privatization in education, these conservatives lament what they characterize as the Balkanization of American identity, and they abhor diversity as a threat to national unity and to a common American psyche. In the minds of cultural conservatives, loyalty, patriotism, and obedience to authority must be rigorously and uncompromisingly taught and can be accomplished by establishing a common curriculum (Hirsch, 1988). The cultural conservative movement also argues that schools must teach specific facts and that these facts must never be challenged, but must rather be accepted as immutable, permanent truth.

For cultural conservatives, the educational crisis is really little more than an indication of a larger crisis—a society that has fractured into diverse points of view, where civility has eroded and where standardized interpretations of the world have been forsaken for what they term a "moral relativism" (Bennett, 1988, p. 9), or values deficit. They blame the "excesses" of the 1960s for what they see as the current crisis in schools and society in general, going so far as to claim, as does P.Y. Pines, that "[f]or the half decade starting with the late 1960's, long established academic standards were abolished wholesale in a spasm reminiscent of the Red Guard's destructive rampage through China's classical cultural institutions" (as cited in Shor, 1992, p. 59).

Despondent over the loss of what they see as the "golden age of pedagogy," where skills and common, unquestioned values were the object of school curricula, cultural conservatives embrace back-to-basics as the panacea for what is wrong with America. One of the best indications of this thrust can be seen in a 1977 article that appeared in *Phi Delta Kappan*. Here, Ben Brodinsky characterized the back-to-basic conservative movement in terms that resonate even more loudly today. According to Brodinsky, back-to-basics proposes, among other things, that the school day be devoted solely to reading, writing, and arithmetic and that phonics be the method used to teach reading. Textbooks should not display "nontraditional values" in sex, religion, or politics, and any criticism of national

identity and "American values" should not be tolerated. Pedagogy is to be teacher-centered with stern discipline, not child-centered with student autonomy. Frequent drills and skill-based curricula, along with teaching facts to students, should be the norm. Academic criteria for promotion must be advocated in place of social promotion. There should be no "frills" in education, such as sex education or controversial discussions of current affairs. The school day should be filled with fewer electives and more required courses in the *basics*. And the elimination of experimental and innovative courses and methods for value clarification, critical discussion, and inquiry should be purged from educational corridors. Finally, back-to-basics, both then and now, advocates the return of patriotism to schools, along with religious instruction (Brodinsky, 1977, pp. 87–94).

Cultural conservatives call for a curricular restoration of authority in schools whereby teachers are to be colonial administrators of an educational plantation. And the same themes that underlie their calls for curriculum restoration can also be found in the attack on what they term "secular humanism." As U.S. Senator Jesse Helms commented not long ago: "When the U.S. Supreme Court prohibited children from participating in voluntary prayers in public schools, the conclusion is inescapable that the Supreme Court not only violated the right of free exercise of religion for all Americans, it also established a national religion in the United States—the religion of secular humanism" (as cited in Duncan, 1979, p. 92).

The movement today toward vouchers for religious schools, home schooling, and the effort to abolish the teaching of evolution in schools has its roots in the Religious Right's efforts to place religion squarely within the sphere of public education. According to cultural conservative Tim LaHaye, "Today public education is so humanistic that it is both anti-Catholic and anti-Protestant—because it is anti-God. . . . The chaos of today's public education system is in direct proportion to its religious obsession with humanism" (LaHaye, 1980, p. 68).

By defining education as training, moral indoctrination, authoritarianism, religious instruction, and back-to-basics, we can easily see why the national debate over standards, from the cultural conservative point of view, is tied to advocating a calibrating apparatus that measures students' progress as the ability to memorize and regurgitate preordained and prescribed facts and data, exercise skills in isolation, digest jingoistic curricula without questioning, read phonetically, and obey authority. William Bennett, the arch–cultural conservative and former educational "czar," stated the cultural conservative position clearly: "We neglected and denied much of the best in American education. . . . We simply stopped doing the right things and allowed an assault on intellectual and moral standards" (Bennett, 1988, p. 9). For Bennett and his cultural conservative cohorts, the assault on intellectual and moral standards has led schools away from their mission—indoctrination and inculcation. These conservatives now rejoice at what they feel is a return to the "real" purpose of education—they see their judgment day as having arrived.

Critical Pedagogy and the Progressive Postmodernist Position

The problem of education in its relation to the direction of social change is all one with the problem of finding out what democracy means in its total range of concrete applications: domestic, international, religious, cultural economic, and political. . . . The trouble . . . is that we have taken democracy for granted; we have thought and acted as if our forefathers had founded it once and for all.

—John Dewey

Radical pedagogy and progressive postmodernism, as pronounced and defined by Brazilian educator Paulo Freire in his landmark book *Pedagogy of the Oppressed* (1970), attaches a completely different and contrary meaning and purpose to education than do cultural conservative, economic conservative, and neoliberal notions of education. For Freire and his progressive postmodern contemporaries, education is not an impartial act, but a conscious political act of freedom and love aimed at subjective exploration and self-reflection, and it should be grounded in an ethical format that embraces human beings, their historicity and their search for emancipation. Much like W.E.B. DuBois, who early on commented that the role of education "is not to make carpenters out of men, but men out of carpenters" (DuBois, 1924, pp. 51), Freire envisioned education and its goals as the eradication of human exploitation, the abolition of human manipulation, the elimination of avarice and greed, the rejection of insipid individualism devoid of individuality, and the rejection of racial, class, and sexual discrimination and exploitation—not capitalist competitiveness. Freire himself was very clear in this regard: "My point of view is that of 'the wretched of the earth', of the excluded" (Freire, 1998b, p. 22).

Radical pedagogy believes that teacher preparation must not be married to training but instead should be attached to a search for personal and social meaning within historical and contemporary understanding. And these teachers believe that knowledge can never be conveyed or transmitted as mere facts and information but must be invented and reinvented through discursive inquiry and a problem-posing curriculum that seeks to help citizens make sense of their cognitive and emotional lives and the world within which they live.

This does not mean that these postmodern theoretical positions define basic skills as unimportant or hold that they should not be taught; rather, their proponents argue that the key is how these skills are taught, the context within which they are taught, and how they are incorporated in the service of enabling the human being to think and act critically. Teaching skills in the context of reasoning, where emotional intelligence and rational thinking are reconnected in the pursuit of intelligent activity orchestrated and incorporated in the service of a problem-posing curriculum that is based on inquiry and discovery, is much different than teaching skills in rote isolation along with indoctrination in the form of culturally legitimized facts disconnected from meaning.

Where conservatives and neoliberals attempt to regulate the world of students through standardization, indoctrination, and the removal of discourse and autonomy, radical pedagogy and progressive postmodernist educational claims assert that education must be interested in the consciousness of human beings and a determination to help them "read the world" through interaction and dialogue (Freire, 1970). Postformalism would advocate teaching ethics *without* indoctrination, in a context where students are encouraged to forge their thinking skills in the fires of controversy and critical scrutiny. Again, Freire states this position clearly: "Problem-posing education affirms men and women as beings in the process of becoming—as unfinished, uncompleted human beings in and with a likewise unfinished reality. The unfinished character of human beings and the transformational character of reality necessitate that education be an ongoing activity" (Freire, 1976, p. 77).

Radical Pedagogy, Progressive Postmodernism, and the Educational Critique of Standards and Assessment

Let us view understanding not as a state of possession of knowledge, but one of enablement. When we understand something, we not only possess certain information about it but are enabled to do certain things with that knowledge.

—David Perkins

As pointed out earlier, in the view of radical pedagogues and progressive postmodernists who embrace democracy and the need for a democratized self as the focus of education, schooling must be linked to what it means to be human. Currently, preparation in school is defined solely as preparation for work, and this preparation for work is sold to the public as preparation for life. Radical pedagogy and progressive postmodernist positions disagree vehemently with this predication and posit the contrary—that preparation in school should be preparation for life, and preparation for life will, by its very nature, enable students to be prepared for the exigencies of work. Certainly rational production is a necessity for human endeavors, but a critical and democratically committed citizenry, they argue, is much more capable of rational production than an unconscious manipulated citizenry grafted onto corporate agendas. They argue that schools should be centers for utopian thinking, laboratories of wonderment, and environments of inquiry available to all students. Yet, progressive postmodernists argue, the unfortunate reality is that amidst all the talk of educational reform, schools are still seeped in the past and thus can do little to help children create and invent their future or the future of society. Because of their emphasis on education as liberation, progressive postmodernists have constructed powerful critiques of economic conservative, neoliberal, and cultural conservative arguments for education and educational standards.

The Standards Debate as Social Prevarication and Myth

Perhaps the greatest tragedy of modern man is his domination by the force of myths and his manipulation by organized advertising, ideological or otherwise. Gradually, without even realizing the loss, he relinquishes his capacity for choice; he is expelled from the orbit of decisions. Ordinary men do not perceive the task of the time; the latter are interpreted by an "elite" and presented in the form of recipes and prescriptions. And when men try to save themselves by following the prescriptions, they drown in leveling anonymity, without hope and without faith, domesticated and adjusted.

—Paulo Freire

Human beings seek to exist in the world, to make sense of their peculiar relationships with external and internal reality. They seek dialogue and relationships with others in order to claim their humanness and become free from the external and internal bonds that bind them. Standards, claim progressive postmodernists, are part and parcel of the sickness, the cognitive dis-ease that is rampant in education today precisely because they reinforce the meaningless of education—giving meaning only to what education can do for one materially, not psychologically or subjectively. They become little more than a prerequisite for accepting and adjusting to a market society.

To begin with, radical pedagogy and progressive postmodern educational theory, hereinafter referred to as *postformalism* (Kincheloe, Steinberg, and Villaverde, 1999), argues that tests and testing do far more than simply seek to measure academic performance or basic skills. From a postformalist point of view, standards and assessment as put forth by both economic and cultural conservatives give a false illusion—an ideological myth of meritocracy and objectivity that really operates deceitfully as technologies of power and control (Foucault, 1977). Standards operate as part of a modernist project, dissecting thinking into minute fragments and then testing the fragments separately from the whole. They also are part of a monocultural or Eurocentric and androcentric tradition that places value on sociocentric truths and cultural claims to superiority.

Postformalism would argue that conservative standards, hereinafter referred to as *universal standards*, are culturally biased, gender discriminative, and class-based sorting and classifying mechanisms that surreptitiously seek to motivate students by holding out the promise of extrinsic material rewards if the standards are met: better jobs, college entrance, higher incomes, and better employment. Universal standards create a false ideology of "fairness" that proclaims that individual effort is the controlling factor in determining success, regardless of one's social class, sex, race, cultural background, or particular place in the social system. Postformalism argues that the current standards debate actually serves to suffocate a truly genuine dialogue about the purpose of education, about the meaning of history and the identity of human beings as subjects seeking their freedom in the enterprise of life; instead, the debate demagogues and couches the controversy over schooling as market competitiveness, global production, better goods and services, and strong national identity.

Unfortunately, and yet understandably, the notion of universal standards resonates with many parents, especially minority parents and the economically and culturally disenfranchised, precisely because they want their children to become successful in a racially and sexually biased class society where wages, for the majority of people, have scarcely risen in more than twenty-five years (Sklar, 1999). And as new jobs emerge and old ones die out, education is increasingly looked upon by our citizenry as a way to endure rapid changes in economic life—to get ahead; education is a way out, or at the very least, a way to stay even and survive. Lower wages, unemployment, and jobs relocated to third-world countries have created economic insecurity, misery, and uncertainty among American citizens, as people scramble and try to avoid becoming the next victim of reorganization, reengineering, downsizing, or restructuring or being caught in the undertow as businesses disappear, merge, and are bought out overnight. The Right exploits these fears and economic uncertainties with the rhetoric of universal standards, falsely arguing that if we only had higher, more normative standards, education would prepare everyone for the "new world order" and ensure that security and equality would be reinstituted in mental and material life. The message is clear: Don't change life, change standards.

The Illusion of Individualistic Meritocracy

The universal standards debate disguises the way that history constructs meaning and defines opportunity by eternalizing standards behind false images of meritocracy, scientific rationality, and truth. By giving illusion to the mythology of meritocracy, standards serve to marginalize, discourage, and disenfranchise, precisely because they propose that those who fail to live up to these technicist standards are individual failures and do not belong in education, that they would be better served in vocational programs, or that perhaps they should not be educated at all. The failure to meet normative standards becomes defined as an individual problem devoid of social context and culpability. The debate refuses to recognize and discuss socioeconomic issues such as crumbling school infrastructures, overcrowded schools, inadequate teaching resources, dys-

functional teacher training programs, the clandestine nature of teaching in isolation without mentorship or guidance, the shortage of qualified teachers (especially among minority communities), poverty, dysfunctional families, the lack of early childhood nutrition, health care, or preschool, low salaries, the dismal state of parental involvement, poverty, low wages, and the economic and political arrangements of postmodern capitalist society that, if they do not create these conditions, certainly allow them to exist. Nor does the debate recognize intellectual diversity, cultural distinctions, epistemological processes and concerns, language disparities and differences, or gender discrimination.

Education is a uniquely public and cooperative activity undertaken in concert with others for the purpose of reading the world, forging loving relationships, living a productive life, and developing personal and social understanding. Yet universal standards create a scarcity mentality—a win-lose situation wherein competition and the ruthless landscape of grade acquisition shape educational discourse and practice under false claims of meritocracy. Standardized tests base themselves on and reinforce an ideology of insipid individualism, where others exist only as rungs on a ladder for one to "get over," to compete with and measure oneself against. Thus, a uniquely public, collaborative activity—*learning*—becomes a privatized, competitive activity—*getting good grades*. For this reason, universal standards are antithetical to human agency and authenticity; they are testimonies to class-, race-, and sex-based privilege and the objectification and reification of human intellectual endeavor. They tear asunder all forms of educational community, pitting students against students, teachers against teachers, and citizens against citizens. Universal standards rigidly enforce hierarchies, acquiescence, and submission in place of cooperation, collaborative problem-solving and shared experience and dialogue. They operate as an ideological moral authority in the hands of an immoral constituency.

Furthermore, the current standards debate gives the false illusion that "we are all in this together" and that the standards proposed are objective, fair, and not culturally, racially, or sexually biased. The debate does this by couching rhetoric in words such as "we," "us," "our," and "together." The discussion provides an individualistic rationale that serves to temper resentment when somebody else gets into college, or gets the "good" job. "After all, *we're* all working under the same standards, aren't *we*? If you just would have done better!" Universal standards impose an "unnatural selection" on citizens by proclaiming their *naturalness*, and in doing so they ideologically manipulate the public with the falsity of their own mythology. All of this serves to surreptitiously beguile students, teachers, and community into believing that there is no political agenda, no advocacy of cultural norms, no prevalence of hierarchical classifying and sorting—that stan-

dards are a neutral, generic conception and operation applicable equally and fairly in the interests of everyone.

Standards and the False Claim to Universality and Objectivity

Human beings come to educational sites with different cultures, backgrounds, opportunities, and constraints. Postformalism alleges that rationalistic universal standards are really sociohistorical constructs, and that at this juncture, they are peculiar constructs allied to the needs of a particular socioeconomic system—postmodern capitalism. Postformalists argue that universal standards are little more than dominant-based claims, scientific, mechanical formulas and regulations that educational elites proclaim as immutable and non-transformatory, but which in actuality are socially and historically created. By masquerading as objective science, standards become a tool for those in power to impose conformity and ideological servitude on people and communities; they become what Foucault termed a "technology of power" (Foucault, 1977)— that is, a way to decimate difference in the interest of privilege and ideological domination by instrumentalist policing. The current standard debate masks difference by failing to acknowledge the diverse epistemological ways of knowing and perceiving the world. Difference, be it cultural, gender based, economic, or otherwise, is sacrificed to a debilitating reductionism that must locate itself within the modernistic conception of scientific, rational, Newtonian thought.

By casting standards as a form of scientific "truth," as a universal techno-rationality, cultural conservatives and neoliberals furtively promise to abolish cultural and class differences by imposing a universal, scientific norm. Imposing uncritical acceptance and passivity through universal assertions of truth, standardized tests cloak prevarication in the clothes of veracity. They foment the idea that there is a preestablished, nonhistorical, universal standard for acceptance into the community of human beings, and in so doing, they attempt to maintain a passive public that refuses to challenge the historicity of cultural norms and the social context and construction of knowledge. Furthermore, current standards teach the hegemonic lesson of obedience by offering ecumenical rules and preordained procedures that must be followed in order for both teachers and students to adapt. Thus, they reduce education to a mere recipe that must be followed, as opposed to an artful process that must be created.

Standards as Instruments of Technocratic Control

Teaching is an act of love, a performance art involving creativity and intelligence. Yet, postformalism argues, universal standards hold students and teachers hostage to an ideology and practice of inauthentic learning and being—a loveless, antiseptic relationship between students and teachers, a

false dualism between the world as an object to be understood and the knower seeking to understand. For this reason standards serve as a straightjacket that binds both the heart and the mind, for they impose teaching as an act of functional, instrumental control—of technological device— not an act of compassion, caring, and love. Standards become a means of covertly managing people and knowledge for private ends. John Fiske reminds us of this when he notes:

> Knowledge is never neutral; it never exists in an empiricist, objective relationship to the real. Knowledge is power, and the circulation of knowledge is part of the social distribution of power. . . . The first is to control the "real," to reduce reality to the knowable, which entails producing it as a discursive construct whose arbitrariness and inadequacy are disguised as far as possible. The second struggle is to have this discursively (and therefore socio-politically) constructed reality accepted as truth by those whose interests may not necessarily be served by accepting it. (Fiske, 1989, pp. 149–150)

Critical consciousness and education for freedom ask men and women to critically examine and scrutinize their social order, not to blindly accept it—to expunge that which oppresses them and embrace that which promises to liberate them. Yet, postformalists would argue, universal standards operate as way of maintaining the inequitable social order, a way of controlling both students and teachers and the production line they work on so that they might blindly and obediently reproduce their own oppression.

Standards as they are currently designed are also a way of controlling, chloroforming, and policing curricula to ensure that what is taught conforms to what the cultural conservative and economic conservative elites feel is important. Teachers are mandated to *teach to the test*, and those who do not are labeled "maladjusted," in need of remediation, and punitively dealt with accordingly. In Delaware, for example, 20 percent of the educational evaluation of teachers will be based on whether students make "progress" within one year with a particular teacher, regardless of whether students have come to the class ready or prepared to learn (George Bush, Speech on education, CNN, September 2, 1999).

"Accountability" becomes the buzz word for those who embrace the need for universal standards. Yet the accountability that is advocated is a one-sided, individualistic accountability, not a shared, socially collaborative accountability, a mutual accountability between socioeconomic arrangements and individual effort and responsibility. Under the rubric of "accountability," individual teachers and their students become individually blamed for the poor academic performance of individual students, regardless of the students' history of achievement, their attitudes regarding learning, or their readiness to learn. George W. Bush made this position quite clear in his

elitist and cynical dismissal of social accountability and culpability when he smugly stated, "Pigment and poverty need not determine performance" (George Bush, Speech on education, CNN, September 2, 1999). The rhetoric appears equitable, responsible, and logical because it seeks to remove issues of race, gender, and social accountability from the debate while putting forth the hidden claim that we all operate on a level playing field.

Universal standards also impose psychological fear among educational community members while simultaneously de-skilling them by turning lesson plans into instrumentalist recipes and antiseptic and generic teaching formulas. The Mid-continent Regional Educational Laboratory, for example, is just one of many think tanks that now have lesson plans available on-line that are linked to any state standard (Mid-continent Regional Educational Laboratory, 1999), further de-skilling teachers by separating them from the conception of their labor and reducing them to simply technical instruments—objects in the service of education as training and slaves to the state standards.

In the United States it was once proclaimed that education is a human right, a Jeffersonian legacy of a common democracy. Yet universal standards insidiously operate as instruments of power, secretly seeking to destroy public schools through economic strangulation in favor of private and religious schools and vouchers. They do this ideologically by feeding the mythological claim that public schools and public school teachers are failing, that they are not living up to the universal standards that elites have imposed. The former president of the Xerox Corporation made this point quite vigorously when he stated, "At a time when our preeminent role in the world economy is in jeopardy, there are few social problems more telling in their urgency. Public education has put this country at a terrible disadvantage" (Kearns & Doyle, 1988, p. 1).

In Florida, universal standards are currently being used to belittle and destroy public schools and the students and teachers who work in them in a particularly disturbing manner. For example, school-by-school report cards have recently been released that assign each public school an A, B, C, D, or F based largely on how the schools and their teachers and students measured up to the state's predetermined standards for competency on the reading and mathematics portion of the Florida Comprehensive Achievement Test. Released on June 24, 1999, these school scores serve as an attention-getting aspect of the new statewide accountability system, and they foster in the public's mind the notion that public schools are failing both students and the public at large ("De Facto National Standards," 1999). They intimate that teacher unions are dismissive of accountability and the idea that teachers should be held responsible and suggest that teachers are interested only in higher wages and benefits for teachers, regardless of their level of competence. The debate rarely focuses on the fact that Florida schools serve 75,000 students who are foreign born, many of them living in situations of high poverty ("De Facto National Standards," 1999). From conservative perspectives, pointing out such facts is simply offering a cultural and class-based *excuse* for individual failure and thus more apologies for lack of accountability and social responsibility.

According to the school reform measures backed by Governor Jeb Bush and passed by the Florida state legislature, the state will now offer vouchers worth $4,000 each to students attending Florida public schools that receive Fs two times in four years. The students may use the vouchers to pay tuition at private or religious schools (*Education Week*, May 5, 1999). Such policies will in turn take more monies from public coffers—bleeding the public schools, economically strangling them, further reducing their ability to function and then hypocritically blaming them for low achievement. This is how universal standards have become an insidious tool, an instrumentalist weapon in the political-conservative fight to dismantle public education by stigmatizing schools and those who teach in them while simultaneously withholding funds and allowing them to hemorrhage to death.

Publicizing test scores is another attempt to shame teachers, to humiliate them, to let low-income and minority students see themselves as incompetent or less educable, while teachers are told that they are dysfunctional and in need of remedial adjustment. This tactic also serves to propagandize and concretize in the mind of the public the idea that unions, in this case teacher unions, are to blame for the problem—that tenure, collective action, or job security rights shield poor teachers and prevent principals, now called CEOs in the vernacular of privateers, from hiring good teachers and firing bad ones. The idea is to cajole the public into an uncritical belief that unions tie reformers' hands, stand in the way of progress, and act in students' worst interests. Certainly this chapter will not serve as an apologist for all that goes on in public schools, from the way they are managed to the way they are operated. However, the universal standards debate is a clear attempt to belittle, rather than intervene and fix, one of the last vestiges of public life in America today—public schools.

Universal standards, prescribed more like mechanical operations and procedures and stripped of all humanness, also become unconscious, ideological features of instrumentalism and technological hegemony. They become the extrinsic reward structures that children in the early years ideologically internalize, reward structures that are echoed later in the economic bonus and incentive systems that will eventually be offered to them to induce them to produce more, to fulfill the future needs of the capitalist workforce. Corporate society needs this psychological, ideological internalization process to begin at an early age in order to prepare citizens for the competitive rigors and inequality of

capitalist life. Cast in this role, universal standards operate in the interests of an authoritarian construction of unconscious assumptions and patterns, as well as strengthening an insidious individualism so necessary to capitalism's material and ideological survival. They become the equivalent of Adam Smith's invisible hand, guiding our privatized self-serving interests within a community of rapacious materialism and operating to diminish relationships, to foment public distrust and disharmony, and to inculcate the ideology of competition within the constructs of the human consciousness. Because of this, they are a form of theoretical, techno-rational control in the hands of a bureaucracy devoted to the desires and needs of a privileged few.

Standards as Big Business

Standards are also big business. The math and reading lists now linked to many state standards have a huge impact on what states can buy with citizens' tax money. The state of California, for example, which recently approved new state standards in reading and math, will spend more than 1 billion dollars of public monies over the next four years on textbooks for classrooms, purchasing texts from corporations such as Houghton Mifflin, Harcourt Brace, and McDougal Little. Yet of this amount, the $250 million spent each year can *only* be spent on textbooks that the state has aligned with the new standards. School districts in California may only spend 30 percent of their grant monies on texts that are not on the state-approved list. And these textbook adoptions are made by a select few, not as a result of a lively community debate or critical examination by the teachers who are forced to use these texts. According to Judy Anderson, the president of the California Math Council, a group that represents 10,000 math educators in California: "If we define mathematics as simply following the rules, that's what this textbook adoption brings about. There's not any thinking going on here" ("California Approves Textbooks," 1999, p. 10). Corporations love the new standards, and so do the nanny state and federal governments that promise that the costs associated with textbook adoption are socialized while corporations and their stockholders privatize the enormous profits.

Standards and the Definition of Intelligence

Critical inquiry, critical perception, and critical consciousness assist human beings to engage the world, to see the world as an object independent of themselves that is capable of being known, changed, and understood in relationship to themselves. Education is responsible for the development of this critical consciousness and engagement, not the rote memorization and indoctrination of universally declared facts and behavioral norms.

As previously discussed, standardized tests, as presently constructed, are based on assessing whether students have digested a set of universally designated facts. And facts are impor-

tant to conservatives, for as Walter Feinberg has noted: "Facts—uninterpreted naked facts—are a sign that the national identity is intact and that local cultural meanings and aspirations are under control. When facts are challenged, when every ethnic and racial group wants its own facts taught in schools, when there are feminist facts, Afro-American facts, and gay facts—then conservatives worry that the school can no longer be counted on to transmit a unified national identity" (Feinberg, 1993, pp. 86–87).

Universal standards liken the intelligent person to a *Jeopardy* contestant: a person who is a repository of facts and information. Intelligence becomes commensurate with having information and basic skills, not with using information and skills to gain knowledge and then empowering oneself through its use. For conservatives, any counterinterpretation of facts, any critical inquiry, questioning, or interrogation of these facts threatens the single conservative national unity, that is, it threatens those in power by stripping naked their moral and mythological political claims about what ideology is, what its implications are, and how it operates to preserve inequality and the status quo.

And of course, universal standards serve another more insidious role: they help to define and reinforce an undemocratic notion of intelligence based on solely Cartesian scientific, rationalistic claims to achievement. The notion of multiple intelligences, as developed by Howard Gardner, which acknowledges that there are multiple ways of knowing including indigenous knowledges, women's consciousness and cognitive processes, emotional intelligence, and so on, are discarded in favor of a logical-mathematical, cognitive intelligence. Any deviation from the universal standard becomes a deviation from the norm, and the rationalistic, Cartesian norm becomes defined as what it means to be human, to be intelligent.

What Might Critical Thinking Standards Look Like and How Might We Link Them to Accountability?

The object of education is to prepare the young to educate themselves throughout their lives.
—**Robert Maynard Hutchins**

There are no eternal facts as there are no absolute truths.
—**Friedrich Nietzsche**

Although postformalism is critical of the current conservative standards debate for the reasons discussed above, postformalists also recognize the need for *authentic* standards to assess and measure progress among students. They too believe that teachers and students should be held accountable and responsible, but they also believe that society itself must be held accountable—that accountability must be shared between individuals and the social structures they live in and that both the objective and subjective conditions of society must be understood to create this shared accountability.

Postformalism is interested in assessing *how* students think, not *what* they think, and they want standards and accountability tied to what it means to be a critical thinker. Postformalists are also committed to helping students develop the ability to assess themselves, the ability to develop and apply criteria to their thinking in the interest of self-improvement and continuous lifelong learning. They begin with the human being—looking to define what it means to be human and intelligent—and then they develop "standards" to assess this humanness and intelligence. These *authentic* standards don't abandon the teaching of basic skills. On the contrary, postformalists seek to teach basic skills within an environment of inquiry that enhances and assesses critical and creative thinking—not simply to teach basic skills in isolation as repetitive, boring activities. They are concerned that skills are best learned and internalized through their use in harmony with the construction of collaborative and individual projects.

Teachers who teach for critical thinking are interested in developing their students' capacity to solve problems, develop empathy and humility, make rational decisions, and continuously assess their thinking to determine its strengths, weaknesses, and limitations. These teachers seek to imbue in their students a sense of imagination and curiosity that calls on them to seek complex answers to complex questions in a world with others—to approach learning as an act of "figuring out what they don't know."

They are particularly interested in helping their students develop effective modes of thinking in the cognitive areas of abstract, systematic, evaluative, and collaborative thinking, and they are aware of the affective dimension of emotional intelligence and its dialectical relationship to creative and critical thought. They endeavor to create a curriculum that helps their students subject what they think they know to critical scrutiny in the interest of achieving the best results, the best decisions, the best thinking, and the best solutions to human problems. They understand that the real curriculum is life, and they work with multiple intelligences and offer varied and interdisciplinary opportunities for students to develop these intelligences. Finally, critical and creative teachers are concerned with all of the above as it affects good judgment, innovation, cooperative living, collaborative problem-solving, and developing a more productive and happier life—not simply making better machines or consumer products.

The following are just examples of what *some* critical and creative thinking standards might look like; they are in no way meant to be definitive or universal. As you will see, they identify what we want our students to do, and so they can be assessed only through performance or portfolio evaluation. They are not offered as a checklist or processes that must be taught in isolation, but as the type of mental processes that critical thinking might employ when solving problems and making decisions.

- Evaluate data and evidence
- Compare and contrast similarities and differences
- Explore actions, decisions, and conclusions of oneself and others
- Evaluate actions, decisions, and solutions of oneself and others
- Clarify generalizations
- Reason inductively, from the particular to the abstract
- Avoid overgeneralizations and oversimplifications
- Recognize the logic of points of view
- Recognize arguments, analyze them, and then evaluate them
- Distinguish between relevant and irrelevant information and data
- Identify sources of information and develop criteria for determining the reliability of these sources
- Develop one's own viewpoint, perspective, and outlook
- Think about one's thinking in the interest of transformative metacognition
- Listen critically to others
- Transfer abstract insights to everyday life
- Reason interdisciplinarily and synthesize subject-matter insights
- Recognize decisions, analyze them, and evaluate them
- Identify, develop, evaluate, and apply criteria to ideas, products, and performances of oneself and others
- Make informed decisions by examining options and anticipating consequences of actions

- Recognize and describe systems and their interdependence
- Work effectively in groups to accomplish goals
- Reason historically, conceiving of places, times, and conditions different from one's own
- Recognize the influence of diverse cultural perspectives on human thought and behavior
- Develop independent thinking and an investigative orientation
- Develop intellectual empathy
- Develop intellectual humility and an insight into egocentric thinking
- Develop intellectual imagination and curiosity
- Develop intellectual efficacy and confidence in one's reasoning abilities
- Develop a tolerance for ambiguity
- Develop intellectual perseverance and discipline when confronting obstacles and problems
- Develop intellectual courage
- Develop intellectual civility when dialoguing
- Develop intellectual integrity

Discussing, questioning, and dialoguing about these and other critical thinking standards would serve to recast the debate that has defined teaching as simply the transmission of information and ideas. Such a discussion would embrace and call attention to the fact that the act of education is at once an act of communication and dialogue in search of significance and meaning. Critical thinking standards

would allow teachers to engage in teaching as an act of love and creativity—as opposed to an act of instrumentality and technological control. And of course, since critical thinking develops and builds character, these standards would help students manage their lives as opposed to having them managed, to author their existence as opposed to having their existence authored, and to govern their personal and social behavior as opposed to having their behavior governed.

These critical thinking *processes* (I use this term to differentiate between these ideas as *processes* and these ideas as *skills*), can be seen as distinctly different from *basic skills*. Both are important and both should be tested. Yet many teachers have never thought about the difference between basic skills and critical thinking processes. Understanding that these processes are uniquely different from what we are told are basic skills is the first step in understanding how they might be taught and assessed. It affords us a starting place from which to dialogue, discuss, and question the development of more authentic standards and assessment.

Developing a Public Language of Literacy and Tools for Assessment

In teaching for thinking, we are not only interested in how many answers students know, but also in knowing how to behave when they don't know. Intelligent behavior is performed in response to questions and problems the answers to which are not immediately known. We are interested in observing how students produce knowledge rather than how they merely reproduce knowledge. The critical attribute of intelligent human beings is not only having information, but knowing how to act on it.

—**Art Costa**

Much has been written within the last ten years about authentic changes in critical thinking assessment tools and techniques—from the use of portfolio assessment to performance assessment. And there is no doubt that some of the most exciting work in authentic assessment today is coming from those who are using it and will use it—classroom teachers. Authentic assessment tools such as reading portfolios, video portfolios, journals, and thinking and listening portfolios can all call upon students to assess their own thinking and the work they are doing while providing the classroom teacher with a documented method for authentic assessment of critical thinking that meets the needs of parents and the public, who correctly search for some accountability in education. This has the dual benefit of allowing students to take responsibility for their learning while at the same time freeing the teacher to become a facilitator of thinking as opposed to a routinized clerk. Teachers who utilize authentic assessment techniques to assess critical thinking know that they are based upon *authentic learning* that asks students to probe the cognitive and affective dimensions of how they come to understand what they think they understand. Furthermore, with authentic assessment, teachers, stu-

dents, and parents can observe student performance and draw conclusions about their literacy from these performances, thereby enabling them to work with students in the interest of continual self-improvement. This process can vary from observing the range of reading and writing skills that students employ to ascertaining what these performances show us as teachers. By observing students' strategies and what they do when they read and write, for example, teachers can deduce students' attitudes and dispositions and help them develop emotional and affective dimensions of intelligence. Authentic assessment also allows educators to continually improve their own instructional techniques, to collaborate as intellectuals as they find out more about how students learn, to integrate this knowledge and attempt to develop their capacity to think critically about their curriculum and how they might work with students to develop knowledge.

How we assess students and what we assess virtually drives, shapes, and influences what happens within the classroom. Assessment shapes the curriculum as much as the curriculum shapes assessment. Understanding the underlying assumptions and inferences that guide the current conservative approach to assessment and contrasting this with an *active literacy*, or postformalist approach to learning and teaching, is essential for increasing our understanding of how students learn. What's more, we must make our postformal positions on assessment understandable and accessible to parents and the community. We must feel compelled to denude the mythology employed by the elite merchants of prevarication and work with parents to construct a vision of what it means to be *actively literate* and educated in today's society—what it means to think critically. This means that the education of children develops simultaneously with the education of parents and communities, as we collaboratively learn to forge a partnership and dialogue within our communities regarding intelligence and learning. We must look for venues to discuss new ideas, whether it is in our unions, our churches, mosques, or temples, at the grocery store, or in the mall. We can never allow the mythology of market-driven forces to script educational theatre. Instead we must struggle to pierce the veil of social and political mendacity and proclaim the conservative standards debate for what it really is—a mythology, a prescription and recipe that is not in the interests of either ourselves or our children.

We also must document students' performances and provide open, public meetings and forums where parents and students are invited to engage in a dialogue with their children about learning and assessment. This will assist parents in understanding what it truly means to be intelligent and how to provide for their children's intellectual growth outside of school. All of this will be essential if we are to rupture the hegemony of the standard mythology and institutionalize authentic procedures for student assessment.

Finally, it is obvious that one cannot assess what one does not understand. We should not take for granted that teachers themselves have been exposed to progressive dialogues regarding intelligence, critical thinking, constructivism, multiple theories of education, or postformalist principles regarding learning, motivation, and teaching. In fact, in light of the disconsolate state of teacher education programs and the demagogic media-driven debate regarding assessment, we probably should assume that the opposite is true.

Similarly, as stated earlier, students must be taught how to assess their own thinking and the thinking of others so they can become life-long learners. They must be motivated to see the logic of what they are studying and to see the relevance of education to their daily lives. Helping students find relevant significance and meaning within a community of learning will not only help them become lifelong learners but will also enable them to monitor their thinking in the interests of self-correction and critical reflection. Students and teachers must understand that *assessing is learning* and *learning is assessing*—that these are not separate and distinct activities, as they have been characterized, but lifelong, ongoing activities.

The table at right can be used to compare and contrast what I refer to as *inauthentic standards assessment* with *authentic standards assessment*.

The implications of these different theories of literacy on assessment, teaching, learning, curriculum devel-

TABLE 1
Comparison of Inauthentic Standards and
Assessment with Authentic Standards and Assessment

Inauthentic Standards and Assessment	Authentic Standards and Assessment
1. Based on isolated items of learning that can be counted and measured	1. Based on orchestrating items of learning for a particular purpose or goal, or to solve a particular problem
2. Focuses on "getting the right answer"	2. Focuses on not just getting the right answer but on uncovering the processes one goes through to get answers
3. Provides a "quick fix" numerical understanding	3. Long-term. Based on insights about what it means to learn and teach
4. Focuses on the trivial aspects of learning	4. Focuses on assessing the broad aspects of literacy, or "the whole person"
5. Skill driven	5. Based on testing skills in the context of critical thinking and problem solving
6. Looks at the surface features of students' performances	6. Looks at the totality of students' performances and serves as a guide for future growth
7. Abstracted and divorced from the real lives of students	7. Relevant and stimulating, motivating students to question and discover
8. Provides misleading information and direction for further learning and teaching	8. Provides complete information that helps to guide and strengthen the curriculum and to provide direction for both teachers and students for further learning and teaching
9. Noninterdisciplinary, failing to help students transfer insights into their own lives	9. Interdisciplinary, helping students to transfer subject insights into their own lives while enabling them to see how disciplines, subjects, and what they are learning relate to each other
10. Provides no understanding for students, teachers, or parents of what it means to be intelligent or educated in today's society	10. Serves as a guide for parents, teachers, and students as to the meaning of intelligence and how intelligence can be cultivated, fostered, and learned
11. Of little use to students, providing them with no direction or standards by which to develop the art of self-assessment	11. Describes literacy as self-assessment and provides students with a profile of their work so that they might develop standards by which to improve their thinking through transformative metacognition

(continues)

TABLE 1   *(continued)*

Inauthentic Standards and Assessment	Authentic Standards and Assessment
12. Fails to account for or assess emotional intelligence or attitudes and dispositions of learning	12. Understands that attitudes and dispositions of learning and emotional intelligence are synergistically related to what it means to be intelligent
13. Serves to control teachers and students, what they teach, and what they think	13. Helps teachers and students control themselves, what they teach, and what they think
14. Tests disciplines	14. Tests disciplined thinking
15. Fails to account for differences in race, gender, and socioeconomic class and refuses to acknowledge the social construction of knowledge	15. Understands that knowledge is socially constructed and conceives of differences as positive
16. Nondialogical	16. Based on communication and dialogue
17. Looks at students as objects or raw materials to be produced and worked on	17. Looks at students as subjects in the process of identity formation
18. Conceives of education as a result only	18. Conceives of education as a process that produces results

opment, and praxis are paramount and cannot be ignored. A reading and writing social studies classroom, for example, that labors under the paradigm of inauthentic assessment or *passive literacy* might ask students to read short texts, answer simple questions, select from multiple-choice answers, and supply missing words in close exercises. The implications of passive literacy are explicit: teachers spend less time on subjects not tested, lecture to students rather than dialogue with them, and are unwilling to stray from the mandated curricula for fear of being humiliated, penalized, and ostracized. As such, passive literacy builds on the model of teacher as all-knowing subject and student as spectator.

In those classrooms working under a paradigm of authentic assessment or *active literacy*, students might be asked to read texts with depth and interest, thereby seeking to understand points of view and assumptions, and to see how people arrive at conclusions and decide to act in a world with others. Students would be animated to problematize their learning and create and answer complex questions that call on multiple intelligences and a host of cognitive and affective abilities in the service of creatively accomplishing a project, or recognizing and solving relevant real-life problems; they would learn to become *participants* in their learning. Multiple choice or limited-response examinations might not be abandoned, but their use would be minimal and only applied to test students' understanding of important basic skills, while performance and portfolio assessment would be recruited in the service of assessing the development of critical and creative thinking and communication processes, along with students' actual application of knowledge and basic skills.

Conclusion

A school should not be a preparation for life. A school should be life.
— **Elbert Hubbard**

From a postformal perspective, what all this means is clear: we must begin to concentrate our efforts on a *public language of literacy*—authentic standards, intellectual diversity, and critical thinking assessment that will enable us to provide a vision of what it means to be actively literate as opposed to passively literate. We must speak to issues of accountability and responsibility in education, but from a postformal point of view. It is important to recognize that institutional and societal support must be cultivated and nurtured in order to create an environment for the achievement of learner outcomes and goals; the current universal standards debate must be seen as inauthentic and antithetical to human development.

Once again, this specifically means that we as educators must come to understand that the debate regarding assessment and standards as it is defined in the popular media is mythological,

jingoistic, propagandistic, and disingenuous; that it does little to foster a healthy, critical discourse regarding student achievement; that it is political. We must reform this debate with a new language of assessment and learning, one tied to what it means to be a human being in search of liberation and subjective emancipation. The standards we adopt should help students become global citizens, not simply global producers and consumers. Standards and assessments should have as their purpose the promotion of healthy individual and social growth through critical reflection. And they must truly offer opportunities to all students, regardless of class, race, culture, or gender.

Societal support and a realignment of economic and cultural priorities and reality would also serve as a means for accomplishing educational goals and commitments. This would mean that the debate regarding education would need to confront objective reality—such as issues of racial, sexual, educational, and socioeconomic equity—directly and honestly, to embrace the necessity for an acute paradigm shift toward general societal humanistic values and changes in forums from the classroom to the workplace, from the family to the state. It would be perfidious to propose that equity can exist within the institutions of education while economic and social inequality pervades major societal institutions as a whole.

For this reason, teachers as intellectuals must become teachers as social activists, collaborating and reoxygenating their unions with vision and struggling for a social commitment to make children the top priority, to preserve and strengthen public education, to provide adequate nutrition and health care to families, to furnish safe schools and neighborhoods, to ensure the development and distribution of fair and adequate funding for public education, to equalize opportunity, and to support local decision making by governing bodies. As society and its institutions forge a partnership for critical thinking and educational opportunities for all students, the primary indicator of our effectiveness will be our ability to achieve our greatest goal: the education of all our nation's children and the creation of a loving world of authentic agency and caring human beings.

References

All quotes not specifically referenced are from *Peter's Quotations*.

Aronowitz, S. (1998). *Pedagogy of freedom*. New York: Rowman and Littlefield.

Bennett, W. (1988). *Our children and our country*. New York: Simon and Schuster.

Brodinsky, B. (1977, October). The new right: The movement and its impact. *Phi Delta Kappan*, pp. 87–94.

California approves math, English textbooks tied to standards. (1999, June 23). *Education Week*, p. 10.

Costa, A. (1994). What human beings do when they behave intelligently and how they become more so. Paper given at the Miami–Dade County Public School conference on Critical Thinking, Miami, Florida.

De facto national standards. (1999, July 14). *Education Week*, p. 36.

Dewey, J. (1916). *Democracy and education*. New York: MacMillan.

Dewey, J. (1997, originally published in 1916). *Democracy and education*. New York: Simon & Schuster.

DuBois, W.E.B. (1924). Diuturni Silenti. In *The education of black people*, ed. H. Aptheker (pp. 50–54). New York: Monthly Review Press.

Duncan, Homer. (1979). *Secular humanism, the most dangerous religion in America*. Lubbock, TX: Missionary Crusader.

Education Week. May 5, 1999.

Executive pay. New York. (1999, April 19). *Business Week*.

Feinberg, W. (1993). *Japan and the pursuit of American identity*. New York: Routledge.

Fiske, J. (1989). *Reading the popular*. Boston: Unwin Hyman.

Foucault, M. (1977). *Discipline and punish: The birth of the prison*. New York: Pantheon.

Freire, P. (1970). *Pedagogy of the oppressed*. New York: Seabury Press.

Freire, P. (1976). *Education for critical consciousness*. New York: Continuum.

Freire, P. (1998a). *The Paulo Freire reader*. New York: Continuum.

Freire, P. (1998b). *Pedagogy of freedom*. New York: Rowman and Littlefield.

Hirsch, E. D. (1988). *Cultural literacy: What every American needs to know*. New York: Vintage.

Kearns, D., & Doyle, D. (1988). *Winning the brain race*. ICS Press.

Kincheloe, J., Steinberg, S., & Villaverde, L. (1999). *Rethinking intelligence*. New York: Routledge.

LaHaye, T. (1980). *The battle for the mind*. New York: Power Books.

Mid-continent Regional Educational Laboratory. (1997). Aurora, CO.

The National Commission on Excellence. (1983). *A nation at risk*. Washington, DC: USA Research.

National Education Goals Report. (1991). Washington, DC: GPO.

The National Skills Standards Board. (1998). Washington, DC: U.S. Department of Education.

Perkins, D. (1995). *Smart schools.* New York: Free Press.

Peter, L. (1977). *Peter's quotations.* New York: Quill.

President Clinton names Paul F. Colz and Alan Wurtzer as members of National Skill Standards Board. (1999, May 5). *The New York State AFL-CIO.*

Ravitch, D. (1996). *National standards in American education.* Washington, DC: The Brookings Institute.

Reich, R. (1992). *The work of nations.* New York: Vintage.

Shor, I. (1992). *Culture wars.* Chicago: The University of Chicago Press.

Sklar, H. (1999). *Shifting fortunes: The perils of the growing American wealth gap.* Boston, MA: United for a Fair Economy.

Sculley, J. (1992). Critical thinking: Why it matters so much. Speech given at 1992 Economic Conference, Arkansas.

Unz, R. (1999, May 3). *Voucher veto. The Nation Magazine,* pp. 6–7.

Wagner, T. (1994). *How schools change.* Boston: Beacon Press.

RESPONDING TO STANDARDS

The Professor of Education's Legacy and Responsibility

William H. Schubert and Thomas P. Thomas

It is our contention that a principal responsibility of professors of education is to create possibilities for the future, to question assumptions, to imagine innovative alternatives and their consequences, to see things as they might be otherwise, to make the strange familiar and the familiar strange, and to keep matters of goodness and justice in the foreground of consideration. The works of eminent educational philosophers such as John Dewey and Maxine Greene are replete with these values. In contrast, the current enthusiasm (mania?) for standards at all levels of education is promoted as a proposal for responsible education, with standards constructed primarily from a narrow historical tradition and faithfulness to an institutional status quo. While we can easily accommodate these standards as intelligent consultants and collaborators in creating a curriculum that is relevant to the lives of learners, we cannot abide its pretentious usurpation as the dominant or even exclusive voice in curriculum construction or teacher education. Standards can and have generated anxiety and exasperation; they do not evoke inspiration or aspirations.

Standards are more prevalent than ever before; there are standards for teachers, for teacher candidates, for students, for administrators, for counselors. Forerunners of standards for teachers and students have been seen before, especially in the post-Sputnik curriculum reform of the 1950s and 1960s, the behavioral objectives movement of the 1960s and 1970s, and the special education emphasis on individual educational plans (IEPs) from the 1980s to present (see Schubert & Lopez Schubert, 1981; Schubert, 1986). Nevertheless, the governmental emphasis on standards is unprecedented at both the federal and state level. Thanks to GOALS 2000 funding, nearly every state has developed statewide goals and tests designed to verify the extent to which standards have been acquired and implemented. Professional associations in a remarkable thirteen different disciplines have designed elaborate statements of standards, most federally funded as well.

The prophet of the movement, the National Council for Teachers of Mathematics, has already approved a second edition of their influential standards. Some school districts have followed suit in developing their own standards with an eye on compatibility and consistency with state and national standards. The Association for Supervision and Curriculum Development (ASCD) has published books summarizing these many standards (e.g., Kendall & Marzano, 1997). Moreover, producers of major commercial achievement tests have adopted national academic standards to blueprint their assessment instruments. These tests, combined with state testing, are often used to compare and rank individual teachers, schools, districts, states, and real estate. This constitutes another kind of standard that the public has come to accept as valid. Such misapplications of standardized (a term that now has *two* meanings) tests have overstepped the bounds of merely providing information that can be used as a basis for curricular and instructional improvement.

Certainly many of these efforts are well intended. Most of the so-called blue ribbon commissions, the special agencies, and particularly the professional agencies claim to be offering guidelines, possibilities to ponder, and even ideas to inspire the work of those who daily influence students. Carefully constructed assessments that offer useful information for personal and program development can be helpful to educators. Something adverse (even perverse) happens, however, as statements of standards move from the drawing boards to the school boards and into the lives of teachers and students. They become *the law*, policies to abide by, mandates that must be implemented, and tests that confer or deny status.

It is not unusual for schools, especially those regularly receiving low test scores (schools that often are located in economically impoverished environments), to feel pressured to direct nearly all of their educational resources and efforts toward raising test scores. Colleges of education are themselves giving increased attention to state teacher certification examinations; recent federal policy mandates that their teacher candidate scores on state certification tests be published for ranking. The transformation that occurs when guidelines become mandates was well depicted by Sir Isaiah Berlin when he said: "The history of thought and culture is . . . a changing pattern of great liberating ideas which inevitably turn into suffocating straitjackets and so stimulate their own destruction" (Berlin, 1980, p. 159).

Heralded by their promoters as liberating possibilities or heuristic devices (e.g., Haertel, 1997), standards have been passed along with such force of requirement as to repress the creativity of teachers, students, and professors of education. The achievement of standards that can be demonstrated by a large-scale test score has become a kind of "bottom line" (to use corporate parlance) for judging all aspects of the educational system. The consequences for students is that a hidden curriculum emerges that makes the test score and the credential more important than genuine learning and human growth.

In past eras of such mandates, there was almost always leeway for school district and teacher interpretation—at least a modicum of faith that local authorities could imaginatively tailor guidelines from the conference rooms of experts and policy makers to the idiosyncrasies and special needs or interests of localities. In *Behind the Classroom Door*, John Goodlad, Frances Klein, and associates (1970) noted, for instance, that the rhetoric of post-Sputnik curriculum reform was present at the surface structure of school-public relations, but the deep structure of classroom life (when the door was closed) represented what teachers really wanted to do. Assessment was not as stringent then as today; there was little if any formative evaluation to indicate whether implementation of reform projects was on track, and in the end, summative evaluation measures were rarely tied explicitly to goals. Some would argue that this was a fault of the reform; reformers failed to *make sure* that practitioners did the bidding of outside authorities. Diane Ravitch, for example, argues that standards must "precede and be linked to student tests" if policy makers want the standards to be taken seriously (Ravitch, 1995, p. 24). Others might argue, as is our ten-

dency, that less stringent connections between standards or goals, implementation, and outcome evaluation gave local administrators and teachers opportunity to apply their craft knowledge to students whose particular lives could not be known by outside authorities.

The current failure to assume that teachers can creatively make good decisions in light of their knowledge of the extant situations in which they live and work has a controlling tone that lacks faith in others, especially subordinates. Lee Shulman (1986) cites the novelist John Fowles for insight into this lack of faith. In Fowles's novel *Daniel Martin*, a political leader is asked why we have governments and laws. He replies that it is to prevent bad dreams about what humans would do without them. Shulman applies this to educational policy, noting that we make and enforce standards to prevent our bad dreams about what teachers and local school administrators will do if we do not control them.

When standards are tied to high-stakes large-scale assessment, a top-down controlling mechanism is put in place that can restrict, indeed subvert, grassroots intelligence (except perhaps the intelligence involved in trying to design motivational and instructional strategies for student attainment of these often unengaging standards). The standards and their large-scale assessments can become autocratic impositions that discourage democratic involvement. Ironically, democratic citizenship is often claimed to be one of the ultimate ends of these standards. Standards advocates have so cluttered the educational landscape with required competencies that they appear to assume that the experts who are removed from educational situations and do not know the teachers, children, and environments in those situations are in the best position to say what is needed there. Thus, they offer the same prescription for all learners—a strange notion that would be intolerable to patients in a medical doctor's office. Susan Ohanian (1999) argues convincingly that one size clearly does not fit all.

The content and competency standards before us today *are* the new curriculum, a curriculum mostly developed by disciplinary learned societies and translated by state and local policy makers. These groups, along with test makers, are more often grounded in psychometrics, not in curriculum studies, and stand ready to provide answers to our fundamental and complex curriculum questions: What is worth knowing, experiencing, needing, doing, being, becoming, sharing, and contributing as individuals and as societies? Implicit in such a complicated question are issues of what it means to live a good and worthwhile life, what a just and fair society is like, and how human beings should interact with their natural environment.

These questions are much greater than mere matters of how to be certified for the next level of schooling or for being a teacher or educational leader. Too, they are greater than the political and economic worry of whether we have the competitive edge

in comparison with other nations. Indeed, the basic curriculum questions embrace the whole of life that *is* the fundamental and pervasive educator of us all (see Foshay, 2000), which includes everything that influences the intellectual, emotional, social, physical, aesthetic, and transcendental purposes of life. Surely, state goals and assessments and standardized tests deal with only a minute proportion of the aspects of life that A. W. Foshay set forth in his *curriculum matrix*.

What Noted Curricularists of the Past Say that Pertains to Standards

We have noted above that standards are constructed from traditional past academic practices and perceived contemporary demands. Curriculum scholars of the past who do not share the curriculum orientations currently in favor in public policy have much to say; they provide a cautionary tranquilizer for the rampant acceptance and implementation of the standards movement as the next "quick fix" for education and especially curriculum. We mention a few who, in our view, are among the most insightful and whose work helps us form salient questions about the standards phenomenon and its potential controlling presence on the lives of students and teachers.

John Dewey

Whole treatises continue to be written on John Dewey's proposal for educational reform (e.g., Simpson & Jackson, 1997). S. M. Fishman and L. McCarthy (1998) have reflected on his contemporary relevance to classroom practice, and William Schubert (2000) has written a chapter on Dewey's philosophy as a basis for more just educational communities. Deeply embedded in Dewey's philosophy of education (see Dewey, 1902 and 1916) is his progressive organization of a curriculum that begins with the *psychological*—the needs, interests, and concerns of students—and moves to the *logical*—public knowledge in diverse disciplines and personal knowledge from lived experience that are effective for deliberation on issues of social significance.

Since standards are tied to Dewey's concept of the *logical*, the standards movement counteracts the main tenet of progressive education, that is, to initiate any educational experience in responding to the concerns and interests of students. The problems, relationships, and mysteries that learners ponder are the basis for introducing them to knowledge and skills in existing subject matter areas, facilitated by an integrated curriculum that pertains directly to student growth (see Beane, 1997). To leave students and their concerns out of the curriculum is akin to Shakespeare writing *Hamlet* and omitting the Prince of Denmark!

In an engaging but little-known piece in the *New York Times*, Dewey elucidated his position on standards and purposes in a fictional conversation with members of a utopian society that is far advanced in its educational practices. Dewey wrote:

Naturally I inquired what were the purposes . . . of activities carried on. . . . At first nothing puzzled me more than the fact that my inquiry after objectives was not at all understood, for the whole concept of the school, of teachers and pupils and lessons, had so completely disappeared that when I asked after the special objectives . . . , my Utopian friend thought I was asking why children should live at all, and therefore they did not take my question seriously. After I made them understand what I meant, my question was dismissed with the remark that since children were alive and growing, "of course, we, as the Utopians, try to make their lives worth while to them; of course, we try to see that they really do grow, that they really develop." (Boydston, 1989, pp. 137–138)

Within a controlling framework of content standards, where can we hear the voice of individual students and small communities of learners? How can student interests and concerns become the basis for their genuine growth and development, instead of the current conception that assumes students are defective adults in need of adult experts whose contrived standards can fix them?

George S. Counts

In 1932, George S. Counts wrote the landmark social reconstructionist book, *Dare the School Build a New Social Order?* Here he asked by implication: what kind of social order is most fair and just, and how can school curricula and teachers contribute to the reconstruction of this order? Given that state standards are geared to perpetuate the existing social order and its value system, we might take his question further to ask, how can a new social order be advanced by states that are fashioned out of the dominant values of the existing social order? Are Counts's reconstructionist ideas, which build on Dewey's reconstructionist orientation (see Dewey, 1948), a warranted hope or an unapproachable ideal?

Carter G. Woodson

In *The Mis-education of the Negro* (1933), Carter G. Woodson anticipated much of today's critical reconstructionist message to standard bearers (see Schubert, 1996 and 1997). In the preface of this work, Woodson starkly depicts how the learning of African Americans perpetuated the enslavement of their mental, emotional, and social lives. He observed, "The problem of holding the Negro down, therefore, is easily solved. When you control a man's thinking you do not have to worry about his actions. You do not have to tell him not to stand here or go yonder. He will find his 'proper place' and will stay in it. You do not need to send him to the back door. He will go without being told. In fact, if there is no back door, he will cut one for his special benefit. His education makes it necessary" (Woodson, 1933, p. xiii).

Given this insight, we might ask, to what extent do content standards re-

enforce social class and privilege? When one set of standards is applied for all, regardless of their origins, treatment, and circumstances, do they then become a measuring tool of status?

Harold Rugg

Had there been statements of standards, state goals, and today's industry for achievement testing in the first half of the twentieth century, Harold Rugg's textbooks would probably have not been published. If we add the controlling interests that direct state adoption policies in Texas and California, it is certain that his textbooks would not have been used in the public school. Rugg's social studies texts, which sold in the millions, eventually were smothered by critics who charged his social inquiry approach was un-American. These texts criticized injustice and the competitive ethos in America, encouraging students to be democratically oriented critical thinkers.

With today's prevalence of textbooks driven by state standards and curriculum frameworks, how possible would it be to have alternative conceptions of the curriculum rise to this level of influence? After publishing *That Men May Understand* (1941), in which Rugg explained the trials and tribulations of this effort to depart from the mainstream, he devoted much of the rest of his career to the study of human imagination from diverse cultural standpoints. This inquiry resulted in the posthumous publication of *Imagination* in 1963 with the assistance of philosopher of education Kenneth Benne. Rugg's interests were consistently focused on the projecting of possibilities rather than the reification of knowledge. What possibilities do content standards invite?

Caroline Pratt

What happens when teachers learn from their students? In the first half of the twentieth century, Caroline Pratt, a dedicated early childhood teacher and later a professor, titled a book, *I Learn from Children* (1948). (Putting this in the parlance of today, William Ayers [1993] admonishes teachers to be students of their students.) Pratt asks that we try to fit the school to the child, not mold the child to the school. To truly see children as having something to teach us, as grown-ups and educators, is not to see children as defective adults. Instead of seeing our work as deciding what is good for children to make them better, how can we help them form the emergent ideas and concepts about life that are within them? Standards as mechanisms of control would not seem appropriate to this kind of philosophy.

Harold Benjamin

A satirist of education, Harold Benjamin wrote *The Saber-Tooth Curriculum* (1939) under the pseudonym of J. Abner Peddiwell. In this work, an old professor of education lectures a young teacher-to-be in a bar in Tijuana on what he had learned from an extended sabbatical leave, during which he studied educational systems of prehistoric men and women. He revealed to his young tutee that among key courses in the prehistoric curriculum were *Saber-Tooth Tiger Chasing with Fire* and *Fish Grabbing with the Bare Hands*. These courses served an immediate practical value. When glaciers arrived, however, the environmental conditions changed, making these skills obsolete. Nevertheless, many of the educational standards-makers urged that these two great time-honored curricular areas continue to be taught, arguing that they helped build the mind and character! This story might lead us to question whether learned societies have ensured through their standards the perpetuation of their discipline—not because all standards they promote have relevance to contemporary communities of learning but rather because they perpetuate academic custom.

In a 1949 book, *The Cultivation of Idiosyncrasy*, Benjamin offered a captivating story called "The Animal School." In this school, all students, for their own good, were taught a "required curriculum. This was a school of no nonsense. It was a good, liberal educational institution. It gave broad general training—and instruction—and education too" (Benjamin, 1949, p. 1). Each of the many kinds of animals in the forest had their strengths, but they also had their shortcomings. For example, the eagle was great in jumping and excelled in flying classes but saw no relevance in climbing classes; the squirrel was a wonderful climber but a poor flyer. The prodigious strengths that each kind of animal possessed, their beautiful idiosyncrasies, were overshadowed by the required standards that each animal had to accomplish in many areas. Old Man Coyote was wise enough to see the leveling effect that this standard curriculum was having on learning and he offered the following advice:

> "These schools start with the things that birds and animals do—or even more often what they did some time ago," explained Old Man Coyote. "Then the teachers hammer these doings—or as much of them as they can handle and as they think high toned enough—into schoolings, courses, curriculums, and subjects. Then they hammered the pups into the schoolings. It's a rough and dopey process, and the teachers have had to invent good explanations to defend it. Discipline, culture, systematic training—things like that—are what the teachers use for this purpose." (Benjamin, 1949, p. 7)

Coyote's alternative is deceptively simple: "Turn it around," said Old Man Coyote. "Start with the pups. See what the pups do. Then see what the school can do for the pups. Then see what the pups and school together can do for all the creatures in the woods. Simple—forwards instead of backwards—right end to instead of wrong end to" (Benjamin, 1949, p. 7). Could this alternative work in schools today?

Alice Miel

A pioneer of action research by teachers during the 1940s and 1950s, Alice Miel wrote of cooperative learning (1952) many years before its contemporary revival. Students working collaboratively on ill-structured problems have received considerable positive attention today, unfortunately often only as an instructional strategy for higher achievement on assessment instruments. Time and again we see teachers help students realize that cooperative learning is important only to have to contradict the message with the arrival of individual large-scale assessments, where we work only as individuals and interaction with others becomes a moral violation. Teachers announce that these events are *really* important, so important as to contradict the admonition to cooperate.

Miel also encouraged teachers to work together to build schools through a social process (see her 1946 book *Changing the Curriculum: A Social Process*). With her colleagues, Miel even encouraged doctoral students to work together to develop dissertation research! If on the one hand students are encouraged to work together on projects, yet on the other hand the events that mean the most for their future are not cooperative but competitive, what message do they receive? Is it the message that what really matters most is not of their making; instead, their challenge is to demonstrate compliance?

Stephen M. Corey

Like Miel a faculty member at Teachers College, Columbia University, in the 1940s and 1950s, Stephen Max Corey called for *Action Research to Im-*

prove School Practices (1953). For both Corey and Miel, the criticism of standards is simple and direct: If teachers are supposed to work together to improve the curriculum, and if this improvement includes reconstructing the standards, how can educators succeed in their craft if the standards are not subject to their influence?

Thomas Hopkins

Author of one of the first book-length treatments of curricular integration, Hopkins combined integration (1937) with democratic interaction (1941) and elaborated on the focus of both with his concept of "the emergent self" (1954) as the most fundamental educational project. To help students pursue the project of self-development, he argued, it is essential to know them well, to help them set forth standards unique to their own emergence and growth. Consistently focused on the development of the individual, Hopkins believed that four convictions (a different approach to standards) constitute the work of the democratic school. These beliefs are:

- All human beings are accepted and respected as ends in themselves, not as means to ends fixed by others to promote their favored institution or fixed system of life.
- Meaningful education assists the individual in the discovery and development of his or her gifts and capacities.
- The potential capacity is released and developed by providing ex-

periences that are responsive to the needs that develop in the life of the learner. The educator must place study of the learner at the forefront of curriculum development.

- This process works to improve the self-acceptance of the learner, not for some external social standard. (Hopkins, 1954)

How can this vision of schooling be effected from afar by policy makers who do not know the students as individuals?

Harold Alberty

Following in the footsteps of his mentor, renowned progressive philosopher of education, Boyd H. Bode (Bode, 1938), Harold Alberty articulated a conception of core curriculum that has similarities with that of Hopkins, although Alberty's work was primarily with the high school curriculum. Alberty presented high school study as a progression of group study units on relevant social issues. The development of the core curriculum was from local immediate problems of contemporary life to broader community problems. The secondary school education culminated with the examination of contemporary socioeconomic issues.

Alberty recognized that most high schools were constructed around traditional academic disciplines (a reminder of how *very* different schools were in 1947). He offered a transition process involving six types of curriculum design, to move from the status quo curriculum to a social core curriculum that integrated disciplinary knowledge around controversial issues deliberated on in democratic discussion toward a majority decision (Alberty, 1947). He pointed out that in Type 6, "the core consists of broad units of work, or activities, planned by the teacher and the students in terms of needs as perceived by the group. No basic curriculum structure is set up." His Type 5 (slightly less radical) "consists of broad, pre-planned problem areas, from which are selected learning experiences in terms of the psycho-biological and societal needs, problems, and interests of students" (Alberty, 1947, p. 119). If either a Type 5 or 6 core curriculum were enacted today, what contemporary problems and purposes would emerge? What then would be the role for externally devised academic standards? Could they assume any role beyond advising the curriculum development process?

Theodore Brameld

Theodore Brameld amplified the social reconstructionist perspective initiated by Dewey and developed by Counts and Rugg, assuming a more structured political and global posture. Unabashed in his promotion of a new economic order, Brameld identified education as one of several endeavors for building new social and global relationships. He wrote, "Education becomes a constructive force only when it fuses with the economic, political, socially creative forces of the culture—when it is the very stuff of

the growing struggling life of every large and small community" (Brameld, 1960, p. 178).

In defending a value base on which to construct a reconstructionist education, Brameld arrived at a different conception of standards for education. Rather than thinking of standards as the knowledge and skills to be attained in academic disciplines, Brameld encouraged educators to think of the standards of human living. He suggested twelve basic needs that are inherent in the human condition:

- sufficient nourishment
- adequate dress
- shelter and privacy
- sexual expression
- physiological and mental health
- steady work and income
- companionship, mutual devotion, and belongingness
- recognition, appreciation, status
- novelty and recreation
- literacy and information
- sharing participation
- order, direction, and meaning (Brameld, 1947, pp. 10–11)

Brameld encouraged educators to place these human standards before the learners and ask them to consider social options for realizing these standards for all members of the society and, extensively, all peoples of the world. The learning community, provided guidance and resources by adults, is asked to come to consensus and act on their deliberation.

With one or more of the social standards at the center of investigation, Brameld suggested a "wheel curriculum" be employed for senior high school and the first two years of college. The hub of the wheel is group consideration of a social issue, based on one or more of the above basic human needs, which require social resolution. The spokes are groups of students concentrating on different aspects of the issue who come together periodically to share research and proposals (Brameld, 1956, pp. 179–192). Disciplinary knowledge (the arts, communication, sciences, mathematics, and the social sciences) are integrated into the processes of inquiry, deliberation, and action.

What would schools look like if they replaced the academic standards with standards for human dignity as the driving force of education?

Another point that is seldom emphasized is Tyler's insistence that curriculum and instruction should pertain to the active social experience of the learner. In order to relate to this experience, educators need to know about learning that occurs in the nonschool lives of their students. In the late 1970s, when asked to reflect on what he might add to his rationale, Tyler (1977) said he would try to emphasize more fully the nonschool dimensions of student lives. In this sense, he was saying that to develop effective curricula, educators must know students well. This pertains to students in particular as individuals. How would standards be transformed if they were opened to philosophic conversations and to the lives of the learners?

Ralph W. Tyler

Ralph Tyler is best known in the curriculum field for his rationale for curriculum development (1949), which consists of questions about four salient topics (purposes, learning experiences, organization, and evaluation). He also insisted that curriculum goals be placed against two intellectual screens, the psychological/developmental and the philosophic. When current standards for teacher performance refer to the role of the teacher in curriculum development, they are uniform in their selective use of the Tyler rationale. They dismiss the philosophical screen as an important process in thinking through what students should know, share, and become.

Joseph J. Schwab

In the late 1960s, Schwab (1969) argued that curriculum inquiry suffered from being too theoretic and should be practical in character. Practical inquiry (drawing from both Aristotelian and Deweyan roots) should derive its problems from difficulties in states of affairs, not generalized states of mind as in theoretic inquiry. Practical inquiry should seek situationally specific knowledge, not the will-o'-the-wisp of lawlike knowledge. Practical inquiry should proceed through interaction with and embeddedness in the lived context being studied, not merely through detached induction and deduction about it. Finally, the end of practical inquiry should not be knowledge *qua* knowledge, rather it should be knowledge that informs morally defensible decision and action.

Schwab (1971) called for eclectic arts that match theoretic knowledge to extant situations, tailoring and adapting such knowledge to situations—especially knowledge derived from a repertoire of experience in comparable situations to enable the anticipatory generation of alternatives. Elaborating still more, Schwab (1973) called for a curriculum that is the dynamic interaction of four commonplaces: teachers, learners, subject matter, and milieu (or environment). He emphasized that the most important curriculum work is to continuously monitor and adapt to changes in the relationships among these commonplaces (Schwab, 1983).

The kind of focus on the situation that Schwab advocated necessitates substantial curriculum decision making at the situational level. Thus, it clearly and substantially diminishes the power and value of generic policy and standards. Should curriculum creation be primarily top-down, grassroots, or a continual work in progress based on the thoughtful consideration of all commonplaces in education?

Phillip Phenix

For those readers who have grown impatient with the persistent criticisms of a traditional academic disciplinary curriculum, Philip Phenix would appear to provide comfort. Phenix divided the "various possibilities of significant experience" into six realms of meaning. Two of the realms—the *symbolic*, which relates to language use and mathematics, and the *empiric*, the method and knowledge of scientific inquiry (encompassing both the social and physical sciences)—are strongly represented in the conventional school curriculum. A third realm, *aesthetics*, including the languages of music, the visual arts, and literature, has a less prominent role in the schools but is also represented in the standards movement.

The fourth realm, *synoetics*, the lived reality of the individual either in personal existence or in relations, is seldom responded to in disciplinary content standards. The fifth realm, *ethics*, "is based on free, responsible, deliberate decision" (Phenix, 1964, p. 7). As described by Phenix, this language is not represented either in the standards movement or in conventional schooling. The sixth realm, *synoptics*, refers to integrative languages, the languages of history (understood as cultural narrative), religion, and philosophy. This realm combines the other realms of meaning into an ever developing statement of the person's understanding of the nature of existence. Synoetics, ethics, and synoptics are seldom represented in the conventional academic disciplinary standards.

Phenix contended that the education of young people in the United States lacked direction because those realms that develop personal expression and understanding, purpose, commitment, and integrity are conspicuously absent. This absence establishes a curriculum that serves a "democracy of desire," a directing of society toward the ends of accommodation and self-gratification. The academic disciplines are mere diversion if the larger questions of human purpose are not given voice. Phenix invited the educational community to take seriously the profound responsibility of its profession. Educators are to transform people who might otherwise be inclined to meet only their own limited interests and distractions to participate in a human adventure committed to drawing meaning from life, considering visions of what is worth living for. He suggested:

> Whatever its visible forms, the important goal is that redirecting of life from finite attachment and acquisitiveness to the active love of the good. To accomplish this change is the supreme end of all teaching and learning. All increase in knowledge and skill that confirm one in his (or her) lust for autonomy is loss, not gain. From this standpoint, much of what has been taught and learned in present day education misses the mark. Studies that increase the power to exploit the earth and other people, that arm one for the struggle for privilege, that prepare one to pursue his advantage more successfully, destroy rather than edify a person. The sovereign test of all education is whether or not it is religious, that is, whether or not it tends towards conversion of the person to unconditional commitment to right and truth. (Phenix, 1961, p. 243)

What would happen to the traditional academic standards if they confronted the fuller realms of meaning that Phenix suggested?

James B. Macdonald

Building from Ivan Illich's (1972) notion of de-schooling society, James Macdonald, B. Wolfson, and E. Zaret (1973) decided to take the debilitating and controlling aspects of schooling out of the schoolhouse and make schools places of meaning-seeking (Macdonald & Zaret, 1975). Macdonald developed a hermeneutic for a democratic praxis in education. It begins in the lived experience of the participants. He wrote: "Our activities, efforts, and expectations should, in other words, be focused upon the ideas, values, attitudes and morality of persons in school in the context of their concrete lived experiences; and our efforts should be towards changing consciousness in these settings toward more liberating and fulfilling outcomes" (Macdonald, 1981a, p. 145).

Macdonald encouraged the critical analysis of repressive or oppressive social structures using multiple perspectives. Language communities (academic disciplines are one expression but are not the only kind of language communities) are encouraged to give theoretical perspective to the problem. It is understood that no one language encompasses the fullness of lived experience. Using the analysis of the languages of inquiry developed by Jürgen Habermas (1968), Macdonald isolated three epistemological languages for framing inquiry. By far the most pervasive is scientific/technical language. Its focus is on control and certainty of outcome, not questions of value. Second, the epistemological language of critical theory seeks social emancipation through historical analysis to decode power interests. The failure of using only these two frameworks is that they are incomplete in their consideration of the human condition. Macdonald calls for the engagement of a third language: "Whatever rests in this category which is truly separate from control or emancipation must rest in the area of poetics. I would propose that there is a third methodology; that of the mytho-poetic imagination, particularly related to the use of insight, visualization, and imagination, which is essentially separate from science and praxis. . . . The mytho-poetic deals with 'why is there being rather than nothing,' at the awe, wonder, and anxiety of this puzzle" (Macdonald, 1981b, p. 12).

Macdonald did not give primacy to any of the three language communities. Rather, he encouraged educators to engage people in all of these forms of speaking, thinking, and knowing. From participation in these discourses, we construct the metaphors that help us to interpret and disclose reality. Continued inquiry causes new metaphors to arise and old metaphors to fall away. The hermeneutic circle of understanding takes place within each of the three language communities and across all of them. Macdonald argued that curriculum theory should be a prayerful act by those who educate, a

statement of confident hope in existence as well as an effort to engage its myriad mysteries (1995). The seeking of meaning and reflection about how to live together in this world is a personal and community endeavor. Can it be governed by externally developed standards?

Paulo Freire

In *Pedagogy of the Oppressed*, a book of immense worldwide influence, Paulo Freire (1970) proposed that education should be a problem-posing experience as opposed to the banking image that he used to criticize most institutionalized education. Drawing from liberation theology, he argued that education as liberation comes about when the oppressed can name their world, identify their oppression and oppressor. Often his pedagogy for teaching literacy started with an artifact from the experience of those with whom he was working. He would not tell them what to write or say about it, realizing that the interpretation of an outside "do-gooder" would not evoke meaning. Instead, he would listen to their experience and learn from it, asking the oppressed Brazilian peasants he worked with to share their understanding.

Education is a process of sharing, not directing. Freire offered, "True humanism which serves human beings, cannot accept manipulation under any name whatsoever. In humanism there is no path other than dialogue. To engage in a dialogue is to be genuine. . . . Dialogue is not to invade, not to manipulate, not to 'make slogans.' It is to devote oneself to the constant transformation of reality" (Freire, 1973, p. 114).

Freire invited educators to advance social transformation by making the art of listening, especially to those who are so often repressed and marginalized, share importance with the making of grand statement. His proposal has spread to many parts of the world, translated and elaborated on in numerous works (see Freire, 1997, and Freire and Macedo, 1998). What kind of standards policy could presume to enable others to name their worlds in ways foreign to the experts and policy makers?

Engaging with Contemporary Curricularists

There are contemporary curriculum thinkers who also challenge the notion of building education and reform around standards for content and performance. Dwayne Huebner, Maxine Greene, Louis Berman, Elliot Eisner, Nel Noddings, David Purpel, Michael Apple, Henry Giroux, Joel Spring, Max van Manen, William Pinar, Madeleine Grumet, Jean Anyon, Gloria Ladsen-Billings, Patti Lather, Joe Kincheloe and Shirley Steinberg, Lisa Delpit, William Ayers, William Watkins, and others are significant critics of the supremacy of standards and offer alternative proposals for educating our youth and ourselves.

Conclusion

If we take seriously the advice of past curriculum scholars, it is evident that conceding a controlling function to standards in directing what is most worthwhile to know, become, and share is detrimental to the positive possibilities of what curriculum could be. It bespeaks a pervasive lack of faith in the ability of human beings to decide and act in good, right, and just ways without coercion. Standards, as usually employed by the educational systems of the United States, seem to be based on the antithesis of a Deweyan faith in human capacity (see Dewey, 1934). A democratic faith in government requires faith in its citizens; similarly, a democratic faith in education demands a faith in students. As an aside, schooling appears to be the only business that does not adhere to the almost universal adage that "the customer is always right." In fact, schools seem to hold that their customers (students and even their parents) are almost always wrong; it is their defects that schools want to clean up and correct!

Drawing upon Abraham Lincoln's Gettysburg Address, as Dewey did, we call for education that is of, by, and for students. Dewey expressed it thusly: "The philosophy in question is, to paraphrase the saying of Lincoln about democracy, of education of, by, and for experience. No one of these words, *of*, *by*, or *for*, names anything that is self-evident. Each of them is a challenge to discover and put into op-

eration a principle of order and organization which follows from understanding what educative experience
signifies" (1938, p. 29). To begin to
enact a faith in human beings that is
the basis for democracy requires education that is genuinely *for* students
because it is first *of* and *by* them (see
Schubert & Lopez Schubert, 1981).
We contend, therefore, that education
that is of and by students, that grows
out of their concerns and commitments, is prerequisite to education
that is truly for them in a relevant way.

We should not be content with
standards that do not involve students
and teachers in their design. The educational process itself should create
standards for authentic living, being in
the world, and relating with it in
meaningful, just, and compassionate
ways. Thus, the fundamental curriculum question (What is worthwhile to
know, experience, need, do, be, become, overcome, and share?) must be
infused into the entire educational
process. It must be the central consideration of teachers and students. If
this ideal were realized, or even ap-
proximated, what then would be the
implication for standards as we usually
see them in education—mandates designed from afar and used to control
local educational leaders, teachers,
students, and thus societal growth?

References

Alberty, H. B. (1947). *Reorganizing the high school curriculum*. New York: Macmillan. (Subsequent editions authored with E. J. Alberty.)

Ayers, W. (1993). *To teach: The journey of a teacher*. New York: Teachers College Press.

Beane, J. (1997). *Curriculum integration: Designing a core of democratic education*. New York: Teachers College Press.

Benjamin, H. (1939). *The saber-tooth curriculum*. New York: McGraw Hill.

Benjamin, H. (1949). *The cultivation of idiosyncrasy*. Cambridge: Harvard University Press.

Berlin, I. (1980). *Concepts and categories: Philosophical essays*. Oxford: Oxford University Press.

Bode, B. H. (1938). *Progressive education at the crossroads*. New York: Newson.

Boydston, J. A. (Ed.). (1989). *John Dewey: The Later Works*. Carbondale, IL: Southern Illinois University Press.

Brameld, T. (1947). An inductive approach to intercultural values. *Journal of educational sociology, 21*(1), 5–20.

Brameld, T. (1956). *Towards a reconstructed philosophy of education*. New York: Dryden Press.

Brameld, T. (1960). *Education for an emerging age*. New York: Harper and Brothers.

Corey, S. M. (1953). *Action research to improve school practices*. New York: Bureau of Publications, Teachers College, Columbia University.

Counts, G. S. (1932). *Dare the school build a new social order?* Carbondale, IL: Southern Illinois University Press.

Dewey, J. (1902). *The child and the curriculum*. Chicago: University of Chicago Press.

Dewey, J. (1916). *Democracy and education*. New York: Macmillan.

Dewey, J. (1934). *A common faith*. New Haven, CT: Yale University Press.

Dewey, J. (1938). *Experience and education*. New York: Macmillan.

Dewey, J. (1948). *Reconstruction in philosophy*. (Rev. ed.). Boston: Beacon Press.

Fishman, S.M., & McCarthy, L. (1998). *John Dewey and the challenge of classroom practice*. New York: Teachers College Press.

Foshay, A. W. (2000). *The curriculum: Purpose, substance, practice.* New York: Teachers College Press.

Fowles, J. (1977). *Daniel Martin.* Boston: Little, Brown.

Freire, A.M.A., & Macedo, D. (Eds.). (1998). *The Paulo Freire reader.* New York: Continuum.

Freire, P. (1970). *Pedagogy of the oppressed.* New York: Continuum.

Freire, P. (1973). *Education for critical consciousness.* New York: Seabury.

Freire, P. (1997). *Pedagogy of the heart.* New York: Continuum.

Goodlad, J. I., Klein, M. F., and Associates. (1970). *Behind the classroom door.* Worthington, OH: Charles A. Jones.

Habermas, J. (1968). *Knowledge and human interests.* Boston, MA: Beacon Press.

Haertel, G. D. (1997). Creating school and classroom cultures that value learning: The role of national standards. *Educational Horizons, 75*(3), 143–148.

Hopkins, L. T. (Ed.). (1937). *Integration, its meaning and application.* New York: Appleton-Century.

Hopkins, L. T. (1941). *Interaction: The democratic process.* Boston: D. C. Heath.

Hopkins, L. T. (1954). *The emerging self in school and home.* New York: Harper & Brothers. (Reprint, Westport, CT: Greenwood Press, 1970).

Illich, I. (1972). *De-schooling society.* New York: Harper & Row.

Kendall, J. S., & Marzano, R. J. (1997). *Content knowledge: A compendium of standards and benchmarks for K–12 education.* (2nd ed.). Alexandria, VA: Association for Supervision and Curriculum Development.

Macdonald, J. B. (1981a). Curriculum, consciousness, and social change. *The Journal of Curriculum Theorizing, 3,* 143–154.

Macdonald, J. B. (1981b). Curriculum theory: Knowledge or understanding? In Wilma Harrington (Ed.), *Proceedings of the second conference of curriculum the-*

ory in physical education. Athens, GA: Unpublished.

Macdonald, J. B.(Ed.). (1995). *Theory as a prayerful act: The collected essays of James B. Macdonald.* New York: Lang.

Macdonald, J. B., Wolfson, B., & Zaret, E. (1973). *Reschooling society: A conceptual model.* Washington, DC: Association for Supervision & Curriculum Development.

Macdonald, J. B., & Zaret, E. (Eds.). (1975). *Schools in search of meaning.* Washington, DC: Association for Supervision & Curriculum Development.

Miel, A. (1946). *Changing the curriculum: A social process.* New York: Appleton-Century.

Miel, A., and Associates. (1952). *Cooperative procedures in learning.* New York: Bureau of Publications, Teachers College, Columbia University.

Ohanian, S. (1999). *One size fits few: The folly of educational standards.* Westport, CT: Heinemann.

Phenix, P. (1961). *Education and the common good.* New York: Harper and Brothers.

Phenix, P. (1964). *Realms of meaning.* New York: McGraw Hill.

Pratt, C. (1948). *I learn from children.* New York: Harper and Row.

Ravitch, D. (1995). *National standards in American education.* Washington, DC: The Brookings Institution.

Rugg, H. (1941). *That men may understand: An American in the long armistice.* New York: Doubleday-Doran.

Rugg, H. (1963). *Imagination.* New York: Harper and Row.

Schubert, W. H. (1986). *Curriculum: Perspective, paradigm, and possibility.* New York: Macmillan.

Schubert, W. H. (1996). Perspectives on four curriculum traditions. *Educational Horizons, 74*(4), 169–176. (Reprinted in *News and Views* [Hudson Institute] *15*(11), November 1996, 25–32).

Schubert, W. H. (1997). Character education from four perspectives on curriculum. In Molnar, A., Ed., *The construc-*

tion of children's character, 1997 NSSE Yearbook, Part II, (pp. 17–30). Chicago: University of Chicago Press and the National Society for the Study of Education.

Schubert, W. H. (2000). John Dewey as a philosophical basis for small schools. In Ayers, W., Klonsky, M., and Lyon, G. (Eds.), *A simple justice: The challenge of small schools* (pp. 53–66). New York: Teachers College Press.

Schubert, W. H., and Lopez Schubert, A. L. (1981). Toward curricula that are of, by, and therefore for students. *The Journal of Curriculum Theorizing*, *3*(1), 239–51.

Schwab, J. J. (1969). The practical: A language for curriculum. *School Review*, *78*, 1–23.

Schwab, J. J. (1971). The practical: Arts of eclectic. *School Review*, *79*, 493–542.

Schwab, J. J. (1973). The practical 3: Translation into curriculum. *School Review*, *81*, 501–522.

Schwab, J. J. (1983). The practical 4: Something for curriculum professors to do. *Curriculum Inquiry*, *13*(3), 239–265.

Shulman, L. S. (1986). Those who understand: Knowledge growth in teaching. *Educational Researcher 15*(2), 4–14.

Simpson, D. J., and Jackson, M.J.B. (1997). *Educational reform: A Deweyan perspective*. New York: Garland.

Tyler, R. W. (1949). *Basic principles of curriculum and instruction*. Chicago: University of Chicago Press.

Tyler, R. W. (1977). Desirable content for a curriculum development syllabus today. In A. Molnar & J. A. Zahorik (Eds.), *Curriculum theory* (pp. 36–44). Washington, DC: Association for Supervision & Curriculum Development.

Woodson, C. G. (1933). *The mis-education of the negro*. Washington, DC: Associated Publishers. (Reprint, Trenton, NJ: Africa World Press, 1990).

HERMENEUTICS' INVITATION TO MEANING-MAKING

The Ecology of a Complexity of Standards, Educational Research, Policy, and Praxis

Marjorie Mayers

The standards movement in education is cause for great concern. One of the more pressing matters is that for the most part, the majority of us are not part of the standards discussions and as a result are also not part of the dialogue about what standards mean for educational policy, research, and praxis. The way we understand and make meaning of the standards issues is to defer our own thinking, values, educational philosophy, and creativity to the "experts" who have devised, planned, and set the standards agendas for our teachers, students, schools, and communities. Many of us are not seen as conversants or contributors to the discussions; we are neither welcome nor invited. But we surely have much to offer.

In an effort to change the aforementioned circumstance, to offer a challenge to standards proponents, and to empower a greater number of people to be involved in this educational debate, this chapter will introduce hermeneutics as a way of seeing the world and our educational work in it in a more ecologically holistic way, and it will serve as an example of how an alternative approach to taking up the world, such as hermeneutics, can act as a catalyst for reframing the standards-of-education discourse and our participation in it. There are many provocative questions that involve our deep engagement with the issues at hand, including: What do standards for practice and pedagogy really mean (to you and beyond you)? What are the values undergirding the standards movement? and In what ways can we become participants in renewed visions of what a complexity of standards might entail? These are the kind of questions a hermeneutic approach to looking at the educational standards movement might raise as critical facets of any complexity-of-standards discussion. These questions demand scrutiny and careful attention to the complicatedness inherent in the standards-of-education issues, and this complexity is what I will take up here.

This chapter is split into two parts. First, I will offer an explication of the central tenets of hermeneutics in terms of educational standards issues so that I can demonstrate how a hermeneutic approach recomplexifies that which has been made simple by the current prostandards rhetoric. Second, I will look at major standards/educational issues hermeneutically to exemplify how a hermeneutic approach deepens the discussions at hand. To do this, however, we must first explore the philosophic attributes that make a hermeneutic approach to living in the world meaningful in the standards debate and beyond.

Hermeneutics as a Way In

One might ask what place a discussion about educational research, philosophy, and methodology has in a conversation about educational standards and other practical questions about education. The answer is: everything. Although the standards issues seem to focus on outcomes and means-to-ends, approaches to educational standards necessarily imply some view or other about knowledge, education, pedagogy, expertise, truth, value, and so on. How we come to know, how we judge what it is worthwhile to know, and how we evaluate knowledge has everything to do with what is happen-

ing in classrooms. For example, how much do you trust numbers as representatives of the truth, as in the case of statistics? Often, people believe that statistical analyses represent truth more than do other kinds of data, such as qualitative information derived from interviews, for example. But even though a statistical study may not say anything explicitly about the truth of its claims, there is behind statistical analysis a belief about the nature of 'truth'. In our culture, statistics are positioned as data that are irrefutable and infallible—potent ammunition for "proving" that a certain thing is the way it is because the numbers say so. The purported objectivity of "science by statistics" is further promulgated by the accompanying values that support the contention that data derived from standardized, quantitative measures are value-neutral, clean, and believable, that they correspond to reality. These positivist assumptions include the ontological (the nature of reality) belief that there is an apprehensible *reality out there*—an obdurate existence independent of the observer—that in order to know, or to come to know, objective and value-free approaches must be implemented to achieve *true* results, and that the aim of methodology is to converge on the truth by methods of deduction.

An alternative vantage point stems from a belief system that suggests that there are no privileged positions of authority, and that all data are connected to the contexts of their creation. In other words, despite statistics' claim to truth and certainty, no approach to evaluation, or knowledge acquisition, or inquiry is safe and free from values, perspectives, and biases. The hermeneutic position posits that 'truth', 'reality', and 'knowledge' are a little more complex than some numerical equivalent of how the world works. Hermeneutics wants to problematize that which has been made simple by simplifying questions and linearizing results. Believing that the lifeworld is continually being interpreted by all of us and that the lifeworld is indeed complex, hermeneutics compels us to name our positions, state our histories, and explore how what we think we already know stands in contrast to what seems foreign to us. It is this hermeneutic conversation that I hope to re-enliven so that some of the more pressing issues about educational standards can be illuminated in a challenging way.

Part I—Hermeneutics and Standards of Education: Learning the Approach

As we find our way through the complexity of our existences together, we knowingly or unwittingly adhere to particular processes and methodologies that help us in clarifying, negotiating, and mediating the meanings of our experiences. Often, we align ourselves with that which makes us feel secure, stable, and certain. In this case that might mean that we are more comfortable in attaching ourselves to the kinds of educational standards that are measurable, linear, tangible, knowable, simplified, and straightfor-

ward. This knowingness assures us of what we know and helps to quiet whatever ambiguities about education, or pedagogy, or learning we might have. This knowingness seduces us into thinking that we have understood something about knowledge, learning, or education in a way that closes the conversation because we believe that the truth has been rendered and the decisions have been made. The discourse of the standards movement in education tends to exemplify such thinking.

Clearly, the unprecedented momentum of the standards revolution suggests that this kind of certainty is what we are looking for. Adopting a certain belief, value, and ultimately an approach to knowledge that we believe can deliver the goods to us in a way that won't confuse us, or scare us, or speak to us too personally has meant that we've suddenly closed the dialogue for further investigation. This kind of stability mythologizes education by equating it with outcome measures or teacher standards, while reinforcing the characteristics of the current educational enterprise as that which is dismembered—comprised of disembodied souls who design curricula, power brokers who set policy, disenfranchised workers who deliver data, and severed young beings who are merely recipients of a predetermined, packaged, authoritative education. In this case, knowledge and truth are seen as static, stable, and obdurate. Education is the passing on of substantive data—nothing more, nothing less. Hermeneutics, on the other hand, is all about meaning-making, not apprehending what is already out there but finding ways to take up how we live in the world together.

Hermeneutics offers us a new opportunity to explore what moves us about education and to dig a little deeper into the complexity of what standards might mean and what education is, or could be, or should be. Hans-George Gadamer says that "we are possessed by something and precisely by means of it we are opened up for the new, the different, the true" (Gadamer, 1977, p. 9). And so it is true of this issue and of this offering to you. The standards movement in education is herein presented to be taken up in a new and different way. It is to be engaged by me and by you. In illustrating and demonstrating what I have come up with in thinking about standards in education, I invite you to explore the hermeneutic perspective that implores me to engage the standards-of-education issues beyond the givens. I ask you here to engage this text in a way that will free you from the constraints that bind scholarly inquiry into a narrow set of acceptable procedural rules and evidentiary standards, with the hope of creating a space that allows an unencumbered understanding about the standards issues to emerge and in order for this discussion to act as a building block toward revisioning a different and more complex set of educational standards.

"[T]he real power of hermeneutical consciousness is our ability to see what is questionable" (Gadamer, 1977, p. 13), and so it is our task to look anew at all that complicates and confounds an understanding of what standards of education mean for educational research, policy, and practice. The central tenet of this kind of approach is to make meaning and in some way to impart that meaning in a pedagogic and transformative way (Gallagher, 1992; Smith, 1994). It is not about separating and holding in abeyance our experiences in life, like the false promises of standardized tests that pretend to correct for all variables that may impinge on the "purity" of the results. To the contrary, hermeneutics understands that it is precisely because of our history that we seek to bring to bear what might be otherwise lurking quietly behind the scenes. That means that education is restored to the life-world in which it lives, in all its endless messiness and with all its many contradictions. It is not about reproducing the world so that there is a finite, obdurate, static truth that can be measured against some other truth, but rather it is about engaging in the dialectic and multilayered conversation that is continually in flux, changing, evolving, and shifting.

Hermeneutics is about a kind of personal acuity that enlists us to take up life and all that is mingled in the complexities of living despite our desires for certainty and predictability. Hermeneutics asks us to be critical and careful, and it demands that we struggle—rigorously—to find a clearing in the thicknesses of life. Understanding through interpretation is the hermeneutic quest and "good interpretation shows the connection between experience and expression" (Smith, 1994, p. 107). This is my goal here. The focus of my efforts is to show you, to engage you, and to help you understand that from a hermeneutic perspective, standards involve much more than just getting teachers to be accountable for their professional performance and ensuring that students achieve in certain substantive areas. The hermeneutic mandate is an important one, and it seems to me to be an articulation of the most natural form of communication, of conversation, of questioning, and of living.

Even though we want to be able to get a handle on what is happening in educational discourse by reducing the discussions to issues of accountability and achievement, a hermeneutic or complexity-of-standards approach directs us to take back the conversations that have been severed from the multivalent and rich textures of life and instructs us to reconnect educational questions to a world beyond educational borders. Perhaps that might mean exploring issues of social justice or looking at questions that address socioeconomic contexts, or access to education, and so on. Hermeneutics is, after all, a philosophy of living, looking at all the complexity that is imbedded in the educational endeavor, not a prescription for inquiry, research, or teaching. But a hermeneutic approach to research and teaching can deliver us back to the entangled, confused, and confounded places and spaces in which we live and learn, and it can offer invaluable insights into why, how, and in what

manner one might take up the complexities of questions and ultimately the messiness of answers.

The first step in adopting a hermeneutic approach is to admit that we are interpretive beings and that we propel ourselves from day to day by using our interpretations as guides. For example, the fact that you're reading this text might suggest that you have some interest in educational standards and that because you have an interest you also probably have an opinion on the subject. In exploring what it means to have an opinion, hermeneutics asks us to leave the metaphysical questions of ontology (the nature of reality) to the philosophers and to admit that the world in which we live is the world to which we must pay attention and the world in which we must make meaning. And so what we want to look at is the lifeworld where standards of education get meted out, where kids get caught up in achievement rankings, and where teachers and teaching get dumbed down by being overbureaucratized. And so, the lifeworld where standards meet people and where standards affect lives is central to and inextricably part of what we are discussing here.

Partly because of my intention to explain what hermeneutics is, partly because the standards complexities need to be addressed in a different manner, and partly because I am hoping to engage you in this discussion, a dialogic conversation has begun. This hermeneutic tenet involves the important relationships that are built when we engage text. From this place of experience and expression, I will lead you, and beckon you, and show you. The text will be our place of meeting; it is here that we will be engaged in the conversation around standards and hermeneutics and here that we will raise the issues of knowledge and rigor in the light of what hermeneutics might bring to the standards debate.

Gadamer (1995) suggests that this intermingling of our knowing and understanding, of our beliefs and perspectives, is a "fusion of horizons" where we reach in for the common ground between us, using language, history, and conversation to mediate our communication. This is done in the spirit of understanding and renovation. In this case, the intention is to get closer to the complexity imbedded in the standards-of-education constructs and to explore the interpretive process of engaging the discussions for all the things that our explorations may tell us, things we might be ready for as well as things that might surprise us. In the hermeneutic process we follow the threads of conversations and ideas that lead to various places and diverse understandings. In this case I am trying to explore the central ideas of hermeneutics so that you can appreciate a different perspective and an alternate worldview, especially as it relates to knowledge, truth, and evidence. But simultaneously, this hermeneutic tenet also frees me to wonder what an education based on this kind of discovery might look like. Like Dewey (1916), who advocated for teachers to meet their students where they are, herme-

neutics invites us to do the same in order that meaning can be made between us. What would a standards discussion look like if meaning-making were a central value for learning, teaching, educational research, administration, and policy development?

As noted earlier, there is no unbiased position from whence to offer up a value-free assessment and to extricate information from its context. We always begin from a perspective and carry with us our history, language, purposes, and convictions. In other words, there is no way of getting behind perspective—there is no place of pristine *tabula rasa* from which to depart. The point of departure is always referential and prejudiced, relational and prejudged, in terms of one's history and all that is invoked by one's tradition (Gadamer, 1977, 1995; Gallagher, 1992; Smith, 1994). This is true of me, of the issues, and of you. Standards of education do not exist in a vacuum and have not come to be all by themselves. There are contexts that frame the standards movement as there are values, beliefs, and aspirations tied into the complexities of the issues, as I will try to show you.

But the admission that there is no objectivity to rely on need not frighten us with the thought that everything is relative and subjective. Rather, this approach demands that we be intellectually honest and rigorous and that we offer meanings and interpretations that lead us to understandings we hadn't conceived of before. Tradition or perspective need not translate into the narcissist's ego fantasy, luring us into her world, separate and cloistered from anything else we might know or understand. Perspective is rather about the interplay between dynamic experiences and understandings, between situating what is new in relation to what we may already surmise and where our understanding may already be. Hermeneutics is, in the end, a practical approach to dialogue, dialectic, and discovery.

And herein lies the point of this chapter. It is to admit that there are multiple perspectives about standards and to cogently offer one here. It is to admit that the advocates of technical standards are offering a perspective on what may improve education—including teacher accountability/ability and student achievement—but that it is only a perspective, not the 'truth'. It is to connect the familiar to the unfamiliar and to find our way through the tensions of both. It is to present a case for an interpretation of what the standards movement is doing to the educational enterprise and to the human beings who are therein involved, and to investigate what that potentially means to me, to you, and to our understanding of how certain views are prized over others when particular perspectives are dawned. And so, despite the misunderstanding that interpretation—including the values, approaches, and worldviews that accompany it—is about the self, the ego, and the solipsistic space of the interpreter, we can see otherwise. Good interpretation is certainly not about these things. Hermeneutical interpretation can never be merely about the

reconstruction of the world as it is (as if that would be possible) or as the narcissist sees it, but rather it is always an open and critical approach to questioning and understanding the meanings that are given as well as those that erupt in the geographies we are exploring (Gadamer, 1995). Hermeneutical interpretation is about understanding ourselves, our cultures, our beliefs, our issues, and our lives by way of understanding others, and I will therefore attempt to show you the manifold ways that these connections encounter the topic.

Gadamer suggests that history and language can act as both inhibitors and liberators in terms of our own understandings (Gadamer, 1995). This does not mean that once you have understood yourself you are all of a sudden able to see things as they actually are—definitively, finally—but rather that constant reflection is a necessary component of exploration, understanding, and knowledge creation. At its core, the careful scrutiny of ourselves, of others, and of the world as it presents itself beyond what we may be prepared for can lead us to take up more complex and critical issues, can free us to challenge the status quo, and can help us negotiate the muddled waters that are representative of a complex life. Does the standards movement allow for teacher self-reflexivity that might enable professional growth? Does it encourage students to be life investigators? Are there spaces to critically question the knowledges that are taken for granted in the classroom? A hermeneutic standards-of-complexity approach enables the richness and multifaceted nature of teaching, learning, discovering, exploring, relating, and knowing to take shape in the opening of a dialogue about what it is that we want education to be about in the first place.

To admit in advance that I have a perspective does not justify saying anything at all about standards and the corollary educational issues. If I want you to see the connections that I have made in our complex world, I need to be able to sway you, to build a case for you that illustrates how more complex perspectives on knowledge production, dissemination, and control illuminate the possibilities of the educational enterprise. This is the hermeneutic task. My perspective is a dynamic energy of thoughts, reflections, learning, questioning, feeling, and assessing. I am continually muddling through to make meaning of the things that are presented to me as well as of the things that I seek out. I must bring these things to light if I am to be successful at making a case.

Gadamer (1995) suggests that this is precisely how I may be able to maintain my openness about the topic. Hermeneutics doesn't ask us to hide how our perspectives position us; it requires that we use that perspective to cogently argue for a certain interpretation. These are tasks, I might add, that require a good amount of investigation, perseverance, intellectual prowess, and strong communication abilities.

Now that we have discussed perspective as an important facet of hermeneutics, I will show you how my history, language, and perspective open me to the possibilities of interpretation, possibilities that erupt in the generative engagement and search for meaning with the topic at hand (Jardine, 1998). As Gadamer notes, "history is only present to us in light of our future" (Gadamer, 1977, p. 9). And so it is that hermeneutics recognizes the centrality of the tradition from whence one speaks, set among and in between the fluid motion of the world. Indeed, it is precisely because of my history, my beliefs, and my ideas that I have come to ask questions about standards and how they impact kids, teachers, and the art of pedagogy. For example, questions about the aims of education explode in front of me when I read about standards that aim to prepare students for the global economy of the twenty-first century. Although I might tell myself that there are economic realities, I wonder what economics and employment have to do with learning?

Perhaps this kind of query comes from my work with kids on the street who vision a different world and who value community over competition, or perhaps this comes from my visceral fear of the kinds of values we are teaching our kids by equating meaning-making with money-making. Whatever the case, this questioning process is an example of how I would begin to explore and interpret the kinds of deep meanings that are associated with education, as I see it. If my exploration takes me down paths that lead back to myself, then the interpretation is about me and not about the question of standards of education and economics. If, however, my exploration leads me beyond myself, leads me to investigate the complexity of these issues, then perhaps I may be able to make a case and show how my fear is "justified." A standards-of-complexity approach would welcome the deep thinking and critical exploration that my perspective would bring.

Understanding and interpretation come from a tension that lives between what is familiar to us and what is unfamiliar. This means that my approach to a topic has been based in part on some familiarity with what I imagine education to be about. But the conversation doesn't end because of my familiarity with the topic. In other words, the goal is not to finally decide anything. I am not trying to fit what I find out into what I already know. Hermeneuts contend that what is familiar to us opens up the topic precisely because it presents itself as unfamiliar (Gadamer, 1995; Gallagher, 1992). As an example, the standards-of-education topic that I am addressing has been opened up because of the interplay between my historical experience as a teacher and my difficulties in understanding the issues at hand. Whatever is familiar to me about education presents itself as needing to be taken up again in relation to what seems foreign to me about the standards movement and the values therein. Thus new questions arise. My questioning leads me to read and talk about what standards mean for education in the future, which in turn leads me to ask more questions.

And so it goes: hermeneutics is pushed and propelled by the questions that we ask and the understandings that throw into question the things we thought we already understood (Gadamer, 1995; Gallagher, 1992). From the technical standards-of-education perspective, the discourses about achievement and teacher accountability seem to be all tied up and closed—already convinced about the relative merit of this kind of standards approach. But for me, the literature about standards is but an opening that allows me to search deeply for clues and ideas about how to make meaning around educational issues beyond what I am currently being offered.

This is where interpretation resides—oscillating between what we understand and what we don't, what is familiar to us and what is not. Gallagher (1992) says that "[i]nterpretation is an attempt to responsibly bridge these two demands [i.e., what is familiar and what is unfamiliar], to resolve or in some way to deal with the tension between them" (p. 150). To that end, taking the standards issues and grappling with all that they present prompts me to ask questions about the aims of education as I have not done before. Vacillating in between what I already understand and what is still foreign to me, I take up the tensions that arise in the in-betweens of the discourses about standards.

As noted earlier, it is my task to artfully bring to bear in expression what has been experienced, and to that end you also play a part. Inasmuch as text engages a reader and from that engagement a relationship is born, the dialectics of understanding, communication, questioning, and thought are initiated between us. That is, the text is restored to a living communication when it is taken up, when it is read, when it is interpreted (Ricoeur, 1981). I offer this text as a pedagogic encounter for all of us. I hope that the relationship that you have with this text, like the relationship that I have had with this text, will be an opportunity for learning. We are engaged, you and I, and our lives will never be the same because we are the accumulations of our experiences and because of our experiences, we are ever changing beings. Above and beyond what we will or want, the lifeworld calls us and we are intertwined in it. We are called, as it were, to pay careful attention. It is to that existential state that hermeneutics invites us. And it is to that flux of dynamics between all that makes this discussion about hermeneutics and standards of education what it is that I invite you.

So how might we take up that invitation? How might we judge an interpretation? What counts as evidence for the interpretation that we offer when we take up the world hermeneutically? In much of his *Truth and Method* (1995), Gadamer refutes scientific claims to truth and authority. He battles with positivist conceptions of objectivity and reason and in their stead offers an alternative view of epistemology. How can we determine the extent to which understanding has occurred, if not in a static measure? How can we be certain that an adequate interpretation has been rendered? There are no better questions to begin with. How might these questions play out if a complexity of standards were adopted as a framework for determining how learning and inquiry, teaching and curricula development take place?

"[G]ood interpretation is a creative act on the side of sharpening identity within the play of differences—and we thereby give voice to and show features of our lives ordinarily suppressed under the weight of the dominant economic, political, and pedagogical fundamentalisms of the time" (Smith, 1994, p. 123). A complexity of standards aims at reinvesting educational research, policy, and praxis with values that acknowledge diversity in its many forms. As Smith (1994) suggests, one of the goals of good interpretation is to lay bare the complexities and underpinnings of the metanarratives that often operate silently but nevertheless influence and constrain the possibilities of our understanding. To make good cases and to provoke and persuade in the hope of renovation and elucidation, hermeneutics offers three central tenets beyond its epistemological position that address the parameters (or the boundlessness) of how we might engage a topic, how we might build a cogent interpretation, and what we might do with the myriad strands and complexities that arise from looking at the world as a complex of interrelated and interdependent ideas, beliefs, circumstances, and so on. Questions, understanding, and the hermeneutic circle are components of a hermeneutic approach that are not clearly delineative, and thus their explication does not lend itself to linear articulation. They need to be understood as a complex of interdependent ideas that reflect the possibilities that the hermeneutic approach offers. Questions and the complexity of openness, issues around understanding and the fertile process by which we reach it, and the hermeneutic circle, understood as the interpretive inertia that continually churns and alters questions and understandings, all of these will enable us to proceed, hermeneutically, in taking up the complexities of standards-based education.

Questions

Questions and openness are central to the hermeneutical endeavor. As Gadamer (1995) contends, "the question is the path to knowledge" (p. 363). For me, this means that a program of inquiry-by-question as opposed to only inquiry-by-methodology opens up doors through which diverse or competing ideas and knowledges can emerge. For example, in terms of this chapter specifically, my questions began years ago when I undertook to become a high school teacher, and they continue to surface as I am engaged in the various roles that connect me to education. As a counselor, educator, scholar, citizen, and student, I question how these roles fit into or rub up uncomfortably against the standards movement. An-

other example of how hermeneutics is driven by questions is the uncertainty that arises when one is investigating how educational issues are dominated and shrouded in neoliberal agendas, rhetoric, and opinion. As the hermeneutic endeavor commands, questions beget questions, and this is true of what we find here. By questioning what seems familiar and final, hermeneutics involves an archaeology of meaning-making. Hermeneutic thinkers understand that taking up a topic involves following the trails forged by the substantive qualities embedded in the topic and by the questions that are raised in the pursuit of its understanding.

Each question directs us toward or away from understanding, but questions also drive what we uncover, what we wonder about, what we admit we do not know. "A question places what is questioned in a particular perspective. When a question arises, it breaks open the being of the object as it were" (Gadamer, 1995, p. 362). Therefore, in the act of inquiry, we must situate our questions within the domains of our own understandings so that they can be laid open to possibilities. The hermeneutical understanding of the foregrounded question is that which stems forth from a position, that which is exposed to whatever hinders or helps propel the question beyond itself. "The important thing is to be aware of one's own bias, so that the text can present itself in all its otherness and thus assert its own truth against one's own fore-meaning" (Gadamer, 1995, p. 269). After all, we are

ultimately concerned with understanding and meaning, and therefore
the extent to which a question reveals
possibilities will determine to some
extent the value of the question itself.

And so in the trajectory of this exploration into the standards movement, I've been compelled by some
questions, while quieting and laying
others aside. Jardine (1998) notes that
knowing in advance which threads to
follow and which to lay aside is inde-
terminable until such time as the leads
lead nowhere. Perhaps this is one of
the aspects of hermeneutics that we
can perceive and judge, that can help
us conclude whether or not an adequate interpretation has been rendered. Are our questions evoking
more questions? Are they leading us
somewhere else—somewhere beyond
the boundaries of what we already
know, or think, or feel?

Language

Language, as Gadamer (1995) emphasizes, is central to the way understanding is experienced. In the first place, a
conversation is always about something, and in the second place, a conversation is dialectically engaged by
languaging about that something.
Hermeneutics prescribes that we enter into multiple dialogues at multiple
levels. Here, for example, I am both
conversing with the texts that explicate the hermeneutic/interpretive nature of conversation, dialectic, and dialogue and, simultaneously, I am
conversing with you and with this text.
Invested in these conversations, there

is an impetus to arrive at some shared
meaning and some shared conception
of what this text is revealing about
hermeneutic understanding, conversation, and standards in education. Language is the foot soldier that helps deliver the "fusion of horizons" I
mentioned earlier.

Similarly, in the course of my conversing with what the standards movement presents, I have initiated multiple conversations with the ideas and
questions that arise from taking a
topic up. I grapple with and sway in
the decisions that direct which questions persist in asking for reconciliation and which understandings I
might follow and explore. I am continually engaged in a dialogic conversation with myself, with others, with
literature, with society, with complexities, and with the world. To that end,
the entire interpretive turn is about
conversation and renovation. Perhaps
we might say that understanding is
temporarily achieved when something
new emerges about a topic, something
that leads us someplace else. In this
case, perhaps we might posit that understanding "of the particular case
leads us to understand the universal"
(Gallagher, 1992, p. 342; Jardine,
1992), all the while knowing that understanding and learning are never
complete or final (Gallagher, 1992;
Gadamer, 1995; Jardine, 1998).

The Hermeneutic Circle

One way of conceiving of this conver-
gence of voice and conversation, understanding and reflection in a herme-

neutic approach is by invoking the hermeneutic circle. The hermeneutic circle is a process in which meaning and understanding unfold through the constant renewal of questions and conversation. This process is fluid. It has movement like the gentle (or maybe not so gentle) ebb and flow of the ocean's tide. The hermeneutic circle refers to the interplay between parts and wholes where, as F. Schleiermacher explains, "the meaning of the part is only understood within the context of the whole, but the whole is never given unless through an understanding of the parts. Understanding therefore requires a circular movement from parts to whole and from whole to parts" (as cited in Gallagher, 1992, p. 59).

And so this process of questioning and understanding, reflecting and questioning again, reveals the unending reciprocity between thinking, feeling, knowing, questioning, experiencing, and interpreting. The hermeneutic circle therefore implies a temporality, a contextual referent or chronological stream of turnings and twistings that contiguously evolve in the processes of education, learning, teaching, inquiring, discovering, arguing, and so on. As a result of each experience that beckons our intention and calls our attention to it, we accumulate a knowing that propels us into the future, all the while incorporating our understandings of the past. The process evolves and revolves, always enlarging itself to incorporate new aspects of understanding, producing more questions and leading into

deeper and more complex directions. As Gadamer (1995) notes: "The art of questioning is the art of questioning even further—i.e., the art of thinking" (p. 367). As Gallagher (1992) concludes, "[t]he more movement in the circle, the larger the circle grows, embracing the expanding contexts that throw more and more light upon the parts" (p. 59) and increasing the potential for a more comprehensive interpretation to emerge. And so it is true of this chapter, of this book, and of the move to reaffirm a standards-of-complexity approach to educational research, policy, and praxis.

Part II—Standards as a Way into Hermeneutics: A New Vision of Complexity

Now that we understand something about the process and importance of hermeneutic exploration and the meaning-making possibilities of good interpretation, and now that we have explored the central tenets of hermeneutics with regard to truth, questions, language, knowledge, conversation, and the hermeneutic circle, we can begin to weave into our hermeneutic conversation specific examples of how a hermeneutic approach would break open, change, expose, and free the standards debate to incorporate a more complex and ecologically full perspective on what standards mean for education and beyond. Questions that beckon some kind of attention might include these: How does current standards rhetoric fix the educational issues under discussion, and to whose advantage? How might standards of complexity embrace a hermeneutic approach in exploring some of the issues that are so presented? Is it even possible, given this rigidity, to enter into the discussion about the relative usefulness of standards of education? Instead of a closed case that claims that standards for teacher accountability and student achievement is the way of the future, a hermeneutic approach to this topic opens and broadens the discussion to include the multitude of particularities, complexities, confusions, and contradictions that are simplified, reduced, and expelled by the current standards movement rhetoric.

If the conversation is already in progress without us, where is our entrée into the fray? I suggest that shifting our way of thinking about truth, knowledge, rigor, research, policy, and practice; altering how we take up the world and restoring the world to its original complexity; and admitting that issues are more complex than we would like them to be will break new ground and will create renewed educational hope and enthusiasm. This is what a hermeneutic approach would count on. How might we take up the issues and how might we re-vision what education is, or could be, or should be? How shall we look at this in all its complexity, a complexity that might be different from what the standards-in-education movement has already uncovered? The answers are simply to dig a little deeper, to search a little harder, to be a bit more reflexive, to understand our own invested interests, to look a little further afield, and to examine in more detail what this standards conversation is really about.

Contesting what the implications of a standards-driven education might actually mean is a complicated venture to undertake. For example, when we speak hermeneutically about perspective, we must acknowledge, as we did earlier, that your engaging this text suggests that something about the question of educational standards intrigues you, compels your attention, or draws you into this topic. Is your reading value-neutral, or are you aware that you have certain beliefs already in place with regard to issues of standards-based education? A great place to begin would be to wonder about what draws you to the topic of standards in the first place? What beliefs, values, and approaches do you already have in relation to educational standards and the goals the standards movement purports? What experience is so deeply a part of you that it positions you in a specific way relative to standards-of-education questions and relative to a hermeneutic approach?

These are important perspectival questions. They are the lenses through which you frame your interpretation of the information, ideas, and suggestions throughout this chapter and throughout this book. We are, after all, the accumulations of our experiences, and our lives cannot be severed from how we might take up a topic such as standards in education. As teachers, administrators, policy planners, academicians, parents, and citizens, we all have a stake in how education is framed in the larger social order, and we all have a responsibility to engage the discussions that sometimes seem beyond our reach.

To this end, the following substantive examples have been raised from the issues about the standards movement that struck me as I undertook to write this chapter. The questions and musings that follow are the result of my hermeneutic approach to this educational debate. These are the issues that a technical standards of education might ignore because they may not relate directly to the outcome-based standards to which this movement is connected, whereas a standards-of-complexity position would welcome the multifarious ways in which one might reframe what is complex about the project of education, as complex. It is my task here not to explore standards issues in depth but rather to invite you to experience the kinds of circular turnings and twistings that a hermeneutic approach brings to the standards topic.

The Seduction of Language

Hermeneutics is about language. It's about the conversations that we have with each other, the way that language can conceal or expose ideologies; it's about all that we do in our lives together, how we make and search for meaning; it's connected to everything that we are, and hope for, and dream of. In looking at the importance of language in a hermeneutic dialogue, I am seduced by the exquisitely crafted documentation that abounds in standards-of-education literature. My own experience with the language of the standards movement often left me wondering what was wrong with teacher standards. When reading about how standards encourage teachers to be next to godly, I loved the language about what teachers could be, or should be. I loved what I was reading about education and the complexity of the educational endeavor. If teachers could be all this with standards, who would dare argue against them? I was hooked, convinced, and captured. Then, after a pause and a question about what might lie behind this beautifully constructed case, I began to wonder how this language had seduced me to buy into what the standards movement proponents are selling. Entitled to make a case for a standards of education, the standards people use language to construct the meanings and persuasive arguments that hermeneuts encourage. For example, the following comes from the documentation of the National Board for Professional Teaching Standards:

What Teachers Should Know and
Be Able to Do

In this policy, the National Board presents its view of what teachers should know and be able to do—its convictions about what it values and believes should be honored in teaching. This expression of ideals guides all of the National Board's standards and assessment processes.

The fundamental requirements for proficient teaching are relatively clear:

a broad grounding in the liberal arts and sciences; knowledge of the subjects to be taught, of the skills to be developed, and of the curricular arrangements and materials that organize and embody that content; knowledge of general and subject-specific methods for teaching and for evaluating student learning; knowledge of students and human development; skills in effectively teaching students from racially, ethnically, and socioeconomically diverse backgrounds; and the skills, capacities and dispositions to employ such knowledge wisely in the interest of students.

This enumeration suggests a broad base for expertise in teaching but conceals the complexities, uncertainties, and dilemmas of the work. The formal knowledge teachers rely on accumulates steadily, yet provides insufficient guidance in many concrete situations. Teaching ultimately requires judgment, improvisation, and conversation about means and ends. Human qualities, expert knowledge and skill, and professional commitment together compose excellence in this craft. The document continues:

The National Board has led the vanguard effort to develop professional standards for elementary and secondary school teaching. The National Board Certified Teachers stand for professionalism in the schools. The National Board's responsibility is not only to ensure that teachers who become National Board Certified meet its professional standards of commitment and competence, but also to maintain standards and assessments that are so well regarded that America's accomplished teachers will decide to seek National Board Certification.

Well, I'm sold—how about you? We can see that there is clearly nothing wrong with what this document tells us about how teachers should be prepared for the classroom. If life were only this simple. But the seduction lies in how the language positions detractors, and also how the standards assumed here are measured.

We all need to be careful with language because it can capture us without our critical selves noticing the circumstances of our capture. In this case, scrutinizing the language of the standards-in-education documents made me question how I feel about the topic at hand. I came to understand two things I had not realized before. In the first place, I realized that the way in which the standards debate is articulated leaves no room for an alternative viewpoint to be taken up. Perhaps we might consider whether or not that is the deliberate positioning of the debate, whether it intentionally frames those people who would take issue with these kinds of standards philosophies as crazy, irrational, and so on. How can you argue when everything has been so neatly tied up? But despite the seemingly Pollyannaish language that beckoned me to abandon my commitments to a hermeneutic, complex, and messy existence and to release myself into the capable hands of those who would make sure that "everything was going to be all right," I realized that no matter how beautiful and promising the language of the technical standards movement is, the bottom lines will continue to be focused on teacher accountability through the evaluation of student achievement.

I recognize that not all standards boards want the same things. Some allow teachers to prepare portfolios to demonstrate their excellence. But I am continually left with the same bothersome questions about who determines excellence and what measures will be used to judge. This hermeneutic lesson about language has heightened my sensibilities. By confirming the importance of language in how we construct meaning, it has shown me how attentive to language we must be as we take up the issues of standards of education.

Standards as 'Truth' and Rigor

Previously I spoke about the nature of 'truth' as it relates to knowledge production and acquisition and its connection to 'reality'. I found examples of this relationship in the documents of the standards movement. In coming to understand something about the standards-of-education movement, I noticed that technical standards literature presents the issue of improving education as largely synonymous with improving students' performance on standardized tests. Improving education is the goal behind the movement. On the surface, that seems fine; who could possibly suggest that improving

education is a bad enterprise? But who sets the standards, what aims of education do the standards represent, and what values undergird the standards reforms? A complexity of standards might situate this approach to educational improvement in the context of exploring how certain appropriations of the 'truth' are represented in numerical representations of achievement and rankings, and it might posit that there are multiple 'truths' to which we might attend.

My investigation has led me to consider that, in fact, the issues are so complex that it is difficult to see a clear path toward encouraging schools, teachers, students, administrators, and so on to do better. In other words, I am restoring the difficulty of taking up a philosophy of science theme in the debate about what achievement tests represent in the complex world in which we live, learn, and teach. The questions above and others rise to the surface because I am circumspect about the assumption that the educational enterprise can be reduced to a focus on outcomes. Similarly, the assumption that rigor comes with high achievement on tests leads me to question what it is we want for our kids. Why do we want them to achieve? The standards argument seems to be based on a reductionist model that implies that if you are not in favor of "achievement" then you are not interested in student well-being, student development, or student learning. I would submit that we first need to explore the values that undergird what we expect achievement to encompass.

Questions about the aims of education need to be reintroduced into the dialogue to help lay bare what we want our kids and teachers to be doing and achieving and for what purposes.

Teacher Standards and Student Achievement: One Happy Family

Of course, when we speak about rigor, the topic that naturally follows is how to ensure rigor for both teachers and students. In the pursuit of teaching excellence, the standards movement purports that rigor equals achievement, and achievement equals teacher accountability. What strikes me as odd is that teacher standards and student standards are often discussed separately. Why is that the case when teachers and students live in relationship in the context of learning, knowing, and exploring? What agendas are the standards proponents meeting by keeping separate these notions of accountability and achievement?

A complexity-of-standards approach would ultimately want to take up the question of how teachers relate with students and vice versa, since they live together in the dynamic flow of relational complexities present in the educational enterprise. Moreover, there are contexts that frame the experiences of both teachers and students, contexts which cannot be severed from the discussions about rigor, achievement, and accountability. To do so would be to claim that the issues presented are not tied into and are not a part of the larger systems of our living together on this planet. Global economic issues or local, state, and national political agendas frame how we see and interpret these standards constructs. In the hermeneutic spirit of seeing parts as relative to wholes and understanding that neither can exist without the other, perhaps hermeneutic inquiries in schools would let these kinds of questions and paths develop and be followed—from the particularities of what is happening in schools to the systemic influences that frame schools in the first place.

At the school level, it seems that students are being rated, and as a result teachers are being evaluated. Teachers' own hermeneutic, creative, inquisitive natures for pedagogy and relationship are lost in the simplified discussions about standards and mired in the fear that they must be accountable for how their students perform on measures that are often created miles away from the lifeworld of the school in which they teach. If this is how we want our teachers to work, is it any wonder that they in turn question the nature and purposes of "education" as we have defined it? Living in the knowledge that their own sense of creativity and pedagogical expertise must be seconded to the "experts" who lay out the curricular agenda, teachers find their roles reduced. They feel it, they know it, and so do we.

At the systemic level, agendas are set by the few to encourage educational endeavors to fit into the dominant educational modality, treated as if everyone and everything should fall in line without question or controversy.

There are incentives for people in all camps and on all sides to simplify arguments so that the "buy-in" is more likely. Perhaps the search for simplicity has to do with a fast-paced, changing world, or maybe it has more to do with the pervasiveness and persuasiveness of the dominant economic, social, and political ideologies that are firmly implanted in the collective psyche. A hermeneutic investigation could expose some of the underlying values that compete in the spaces and places of educational reform and could create a conversation that is more fully ready to accept the complexities and confusions that abound in the teacher-student-pedagogy-school-system-society-values matrix.

This says nothing about the fact that in all of these various discussions, students seem to be left out of the picture and out of the conversation. These are unnegotiable spaces for kids. I can't help wondering what their aspirations are relative to their own educational dreams and hopes. Can we not trust their input, their answer to the question Why is education important? Are we not interested in how they perceive the "achievement" regime that is currently being pushed?

To my mind, this seems to be another example of a top-down approach to getting the education equation neatly tied up and linearized. Herbert Marcuse (1964) would suggest that the standards agenda for educational reform is a part of a larger vortex that reduces possibilities for complexity, diversity, controversy, and change. He would offer that the system seeks to rationalize people into the dominant ideology to reduce resistance and perpetrate the status quo. Could he be right?

Gadamer (1995) says that the strength of an interpretation lies in the very act of trying to see whether or not the other person's perspective might be valid. Can we allow ourselves the freedom and flexibility to engage that kind of educational debate and that kind of serious deliberation? What room does a technical standards-of-education value system open for resisters, dissenters, and those who otherwise want to challenge the systems that we take for granted? How might I respond to the reality that we are ready now to reward teachers and schools, financially and otherwise, for high achievement scores? What value system is being prized in this instance?

Substantive Severings

In addition to the ways in which teachers and students are severed from each other and asked to fall into line in a technically standardized modality of education, I have also noticed that the organization of the standards movement is both convoluted and compartmentalized. In the first place, standards boards abound, all racing to "nail it down" and "get it settled" once and for all. These include the National Assessment of Educational Progress Board, the National Board for Teaching Standards, and dozens of state boards of education that are joining the standards-based education reform frenzy. Even though teacher accountability is set up to ensure that teachers are rigorous, serious, and faithful servants of the curriculum, teacher standards are completely intertwined in the substantive dictates of standards-based education.

There is a plethora of information that defines, delineates, and describes curriculum-based standards for the various subjects taught in school. Although I am in favor of the rigorous pursuit of knowledge, I must pause and ask myself if these prefabricated, severed, and compartmentalized snippets of what kids should know are reflective of the kind of broad-based education that we should arguably be valuing. One of the questions that keep surfacing as I think about the myriad questions and confusions I have about the standards movement is: What happens when something erupts in a classroom that is beyond the dictates of the standards but is worth following because the students are invested in and interested in understanding their experiences?

More specifically, let's imagine that a geography class takes up learning about Ethiopia, and in the course of that learning, territorial claims by surrounding countries are reported in the local newspaper. Imagine that the class wants to understand how space and politics merge in complicated ways in the politics of nationhood. The traditions, cultures, histories, religions, politics, economics, and social configurations of Ethiopia's placement, literally and figuratively, inspire the kids to look at Ethiopian litera-

ture, eat Ethiopian food, and listen to Ethiopian music. Clearly, our class has digressed away from the set geography curriculum and the teacher is chomping at the bit because in four weeks' time the kids are going to take an exam that is not going to ask them to comment on what kinds of investigations, questions, curiosities, intrigues, and excitement their inquiry into Ethiopia had for them. So the teacher presses on to fulfill the curricular mandate, feeling pressured to cover what the state has set out as the standard.

This hypothetical example highlights how severed substantive standards alienate and constrain the potential for complex configurations of learning. Taken to the extreme, technical standards sever substantive topics and reduce them to dead knowledge—that is, knowledge that is severed from the lifeblood of the lived world. There is no doubt that there are many teachers who would take the opportunity to journey down the aforementioned Ethiopian path, but what are the ramifications of diverting from the set agenda? What happens to teacher accountability when students don't cover the curriculum?

This example illustrates the potential for a hermeneutic learning that has the depth and breadth of a complex knowledge. Requiring the kids to follow trails of inquiry that are propelled by questions, encouraging the study of systems that may be foreign to our own, and renovating what we understand by means of what we don't—this kind of hermeneutic, complexity-of-standards approach requires high quality and rigorous study.

Furthermore, I wonder how the world is perceived by students who are taught that the world is compartmentalized very much like the subjects they take up in school. Is geography really only about geography, or is it otherwise connected to how we make space for ourselves in the world? This kind of ecological perspective calls on students, teachers, policy planners, and administrators to view education as an endeavor that promotes learning, questioning, and exploring. Standards of complexity recognize the need for teachers to be invested with the kind of scholarly trust that promotes excellence in classrooms and beyond, while simultaneously recognizing that the issues around substantive standards are difficult to tackle since we continually have to engage the complex question, what do we want our kids to be learning?

The standards-of-education movement lures us into believing that everything we can know is definable, measurable, and quantifiable. The overriding impressions that I am left with are that the standards movement pays a lot of attention to "what" and less time on "why". The "why" slips silently away because the "what" represents the status quo and the dominant neoliberal ideologies that have fast-tracked the educational debate into a discussion about how to prepare our students to be the workforce of the twenty-first century.

Educational Research and Colleges of Education

Of course, all that we name as problematic about technical standards in education has monumental implications for colleges of education and educational research. Although the standards discussions are situated far away from university classrooms and are often cloistered in their own kind of "practical," "real world" spaces, universities are still the places where teachers are taught about teaching, and they are likewise the places where much of educational research gets done. The hermeneutic circle that takes me from the particularities and practicalities of the geography example spirals me out to the more philosophical spaces where education is connected to research and practice at the university level.

One observation about the standards movement is that there is a movement afoot for a voluntary national teacher certification program. What, then, are colleges of education doing if not preparing competent, skilled, bright, committed, scholarly, complicated, teachers? What is implied by a standards board on top of a state board? How much bureaucracy can the system sustain?

These questions burn to be answered as the standards movement makes a case for national teacher certification. Why are colleges of education being positioned out of the process of preparing excellent teachers? Do some believe that colleges of education are producing bad teachers? Or is this move about making a hierarchy of teachers, to establish rankings much like those created by student standards? What other elements could be operating covertly that beckon some investigation? Are these things connected to the publication of school rankings, promoting "success" as the end-all and be-all in learning? I suspect so.

Further, what questions about educational standards do not ultimately affect how we train future teachers and encourage innovative educational research initiatives? Why should we prepare excellent teachers if their jobs are really about meting out a standards-based education? How are the worlds of the high school classroom similar to or different from the worlds of the university classroom, and what values are being perpetuated by the approaches that we take with respect to educational research and its impact on educational practice?

Hermeneutics, as we have been discussing, is centered on the experiences and expressions of the lived world. This kind of approach to inquiry demands a complex research method that cannot be rendered in reductionist models of epistemology. To that end, educational research needs to be more closely aligned with the lived world and must also work in conjunction with real schools. The research issue is complex because there is a place for inquiries that may not take place directly in the schools but that nonetheless have an educational impact. However, a research agenda that

is wholly severed from the lifeworld of education might not bear the same kind of complex fruit that a more integrative agenda could.

What a hermeneutic approach offers is its generative and transformative goals in meaning-making. It is always about seeing things anew and making that which has become familiar unfamiliar, thereby creating an opportunity to look again at the world; it is always about making connections beyond the small systems of which we are a part.

Knowledge Producers and Knowledge Production in the Classroom and Beyond

What would it be like if teachers were trained to see themselves as researchers, inquirers, and knowledge producers? What kinds of information might emanate from a teacher education that instilled scholarly identities into those who go into the classrooms to teach and mentor our kids? In the first place, that kind of endeavor could only come to light if a complexity-of-education approach were adopted. Standards of complexity recognize that teachers and students are themselves researchers. Hermeneutics can invite them to ask questions and can encourage them to look at all that is complicated about their learning, about the contexts in which they learn, about the subject matter that they are asked to engage, and about the values of knowledge that they encounter.

Because the new pedagogical hermeneutic requires of teachers first and foremost that they be *interpreters* of culture, rather than merely *transmitters* or managers, it is imperative that they be as widely and deeply educated as possible so that they can speak across disciplines, across cultures and national boundaries. The pedagogical modus of the hermeneutic classroom is *dialogue*, in which the teacher has the capacity to interpret culture and information so that students can appreciate their participation in it, as in a living stream that both flows through life and is the source of its sustenance (Smith, 1999, p. 5).

If technical standards of education take root, will teachers be able to be what Smith is suggesting? Will they have the freedom? Will the complexity of the world as it presents itself be simplified and concretized for an achievement-based educational system?

Hermeneutics in the classroom might entail a complexity-of-standards approach that would hermeneutically explore the cultures of schools, the breadth of social, political, psychological, relational, and substantive learning that happens simultaneously in the educational space. What about children who are becoming fine citizens and well-adjusted individuals but who are doing only marginally well on their achievement tests? A hermeneutic approach might investigate all the complexities and surprises that might be operating in classrooms that don't make the "grade." Such an approach would include and encourage questions about our lives together, about our purposes for engaging with children, for being part of learning.

Standards, Hermeneutics, Administrators, and Policy Makers

The kind of broad questions that I have raised throughout this chapter demonstrate how a hermeneutic perspective might take up the standards-of-education issues, for teachers and students, in classrooms and universities, for teaching and learning. A hermeneutic perspective does not alienate anyone who is interested in the complexity of our lives together. Open, critical, and difficult queries about our lived educational experiences can be undertaken at all levels of the educational enterprise. Requiring investigation that involves looking critically at all that plays into educational, pedagogic, psychological, and social interactions, the learning endeavor is deeply connected to the policy that frames it. I wonder what it would take for policy makers and administrators to also re-vision themselves as questioners, researchers, and educational practitioners who, like detectives, look for the things that strike them beyond the simple task of enforcing a standards-of-education agenda. Perhaps this explication of a hermeneutic approach might elucidate, to some extent, how we might begin to do that.

Questions as Conclusions

The standards issues are complex, as I've tried to demonstrate. Part of what makes the topic so complicated is that there seems to be an easy answer waiting for us in the standards-of-education movement, an answer that will allay our fears about what we're doing with teachers, students, scholars, and schools by replacing complexity with complacency in education. Hermeneutics wants us to resist that temptation and to commit ourselves to the original difficulties of the lived world. Hermeneutics offers us the opportunity to get into the lived world where these issues play out and where we are offered the opportunity to make the world a better place, to come to know ourselves and our values, and to articulate those values and beliefs as they relate to education in general and educational standards in particular.

The questions that I've raised throughout this chapter are meant to serve multiple purposes. In the first instance, they teach what hermeneutics is. In the second instance, they demonstrate how hermeneutics can break open the standards-of-education debate by offering an approach that encourages us to get in the business of making meaning in the messiness of our lives together.

References

Dewey, J. (1916). *Democracy and education.* New York: Macmillan.

Gadamer, H. G. (1977). *Philosophical her-* *meneutics.* Berkeley and Los Angeles: University of California Press.

Gadamer, H. G. (1995). *Truth and method* (2nd ed.). New York: Continuum.

Gallagher, S. (1992). *Hermeneutics and education.* Albany, NY: SUNY Press.

Jardine, D. (1992). The fecundity of the individual case: Considerations of the pedagogic heart of interpretations. *Journal of Philosophy of Education, 26,* 51–61.

Jardine, D. (1998). *To dwell with a boundless heart: Essays in curriculum theory, hermeneutics, and the ecological imagination.* New York: Peter Lang.

Marcuse, H. (1964). *One-dimensional man.* Boston: Beacon. (Reprint, with introduction by D. Kellner, Beacon, 1991).

National Board for Professional Teaching Standards. (2000). NBPTS Report—Introduction: What teachers should know and be able to do. *National Board for Professional Teaching standards* [On line]. Available: http://www.nbpts.org/nbpts/standards/intro.html

Ricoeur, P. (1981). Hermeneutics and the human sciences. In J. B. Thompson (Ed. and Trans.), *Paul Ricoeur—Hermeneutics and the human sciences: Essays on language, action and interpretation* (pp. 145–164). London: Cambridge University Press.

Smith, D. (1994). *Pedagon: Meditations on pedagogy and culture.* Bragg Creek: Makyo Press.

Smith, D. (1999). Globalization and education: Prospects for postcolonial pedagogy in a hermeneutic mode. *Interchange, 30*(1), 1–10.

CHALLENGING HIGH-STAKES STANDARDIZED TESTING

Building an Antiracist, Progressive Social Movement in Public Education

Alex Caputo-Pearl

In 1997, I returned to teaching in Los Angeles. I had taken a three-year hiatus from the public schools to focus on community organizing and graduate work in urban planning. As I watched the halls buzz with students eager to see their friends, I was filled with excitement and was sure that I had made the right decision. I would once again be a white teacher in a low-income community of color. But this time, in addition to taking on the challenges of teaching young people, I would look for opportunities to build labor/community coalitions for social justice with parents, teachers, and students. Peering into the corridor from a classroom that had cracked chalkboards, a leak in the ceiling, and no books, I did not have to look far for injustice.

Simultaneous with my return to the classroom, the momentum behind racist and class-biased high-stakes tests—those that are tied to student promotion, student scholarships, funding for schools, and tracking—began to grow in educational public policy circles. As my students face another year of narrow "drill and kill" and "test preparation" exercises amidst appalling learning conditions, it has become clear that the crisis in public education requires intervention by a social movement that challenges racism and class bias. To be effective, this movement must challenge the dominant ideas and myths—the ideology—that perpetuate systematic discrimination in schools and other institutions.[1]

This article first explores three major questions. First, what is the dominant ideology at the foundation of U.S. public education? Second, how has standardized testing historically supported this ideology? Third, how is the current high-stakes testing policy in Los Angeles both rooted in and

577

supportive of ideology that perpetuates racism and class bias?

The last section will be devoted to exploring an experimental political organizing model that is being used in Los Angeles by the Coalition for Educational Justice (CEJ). Several questions will be addressed: What dilemmas are presented to this kind of organizing at a historical moment when racist and biased ideology is so powerful? Given these dilemmas, what kind of educational reforms should CEJ be fighting for? What kind of organizing model should be used to build a grassroots base of power? Are there reforms that can legitimately improve quality of education for low-income students of color and simultaneously open space for transformative social movements?

Dominant Ideology in U.S. Public Education

The dominant ideology and mythologies surrounding U.S. public education contradict the real purposes of schools in a capitalist and racist society. The myths of meritocracy and "educational attainment" as the avenue for overcoming poverty and racism are at the foundation of support for U.S. education. If you walk into any public school, you will see some version of the incantation "All Students Can Succeed" posted visibly. Chances are that you will also see eye-catching posters encouraging students to "Stay in School" so they can "Go to College and Get a Good Job." These invocations are central to reproducing

the dominant ideology, which assumes that (1) U.S. schools, from a level playing field, objectively determine who merits social privileges, thereby giving us a meritocracy, (2) everyone can receive these privileges if they can show that they are deserving, and (3) no matter what conditions surround a person, "educational attainment"—understood sometimes as high school graduation, at other times as high standardized test scores—is the true avenue to overcoming poverty and racism.

This ideology conceals profound racism and class bias in education and employment, particularly affecting low-income African-Americans, Latinos, Native Americans, and Asian-Americans. Factually, educational attainment—for example, getting a high school diploma—is not as important a determinant of job and university access as race and class are.[2] Similarly, race and class are tightly correlated with school drop out, a phenomenon that, when allowed to occur, violates students' rights to equal educational access. Many dropouts are in reality "push outs" because of the retention, or mandatory "flunking," policies popular today under the euphemism of "No Social Promotion." Rather than improving students' academic performance, these policies tend to disproportionately encourage low-income students of color to quit their underresourced and often hopeless schools.[3]

Racist and class-biased school funding policies are a primary cause of these inequalities. A 1999 study by the

Civil Rights Project at Harvard University found that public education in the United States is becoming increasingly segregated by race and income. Nationally, segregation has increased for African-American students since the 1980s and for Latinos since 1960. Students in the most racially segregated schools are ten times more likely to be poor than students in all-white or nearly all-white schools (Colvin, 1999a). Their schools are also more likely to be poor. Though reliance on regressive property taxes to fund schools has diminished slightly, vast disparities in per-student funding still exist between majority white and middle-class schools and those that serve low-income communities of color.[4]

A racist and class-biased job opportunity structure is also a primary cause of such inequalities. At the turn of the twenty-first century, the U.S. economy is as bifurcated as ever. The expanding high-tech "informational," financial, electronics, and "dot-com" sectors have generated high-paying, high-prestige jobs, disproportionately for white people.[5] Concurrently, there has been an increase in low-paying service and light manufacturing jobs and contracted-out, lower-paying public-sector jobs, where people of color are heavily overrepresented. In this context, it is clear that all students are not meant to succeed.

Yet only by placing these trends into a broader political and educational context do we see the full extent to which the "All Students Can Succeed" mantra is a lie. City police departments in New York, Los Angeles, Philadelphia, and other cities regularly violate the rights of people of color (Seeley, 2000; Hayden, 2000; Getlin, 2000), who have been criminalized throughout the 1990s, with many thrown into an expanding prison-industrial complex for nonviolent offenses. Simultaneously, social services have been attacked, defunded, or willfully neglected. Welfare and related services have been deformed, leading to an increase in hunger and poverty. Inadequate monies have been devoted to inner-city transportation, and in the health care sector, the ranks of the uninsured continue to rise. Simultaneously, decent-paying jobs have left working-class neighborhoods and communities of color. Affirmative action is under attack, and representation of Latinos, African-Americans, and Native Americans is falling in many universities (Jenkins, 2000; Weiss, 1999a).

This oppressive broader context extends to youth and educational policy. States are passing legislation that would allow teenagers to be tried as adults and placed in jail for longer periods of time (Giroux, 2000; Cooper, 2000). The police presence in inner-city schools is unprecedented. Zero-tolerance discipline policies in schools have a racially discriminatory impact as students of color are suspended and denied equal access to education at levels many times that of white students (Ayers & Dohrn, 2000). Understanding the desperation for employment options in low-income communities of color, the U.S. military concentrates its recruitment in the inner cities, eager to place youth at the front lines of the "drug war" in Latin America and other excursions abroad. Low-income parents of color are routinely treated like second-class citizens on school campuses, stereotyped as lazy welfare queens, violent offenders, or immigrants "taking advantage of the system." Immigrants' languages have been denigrated, deemed inappropriate for school.

Fundamentally, contrary to the mantra, all students are not meant to succeed in a capitalist and racist society. Meritocracy, equal opportunity, and "educational attainment" ladders do not exist. Rather, a race and class hierarchy exists. Separate and unequal schools and separate and unequal job/university opportunity structures comprise a linked setup for students of color and low-income students. Not surprisingly, capitalism needs exactly this type of setup to function. The capitalist school system has always played an important role in (1) sorting people into the socioeconomic hierarchy, for the most part along racial, gender, and linguistic lines, and (2) socializing people to accept hierarchical relationships by perpetuating the dominant ideology, such as white male superiority and meritocracy (see Bowles & Gintis, 1976; Morrow & Torres, 1995).

Yet the victories of the civil rights, workers', and women's movements against some of the most egregious racist, classist, and sexist barriers have been both forceful and real. These victories, in combination with the in-credible perseverance and brilliance of many individuals, have helped some low-income people of color reach middle- and upper-class status. In fact, enough have reached this status to help the media to perpetuate and strengthen the myths of meritocracy and "educational attainment" as the avenue to overcome poverty and racism. But the reality is that structural forms of discrimination—those that systematically violate human rights—still stand in the way of the majority of low-income people of color. To challenge these structures, we must combine sophisticated political analysis with a strategy to build a social movement.

The Historic Role of Standardized Testing in Supporting the Dominant Ideology in Education

For decades, standardized intelligence and achievement tests have served as a racist and class-biased tool for the sorting and socialization process that capitalist and racist schools perform. They have also served as a vital tool in the perpetuation of ideology that posits the inferior intellectual abilities of people of color, immigrants, and low-income people. The racist eugenics movement in the early 1900s substantially contributed to the development and administration of the first standardized tests. In 1923, Princeton professor Carl Brigham's U.S. Army intelligence tests laid the foundation for the creation of the Scholastic Aptitude Test (SAT), a variation of which now determines college entrance. His all-English standardized testing of army recruits—81,000 "native born" whites, 12,000 foreign-born immigrants, and 23,000 African-Americans—led him to conclude that (1) "the foreign born are intellectually inferior to the native born," (2) intelligence rises as the recruit spends more time in the United States, and (3) relative quantities of Nordic blood determine a person's intelligence. Not surprisingly, beyond the clear language bias, the tests were culturally and socioeconomically biased, including questions about U.S. postage rules, bowling, and tennis (Sacks, 1999, pp. 29–32).

Also in the 1920s, Lewis Terman, Stanford University professor and originator of the Stanford-Binet intelligence test, began to perfect the role of tests in sorting and socialization. He convinced many school districts to use high-stakes and culturally biased tests to place students onto gifted and talented tracks, "slow" tracks, or entirely separate schools. For example, in the 1920s an educational consultant for the San Jose school system recommended that the district use Terman's tests to guide "children for their proper economic life activities in accordance with their abilities." The vast majority of Mexican-American children in the district went to lower academic tracks because of "inferior intellectual quality." By the mid-1920s, more than 2 million school children across the United States were tested primarily for academic tracking purposes (Stoskopf, 1999, p. 12).

Today, politicians and business leaders have increasingly advocated standardized testing. They argue that this emphasis will ensure that (1) schools and teachers are accountable to communities and students are made accountable for their lessons, (2) the quality of education is increasing when scores are increasing, and (3) economic and academic opportunities are expanding for students who attain higher scores. Using standardized tests as a hammer, they tell students to be accountable for their classwork and homework, parents to be accountable for their children's performance, and teachers to be accountable for their students' performance. In doing so, they effectively marginalize discussion of the real problems—that government and corporations refuse to be held accountable for the provision of decent public services, jobs, school supplies, and resources to low-income people and communities of color.

Wearing the dual masks of "objectivity" and the "need for a tool that precisely measures educational attainment," the rhetoric of government and business leaders surrounding the use of high-stakes standardized tests is more subtle today than it was in the 1920s. However, the objectives and effects of the tests, specifically around sorting and socialization, remain largely the same. Now, as during the 1920s, white and middle-class students are disproportionately rewarded with the top of the test score tallies. Low-income students of color who live in underresourced communities, attend underresourced schools, and experience racism on a daily basis are punished and neglected at the bottom, many of them tracked into low-wage jobs or "pushed out" of school into prison and the military.

How High-Stakes Standardized Testing Supports Dominant Ideology, Racism, and Class Bias in Los Angeles

Political-Economic Context

The nationwide crises in job stratification and government cuts are explosively magnified in Los Angeles. Los Angeles is considered a "world city," with a corresponding bifurcated, unequal job structure.[6] On the high end of employment, LA's job growth rate in the financial, real estate, and business services sectors—including advanced services provided to corporations involving financial innovations, transactions, accounting, computer programming, and management consulting—was over 50 percent between 1972 and 1984. In addition to the consistency of the primarily white-collar film industry, growth in electronics and telecommunications is also driving the economy, with firms clustered in the suburbs of Northern Orange County, El Segundo, Chatsworth, and Burbank-Glendale (Keil, 1998, pp. 99–112).

At the same time that these primarily white-collar sectors have boomed, wealth disparity and poverty have been increasing and continue to be overwhelmingly race based, that is, concentrated in communities of color.[7] Two hundred eighty thousand manufacturing jobs—many of them union and overwhelmingly held by people of color—were torn away from working class areas of LA County between 1979 and 1993, as corporate leaders in the auto, rubber, steel, and glass industries sought consolidation and lower-wage locations (Wolff, 1994). Public sector cuts have resulted in layoffs for thousands in the government workforce, also disproportionately made up of people of color and women. "Reindustrialization" that has occurred since the loss of heavy manufacturing has been in low-wage, nonunion sectors such as garment making, food processing, and restaurant and hotel services (Keil, 1998, pp. 95–112. See also Soja, 1991).

Meanwhile, government spending and programs for social needs have been under attack. Women of color in particular have been punished by President Clinton's welfare reform. Of the thousands of women in LA County who have had their welfare cash grant reduced, half have not been able to pay for food. Just under 50 percent of those women affected by welfare reform have become homeless, and 25 percent have not been able to find child care. Moreover, 58 percent of women in LA County who have been removed from the welfare system are currently unemployed. Of those who have jobs, over 50 percent earn less than seven dollars per hour, substantially shy of a living wage (Welfare Reform Monitoring Project, 2000).

Health care is also in crisis. Approximately 2.7 million of the 9 million residents of LA County do not have health insurance, 700,000 of them children. Forty-six percent of Latinos and 26 percent of African-Americans do not have health insurance. Meanwhile, hospitals are downsizing, and the entire county health system is in permanent financial crisis (LA County Dept. of Health Services, 2000; Riccardi, 2000). The Los Angeles Metropolitan Transportation Authority has defied a court order to buy more buses to serve its ridership, which is overwhelmingly low-income and of color, focusing instead on building corporate rail projects to suburbs and the port (Rabin, 2000a, 2000b; Mann, 1996).

On top of this, anti–working class propositions based on racist campaigns of misinformation about the undeserving poor have devastated communities of color. Affirmative action and bilingual education have been banned through passage of Propositions 209 and 227. Jail construction is exploding with the passage of Proposition 184's "three strikes" and Proposition 21's "juvenile justice."[8] Meanwhile, it is not crime that is increasing, but the desire to criminalize the poor and people of color. As evidence of this, the top two reasons that people are entering California jails are nonviolent offenses—possession of a controlled substance and possession of a controlled substance for sale (Irwin, 1999). Thirty-two percent of the California prison population is African-American and 34 percent is Latino, far

disproportionate to their share of the California population (Southern California Criminal Justice Consortium, 1999). The Los Angeles Police Department is under federal investigation for beating, shooting, and stealing from people of color.

At the same time, the California state university system has been cutting its remedial programs, which have historically helped students who come from underresourced K-12 schools (Weiss, 1999c). The University of California system has become more exclusive. The 1999 freshman class at UCLA had an average GPA of 4.24 and an SAT score of 1330. Representation of African-Americans, Latinos, and Native Americans is decreasing, down to 13 percent (Weiss, 1999a). Its student body came mostly from families that earn between $100,000 and $150,000 per year (Weiss, 1999b).

Public Education Context

The separate and unequal job/university opportunity structures in Los Angeles are supported by separate and unequal schooling. California's ranking of forty-first in the United States in per-pupil spending (Yates, 1999) and the 1978 passage of Proposition 13, which permanently reduced property and corporate tax rates, have been substantial causes of the inequalities and inadequacies of schools. Beyond this, California state policy is in place for Basic Aid Districts, allowing the wealthiest areas in the state to keep a higher-than-average percentage of their property tax money in their own districts, thereby further concentrating wealth and privilege (for more information, see Odden, 1992). Further, PTA groupings from wealthy areas routinely put thousands of dollars into their school systems to buy new teachers or supplies. But beyond these policies, the inequality has been driven by the consistent and racist neglect of urban poverty and institutions and the refusal of policy makers to understand that creation of first-class education in crowded, historically oppressed, inner-city communities will require massive investment, well beyond what is invested in middle-class suburbs.

Over 80 percent of students in the Los Angeles Unified School District (LAUSD) are people of color and 70 percent are poor (Kantor, 1997, p. 21). Many of the over 700 schools in LAUSD, the second-largest district in the country, are literally crumbling. Since 1978, only eight new schools have been built, while enrollment has expanded by 10,000 students per year (Colvin, 1999b). Class and school sizes have soared, making it virtually impossible for regular, engaged student-teacher interaction to occur (Blume, 2000; Smith, 2000). Over one-quarter of the teachers in LAUSD are non-credentialed and lack the professional support they need. Many classrooms have no permanent teacher (only rotating substitutes) and no teaching assistants, especially in the most racially and economically isolated areas (Colvin, 1999b). A severe textbook shortage exists across several subject areas

(Smith, Sahagun, & Sauerwein, 2000). These conditions present a portrait of inequality when compared to those in the predominantly white public schools of Beverly Hills, Santa Monica, La Jolla, Mountain View, or Santa Cruz.

Amidst this political economic and educational context, independent and progressive movements fighting for social justice have been profoundly weak (for an analysis of different types of movements see Wypijewski, 1997). Many movements are of the narrow "Not In My Back Yard" (NIMBY) nature, focusing on community-specific issues—for example, struggling to keep a landfill from being built—without determining whether a problem is extinguished or merely relocated to another neighborhood. Other movements are tied to and dependent upon Democratic Party or AFL-CIO (American Federation of Labor) officials, thereby confined only to the narrow, often racist and class-biased politics of these organizations. Still other grassroots mobilizations are temporary in nature, formed only for short-term struggles to defeat propositions or candidates. And finally, other movements have been under consistent threat of police repression, such as the Justice for Janitors movement of Los Angeles (Olney, 1993). Notwithstanding these obstacles, the rise of high-stakes testing in Los Angeles—and the necessity of opposing it—may open political space for a new, transformative social movement in public education to emerge.

The Rise of High-Stakes Standardized Testing

The California and Los Angeles governments' preferred "solutions" to the educational and economic crises have been to implement high-stakes testing and retention rather than to invest heavily in schools and attack racism. In 1997, California's Republican governor, Pete Wilson, sponsored legislation requiring the statewide administration of the Harcourt Brace Corporation's Stanford 9 test. It would be administered in English to the vast majority of students, regardless of English fluency levels. This racist attack by Wilson on immigrant students was consistent with his support for Proposition 187, which threatened to remove undocumented immigrant students from schools, and for Proposition 227, which effectively banned bilingual education.

Stanford 9 tests—acknowledged by prominent academics and educators to be culturally and socioeconomically biased—have included questions about foods, furniture, television programs, legends, computer usage, and views of private and public property that would favor students from white, middle-class backgrounds and those who grew up in the United States (Groves, 2000a). These are the students who have the highest degree of access to resources and to the "cultural capital" that is valued by the dominant white, middle-class strata. Most importantly, on top of the language and cultural bias, the Stanford 9 is administered in

an unequal educational and employment context—where students in low-income communities of color who go to schools without resources are at a severe disadvantage.

In 1998, "No Social Promotion" legislation passed the California Assembly and Senate, receiving support from Governor Wilson, LA Mayor Richard Riordan, and other politicians looking for a quick fix to the public's concern about schools. This legislation was separate from the earlier statewide Stanford 9 law, but the two laws would come together to create explosive high-stakes testing policies. Under the 1998 law, the practice of socially promoting students would be ended, and districts would be required to retain, or "flunk," students not considered to be at grade level. This policy sailed through Sacramento with strong bipartisan support and constant political grandstanding around a "new era of accountability" for the schools.

This political support came despite the fact that virtually all research on student retention shows that it does not have positive academic effects, instead dramatically increasing the chance of student drop out. Experiences in New York City and Georgia in the 1980s and in Chicago and Texas in the 1990s have shown that, predictably, low-income students of color are the most likely to be "flunked" and to be "pushed out" because they are the most likely to attend schools that do not serve them.[9] Despite this, in a rush to score political points locally and in Sacramento, LAUSD put a retention plan in place a year early. In LAUSD and all over the state, the Stanford 9 and other standardized tests would be phased in as criteria for retaining students, creating a triple hit on low-income students of color in the form of a biased test given in a context of inequality that is linked to discriminatory policies like retention.[10]

Democrat Gray Davis—dubbed a right-wing, "Crackdown Democrat" by the *New York Times*—was elected governor of California in 1998 on a platform of education "reform" and law-and-order politics that demonized youth of color and promised more police and status quo economic development policies (Nieves, 2000). Davis immediately outlined more punishments and rewards for students, teachers, and schools based on Stanford 9 results. At the same time, he guaranteed that he would not raise per-pupil spending to the national average. The politically ambitious Davis offered this guarantee as a clear signal to right-wing and business interests that he would not move to implement even remotely progressive tax measures to fund schools (Pyle, 2000).

Instead, Davis created the Academic Performance Index (API), based on Stanford 9 scores, in order to rank schools statewide. Low-ranked schools that remain low-ranked are threatened with the stigma of "reconstitution"— the involuntary transfer of all staff. Moreover, Davis and his staff have taken measures that virtually ensure a narrowing of curriculum around the Stanford 9, rampant "teaching to the test," and racist and class-biased re-

warding of the privileged. In his 2000–2001 budget the governor included (1) financial rewards and punishments for entire schools depending on changes in their Stanford 9 and API scores, (2) scholarships for students in the top percentiles of the Stanford 9 and for some others who markedly increase their scores, and (3) financial rewards for individual teachers—up to $25,000—who improve the scores of their classes (Colvin & Helfand, 2000).

As these policies were sailing through Sacramento, another leading force in Los Angeles education, United Teachers-Los Angeles (UTLA), an affiliate of the AFL-CIO, was the center of great contestation regarding high-stakes testing. The union leadership had lobbied in Sacramento for the student retention legislation in 1998, worried that union opposition would give the impression to the public that teachers were against "school accountability." Since then, union leadership has been very involved in helping the district implement high-stakes testing and retention, arguing that it is a moving train with public support and that the union should jump aboard to impact its direction. As the policies have moved forward, UTLA's most visible official critiques of testing and retention have focused narrowly on teacher rights—how the policies create too much paperwork for teachers and how teachers should not be held accountable to only one measurement device, in this case the Stanford 9.

But rank-and-file activists—many involved in the CEJ—passed motions at the UTLA House of Representatives to oppose the Stanford 9. Further, motions were passed in some UTLA area meetings to reverse union policy and oppose the retention plan. Predictably, union leaders delayed any public opposition to the Stanford 9 test, even with motions in place. But to their credit, they eventually did take action.

Meanwhile, portions of the union leadership and significant sectors of the rank and file continue to argue that if UTLA militantly opposes the Stanford 9 and student retention, the union's current efforts to advocate for a pay raise will be defeated. The union's prioritization of the demand for increased teacher pay and benefits and its primary focus on teacher rights in its critiques of testing and retention reflect an economistic strategy. In this way, UTLA has continued the long tradition of labor union leaderships subordinating antiracist, community-based, antipoverty, and antisexist demands to narrow, economistic demands that overwhelmingly benefit union-organized, upper-strata working class, and middle class constituencies rather than the most vulnerable in society (for discussion, see Mann & Ramsey, 1996; Mann, et al., 1994).

Meanwhile, a third leading force in education—corporations and business interests—advocated strongly for standardized testing. Harcourt Brace, Inc., which develops the Stanford 9, receives millions of dollars in contract money from the State of California. McGraw-Hill, Inc. and other companies make millions in publishing year-round test-preparation materials.

Other companies have contracts with districts nationwide to provide narrow, test-coaching tutoring to a handful of students (for more on the money in testing, see Sacks, 1999, pp. 12-13, 221-230). Lobbyists for these companies can often be found in Sacramento and at district offices. Further, business leaders from Hewlett-Packard, Boeing, IBM, Pacific Bell, and other corporations formed the California Business Consortium for Educational Excellence. The consortium has a full-time staff devoted to lobbying in Sacramento for standardized testing, among other policies (Colvin, 2000).

On another front, Eli Broad—a financial services/real estate millionaire and a key member of LA Mayor Richard Riordan's inner policy circle, made up of white male millionaires—recruited and helped to hire former Colorado Governor Roy Romer as LAUSD's new superintendent.[11] Time will tell what Romer's policies will be, but the former cochair of the National Committee on Educational Standards and Testing has expressed support for retention programs and test-based rewards and consequences. In his early days as superintendent, he has offered very few ideas that might address inequality, institutional racism, and adequacy of resources ("Roy Romer's," n.d.; Callan, n.d.). However, now with the beginnings of a movement called the Coalition for Educational Justice (CEJ), the debate about high-stakes testing is taking new directions within the UTLA. This group has mobilized an antiracist, multicultural coalition of thousands of parents, students, and teachers to achieve victories forcing the LAUSD to allow parental waivers of these high-stakes tests and notification by the district that waivers are available. They have also moved the debate from accountability to educational and social justice.

For their part, however, business leaders have four major interests in public education, all of which are supported by policies that emphasize standardized testing. First, they are interested in tapping into new markets in which they can make profits. Thus, the more services within public education—from testing and evaluation to food services—that can be "spun out" to private companies for lucrative contracts, the better.

Second, business leaders are interested in having at their disposal an appropriate workforce. Looking beyond their feel-good rhetoric of "raising all standards and levels," we can see that most business leaders want a labor market that is stratified and segmented, like that which is supported by unequal education and standardized testing. This type of labor market contains both highly skilled and highly paid workers and those workers that would accept lower-paying, unsatisfying jobs.

Third, most business leaders wish to push public agencies to "run more like businesses"—where the guiding dirges dictate cost-benefit analysis and more investment in the private sphere than the public sphere. Thus, business leaders advocate for fiscal austerity in the use of public money for the schools. To this end, they advocate financial discipline through tools such as standardized test results to determine which schools and employees should get public money and which should not. Business leaders' key objective in advocating that schools be "run like businesses" is that corporations be shielded from progressive taxation measures that would substantially redistribute wealth and place more money in the public sphere.

Finally, business leaders are often in the forefront of advocating a narrow "core curriculum." Because so much power in the United States is concentrated in the hands of corporations, curricula that engage students in interrogating, dissecting, and "speaking truth to power" are dangerous. So social movement histories, labor histories, civil rights histories, and other histories that deal with the struggles of working people against powerful institutions are often excluded from curricula.

The majority of these political players—politicians, union officials, and business leaders—promise that raising test scores will attack income inequality and racism. Yet if that is truly the intention of some, it stands in direct contradiction to many of their other policy choices. More likely, for many it is a cynical ploy to divert attention from real problems and from the need for massive investment. The "rising test scores equals an attack on poverty and racism" formulation is the newest reflection of the "educational attainment" recitation.

The Real Impacts of High-Stakes Standardized Testing

As I've pointed out, the proponents of high-stakes standardized testing argue that testing will ensure that (1) schools and teachers are accountable to communities and students are made accountable for their lessons, (2) the quality of education is increasing when scores are increasing, and (3) economic and academic opportunities are expanding for students who attain higher scores. The *real* impacts of high-stakes standardized testing in Los Angeles refute what the proponents argue and, in fact, deepen existing inequalities.

First, high-stakes testing strengthens racism and class bias. Also, because the Stanford 9 test is culturally and linguistically biased and administered in an entirely unequal context, test results have duplicated the patterns of standardized test results throughout history—they have left whites and middle-class students at the top of the test score tallies and have left a disproportionate number of students of color and low-income students at the bottom of the tallies. In 1999, among low-income students in California the average API score—based entirely on Stanford 9 scores—was 499, 118 points below the statewide average. The scores for students whose parents did not go to college—a right that has been abrogated for most Latinos and African-Americans in LA and elsewhere—were approximately 50 points lower than those whose parents did go

to college. Further, API rankings dropped as the percentage of non-credentialed teachers in the school rose (Friedman, 2000; Groves, 2000; Helfand & Sahagun, 2000).

Though Los Angeles and California are in the early stages of doling out the high stakes attached to Stanford 9, a pattern is clearly being set. The majority of punishments set by Davis and the districts will be directed at low-income students of color and those who don't speak English—and their schools. Rewards will primarily go to middle- and upper-class white students with good schools and access to cultural capital—and to their teachers and schools (see Zamichow, 2000).

Second, particularly in schools that serve low-income students of color, uncritical, unimaginative work on basic skills and "test prep" is glorified, serving a corporate agenda to prepare entry-level workers. The curriculum has been narrowed at many inner-city schools in LA, further marginalizing the histories of women, national liberation and anti-imperialist movements, labor, gays and lesbians, and so on—as appointed testing coordinators hold unprecedented power, requiring homerooms, study halls, and entire classes for Stanford 9 test coaching. Racism is further embedded in the curriculum as languages, experiences, and information that are deemed unrelated to "standards" and tests are devalued. Separate and unequal schooling takes another parallel form as inner-city LA schools focus on disengaging "drill and kill" test coaching exercises while suburban, primarily white schools—less worried about test score punishments—engage their students with project-based and critical thinking–based learning (see Caputo-Pearl, 1999; Groves & Richardson, 2000; Berlak, 1999; Aratani, 2000).

This discussion reveals the third major impact of high-stakes testing in Los Angeles. One result of test coaching, according to virtually all education researchers, is a predictable "bounce" upward in test scores, even at underresourced schools, as we have seen over the last two years in LAUSD (Groves, 2000b; Helfand & Sahagun, 2000). Educational researchers further agree that rising test scores are not tightly correlated to academic achievement or improvements in school quality. They equate to student knowledge of the test and test format, not to real learning or expansion of student economic opportunity (see Kohn, 1999, pp. 73-92; Groves, 1999). Despite this research, much of the public believes that rising scores indicate healthier schools. The media and the LAUSD's focus on this "improvement" smokescreens the need for a much broader discussion of what is needed for real educational reform.

Fourth, new forms of tracking, or "educational triage," have been institutionalized in LAUSD, primarily at schools in low-income communities of color. District officials, under pressure to improve the lowest-scoring schools, have directed teachers in these communities to focus their attention on those students who have already scored relatively high on tests.

These students, the district contends, have proved they take tests well. If they receive more attention, so the argument goes, their test-taking abilities are bound to improve. Their resulting higher individual scores can pull up the entire school's average, thus creating the illusion of reform and opening the possibility for test-based rewards (Caputo-Pearl, 1999; Moberg, 1998).

Fifth, corporate and private influence over LA's public schools has deepened, privatization forces have been strengthened, and school accountability to communities has been weakened. Because of the Stanford 9, much of the LAUSD curriculum is now influenced by Harcourt Brace, Inc. and its economic and political allies in national business consortiums. Sylvan, Kaplan, and other companies have signed contracts with several LAUSD schools to provide "test preparation," thus cracking open the door of the public schools to privatization and advocates of "contracting out." Students all across LAUSD are treated like numbers (test scores) and commodities (with value based on test scores).

Test scores influence more and more school site decisions, playing the same role as profit in disciplining financial decisions and workers and promoting fiscal austerity. Business leaders and CEOs have unprecedented power over LAUSD. Mayor Riordan and his inner circle have advocated for the corporate-inspired and test-frenzied LEARN reform program, for the inclusion of McKinsey International Business Consulting Firm into the top circles of decision making in the district, and for an expansion of the role of the UCLA Business Program in the training of principals, teachers, and top administrators. Further, there is less and less school accountability to communities in LA as more and more district policy is determined by state mandates, such as the Stanford 9, retention, and bilingual education laws.

Sixth, and perhaps most importantly, dominant ideology in public education has been strengthened by high-stakes standardized testing. Many more people have bought into the ideas that students must compete for limited resources and that they will have better life chances if their test scores rise—legitimating the supposed "objectivity" of the tests and reflecting adoption of the meritocracy and "educational attainment" myths. As a result, many youth of color and low-income youth have internalized low test scores as objective proof that they should not expect to get into universities or satisfying jobs.

Media accounts of LAUSD's eighth-grade retention plan this year were filled with the angst and anxiety of many students who were attending underresourced schools and threatened with failure. For example, one student said, "I keep thinking, 'What if I fail? What if I don't make it to high school?' It would be so embarrassing. I sometimes get mad and break down and cry." Another eighth-grade student who was interviewed clearly stated her intention to drop out of school because of the high-stakes testing, and a third summed it

up: "I don't think the end of social promotion is fair because some students come from bad elementary schools. They've had bad training and now they're going to be punished?"[12]

It is in this realm that a model for building social movements must be tested. The nascent movement must first carve out the political space to engage with an alternative vision of education. Leaders who emerge from that space must then begin to build a base of support around a collective, alternative vision. The organizing of a base of support must be rooted in the dual premises of qualitatively breaking from dominant ideology and respectfully engaging parents, students, and teachers in authentic dialogues on concrete educational issues.

Experimenting with an Organizing Model: Building a Transformative Social Movement for Educational Justice in Los Angeles

The introduction of this chapter included key questions about social movements. What kind of educational reforms should a social movement be fighting for? What kind of organizing model should be used to build a grassroots base of power? Are there reforms that can legitimately improve quality of education for low-income students of color and simultaneously open space for transformative social movements?

This final section explores some responses to these questions through an examination of an experimental grassroots organization in Los Angeles. The views in this section do not represent the views of the organization, Coalition for Educational Justice (CEJ). Rather, they are my views as one of the founders of the organization and a member of the CEJ Steering Committee.

In September 1999, a group comprised mostly of teachers but also including parents and university-based activists came together to form CEJ. The organization established unity around a strategy of building a long-term, multiracial, grassroots parent-student-teacher social movement to change public education. Further, the organization established unity around a broad political program that challenges racism and class bias in education with the following demands:

1. A moratorium on high-stakes testing and retention,
2. A massive infusion of resources for schools—particularly those in low-income communities of color—through a shift of state funds away from prisons and the implementation of progressive taxation measures,
3. The reinstatement of bilingual education and devotion of resources toward meeting the language needs of African-American students,
4. The creation of well-paid, meaningful, socially useful jobs in low-income communities of color, starting with an expansion of LAUSD's Teaching Assistant Career Ladder, which subsidizes

predominantly students of color in their training to become teachers,
5. Massive expansion of university access for low-income students of color,
6. The creation of a community- and teacher-developed curriculum that is progressive, student-centered, and founded upon critical thinking and alternative assessments.

The moratorium on high-stakes testing and retention has emerged as the leading, or most high-profile, CEJ demand for several reasons. First, the testing policy is the latest egregious attack against low-income people of color. Building a strategic alliance to hinder the policy is the conscionable thing to do.

Second, because the impact of high-stakes testing will fall most heavily on low-income communities of color, opposing the testing policy opens space to organize new constituencies of low-income people, women, and people of color. These constituencies, with the active participation of antiracist whites and men, must form the leading core of transformative social movements. It is the collective life experiences of these constituencies that situate them as the main force in opposition to market-based, transnational capitalist, racist, and sexist principles—exactly those principles that must be frontally challenged in order to fight the multiple axes of oppression in society (Mann & Ramsey, 1996; Mann, 1998).

Third, the testing policies constitute the major "reform" in public education today, advocated by Democrats, Republicans, and independents alike. Without discrediting this "reform" that occupies so much political space, it will be very difficult for CEJ and other educational advocacy organizations to successfully put an alternative political program forward into the public debate.

Fourth, attacking high-stakes testing can unmask the bankruptcy of the dominant ideology in education today. High-stakes testing is both rooted in and supportive of ideas around meritocracy, racism, and faulty premises such as "rising test scores are an avenue to overcoming poverty and racism," "low-income people of color should be the ones who are held accountable," and "government functions better when it is run like a business." We must wage battle against these ideas if we truly seek to build a transformative social movement in public education—one that is putting forward an alternative model for public education that is qualitatively breaking from existing ideology and indicative of a radical restructuring of societal priorities. Waging ideological battle is most effective when the context is a concrete struggle over policy—like high-stakes testing—that deeply affects people's lives and a city's trajectory.

Fifth, opposing high-stakes testing opens great tactical opportunities. In the everyday operation of schools there is tremendous reliance on testing and "test preparation." There is also a frenzied political attachment, from a variety of forces, to testing policies. The possibility exists, therefore, that coordinated protest against testing policies could create a political crisis in schools and policy circles, opening new points of leverage against policy makers and new spaces for building political consciousness.

Though the nuances in CEJ's work will be shaped by cycles of action and reflection within the organizing, we must pay attention to central dilemmas and key strategic elements over the long term. Two sets of dilemmas will be discussed in detail here, and then others will be flagged in the course of the discussion on strategic elements.

Dilemmas

First, how do we assure that teachers will not dominate CEJ over the long term? Many teachers are from relatively privileged backgrounds, where their voices in public—including in front of classrooms—have been granted respect. Partially as a result of this, many teachers are comfortable speaking in front of groups. On the other hand, many parents and students have not had as many opportunities to speak publicly. Further, in a context where national teacher organizations are advocating that educators view themselves as "professionals," many teachers adopt elitist attitudes that justify talking over rather than listening to youth and parents, especially those from low-income backgrounds. In addition, teachers have easy access to information about schools and district policies that many parents and students do not have.

If these inequalities and attitudes are not addressed in a straightforward manner, teacher domination of meetings and organizational decisions will flow unchecked. Given this, CEJ must reflect upon and be willing to change dynamics in parent-student-teacher interactions, organizing styles, and meeting and committee formats and must make efforts to create a culture of language equality.

Second, how does CEJ concretely build genuine parent-student-teacher trust and collaboration? This question is particularly problematic because schools—and by extension, teachers— have been legitimately viewed by many in low-income communities of color as oppressive and authoritarian. Further, many politicians subtly and explicitly encourage distrust and mutual blame among teachers, parents, and students. In order to address these obstacles, can CEJ effectively acknowledge historic tensions, explore feelings generated by these tensions, and seek solutions?

One flashpoint of tensions within and outside of CEJ might be around the issue of teacher pay raises. UTLA and other teacher unions all over California are currently seeking double-digit pay raises. Many rank-and-file teachers, including many members of CEJ, have become involved in mobilizing support behind this contract demand. Personally, I would not oppose pay increases for teachers. However, I do not believe that a demand for

teacher pay raises should be part of an antiracist, progressive political program such as the one developed by CEJ. Teacher pay, benefits, and protections provide for a relatively comfortable quality of life, especially when compared to that of the majority of families with students in LAUSD. Although teacher compensation is an important issue, a progressive, antiracist movement's mission is to expose and challenge the most egregious forms of oppression, which do not include the undercompensation of teachers.

Throughout history, substantial sectors of the organized upper strata of the working class and the middle class, including teachers, have *philosophically* supported progressive and even antiracist political change. But when achieving elements of that progressive change has depended upon sacrificing pay or comfort, the majority in these classes, led by their union leaderships, have dispensed with philosophical support and protected what they have perceived to be in their economistic self-interest—pay raises and benefits. Given this, where will teachers, parents, and youth within CEJ fall when the LAUSD is deciding between devoting money to teacher pay raises or to books for low-income students? How will levels of trust be affected? If teachers and others within CEJ are not clear that teacher pay raises are *not* a part of the organization's political program, will parents, students, and community members see CEJ as an organization that is tied to the narrow teacher union agenda?

Key Elements of a Strategy for Building a Social Movement

Let's begin by asking what might constitute a progressive social movement. What might some strategies for building such a movement entail?

A Political Program That Constitutes a Challenge to Dominant Ideology and Requires Structural Change but Also Creates Space for Related Short-Term Demands

As argued earlier, a transformative movement must develop its long-term political program so that it constitutes an ideological challenge to racist, capitalist, and sexist structures. It is only through a qualitative break from existing capitalist, racist, and sexist ideology—rather than a quantitative, gradualist extension that is consistent with existing ideology—that a new vision of society, a new consciousness, and a new militancy can be built. The political program must also require structural change in government funding, distribution of wealth, urban power dynamics, and urban and industrial planning.

Yet short-term demands will emerge from the political program, and at different moments, these must be highlighted. These shorter-term demands may not in and of themselves require structural change in order to be implemented. But they may be very important to the immediate improvement of people's quality of life and to the opening of more political space for the movement as it builds support for its broader program.

For example, the six planks of CEJ's transformative political program always provide a broad framework communicated in CEJ's organizational leaflets and materials. However, we also highlighted the following short-term demands at a May 2000 CEJ press conference and through subsequent delegations to school board members: (a) LAUSD must accept all forms of Stanford 9 test exemptions from parents, (b) through all district media, LAUSD must inform parents and students of these exemptions, and (c) LAUSD must cease and desist from intimidating parents into not signing exemptions and from intimidating teachers into not talking about exemptions.

We felt that pressuring the LAUSD School Board to accede to these short-term demands would concretely support the rights of students and parents. Winning the demands would also open political space for CEJ—winning media attention, allowing for unhindered discussions with parents and students about test exemptions, and allowing for the possibility of creating short-term alliances with some board members.

Political Objectives

The central objectives of a transformative movement must be to (a) build political consciousness, (b) build leadership, (c) build long-term organization, and (d) win reforms that improve the lives of the most vulnerable in society.

CEJ has been developing an experimental organizing model in which we put forth to parents, students, and teachers an analysis of education that is based explicitly on antiracist and antibias politics—centered around the six planks of our political program. We have viewed consciousness-raising as a process that emerges from dialogue around these explicit politics.

Many of us have disagreed with progressives who argue that we must organize with a "lowest common denominator" or "electorate focus group" politics. These progressives seek to avoid alienating middle-class people, especially whites. They therefore avoid using words like "racism" and censor themselves when it comes to describing what their long-term political vision is, out of fear that they might seem "too radical." Further, many of us in CEJ have rejected the argument that offering explicit political analysis in the organizing process is a form of undemocratic imposition of views upon people.

Rather, we see the necessity of explicitly naming racism and other forms of oppression. Though the group of people attracted to these politics may be small at first, the theory is that they will be strong ideologically and passionate about the mission to broaden the base and build power. Our confidence that an initial leadership core can build a broad movement over time is based on the belief that there is an existing constituency in Los Angeles—though largely unorganized—that is seeking political forms through which to engage in antiracist and antibias struggle.

Moreover, we have viewed the re-luctance of many progressives to engage working-class people with explicit political analysis as, at best, an indication of an unwillingness to engage in authentic dialogue and debate and, at worst, a sign of disrespect for and underestimation of working-class people. Do these organizers believe that low-income people are not able to handle the assertive presentation of deep political beliefs or that they will simply adopt a politics that is presented to them with no debate or dialogue?

Toward the goal of building a long-term organization, CEJ is attempting to cultivate new leadership by creating a committee structure that gives people (so far, mostly parents and teachers, with a real weakness in youth participation) many spaces and manners in which to participate. Further, we are seeking to self-consciously rotate responsibilities and "project leads" so that as many people as possible may obtain a breadth of experience. Perhaps most importantly, CEJ has begun to institutionalize a process for self-reflection. We regularly assess and criticize our organizing and outreach work through report-backs, debriefings, and goal-setting sessions.

In its very limited existence, CEJ has won small reforms in LAUSD and union policy. We have struggled to find a balance between the desire to celebrate these modest victories and the necessity of theorizing the reforms, that is, seeing them only as beginning steps toward a long-term transformation. We are developing a social movement theory of education reform, where reforms for the sake of reforms and unconsolidated reforms are critiqued, and structural reforms that open political space for transformative social movements are sought.

In February 2000, CEJ organized behind a motion that overwhelmingly passed through the UTLA House of Representatives. The motion made it union policy to oppose the administering of the Stanford 9 test on the basis of its high-stakes, racist, and class-biased character. With ongoing CEJ pressure and the new policy in hand, the union leadership appealed to LAUSD Interim Superintendent Ramon Cortines to cancel non–state mandated portions of the Stanford 9 for the 1999–2000 testing year. Within days after CEJ and UTLA leadership collaborated on collecting petitions from around the district, Cortines acceded, assuring that students would endure fewer hours of testing and "test prep," thereby protecting more instructional time.

CEJ claimed the limited victory and attempted to publicize the organization and the political message in the days afterward. Yet an ongoing process of critical self-reflection has been necessary to assure that (1) CEJ members do not fall under the illusion that the victory brings us substantially closer to the realization of our broad political program, and (2) CEJ members avoid seeing UTLA as a long-term ally, instead seeing the union leadership as a force that, for a moment, flowed in a direction similar to ours for a variety of reasons, including our pressure.

Main Base

The main base of transformative movements must be composed primarily of the most vulnerable in society—low-income people, people of color, and women. There are five major reasons for this. First, as stated earlier, their objective life experiences situate them as the main force in opposition to market-driven politics, transnational capitalism, racism, and sexism. Second, the building of progressive movements with acknowledged and celebrated multiplicity creates the space to reconstruct race, class, and gender categories. These categories must be newly understood for a viable progressive movement to be sustained (see Kelley, 1998). For example, white people must, through the practice of engaging in meetings and political actions, understand the myriad ways in which they have benefited from white privilege. In a multiracial group context, then, they must struggle to find the appropriate roles for themselves within organizations (Lipsitz, 1998).

Third, placing a priority on the leadership of low-income people of color—with a focus on women—creates a space in which whites and males can be challenged to reject sexism and privilege in favor of broader politics. Fourth, by acknowledging the priority of winning reforms that specifically benefit the most vulnerable, a space is created in which narrow self-interest can be challenged as the primary motivator in politics. In the broader context, the most vulnerable people in the

United States and in the world need loyal political allies among the middle classes in order to win a massive redistribution of resources. Such allies will not emerge primarily out of self-interested motives. This quality of ally will emerge only through a spirit of altruism—of choosing to give up fruits of privilege. Fifth, victories that benefit the most vulnerable, while the hardest to win, can benefit the whole society. Expansion of a bus system that serves primarily low-income people of color may end up creating an infrastructure for real transit access for all; the creation of tutoring programs in inner-city schools may end up being extended to an entire district, benefiting white, middle-class students as well (on the main base in organizing, see Mann & Ramsey, 1996; Mann, 1998).

After nine months of organizing, in early 2001 CEJ had a small but expanding base and our active base—which participates in committees, actions, and petition collecting—consisted of approximately seventy-five teachers and thirty to forty parents citywide. Hundreds more teachers have come to meetings, know of CEJ, and consider themselves loose allies. Through a series of community meetings, we have engaged approximately 400 parents in conversation about the CEJ political program. In addition, we have tight links with a youth group that helps to bring high school students into the work. Most of our resources now go into building our parent and student base to address our weaknesses in those areas. For many of us, it is a major goal to have

equal representation of teachers, parents, and students in the organization in the next year.

Political Independence from Parties and Unions, with a Policy of Unity and Struggle

A transformative movement must assert its political independence. For those of us attempting to build progressive, antiracist movements, two of the main forces that we must challenge and differentiate ourselves from are the Democratic Party and the AFL-CIO leadership. Both of these forces have been apologists for and, ultimately, defenders of the inequalities inherent in U.S. capitalism, racism, and male domination. They have advocated "getting a bigger piece of the pie" for workers and electoral interest groups while not only avoiding challenges to the most central elements of institutional racism and class domination but also becoming a leading force in regressive politics such as support for an imperialist, prointervention U.S. foreign policy, anticommunist hysteria, or anti-immigrant policy.

However, there are also more progressive strands within the histories of the Democratic Party and the labor movement, reflected in the Democrats' support of abortion rights and the creation of New Deal poverty programs. These strands give them a particular hold on the political allegiances of many low-income people, people of color, and women. CEJ must seek to point out these very contradictions in the politics of the Democratic Party and AFL-CIO leadership in the realm of struggle over concrete policies.

A recent example of a struggle over the destructive "pragmatism" and regressive politics of these forces could be seen in their relationship to Proposition 227, the referendum that effectively banned bilingual education. A substantial group of teachers, parents, and students—many of whom are now involved in CEJ—staked out a position that affirmed bilingual education after the referendum passed. This group prepared to take militant action in organizing support for the reinstatement of bilingual programs.

However, the UTLA leadership threatened those teachers who were advocating noncompliance with the 227 law, claiming that such teachers would not be defended by the union, thereby opening them to potential lawsuits and dismissal. Meanwhile, Democratic Party leaders recommended that we make the best of a bad situation. Before the election, they advocated a "compromise bill" that would have ceded the antibilingual and anti-immigrant ideological victory to the pro-227 forces but protected some elements of local school control. In a startling move, the Democratic speaker of the California Assembly, Antonio Villaraigosa, counseled that "racism" not be discussed in opposing 227.

This was only the most recent reflection of the flawed Democratic Party strategy of capitulation and appeasement—going quietly on record against racist initiatives while not re-

ally fighting against them, saying they cannot be allowed to become "make or break" issues for the party. This strategy has led to an immeasurable level of demoralization among progressives who have found themselves struggling against racist propositions that use the terms of the Right while being expressly prohibited by the Democratic/AFL-CIO coalition from using terms like "immigrants' rights" or even "affirmative action" (for more on this struggle see Caputo-Pearl, 1998).

If CEJ holds to a position of independence from the Democratic Party and AFL-CIO, this does not mean that there is to be no interaction with these forces. On the contrary, a policy of independence must be merged with one of unity and struggle. Short-term alliances and unity with the Democrats and AFL-CIO should be sought wherever possible, but independence and political struggle should be asserted whenever necessary.

Long-Term Strategic Planning with Targets, Allies, and Tactics

A transformative movement must choose as main targets the institutions and individuals who have the power to meet the movement's demands. In the case of CEJ, Governor Gray Davis, the LAUSD School Board, and the LAUSD superintendent are the main targets.

To build pressure against these targets, a transformative movement must seek strategic and tactical allies in all forums—including labor leaderships, political parties, small businesses, and so on. Strategic allies are those that share the movement's political demands and strategic vision over the long term. CEJ is beginning to explore a strategic alliance with some youth groups based in communities of color who are fighting against the prison-industrial complex. Tactical allies are those that may support one movement demand in a particular moment, as UTLA leadership did when helping CEJ pressure Interim Superintendent Cortines.

A transformative movement must develop political tactics that pressure targets to accede to demands. Tactics are concrete events, such as press conferences, demonstrations, civil disobedience, poster campaigns, letters, petitions, meetings, motions within union structures, and the like. The primary tactics that CEJ has used in its very young campaign are motions within UTLA, a press conference at the school board, a new petition drive targeting the LAUSD School Board, and delegations to school board members.

Conclusion

At the writing of this chapter, there is much conjecture about the emergence of a new progressive social movement across the United States, given momentum by the protests at the World Trade Organization in Seattle and the International Monetary Fund in Washington, D.C. While there are certainly positive aspects to this new movement, two of its weaknesses have been its over-focus on challenges to corporate power—somewhat to the exclusion of challenges to racism and sexism—and its emphasis on short-term anti-institutional civil disobedience rather than long-term political strategy.

It has been the goal of this chapter to provoke debate in progressive, Left, and liberal circles around issues of educational reform and social movement building. I have attempted to address the explosive intersections of class and racial oppression in education—at the nexus of dominant ideologies and high-stakes testing—and the necessity to challenge both along with gender oppression.

Further, I have attempted to provoke discussion around what is needed to build a long-term political strategy in education. The strategy that I hint at is one that goes beyond short-term actions of civil disobedience. Rather, it attempts to blend anti-institutionalism with a "through the institutions" approach that sees ongoing engagement with "the powers that be" as vital to winning reforms, building a multiconstituency movement, challenging dominant ideology, and achieving moral legitimacy. I hope that this article contributes to these much needed debates.

TABLE 1
Coalition for Educational Justice (CEJ)

This year, LA Unified School District will hold students back a grade (retention) in the 2nd and 8th grades if they don't pass certain "standards." By 2001 and 2002, LAUSD will hold students back in all grades based substantially on the Stanford 9 standardized test and others (given in English). Why should we oppose this?

High-Stakes Testing and Retention Are Class-Biased and Racist

1. Low-income students, who have fewer resources at their schools, aren't given an equal chance on these tests. Retention policies tied to test results, therefore, are class- and racially discriminatory because poverty mostly affects immigrants and communities of color. For example, LA County schools are hyper-segregated and students in communities of color are 12 times more likely to be low-income than students in white communities. Low-income students of color are also more likely to lack basic materials at their schools, and are 6 times more likely than white students to have less experienced teachers.

2. When given only in English, tests measure national origin more than mastery of school material. When tests are language-biased, otherwise competent students are punished for not speaking English fluently.

3. The tests are culturally biased as mostly middle-income, white test makers produce tests that measure the knowledge and experiences valued by middle-income whites. They ignore the knowledge and experiences valued by other cultures.

4. Schools in low-income communities of color in particular, where test pressure is highest, focus on destructive "Back to Basics" lessons and testing drills. They also "track" students. "Back to Basics" does not have high learning standards. Wealthy schools more often do rigorous, project-based learning.

5. Low-income students are retained twice as often as high-income children. Students of color are retained in large numbers. Retention contributes to the high dropout rate among African-Americans and Latinos, as compared to whites. The gap between white students and students of color is widened, not narrowed.

High-Stakes Testing and Retention Hurt Learning, Students, and Teachers

1. Standardized tests do not measure creativity, problem-solving abilities, ethical thinking, and many other things central to learning. They mostly measure what is crammed into students' short-term memories.

2. Positive jumps in test scores are often due to narrow test coaching rather than real learning.

3. Most students like school less when their classes and time are focused on standardized tests.

4. Retention contributes to academic failure rather than to success in school. A single grade retention increases the chances that a student will drop out by 50%. A second retention increases the risk by 90%.

(continues)

TABLE 1   *(continued)*

5. Retention blames poor performance on children, not on the school district. Rather than transform schools, retention policies make students repeat an experience that failed them before.

6. Testing hype puts negative pressure on teachers and stifles their creativity.

7. Ongoing tutoring without retention should be greatly expanded for students with academic needs. The focus on retention ensures that only narrow, pressure-filled tutoring programs will exist.

TESTING AND RETENTION PUNISH MOSTLY LOW-INCOME STUDENTS OF COLOR FOR THE FAILURES OF SCHOOL DISTRICTS. GET INVOLVED IN CEJ. *Call Alex Caputo-Pearl (310–452–3310), Ramon Martinez (213-389-3418), or a campaign representative at your school for more information.*

TABLE 2
Coalition for Educational Justice (CEJ):
Six Demands That Would Really Improve Schools

1. Place an Immediate Moratorium on High-Stakes Standardized Testing and Retention.

2. Devote More Resources to Classrooms. Reduce class size, build more environmentally safe schools, develop teacher peer assistance, hire and train more teaching assistants and other staff, raise school workers' pay, fully stock classrooms with culture- and language-appropriate books and materials.

Why? Smaller class and school size, as well as competent teachers, are important for all students, especially low-income students of color. The *LA Times* has documented severe textbook shortages in LAUSD. Little is being done to provide thousands of new LAUSD teachers without credentials with adequate assistance, while poor conditions and low pay discourage the hiring of credentialed teachers and other school staff.

3. Reinstate Bilingual Education in the Whole District and, in the Meantime, Protect Existing Bilingual Education Programs. Devote Massive Resources to Supporting the Language Background and Needs of African-American Students.

Why? LAUSD attacks immigrants' language rights by promoting monolingualism and the dominance of English over other languages. It marginalizes African-American students around issues of language. Further, educational access rights are denied to immigrants who would do better in bilingual classes. Bilingual programs in LA's Eastman Elementary and other states teach content, English, and other languages. In an increasingly small world, we can celebrate multilingualism rather than narrow our language choices by developing Early Second Language Development Programs for all students.

4. Raise Student Achievement Through University Access and Job Development. Build university affirmative action programs and expand Paraeducator Career Ladder and Multilingual Teacher Academy.

(continues)

TABLE 2   *(continued)*

Why? UCLA and other universities are more and more exclusive. The 1999 UCLA freshman class had an average GPA of 4.24 and SAT of 1330. Its student body came mostly from families that earn between $100,000 and $150,000 per year. Representation of African-Americans, Latinos, and Native Americans is decreasing, down to 13%. High Potential Programs, like that of the 1960s at UCLA, can open university access to student leaders from low-income communities of color who could not meet requirements because of poor conditions at their schools. Secondly, over 300,000 medium-wage jobs left LA County between 1979 and 1993, as corporations went elsewhere and government cut jobs. Working class people of color held many of these jobs. Expansion of the program that prepares teaching assistants (paraeducators) to become teachers could create jobs in low-income communities of color and address the teacher shortage.

5. *Build a Student-Centered, Activity-based, Teacher- and Community-Developed Curriculum That Uses Alternative Assessments to Measure Student Growth, and That*

Brings Out Intellectual Curiosity, Critical Thinking, Cooperation, and Democratic Values
   Why? Students do better in activity- and project-based classrooms that use performance-based assessments than in the "Back to Basics" classrooms that focus on drilling and standardized testing. Activity-based classes help students build their own points of view, rather than just hear the narrow points of view in the standard curriculum. The LAUSD Board approved reading programs that use "Back to Basics" approaches that are not good for students, particularly English Language Learners. Second, real local control of schools results when parents, students, and teachers can develop the learning programs rather than government and business people in Sacramento.

6. *Shift Spending to Education.* Reallocate money from standardized testing contracts, prisons, military, and corporations to schools.

Why? We need money to transform our schools. We can challenge the explosive growth in prison and military spending, fight for higher corporate taxes, and redistribute money that LAUSD already has.

To get involved in the Coalition for Educational Justice (CEJ), call Alex Caputo-Pearl (310-452-3310), Ramon Martinez (213-389-3418), or a campaign representative at your school.

Notes

1. Italian political theorist Antonio Gramsci believed that dominant social classes would advocate sets of assumptions, ideas, and myths—sometimes incoherent and contradictory—that eventually would become adopted by the majority of society as foundational. Regardless of its morality or lack thereof, this "dominant ideology" becomes hegemonic, or extremely influential, across all sectors of society. Once dominant ideology is embedded as "common sense," it can guide policy and lead to political consent from

the majority of all sectors of society even when its policies may be destructive in particular sectors (Sassoon, 1982, pp. 12–17).

2. In 1994, white high school dropouts had a higher employment rate than African-Americans and Latinos with high school diplomas. Seventy-three percent of white high school graduates not enrolled in college were employed, twice the percentage for African-Americans and almost triple the percentage for Latinos. Further, wage rates for white high school graduates far exceed those for high school graduates of color (U.S. Department of Commerce, 1994).

3. While well over 90 percent of white students finish high school, fewer than 85 percent of African-Americans and 61 percent of Latinos finish. In most low-income inner-city districts that disproportionately serve students of color, the dropout rates are two to four times as high as the rates in the surrounding suburbs that disproportionately serve white and middle-class students (Macias Rojas & Gordon, 1999) Nationwide, students of color and low-income students are retained at rates much higher than those of white and middle-class students. A single grade retention increases the chances that a student will drop out by 50 percent. A second retention increases the risk by 90 percent (Roderick, 1995).

4. In the 1980s, the ten highest per-pupil-spending elementary school districts in Illinois, New York, Ohio, and Texas—vastly white—outspent the ten lowest per-pupil-spending districts—vastly of color—by more than two and a half times (Lowe, 1997, p. 16).

5. Heavy concentrations of these jobs exist in southern California, Silicon Valley, Wall Street, the Boston suburbs, and Seattle.

6. Los Angeles is a major center of international trade and banking; a command and control point for the organization and functioning of the world economy; home to dramatically expanding white-collar financial, legal, and business services sectors; a major center of both international tourism and immigration; and home to both a transnational corporate elite—a well-paid sector of professionals working in government, business, and international organizations who support the transnational corporate agenda—and a growing multinational working class that is disproportionately represented in low-wage service sectors, low-wage manufacturing, the penal system, or unemployment lines (for more on world city theory and Los Angeles political economy, see Keil, 1998; Friedmann & Wolff, 1982; Friedmann, 1995; Soja, Morales, & Wolff, 1983.)

7. In Los Angeles, average real earnings for male full-time, full-year workers dropped from $32,000 in 1969 to $25,000 in 1990. In 1969, 7 percent of full-time, full-year workers made less than $15,000, while by 1990 the figure had risen to 19 percent. In 1989, wages for the poorest fifth of families as a percentage of wages for the wealthiest fifth was lower in LA than in any part of the United States (Mosely, 1996). In South Central LA, which is overwhelmingly African-American and Latino, unemployment rates annually stand at 30 percent or above, with portions of the African-American community hovering around 40 percent to 50 percent (Keil, 1998, p. 218). From 1993 to 1997, the average income of California's richest 1 percent grew by 57 percent to almost $900,000. For California's poorest working families, the average income in 1997—$13,000—reflected a 13 percent drop since 1989 (Arax, Curtius, & Nelson, 2000).

8. California has committed over $4.6 billion to building more state prisons, county jails, and youth facilities in the past fifteen years, plus $3.4 billion in interest. Since 1986, state prison costs have grown from 3 percent of California's General

Fund to 9 percent (Southern California Criminal Justice Consortium, 1999).

9. In New York's retention program, called Promotional Gates, many students were "flunked" repeatedly because they could not pass a reading or math test. The retained students had lower achievement, higher incidences of disciplinary problems, and higher dropout rates. Georgia implemented a retention program in 1980, based significantly on standardized tests. The high school completion rate in Atlanta, where the most underresourced schools were, dropped from 75 percent in the late 1970s to 65 percent by 1982 and then to 61 percent in 1988. In Texas, under high-stakes testing and retention policies, African-American and Latino graduation rates dropped from 60 percent in 1978 to below 50 percent in 1999, compared to 75 percent for whites. In Chicago, thousands of retained eighth-grade students are "unaccounted for," assumed to have dropped out after repeating grades under horrible conditions (Darling-Hammond & Falk, 1997; McNeil, 2000; Woestehoff, 1999).

10. Some of these tests, like the STEPS, are better than the Stanford 9 as performance assessments because they rely less on multiple choice and more on problem-solving and open-ended answers. However, the use of them as high-stakes tests determining grade promotion makes them as racially and economically discriminatory as the Stanford 9.

11. Riordan's inner circle also put $2 million into the 1999 LAUSD School Board elections in support of four candidates. Each candidate won, establishing a majority, and the election went on record as the most expensive school board race ever in U.S. history.

12. Other comments by different eighth graders included: (1) "The gifted kids already say I'm a slow-brain. I've told my mom that I don't want to go to school because I don't want to fail. I don't want to be stupid. I cry thinking about it." (2) "I

told my mom I was seriously thinking about not going to high school but she told me about the consequences, so I told her I would try it" (Sauerwein, 2000).

References

Aratani, Lori. (2000, February 21). Teaching to the test. *San Jose Mercury News*, p. 1A.

Arax, Mark, Mary Curtius, & Nelson, Soraya Sarhaddi. (2000, January 9). California income gap grows amid prosperity. *Los Angeles Times*, p. A1.

Ayers, William, & Dohrn, Bernardine. (2000). Resisting zero tolerance. *Rethinking Schools*, *14*(3), p. 14.

Berlak, Harold. (1999). Standards and the control of knowledge. *Rethinking Schools*, *13*(3), p. 10.

Blume, Howard. (2000). No vacancy. *LA Weekly*, *22*(29), p. 26.

Bowles, Samuel, & Gintis, Herbert. (1976). *Schooling in capitalist America: Educational reform and the contradictions of economic life*. New York: BasicBooks.

Callan, Patrick M. (n.d.). An interview with Roy Romer. *Policy Center Journal*. [On-line]. Available: www.policycenter.org/ct_0495/ctqa_0495.html.

Caputo-Pearl, Alex. (1998). A teacher's strategy: Un programa antiracista para la reforma de la educación pública. *AhoraNow*, *6*, pp. 10-12.

Caputo-Pearl, Alex. (1999, May 2). How the Stanford 9 Test institutionalizes unequal education. *Los Angeles Times Opinion*, p. M6.

Colvin, Richard Lee. (1999a, June 12). School segregation is growing, report finds. *Los Angeles Times*, p. A1.

Colvin, Richard Lee. (1999b, October 17). How LA Unified got into this fix. *Los Angeles Times*, p. A1.

Colvin, Richard Lee. (2000, July 1). Businesses get behind standards in schools. *Los Angeles Times*, p. B2.

Colvin, Richard Lee, & Helfand, Duke. (2000). Millions for schools tied to Stanford 9 test scores. *Los Angeles Times*, p. A20.

Cooper, Louise. (2000). Youth activists fight Prop 21. *Against the Current*, *15*(2), p. 12.

Darling-Hammond, Linda, & Falk, Beverly. (1997, November). Using standards and assessments to support student learning. *Phi Delta Kappan*, pp. 190-199.

Friedman, David. (2000, March 26). The economic root of low test scores. *Los Angles Times Opinion*, p. M1.

Friedmann, John. (1995). Where we stand: A decade of world city research. In Paul L. Knox and Peter J. Taylor (Eds.), *World Cities in a World System*, pp. 21-47. Cambridge: Cambridge University Press.

Friedmann, John, & Wolff, Goetz. (1982). The world city hypothesis: An agenda for research and action. *IJURR*, 6, pp. 309-344.

Getlin, Josh. (2000, March 20). Despite pressure, NYPD resists call for reforms. *Los Angeles Times*, p. A1.

Giroux, Henry. (2000). At war against the young. *Against the Current*, *15*(2), p. 17.

Groves, Martha. (1999, April 6). Stanford 9 a test of nerves as well as achievement. *Los Angeles Times*, p. A1.

Groves, Martha. (2000a, July 14). Two experts say Stanford 9 test has many flaws. *Los Angeles Times*, p. A3.

Groves, Martha. (2000b, July 18). State's students score key gains on Stanford 9 Test. *Los Angeles Times*, p. A1.

Groves, Martha, & Richardson, Lisa. (2000, April 1). Test prep moving into primary grades. *Los Angeles Times*, p. A1.

Hayden, Tom. (2000). Gato and Alex— No safe place: The human story of the Los Angeles police scandal. *The Nation*, *271*(2), p. 24.

Helfand, Duke, & Sahagun, Louis. (2000, July 18). How LA County schools fared on statewide exams. *Los Angeles Times*, p. S1.

Irwin, John. (1999). *America's one million nonviolent prisoners*. Produced for the Justice Policy Institute and the Southern California Criminal Justice Consortium, Pasadena, CA.

Jenkins, Alan. (2000). Leveling the playing field: An opportunity agenda. *The Nation*, *270*(9), p. 16.

Kantor, Harvey. (1997). Equal opportunity and the federal role in education. In *Funding for justice: Money, equity, and the future of public education*, p. 21. Milwaukee, WI: Rethinking Schools.

Keil, Roger. (1998). *Los Angeles: Globalization, urbanization, and social struggles*. England: John Wiley & Sons.

Kelley, Robin. (1998). *Yo' Mama's dysfunktional: Fighting the culture wars in urban America*. Boston: Beacon Press.

Kohn, Alfie. (1999). *The schools our children deserve*. Boston, New York: Houghton Mifflin.

Lipsitz, George. (1998). *The possessive investment in whiteness: How white people profit from identity politics*. Philadelphia: Temple University Press.

Los Angeles County Department of Health Services. (2000). *The health of Angelenos: A comprehensive report on the health of the residents of Los Angeles County*. Available through LA County Department of Health Services, Los Angeles, CA.

Lowe, Robert. (1997). Race, power, and funding: An historical perspective. In *Funding for justice: Money, equity, and the future of public education*, pp. 16–42. Milwaukee, WI: Rethinking Schools.

Macias Rojas, Patrisia, & Gordon, Rebecca. (1999). Just facts: Racial resegregation and inequality in the public schools. *ColorLines*, *2*(1), 11.

Mann, Eric. (1996). *A new vision for urban transportation*. Los Angeles: Strategy Center Publications.

Mann, Eric. (1998). Workers of the world unite: The struggle against imperialism is the key to Marxism's reconstruction. *AhoraNow*, 5, pp. 1-7.

Mann, Eric, Duran, Lisa, Gallegos, Bill, Omatsu, Glenn, & the Urban Strategies Group of the Labor/Community Strategy Center. (1994). *Immigrant rights and wrongs*. Los Angeles: Strategy Center Publications.

Mann, Eric, & Ramsey, Kikanza. (1996). The left choice is the best choice. *AhoraNow*, 1, pp. 1-5.

McNeil, Linda. (2000, June). Creating new inequalities: Contradictions of reform. *Phi Delta Kappan*, pp. 729-734.

Moberg, David. (1998). Chicago's 4 R's: Reading, 'Riting, 'Rithmetic and Reform. *In These Times*, 22(21), pp. 10-13.

Morrow, Raymond Allan, & Torres, Carlos Alberto. (1995). *Social theory and education: A critique of theories of social and cultural reproduction*. Albany: State University of New York Press.

Mosely, Kevin. (1996). *Low wage poverty in Los Angeles*. Article written for use by the Los Angeles Living Wage Coalition, Los Angeles, CA.

Nieves, Evelyn. (2000, May 23). California governor building a 'tough on crime' record. *New York Times*, p. A1.

Odden, Allan R. (Ed.). (1992). *Rethinking school finance: An agenda for the 1990's*. San Francisco: Jossey-Bass.

Olney, Peter. (1993, July/August). The rising of the million. *Crossroads*, pp. 13-15.

Pyle, Amy. (2000, January 6). State school spending gap debate grows. *Los Angeles Times*, p. A1.

Rabin, Jeffrey. (2000a, May 1). Much is at stake in showdown for bus riders, MTA. *Los Angeles Times*, p. B1.

Rabin, Jeffrey. (2000b, May 3). Bus battle rages in federal courtroom. *Los Angeles Times*, p. B3.

Riccardi, Nicholas. (2000, June 28). US to Extend Waiver on LA County Health Funds. *Los Angeles Times*, p. A1.

Roderick, Melissa. (1995). Grade retention and school dropout. *Research Bulletin of the Center for Evaluation, Development, and Research*, 15.

Roy Romer's 12-step program to true reform. (n.d.). *Chief Executive Journal*. [On-line]. Available: www.chiefexecutive.net/mag/149/article1a.htm.

Sacks, Peter. (1999). *Standardized minds: The high price of America's testing culture and what we can do to change it*. Cambridge, MA: Perseus Publishing.

Sassoon, Anne Showstack. (Ed.). 1982. *Approaches to Gramsci*. London: Writers and Readers Publishing Cooperative Society.

Sauerwein, Kristina. (2000, February 15). Fears of failure hit eighth graders. *Los Angeles Times*, p. B1.

Seeley, John. (2000). Philadelphia story. *LA Weekly*, 22(35), p. 15.

Smith, Doug. (2000, May 27). Lack of classrooms a looming crisis for LA Unified. *Los Angeles Times*, p. B1.

Smith, Doug, Sahagun, Louis, & Sauerwein, Kristina. (2000, July 16). With state checkbooks open, some students still lack texts. *Los Angeles Times*, p. A1.

Soja, Edward. (1991). Poles apart: Urban restructuring in New York and Los Angeles. In John H. Mollenkopf and Manuel Castells (Eds.), *Dual city: Restructuring New York*, pp. 361-375. New York: Russell Sage Foundation.

Soja, Edward, Morales, Rebecca, & Wolff, Goetz. (1983). Urban restructuring: An analysis of social and spatial change in Los Angeles. *Economic Geography*, 59(2), pp. 195-230.

Southern California Criminal Justice Consortium. (1999). Pasadena, CA.

Stoskopf, Alan. (1999). The forgotten history of eugenics." *Rethinking Schools*, 13(3), p. 12.

U.S. Department of Commerce, Bureau of the Census. (1994). *October Current Population Surveys*. Washington, DC: GPO.

Weiss, Kenneth. (1999a, April 3). Minority admissions at UC almost at 1997 level. *Los Angeles Times*, p. A1.

Weiss, Kenneth. (1999b, June 17). Heard the latest one about USC and UCLA? *Los Angeles Times*, p. A1.

Weiss, Kenneth. (1999c, November 18). Cal State cracks down on remedial students. *Los Angeles Times*, p. A1.

Welfare Reform Monitoring Project. (2000). Produced by Los Angeles Coalition to End Hunger and Homelessness, Los Angeles, CA.

Woestehoff, Julie. (1999). Chicago flunking policy gets an F. *Rethinking Schools*, *13*(3), pp. 20-21.

Wolff, Goetz. (1994). *Los Angeles plant closures of the late 70's and early 80's*. Produced by Resources for Employment and Economic Development, Los Angeles, CA.

Wypijewski, JoAnn. (1997, September 8/15). A stirring in the land. *The Nation*, pp. 17-25.

Yates, Nona. (1999, October 27). How California compares. *Los Angeles Times*, p. B2.

Zamichow, Nora. (2000, April 18). Merit-based scholarships draw support of affluent. *Los Angeles Times*, p. B1.

RAISING THE STANDARDS FOR DEMOCRATIC EDUCATION

Research and Evaluation as Public Knowledge

John Willinsky

The standardized testing movement in the schools may be the product of educational research, but our growing reliance on these tests is scientifically shortchanging the education system and the nation. The tests are developed through advanced statistical methods, subjected to reliability and validity assessments, and utilize controlled conditions and sampling principles, all to ensure a measurement of student achievement that is as accurate as possible. They represent another reassuring application of the modern scientific methods that deliver clean water to our taps and cool air to our air-conditioned homes on a hot day.

Yet the one-size-fits-all approach of standardized testing may be misaligned with today's diverse economy, as labor economist Robert B. Reich (2000) has pointed out, and I would also add that they set far too low a standard for the scientific contribu-

tion to an education system that serves the nation well. Given all that the realm of educational research has to offer, the tests represent a decidedly retarded view of research and a diminished conception of the democratic character of public schooling. That is, while most everyone would agree that test performance does not encompass the whole of what it means to learn or to be educated, we also need to recognize that the tests do not encompass the whole of the truth that research has to offer on the school experience, just as a faith in testing does not deliver what should be expected from an education system in a democratic society. We need to raise the standards of accountability for research and education so that we are working from a far more complete and diverse picture of what is required to create a democratic and educated society.

Educational research rarely tells a singular story and rarely offers but one answer, and even then, it is certainly not the sort of answer that test scores offer, in which a single number, sitting in comparison with others, determines the fate of a child, a teacher, a principal, a school, a district. In the face of public faith in what the test scores say about the schools, people need to appreciate that research already affords, largely at public expense, a far-reaching understanding of what it means to send children off for a dozen years to learn about as many subjects, across a handful of public and private schools. Contrast that understanding with this current focus on a singular measure of how our children are learning, whether a school is good or bad, which provides little public incentive for discussing questions of educational means and ends. Thinking about test score standards, measured against national curriculum standards, displaces local and global thinking about what the school should be like and how it can serve the children and the community. Poor test results suggest the need for test mechanics to come in and tune the schools for better performance, better results.

The tests may well reassure the public that they know how this school compares to that school on a single measure, but they do little to inform the public about the nature of education and about the risks and possibilities of learning, which is something that educational research is good at, something that could go some distance in developing the conditions of a more deliberative democracy. We want to set a standard of accountability for education and the research that supports democracy, that allows—to call on one of public education's most traditional goals—for a strengthening of democratic purpose and process, especially as that purpose and process concerns the schools themselves.

Let us raise the standards, then, of educational accountability. The public deserves to know more, far more than standardized test results can tell. People deserve to know more not only because they have already paid for this wealth of educational research, not only because their children's and their own future depends on what it has to tell us about the education system, but also because such knowledge is vital to democracy, and because people might well wish, as a result of this education, to learn more about learning. This is a call for strengthening the basis of participation, of informed advice and consent. If the current standardized achievement standards do not help us think about different approaches to educating bilingual children, about creating an appreciation of literature and other arts, about developing critical thinking skills, about improving the health and well-being, the different talents of students, then those measures are not helping education's democratic project.

We need not abandon the standardized tests. They are one of the several sources of information that are needed within the context of the larger process of inquiry in order to examine what it means to learn and teach, and how that relates to the economy and the welfare, the culture and the health of the nation and the planet. The goal is to raise the standards of public reason and deliberation as a means of increasing the quality of democratic life.

The challenge in adhering to and developing these standards of more democratic forms of education and governance resides in developing new expectations—and the corresponding information technologies—for the public value of this research among educators, researchers, policy makers, and the public. To make standardized test results the sole public face of educational research and evaluation, as we have at this point, is like making a baseball player's weight the sole statistic available not only to those watching the game but to the team's manager, coaches, and owners.

The research community needs to take far greater responsibility for bringing into the public discourse about education the complex and varied understandings afforded by research into how students learn. The lack of talk about any research except test results is not a failure on the part of the public, the policy makers, or the educators. Researchers have not made access to this understanding easy; research standards have yet to include consideration of a work's contribution to public deliberations. It is time to focus on how educational research constitutes a public good.

The standards for public reason and deliberation, informed by research, can only be raised, however, through support from both the research community and the public. As with any

work or performance, the relationship between the producer and the audience can build an experience that goes beyond what either had thought possible, an experience that creates, in effect, a new standard for both parties. So this plea for raising the standards by expanding the expectations for the public value of educational research and evaluation is addressed to both the research community and the public, in the knowledge that an appreciation of its critical contribution to extending the educational reach of democratic possibilities will need to come from both.

As things now stand, with the public regarding a singular standard for student achievement as the whole of the educational question, not only is the democratic basis of education diminished but the entire research-into-policy system is open to large-scale abuse. In fact, I offer a case study in the misuse of research, in the vital area of teaching the young to read and write, to demonstrate just how critical it is to set this new standard for educational research as a viable form of public knowledge. This case study will demonstrate that while researchers are very good at policing the standards for research as professional practice, they have a distance to go in appreciating the standards for research as a democratic form of public knowledge. And until the whole of educational research becomes part of that public standard, the schools are left to the dictates of research's most singular and narrow form of inquiry, the achievement test.

Research and Democracy: A Case Study

In 1997, Bonita Grossen published the influential white paper, *Thirty Years of Research: What We Know about How Children Learn to Read*, through the Centre for the Future of Teaching and Learning in Santa Cruz, California (Grossen, 1997). Her synthesis of reading research was intended to demonstrate that a consensus had been reached on the value of "code-oriented" or phonics curriculums when it came to teaching children to read. The paper, which drew on a good deal of research from the National Institute of Child Health and Human Development (NICHD), delivered an assured and singular answer to the question of what we know about reading, and it has played a significant role in successful efforts to shift the educational programs of Texas and California.

Yet it was not long before the paper's claims were called into question by Richard Allington and Haley Woodside-Jiron, two educational researchers at the National Research Center on English Learning and Achievement at the University of Albany (1999). They found Grossen's white paper to have misrepresented the research and thereby to have proposed essentially unsubstantiated instructional recommendations for teaching reading. Allington and Woodside-Jiron then argued that this "misuse of educational research" was grounds for questioning "the reliability of any 'consensus' document

whenever 'research' is used as a policy lever," and they advised the American Educational Research Association (AERA) to "develop an early-warning system and a viable procedure for responding to similar advocacy events in the future" (1999, p. 11). Their Cold War rhetoric of early-warning defense systems suggests just the sort of boundary between university-based research and the public arena of policy making that needs to be overcome.

Allington and Woodside-Jiron were obviously concerned that "consensus documents" such as *Thirty Years of Research* can distort the autonomous and independent nature of research and researchers in the name of having a greater public impact. My concern here is that the shroud of suspicion that they would cast over public *advocacy* and *consensus* only serves to absolve researchers of their civic responsibility for ensuring that their work informs democratic deliberations about education. Such suspicion lowers the researcher's public accountability, and it reduces, in turn, the prospect that research might contribute to the public's thinking about education, leaving that field to the narrow channel of standardized test results as the sole scientifically based measure of what schools are doing. While I have no objection to AERA setting up a committee to monitor the public uses of research in an effort to prevent misrepresentations of research results, I think this should be only the first and not the final step in increasing the public presence of educational research, especially at this time of great changes in scholarly publishing.

It does seem apparent that academic journals will inevitably migrate to the Web over the next decade for reasons of economy, productivity, and plain convenience (Ekman & Quandt, 1999). However, in a field such as education, researchers face a critical choice in this process. They can simply let it happen so that the basic process by which researchers publish research for other researchers goes unaltered, or they can actively work with these new technologies and our own research practices to improve the public presence and value of educational research, with an eye to making this research more accessible, coherent, and comprehensible on a public scale (Willinsky, 1999, 2000). Researchers in education should be encouraged, for example, by how quickly the public, in considerable numbers, has taken to using on-line medical and financial research services.[1] The research community should see this process of "going public" as a way of limiting the political misuse of research, as a way of raising educational standards by enabling the public to learn far more than it could before about the risks and possibilities of schooling—knowledge that can be shared on a global basis. Where should reliable and rigorous educational research stand with principled, progressive advocacy, consensus, and public concern when it comes to such critical educational issues as literacy? At stake is the very integrity of the research enterprise.

Research's Public Value

Whether it represents industry alliances, social issues, environmental concerns, or consumer groups, the interest group has increasingly come to represent the forceful public voice of advocacy with significant political clout.[2] Interest groups have been particularly active around educational issues, getting behind state referendums on bilingual education and affirmative action, for example, as well as the teaching of evolution.[3] Now, it may be tempting to think of interest groups as a distortion of the natural course of democratic processes, to see them as the opinionated and vested ganging up against the individual expression of equal citizens, but interest groups also represent a freedom of association around deeply felt values, issues, and interests, if only in response to a politics of issue-less candidate consumerism.

What we need to recognize is that advocacy has raised the public profile and deliberative role of research. Allington and Woodside-Jiron make this clear in identifying three forms of advocacy in their questionable case against Grossen's work: "(a) The appearances of NICHD staff and NICHD-supported researchers before policymaking forums, (b) the widespread dissemination of this research through the popular print media, and (c) the use of a particular policy tool—a white paper (Grossen, 1997)—that purports to summarize the NICHD-supported research" (1999, p. 4). The flaws of the Grossen paper aside, my concern is that the public uses of research are not inimical to the goals or quality of scholarship. Researchers have long been advocates, especially with literacy—whether for or against code-oriented curriculums (Stahl, 1999). However, the research community, rather than reinforcing its defenses against the political use of flawed work, needs to do more to make its work part of the public domain, which would provide, among other things, its own check on such abuses.

What might the increased public presence of educational research look like? Let me offer a quick-sketch version. Think of a public access Web site developed in conjunction with post-print journal publishing that would enable educators, policy makers, and researchers to survey related studies. This would need to be more than AskERIC, which provides a list of authors and titles linked to abstracts, although it could start that way.

Say one was interested in research on learning to read and chose Grossen's *Thirty Years of Research*. To appreciate what research has to offer in this on-line universe of knowledge, one should then be able to link not only to the studies that Grossen cites but also to the subsequent studies that have cited her study and the studies she cites, through a two-way citation process. This would enable readers to see how well these works have stood up to critical comment. It would enable one to access formal reviews of Grossen's work (such as that by Allington and Woodside-Jiron) and to

join informal discussions that have referred to it. One should also be able to link to the relevant policies and practices in various states, to appreciate how this research works.[4] Such a public knowledge Web site could be supplemented by specialized dictionaries and sites about practice and application, much as the National Library of Medicine's MEDLINE*plus* provides for health research.[5]

It would take much experimentation, collaboration, and research to develop an accepted and sustainable standard for a public-access site like this. But such a site would drive up the level of debate among interest groups while providing people and policy makers with greater confidence in using research as part of the deliberative process. Thus it would speak to Penelope L. Peterson's concerns, expressed a few years ago in her presidential address to the AERA, "Why Do Educational Research?" wherein she insisted that the goals of this association and thus of its membership were not only to "ensure the continued funding for research" but to "communicate the findings of high-quality research in ways that influence policy and practice" (1998, p. 9).

The current standard of the value or quality of research assesses its internal consistency, the validity and reliability of its measures, and the soundness of its conclusions. Yet what we just as often herald in our work, from the initial funding proposal to the study's conclusions, is the claim that our research offers practitioners and policy makers, parents and the public, the nation and the world a better understanding of, say, students' reading and writing. This may not apply to all educational research, but when we are pursuing a scholarly understanding of literacy, at some point it seems fair to ask whether what we know could offer more to people who want to understand more about literacy and to act on that understanding. We are educators, after all, and this element of *public* education seems worth our attention at a time when the very medium of scholarly communication is changing.

This does not mean abandoning peer review and other methods of ensuring the distinguishing quality of research as a form of knowledge, however imperfect these might be. However, it does mean thinking more about how research works in public and whether, by design and publication, it could work better in helping people think about what they want from schools. It may be too soon to argue that the public's capacity for research is increasing with this Web-borne age of information, but to judge from the medical and financial research sites at least, people are hungry for knowledge that once was the sole domain of experts and professionals.

The contribution of educational research to policy making need not be seen as external to its scientific claims. Rather, it can be seen as another potential validation of these claims. As literacy research often seeks to better understand how educators can improve children's reading and writing, it seems appropriate to judge its effec-

tiveness as it informs those involved in the democratic process of setting and enacting educational policies.

We may refer to this process, a little self-righteously I find, as "talking truth to power," and yet it calls for more than keeping a watchful eye on public uses of this knowledge like librarians who see themselves as, above all, protectors of the books. It calls for improving the public's ability to tap into the truths and powers that this knowledge offers as if that were the very object of undertaking this research. This, in turn, will raise the standards of both the schools and the talk about the schools. It will also lead us to expect more educational work from both researchers and the public. Research into educational practices should matter to people, all the more so in an age of interest-group politics. The public quality of this knowledge is surely the best protection against its abuse by the politics of expertise.

Knowledge without Consensus

A critical point for raising the standards of educational accountability—which I am proposing we do by increasing the public quality of research on the schools—is whether the public has a stomach for results that do not reflect a consensus among researchers. To stay with our case study, Allington and Woodside-Jiron's critique of *Thirty Years of Research* is principally based on its pretense to represent a consensus among literacy researchers. As I noted above, Allington and Woodside-Jiron end up calling the very concept of consensus into question, at least in policy settings: "The research community, in our view, should be concerned about the reliability of any 'consensus' document whenever 'research' is used as a policy lever" (1999, p. 11). I agree, and I hope to see that concern extended to the public's own regard for consensus among researchers. The value of research's contribution lies in the detail, in how it renders the differences among programs, the overlooked consequences, and the nature of students' and teachers' experiences.

Yet a consensus is also at work here, a consensus on the validity of such differences in research approaches and findings. Researchers are trained very well to scrutinize each other's work, with its divergences and distinctions, identifying its strengths and weaknesses. This ability to judge the quality of divergent work is surely part of what the research community has to offer, part of what makes this form of knowledge interesting and potentially helpful. While it may seem that the public and the policy makers will balk at any research that does not represent researcher consensus, policy makers at least have learned to work with a range of what Barker and Peters call "cognitive difficulties" posed by the relevant research, from the merely complex to the scientifically unknown and perhaps unknowable (1993, p. 2).

If the public can set aside the idea that research is a process of arriving at a singular, universal truth, at least with something as complex as learning to read and write, it will have the chance

to better understand how literacy can be encouraged and studied in different ways. Rather than bolster the impression that research seeks a consistent and single-minded body of findings that would dictate, in effect, how to teach literacy—as if the decision of how to teach should be left up to the experts—we would do better to develop ways of representing the divergence and the agreement within this field of inquiry. Knowing the possibilities and risks identified so far, knowing the challenges that research still faces, provides its own comfort, its own basis for taking action in the face of always partial knowledge.

On the one hand, presenting this consensus about divergence seems simple enough. We make plain for people how the research has been divided, neatly so at times—much as is the field of practice—between code- and process-oriented, phonics and whole language. Go back to that public access Web site I sketched out earlier and imagine a series of concept maps and summaries representing the division between code and process studies, with commentaries bringing into juxtaposition comparable studies between the two schools of thought.

This division is made abundantly clear by Stephen Stahl, a professor of reading education at the University of Georgia (1999). Stahl's own tireless research efforts over the years capture the divergent literacy goals that divide the two approaches, while demonstrating that the impact on learners, whether in motivation or achievement, has often failed to differ, apart from signs that whole language, for example, favors voluntary use of reading strategies, while its lack of interest in reading achievement diminishes test scores. Stahl also demonstrates how either of these reading programs appeals to a worldview among educators and researchers that encompasses more than the impact of test scores. Researchers need to help people see why studies might differ; they need to help people see the difference made by those differences. But this brings me to the more difficult part of representing this consensus over the divergent state of the research.

For, as things stand, these differences diminish the public impact of research. While he was editor of *Educational Researcher*, Robert Donmoyer wrote on the topic of talking truth to power: "As long as the research community tells the policy community contradictory things, the research community cannot expect to have much influence in decision making" (1997, p. 2). One challenge is to find ways of presenting studies that challenge and contradict what has come before in a way that enables people to judge for themselves, or in a way that invites additional studies to further resolve the matter. Another challenge is to design and present studies that support ready comparisons and contrasts among divergent stances, as Stahl, for example, notes how less than half of the forty whole language studies he examined used achievement measures favored by code studies, although in fairness adequate assessment would require that mutually acceptable

measures be used (1999, p. 17). It should be obvious, then, that rendering research as a public resource of greater coherence and comprehensibility, even in its differences, will take far more than a nifty Web site. It will require a rethinking of the standards and practices that guide our scholarship; however, such a rethinking seems appropriate to this whole question of what we want to do with these new technologies for managing and sharing knowledge.

We might think of this enterprise as extending the example of the open inquiries of the National Academy of Sciences, which are making "going public" a regular part of what it is to do in publishing research. This could well augment public confidence in research, policies, and resulting practices while offering researchers a concrete relationship with an expanded audience. This is to use the Web as the printing press was originally used when scientific journal publishing began somewhat more than three centuries ago, to expand the reach and usefulness of knowledge (Eisenstein, 1979, pp. 543–566).

Up to now, this new medium has been largely directed at making it easier for researchers to publish their research for other researchers, which may well increase access among researchers on a global scale. But as we take this initial step, I want to ask whether we should not explore ways of using the increased access offered by the Web to make research a greater part of the larger social process of sense-making, which in turn could only make this larger sense-making a greater part of the research process.

I recognize what I am asking of a lot of researchers who have grown wary of politics. I hear the resistance in Stahl, for example, when in concluding his perhaps premature obituary for whole language he lends his support to Allington and Woodside-Jiron by insisting that "we need to understand the nature of political movements in education so that we can transcend them to provide effective instruction to the young" (1999, p. 21). Nonetheless, I respectfully counter, researchers need to understand political movements in education so that they can increase the presence and play of publicly funded research in the necessarily political processes of organizing and directing education in a democratic state. Researchers need to understand political movements in education so that their work contributes to the scope and informed basis of democratic participation—be it the participation of individuals or political movements—by equipping people with the knowledge that can improve instruction in directions decided through public processes. Researchers need to do this because they believe, in their own form of research consensus, that the knowledge that they are so carefully pursuing through research has a valuable contribution to make to people's understanding and to the potential level of "public reason," a phrase borrowed from Kant and more recently worked by John Rawls (1999).

Effective instruction for the young does not require us to transcend the politics of democratic participation in education, as if to finally separate the singular researched truth of reading, as ascertained by a test score, from the rabble-rousing politics of education. What research can tell us about *effective* instruction and *the effects of instruction* should help us realize the consequences of those politics, should help us appreciate the risks and possibilities of coming together to create an education system for the young. The research should help educators and the public make sense of what is at stake in how we understand and approach the teaching of reading and writing. Our expectation that this research contributes to democratic processes raises the educational standards for both researchers—in rendering their work incisive, coherent, and intelligible—and the public—as people's use of this knowledge to increase their democratic and civic engagement adds to the very reasons for the public's investment in education.

Innovative experiments are already under way in the publication of research in electronic forms (Pea, 1999; Kiernan, 1999; Norris, Smolka & Soloway, 1999).[6] And if there is no telling what shape this medium will take in the years ahead, or what impact it will have on the role that educational research plays in public forums, we should not let this uncertainty dissuade us from experimenting with new technologies that can increase the play of knowledge in the public sector, encouraging people to democratically engage with the institutions that govern their lives. A consensus among researchers on the value or possibility of improving the public value of research is as unlikely as is a consensus on how to teach reading and writing. But we might still agree that we should at least test the possibility that educational research can do more to inform the public and that professional talk about education falls within the public responsibilities of a research enterprise devoted to understanding educational processes. That is just the sort of cautious and concerned consensus that would advance the interests of democratic deliberation.

We should attempt, then, to set new standards for public knowledge so that people are able to readily draw on research findings, and we should set new standards for what educational research can contribute to our understanding of the schools, standards that go well beyond the narrow scope of a standardized test score. Such standards will contribute to an increase in effective democratic participation; they will help people realize the full value of publicly funded research; and perhaps most importantly, they will speak to the very value of public education in all of its contributions to the civic and political responsibilities that constitute a democratic state.

Notes

1. Donald A.B. Lindberg, Director of the National Library of Medicine, reports that "when the Library discovered that one third of the almost 200 million MEDLINE searches per year are being done by the public, for their personal health and the health of their families, the Library im-

mediately began planning a new program to help consumers easily access health information on the Internet and MEDLINE*plus* was created as part of this effort" (Lindberg, 2001). This new service provides access to extensive information about specific diseases and conditions and also has links to consumer health information from the National Institutes of Health, as well as to clearinghouses, dictionaries, lists of hospitals and physicians, health information in Spanish and other languages, and sites related to clinical trials.

2. A front-page story in the *New York Times* explains the current political climate as follows: "So many independent interest groups are poised to spend large sums on advertising to influence elections this year that Republicans and Democrats alike fear the candidates may find themselves playing bit parts in their own campaigns" (Berke, 1998, p. A1).

3. The most recent example of interest group impact is found in the Kansas Board of Education's 1999 decision to make the teaching of evolution optional in science classes. As Stephen Jay Gould has pointed out, it took the fundamentalists behind that vote three elections to secure a one-vote majority on the ten-member board (Dreifus, 1999). But then journalist Richard Wright has accused Stephen Jay Gould's popular work on evolution of feeding the creationists' cause, as creationists "love the conspiratorial aura of Gould's description of these gaps [in the fossil record] as the 'trade secret of paleontology'" (Wright, 1999, p. 61). This risk of misuse that follows from the very accessibility of Gould's work is a necessary aspect, I am arguing, of research playing a greater public role.

4. These ideas are based on the two pilot projects of the Public Knowledge Project (see http://www.pkp.ubc.ca/) at the University of British Columbia. The first was a collaborative effort with the *Vancouver Sun*, a daily local newspaper, examining how print journalism could be

extended by providing links to related research, policies, practices, programs, and organizations available on the Internet. A Public Knowledge Policy Forum was then created with the British Columbia Teacher's Federation (see http://pkp.bctf.bc.ca) to facilitate public participation in the policy-making process of the British Columbia Ministry of Education, supported by access to the relevant educational research and the government policies and plans.

5. MEDLINE*plus*, National Library of Medicine. [On-line]. Available at: http://www.nlm.nih.gov/medlineplus. See note 1.

6. For more on the work of the Public Knowledge Project in this regard, see note 4 above.

References

Allington, R., & Woodside-Jiron, H. (1999). The politics of literacy teaching: How "research" shaped educational policy. *Educational Researcher*, *28*(8), 4–13.

Barker, A., & Peters, B. G. (1993). Introduction: Science policy and government. In A. Barker & B. G. Peters (Eds.), *The politics of expert advice: Creating, using and manipulating scientific knowledge for public policy* (pp. 1–16). Pittsburgh, PA: University of Pittsburgh Press.

Berke, R. L. (1998, January 11). Interest groups prepare to spend on campaign spin. *New York Times*, pp. A1, A14.

Chang, M., Witt-Sandis, D., Jones, J., & Hakuta, K. (1999). *Compelling interest: Examining the evidence on racial dynamics in higher education*. Report of the AERA Panel on Racial Dynamics in Colleges and Universities. Stanford, CA: Stanford University Center for Comparative Studies in Race and Ethnicity. [Online.] Available at: http://www.aera.net.

Donmoyer, R. (1997). Revisiting the "talking 'truth' to power" problem. *Educational Researcher, 26*(3), 2.

Dreifus, C. (1999, December 21). Primordial beasts, creationists, and the mighty Yankees: A conversation with Stephen Jay Gould. *New York Times*, D3.

Eisenstein, E. L. (1979). The printing press as an agent of change: Communications and cultural transformation in early-modern Europe. Cambridge: Cambridge University Press.

Ekman, R., & Quandt, R. E. (1999). *Technology and scholarly communication*. Berkeley and Los Angeles: University of California Press.

Grossen, P. (1997). *Thirty years of research: What we know about how children learn to read*. Santa Cruz, CA: Centre for the Future of Teaching and Learning.

Kiernan, V. (1999, December 3). "Open Archives" project promises alternative to costly journals. *Chronicle of Higher Education*, pp. A43-A44.

Lindberg, D.A.B. (2001, January 31). About MEDLINE*plus*. [On-line]. Available: http://www.nlm.nih.gov/medlineplus/aboutmedlineplus.html.

Norris, C., Smolka, J., & Soloway, E. (1999). Convergent analysis: A method for extracting the value from research studies on technology in education. The Secretary's Conference on Educational Technology, July 12–13, Washington, DC. [On-line]. Available: http://www.ed.gov/Technology/TechConf/1999/whitepapers/paper2.html.

Pea, R. D., (1999). New media communication forums for improving education research and practice. In E. C. Lagemann & L. S. Shulman (Eds.), *Issues in education research: Problems and possibilities* (pp. 336–370). San Francisco, CA: Jossey Bass.

Peterson, P. L. (1998). Why do educational research? Rethinking our roles and identities, our texts and contexts. *Educational Researcher, 27*(3), 9–12.

Rawls, J. (1999). *The law of peoples with the*

idea of public reason revisited. Cambridge, MA: Harvard University Press.

Reich R. B. (2000, July 11). One education does not fit all. *New York Times*, p. A18.

Stahl, S. (1999). Why innovations come and go (and mostly go): The case of whole language. *Educational Researcher*, *28*(8), 13–22.

Wright, R. (1999, December 13). The accidental creationist: Why Stephen Jay Gould is bad for evolution. *New Yorker*, pp. 56–65.

Willinsky, J. (1999). *Technologies of knowing: A proposal for the human sciences*. Boston: Beacon.

Willinsky, J. (2000). *If only we knew: Increasing the public value of social science research*. Routledge: New York.

MOVING BEYOND COGNITIVE FORMALISM

The Democratic System of Meaning and New Modes of Thinking

Joe L. Kincheloe

The crisis of modernist reductionism can be conceptualized as a crisis of cognition, of thinking. Modernism has been marked by a way of thinking obsessed with the rational management of the lives of individuals. In this frame, technical standards can be better conceptualized as part of a culture of manipulation that wants to covertly teach us what and how to think. Indeed, technical standards are part of a larger process that involves powerful groups producing an educational experience and a way of thinking that serves their own interests. Technical standards are not designed to protect the sacred human spirit as much as they are meant to control that very spirit. Students often sense this purpose and sometimes rebel or resist the effort in a variety of creative ways. Such resistance is viewed by educators as a *motivational problem*. Maybe by understanding its genesis, we might

come to see it differently—possibly as a sign of hope in the ethical sense of many of our students.

No matter how we view such student behavior, it is safe to argue that most students are not very interested in the memorization rituals of top-down technical standards. They are not motivated to explore the possibilities of the human mind, not because they are uninterested but because they have never heard or seen anybody make such a reference. What do we mean, they ask, by such exploration? Devoid of a meaningful justification for the pursuit of learning, teachers and students in these reductionistic situations wander aimlessly in a maze of fragmented information and unchallenging thinking. Classrooms in technical schools become spiritless places where nervous, rule-following teachers face students who have no conception of any intrinsic value in the lessons being taught. Everything that goes on in such schools seems irrelevant in regard to its intrinsic value—those students who are motivated are typically moved by the extrinsic values of education, including its role in pathways to economic and social success. If the path to such success involved proficiency at picking raspberries, such success-motivated students would excel at that task.

The Cognitive Crisis

American society's inability to understand the limitations of reductionism and positivism is a part of a larger cognitive crisis. This crisis is characterized by a difficulty in understanding the social construction of self, the contradictions of what we label progress, the complexity of cultural difference, and the limitations of Western reason. Often when delineating a particular outcome as progress, for example, positivist observers are compelled to remove from view everything that falls outside the specific outcome in question. Thus, when we argue that a school's standards test score improvement is a sign of progress, we focus only on the scores. If the numbers are to constitute our proof, we cannot explore the simultaneous deterioration of students' sense of well-being, their inability to find significance in the everyday life of the classroom, or their lack of cognitive improvement as a result of the learning experience. A complex critique of standards-driven test score improvement reveals concurrent negative effects on the learning climate and the cognitive aspects of the school.

Complex analysis uncovers repressive contradictions in such pronouncements of progress. In one of the most important contradictions, the map of what is being studied is confused with the terrain itself. Standards-driven tests do not measure the educational competence or cognitive ability/accomplishment of students. Many political and educational leaders, however, believe that they do provide an accurate portrayal of what is happening in school. It is important to note that such scores tell us simply how well students have learned to take standardized tests and to engage in the specific type of thinking standardized tests require. Such a cognitive style is rarely required in academia or in the workplace. Two of the few places such thinking might be rewarded outside of the testing situation might be on *Who Wants to Be a Millionaire?* or *Jeopardy*.

Lost, of course, in these tests and the technical standards that drive them are the higher-order cognitive functions that help us see behind the curtain, beneath the surface. Such a cognitive ability helps students and teachers discern the processes in which knowledge is implicated. When reductionists fail to see the *process*, they view a misleading world of discrete entities, each separated from all others. Technical standards–driven schooling and the thinking it promotes reflect this isolating tendency as they search for fundamental essences, an understanding of "things-in-themselves." Thus, the possibility of a process-oriented cognition that views an entity as part of a larger set of temporal, spatial, and conceptual relationships is severely reduced by technical standards. No one is examining these types of cognitive issues in the literature on standards floating around in the first years of the twenty-first century. Standards of complexity make sure that these cognitive dynamics are always addressed in the conversation about educational reform.

The cognitive crisis of modernism reveals itself in the tyranny of the unexamined word and unexamined cognitive styles. Any discussion of educational standards and the goals of education would seem to require an analysis of what academic abilities and cognitive skills contribute to the production of an educated person. So far such a conversation has not taken place. Voices that challenge the mentality of technical standards both inside and outside the United States have been silenced. The narrative of progress based on a reductionistic form of reason and its obsession with things-in-themselves have served to overpower dissenters. In the process, American society has suffered, cognition has stagnated, and schools have become more concerned with honoring the past than inventing the future. Questions of justice and fairness in light of the contextual experiences of different students are represented by advocates of technical standards as manifestations of the forces that are undermining the quality of our schools. Such a perspective reflects the reductionists' inability to think in

terms of context and the influences it exerts on our relationship to the world.

As referenced elsewhere in this volume, technical standards promote a cognitive reductionism that finds it difficult to study the cognitive process, consciousness, and identity formation because of their immateriality, their refusal to be neatly characterized as things-in-themselves. How do we know for certain the nature of cognitive ability? Such a complex entity does not lend itself to concrete delineations of its nature. Just when positivistic scientists believe they have nailed it down, cognitive ability changes as a result of its contact with different cognitive forms. Such diversity changes what was previously viewed as cognitive ability because it induces reflection, which moves cognitive ability to a new space. This process of cognitive change continues, based on the experiences encountered and the new contexts negotiated.

Technical standards demand a twelve-to-sixteen-year training program for the fragmented positivistic mindset. Requiring an emphasis on quantities, distance, and location, technical standards ignore thinking that focuses on qualities, relationships, and context. Modernist assumptions are deeply embedded in various aspects of technical standards–driven school life. Standards-driven tests prepare students to think in terms of linear causality and quantification—the foundation of positivism. Because we are not taught to think in complex terms, in terms that expose the tacit assumptions that shape our conventions, institutions, and everyday practices, many educators are not aware that they are promoting a particular ideologically inscribed cognitive style when they design, implement, and assess standards. Such naiveté exacerbates the cognitive crisis that undermines us.

Technical standards are handcuffed to a bed covered with a crazy quilt of unexamined assumptions. Because reductionistic observers are blind to these ideological, epistemological, and cognitive presuppositions, the questions they ask, the policies they formulate, the goals they pursue in relation to standards-driven educational reform are not very academically sophisticated. These tacit assumptions dictate the nature of the reform conversation without the participants' awareness. Often, standards advocates are oblivious to the implications and effects of their proposals.

Other times, however, standards advocates are acutely aware of the ideological, political, and cognitive dynamics involved and the interests they serve. In the back-to-basics proposals of the 1970s and 1980s, the same dynamics were at work that operate in the standards movement of the early twenty-first century. Presidents Reagan and Bush in the 1980s turned to increased standardized testing, strict accountability measures for teachers, and more business and school partnerships in their reform proposals. President Clinton continued these types of reform during his two administrations, and President W. Bush pushes them even more aggressively in his administration. Thus, current technical standards proposals are merely a continuation of policies already in place. A similar policy pattern was present in Great Britain under Margaret Thatcher and John Major.

The Reagan-Bush-Clinton-W. Bush/Thatcher-Major proposals emphasized the training of competitive and productive workers. While the production of good workers is not in itself a problematic goal of education, such a task is far more complex than envisioned in these reforms (see Kincheloe, 1995). Instead of educating smart workers and courageous citizens dedicated to the social good, the Reagan-Bush-Clinton-W. Bush proposals have often attempted to produce workers who are compliant and loyal to their companies, that is, passive thinkers. Such "team players" do not pose any significant challenge to the injustices and myopia of the reductionist mode of education. Of course, technical standards as the latest chapter of educational reductionism perpetuate these ideological and cognitive dynamics. The cognitive crisis is exacerbated.

Reductionism in the Cognitive Space: The Limitations of Formal Thinking

"Teaching the basics" is one aspect of the public conversation about standards that allows reductionists to score public relations points. Over and over again, they speak of teaching children to read and write, as if those who oppose their oversimplifications were opposed to such teaching. Let it be stated clearly at this point: no advocate of standards of complexity is opposed to the teaching of reading and writing. The point for standards of complexity is not whether to teach such abilities, but how you teach such abilities without squashing children's desire to learn, without diminishing their understanding of how such academic skills affect their lives. How such skills are taught, how they are connected to a child's life so he or she will use and expand upon them, is a much more complex question. In the context of formal thinking, the same concept is applicable. Students, however, should not be taught formal thinking skills in a rote, simply-follow-the-procedure manner. Students must understand where such a way of thinking came from and what it can and cannot do. Such larger understandings or meta-awarenesses are central to standards of complexity (Spring, 1994).

Though we have alluded to positivism—the way of seeing that forms the foundation for formalism/formal thinking—throughout this volume, a quick overview of positivism is important in this cognitive context. Positivism is the epistemological extension of the modernist revolution initiated by Descartes, Newton, and Bacon. The assumptions of positivism are drawn from the logic and methods of investigation associated with reductionistic physical science. In such a context hermeneutical principles of interpretation hold little relevance. The meanings of the scientific data produced are rather obvious, positivists contend, so what need is there for interpretation? What is important in the positivistic context involves explanation, prediction, and technical control. How we decide what constitutes a desirable state of affairs—for example, a well-educated person—is of little consequence. To the positivist, knowledge is worthwhile to the extent that it describes objectified data; it does not involve imagining what could be.

Complex questions concerning the social construction of knowledge—the codes, media, ideologies, and socioeconomic structures that shape facts and the political interests that direct the selection and evaluation of data—are irrelevant when knowledge is assumed to be objective and value free. Since the hidden values of knowledge are unexamined by the positivistic tradition, the positivistic cult of objectivity suppresses political discussion in the public sphere. For example, who benefits and who is harmed by technical standards is not a political (power-related) question in the public conversation about standards. Since, in the eyes of positivists, technical standards have been identified in a value-free manner, then they are immune from such political questioning. Positivism and the forms of thinking it supports do not attempt to expose the power imbalances hiding in the languages of knowledge production, teaching, and everyday life. Since it is incapable of reflecting on the political dimensions that infiltrate it, positivism ultimately offers uncritical support for the status quo (Scholes, 1982; McLaren, 2000; Hinchey, 1998).

Formalism and the Limitations of Cognitive Growth

Cognitive strategies that positivism appropriates from the physical sciences do not neatly fit into the social, psychological, and educational domains. Focusing on the goals of prediction and control, physical science–oriented positivism emphasizes exactness and precision. In an educational context operating within the orbit of positivism, the concern with exactness and precision overrides the flexibility needed for cognitive growth and self-direction, learning to teach oneself. Thus, positivist educational and political leaders attempt to produce exact forms of empirical proof for concepts that are nonempirical in nature. How might we quantitatively measure one of the most important goals of a complex education: students' ability to teach themselves? Madeline Hunter (1987) extended this notion when she admitted that the purpose of education may be to develop creative problem solvers and responsible, productive decision makers. But, thinking as the positivist she was, she said, "I can't cite any research to support that statement" (p. 53).

Just what kind of research would "support" such a statement? Indeed, such a statement involves making a value judgment about what constitutes educational goals. Such a judgment cannot be articulated as an empirical question. Positivists have terrific diffi-

culty with issues, questions, judgments, concerns, and feelings that don't lend themselves to an empirical framing. When these dynamics are forced into the empirical framework, logical errors are committed that hold profound negative consequences. Thus, the complex question of educational purpose omnipresent in the standards debate is reduced to an empirical question of test scores. In such a move, all of the ethical, cognitive, political, spiritual, and social features inherent in the issue of educational purpose are erased without any contemplation. A complex question— what is a good education?—is reduced to a simple question—how do we raise standards-driven test scores? The cognitive reductionism inherent in this reductionistic formalism seems rather obvious.

Within much of what passes for cognitive theory, Jean Piaget's notion of formal thinking is viewed as the highest level of cognition that can be reached. Yet analysts operating in the zone of complexity do not accept such a perspective; they recognize the limitations of formal thinking. Adults do not reach some cognitive ceiling, a state of cognitive equilibrium beyond which no new levels of thinking can emerge. There have to be modes of cognition that move beyond the Western culturally inscribed formal operational ability to formulate abstract conclusions, understand cause-effect relationships, and to produce a reductionistic view of reality. Advocates of complexity maintain that we now know too much to define formalism as the zenith of human cognition (Arlin, 1975; Kincheloe & Steinberg, 1993; Kincheloe, Steinberg, & Hinchey, 1999).

Formalism implies acceptance of a Cartesian mechanistic worldview and of a cognitive mode that is trapped within a cause-effect, hypothesis-generating, deductive system of reasoning. The formal operational thinker employs a science that breaks a physical, social, psychological, or educational system into its basic parts to understand the way it works. Emphasizing certainty and prediction, formal operational thinking organizes verified facts into a theory. The facts that do not fit into the theory are eliminated, and the theory developed is the one best suited to eliminate contradictions in knowledge. Thus, formal operational thought and its attendant mode of inquiry operate on the assumption that contradiction resolution is an important objective (Kramer, 1983). Many technical standards devisers, assuming that formal operational thought represents the highest level of human cognition, focus their efforts on its cultivation and measurement. Students and teachers who understand the limitations of formalism are often criticized for their lack of rigor, their subjectivism (Sternberg, 1985). (It is important to note here that many technical standards fail to get to formal operations, resting instead at a concrete level of thinking.)

Postformal thinkers are comfortable with the uncertain, tentative nature of knowledge as it emerges from complex research. They are tolerant of contradiction and value the attempt to integrate ostensibly dissimilar phenomena into new, revealing syntheses. In other words, postformal thinkers escape the confines of Cartesian-Newtonian reductionism and venture into the zone of complexity. Postformalism underpins a form of cognition suitable for an electronic world; only a postformal thinker is cognitively and conceptually equipped to handle the uncertainty of the contemporary. Where the formal operational orientation functions on the basis of the Cartesian assumptions of linear causality and determinism, the postformal perspective assumes reciprocity and holism (the complex, nonlinear interconnection of events) (Van Hesteran, 1986; Kramer, 1983).

Thus, simple, privileged vantage points from which to view socioeducational phenomena are rejected by postformal thinkers, as they come to realize that there are many ways of approaching an event. Teachers operating in the zone of complexity will see multiple depictions of the phenomenon, depending both on the context from which it emanates and the system of meaning they employ to help formulate their questions and research strategies; for example, do they adopt a view from above or a view from below? Traditional Marxism, for example, argued in its own deterministic way that humans see only what their conceptual lenses allow them to see, and that they understand what the context for understanding permits.

In the spirit of hope, possibility, and antideterminism, complex teachers seek to liberate themselves from such determinism by taking control of their perceptual abilities, by transcending what the context permits. In this way we cognitively free ourselves from the constraints of Cartesian dualism and from the structural forces that limit our ability to see the world from outside our restricted vantage point. In its logocentrism, modernity discounted the terrain of private inner reality. What good was such a landscape in the process of industrialization, material progress, and the conquest of nature? As postformalism rediscovers the sensuous and complex, it incorporates such notions into new ways of exploring and perceiving the social, educational, and even physical world (Gordon, Miller, & Rollock, 1990; Kramer, 1983; Slaughter, 1989).

Such new modes of thinking and exploring the world incorporate sensual knowledge and self-knowledge in interesting ways. Researchers who do not understand themselves tend to misconstrue the pronouncements and feelings of others. The complexity and multiple readings characteristic of postformal analysis are remote to formal thinkers, as they seek comfort in the prescribed methods, the objectivity, the depersonalization of traditional social-scientific, educational research and positivist cognitive approaches (Van Hesteran, 1986). In a sense, the Cartesian objectivist tradition provides a shelter in which the self can hide from the deeply personal issues that permeate all socioeducational phenomena—personal issues, which, if it were not for the deperson-

alization of traditional inquiry, would force an uncomfortable element of self-revelation.

Postformal thinkers/inquirers seek insight into how their own assumptions (as well as those of the individuals they study) came to be constructed. They transcend formalism's concern with problem solving by seeking to determine the origins of the problem; in other words, they seek to learn to think about their own thinking. "How did I come to think this way?" they ask. "What might I do to capture a more complex perspective on the world?" Formalism is uncomfortable in this domain and attempts to squash questions such as these that merely "complicate the matter." In the simplification process that occurs at this point, meanings are distorted and multiple viewpoints are erased. Awareness of the systems of meaning assumed within knowledge production is lost in this formalist process. The possibility of cognitive growth is undermined.

What Does a System of Meaning Have to Do with Cognition? Analyzing Formalism via a Democratic System of Meaning

I referred above to the concept of a "system of meaning" and its relationship to the way we "see" and "think about" the world. Our understanding of the limitations of formal cognition is based upon the system of meaning that we bring to the analytical process. Thus, before we go any further in our discussion of cognition and educa-

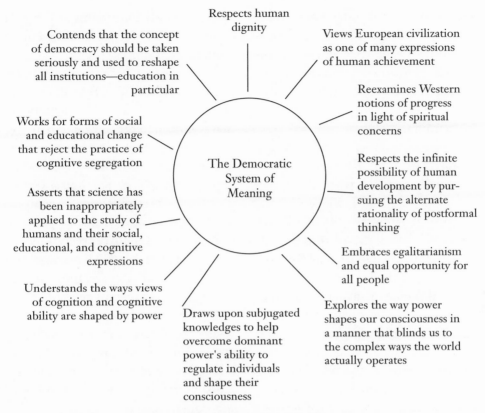

Respects human dignity

Contends that the concept of democracy should be taken seriously and used to reshape all institutions—education in particular

Views European civilization as one of many expressions of human achievement

Works for forms of social and educational change that reject the practice of cognitive segregation

Reexamines Western notions of progress in light of spiritual concerns

The Democratic System of Meaning

Respects the infinite possibility of human development by pursuing the alternate rationality of postformal thinking

Asserts that science has been inappropriately applied to the study of humans and their social, educational, and cognitive expressions

Embraces egalitarianism and equal opportunity for all people

Understands the ways views of cognition and cognitive ability are shaped by power

Draws upon subjugated knowledges to help overcome dominant power's ability to regulate individuals and shape their consciousness

Explores the way power shapes our consciousness in a manner that blinds us to the complex ways the world actually operates

Moving Beyond Cognitive Formalism

tional standards, it is important to specify the system of meaning we are using. The above figure is a brief outline of our democratic system of meaning.

A democratic system of meaning respects human dignity. A democratic system of meaning examines ways of thinking and cognitive styles in light of how they contribute or do not contribute to the production of human dignity. To develop this idea I draw upon the same principles I used to develop the idea of "good work" in *Toil and Trouble: Good Work, Smart Workers, and the Integration of Academic and Vocational Education* (1995) and *How Do We Tell the Work-*

ers? The Socio-Economic Foundations of Work and Vocational Education (1999).

1. *The principle of self-direction—a cognition of risk.* Does the way of thinking help individuals direct their own lives? Does it help them identify and solve problems by making use of skills, knowledge, reasoning, and intuition? A democratic system of meaning respects human dignity and promotes a form of cognition that assumes that the promotion of human dignity is worth the risks such promotion often involves.

2. *The principle of a life grounded around active learning.* A democratic system of meaning maintains that individuals should never be allowed to

become passive instruments of power wielders. In this context, the democratic system explores cognitive forms and asks Do they promote active learning? Do they encourage individuals to take responsibility for their own learning?

3. *The principle of cooperation and community building*. Recognizing that the social relationships of the world are too often fractured, the democratic system of meaning works to discern how particular modes of thinking affect such fracture. Do they simply promote competition, where I use my mind to promote my gain over another person's loss? The form of thinking promoted with this principle attunes individuals to the needs of others.

4. *The principle of individual learning and activity that contributes to the social welfare*. If the cognitive forms that support teaching and learning do not contribute to the public good, then they must be made to do so. Often this feature of learning or studying cognition is not taken into account. A democratic system of meaning always examines the consequences of individual conceptualization and learning for the public well-being.

5. *The principle of support for people's need to express their individuality*. In a positivistic world, too often individuals face their superiors' attempts to regulate them. The democratic system of meaning makes sure that particular cognitive modes protect the need for self-expression while also shielding individuals from the pathologies of domination. The democratic system of meaning often helps individuals discern previously unrecognized forms of domination and recognize their effects on individual consciousness.

6. *The principle of incorporating play into work and learning*. Standards rhetoric has created a climate in schools that is hostile to the notion of play. Yet play seems to be basic to human civilization and constitutes one of the highest human endeavors. Play principles can be extended into learning in the following ways: rules of play are not constructed to repress freedom but to constrain authoritarianism and thus to promote fairness; the structure of play is dynamic in its relation to the interaction of the players, and by necessity this interaction is grounded on the equality of the players; the activity is always viewed as an autonomous expression of self, as care is taken not to subordinate imagination to predetermined outcomes. Thus, play does not produce a deadening exhaustion since the activity refreshes the senses and celebrates the person. In this context we can learn to think as collaborators rather than as competitors in the learning process. Rigorous learning in schools shaped by standards of complexity can be viewed as a form of play when teachers and learners work together for shared purposes (Aronowitz, 1973).

A democratic system of meaning views European civilization as but one of many expressions of human achievement. While there is no doubt that Europeans have produced great cultural achievements and ways of thinking that have led to great changes in the course of human history, our system of meaning moves us to explore other cultures' achievements and cognitive styles as well. In this context, standards of complexity do not uncritically embrace the formal thinking that emerges from European epistemological assumptions. The scientific methods of European ways of seeing do not produce universal, neutral, and objective knowledge. From the perspective of European positivism, individuals from non-European cultures are often viewed simply as inferiors who don't share "our" values and are thus dismissed. Such Eurocentric ways of seeing produce an epistemological power that induces individuals to acquiesce to modernist criteria for judging what is of worth in human experience.

Across the centuries, this epistemological colonialism moved Europeans to see themselves as producers and purveyors of truth. Through their science and rationality they often came to think that they possessed the solutions to all earthly (and sometimes unearthly) problems. As agents of truth, Europeans were able to justify a variety of crimes against humanity—especially nonwhite humanity (Dion-Buffalo & Mohawk, 1992). Understanding this historical reality and its consequences becomes even more important for Americans after the tragic events of September 11, 2001. Our democratic system of meaning attempts to get beyond this ethnocentric form of thinking and to draw upon the power of cultural difference to move to a new cognitive domain. Central to this move is the effort to

see the world from a variety of cultural and historical vantage points. The cognitive and pedagogical implications of such a move are dramatic, as multiple accounts and ways of seeing replace the monolithic "truth."

In light of the ways African, Latino, Muslim, Asian, and indigenous lives are misrepresented in both schools and the media, such a way of seeing is profoundly needed by non-European students with understandably low self-esteem, not to mention students from the dominant culture whose anger toward the marginalized grows daily. A curriculum that *sees* from the margins operates differently from the dominant curriculum, starting, for example, a study of race in the United States not with slavery but with the pre-fifteenth-century civilizations in West Africa. Such an approach tells a different story, as it frames the African American struggle as one to regain its original strength, not as a story of a traditionally weak, enslaved people trying to *develop* a sense of dignity.

The subjugated curriculum of the marginalized does not attempt merely to replace Eurocentrism with Afrocentrism, or androcentrism (male centeredness) with gynocentrism (female centeredness). Proponents do maintain, however, that the study of various marginalized peoples should be emphasized because they have been ignored or distorted. They also contend that dominant groups such as white people should be viewed from other angles, from non-Eurocentric epistemological assumptions. Such analysis does not mean that we simply demonize whiteness; it does mean that we treasure subjugated ways of knowing and thinking. Subjugated stories become a valuable resource for building a better future for individuals from diverse groups, a collective future based on the principles of communitarianism, power sharing, and social justice. In a cognitive context such goals are most easily reached when our thinking is informed by the perspectives of a variety of cultural traditions. Standards of complexity emphasize this type of rigorous diversity.

A democratic system of meaning reexamines Western notions of progress in light of spiritual concerns. The scientific revolution in Western Europe in the seventeenth and eighteenth centuries promoted ways of thinking grounded on particular values and worldviews. *Progress* was central to this cognitive format—and this term implied a specific type of meaning making. Cartesian-Newtonian progress involved a belief in centralization, concentration, accumulation, efficiency, and speed. Bigger became better as the dualistic way of seeing reinforced a patriarchal, expansionist sociopolitical order grounded on a desire for power and conquest. Such a worldview often served to dehumanize, to focus attention on concerns other than the sanctity of humanity.

A foundation was laid that allowed science and technology to transform the world. Commerce increased, nationalism grew, and European civilization could conquer at a rate previously unimagined. Rationality became a new deity, and around this god the credo of modernity was developed: the world is rational and there is only one meaning of the term. All phenomena can be described within the boundaries of this monolithic rationality, whether we are studying atoms or the solar system, dreams or engines, learning or gunpowder, electricity or forms of government. Rationality applied to politics and government nourished the most progressive aspects of modernism—its ideals of freedom, justice, and equality. In the attempt to develop ways of transcending the regressive features of modernism, this progressive dimension must not be forgotten (Leshan & Margenau, 1982; Hannam, 1990).

On the whole, however, regressive modernism's hyperrationality served to reduce and fragment the world until individuals were blinded to particular forms of human and even physical experience. Attempting to study the world in isolation, bit by bit, economists studied the economy separate from human beings, educational scientists studied the schools separate from society, and psychologists studied the concept of mind separate from the cultural experiences that shape it. In this way cognition was viewed as some innate process that has little to do with one's lived experiences. Intelligence was defined as a thing-in-itself, a measurable quantity with a substance similar to other physical objects like gasoline, soil, or asteroids. In this view, a person has some measurable quantity of intelligence, rather like cholesterol. In the Cartesian context, few seemed to consider the possibility that the way cognitive ability is defined shapes how much of it a particular individual is deemed to have.

This formalization and quantification of humanness demeaned the spiritual aspect of human life. Spiritual, in the sense I am employing here, involves the "immaterial, intelligent, and sentient" (involving the ability to perceive) aspects of humans. As Aoestre Johnson (1999) puts it, spirituality involves the "animating or vital principle held to give life to physical beings," an entitlement to "reverence, honor, and respect" (p. 105). Our democratic system of meaning embraces this spirituality, and the cognition promoted in this context seeks forms of thinking that contribute to the protection of human spirituality. One of the reasons that I am uncomfortable with modernist cognitive forms is their lack of concern for this spiritual aspect of human beings. Standards of complexity assume that Cartesian formal thinking and the education that emerges around it do not respect the sacredness of students. Progress in this context involves human spiritual enhancement.

A democratic system of meaning respects the infinite possibility of human development by pursuing the alternative rationality of postformal thinking. The new forms of democratic living and thinking that postformalism attempts to make possible are inextricably linked to an alternative rationality. Contrary to the claims of some scholars in mainstream educational psychology, postformalism does not seek to embrace irrationality or to reject the entire enterprise of empirical research. I borrow the phrase "alternative rationality" from Stanley Aronowitz (1988), whose critique of mainstream science helps shape our vision of postformalism. In this schemata, new rationalities employ forms of analysis sensitive to signs and symbols, the power of context in relation to thinking, the role of emotion and feeling in cognitive activity, the value of the psychoanalytical process as it taps into the recesses of (un)consciousness, and our system of meaning's spiritual concerns. The effort to extend higher-order cognition extends Aronowitz's powerful alternatives by asking ethical questions of cognition and action. Such inquiries induce educational and cognitive psychologists to study issues of purpose, meaning, and ultimately worth. Do certain forms of thinking undermine the quest for justice? Do certain forms of research cause observers to view problematic ways of seeing as if they involved no issues of power and privilege (Shotter, 1993; Cannella, 1997, 1999)?

Our democratic system of meaning is dedicated to postformal principles of cognition simply because they challenge the limited cognitive imagination of psychological reductionism. Human beings, postformalists contend, can be so much more than they are now. Postformal educators operating with these understandings in mind are ready to take part in schools that are shaped by standards of complexity. They stand ready to engage in the revolutionary process of reconceptualizing comfortable Western notions of reason.

Postformalism is grounded on the understanding that reason is a social construction, culturally mediated by signs, symbols, and codes. In this context, Cartesian-Newtonian reason is not transhistorical and transcultural but merely one of many sophisticated forms of meaning making. The traditional scientific aim of its own rational universalism is rejected, along with its abstract reason divorced from experience and its concern for adjusting individuals to the status quo. This dynamic of adjustment reveals itself in functionalist theories that reinforce the legitimacy of the status quo rather than engaging students in a critique of its shortcomings. Mainstream educational psychology fits in this functionalist context, as it identifies deficiency and/or pathology in the marginalized student. The possibility of cultural mismatch or conflicting social values among the climate of school, the psychological criteria for assessment, and the student is rarely considered.

The postformal reconceptualization of Cartesian-Newtonian reason challenges the mainstream educational psychological construction of autonomy and isolated self-direction as the ultimate manifestations of the reasonable individual. In this context, the abstract individualism of Cartesianism inscribes cognitive theory with a validated set of procedures for attaining rational autonomy, called formal thinking. Known, of course, as the scientific method, these procedures provide modernist educational psychologists with the yellow brick road to rigor, context-freedom, protection from the bias/distortion of subjectivity, and truth. The teaching that emanates from these assumptions asserts that the purpose of instruction is to impart this procedural form of thinking and to measure students' capacity to employ it. As postformal teachers rethink reason, they embrace intimacy and interpretation rather than distance and proof. Such teachers value the personal knowledge of students and the ways of understanding that draw individuals together. Such an emphasis is not a retreat to irrationality but an effort to push the boundaries of reason beyond a limited set of procedures and the confines of abstract principles.

In this critical pursuit, postformal teachers seek to engage their students in the understanding of the world in general and everyday life in particular—both in relation to one another and from as many vantage points as possible. A central feature of the postformal teacher's expansion of reason involves the ability to uncover new perspectives, new angles on the world, everyday life, and self. In this arena, students and teachers learn to contextualize in new and exciting ways. In a postformal classroom studying the Gulf War, students would study not only U.S. accounts of the conflict but Iraqi perspectives. They would interview gung-ho U.S. Army veterans, war protesters, Iraqi victims, and observers from Africa and Latin America. Students would analyze the war in a geopolitical context, a multinational economic context, an environmental context, and a medical context. The role of the postformal teacher would involve devising new contexts and new perspectives from which to explore the meaning of the war in a historical and a lived context. Moral and ethical questions would be raised and student interpretations of the event and analysis of its personal meaning in their lives would be encouraged.

As students studied the war in a variety of contexts, they would simultaneously engage in a meta-analytical cognitive analysis of contextualizing itself. Such an analysis would help students understand that postformalism frees us to conduct inquiry in ways that match the special needs presented by specific contexts. Such a position concerning knowledge production is emancipatory in that it frees us from the limitations of Cartesian-Newtonian procedural thinking. It also illustrates the relationship between research method and cognitive strategy, a relationship rarely noted in mainstream cognitive and educational psychology. Such insights induce democratically grounded postformal educators to become researchers of unique manifestations of cognitive sophistication, of new forms of intelligence. In a recent book entitled *What Is Indigenous Knowledge? Voices from the Academy*, Ladi Semali and I take up this postformal notion of researching new forms of intelligence. Indeed, we argue that an important justification for studying indigenous knowledges around the world is that it helps educators break away from the cognitive

limitations of Western reason (Semali and Kincheloe, 1999).

A democratic system of meaning embraces egalitarianism and equal opportunity for all people.   Without the guidance of a democratic system of meaning, educators, especially advocates of technical standards, do not understand (and many times do not even try to understand) the institutionalization of inequality in schools. Dominant power produces and validates modes of cognition, sets of content standards, systems of instruction, methods of evaluation, definitions of teacher and student success, and classification and tracking systems that arrange students into advanced, college-bound, general, or vocational tracks. Such divisions provide the knowledge, social practices, cultural capital, and skills required by the class-driven hierarchy of labor in the workplace.

In this case, dominant power interacts with personal behavior when school leaders induce students to believe that such class-based divisions of students and workers are natural and necessary. Students from outside the mainstream, the nonwhite and the poor, are convinced that they do not possess the ability to move into upper levels. They are entangled in the myths of their cultural and academic inferiority as outsiders. Black students, for example, who are often very successful in college, report that by the time they were junior high students, the culture of the school had convinced them that college was out of the question. Thus, students and their teachers come to accept the myths of inferiority. "How can we expect these students to understand physics?" teachers and guidance counselors ask as they channel the outsiders into nonacademic vocational tracks.

Advocates of the democratic system of meaning and standards of complexity study these power dynamics and their relation to student performance. They understand that when psychometricians act on the assumption that the contents of the mind are more important than the environmental influences that construct it, the possibility of difference being mistaken for deficiency increases. In this formalist context, the social, the cultural, and the economic are erased in cognitive evaluation. Positivistic cognitive scientists take a social and historical dynamic and turn it into a natural process. Indeed, this prestidigitation has ancient origins—since the time of Plato, theories of intelligence have been used to justify socioeconomic disparity. The "dregs" at the bottom have always been said to be deficient and/or pathological. Reductionistic elitists blame the poor for being poor. It is an academic and logical outrage to separate environmental factors from any effort to measure ability or intelligence.

It doesn't take a sociologist to uncover the strange alchemy that occurs when a culturally different and/or poor student encounters the culture of school, grounded as it is in middle-class, white culture, and the conservative wing of the testing psychology establishment. This middle-class mind-set often views poverty as a badge of failure. One African American child absorbed this lesson in her first experiences in school, as evidenced by her response to the question, What is poverty? "Poverty," she said, "is when you aren't living right." Positivist psychologists seem to be oblivious to the psychic toll of such lessons and the ways they move marginalized young people to reject the academic world and the experiences that surround it as a matter of self-protection.

In this situation, teachers and students of educational sociology come to understand that children from lower socioeconomic and nonwhite homes do not ascribe importance to school work in the same way as do upper-middle-class white students. Poor and racially marginalized children often see academic work and the information and skills tests seek to measure as unreal, as a series of short-term tasks rather than something with long-term significance for their lives. Important work is something you get paid for after its completion. Without such compensation or long-term justification, these students display little interest in the "academic." This lack of motivation and its consequences, involving reduced understanding of certain knowledge forms and discursive formats, are interpreted by many educators and psychologists as a lack of intelligence. Poor performance on standardized tests scientifically confirms the "inferiority" of such students.

Unfortunately, this happens every

day. Too many educators and psychologists (though certainly not all) mistake cultural and class differences in manners, attitudes, speech, and school performance for a lack of cognitive ability. Some teachers and counselors report that they place some students in low-ability tracks because of their cultural or class backgrounds. Their rationale involves the marginalized student's social discomfort around students from a "higher status/ability background." These students should be with their own kind, they maintain. Advocates of technical standards also worry that the presence of such students in high-ability tracks would subvert the quality of education received by more "intelligent" students. Such beliefs constrict the educational establishment's view of the human capacity for development and the understanding of multiple dimensions of human diversity. Reductionists and their ideological compadres miss these social complexities. As they reduce intelligence to one's performance on an IQ test, they ignore the unique and creative accomplishments one is capable of in diverse venues and contexts.

Research on the educational performance of low-status groups in other countries provides important insight into the shortcomings of cognitive elitism. In Sweden, Finnish people are viewed as inferior—the failure rate for Finnish children in Swedish schools is very high. When Finnish children immigrate to Australia, however, they do as well as Swedish immigrants. Koreans do poorly in Japanese schools, where they are viewed as culturally in-

ferior; in American schools, on the other hand, Korean immigrants are very successful.

The examples are numerous, but the results generally follow the same pattern: racial, ethnic, and class groups that are viewed negatively or as inferiors in a nation's dominant culture tend to perform poorly academically. Reductionists don't want to understand that power relations between groups must be considered when individuals' abilities are analyzed. Without the insights derived from such environmental understandings, brilliant and creative people from marginalized backgrounds will continue to be relegated to the vast army of the inferior and untalented. Our democratic system of meaning alerts us to these harmful processes, as it grounds our formulation of new cognitive insights that confront these exclusionary and elitist ways of seeing. This is a central feature of standards of complexity.

A democratic system of meaning explores the way power shapes our consciousness, blinding us to the complex ways the world actually operates. The democratic system of meaning is dedicated to helping educators and the public understand the ways that dominant power operates to distort our understanding of how the world works. In this effort, standards of complexity help individuals discern how technical standards create and teach cognitive modes that paint a picture of the world that supports existing power relations. One cannot talk of securing social justice and promoting democracy without challenging the way this dominant power operates on both the contemporary educational and cultural landscape. The cultural realm has become a more and more important location in the shaping of both historical and everyday experience. No longer exercised simply by physical force, dominant power now works also through cultural institutions such as the schools, the media, the family, and the church, which exert sociopsychological pressure to win people's consent to domination.

In his notion of hegemony, developed in Mussolini's Italian prisons of the 1920s and 1930s, Antonio Gramsci recognized that the winning of popular consent is a very complex process. The dominant power bloc wins popular consent by way of a pedagogical process, a form of learning that engages people's conceptions of the world in such a way that transforms (not displaces) them with perspectives more compatible with those of the elite. The existence and nature of hegemony is one of the most important and least understood features of early-twenty-first-century life. Students of power, educators, sociologists, researchers, all of us are hegemonized, as our field of knowledge and understanding is structured by limited exposure to competing definitions of the sociopolitical world. The hegemonic field, with its bounded sociopsychological horizon, garners consent to an inequitable power matrix—a set of social relations that are legitimated by their depiction as natural and inevitable (Goldman, 1992;

West, 1993; McLaren, 1994; Giroux, 1997).

The technologies of hegemony (the methods by which social consent is garnered) move the state of social domination from condition yellow to condition red. Advocates of standards of complexity and postformalism find themselves in a state of full alert in regard to the exacerbation of domination in the postmodern condition. This technology of hegemony, termed *hyperreality* by postmodernist theorist Jean Baudrillard (1983), is marked by a blurring of the distinction between the real and the unreal. Such a blurring produces a social vertigo precipitated by a loss of contact with traditional notions of time, community, self, and history. New structures of cultural space and time generated by bombarding electronic images from local, national, and international venues shake our personal sense of place (Aronowitz & Giroux, 1991; Gergen, 1991; Kincheloe, 1995).

This proliferation of signs and images characteristic of media information–soaked hyperreality functions as a mechanism of control in contemporary Western societies. The success of a counterhegemonic education hinges on: (1) its ability to link the production of the representations, images, and signs of hyperreality to power blocs in the political economy and (2) its capacity, once this linkage is exposed and described, to delineate the highly complex and ambiguous cognitive effects of the reception of these images and signs on individuals located at various race, class, and gender coordinates in the web of reality. No easy task, this effort—but to avoid it is to turn our backs on the democratic experiment, educational rigor, and the possibility of social justice. This is why the effort to trace the effects of power in the ways the power bloc represents reality is so important.

We must be very specific about the nature of domination in contemporary life. Hyperreality, in its obscured yet ubiquitous guise, amplifies power by corporate control of the means of simulation and representation. By determining what is important (what is worthy, for example, of time on TV) and what is not, corporate-owned media can set agendas, mold loyalties, depict conflicts, and undermine challenges to the existing power bloc without a modicum of public notice. Students of cognition operating in the zone of complexity face the task of analyzing power/domination; the importance of this task cannot be overemphasized, for it is not addressed on the mediascape.

CBS will not present a two-minute story on domination in hyperreality on tomorrow night's evening news, nor will a single local affiliate discuss such a thing in any of its news programming in the foreseeable future. Electronic media will make programming decisions on the basis of commodity exchange issues; that is, cultural codes will be conveyed to the viewing audience on the basis of their capacity to engage men, women, and children in their *duty* to consume (Luke, 1991). The constituency of hyperreality serves the needs of the

power bloc with honor and civic reverence—its "patriotic" acts of consumption constitute the life-affirming productive energy of twenty-first-century capitalism.

The conditions under which knowledge is produced, consciousness is shaped, cognitive modes are fashioned, and hegemonic consent is won have dramatically changed over the past two decades. Power is now produced and exercised in a way that allows it to penetrate national and global boundaries. Western corporations transmit hegemonic power to Third World countries through advertising images sent by satellites; through the work of experts sent to speed "development" in agriculture, education, and the physical sciences; and through cultural representations plastered on billboards throughout the countryside. Advocates of standards of complexity and postformal modes of cognition understand that these are central educational issues of the twenty-first century. Proponents of educational reform, especially top-down technical standards, fail even to acknowledge the existence of these issues, as they hide behind their formalist barricades. Such political and educational leaders are simply not concerned with the way individuals learn and think, as long as existing power relations are not threatened and democratic dissent is suppressed.

Those who appreciate the democratic system of meaning understand that hegemonic power wins consent through the production of pleasure, as popular culture in the form of advertisements, TV shows, popular music, movies, and computer games induces individuals throughout the world to make emotional investments that tie them to such cultural productions. Such investments produce meaning and ways of thinking as they shape identity and an individual's view of the world. Individuals always view power, no matter how or where it is produced, through their own histories and their own race, class, and gender filters. Understanding contemporary power production and the cognitive filters everyone possesses, advocates of standards of complexity appreciate the need for more nuanced understandings of the way hegemonic messages are received, incorporated, and resisted.

Such understandings provide important insights into the effects of power, the ways the individual interfaces with sociopolitical structures, and the way meaning is made on power-produced terrains of representations and dominant culture formations. Concern with the phenomenological (having to do with the nature of consciousness) experience of the individual through the influence of social power allows scholars to focus on the moment of self-creation, the way belief structures are formed, and in a hegemonic context, the way consent is elicited. In their analysis of this process, democratic analysts want to know how power leaves its hegemonic imprint on individual consciousness. The better such a process is understood, the more we are empowered to understand what white supremacy, patriarchy, and rule by class elite have

done to individuals from all cultural spheres and how these factors have shaped their educational experience, their cognitive facilities, and their views of the way the world operates. In this power-driven context, democracy is under threat, as new forms of cognitive regulation invisibly work their malevolent magic.

A democratic system of meaning draws upon subjugated knowledge to help overcome the regulation of individuals and the shaping of their consciousness by the dominant power. The democratic system of meaning works to make cultural, gender, and class differences visible. Understanding the power asymmetries in these differences, the democratic system of meaning explores these dynamics in the context of disciplinary content knowledges, methods of teaching, standards, and modes of cognition. Understanding these dynamics in social and historical context, standards of complexity engage those who have been deemed different in the investigation of how institutions can be reformed in a way that is just, democratic, and rigorous. In a democratic system of meaning, difference is connected to democracy in that it understands schools as contested public spaces, pushed and pulled by forces of power. Curriculum, pedagogy, and acceptable modes of cognition are always shaped by these power struggles.

Attention to difference demands that teachers be aware of the specific histories and struggles of oppressed peoples in a variety of arenas. One of these arenas involves the school itself, as many scholars contend that the classroom is a central site for the legitimization of myths, lies, and silences about nonwhite, poor, and other marginalized individuals. If educators were actually to teach the specific histories and struggles of Latinos in America, for example, they would have to rethink the history of Anglos in America. When history books lie about the history of an oppressed group, they concurrently lie about all history—the entire curriculum is distorted by such duplicity. Teachers in the zone of complexity understand these historical and curricular insights and use them to move the recognition of difference into a politically transformative form of education. Such a pedagogy does not accept the inevitability of social privilege and social inequality. Instead, our democratic system of meaning understands Western societies as collectivities of difference, where the potential exists for all people to be edified by interaction with the "other" and the ways of knowing he or she brings to an encounter.

The benefits of a contextualized understanding of difference are multidimensional. Standards of complexity move beyond the "difference-is-spice" curriculum to the use of difference to reformulate the basic concepts of a discipline. In addition, standards of complexity use difference to debunk the myth, perpetuated by conservatives, that Western societies are grounded on a social, political, and cultural consensus. If the consensus myth is accepted, then standards of

complexity can be positioned as a divisive discourse that tears the social fabric apart with charges of injustice. In this context complex teachers are careful to situate different social groups *in relationship to* one another, not *in opposition to* one another.

Contrary to conservative charges, the point is not to pit groups against one another but to emphasize the importance and specific nature of oppressed cultures. Such an emphasis helps to expose the specific nature and commitments of a dominant culture that often hide behind its proclamation of neutrality. Using difference in this way precludes Anglo, European, male, and heterosexual culture from representing its norms as beyond history and culture. No longer can dominant culture celebrate its neutrality and universality while condemning the abnormality and deviancy of the marginalized (McCarthy & Apple, 1988; Frankenberg, 1993; McLaren, 1993; Zinn & Dill, 1994).

If difference is more empowering than homogeneity, its power emanates from its ability to expand each person's horizon and social understanding. Students who belong to divergent socioeconomic groups can learn much from one another if provided with the space to exchange ideas and analyze mutual difficulties. As such a powerful force, difference must be not simply tolerated but cultivated as a spark to human creativity. Any description of critical thinking must include an understanding of difference that nurtures a critical sense of empathy. Cornel West (1993) argues that empathy involves the ability to appreciate the anxieties and frustrations of others and never to lose sight of the humanity of the marginalized, no matter how wretched their condition.

The point emerging here, of course, involves the ethical and cognitive benefits derived from the confrontation with diversity and the different vantage points it provides us for viewing the lived world. Taking a cue from liberation theologians in Latin America, complex teachers often begin their analysis of an institution by listening to those who have suffered most as a result of its existence. These "different" ways of seeing allow such teachers to tap into the cognitive power of empathy—a power that allows individuals access to deep patterns of racism, class bias, and sexism and the way they structure oppression in schools. In this context, students and teachers begin to see other ways of thinking, and this recognition leads to a reexamination of how they themselves have come to think and view the world in the way they do.

Using this reflective process, teachers in standards of complexity seek a dialogue between Eastern cultures and Western cultures, as well as a conversation between the relatively wealthy northern cultures and the impoverished southern cultures (Bohm & Peat, 1987; Welch, 1991). In such a context, forms of knowing that have traditionally been excluded by the modernist West, such as the understandings of blue-collar workers, move educators to new vantage points and unexplored planetary perspec-

tives. Understanding derived from the perspective of the excluded or the culturally different allows for an appreciation of the nature of justice, the invisibility of the process of oppression, and the difference that highlights our own social construction as individuals.

In this spirit, all individuals who appreciate the insights of diverse knowledges begin to look at their work from the perspectives of their Asian, African, Latino, and indigenous colleagues around the world. Such cognitive cross-fertilization often reveals the tacit assumptions that impede innovations. For example, home builders and architects who study Native American, Japanese, or African ways of building houses may gain creative insight into their crafts. After studying the way Zuni pueblos addressed problems of living space, they might be empowered to tackle space problems creatively in ways conventional builders hadn't considered.

In the context of cognitive development, Piaget argued that conceptual change takes place when learners engage in the process of accommodation. He described accommodation as the restructuring of one's cognitive maps to take care of an unanticipated event—that is, to deal with difference. In order to accommodate, an individual must actively change his or her existing intellectual structure to understand the dissonance produced by the novel demand. Accommodation is a reflective, integrative behavior that forces us to realize that our present cognitive structure is insufficient to deal with the changing pressures of the environment (Kaufman, 1978; Fosnot, 1988).

In a sense, accommodation becomes a subversive agent of change leading an individual to adjust whenever and wherever it might be necessary. When Piagetian accommodation is connected with the Frankfurt School's concept of negation in a context that appreciates the notion of difference suggested by the democratic system of meaning, interesting things begin to happen. Common to both critical theory and accommodation, negation involves the continuous criticism and reconstruction of what one thinks one knows. For example, critical theorist Max Horkheimer argued that through negation we develop a critical consciousness that allows us to get beyond old, ossified worldviews and to incorporate our new understandings into a new reflective attitude (Held, 1980).

As teachers recognize the cognitive potential of critical accommodation, they structure learning situations wherein individuals come to understand previously unrecognized aspects of the environment and to expose the cognitive limitations that precluded insight in the past. Horkheimer maintained that through the awareness gained by way of critical negation (the philosophical analogue to the cognitive act of accommodation), an individual develops and becomes open to democratic change. In this context, critical accommodation can be described as a reshaping of consciousness consonant with an understanding of democracy and social justice. Thus,

educators see the diversity of classroom experiences as an opportunity for cognitive growth. An example from complex democratic classrooms might help to ground this concept. Teachers exploring the meaning of intelligence would develop (or *assimilate*, in Piagetian theory) an understanding of the concept based on their personal experience and the coverage of cognition in their teacher education. They would accommodate the concept as they began to examine students who were labeled unintelligent but displayed sophisticated abilities in the manual arts or in the practical understandings of the trades and crafts.

At this point the teachers might take note of this contradiction and begin to integrate this recognition of exception (accommodation) into a reconceptualization of the prevailing definition of intelligence in the culture of school. The old definition of intelligence would have been negated; through exposure to diverse expressions of intelligence, new ways of seeing it would have been accommodated. Our democratic system of meaning might have alerted teachers to the mainstream dismissal of the talents of students from the margins, nonwhite and economically disadvantaged young people. Picking up on these concerns, teachers would critically accommodate nontraditional expressions of intelligence that would free them from the privileged, racist, and class-biased definitions that were used to exclude cognitive styles that transcended the official codes. In this and many other situations, accommodation becomes the emancipatory feature of the thinking process. In a standards of complexity context, educators recognize this and use accommodation in the struggle for democratic economic, social, educational, and cognitive change (Hultgren, 1987; Lather, 1991).

Derived from dangerous memories of history that have been suppressed and information that has been disqualified by social and academic gatekeepers, subjugated knowledge plays a central role in standards of complexity. Through the conscious cultivation of these low-ranking knowledges, alternative democratic and emancipatory visions of society, politics, education, and cognition are possible. In a complex democratic curriculum, subjugated knowledge is not passed along as a new canon but becomes a living body of knowledge open to different interpretations. Viewed in its relationship to the traditional curriculum, subjugated knowledge is employed as a constellation of concepts that challenge the invisible cultural assumptions embedded in all aspects of schooling and knowledge production. The subjugated knowledges of African Americans, Native Americans, working-class people, women, and many other groups have contested the dominant culture's view of reality.

Confronted with subjugated knowledge, individuals from white mainstream culture begin to appreciate the fact that there are multiple perspectives on all issues. Indeed, they begin to realize that textbooks and content standards discard data about unpopu-

lar viewpoints and information produced by marginalized groups. Curricula that include subjugated perspectives teach a lesson on the complexities of knowledge production and how this process shapes our view of ourselves and the world around us. The curriculum cannot stay the same if we take the knowledges of working-class men and women seriously; if we get beyond the rosy, romanticized picture of immigration to North America and document the traumatic stories of the immigrants; if we seek out women's perspectives on the evolution of Western culture; or if we study the culture enslaved Africans brought to the New World.

The dominant cultural power blocs that often dictate technical, top-down content standards at the beginning of the twenty-first century seem oblivious to the need to listen to marginalized people and to take their knowledge seriously. Western power wielders are not good at listening to information that does not seem to contribute to hegemony, that does not enhance their ability to win the consent of the subjugated to their governance. Knowledge that emerges from and serves the purposes of the subjugated is often erased—made to appear dangerous and pathological to other citizens.

Drawing upon work within the discipline of cultural studies that seeks to reverse conditions of oppression, subjugated knowledge seeks new ways of validating the importance and relevance of divergent voices. Such voices are excluded not merely from schoolrooms, curriculum guides, and content standards, but from other sites of knowledge production, such as popular culture. Having become a major pedagogical force in Western societies over the past few decades, the popular culture "curriculum" is monitored for emancipatory expressions of subjugated knowledge. Though not always successful, power wielders attempt to neutralize the subjugated knowledges that find their way into TV, movies, popular music, the Internet, and other popular cultural sites (Dion-Buffalo & Mohawk, 1992; Fiske, 1993; Mullings, 1994; Nieto, 1996; McLaren & Morris, 1997).

But the value of subjugated knowledges is not contingent on the blessings of power wielders and standards devisors in the dominant culture, and so purveyors of subjugated knowledge can confront individuals from the white, upper-middle-class cultural center with the oppressed's view of them. Some of the pictures are quite disconcerting for mainstream individuals who have never given much thought to the way they are seen from the social margins. Individuals from dominant social formations have never developed their imagination about how they look to marginalized others, while the marginalized have been forced to give their appearance to the mainstream a great deal of attention. As a result, women often make sense of men's image of women better than men understand women's view of men; individuals with African heritages understand the motivations of whites better than the reverse; and low-status workers figure out how

they are seen by their managers more clearly than the managers understand how they appear to workers.

Obviously, such insights provide us with a very different view of the world and the processes that shape it. Teachers who employ subjugated viewpoints become transformative agents who alert the community to its hidden features, its submerged memories—in the process helping individuals to name their oppression or possibly understand their complicity in oppression. Such a naming process helps students, teachers, workers, and other community members to reflect on their construction of their lived worlds so that they develop the ability to take control of their own lives and move to a new cognitive domain. In this new cognitive domain, teachers and students explore dangerous knowledges that often change their perceptions of the forces that shape them. In this context, they redefine their ways of seeing with a new level of self-knowledge.

Teaching that is committed to subjugated knowledge has "friends in low places." In standards of complexity, the view from above of the traditional Eurocentric upper-middle-class male curriculum makes way for the inclusion of views from below. Emerging from an understanding of and respect for the perspective of the oppressed, such an epistemological position uses the voices of the subjugated to formulate a reconstruction of the dominant educational structure. It is a radical reconstruction in the sense that it attempts to empower those who are presently powerless and to validate oppressed ways of thinking that open new cognitive doors to everyone.

As democratic teachers expose the way dominant power invalidates the cognitive styles of marginalized groups, we begin to examine the testing procedures of technical standards and their political effects. Eurocentric psychometricians devise tests to evaluate student performance, forgetting in the process that evaluation is based on unquestioned definitions of intelligence and performance. Thus, the winners and losers will line up in predictable ways, with those from groups with high levels of social power performing better than those with low levels of power.

The advantage of subjugated perspectives, the views from below, involves what has been termed the "double consciousness" of the oppressed. If they are to survive, subjugated groups develop an understanding of those who attempt to dominate them; at the same time they are cognizant of the everyday mechanisms of oppression and their effects. W.E.B. DuBois (1973) called this double consciousness of the oppressed a form of "second sight," an ability to see oneself through the perception of others. A complex cognitive curriculum of second sight is grounded on the understanding that a rigorously educated person knows more than just the validated knowledge of the dominant culture.

For example, understanding science from a complex perspective would involve analysis of its specific historical origins (the seventeenth and eigh-

teenth centuries) and its cultural location (Western Europe). A complex science curriculum would appreciate that, like other ways of understanding and studying reality, Western science is a social construction of a particular culture at a particular time. Such a cognizance would not induce us to dismiss and discard the accomplishments of Western science—that would be silly. But it would induce us to study other ways of knowing, such as the scientific theories of Native Americans and other cultural groups. In this way we would gain the cognitive abilities of a variety of cultural insights. Here rests the benefits of a truly globalized curriculum.

A democratic system of meaning understands how views of cognition and cognitive ability are shaped by power. Educational leaders and standards developers understand cognition, cognitive ability, and intelligence in a distinct way, and this understanding exerts a dramatic impact. Classrooms that accept decontextualized, reductionistic, psychometric views are organized and evaluated very differently from classrooms that understand the multiple expressions of cognitive ability found within Western societies, in other cultures, and in different places and times. Technical standards reduce student learning to the notion of replication rather than interpretation. Here students "know" only when they can display a decontextualized fragment of data at the bidding of the test.

Assuming that the most significant aspects of school performance and cognitive activity can be quantitatively measured, the psychometric discourse discourages students and teachers from connecting their lived experience to academic knowledge. Students learn to lay aside their creative and interpretive predispositions and focus only on the data that will be included on the examination, regardless of its relationship to the meaning of the subject matter or to their attempts to make sense of the world. In this context, students are rewarded for their ability to present test makers with what they have been taught in the exact manner it was first presented to them. The ability to engage information critically, creatively, or analytically is often irrelevant—even, it could be argued, harmful—to the quest for high evaluations (Pinar, 1994; Maher & Rathbone, 1986; Bozik, 1987; Lawler, 1975; Gallagher, 1992; Hanson, 1994).

Used in the name of rigorous science in conjunction with technical standards, psychometrics leaves destruction in its wake. The discourse of testing trivializes cognition, focusing attention on dynamics that are not necessarily important but that lend themselves to quick and easy measurement. Professional prerogative is stolen from teachers who are forced to make curricular decisions not on the basis of their professional evaluations of student needs but on the demands of a test. In this context, the standardized test becomes "the tail that wags the dog," as the exam (not the teacher) determines what is taught and learned (Kincheloe, 1991; Rivlin, 1971; House,

1978). The *social* relationship of the student to the school, the teacher, the curriculum, and the tests is irrelevant in positivistic educational psychology. Yet a student's membership or lack of such in what Jean Lave and Etienne Wenger (1991) call "a community of practice" exerts a profound impact on how he or she performs in testing situations in particular and school in general.

Any evaluation of student progress and potential must ask, How integrated is a child into mainstream education's discourse community? School activities, tasks, functions, and understandings are inseparable from wider cultural relationships that grant them *meaning*. For students who live outside these wider cultural relationships, it becomes extremely difficult to understand why the school requires particular tasks to be performed or why certain knowledge is important. A cultural outsider may feel bewildered by the demands of the school. Growing up in the mountains of rural Tennessee, I witnessed dirt poor but savvy mountain children capable of brilliant out-of-school accomplishments fall victim to their cultural exclusion from the discourse community of schooling. "What is she talking about?" such students often asked in regard to the teacher's explanation of an assignment. Needless to say, such students— no matter how brilliant—typically performed poorly in my school.

Positivistic educational psychology and advocates of technical standards exhibit little compassion for those excluded from the educational discourse community—such students are mere pebbles in the great sea of the low-IQ incompetent. Here is where cognitive reductionists confuse high IQ with cultural advantage. Such an error is the direct result of their social decontextualization of the study of intelligence. Unable to realize the academic benefits gained through access to the school's discourse community, they unabashedly continue to see high intelligence only in people who are most like them—white, privileged, and profoundly immersed in the discourse community of education.

Such understandings provide great insights for those committed to the promise of a democratic system of education. Indeed, egalitarian reform of American education may have to begin with the identification of those students who reside both within and outside the discourse community of the school. For the outsiders, democratic intervention would not involve "remedial" drill and recitation but a cultural immersion into the assumptions and codes of the discourse community. Democratic reformers well understand the ways biology and environment limit our choices and performances, but, unlike cognitive reductionists, they maintain that progress is possible. Individuals can with facilitation achieve far beyond what the dismal pseudoscience of psychometrics allow.

As opposed to technical standards and their positivistic, reductionistic view of cognitive ability, the democratic system of meaning that grounds standards of complexity maintains that

there is great hope for cognitive growth and improved educational performance for more than a privileged few. Psychometrics and technical standards rob economically poor and racially marginalized students of future promise. An entire school of psychological analysis has emerged over the last two decades that views the development of higher orders of thinking in terms of and seated within sociocultural interaction (Bohm & Edwards, 1991; Gardner, 1983, 1991; Hultgren, 1987; Kincheloe, 1993; Lave, 1988; Raizen, 1989; Vygotsky, 1978; Walkerdine, 1984, 1988; Wertsch, 1991; Wexler, 1992; Cannella, 1997, 1999; Weil, 1998; Weil and Anderson, 2000).

With these compelling psychological understandings at our fingertips, democratic educators and citizens find it necessary to respond to the assertions of positivistic psychometrics. Our response is meant to put these pseudoscientific dalliances behind us so that we might turn our attention to the important work of educating students of all races, ethnicities, creeds, and socioeconomic classes for personal fulfillment, social justice, and higher orders of cognition. One of the first steps of such a project involves rethinking educational psychology in a manner that appreciates the cultural dimensions of intelligence, that expands the guidelines for what can be labeled as intelligence.

Viewing cognition from this vantage point, we are drawn to the validation of a variety of thinking styles. We don't have to look very far to find forms of intelligence dismissed by psychometricians. Different forms of intelligence surround us. If we read *Frames of Mind: A Theory of Multiple Intelligences* (1983) by Howard Gardner (dismissed by positivist psychometricians as a radical who doesn't present his findings in the language of statistics), or if we observe individuals that schools have labeled as "slow," more likely than not we will discover fascinating and sophisticated forms of intelligence. Educator John Goodlad (1992) writes eloquently of the brilliance of the individuals he encounters in his everyday life outside the academy and the humility he experiences in their presence. When we avoid cognitive reductionism, a new world is opened to us—in the strangest places we uncover forms of valuable thinking. In no way are we attempting to romanticize the unschooled, but we appreciate the insights the unschooled may provide us.

The point is simple: as our democratic system of meaning embraces unrecognized manifestations of intelligence, it challenges the reductionism and mechanism of psychometrics. Indeed, the democratic psychology of standards of complexity confronts the status quo, rejecting the evaluation of students against a single standard of higher-order cognition. Threatened by an expanded definition of intelligence, right-wing advocates of elite technical standards will be agitated. They will frame our arguments as examples of the breakdown of academic standards, the vulgarization of society. When positivist psychometricians assert their theory of dysgenesis (racial decline based on higher rates of reproduction of *inferior peoples*) or when Dinish D'Souza (1991) claims that an appreciation of cultural diversity undermines traditional academic excellence, they express an ethnocentric and privileged fear of losing control of the cultural discourse, of losing their "natural" right to define "quality." In this context, we can clearly see how power wielders shape the definition of valid cognitive ability.

A democratic system of meaning asserts that science has been inappropriately applied to the study of humans and their social, educational, and cognitive expressions. While Western science has provided innumerable benefits and profound insights to the inhabitants of the planet, there are some areas where its perspective runs into problems. One of those areas is the study of cognition. The democratic system of meaning exposes the ways Western science becomes oppressive in its definition of cognition. While understanding progressive uses of Western science and the complexity of its sociopolitical role, we emphasize the problematic nature of Western science in this context and its power-saturated relationship with cognition.

Western modernism has often understood the experience of various "others" and their ways of thinking from a narrow Eurocentric perspective. The story of the Scientific Revolution in Europe itself is framed in the ethnocentric West-is-best discourse of colonialism. The irony of the story is that Western science is not simply a

European achievement, as knowledge interchanges between Europe and various non-Western cultures had taken place for hundreds of years preceding the Western Enlightenment. Non-Western scientific and technological ideas and inventions traditionally attributed to the West include, for example:

- China—magnetic science, quantitative cartography, cast iron, the mechanical clock, and harnesses for horses
- Polynesia—knowledge of navigation and sea currents
- Aboriginal peoples—knowledge of flora and fauna of Australia (Scheurich & Young, 1997; Hess, 1995; Baker, 1996)

As my colleagues and I put together this volume on educational standards, we witness around us a retrenchment of many Westerners' commitment to modernist ways of seeing. Reacting to threats of social changes; the criticisms of non-Western spokespeople; calls for race, class, and gender justice; and scholarly analyses of the failures of modernist psychology; neoconservatives and liberals alike have sought to deflect criticism with educational and political appeals to a new Cartesianism. Such forces will undoubtedly attack our analysis of a cognition of complexity as merely one more example of "irrationality," of a "return to a new Dark Age," of "barbarians at the gate of civilization." We hope they can get beyond their invective to a careful reading of what happens when multi-

ple ways of seeing and diverse knowledges engage in a dialogue. Such a process, we believe, holds dynamic possibilities.

Western science, like any system of knowledge production, constructs or makes the world it studies and describes. Epistemologies emerge from the cultural experiences of particular groups, not as an unexpected vision on the road to Damascus. Thus, the Western modernist way of producing knowledge and constructing reality is one of a multitude of local ways of knowing—it is a local knowledge system that denies its locality, seeking to produce not local but translocal knowledge and "the correct" way of thinking. Such knowledge is deemed true regardless of context and is the product of the process we previously labeled Cartesian reductionism. This mode of cognition breaks problems down into isolated components. They are then examined separately from one another, categorized, and pronounced "true."

This validation endows both the process and the knowledge it produces with high status that can be used to wield power over people with limited access to such cognitive and epistemological features. When this occurs, Western science promotes a hierarchical and linear form of thinking and knowledge production, dismissing questions of context that provide information with meaning and potential application. Questions concerning the cultural assumptions implicit in the production and use of such knowledge are not deemed important in such a process (Kloppenberg, 1991; Scheurich & Young, 1997; Freire & Faundez, 1989).

As it pronounces Western ways of thinking as the highest order of cognition, this regulatory science degrades subjugated and indigenous knowledges and subjugated and indigenous peoples. Indeed, modernist science in the guise of anthropology, for example, has been deployed as a weapon against indigenous peoples. The Bureau of American Ethnology produced knowledge about Native Americans that was used to better control their behavior, exploit their labor, and confiscate their land and resources. Indeed, modernist science not only shapes the consciousness of those who operate within its pedagogical orbit, but it also helps determine the social, political, economic, and cognitive conditions of the contemporary world. Whether we feel philosophically comfortable with it or not, modernist science is a powerful force at work both at the macrostructural level and in the everyday microdynamics of our lives. We maintain that a key aspect of a rigorous education involves an understanding of this sociopolitical role of science. Without such an understanding, we may be blind to the role of science as an instrument of colonialism (Sponsel, 1992; Levine, 1996).

To comprehend the power of Western science we must understand its ability to depict its findings as universal knowledge. Modernist science produces universal histories, defines civilization, and determines reality; such capabilities legitimate particular ways of seeing and, concurrently, delegitimate others. Such an ability is imperialistic, as it operates to characterize non-Cartesian knowledges as inadequate and inferior. Too often these power-related features of knowledge production are ignored in the mainstream philosophical study of epistemology. Epistemology, such scholars contend, is a philosophical issue—nothing more.

Such scholars fail to appreciate how modernist scientific universalism excludes "white science" as a cultural knowledge, a local way of seeing. Ethnoscience, like ethnicity itself, falls within the category of "otherness." Indeed, whiteness itself took shape around the European Enlightenment's notion of scientific rationality, with its privileged construction of a transcendental, universal, white, male subject who operated at the recesses of power and who, even in this central position, gave the impression of escaping the confines of time and space (Ashcroft, Griffiths, & Tiffin, 1995). Non-Western modes of cognition are produced at a particular time and in a particular space and reflect the limitations of their venue and time. In the reductionist mode, Western ways of thinking, like diamonds, are forever.

In this context, whiteness was naturalized as a universal entity that operated as more than a mere ethnic positionality emerging from a particular time, the late seventeenth and eighteenth centuries, and a particular space, Western Europe. In this historical configuration, reason is whitened and human nature itself is grounded upon this Cartesian reasoning capacity. Lost in the defining process is the socially constructed nature of scientific reason itself, not to mention its emergence as a signifier of whiteness. Thus, in its rationalistic womb, whiteness begins to establish itself as a norm that represents an authoritative, delimited, and hierarchical mode of thought. In the emerging colonial contexts in which whites would increasingly find themselves in the decades and centuries following the Enlightenment, the encounter with nonwhiteness would be framed in rationalistic terms—whiteness representing orderliness, rationality, and self-control and nonwhiteness representing chaos, irrationality, violence, and the breakdown of self-regulation.

Rationality emerged as the conceptual base around which civilization and savagery could be delineated (Alcoff, 1995; Keating, 1995). This rationalistic, modernist whiteness is shaped and confirmed by its close association with science. As a scientific construct, whiteness privileges mind over body; intellectual over experiential ways of knowing; mental abstractions over passion, bodily sensations, and tactile understanding. In the study of cognition and education such epistemological tendencies take on dramatic importance. In educators' efforts to understand the forces that drive the curriculum and the purposes of Western education, modernist whiteness is a central player. The insight it provides into the social construction of schooling, intelligence, and the disciplines of psychology and educational

psychology in general opens a gateway into white consciousness and its reactions to the world around it. White consciousness morphs into white cognition in the hands of reductionists. Everyone quickly learns what groups "have ability" and what groups do not. Students from the groups that supposedly do not have ability are academically damaged.

These Western rationalistic dynamics of whiteness as a colonial impulse were well articulated by Sir Francis Bacon in his ruminations on the scientific method. Bacon conceptualized science as an entity that would "bind" nature and reduce her to a slave. As a slave, she could perform useful services for Europeans. This dominant-submissive relationship between scientist and nature is reproduced in the colonial relations between European and non-European, in the power relations between universal and local knowledge. Such political dynamics have been rarely addressed in the literature of Western scholarship—psychology and cognition in particular. Of course, great anger is elicited when non-Western or Western analysts point out the assumptions of Western cognitive superiority, racial hierarchy, and colonial relationships inscribed in Cartesian epistemologies. Since such assumptions are seen as natural or even God-given, critics who expose their social construction and ethnocentrism are viewed as enemies of the Western "regime of truth" or of the culture itself. Advocates of technical standards have worked hard to demonize those who would challenge positivistic proclamations of Western European superiority.

A democratic system of meaning works for forms of social and educational change that reject the practice of cognitive segregation. Our democratic system of meaning is grounded on a humility that refuses to see Western, male, Cartesian, upper- and upper-middle-class, and white ways of thinking as superior. Thus, with this cultural humility in mind, the democratic system of meaning subjects dominant forms of cognition to analysis that had previously been excluded by the modernist ethos. It admits to the educational conversation previously forbidden ways of seeing derived from new questions asked by previously excluded voices. Standards of complexity thus challenge hierarchical structures of cognition, knowledge, and power as they seek new ways of conceptualizing self and world and the relationship between them. When educational standards are grounded on a democratic system of meaning that is concerned with first naming, then changing social situations that impede the development of just, inclusive, democratic communities marked by a commitment to economic and social justice and contextualizing historically how worldviews and self-concepts come to be constructed, then schooling becomes a powerful tool for progressive cognitive and social change.

In the middle of the nineteenth century, schools began to develop into state-supported institutions used in the attempt to discipline future workers and citizens in general. As envisioned by many socioeconomic and political leaders, schools would normalize students so they would fit into the existing socioeconomic structure. Such efforts, of course, collided head on with the efforts of democratic reformers who saw the school as a site for the empowerment of democratic citizens. The conflict between the regulatory and the democratic purposes of school constitutes a main theme in both historical and contemporary schooling. Obviously the debate between technical standards and standards of complexity reflects this traditional American disagreement.

Locating the cause of school failure in the individual pathology of the student, the disciplinary/regulatory educational impulse has assumed that there are rigid right and wrong ways of cognitive development—and poor and nonwhite children's ways of operating are usually seen as wrong. This is only one of countless ways a Eurocentric hegemonic norm structures the lived experience of students and the everyday life of school. Such a norm invisibly establishes a school culture that subtly validates white supremacy, patriarchy, and class elitism.

These dynamics always work within a commonsense framework and so they are often missed by teachers, educational leaders, educational scholars, and standards developers. For example, many educators assume—falsely, Jeanne Oakes (1985) argues in *Keeping Track*—that the presence of lower-performing students in a classroom will hold back smarter students. Thus, a tracking system is justified on the assumption that higher-order scholarship can take place only in a cognitively segregated classroom. Such cognitive segregation almost always takes place in a race- and class-oriented manner. Such "common sense" eventuates in a situation where privileged, predominantly white students from upper- and upper-middle-class homes receive privileged educational experiences. Such unfair practices are combined with the curricular content discussed previously, which validates existing inequality and suppresses conflict and dissent. So we find that the power bloc often uses schools as a part of a larger strategy to defend its interests against the social discord its policies have produced.

Hegemony is never a simple process where power wielders merely force their subjects to comply. Instead, it works via negotiation, compromise, and struggle to elicit the compliance of the oppressed to the structures that oppress them. By convincing non-white and poor students that they don't meet the standards required by educational excellence, the power bloc induces such students to consent to their own degradation. "I'm not good in academics," scores of brilliant workers in the trades and the clerical domain tell us, reflecting the pronouncements of school personnel who had no idea what such individuals can do beyond what the standardized test scores said they should do. Hegemony is an unequal struggle between groups and individuals with disparate power

and authority. What power did our friends in the trades and in clerical work have to fight the authority of the school, with its experts anointed with the mantle of science?

Experts too often carry with them the interests of the power bloc, for the knowledge they possess typically comes from a Eurocentric, white, class elitist, male academic domain. Draped with authority, their pronouncements are difficult to oppose (Denzin, 1987; Fiske, 1993, 1994; Christian-Smith & Erdman, 1997; Jipson & Reynolds, 1997). Every year I hear brilliant students, typically from racially or economically marginalized homes, talk about how they failed in school because they were "not very smart." Standards of complexity promote a cognitive approach that understands the origins and untruthfulness of such damaging internalizations.

Mainstream schools structure the hegemonic terrain on which students operate by validating and invalidating competing definitions of reality. The worldview of poor students is often viewed by schools as an absence of "class" and proper breeding. When students resist this characterization and assert their worldviews, they may act on particular values that further disenfranchise them in the classroom. Clinton Allison (1998) reminds resistant students that their silence, disruption, nonperformance, lateness, and absence may "cost them the possibility of using school for their own liberation" (p. 36). Paul Willis (1977) taught us in his study of the "working-class lads" in Birmingham, England, that their resistance to the class inequities helped to reinforce the class structure by locking them into their working-class status. Marginalized student resistance to mainstream norms is often expressed as a cultivated ignorance of information deemed important by the so-called "cultured." It is, of course, the dominant culture, not the students, who benefit from this cultivated unawareness, as young people lose the ability to critique, to make sense of the world around them.

Such resistance leaves them no escape, no way out. Many times in the last ten decades, students have been unable to enjoy a sense of solidarity with their fellow resisters because of race, ethnic, or gender antagonism. Their disempowerment and isolation in this context is complete (West, 1993; McLaren, 1994). Employing the democratic system of meaning, standards of complexity throw a monkey wrench into this disempowerment process, as they construct classroom activities that help all students—marginalized ones in particular—find their own cognitive abilities. Once such abilities are discovered and validated, they are then used to help students gain a new and positive relationship to academic work. In the standardized one-size-fits-all world of technical standards, the opportunity to help students in this manner would never present itself. Standards of complexity offer a better and more just way to educate our children.

A democratic system of meaning contends that the concept of democracy should be taken seriously and used to reshape all institutions—education in particular. Technical standards from Texas to Minnesota attempt in the name of political neutrality to adjust students to the status quo. In this technicist context, the complex concept of learning how experience is named and rewarded and how consciousness is constructed in schools is not a part of education. The realization that democracy is fragile and must be zealously protected by schools and other social institutions is lost in the technical concern with the inculcation of lower-order cognitive skills. Critical thinking, empowerment, and cognitive improvement are often viewed with fear by the reductionists and are represented to the public as impediments to the "real" learning of "the basics." Technicists contend that advocates of complexity are "concerned with critical thinking and higher order skills" while they "want to teach children to read, write, and master arithmetic."

What they fail to say is that standards of complexity not only teach students to think and function at a higher order of cognition but also teach students to read, write, and do arithmetic at the same time. An important distinction between the pedagogical orientations is that in standards of complexity students *want* to read, write, and do arithmetic and to understand the relationships of such skills to their lives. Such students understand how such skills empower them, as they learn to teach themselves. In this context, students become both self-sufficient and contributing community members. There is no conflict between learning reading, writing, and arithmetic and gaining the ability to appreciate the processes of consciousness-construction, engaged citizenship, knowledge production, primary and secondary research, and higher-order cognition.

Without a democratic system of meaning and a vision of an egalitarian future, students in top-down, technical standards–driven classrooms are merely adapted to the brutal competition of the existing school and society. Even while acknowledging that teachers and students need to be able to "get by" or "make it" in the everyday world of the twenty-first century, we can still see that it is essential that such individuals be exposed to alternatives, to visions of what can be. Without such visions we are doomed to the perpetuation of the structural inequalities and the cognitive passivity of the status quo. Democracy will struggle to survive under such circumstances. The cognitive work of William Perry (1970) on adult thinking and Mary Field Belenky, Blythe McVicker Clinchy, Nancy Rule Goldberger, and Jill Mattuck Tarule (1986) on women's ways of knowing helps us theorize four levels of adult cognition that hold profound implications for understanding the relationship between cognition and democracy. Standards of complexity examine these levels carefully and work to apply them to the construction of a democratic system of meaning and empowered teaching and learning.

The levels break down in the following manner: Level one, dualism/received knowledge, views knowledge as a compilation of isolated facts to be committed to memory. The text becomes the authority, information is dualistic (either right or wrong), and interpretation is irrelevant. Level two, multiplicity/received knowledge, understands that conflicting interpretations and multiple perspectives are inevitable. Even though level-two thinkers recognize ambiguity, they don't know how to deal with it. Thus, they retreat to the position that knowledge is simply opinion. Level three, reflective skepticism/procedural knowledge, appreciates the notion that interpretations of information vary in quality and that some means of assessing their worth is necessary. Thus, they develop a set of procedures, often the scientific method, to evaluate knowledge.

Level four, commitment in relativism/constructed knowledge, accepts the idea that individuals must take a position and commit themselves to it though they cannot be sure that it is correct. Personal knowledge is integrated with knowledge obtained from others, as thinkers on this level move beyond the procedural thinking of level three. At stage four, forms of meta-analysis begin to develop as thinkers ask, Who asks questions? Why are the questions asked? and What are the procedures by which questions are answered? Postformal sociocognitive theory picks up at level four and attempts to socially and politically situate and thus sophisticate the types of thinking cultivated by teachers operating in the zone of complexity (Kurfiss, 1988; Belenky, Clinchy, Goldberger, & Tarule, 1986; Bobbitt, 1987; Downing, 1990; Maher & Rathbone, 1986).

While resisting the reductionistic tendency to transform these stages into a master narrative that is universalized to all human experience, the stages are useful as heuristic devices, or ways of viewing that promote understanding. Used to help us understand the connections between thinking and politics, they become valuable in theorizing about complex democratic forms of curriculum and instruction. They help us see more clearly the ways in which pedagogy is a form of cultural politics. When a democratic citizenry analyzes written and television/media texts only at levels one or two, serious political consequences result. They may not possess the ability to assess political arguments or to understand why particular positions are taken.

Even at level three, when procedural thinking is applied to textual reading, the thinking strategies learned may be inadequate for reading the messages transmitted at the level of intended coding and signing. Thus, the affective and subliminal impact of the text's semiotic dimensions may remain unchallenged by the literal procedural reading. In the contemporary electronic hyperreality, with its proliferation of encoded communications, a postformal ability to extract meaning from persuasive information forms, such as political communiqués, commercial and political advertising, and

pictorial images, becomes a survival skill. The notion of ideological disembedding and deep reading are contingent on such abilities; indeed, our complex notion of an educated person must eventually accommodate them.

The ethical and political demands of the attempt to preserve a democratic culture are on the line. All the talk about extending democratic possibilities, combating political tyranny, preventing assaults on human dignity and freedom, and promoting social justice is of little benefit if citizens are cognitively unable, for example, to deconstruct and expose the encoded intentions of Charlton Heston's appeals for handgun ownership on television advertisements for the National Rifle Association. Educational visions that simply attempt to reveal fixed, external truths or the great ideas of America (which typically include celebrations of white-male military and political victories) fail to engage students with living arguments and with practical forms to act democratically; to uncover power relations, to expose hegemonic intentions is a moral enterprise, a higher-order cognitive maneuver, a courageous act of democratic citizenship.

Conclusion

Drawing upon postformalism, the democratic system of meaning sees the development of a democratic social and educational vision as the foundation for standards of complexity. In this context, teachers and students ask if thinking should be shaped in accord with the perceived demands of economic production or nurtured by those who are interested in democratic personal and social development. The modernist concern with human development in terms of human capital and productivity allows for mass acceptance of Reagan-Bush-Clinton-W. Bush/Thatcher-Major educational reform as merely one step in a government-directed economic-technological competitive strategy. Like other aspects of the contemporary landscape, thinking has been commodified—its value measured only in terms of the logic of capital. The democratic and ethical dimensions of thinking have grown increasingly irrelevant.

Although aware of the need to avoid oversimplification, I might argue that much of contemporary cognitive education can be divided into one of two classifications: (1) education for cognition manipulation or (2) education for cognitive growth and democratic emancipation. The one-truth epistemology of positivism has dovetailed seductively with the scientific-management orientations of the proponents of human capital development. Both viewpoints have overcome any moral qualms with the manipulation of human beings for desired ends. The controlled labor of the twenty-first-century factory, with its "team players" exercising their "democratic" control of the workplace by making decisions about the most trivial dimensions of the operation (e.g., where to locate the water cooler), is similar to the controlled teachers shaped by technical standards. Such teachers follow top-down administrative edicts as they teach from their prepackaged, teacher-proof materials and reward students for devotion to memory work that studiously avoids the encouragement of questioning attitudes about the entire process (Koetting, 1988; Young, 1990).

Advocates of standards of complexity, buoyed by their concern with the sociopolitical factors that destroy democracy and democratic modes of thinking, provide a perspective on school reform usually missed by other perspectives. With their awareness of cultural context and its attention to race, class, and gender oppression, they think in terms of educational alternatives that are equitable and responsive to the lived needs of marginalized students. As such, standards of complexity transcend simple modernist, rationalist attempts to raise test scores or to transfer skills.

Such democratically sensitive reforms are central to the concept of student, teacher, worker, and citizen empowerment. Complex teachers, therefore, want to educate students who are ready, willing, and able to take charge of their own worlds, as they seek to build communities of active citizens dedicated to universal education and social justice. They seek to emancipate students, empowering them to free themselves from efforts by dominant power to shape their consciousness (Solorzano, 1989; Nieto, 1996).

The emancipatory confrontation with power allows us to glimpse who we want to be, as we struggle to understand how we come to see the world. In our emancipatory journey toward self-direction, our interactions with the democratic system of meaning alert us to the complexity of the task. Democratic teachers come to understand that human identity is such a chaotic knot of intertwined forces that no social agent can ever completely disentangle it. Using Michel Foucault's concept of genealogy, we trace the formation of our subjectivities. We begin to see ourselves at various points in the web of reality, ever confined by our placement but liberated by our appreciation of our predicament. Thus, in the spirit of postformalism we begin to understand and disengage ourselves from the power narratives that have laid the basis for the dominant way of seeing.

Our ability to see from a variety of perspectives forms the basis of a long-running metadialogue with ourselves. This inner conversation leads to a perpetual redefinition of our images of both self and world. Emancipation/empowerment doesn't take place by merely wishing it so. The emancipatory process is long, difficult, and too often unrewarded by others. It takes courage, fortitude, analytical ability, time, and rigorous research and study to exercise power over one's own life and to encourage such dedication in others. Gaining these abilities is the reason we learn to read, write, do arithmetic, and think at a higher level.

With this understanding we have developed a sense of purpose, an educational philosophy.

References

Alcoff, L. (1995). Mestizo identity. In N. Zack (Ed.), *American mixed race: The culture of microdiversity*. Lanham, MD: Rowman and Littlefield.

Allison, C. (1998). Okie narratives: Agency and whiteness. In J. Kincheloe, et al. (Eds.), *White reign: Deploying whiteness in America*. New York: St. Martins.

Arlin, P. (1975). Cognitive development in adulthood: A fifth stage. *Developmental Psychology, 11*(5), 602–606.

Aronowitz, S. (1973). *False promises*. New York: McGraw-Hill.

Aronowitz, S. (1988). *Science as power: Discourse and ideology in modern society*. Minneapolis: University of Minnesota Press.

Aronowitz, S., & Giroux, H. (1991). *Postmodern education: Politics, culture, and social criticism*. Minneapolis: University of Minnesota Press.

Ashcroft, B., Griffiths, G., & Tiffin, H. (Eds.). (1995). *The post-colonial studies reader*. New York: Routledge.

Baker, D. (1996). Does "indigenous science" really exist? *Australian Science Teachers Journal, 42*(1), 18–20.

Baudrillard, Jean. (1983). *Simulations*. New York: Semiotext(3).

Belenky, M., Clinchy, B., Goldberger, N., & Tarule, J. (1986). *Women's ways of knowing: The development of self, voice, and mind*. New York: Basic Books.

Bobbitt, N. (1987). Reflective thinking: Meaning and implications for teaching. In R. Thomas (Ed.), *Higher-order thinking: Definition, meaning and instructional approaches*. Washington, DC: Home Economics Education Association.

Bohm, D., & Edwards, M. (1991). *Changing consciousness*. San Francisco: Harper.

Bohm, D., & Peat, F. (1987). *Science, order, and creativity.* New York: Bantam Books.

Bozik, M. (1987). *Critical thinking through negative thinking.* Paper presented to the Speech Communication Association, Boston.

Cannella, G. (1997). *Deconstructing early childhood education: Social justice and revolution.* New York: Peter Lang.

Cannella, G. (1999). Post-formal thought as critique, reconceptualization, and possibility for teacher education reform. In J. Kincheloe, S. Steinberg, and L. Villaverde (Eds.), *Rethinking intelligence: Confronting psychological assumptions about teaching and learning.* New York: Routledge.

Christian-Smith, L., & Erdman, J. (1997). Mom, it's not real: Children constructing childhood through reading horror fiction. In S. Steinberg and J. Kincheloe (Eds.), *Kinderculture: Corporate constructions of childhood.* Boulder, CO: Westview Press.

Denzin, N. (1987). Postmodern children. *Caring for Children/Society, 1,* 32–35.

Dion-Buffalo, Y., & Mohawk, J. (1992). Thoughts from an autochthonous center: Postmodernism and cultural studies. *Akwe:kon Journal, 9*(4), 16–21.

Downing, R. (1990). *Reflective judgment in debate: Or, the end of critical thinking as the goal of educational debate.* Paper presented to the Western Forensic Association.

D'Souza, D. (1991). *Illiberal education: The politics of race and sex on campus.* New York: The Free Press.

DuBois, W.E.B. (1973). The education of black people: Ten critiques, 1906–1960. H. Aptheker (Ed.). New York: Monthly Review Press.

Fiske, J. (1993). *Power plays, power works.* New York: Verso.

Fiske, J. (1994). *Media matters: Everyday culture and political change.* Minneapolis: University of Minnesota Press.

Fosnot, C. (1988). *The dance of education.*

Paper presented to the Annual Conference of the Association for Educational Communication and Technology, New Orleans.

Frankenberg, R. (1993). *The social construction of whiteness: White women, race matters.* Minneapolis: University of Minnesota Press.

Freire, P., & Faundez, A. (1989). *Learning to question: A pedagogy of liberation.* New York: Continuum.

Gallagher, S. (1992). *Hermeneutics and education.* Albany, NY: SUNY Press.

Gardner, H. (1983). *Frames of mind: A theory of multiple intelligences.* New York: Basic Books.

Gardner, H. (1991). *The unschooled mind: How children think and how schools should teach.* New York: Basic Books.

Gergen, K. (1991). *The saturated self: Dilemmas of identity in contemporary life.* New York: Basic Books.

Giroux, H. (1997). *Pedagogy and the politics of hope: Theory, culture, and schooling.* Boulder, CO: Westview Press.

Goldman, R. (1992). *Reading ads socially.* New York: Routledge.

Goodlad, J. (1992, February 19). Beyond half an education. *Education Week, 11*(22), 34, 44.

Gordon, E., Miller, F., & Rollock, D. (Eds.). (1990). Coping with communicentric bias in knowledge production in the social sciences. *Educational Researcher, 19*(3), 14–19.

Hannam, M. (1990). The dream of democracy. *Arena, 90,* 109–116.

Hanson, F. (1994). *Testing, testing: Social consequences of the examined life.* Berkeley and Los Angeles: University of California Press.

Held, D. (1980). *Introduction to critical theory: Horkheimer to Habermas.* Berkeley and Los Angeles: University of California Press.

Hess, D. (1995). *Science and technology in a multicultural world: The cultural politics of facts and artifacts.* New York: Columbia University Press.

Hinchey, P. (1998). *Finding freedom in the classroom: A practical introduction to critical theory.* New York: Peter Lang.

House, E. (1978). Evaluation as scientific management in U.S. school reform. *Comparative Education Review, 22*(3), 388–401.

Hultgren, F. (1987). Critical thinking: Phenomenological and critical foundations. In R. Thomas (Ed.), *Higher-order thinking: Definition, meaning and instructional approaches.* Washington, DC: Home Economics Education Association.

Hunter, M. (1987). Beyond rereading Dewey . . . what's next? A response to Gibboney. *Educational Leadership, 35,* 51–53.

Jipson, J., & Reynolds, U. (1997). Anything you want: Women and children in popular culture. In S. Steinberg and J. Kincheloe (Eds.), *Kinderculture: Corporate constructions of childhood.* Boulder, CO: Westview Press.

Johnson, A. (1999). Teaching as sacrament. In J. Kincheloe, S. Steinberg, L. Villaverde (Eds.), *Rethinking intelligence: Confronting psychological assumptions about teaching and learning.* New York: Routledge.

Kaufman, B. (1978). Piaget, Marx, and the political ideology of schooling. *Journal of Curriculum Studies, 10*(1), 19–44.

Keating, A. (1995). Interrogating "whiteness," (de)constructing "race." *College English, 57*(8), 901–18.

Kincheloe, J. (1991). *Teachers as researchers: Qualitative paths to empowerment.* New York: Falmer.

Kincheloe, J. (1993). *Towards a critical politics of teacher thinking: Mapping the postmodern.* Westport, CT: Bergin and Garvey.

Kincheloe, J. (1995). *Toil and trouble: Good work, smart workers, and the integration of academic and vocational education.* New York: Peter Lang.

Kincheloe, J. (1999). *How Do We Tell the Workers? The Socio-Economic Foundations of Work and Vocational Education.* Boulder, CO: Westview Press.

Kincheloe, J., & Steinberg, S. (1993). A tentative description of post-formal thinking: The critical confrontation with cognitive theory. *Harvard Educational Review, 63*(3), 296–320.

Kincheloe, J., Steinberg, S., & Hinchey, P. (Eds.). (1999). *The post-formal reader: Cognition and education.* New York: Falmer.

Kloppenberg, J. (1991). Social theory and the de/reconstruction of agricultural science: Local knowledge for an alternative agriculture. *Rural Sociology, 56*(4), 519–48.

Koetting, J. (1988). *Educational connoisseurship and educational criticism: Pushing beyond information and effectiveness.* Paper presented to the Association for Educational Communications and Technology, New Orleans.

Kramer, D. (1983). Post-formal operations? A need for further conceptualization. *Human Development, 26,* 91–105.

Kurfiss, J. (1988). *Critical thinking: Theory, research, practice, and possibilities.* Washington, DC: Association for the Study of Higher Education.

Lather, P. (1991). *Getting smart: Feminist research and pedagogy with/in the postmodern.* New York: Routledge.

Lave, J. (1988). *Cognition in practice.* Cambridge: Cambridge University Press.

Lave, J., & Wenger, W. (1991). *Situated learning: Legitimate peripheral participation.* New York: Cambridge University Press.

Lawler, J. (1975). The Marxian dialectic—dialectic investigations by Bertell Ollman. *Monthly Review, 46*(9), 48–51.

Leshan, L., & Margenau, H. (1982). *Einstein's space and Van Gogh's sky: Physical reality and beyond.* New York: Macmillan Publishing Company.

Levine, G. (1996). What is science studies for and who cares? In A. Ross (Ed.), *Science wars.* Durham, NC: Duke University Press.

Luke, T. (1991). Touring hyperreality: Critical theory confronts informational society. In P. Wexler (Ed.), *Critical theory now*. New York: Falmer.

Maher, F., & Rathbone, C. (1986). Teacher education and feminist theory: Some implications for practice. *American Journal of Education, 94*(2), 214–35.

McCarthy, C., & Apple, M. (1988). Race, class, and gender in American educational research: Toward a nonsynchronous parallelist position. In L. Weis (Ed.), *Class, race, and gender in American education*. Albany, NY: State University of New York Press.

McLaren, P. (1993). Border disputes: Multicultural narrative, identity formation, and critical pedagogy in postmodern America. In D. McLaughlin and W. Tierney (Eds.), *Naming silenced lives: Personal narratives and the process of educational change*. New York: Routledge.

McLaren, P. (1994). Multiculturalism and the postmodern critique: Toward a pedagogy of resistance and transformation. In H. Giroux and P. McLaren (Eds.), *Between borders: Pedagogy and the politics of cultural studies*. New York: Routledge.

McLaren, P. (2000). *Che Guevara, Paulo Freire, and the pedagogy of revolution*. Lanham, MD: Rowman and Littlefield.

McLaren, P., & Morris, J. (1997). Mighty Morphin Power Rangers: The aesthetics of macho-militaristic justice. In J. Kincheloe and S. Steinberg (Eds.), *Kinderculture: Corporate constructions of childhood*. Boulder, CO: Westview Press.

Mullings, L. (1994). Images, ideology, and women of color. In M. Zinn and B. Dill (Eds.), *Women of color in U.S. society*. Philadelphia: Temple University Press.

Nieto, S. (1996). *Affirming diversity: The sociopolitical context of multicultural education*. White Plains, NY: Longman.

Oakes, J. (1985). *Keeping track: How schools structure inequality*. New Haven, CT: Yale University Press.

Perry, W. (1970). *Forms of intellectual and ethical development in the college years: A scheme*. New York: Rinehart & Winston.

Pinar, W. (1994). *Autobiography, politics, and sexuality: Essays in curriculum theory, 1972–1992*. New York: Peter Lang.

Raizen, S. (1989). *Reforming education for work: A cognitive science perspective*. Berkeley, CA: NCRVE.

Rivlin, A. (1971). *Systematic thinking for social action*. Washington, DC: The Brookings Institution.

Scheurich, J., & Young, M. (1997). Coloring epistemologies: Are our research epistemologies racially biased? *Educational Researcher, 26*(4), 4–16.

Scholes, R. (1982). *Semiotics and interpretation*. New Haven, CT: Yale University Press.

Semali, L., & Kincheloe, J. (1999). *What is indigenous knowledge? Voices from the academy*. New York: Falmer.

Shotter, J. (1993). *Cultural politics of everyday life*. Toronto: University of Toronto Press.

Slaughter, R. (1989). Cultural reconstruction in the post-modern world. *Journal of Curriculum Studies, 3*, 255–70.

Solorzano, D. (1989). Teaching and social change: Reflections on a Freirean approach in a college classroom. *Teaching Sociology, 17*, 218–25.

Sponsel, L. (1992). Information asymmetry and the democratization of anthropology. *Human Organization, 51*(3), 299–301.

Spring, J. (1994). *The American school: 1642–1993*. New York: McGraw Hill.

Sternberg, R. (1985). *Beyond I.Q.* New York: Cambridge University Press.

Van Hesteran, F. (1986). Counseling research in a different key: The promise of human science perspective. *Canadian Journal of Counseling, 20*(4), 200–234.

Vygotsky, L. (1978). *Mind in society: The*

development of higher psychological processes*. Cambridge, MA: Harvard University Press.

Walkerdine, V. (1984). Developmental psychology and the child-centered pedagogy: The insertion of Piaget into early education. In J. Henriques, W. Hollway, C. Urwin, C. Venn, and V. Walkerdine (Eds.), *Changing the subject*. New York: Methuen.

Walkerdine, V. (1988). *The mastery of reason: Cognitive development and the production of rationality*. New York: Routledge.

Weil, D. (1998). *Towards a critical multicultural literacy. Theory and practice for education for liberation*. New York: Peter Lang.

Weil, D., & Anderson, H. (Eds.). (2000). *Perspectives in critical thinking: Essays by teachers in teachory and practice*. New York: Peter Lang.

Welch, S. (1991). An ethic of solidarity and difference. In H. Giroux (Ed.), *Postmodernism, feminism, and cultural politics: Redrawing educational boundaries*. Albany: State University of New York Press.

Wertsch, J. (1991). *Voices of the mind: A sociocultural approach to mediated action*. Cambridge, MA: Harvard University Press.

West, C. (1993). *Race matters*. Boston: Beacon Press.

Wexler, P. (1992). *Becoming somebody: Toward a social psychology of school*. London: Falmer.

Willis, P. (1977). *Learning to labour: How working class kids get working class jobs*. Farnborough, England: Saxon House.

Young, R. (1990). *A critical theory of education: Habermas and our children's future*. New York: Teachers College Press.

Zinn, M., & Dill, B. (1994). Difference and domination. In M. Zinn and B. Dill (Eds.), *Women of color in U.S. society*. Philadelphia: Temple University Press.

DYNAMIC ASSESSMENT AND MEDIATED LEARNING

Teach Them All to Fish

Judi Hirsch

Give them fish, they eat for a day; teach them to fish, they eat for a lifetime.

As we enter the twenty-first century, poverty and discrimination continue to affect more and more members of our society; especially impacted and vulnerable are students of color and immigrants from low-income families whose presence is changing the demographics of our public schools. The increasing use of static, norm-referenced standardized tests in the United States, which purport to measure academic progress, neither reflects nor supports the authentic abilities of our young people. Too many students are being failed by our educational system. Given this situation, it is critical that we decide to focus on helping our students to see themselves as they really are: fully intelligent and capable of learning and leading. Acting on this belief will serve our young people well and assure them a future as viable and productive citizens. As parents, educators, and stakeholders working for equity and social justice in an increasingly multilingual and multicultural context, we must decide that the time has come to change the schools and teach them all to fish.

This chapter will introduce dynamic assessment and mediated learning as alternatives to current methods of evaluation. Dynamic assessment and mediated learning are methods of assessing, teaching, and interacting with young people that reveal and enhance the many things they already know and can do. Because it offers a more accurate and optimistic picture of a student's potential for learning, dynamic assessment is a promising method for assisting those students who are presently underachieving and find themselves disenfranchised from the system, but who will soon constitute a majority of our population and thus need to be supported as they take on their new role as leaders. This chapter will focus primarily on under-achieving students, first giving a brief history of the development of dynamic assessment and mediated learning and comparing dynamic assessment to standardized tests. Then I will discuss the role of the mediator and mediated learning experiences (MLEs), talk about what happens to students who do not receive enough MLE, suggest ways to apply MLE to our youth of today, present a case study, and then look at how we might use this approach to change our schools.

The personal and professional experiences that inform my beliefs about young people are varied and somewhat unusual. After graduating from college in 1964 with a degree in political science, I was able to work in an elementary school because New York had a shortage of teachers. After that first year, I got a job in "special education" and have remained in this field ever since. In 1970, I moved to Israel where I worked with Reuven Feuerstein, sharing his methodology with teachers and students throughout that country. When I returned to the United States in 1979, I continued to use his ideas at both the public school and university level, eventually earning a doctorate in multicultural education. My research showed that African American and Mexican American students labeled "learning disabled" who were exposed to Feuerstein's remedial program in junior high school showed significantly greater improvement in their academic and social skills than did a control group of matched pairs who received a more traditional remedial education.

For the past twenty years I have been a resource specialist in urban secondary schools, working mostly with students identified as "learning disabled." I also have a small private practice devoted to assessment, and I offer classes to teachers both through my district and a local university. For the past three years, in addition to having my own classroom at a local high school, I have been visiting other schools, spreading the word about mediated learning to regular and special education teachers and their students. Over the years, I have traveled widely as a consultant and have shared these ideas with many hundreds of educators. These experiences have helped me solidify my ideas about how best to teach, assess, and encourage our youth, as well as how to help those who are hired to perform these critical and challenging tasks—often without receiving much preparation, support, or remuneration.

Static vs. Dynamic Assessment

Let's begin with a basic question. Why do we assess children? What are we trying to learn? The justification for the use of an educational assessment tool should be its contribution to teacher (and student) awareness of how to improve student achievement in school and thus, how to contribute to a student's success in life. The results of any evaluation should enable educators to link remediation to the problems uncovered by the assessment. Static assessment does not facilitate remediation.

Currently, all students are given standardized tests under the same conditions, and the results for most of our children in public school are predictable because test scores are known to correlate with parental income, or zip code. The scores for low-income children of color and immigrants are often quite low, even in the single digits. Further, the testing experience for these children is so devastating that they often emerge convinced that they are stupid. I have seen children cry or sit with their heads covered during a test because it is "against the rules" for us to give them any form of assistance. (One can only speculate about what students think happens to their teachers during tests, since at all other times we are so eager to help them).

If you are an adult who went to public school, chances are you have taken many norm-referenced, standardized tests, which have been carefully designed to sort, rank, and place everyone on a bell-shaped curve. Many people have internalized the belief that this bell-shaped curve truly represents society, but it is only an artificial statistical construct and not real at all. It is carefully designed so that only a few students can get very high or very low scores—which is usually taken to mean that only a few people are very bright and only a few very slow—while the great majority languish somewhere in the middle. In addition, half of those taking these tests will end up below the norm, or below "average." It is just as plausible, how-

ever, that all of us are very bright, which would mean that the shape of the curve would be a gentle upward curve rather than a bell shape, more like the (in)famous Nike swoosh.

The results of static, standardized, norm-referenced tests tell us nothing about the person we are trying to reach. What can a teacher do knowing only that a child's reading score is at a grade level of 3.6? Or that their math score is 4.8? Given nothing but the test scores, will the teacher know what students like to read or what kind of math problems are hard for them? Or why they received the score they did? Were they scared? Was there a word they didn't understand? Did they have a traumatizing experience that morning before the test? At what critical point did they need to hear a word of encouragement?

Test scores answer none of these questions. There are so many reasons students do poorly on tests—all tests but especially the "high-stakes" tests that determine whether or not they'll graduate or go on to the next grade— that it's a useless and hurtful way to try to learn something about the youngsters we teach. There must be a better way of assessing our youth.

Those of us who attended school in the United States probably remember the experience of taking a standardized test. Start time is the same for everyone, and in each room the familiar words sternly sound: "When I say 'Go!' open your booklets and begin to work. No talking! Make sure you mark only one answer for each question on your answer sheet. If you make a mistake, be sure to erase your first answer completely. When I say 'Stop' put your pencils down. . . . " Not only is this procedure unpleasant for most young people, but neither the teachers nor the parents, and certainly not the students, will ever know any more about how to improve performance after the test than they did before, even if the results arrive sooner than the usual three months' delay.

There are other options, other ways of testing people and reporting the results. One alternative is to use criterion-referenced tests, which are designed so that everyone who learns what's being tested can pass. Driving tests are a common example; people are evaluated based on whether or not they can drive a car, and everyone who can drive passes the test. We don't need a norm-referenced test for driving, so why do we need one for academic subjects? People don't feel as bad about themselves in relation to driving as they do in relation to math or spelling or any of the areas in which they've been tested on norm-referenced tests.

Another option is to use dynamic assessment. This approach provides much insight into the cognitive functioning of young people; all that is required is time, persistence, and commitment from both sides. In this context, usually initiated by the adult, we ask underachieving students to trust the teacher/examiner enough to risk exposing their weaknesses and to experience the fear that we might not always be there to support them. In

return, as caring adults, we must make a commitment to support students as they struggle to gain control of their lives. Often they need to be repeatedly reminded of the truth about their intelligence. I have never met a student, or an adult for that matter, who has been able to totally free themselves from the fear that they're not smart enough.

What follows is a very abbreviated example of an item from a dynamic assessment, which, unlike norm-referenced standardized tests, is designed precisely to provide immediate, authentic feedback to everyone present. We learn how a student thinks—which cognitive skills are in evidence and which ones aren't. Here are the results of an assessment performed with a high school student, let us call her "M.," who was interested in knowing how to improve her thinking. If you like, you can follow along as directed; however, if you choose to do that, you must not look ahead. At the end, you can compare your work with that of the student. Are you ready?

Step 1: Copy the following, known as Rey's Complex Figure Drawing (CFD) and label it #1.

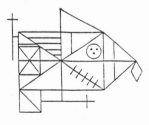

Step 2: When you are done, turn the page over and make the same

drawing from memory. No peeking! Now, compare your second drawing with the original and notice how well you remembered what you drew.

Here is what M. remembered:

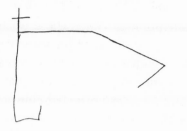

As you can see, M. barely remembered anything, and if we stopped the assessment at this point, the prognosis would be rather dismal. If this were all she was able to do at the age of sixteen it would appear that she had (measurable?) cognitive deficits, and she certainly wouldn't be encouraged to pursue an academic career. This assessment, which is currently used by many psychologists, can cause a great deal of hurt and damage if we look only at the evidence we have thus far and decide that what we see represents the student's cognitive functioning. It appears as if M. has no "short-term memory," which might explain why she isn't doing well in school. (For those of you who tried this on your own, I would imagine that your memory drawing was better, and that M.'s results may shock you.) However, dynamic assessment involves students in a test-teach-test situation, so our work is just now beginning. All we have established is a baseline; all we know is what M. can do without any help, support, or encouragement.

What happens next involves medi-

ated learning, the part of the assessment where I suggested to M. ways she could improve her performance. There is no "failure" because both of us are in a learning situation. We both want to figure out how to help her do a better job, and M. knows that this is the purpose of the MLE. After mediation, I ask her again to make a copy of the drawing and, following that, another drawing from memory. If we look at her last attempt, and compare it with her first, we can see that her second memory drawing is far superior even to her first copy.

M.'s second memory

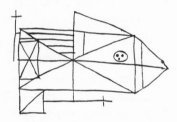

M.'s first copy

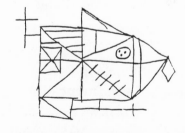

The reason for this vast improvement is that M. has learned to make a plan and is now using this cognitive ability to complete the drawing. Both she and I learned valuable information about the way she thinks, which will help her improve her academic achievement and organize her life. The results of this assessment will be the guiding principles around which we will work until she graduates. Of course, this is a very condensed vignette. Remediating a student who is functioning as much as six to eight years below her peers requires ongoing vigilance, attention, and encouragement.

When M. started high school as a sixteen-year-old ninth grader, she was truly unable to perform at any reasonable academic level; her standard scores were in the 60s and 70s (where 100 is considered average), and her grade equivalents were no more than 4.0 in any academic subject—some were even less. Her cognitive skills were also quite low. Not only that, but she was also a "noodle," totally unable to take responsibility for anything, including things that were very central to her life. After three years of mediated learning, she graduated from high school, got a job, and is now attending a local college; the last two accomplishments were done on her own.

A Brief History of Dynamic Assessment

Reuven Feuerstein, a refugee from Romania, was the chief psychologist for Youth Aliyah, the agency responsible for the care of teenagers who came to Israel after it achieved independence in 1948. Feuerstein worked alongside other Jewish doctors, teachers, and psychologists to help examine the flood of adolescents arriving from Europe and North Africa after World War II. He had trained in France with Jean Piaget and had become familiar with what was then thought to be normal child development. Under Feuerstein's supervision, these young immigrants were assessed to determine their suitability for either farming or academic life. When these uprooted teens were assessed on standardized tests of intelligence, much to his dismay their scores were so low that most of them, under normal circumstances, would have been consigned to custodial care, an unthinkable option after 6 million Jews had just been lost during the war.

Fortunately, Feuerstein understood that there were compelling reasons underlying these low scores, having more to do with the traumatic experiences the young people had just been through than with their inherent abilities. He refused to accept that their current levels of performance might be permanent, and he reflected upon what could be done to improve them. Criticizing the test process and results rather than the children, Feuerstein devised a more useful and promising way to look at human intelligence. He focused on the process of learning rather than on its product—that is, on noticing how people learn rather than on measuring what they already know. To evaluate the potential for learning of these educationally, emotionally, and culturally deprived immigrant youth, Feuerstein developed the Learning Potential Assessment Device (LPAD). The LPAD is a powerful tool based on mediated learning, the theory that people learn best when taught by someone who is deeply committed to their success, with the goal of fostering the learner's independent thinking strategies. In mediated learning, the teacher does not dispense information, but instead encourages a student to think and to struggle with the task at hand.

The LPAD puts students into a dynamic learning situation and focuses on improving their thinking by identifying the strategies that enhance student learning and the cognitive deficits that need to be overcome. The focus is on noticing the change (or modifiability) in the student's receptivity, as well as the extent to which this receptivity can be magnified. This outcome can only result if we never give up on the student and continue to have faith in their ability—the basic prerequisite to being a good mediator.

Feuerstein's theory, called structural cognitive modifiability, informs dynamic assessment. It maintains that if we can change the basic way in which people think (i.e., their cognitive structure), then we can effect a permanent change in their learning. This is different from giving a person a piece of information, which may or may not be remembered. That is why it is important to keep reminding students to focus on improving their cognitive strategies. Successful thinking requires the ongoing use of many cognitive strategies. Thus, in order to effectively remediate a student who is doing poorly, we must look for underlying deficiencies, weak or missing cognitive function(s) rather than focusing on superficial content. (A complete list of Feuerstein's cognitive

functions can be found at the end of this chapter.)

Although he sees the thinking process as a whole, Feuerstein separates cognitive functioning into three interrelated phases of the mental act: the input phase, where information is gathered; the elaboration phase, where information is processed; and the output phase, where solutions to problems may be expressed. This categorization helps focus intervention at the appropriate phase. The aim is always to identify the type of error rather than the fact that an error was made. We hypothesize about which cognitive deficiency needs to be addressed and in which phase it is located in order to make the student more aware of his or her thinking.

For example, suppose a child wrote "6 x 2 = 8." Marking the equation wrong by putting a big red "X" next to it or circling it implicitly says that the answer is wrong without involving the student in the assessment process. However, if we are interested in finding out how the student got this answer, then we might simply ask. If the student says, "six plus two equals eight," we can then try to help the student notice that the real problem (the cognitive deficiency) is located in the input stage. We might hypothesize that it is a "lack of or impaired spatial orientation" because the student moved the "x" in space, making it into a "+" sign. Clearly, if the child knows both that 6 + 2 = 8 and 6 x 2 = 12, we don't have an incorrect answer but rather a misunderstood problem. It is important to communicate with students and listen to them if we really want to help. Sharing this information with students increasingly allows them to check their own work and rely less and less upon the teacher; it also facilitates their participation in the enhancement of their achievement, making them more self-confident, responsible, and independent.

Dynamic Assessment of Learning Potential

When dynamic assessment is used to evaluate students' learning potential, the procedures, goals, and experiences are quite different from those associated with standardized tests. Below are ten principles that form the backbone of dynamic assessment:

1. The instrument of assessment is the assessor, not the test. Results are based on the well-trained examiner's judgment regarding the manner and modality through which the student's learning is best achieved—oral or written language, words, pictures, numbers, and so on—in addition to any idiosyncratic information available that can be used to enhance student success.

2. The structure of the test situation is unique. Static test situations, such as are required for administering the PIAT, WRAT, SAT 9, Woodcock Johnson, SAT, and WISC, give students only one chance to answer each question; they are allowed no assistance at all in understanding the questions, nor is any feedback given regarding their answers. Dynamic assessment uses a test-teach-test approach. We are interested in knowing how students solve problems so that they'll do better on the next challenge facing them.

3. Students have unlimited time. We may note how much time the young person "invests" in solving the problem at hand and compare it to the next time the student is similarly involved, but if we want students to struggle until they succeed, they need to know they'll have as much time as they need to work on a problem.

4. The examiner is interested in maximizing the student's success. Instead of a large impersonal arena with separate desks for each of the many students in the room, none of whom are ever allowed to talk, dynamic assessment is based on the intimate interaction between the examiner and the examinee. The focus is on immediate mediation-observation, discussion, intervention, and reinforcement, as well as on ongoing verbal interaction and feedback.

5. The focus is on learning where the student's strengths lie and how to enhance the student's ability to learn. There is a shift in orientation from product to process; our focus is on assessment, not on measurement. We seek reasons for success and failure and see these explanations as more important than the number of correct answers. Often, in the process of explaining an incorrect answer, the student will self-correct, revealing comprehension that can only be observed in the presence of an interested and supportive listener.

6. There is no manual for converting raw scores because there are no

raw scores, nor are there any standard scores, quartiles, percentiles, or grade level equivalents with which to compare them. Peaks are sought rather than ignored, and "average" scores are never used. Each person is unique and grows up with a particular set of circumstances—including hurts like classism, racism, sexism, and so on—and needs to be related to and valued as the unique person he or she is. Students can only be viewed in relation to themselves. We don't compare or report on how well students perform in relation to other children. Dynamic assessments are not norm referenced. Comparisons are quite meaningless for they don't tell us anything about this particular child, why he or she is having a difficulty or how to remediate it.

7. When interpreting results, the examiner focuses on indications of cognitive strengths and weaknesses. The examiner tries to identify and describe the successful strategies students use in approaching the work, strategies that will influence their future thinking and learning. In addition, the examiner tries to locate these strengths, along with weaknesses, at one of three phases of the thinking process: at the input level, at the elaboration level, or at the output level.

8. Dynamic assessment presents a learning opportunity for both students and teachers. This dynamic diagnostic process develops students' ability to reflect on their own learning and examine their own thinking in the process of being assessed. It is not something that the teacher or examiner does *to* the student. Student and teacher are both engaged together in this ongoing, collaborative enterprise. Thus the "testing" process is really a learning process that drives the student's intellectual development.

9. The examiner is interested in knowing how receptive children are to intervention. Some students allow and even invite teachers to support them in their learning struggles, and they thrive with teacher assistance, while others put up a wall of resistance that makes helping them very challenging. Often, this is the most important piece of information a teacher can have because it will determine what kind of intervention and support—academic and/or emotional—a student needs in order to succeed.

10. During the assessment an attempt is made to connect what is noticed about the child's cognitive functioning with life outside of school. The assessor focuses on the child's thinking process and not on some separate, unrelated skill.

The intent of these principles is not to ascertain the child's ability to read, write, or compute, but to find the underlying cognitive reasons that may explain why these skills are not being well developed. These cognitive deficits manifest themselves in all areas of a child's life, which is why remediation is both so crucial and so powerful. Getting children to successfully implement a cognitive strategy will have a more far-reaching impact on their life than mastering any specific skill, like long division, that we could possibly teach them.

For example, if we notice that a student is having a hard time organizing information, we might ask what his or her room looks like at home. This usually elicits a laugh from a parent (if it's possible to arrange for one or both of them to be present during the assessment). When we take the time to discuss how one might remedy this situation, students often begin to apply what they are learning about themselves to other situations in life, like organizing a notebook or backpack or scheduling their weekend activities. Parents can get insight about how to support their children at home in order to reinforce what's being done at school. The key lies in learning how to mediate the world for their children rather than in telling them what to do.

The Role of the Mediator

Feuerstein was influenced by Lev Vygotsky, a Russian psychologist and early contemporary of Piaget, whose major contribution to learning theory is the recognition that children learn best in a social context when assisted by a caring adult, or mediator, who engages with them in their zone of proximal development (ZPD), the "distance between the actual developmental level as determined by independent problem solving and the level of potential development as determined through problem solving under adult guidance or in collaboration with more capable peers" (Vygotsky, 1986, p. 86). Vygotsky was much more concerned with the qualitative assess-

ment of psychological processing and the dynamics of the student development than he was with the quantitative assessment of "intelligence." Based on the learning theories of Vygotsky, which remind us that children come to school with a powerful knowledge base from their own lived experiences, mediated learning focuses on how people process new information rather than on what they already know and can do.

In Feuerstein's work with young immigrants he became their mediator. He helped these teenagers regain their ability to think by providing them with a caring adult who saw each of them as bright and capable. His decision to assess their learning potential instead of their amassed knowledge represents a critical break in psychometric evaluation. Feuerstein used a cyclical approach to teaching and remediation. Based upon the initial interaction, Feuerstein would make a tentative hypothesis about a child's cognitive functioning and then act on this assumption when remediating, noticing how well this intervention was received by the child. He would then use this evidence to inform and refine his thinking before the next encounter. As mediators, we help children to recognize the thinking patterns that they use when successfully solving a problem and then we encourage them to apply these approaches to other, similar situations, thus building up a repertoire of cognitive strategies that can be generalized to other situations in their lives. Teaching young people to generalize is one of the cornerstones of Feuerstein's remediation and sets it apart from other types of remedial methods.

It is important to remember that it is the young person who is doing the learning, that mediators are only there to provide the necessary structural support, information, and encouragement. We are midwives—vital as catalysts, yet outside of the learning process. If a child can crawl and needs a hand in learning to walk, we would be there as mediators, cheering her on, holding out our hands and saying lovingly, "Come here, sweetheart." We wouldn't insist that she continue to crawl, nor would we demand that she begin to skip; we certainly wouldn't give her a "walking" test.

Mediated Learning Experiences

People learn in two basic ways: They learn from direct exposure to the world, and they learn from being taught about the world. When the latter is done with intention, or *conscientiousness*, to borrow a term from Paulo Freire, Feuerstein calls it a mediated learning experience (MLE). The main characteristic of an MLE is that the mediator mentally transcends the content of the moment, thinks about the future, and focuses on the learner rather than on the problem that's being addressed; the emphasis is on how the child will remember this experience rather than on what we are doing at the moment.

There is a quick and easy way for parents, teachers, and caregivers to ascertain whether or not they are offering a child an MLE: If the focus is on the here and now, on getting the job done or providing an answer, chances are good that there is little mediation going on. On the other hand, if the focus is on having the child learn something that he or she can use in the future, the likelihood is that the child is being taught a cognitive strategy that will empower him or her to take more responsibility the next time a similar situation occurs. For young people to become more responsible, the intentions of the mediator must be made clear, the desired behavior must be explained and its connections to the future made explicit; children need to know why they are being asked to behave in a certain way.

Many teachers, parents, and caregivers are very pressed for time, always trying to meet the perceived immediate needs of the children in their care. So they are often unaware of how important and far reaching this concept of mediated learning can be. Adults are often overwhelmed by the needs of the moment and may think that mediating is too time consuming, not realizing the ramifications of their actions. This is true for parents who are trying to get their children ready for school, who may be struggling with them about eating breakfast, cleaning up after themselves, brushing their teeth, or dressing and getting out of the house on time; it may seem quicker for parents to just do the job themselves. Or, perhaps a teacher is trying to get class dismissed and there seems to be no time to have the students help with cleaning up or with checking to see that they have everything they need in their backpacks. Maybe the teacher would like for each student to proofread all papers before handing them in, but there doesn't seem to be enough time, and the teacher can do it faster alone. Yet it is better for everyone if a mediational environment is established because the children will begin to take on more responsibility and the adults will get to have a life.

Unfortunately, if the aforementioned routines continue unchanged, the adults can become frustrated and the young people can experience cognitive stagnation. A common theme in all of these situations is a missed opportunity for modifying behavior so that the young people become more responsible. Another positive side effect of using mediation is that once new behaviors are in place, the adults can rest easy knowing their children are on their way to becoming thoughtful, caring adults and that they themselves don't have to work so hard. We get to do less worrying and also less actual work because the responsibility for making their lives go well is being slowly internalized and acted upon by the young people.

Perhaps it would help if we were to remember that humans are part of the animal kingdom, and that as such, it is the adults' duty to teach the young ones to fend for themselves so that they will eventually be able to do so successfully. This is why we must take the time to mediate and remediate until the job is done. Every time we take over for the children, we are not only

depriving them of opportunities to learn, but we are working overtime at a job that rightfully belongs to someone else. Again, the quick "test" of whether some intervention is "mediated" or not is to look at the purpose; if the purpose is to get the immediate job done, we are not only not mediating, but we may also be very subtly conveying to the young people that we have no confidence in them. This leads to a condition known as "learned helplessness," which in turn requires more intervention, thus making us work harder while actually setting the young ones back, sometimes with dire consequences.

It is worth the initial investment of time, both for their sakes and ours, to decide to act as mediators rather than as dispensers of information. While this may take more time in the beginning, once the young ones learn what is expected of them (and the amount will grow exponentially), they will rise to the occasion. The only caveat we must bear in mind is that those who have had more MLEs will become independent sooner. In the beginning, teachers may have to work harder because they will need to be thinking in new ways about what they are doing and modeling, (called *metacognating*), but they will soon see less and less need to stay up late making lesson plans or grading papers, and they will come to work tired and full of resentment less and less often. Instead, teachers will have the focus required to notice where their students need a hand, and they will actually be able to give them the attention they need because the other students will be busily working on solving problems that they know they can do because of their previous exposure to MLE. Furthermore, as time goes on, students will begin to mediate for each other.

For example, suppose a child wants to know how to spell a particular word. Many teachers are so busy and overwhelmed by large classes that they just tell the student the correct spelling, which of course sets in motion a whole lot of precedents: the next time that child wants to know something, the teacher, who has already established herself as the repository of all knowledge and wisdom in the classroom, will be asked, and if other children witness this interaction, they too, will seek out her wisdom. More damaging, though, is the effect on students, who are never given a chance to see if they know anything.

The MLE alternative is not difficult. For spelling inquiries, for instance, I always ask, "How do you think it starts?" and often suggest that they say the word in syllables and think of words that sound the same that they already know how to spell. This is important; I want my students to know that they have lots of right answers lurking inside them, as I remind those who rush to help others by telling them instead of letting them struggle. The same thing happens when someone asks me what day (or date) it is. I ask, "Where would I look?" or "How would I find out?" They always look at the calendar and understand what I'm saying. They definitely do not ask me

again! One thing I can say about my students with learning disabilities is that they are more able to struggle independently than many regular education students I have encountered. Just today, D., who used to be one of my most challenged spellers, did not ask me how to spell "backwards" but asked me if the correct way to spell the word was "b-a-c-k and then w-o-r-d-s." I told her about the "a" in the second syllable, but otherwise, she got it perfectly right.

What Happens When Children Are Deprived of MLE?

All cultures prepare the next generation to become competent, flexible adults, able to carry on their traditions. Because they are already competent at doing many things, people thus trained can more easily adapt to new ways. This has enabled cultures to survive for many thousands of years and also to accommodate to change. People whose culture is intact seem to have some inner regulatory mechanism controlling their behavior. They were probably raised in a family or group that had specific ways of doing things, such as preparing for celebrating life events, obtaining and preparing food, and so on, or perhaps they came here from another country and kept their former ways, which might include speaking their native language or maintaining their manner of dress or customs.

Feuerstein describes how easily the Bedouins, a nomadic people living in the Negev desert in southern Israel, were able to adapt to modern life as compared to some of the European immigrants who had come to Israel so traumatized by the chaos during and after World War II that they had no set way of doing anything, no culture to fall back on. For the Europeans, everything had to be retaught, remediated. The same was true of the Mien and the Hmong who immigrated to the United States from Southeast Asia after the Vietnam War. For them, learning to read and write English was very challenging since they had no written language with which to compare it.

The trauma suffered by Jewish children in war-torn Europe is in many ways comparable to the trauma faced by many of today's immigrants who have recently come to the United States from Southeast Asia and Central America as victims of political or economic oppression. The same is true for many African Americans, Mexican Americans, Native Americans, and others, including poor whites, who are living in the toxic environments of our nation's ghettos. Feuerstein teaches us that it is crucial that we never give up on any of our students. Even if we first encounter them when they are in their teens, perhaps not exhibiting much in terms of a cognitive repertoire, they can always benefit from our efforts at remediation. As Martin Buber has said, "It is the duty of a teacher to see children as they can be, not as they are." This working hypothesis is consistent with the research (Rosenthal & Jacobson, 1992) that shows the best predictor of

student success to be teacher expectation. And if one asks what correlates most with success, the answer, of course, is success!

Feuerstein knew that early and frequent exposure to MLE would increase a child's capacity to learn from direct contact with the world, including learning from their teachers at school. However, he also knew that racism, extreme poverty, war, serious physical and mental illness, and various forms of abuse, neglect and deprivation could interrupt opportunities for providing and receiving MLE. As a result, children's intellectual development is frequently suspended when they don't have either the stability of caring adults or the physical continuity of place. Sometimes the ravages of extreme poverty and other forces that destroy the integrity of the family make it almost impossible for parents and caregivers to transmit the powerful cultural wisdom that has sustained their people in the past. When patterns of disruption persist over succeeding generations, people can lose their ability to cope with daily problems. Their culture begins to die, and because of their special vulnerability, the young ones become the first casualties.

We frequently see this phenomenon in schools that serve poverty-ridden, marginalized, and immigrant populations. Children who appear to be bright and intelligent are often unable to make any progress in school. They may be present in class and even participate in a learning experience, but if they remember events at all, they remember them as isolated occurrences rather than part of a coherent and sequential body of knowledge. Teachers complain about giving tests based upon material recently taught and finding that some children seem genuinely unable to remember anything, despite the fact that they were in class. Feuerstein calls such behavior an "episodic grasp of reality" and describes it as a cognitive deficiency. The best intervention in this case is to remediate by helping to build the cognitive structures that will help the children to see that things are related; perhaps, due to a lack of MLE, they never learned how to make connections because it was never modeled for them. It may be that teachers will have to stop putting more information into children's heads until they have helped the children to construct a kind of mental filing cabinet in which to store the accumulated data so that it can be easily retrieved.

The inability to transmit one's culture is especially poignant for those immigrants who are innocent victims of war. For example, Cambodian children who were born in Thai refugee camps often couldn't receive anything from their parents, not even water, because it was trucked in and doled out by the United Nations workers. (It's too bad that UN personnel weren't aware of the ramifications of their actions.) Such experiences severely impacted those families' ability to pass on their traditions, and for children who haven't been taught the ways of their people, there is little cognitive foundation upon which to build. These children become intellectually vulnerable and are often prey to the allure of quick and slick attention-getters like fads, junk food, TV advertisements, video games, and the like. Young people who grow up without any rituals around mealtime, bedtime, or holidays are frequently unsuccessful in school. Because routines are unfamiliar to them, they are unable to remember to come to class on time, prepared to learn. They live for the moment and clearly lack planning behaviors because there are few ritualized, sequential events in their lives. Alienated from (and sometime rejected by) the mainstream culture, these youth often drop out or get pushed out of school, and they all too often end up hopeless and incarcerated.

In order to prevent such dreadful outcomes, we need to help these young people rebuild their cognitive structures so that they can learn about the world and make sense of it. Once these structures are in place and they learn to use them, the young people will be able to direct their own learning. We can accomplish this in two ways: we can try to reconnect these students to their culture, so that they can benefit from the ancient wisdom and take pride in who they are, and we can simultaneously provide MLE to help them make up for what they missed as young children.

How Can We Offer MLE to Underachieving Youth?

What can we do for children who haven't had enough MLE to benefit from what we are offering them at school? How can we provide opportunities for young people to succeed when in many of today's urban classrooms, teachers are overwhelmed and students keep falling further behind? How do we bridge the gap between nonmainstream cultures and our own? We need to find answers without blaming the victims of this unjust system: the students, the parents, and the teachers who go home crying about the children they haven't been able to reach.

Helping our youth would be easier if our culture were more child-centered. Unfortunately, certain groups in our society are looking for a quick fix, and few of those in power seem to have the courage to take the responsibility for making real change, which would require both a reassessment and a realignment of our priorities and fiscal allocations. Pointing fingers at youth, especially those who are poor, immigrants, and/or people of color, has become more and more common. One example is the recent spate of legislation in California that was anti-youth (Proposition 21), anti-immigrant (Proposition 187), antibilingual education (Proposition 227), and anti–affirmative action (Proposition 209). We must find positive ways to counter this oppressive and discriminatory trend.

Sometimes in our zeal to discover the cause of a student's difficulty we find a culprit instead. Frustrated by our inability to help, we often blame the student, saying, "If you'd only try harder!" This implies that the student is lazy, but we must assume that all of us, including our students, are always doing the very best we can, given our life circumstances. Perhaps the student has been living in poverty, in humiliation, or in an abusive situation; perhaps they have had to care for siblings and do the chores because no parent was around; or perhaps they have had to put up with an alcoholic or a drug abuser in their life. We must make the assumption that there are very good reasons why people behave the way that they do, even if we don't know what these reasons are. We must keep on supporting our youth until they get strong enough, until they believe in themselves enough to liberate themselves from where they are stuck, whether the cause is external, like racism, or some form of internalized oppression, like believing they're not smart enough.

In many cases, before we can even begin to address the remediation of cognitive functioning, we must first penetrate the veil of hopelessness that seems to surround many of our youth. One way for teachers to contradict their students' negative feelings is to become involved in their lives. I really like my students and enjoy spending time with them and showing them that I care. When I am with them I always act on my belief that they are brilliant in a way that gives them hope, so they can find the courage to use their cognitive skills to tackle the work before them. I compliment them and brag about them to others; I go over to where they are sitting and have them read each other's work; I am demonstrative when working with them; I call them at home and tell their parents wonderful things about them; I bring them newspaper articles that have bearing on their lives; I take lots of photos of them and always make extra copies for them; I bring in books I've bought just for them; and I invite people I've met to come in and hang out with them. These actions help them to start believing in themselves and give them the fuel to begin to make efforts on their own behalf. Eventually, they have enough confidence in themselves to take on new challenges.

Of course, getting these young people to believe in themselves is neither quick nor easy, and depending upon how long the child has been mired in despair and what kind of support system he or she has outside of school, this process could take a long time. In school, it helps if children can stay with the same teacher for more than one year. It also helps if we set up our classrooms so that the students' peers, people they can count on, become part of their support system, always reminding them of the truth about themselves. The path to self-confidence is not necessarily straight, but filled with setbacks and plateaus; each time a new challenge appears, I often need to remind the students once again of their innate goodness and intelligence. Usually, the "reminding" takes less and less time with each new challenge, and the more the young person is surrounded with supporters, the less likely the fear will endure. The trick is to outlast the stu-

dents' hopelessness; we can never give up on them, but we must remember to be their ally, not their caretaker.

My experience has been that students don't really get stuck in subject matter. They don't get bogged down, say, in reading or in math. Rather, they become paralyzed by fear and hopelessness when faced with a task they think they can't do, in schools that pay little attention to their needs. They get stuck when they forget that they are really brilliant and capable of knowing what to do when they don't know an answer right away, that they do know how to approach a problem.

In order to provide more MLE in our schools and homes, we need to find out where the young people are challenging themselves so that we can give them a hand exactly where they need it. In order to find that place, we need to know our youth well and develop real relationships with them. Right there, in Vygotsky's ZPD, is where we want to be, supporting the young people as they struggle to learn. The struggle for us, as teachers, is to refrain from interfering with that process while at the same time being totally there for the students, cheering them on as they learn that they can learn. I actually tell my students that I get paid to remind them that they're brilliant when they forget.

For many of today's teens, it is more acceptable to be seen as a troublemaker than as someone who doesn't understand; this is especially true for boys. It's the rare student who will ask an adult for help. This apparent lack of interest is often seen as apathy or defiance by parents and teachers who aren't aware of the humiliation associated with requests for assistance. It is the wise adult who can figure out a way to give young people support without making them appear weak or needy in front of their peers; this is especially relevant for students who struggle with language or academic skills because they already feel so inadequate. Sometimes, the best we can do is work with them away from other students, either one-on-one or in small groups, until their confidence is built up enough for them to allow their needs to be seen in a regular classroom.

As adults, one of the most meaningful things we can do (for ourselves and for our children) is to continually express belief in our youth, even if people gave up on us when we were young. This is difficult to do because adults no doubt inadvertently hurt us when we were young, and much of this probably occurred at school. Many of us have internalized the mistaken notion that we aren't smart or that we can't learn something like math or a foreign language, how to swim, how to sing, or whatever. In fact, the more that teachers (or parents) believe that they, as adults, can't do something or learn something, the more readily they are willing to accept that some of their students (or children) can't learn either. Even those of us who aren't aware of this internal dynamic unconsciously perpetuate it. One positive side effect of believing in the healing power of our actions toward young people is the possibility that we will see

that we, too, can learn something we never thought we could.

Schools should be reorganized to help students at the moment they need help, rather than first waiting for them to become humiliated and defeated. I try to be with my students every step of the way rather than waiting until an assignment is ready to be handed in—or more frequently, *not* handed in—before checking their work. It is important to me that they get help right away and whenever they need it, like having training wheels that are left on for security's sake long after they've outlived their usefulness. It must be the child who decides when to remove these supports, not the adult. We may see that the young person is brilliant long before they recognize this truth, but they have lived so long with their humiliation that we must be patient and wait until they see it for themselves. (Many of us still carry around old hurts that we have decided are real just because nobody was around to prove us wrong; we can decide that this won't happen to our children).

Another way to be supportive of these students is not to hold them too tightly to time constraints. Even in the "real world" people are both forgiving and understanding when someone misses a deadline; very few decisions are so crucial that they must be made within a circumscribed time limit. Many adults I know are late or forgetful and the penalty, if any, is minuscule. So why is it that deadlines are so inflexible and holy at school? Why must students fail before being allowed to get some extra time on a test or an assignment? What craziness! Are morning newspapers snatched from people's hands before they're done reading? Are showers turned off in midstream? Have parents been told they're spending too much time playing with their children or taking too long to complete a crossword puzzle? Why tell students they'll fail if they don't finish a test or an assignment in a certain amount of time? Why do we need such a rigid system of winners and losers?

Today, many of these "losers" are referred for special education in the hopes of getting them some individual help, but there are many problems with this option; it is not a panacea.

1. The process is very lengthy and very costly; many people need to "test" the student, including nurses, psychologists, regular teachers, and any specialists whose opinions might be needed.

2. In order for students to "qualify" for services, a "discrepancy" needs to be found between their IQ and their academic achievement, both as measured by standardized tests. Unfortunately, many low-income students of color and immigrants don't get high enough scores on IQ tests to reflect at least average intelligence, so when the test results are compared, no discrepancy is found. (Until 1975, the situation for African American children referred for special education in California was such that most were put into classes for the retarded because of low IQ scores. Since that time, in California, IQ tests cannot be used to place African American children in special education.)

3. Many children and parents are too humiliated to make use of these services and refuse to participate because of the teasing and mistreatment often suffered by the children and the stigma parents may feel about having a child in this program.

4. Special education services are extremely costly because of the mandate for one-on-one services by a credentialed specialist.

5. Few people know how to support these students, and the few who do are in high demand; they are stretched very thinly, work very hard, and receive low pay and little respect. They have a high burnout rate and many leave public education for private practice.

6. Much of the teaching that is done in special education classes involves direct instruction rather than mediated learning, so children's underlying cognitive needs aren't addressed; thus they don't really make much progress.

7. Annual testing in special education is static rather than dynamic. Thus, student progress, when it occurs, often isn't reflected in test scores. Sadly, most students who do qualify for special education rarely leave their placements to return to regular education and thus continue to fall further and further behind.

8. Most teachers who go into this field really want to help students, but half of the special education teacher's time is consumed by paperwork, which drives many from their jobs.

9. There is really not much difference between the needs of those who qualify for special education services and other low-performing students, many of whom would qualify for services if tested.

10. All those who need academic support should be able to get it. It would save time, money, and young people's self-esteem if every school had a Learning Center where students could go to get help whenever they needed it. Teachers trained in using MLE could staff the room on a rotating basis. All that would be needed are some basic resources such as books to read, computers for word processing, and tables to work on (individual desks being too isolating).

Another way to offer our students more MLEs is to expand the role of school psychologists. Often, their activities are limited to testing children for possible inclusion in special education programs using static assessments, which have resulted in some students being classified as retarded. I can't tell you the number of times students of mine with low IQs or the word *retarded* (or the euphemism *borderline*) in their files went on to graduate, go to college, and succeed in the world of work. How dare we assume that these norm-referenced, standardized tests reveal any more than they do! All they demonstrate is how a frightened, usually marginalized child performs on a white, middle-class test, given by a white middle-class psychologist who isn't interested in finding out how children learn by actually trying to work with them.

It is especially in these situations that dynamic assessment should be used. Psychologists should be trained in this technique so they can provide "videos" of young people in the process of learning rather than offering a "snapshot" version of their failure. When the results of a dynamic assessment are then shared with teachers, they will have accurate and immediate information about how to intervene to improve a child's academic performance. By using mediated learning and continuing to use dynamic assessment, teachers and students can form a partnership that will lead to student success that will last for the rest of their lives!

A Case Study in Assessment and Mediated Learning

N. is a handsome immigrant from a war-torn Central American country who lives with his mother and two younger siblings in a densely populated neighborhood that has a very high crime rate and a lot of gang involvement. By the time he got to junior high, he had very poor attendance and low academic skills; he dropped out of school. It was only due to the efforts of a local padre and the suggestion of a friend that he found our school: a small, alternative public high school with 100 students taught by four regular education teachers and myself.

N. was first placed in my room about a year ago because he and his world cultures teacher weren't getting along. Since there weren't many options, I became his world cultures teacher. I gave him a workbook I thought he might be able to read, but when I checked his work, most of the answers were wrong or incomplete. Furthermore, his handwriting demonstrated an awkward mixture of cursive and print, each letter slanting in a different direction. He seemed quick and bright, always asking questions and fixing our computers, so I asked him why, at the age of sixteen, he was only in the ninth grade and failing most of his classes. As I learned more about him, I began to understand more about some of the challenges facing our youth.

Little by little, N. became part of our Learning Center, the place where I work as a resource specialist, and began asking me if I could give him assignments for his other classes. He was failing all of his academic classes, so his teachers were pleased to see that he was now starting to attend school and do some work. They gladly agreed to let him stay with me. Soon thereafter, he asked me how students got to be in my program.

I asked N. to look at the other students in the Learning Center and to notice that each of them was very smart and also that each of them had some challenge, some area that represented struggle. I said, "You probably notice that I push them and encourage them to struggle, and eventually, as they begin to 'get it' that they really are brilliant, they need me less and less. N., that's how these students got into the program—someone noticed that they were smart but that they

weren't doing well in school and suggested that they be tested."

At the request of N.'s mother's, we began the assessment process, thinking that perhaps he had so much difficulty in school because of a "learning disability." By May, the testing process had been completed, and the psychologist and I met to compare notes, as we always do before an individual educational plan (IEP) meeting in order to identify the "disability" and see if the student qualifies for special education. I showed her my results, which were what we expected: low academic scores across the board and evidence of a processing problem.

It came as no surprise to me that N. got 100 percent correct on the tests of auditory and visual memory, but fewer than half right when asked to write down what he remembered. I knew that these results, combined with at least an "average" IQ and low academic scores, should make him a shoo-in for the program. His case was "classic." Unfortunately, the psychologist's results did not bode well for N. She found his score on cognitive tests to be "borderline," a euphemism for retarded, which would mean that there was no discrepancy, not enough difference between the scores on tests of his intelligence/inherent ability and his academic achievement to qualify calling him "learning disabled." Only because I continued to advocate strongly for this student did she review her notes and finally found one subtest that could be used to help us find a discrepancy.

When N.'s IEP was completed, he

and his mother and most of his teachers were pleased to learn both that there was a reason for his behavior, and more importantly, that we could hope for some improvement. As I always do with new students, I started mediating and explained how important it was to come to school on time, eat healthy foods, watch PBS, take home books to read, do homework, floss his teeth, get a physical and a vision test, and so on. He actually did manage to pass world cultures with me and one other nonacademic class, though he failed the rest because of his previous poor attendance.

Our school counselor arranged for him to take some independent study summer school classes so that he would start to accumulate credits and have a fighting chance of graduating before his twenty-fifth birthday. He passed both summer classes and also held down a summer job at a prestigious technology center. In the fall, he concurrently enrolled in a local community college along with another of my resource specialist students. They took a course in American labor history for high school credit in which they both got As. Filled with new confidence, they now see themselves as capable of doing something that nobody in their families has ever done: graduate from high school and go to college.

N. also did another amazing thing. While visiting my house last summer, he asked for a book to read and I lent him a favorite of mine, Eduardo Galeano's *Book of Embraces*. I chose it because it is composed of short paragraphs and because the author is from Uruguay, and thus writes in Spanish, N.'s native language. N liked it so much that he carried it around for months, pondering its depths. Recently, this former nonreader showed me a book of poetry he was reading by Luis Rodríguez, author of *La Vida Loca/Always Running*, in which there was a poem that author had dedicated to Galeano. N. had discovered the poem himself; while reading *La Vida Loca*, he had ordered the author's volume of poetry from another branch of the library (which he found by using the library's computer) and then, when reading the book, noticed this particular poem. Galeano is a very political and sophisticated author who is highly respected by many intellectuals and exiles from South American countries. This young man is on his way to success, no thanks to norm-referenced standardized IQ tests.

A year has passed since N. first began working with me. This June he turned eighteen. He is determined, despite a dearth of credits, to graduate next year. I explained to him that he'd need to pass every single class—which means not only attending them but also doing the work—and that he would need to take some independent study classes and perhaps even more courses at the local community college. He agreed. So far, he's pretty much stayed on track, though he needs a lot of mediating, or reminding. He recently requested to return to regular English class because the students are reading a book by an author he likes. By working after school he was able to buy a car, which has helped him to improve his attendance. (He lives at the other end of the city, and it takes an hour and a half to get here by bus. His mom used to drive him, but she got laid off . . . the story is all too familiar.)

What Can We Do?
We Can Change the Schools

Given the current situation and the increasing reliance on "high-stakes" tests across the nation, what can we do to help our students and ourselves? As Tatanka Iontanka (Sitting Bull) said, "Let's put our heads together and see what we will make for our children." We can change the relationship between teacher and student from an authoritarian, top-down, "I teach, you learn," model to one of mutual collaboration. Each teacher could be, as Australian educator Julia Atkins says, a "guide from the side" rather than a "sage on the stage." Not only will this move the children to the center of our enterprise, but it will help us to avoid the burnout that drives far too many of us away from the joy of working with young people as they struggle to make sense of their world.

I've been lucky to work at a K-12 school where I often got to spend many years with students, either working one-on-one with them in my Learning Center or visiting them in their classes. This situation is ideal and perhaps unusual, but it is becoming less so; there seems to be a trend toward creating more small schools and multi-age classes. But what about regular teachers who work in regular

schools—what can they do to make things better for themselves and their students? How can they incorporate mediated learning and dynamic assessment?

As long as teachers understand that it is the children who are supposed to be doing the learning, any classroom can be set up to offer MLE. Teachers can decide to become mediators rather than remain traditional "teachers" who stand in front of the class and "perform." Given the three main components of a classroom—the teacher, the students, and the curriculum—when we use mediated learning, the teachers get to relate to the students and encourage the students to relate to the content.

By slowly transferring the responsibility for learning to their students, teachers will make life easier for themselves. They can use the same books and curricular material they always have, but in a different way. They need to "tweak" assignments so the focus is on the students; curriculum should be used to enhance students' cognitive skills, not as an end in itself. Assignments, projects, and investigations can be devised that respect the increasing cultural diversity of our students and their need for cognitive remediation. Once teachers know the students' cognitive strengths and challenges, they won't need to reinvent the wheel with each new assignment. They don't need to become specialists in curriculum because the children are their subjects. Yes, we need to know our content area, but we need to know our kids more; we need to know how they learn, what they do when they're stuck, and the like.

Many elementary and middle school teachers work in self-contained classrooms and would find it relatively easy to implement a mediational style with their students, if they don't already do so. MLE can also be introduced in high school classes where teachers and students often only see each other once daily for short periods of time. While it is true that teachers should not take on the teaching of a subject area that is unfamiliar to them, I don't believe that teachers need be subject matter experts in order for their students to learn. A teacher has to know enough to guide student inquiry and ask provocative questions, but subject matter expertise is meaningless unless teachers know how to relate to students, how to mediate. In fact, teachers who demonstrate impressive mastery of their content area are often in danger of making this the focus of the class rather than their students. It is far more important to the intellectual and emotional life of students that they learn something that will be remembered and used for a long time—such as learning that they can learn, or being able to incorporate the cognitive skill of planning into their daily life—than it is to get 100 percent on a test of facts which will soon be forgotten. If we think back to those teachers who made a difference in our lives, we'll find that it wasn't those who only dazzled us with their intellectual prowess; it was those who sparked something in us. The best teachers are the ones who understand that they teach children, not math or science or history.

Using mediated learning will make school more meaningful, cut down on boredom and behavior problems, encourage students to collaborate, and thus give teachers time to work individually with the students in their ZPD. We need to know how these students see themselves as learners, how their families see them, and how family members see each other. This is much more important than knowing what they know or are able to do at the moment because it will inform us of how they will deal with challenges in the future.

Mediated learning will give us time to ask the many questions that teach us about our students: What kinds of books they like to read (adventures? biographies? poems? picture books? encyclopedias?). What they want to learn in mathematics (fractions? money? algebra? long division?). What do they do when they're stuck? Do they give up and stop working? Skip that problem or word? Ask for assistance? Do they ask for help from their peers? From adults? Which ones? From no one?

Which do students care about more, the process or the product? Are they likely to copy from a neighbor or do they enjoy figuring things out on their own? If the objective of the assignment is getting the right answer (rather than understanding what they are doing), then students will often copy from a book or from another student in order to turn in a completed assignment. Little has been learned.

That's the disadvantage of giving one nonnegotiable assignment to an entire class, as is usually suggested in teacher's manuals. The assumption that one size fits all is erroneous.

We also need to know how students see school. Is it a place where they are constantly fearful and humiliated or is it a place to learn, to play, and to make friends? Do they like to be the center of attention or do they try to slide through unnoticed? How important are grades to them and their families? Does anyone care? If so, who? Are there rewards or punishments attached? What is the educational history of family members? What is their class background? How long have they lived here? Where did they come from and why? Who in the family speaks English? Can they read and write in their own language? Did everyone or anyone graduate from high school? Do their parents have unreasonable expectations of their children? Are there problems with literacy, abuse, neglect, or denial in their homes? What kind of support do they have?

The answers to these questions will also help educators learn how best to communicate with the child's family; this kind of knowledge can make a huge difference in the way the young person responds to us and to the whole business of school. Often, when I call a student's home, parents expect to be blamed for how they raised their child. Calling to complain only makes parents feel like failures. A wise teacher can build bridges and relationships so that we become allies with the parents, as we work together to help

their children succeed. One of the worst things that can befall a child is to become a pawn in the power struggle between home and school.

When we move curriculum away from prepackaged pablum toward content that is relevant to the lives of our children, students can be challenged and allowed to construct meaning in a way that makes sense to them. If we focus more on the children and do away with grades and standardized tests, the likelihood is that more of our underachieving students would be removed from the "endangered species list," a goal near and dear to the hearts of many educators, parents, and community members.

When we are able to relate to the students and get them to relate to the content, we avoid the tedium and burnout that often burden those who focus on content and paperwork rather than on students and their very real struggles. If you embrace the principles laid out here, young people will learn and you'll get to have a life. The beauty of using mediated learning and a dynamic approach to assessment is that we get to become close to the young people as we support them in their struggles to make meaning out of chaos. What could be a better way to invest in their futures? Teach them all to fish!

Following is a list of Feuerstein's cognitive functions. A discussion of their implementation is beyond the scope of this chapter; those who are interested may contact the author at judih@ousd.k12.ca.us or Feuerstein himself for further information.

Feuerstein's Cognitive Functions

I. Gathering all the information we need (Input)

1. Using our senses: Listening, seeing, smelling, tasting, touching, and feeling to gather clear and complete information (clear perception)
2. Using a system or plan so that we do not skip or miss something important or repeat ourselves (systematic exploration)
3. Giving the thing we gather through our senses and our experience a name so that we can remember it more clearly and talk about it (labeling)
4. Describing things and events in terms of where and when they occur (temporal and spatial references)
5. Deciding on the characteristics of a thing or event that always stays the same even when changes take place (conservation, constancy, and object permanence)
6. Organizing the information we gather by considering more than one thing at a time (using two sources of information)
7. Being precise and accurate when it matters (precision)

II. Using the information we have gathered (Elaboration)

1. Defining what the problem is, what we are being asked to do, and what we must figure out (analyzing disequilibrium)
2. Using only that part of the information we have gathered that is relevant, that is, taking what applies to the problem and ignoring the rest (relevance)
3. Having a good picture in our mind of what we are looking for, or what we must do (interiorization)
4. Making a plan that will include the steps we need to take to reach our goal (planning behavior)
5. Remembering and keeping in mind the various pieces of information we need (broadening our mental field)
6. Looking for the relationship by which separate objects, events, and experiences can be tied together (projecting relationships)
7. Comparing objects and experiences to others to see what is similar and what is different (comparative behavior)
8. Finding the class or set to which the new object or experience belongs (categorization)
9. Thinking about different possibilities and figuring out what would happen if we were to choose one or another (hypothetical thinking)
10. Using logic to prove things and to defend our opinion (logical evidence)

III. Expressing the solution to a problem (Output)

1. Being clear and precise in our language so that there is no question as to what our answer is; putting ourselves into the "shoes" of the listener to be sure that our answer will be understood (overcoming egocentric communication)
2. Thinking things through before we answer instead of immediately trying to answer, making a mistake, and then trying again (overcoming trial and error)

(continues)

Feuerstein's Cognitive Functions *(continued)*

---

3. Counting to ten (at least) so that we don't say or do something we will be sorry for later (restraining impulsive behavior)
4. Avoiding panic when we can't answer a question for some reason, even though we "know" the answer; leaving the question for a little while and then when returning to it, using a strategy to help us find the answer (overcoming blocking)

References

Feuerstein, R., Rand, Y., & Hoffman, M. (1979). *The dynamic assessment of the retarded performer: The learning potential assessment device, theory, instruments and techniques.* Baltimore, MD: University Park Press.

Rosenthal, R., and Jacobson, L. (1992). *Pygmalion in the classroom: Teacher expectation and pupil's intellectual development.* New York: Irvington Publishers.

Vygotsky, L. S. (1986). *Thought and language.* (A. Kouzoulin, Ed.). Cambridge, MA: MIT Press.

STANDARDS AND MULTICULTURALISM

Bill Bigelow

Proponents of "higher standards" and more testing promise raised expectations for all students and increased "accountability." In practice, their reforms are hostile to good teaching and pose a special threat to multiculturalism.

The state where I teach, Oregon, has joined the national testing craze. This fall, the Oregon Department of Education field-tested its first ever statewide social studies assessments. Many teachers were dismayed to discover that the tests were a multiple-choice maze that lurched about, helter-skelter, seeking answers on World War I, constitutional amendments, global climate, rivers in India, hypothetical population projections, Supreme Court decisions, and economic terminology. Evidently, for the state of Oregon, social studies knowledge is little more than piles of disconnected facts about the world.

If it prevails, Oregon's brand of standardization will undermine a multicultural curriculum—one that de-scribes and attempts to explain the world as it really exists, speaks to the diversity of our society and our students, and aims not only to teach important facts but to develop citizens who can make the world safer and more just. In a sense, the entire effort to create fixed standards violates the very essence of multiculturalism. Multiculturalism is, in the words of Harvard professor Henry Louis Gates Jr. (1995), a "conversation among different voices," a search for perspectives that have been silenced in traditional scholastic narratives. Multiculturalism attempts to uncover "the histories and experiences of people who have been left out of the curriculum," as antiracist educator Enid Lee (1995) emphasizes. Because multiculturalism is an undertaking that requires new scholarship and constant discussion, it is necessarily ongoing. Yet as researcher Harold Berlak points out, "standardization and centralization of curriculum testing is an effort to put an end to a cacophony of voices on what constitutes truth, knowledge, and learning and what the young should be taught. It insists upon one set of answers." Curriculum standardization is, as Berlak indicates (2000), a way to silence dissident voices, "a way to manufacture consent and cohesion."

Creating official, government-approved social studies standards is bound to be controversial, whether at the national or state level. Thus, according to the Portland *Oregonian*, state education officials "tried to stake a neutral ground" in order to win approval for its version of social reality. "We have tried so hard to go right down the middle between what teachers want, what parents want, and what the [Republican-dominated] Legislature wants," said Dawn Billings, a Department of Education curriculum coordinator. Not surprisingly, as a result of this attempt to be "neutral" and inoffensive, the standards lack a critical sensibility—an emphasis on conflict and diversity of interpretation—and tend toward a conservative, *Father Knows Best* portrait of history and society. For example, one typical tenth-grade benchmark calls for students to "understand how the Constitution can be a vehicle for change and for resolving issues as well as a device for preserving values and principles of society."

Are these the only options? Is this how, say, Frederick Douglass or the Seminole leader Osceola would have seen the Constitution? Shouldn't students also understand how the Constitution can be (and has been) a vehicle for preserving class and race stratification and for maintaining the privileges of dominant social groups? For example, in the 1857 Dred Scott case, the Supreme Court held that a slave could not sue for his freedom because he was property, not a human being. Chief Justice Roger Taney declared that no Black person in the United States had "any rights which the white man is bound to respect." In response, the Abolitionist William Lloyd Garrison called the Constitution an "agreement with Hell" for its support of slavery. But then, in 1896, the Supreme Court ruled in *Plessy v. Ferguson* that segregation—"separate but equal"—did not violate the Fourteenth Amendment. Seating this understanding historically is crucial.

Historical Realities vs. the Limited Perspective of Standardized Tests

Almost 40 percent of the men who wrote the Constitution owned slaves, including George Washington and James Madison. In my U.S. history classes, we look at the adoption of the Constitution from the standpoint of poor white farmers, enslaved African Americans, unemployed workers in urban areas, and other groups. Students create their own Constitution in a mock assembly, and then compare their document to the actual Constitution. They discover, for example, that the Constitution does not include the word "slave," but instead refers to enslaved African Americans euphemistically, as in Article 4, Section

2: "No person held to service or labor in one state, under the laws thereof, escaping into another, shall in consequence of any law or regulation therein, be discharged from such service or labor, but shall be delivered up on claim of the party to whom such service or labor may be due." It's a vicious clause that cannot be made to fit in the "preserving values and principles" rhetoric of the benchmark mentioned above.

It is probably inevitable that school curricula will reflect the contradictions between a society's myths and realities. But while a critical multicultural approach attempts to examine these contradictions, standardization tends to paper them over. For example, here is another benchmark that similarly fails the multicultural test: "Explain how laws are developed and applied to provide order, set limits, protect basic rights, and promote the common good." Whose order, whose basic rights, are protected by laws? Are all social groups included equally in the term "common good"? Between 1862 and 1890, laws in the United States gave 180 million acres (an area the size of Texas and Oklahoma combined) to privately owned railroad companies but gave virtually no land to African Americans freed from slavery in the South. Viewing the Constitution and other U.S. laws through a multicultural lens would add texture and depth to the facile one-sidedness of Oregon's "neutral" standards.

Indeed, the "R" word, "racism," is not mentioned once in any of the seven 1998 eleventh-grade field tests or in the social studies standards adopted in March 1998 by the state board of education. Even if the only yardstick were strict historical accuracy, this would be a bizarre omission: the state was launched as a whites-only territory by the Oregon Donation Act and in racist wars of dispossession waged against indigenous peoples; the first constitution outlawed slavery but also forbade Blacks from living in the state, a prohibition that remained on the books until 1926.

Perhaps state education officials are concerned that introducing the concept of racism to students could call into question the essentially harmonious world of change and continuity over time that underpins the standards project. Whatever the reason for the absence of this concept in the tests, there is no way that students can make sense of the world today without the idea of racism in their conceptual knapsack. If a key goal of multiculturalism is to account for how the past helped shape the present, and if an important part of the present is social inequality, then Oregon's standards and tests earn a failing grade.

Despite the publication of state social studies standards and benchmarks, teachers and parents don't really know what students are expected to learn until they see the tests, which were developed by an out-of-state assessment corporation, MetriTech. As Wade W. Nelson (1998) points out in a delightfully frank article, "The Naked Truth about School Reform in Minnesota" (which might as well have been written about Oregon), "The content of the standards is found only in the tests used to assess them. Access to the tests themselves is carefully controlled, making it difficult to get a handle on what these standards are. It seems ironic to me that basic standards—that which every student is expected to know or be able to do—are revealed only in tests accessible only to test makers and administrators. This design avoids much of the debate about what these standards ought to be," and this debate is essential to the ongoing struggle for a multicultural curriculum.

Discrete Facts

It's when you look directly at the tests that their limitations and negative implications for multiculturalism become most clear. Test questions inevitably focus on discrete facts, but they cannot address the deeper, multifaceted meaning of facts. For example, in the field tests Oregon piloted in the fall of 1998, one question asked which constitutional amendment gave women the right to vote. Students could get this question right even if they knew virtually nothing about the long struggle for women's rights. On the other hand, they could know lots about the feminist movement and not recall that it was the Nineteenth and not the Sixteenth, Seventeenth, or Eighteenth Amendment (the other test choices) that gave women the right to vote. Further, because there is no way to predict precisely which facts will be sought on the state tests, teach-

ers will feel pressured to turn courses into a "memory Olympics"; teachers simply will not be able to afford to spend time probing beneath the headlines of history.

Last year, my students at Franklin High School in Portland performed a role play on the 1848 women's rights conference in Seneca Falls, New York, the first formal U.S. gathering to demand greater equality for women. The original assembly was composed largely of middle- to upper-class white women. I wanted my students to appreciate these women's courage and to understand the issues that they addressed but also to consider the limitations imposed by their race, class, and ethnicity. Thus, in our simulated 1848 gathering, my students portrayed women who were not at the original conference—enslaved African Americans, Cherokee women who had been forcibly moved to Oklahoma on the Trail of Tears, Mexican women in the recently conquered territory of New Mexico, and poor, white New England mill workers—as well as the white, middle- and upper-class reformers like Elizabeth Cady Stanton and Lucretia Mott who were in attendance.

In this more socially representative fictional assembly, students learned about the resolutions adopted at the original gathering and the conditions that motivated them, but they also saw firsthand how more privileged white women ignored other important issues that a more diverse convention might have addressed, such as treaty rights of Mexican women, sexual abuse of enslaved African Americans, and the workplace exploitation of poor white women.

The knowledge that my students acquired from this role play consisted not only of "facts"—although they learned plenty of these. They also exercised their multicultural social imaginations—listening for the voices that are often silenced in the traditional U.S. history narrative and becoming more alert to the importance of issues of race and class. However, this kind of teaching and learning takes time—time that could be ill afforded in the fact-packing pedagogy required by multiple-choice tests. And after all their study, would my students have recalled whether it was the Sixteenth, Seventeenth, Eighteenth, or Nineteenth Amendment that gave women the right to vote? If not, they would have appeared ignorant about the struggle for women's rights.

Likewise, my global studies students spend the better part of a quarter reading, discussing, role-playing, and writing about the manifold consequences of European colonialism. They read excerpts from Okot p'Bitek's poignant book-length poem, *Song of Lawino*, which is about the lingering psychological effects of colonialism in Uganda. They role-play a trial on the colonial roots of the potato famine in Ireland, and they examine how Asian economies were distorted to serve the needs of European ruling classes. But when confronted with Oregon's multiple-choice question that asks which continent was most thoroughly colonized in 1914, would my students answer correctly?

As these examples illustrate, in a multicultural curriculum it's not so much facts as it is perspective that is important in nurturing a fuller understanding of society. And sometimes considering new perspectives requires imagination as much as or more than memory of specific facts. For example, my history students read about the people Columbus encountered in 1492, the Tainos—who themselves left no written records—in excerpts from Columbus's journal and articles like Jose Barreiro's "Tainos: Men of the Good" (1998). I ask students to write a story or diary entry from the point of view of a Taino during the first few days or weeks of their encounter with Spaniards, drawing on information in the readings but then going further. Although necessarily a speculative undertaking, this project invites students to turn the "Columbus discovers America" story on its head and encourages them to appreciate the humanity in the people usually marginalized in tales of "exploration." In response, students have written pieces of startling insight. Sure, a multiple-choice test can assess whether students know that Columbus first sailed in 1492, where he landed, or the name of the people he encountered. But such a test is ill equipped to assess what students truly understand about this encounter.

Not surprisingly, Oregon's "one best answer" approach vastly oversimplifies and misrepresents complex social processes and entirely erases ethnicity and race as categories of analysis. One question on a recent test reads: "In 1919, over 4.1 million Americans belonged to labor unions. By 1928, that number had dropped to 3.4 million. Which of the following best accounts for that drop?" It seems that the correct answer must be A.: "Wages increased dramatically, so workers didn't need unions."

All the other answers are clearly wrong, but is this answer "correct"? Since when do workers leave unions when they win higher wages? Weren't mechanization and scientific management factors in undermining traditional craft unions? Did the post–World War I red scare, with its systematic attacks on radical unions like the Industrial Workers of the World and deportations of foreign-born labor organizers, affect union membership? And how about the Oregon test's reductive category of "worker"? Shouldn't students be alert to how race, ethnicity, and gender were and are important factors in determining one's workplace experience, including union membership? For example, in 1919, professional strikebreakers, hired by steel corporations, were told to stir up as much bad feeling as they possibly could between the Serbians and the Italians. And more than 30,000 Black workers, excluded from AFL unions, were brought in as strikebreakers. A multicultural awareness is vital if we're to arrive at a satisfactory answer to the Oregon field-test question above. But instead, the state would reward students for choosing a historical sound bite that is as shallow as it is wrong.

This leads me to an aspect of these tests that is especially offensive to teachers: they don't merely assess, they also instruct. The tests represent the authority of the state, implicitly telling students, "Just memorize the facts, kids. That's what social studies is all about—and if teachers do any more than that, they're wasting your time." Multiple-choice tests undermine teachers' efforts to construct a rigorous multicultural curriculum because they delegitimate that curriculum in students' eyes by suggesting that "if it were important it would be on the test."

The Core of Multiculturalism

At its core, multicultural teaching is an ethical, even political, enterprise. Its aim is not just to impart lots of interesting facts, to equip students to be proficient Trivial Pursuit players, but to help make the world a better place. It highlights injustice of all kinds—racial, gender, class, linguistic, ethnic, national, environmental—in order to make explanations and propose solutions. It recognizes our responsibility to fellow human beings and to the earth. It has heart and soul.

Compare that aim with the sterile, fact-collecting orientation of Oregon's standards and assessments. For example, a typical forty-nine-question high school field test piloted in 1998 included seven questions on global climate, two on the location of rivers in India and Africa, and one on hypothetical world population projections for the year 2050. But not a single question in the test concerned the lives of people around the world or environmental conditions—nothing about increasing poverty, the global AIDS epidemic, the disappearance of the rain forests, rates of unemployment, global warming, and other crises; nor were there any questions on efforts to address these crises. The test bounded aimlessly from one disjointed fact to another. In the most profound sense it was pointless.

Indeed, the test's random amorality may reveal another of its cultural biases. Oregon's standards and assessments make no distinction between knowledge and information. The state's version of social education would appear to have no raison d'être beyond the acquisition of large quantities of data. But for many cultures, the aim of knowledge is not bulk, but wisdom—insight into meaningful aspects about the nature of life.

Peter Kiang (1998/1999) makes a similar point about the Massachusetts teacher test that calls into question the validity of enterprises such as these. He writes that "by constructing a test based on a sequence of isolated, decontextualized questions that have no relationship to each other, the underlying epistemology embedded in the test design has a Western-cultural bias, even if individual questions include or represent 'multicultural' content. Articulating and assessing a knowledge base requires examining not only what one knows, but also how one knows."

Students "know" in different ways, and these differences are often cultural. Oregon nonetheless subjects all students to an abstract, data-heavy assessment device that does not gauge what or how they have learned. As Kiang points out, test makers address multicultural criticism by including individual questions about multicultural content—for example, by highlighting snippets of information about famous people of color like Martin Luther King Jr., Cesar Chavez, and Harriet Tubman. But these "heroes and holidays" additions cannot mask the fundamental hostility to multicultural education shown by standards and assessments like those initiated by Oregon.

Spelling out an alternative to Oregon's culturally biased, superficial "accountability" plan would require another chapter. In brief, I want the state to abandon its effort to turn me into a delivery system of approved social information. I want it to support me and other teachers as we collaborate to create curriculum that deals forthrightly with social problems, that fights racism and social injustice. I want it to support teachers as we construct rigorous performance standards for students that promote deep thinking about the nature of our society. I want it to acknowledge the legitimacy of a multicultural curriculum of critical questions, complexity, multiple perspectives, and social imagination. I want it to admit that wisdom is more than information—that the world can't be chopped up into multiple-choice

questions, and that you can't bubble-
in the truth with a number-two pencil.

References

Barreiro, J. (1998). The Tainos: "Men of
the good." In B. Bigelow & B. Peterson
(Eds.), *Rethinking Columbus: The next
500 years* (2nd ed.). Milwaukee: Rethinking Schools.

Berlak, H. (2000). Cultural politics: The
science of assessment and democratic
renewal of public education. In A. Filer
(Ed.), *Assessment: Social practice and social product.* London: Falmer Press.

Gates, H. L., Jr. (1995). Multiculturalism:
A conversation among different voices.
In D. Levine, et al. (Eds.), *Rethinking
schools: An agenda for change*, p. 7. New
York: The New Press.

Kiang, P. (1998/1999.) Trivial pursuit testing. *Rethinking Schools*, *12*(2), 23.

Lee, E. (1995). Taking multicultural, anti-
racist education seriously. In D.
Levine, et al. (Eds.), *Rethinking schools:
An agenda for change*, p. 9. New York:
The New Press.

Nelson, W. W. (1998). The naked truth
about school reform in Minnesota. *Phi
Delta Kappan*, *79*(9), 681.

A SWORD OVER THEIR HEADS

The Standards Movement as a Disciplinary Device

Ivor Goodson and Martha Foote

It is a common adage in education: school reforms never endure but, like a pendulum, merely sway back and forth, clocking in and out and then back into our schools in a perpetual cycle (Kliebard, 1995). As a result, the wisdom goes, it is pointless for teachers to try to transform their practices because no reform lasts for long, and time and energy are merely wasted in the capricious pursuit of the latest educational fad. Additionally, if teachers simply wait long enough, they can even witness the return of past efforts, repackaged and recycled over and over and over again. Assuming that the fleeting nature of school reform is a problem, we might ask ourselves just how far reform advocates would be willing to go to solve it, to ensure sustainable reforms? To what extent would they compel teachers to comply with a new reform effort? And would these methods of compulsion work?

Proponents of the standards movement, the most pervasive reform effort in education today, seek to end the perceived transient nature of reform undertakings through the use of legislated consequences and rewards. New state standards are tied to mandatory high-stakes state exams, requiring students to attain a certain minimum score on these exams to be allowed to continue to the next grade level or even to receive a high school diploma, regardless of their academic record. The expectation, then, is that teachers, fully aware of these ramifications, will be compelled to alter their teaching practices in order to prepare their students for these exams, thus helping them reach the new high standards. (And to augment the incentives, some states also tie these test scores to teacher bonuses and/or the threat of state seizure of schools.)

In other words, a disciplinary device is put into place to ensure the implementation of the new reform. What is simply assumed, or often left unexamined, however, is whether (1) particularly high standards are educationally sound and (2) the exams validly measure the attainment of the standards. Both points are hotly disputed by researchers and educators (Heubert & Hauser, 1999; McNeil, 2000; Neill, 1997; Ohanian, 1999). Yet, despite these controversies, many states continue to make high-stakes decisions on the basis of a single standardized exam, while proclaiming teachers accountable for the critical test score that can determine a child's future.

This chapter provides a look into the effects of mandated high-stakes exams on the teachers in one particular high school, the Durant School, located in a small industrial city in the northeast section of the United States. With its distinct learner-centered philosophy and performance-based assessments, the Durant School has long had a reputation as a haven for students seeking alternatives to traditional high school programs. Through the years, it has also been supported by its city school district as a magnet school and permitted to operate with substantial autonomy, shielded from the vagaries of periodic mandates and entrusted to uphold its particular, and successful, mission. (Within the district, the school has higher-than-average attendance and college acceptance rates, and lower-than-average suspension and dropout rates.)

This autonomy, however, came into question in 1996, when the state adopted a series of five high-stakes exams to measure its new high standards. The first exam, on English language arts, was to be introduced in June 1999, followed by math, world history, American history, and science; the passage of all five would be required for graduation. Though the Durant School at first assumed it would be given an exemption from these new mandates, it soon discovered that this reform was different: all schools and all students were to be subjected to the same terms. The state was allowing no exemptions.

The school now found itself in the middle of an excruciating dilemma: teach to the new high-stakes tests or preserve its program; give kids the best chance possible to pass these state exams or risk their ability to graduate by upholding the school's philosophy; compromise the school's integrity or possibly compromise their students' futures. Because the reform was directly tied to a student's eligibility to graduate, the teachers felt they could not ignore it. They were going to have to alter their practices, because in their eyes, their students' lives were at stake. The disciplinary device was working.

The Effects of the High-Stakes State Mathematics Exam

At the beginning of the 1997–1998 school year, the staff at the Durant School instituted a new policy that required all incoming freshmen to take a state-designed mathematics course to help prepare them for the future state math exam. This course was a radical departure from the school's usual approach to curriculum, in which teachers develop their own courses incorporating student interests, their real-life, contextual experiences, and in-depth projects and investigations. However, the staff believed that this departure was inescapable, given that these freshmen would be the first class required to pass the state math exam in order to graduate. They felt that it was necessary to concentrate on teaching specifically to the state math standards and to cover as much content that might be on the exam as possible. In other words, they were compelled to alter their methods not to improve practice but to keep their students out of harm's way.

Our research at the Durant School began in the 1998–1999 school year, the second year of the new math policy. Our interviews and participant observation made it evident that this change was exacting a toll on Rob, the teacher of the freshman math course. At a staff meeting in January 1999, Rob said that his teaching had changed, that he was now "teaching to the test"—specifically, the current state test that would be administered in June at the course's end. (The new high-stakes state math test had not yet been developed; however, the state exam for this particular course was considered its closest model.)

Rob explained that he saw it as his responsibility as an educator to teach this way; to do otherwise would be "educational malfeasance," as it would hinder his students' ability to pass the state exam. He then said: "And I hate it," quickly adding, "I don't like it here [at the school] this year. I'm tense. I'm impatient." In an interview later that spring, Rob elaborated on the change in his teaching practices: "In the past I would teach based on making sure kids understood things. In my class, where the kids are preparing for the [state exam], I realize my dissatisfaction is making sure I get through the curriculum, and I find that very frustrating."

A year later, the change was no easier for Rob. At a staff meeting in January 2000, he explained that because of the pressure to cover all the content necessary to meet the state standards, he could no longer take the time to listen to his students and respond accordingly, as he used to do. "I feel like I'm disconnecting from my students," he announced in distress. A few months later, he again exclaimed in staff meeting, "I don't want to teach to the stupid thing [the state exam], but I can't not."

As evidenced by these statements, Rob, a teacher with over twenty years' experience in the classroom, had indeed altered his teaching. However, this change occurred not in order to improve his practice, but solely to prepare his students for a state exam, a state exam that he sees as a "stupid thing." He does not see merit in covering all the content of the math standards. To the contrary, he finds that the pressure to teach it all has a negative effect on his classroom because his focus has switched from his students to the standards. He can no longer take the time to make sure that students understand. He can no longer take the time to listen and respond to them. Instead, he is compelled to sweep through an imposed curriculum of math standards in order to prepare his students for a single exam, an exam they must pass in order to graduate from high school. Ironically, the high standards reform effort, an effort designed to improve the level of teaching, is, in Rob's experience, having just the opposite effect.

The Effects of the High-Stakes State World History Exam

The next high-stakes state exam to alter the Durant School's program was the world history exam, passage of which was to be required of all students beginning with the class of 2002. In staff meetings throughout the spring of 1999, the staff extensively debated whether to begin teaching this state-designed "high standards" curriculum to which the exam was to be aligned. This curriculum, described by the principal as "a mile wide and an inch deep," is antithetical to the school's philosophy of in-depth learning. As a result, most staff was vehemently opposed to its implementation, preferring to stall until the state had reached a decision on the school's formal request for a variance from the exams (see Goodson and Foote, "Testing Times"). A few, however, felt that the risk to students' futures was too great to count on a favorable decision and to delay teaching to the test. This argument became even stronger after the summer passed and the state had still not issued a decision.

In a staff meeting in early Septem-

ber 1999, as the new school year was about to begin, the two history teachers, Nathaniel and Eve, announced that their world history classes this year would be geared specifically to the upcoming high-stakes state exam. They explained to their sympathetic colleagues that they needed to make this change because no decision on a variance had yet been made by the state. Therefore, the freshmen and sophomores, for whom these classes would be required, would have to pass the state exam in world history in order to graduate from high school.

Nathaniel, a teacher with over twenty years' experience, further explained that he and Eve were making this change because "the state is breathing down our necks." They had decided that what was best for the kids was giving them the best chance to pass, adding, "We're stuck." He later said that he was torn between how he wants to teach and how he must teach to get kids to pass the exam.

Eve stated that it would be irresponsible *not* to prepare the kids now because not only would the exam cover two years' worth of content but the kids would also have other high-stakes exams to prepare for and pass in their junior and senior years. She said that they could not wait. As a result of this decision, there was no longer room in the schedule for such previously popular courses as African-American history; the history teachers would be tied up teaching the state course for the state exam.

In an interview later that autumn, Nathaniel spoke about the changes in his world history course now that he was gearing it to the state exam. He said that instead of employing cooperative learning and in-depth, critical analysis of materials, his preferred methods of teaching, he was now using the overhead and giving class notes. He added that when students had asked in consternation whether he was going to teach like this all year, he had responded affirmatively, explaining that in order for them to pass the state exam, they were going to have to learn a lot of content. He said that he had told them, "Kids, I'm not any happier than you are about this, but I could not live with myself knowing that I did not teach you in a way that would prepare you to jump through that hoop. I couldn't do it personally and professionally."

He further explained in the interview that though he tried to insert some things that would "make history come alive" for his students, he only had limited time for it as there was so much content to cover. He then spoke emotionally of his decision to teach to the test:

I cannot put my head in the sand and ignore the political realities that are looming over the horizon. I've got to deal with it. I just cannot put up a stone wall and deny what's happening. So that's what pushed me to (pause), well, I read the handwriting on the wall and I cannot let these kids go and take the test, which I think they are going to take. You have to prepare them to take the test. What are you going to do? It's a hell of a catch-22. It's the worst one

I've ever faced since having to go into the army. Really, I compare that to when I was like 19–20 years old and got my draft notice [to serve in the Vietnam War]. . . . So I look at this and this is just (pause); you know you can't play with people's lives. I can play with my own, but I can't play with young people's lives. There's too much at stake, way, way too much.

Again, the disciplinary device of a high-stakes exam proved successful in compelling Nathaniel to teach to the new standards. He went from providing experiences designed to foster critical thinking and cooperative learning to using an overhead and giving his students the myriad content standards to copy, because he knew these standards would be covered by the high-stakes test. It was a disciplinary device that he could not ignore because, in his words, he couldn't "play with young people's lives." Like Rob, Nathaniel also believes that his classroom has suffered from the changes he has been forced to make in order to comply with the state mandates. Yet he feels that he has no choice because it is not his life that is at stake; it is his students' lives. And he bears too much responsibility for their futures.

From Trust to Compliance

In addition to the examples provided above of specific classes and teachers affected by the high-stakes tests, a range of more general, yet crucial, issues about the standards reform were frequently raised by Durant School staff throughout our two years of research. One recurrent concern was that trust in teachers and schools had been replaced by enforcement and compliance as a result of the standards initiatives.

In a conversation with the principal, Ed, in December 1998, we discussed an incident in 1986 when the Durant School successfully sought an exemption from a city school district testing mandate. Ed said that back then, the district basically trusted the school to do its own thing, but that times had changed. He said that now it is the state, not the city school district, that makes the mandates, and everyone must comply. He compared it to the military: the state makes the mandates, the city has to comply, and the city has to make all its schools comply as well.

A year later, a teacher named Alan echoed this sentiment during a staff meeting discussion about compliance with the state mandates and the consequent erosion of trust: "The kids have a sword over their heads that we [staff] put there. We have a sword over our heads that Ed puts there. He has a sword over his head that Central Office puts there. And it goes up and up." Alan explained that state methods of enforced compliance interfere with the development of trusting relationships among students, teachers, and administrators. For the staff at the Durant School, these methods threaten to transform the school into an authoritarian institution where the threat of dire consequences compels

one to conform. It is also a wrenching change at a school that has thrived on a philosophy in which both teachers and students have been trusted and respected to pursue their interests responsibly and assiduously.

In fact, the city school district overtly wielded this "sword" in October 1999, when it initiated a policy of sending personnel, unannounced, to schools and classrooms to determine whether (1) teachers were indeed teaching to the standards and (2) a copy of the state learning standards was posted in every classroom as per district mandate. While Ed, in announcing this new policy at staff meeting, saw these visits as a possible opportunity to educate district personnel about the Durant School's philosophy of learning and assessment, the school's guidance counselor, Karl, disagreed. He doubted whether these visitors would care about anything beyond whether the school "is stepping in line." After much discussion, Ed left it to each teacher to decide how to engage with these visitors, as long as they showed how their lesson was aligned with the standards. Meanwhile, he passed out copies of the standards for each teacher to post in their classrooms. Compliance with district policy was upheld.

A few weeks later, the state's commissioner of education visited the district and held a community forum on the new standards in a neighboring school. He told the teachers in the audience that "all eyes are on you" as witness to whether the students are meeting the standards and passing the state exams. He added, "I am watching you, too." Trust to teach appropriately and professionally did not enter the equation. For this commissioner, teachers would teach to the standards because they would know they were being monitored and scrutinized. The high-stakes exams, then, became the high-profile tool through which the surveillance could occur and compliance could be achieved.

Concluding Remarks

At the Durant School, the use of high-stakes exams did ensure compliance with the state's new "high standards." Even though the staff was both confident that their existing program was educationally sound (and district statistics on the school supported this sentiment) and also critical of the content standards and exams, they were compelled to make changes. Why? Because the staff felt too professionally and personally responsible to their students to allow them to take high-stakes exams unprepared. These teachers saw their students on a chopping block, placed there by the state. As the immediate keepers of the standards, then, they saw it as their responsibility to lead their students out of danger. They had to teach to the high-stakes tests. Proponents of the standards movement call this "accountability." In other circumstances, it is called extortion.

In April 2000, during a staff meeting discussion on the tremendous difficulties many Durant School students face in their home and personal lives, a teacher, Doug, pointed out the dilemma of trying to reach out to his students when feeling pressured to teach to the standards. He wondered out loud, "Do I put my kids in danger when I say that we don't have time to discuss their issues?" He explained the dilemma: if he is not concentrating on the state standards, then he is not preparing the kids to pass the exams; however, if he is teaching to the standards, then he is reducing the students' school experience to something trivial for them. He concluded, "We're caught between the devil and the deep blue sea." The staff agreed.

References

Heubert, J. P., & Hauser, R. M. (Eds.). (1999). *High-stakes: Testing for tracking, promotion, and graduation.* National Research Council. Washington, DC: National Academy Press.

Kliebard, H. M. (1995). *The struggle for the American curriculum* (2nd ed.). New York: Routledge.

McNeil, L. M. (2000). *Contradictions of school reform: The educational costs of standardized testing.* New York: Routledge.

Neill, M., & FairTest Staff. (1997). *Testing our children: A report card on state assessment systems.* Cambridge, MA: FairTest.

Ohanian, S. (1999). *One size fits few: The folly of educational standards.* Portsmouth, NH: Heinemann.

THE SPECTACLE OF STANDARDS AND SUMMITS

E. Wayne Ross

In 1989, President George Bush called the nation's governors together for the first National Education Summit.[1] They set goals and tried to develop ways to measure progress, but they were stymied by resistance to federal interference in local school decisions. Seven years later, governors and forty-four top corporate leaders met at IBM's conference center in Palisades, New York, and set up an approach for states to accomplish what had eluded participants in the first summit, namely, defining what should be taught in local schools and enforcing curriculum standardization through state-mandated tests—what is now called the "standards movement."

Like the summit itself, the report on standards given to summit participants by Public Agenda, a public opinion research organization, is a quintessential example of how neoliberal democracy works to thwart meaningful participation of the many by allowing the few to speak for all. Standards-based educational reform exemplifies how elites manufacture crises (e.g., the widespread failure of public education[2]) and consent (e.g., "everyone" agrees that the way to save public education is through standardized schools driven by high-stakes tests).

The objective appearance of standards-based reforms, which aim to reform schools by focusing on test scores, is designed to conceal (partially) the fact that these reforms are the result of deepening economic inequality and racial segregation, which are typically coupled with authoritarianism. For example, in Chicago, public schools have been militarized—six schools have been turned into military academies and over 7,000 students in forty-one schools are in Junior ROTC —and teachers have been given scripted lessons, keyed to tests, to guide their instruction. In a dramatic shift away from democracy, the Detroit school board was disbanded in 1998 by the Democratic mayor and

Republican governor, who then appointed a new board whose members represent corporate interests and of whom only one is a city resident (Gibson, 1999).

The primary justification for the seizure of schools and the imposition of standardized curriculum has been poor test scores and high dropout rates. But standardized test scores are less a reflection of ability or achievement than measures of parental income. For example, recent data show that someone taking the SAT can expect to score an extra thirty test points for every $10,000 in his parents' yearly income (Sacks, 2000). Dropout rates are directly related to poverty, and none of the powers demanding school seizures or standardization are prepared to address the question of poverty.

When IBM CEO Louis Gerstner Jr. convened the third National Education Summit in September 1999, media attention focused on the laudatory monologue provided by an alliance of conservative and liberal politicians, corporate elites, chief school officers, and teacher union leaders about the "gains" made since the last summit, three years earlier. Specifically, forty-five states had adopted standards in social studies, English, math, and science, up from fourteen in 1996. Forty-eight states had instituted mandated standardized tests, up from thirty-nine in 1996. Over 10,000 employers now used student school records to identify behavior and work habits as part of their hiring process, up from the 3,000 business that previously used transcripts. The media, and the participants themselves, heaped praise on the spectacular achievements of the past three years.

Public Agenda reported to summit participants that the movement to raise standards in public schools strikes a responsive chord with the public,[3] but it also warned that the issue of standards is not immune to the "normal controversies and complications that accompany any large-scale policy change" (Johnson, 1999, p. 1).

What is noteworthy about this report, *Standards and Accountability: Where the Public Stands*, is its straightforward description of the agenda that must be pursued if the economic and political elites are to maintain legitimacy and respond to opposition as they define the curriculum and pedagogy of public schools. The number-one task, according to Public Agenda, is effective propaganda. As they put it: "Experts and decision-makers often must concentrate on the labyrinth of details needed to make a policy work in real life. But to sustain change . . . that touches people's families and daily lives, leaders need to take time periodically to restate the basic rationale, to remind people of the beliefs and values that underlie reform. When the going gets a bit rough, people need to be reminded of why we're here" (Johnson, 1999, p. 2). It is important to note that the "we" in this case refers to the summiteers and other opinion makers like Public Agenda and *Education Week*, the trade weekly that has been an ardent proponent of the standards movement and that collaborated with Public Agenda on its survey of public opinion regarding the standards movement.

While the author of *Standards and Accountability* make much of the "established and remarkably stable" support for standards-based educational reform in the United States, they are mindful of "pitfalls that could derail or unsettle support." First, the report warns that standards advocates should expect unhappiness when the rubber hits the road and students are retained in grade or denied diplomas.

Pointing to the dramatic shift in public support for managed health care as people experienced "drive-by surgery" and denial of treatment options, Public Agenda warns standards advocates that success in delivering test score increases must be accompanied by the "appearance of fairness" in managing the reform effort. Now that thousands of students are being forced to repeat a grade or are denied a diploma, it is likely that the mere appearance of fairness will not be enough to stave off opposition to standards and the high-stakes tests that accompany them. Parents and teachers are the two groups most likely to derail the standards train.

However, in a somewhat quixotic claim, the Public Agenda report declares that parents are insignificant players in the standards movement. Public Agenda says that while parents generally support standards-based reform, "most are not especially well-informed or vigilant consumers, even concerning their own child's progress" (Johnson, 1999, p. 5). This claim con-

flicts with reports that the once-sporadic resistance to standards-based educational reforms is blossoming into a broader rebellion involving parents (e.g., Ohanian, 1999; Ross, 1999; Whitmire, 1999). For example, as a result of parent protests, Los Angeles school officials recently backed off of a plan to end "social promotions," and in Massachusetts, officials were forced to redefine passing scores on state tests that otherwise would have prevented as many as 83 percent of Latino and 80 percent of African American students from receiving high school diplomas.

Perhaps the best example of parental "pushback" is in Virginia, where Parents Across Virginia United to Reform Standards of Learning is a rapidly growing group working to dump the state's curriculum standards and testing program. Virginia's unrealistically broad standards of learning (SOL) includes this standard for third graders: "Students will explain the term *civilization* and describe the ancient civilizations of Greece and Rome in terms of geographic features, government, agriculture, music, art, religion, sports and the roles of men, women and children." Starting in 2004, Virginia high school students must take a series of eleven exams, based on the SOL, in order to graduate. In 2007, 70 percent of a school's students must pass SOL tests for it to remain accredited—last year only 2.2 percent of Virginia schools met this standard.

Beyond the unrealistic nature of the SOL and the deleterious effects of high-stakes testing on teaching and learning, a primary concern of the Virginia parents group is that the state's reform efforts have not included local input on what students should be learning. They argue that many test items are more like Trivial Pursuit factoids than essentials and that Virginia's standards reflect the views of only a few members of the state board of education rather than a consensus of broad-based groups of educators and parents.

The absurdity of many standards and test questions is not limited to Virginia. In Chicago, George Schmidt —a thirty-year veteran of Chicago Public School classrooms and publisher of a monthly newspaper written by and for people who work in Chicago's public schools—is being sued for $1 million by the Chicago Board of Education for publishing questions from the Chicago Academic Standards Examinations (CASE) after students took the tests. This item is from a social studies CASE:

> 23. All of the following activities are part of a typical African woman's life in rural areas *except*:
> A. preparing food
> B. taking care of children
> C. helping her husband grow cash crops
> D. selling crops at the market.

While Public Agenda—and perhaps the corporate leadership of the standards movement—considers parents to be little or no threat to standards-based educational reform, politicians appear more sensitive to the growing antistandards, antitesting pressures. Test boycotts and other forms of resistance have moved the governors of Michigan and California to offer students money ("scholarships" of up to $2,500) for taking or scoring well on state-mandated tests (Aratani, 2000). Indiana politicians are bracing for an enormous backlash against the state graduation test, which threatens to keep 50 percent of the seniors in urban districts and a quarter of seniors state-wide from graduating this year.

Resistance from teachers presents the most significant potential pitfall to the standards movement, according to the Public Agenda report. Many school administrators and the top leaders of the teacher unions are solidly on the standards bandwagon, but the support of rank-and-file teachers is also crucial if the standards movement is to succeed, as is rightly acknowledged in the report:

> If teachers believe that standards policies are important and well thought out, they can sustain and nourish parental support. If teachers are convinced that standards policies are unfair or destructive, they can undercut parental support with extraordinary speed. . . . District directives are often ridiculed or resented, and experienced teachers have already been through waves of reform, which in their minds produced very little of value. Public Agenda's research strongly suggests that bringing the nation's teacher corps

firmly inside the movement to raise standards could be the most pivotal challenge of all. (Johnson, 1999, p. 4)

Following the lead of Public Agenda, the top agenda item at the summit was teaching—in particular, devising ways in which teacher preparation and pay can be tied directly to the standardized curriculum and tests developed by states. For their part, education leaders promised to align college admissions requirements with state curriculum standards. The standards, which threaten academic freedom in K-12 classrooms, are now being applied to university teacher preparation programs as advocates work to create a rigid system in which the education of students *and* teachers is defined by interests accountable only to corporate America. As a result, the standards movement threatens the ability of parents, teachers, students, and other members of local communities to define their own interests and desires and use them as platforms for deciding the content and pedagogy used in public schools.

The idea of paying teachers based on their students' test scores, which was endorsed at the summit, is backed by Bob Chase and Sandra Feldman, the presidents of the National Education Association and the American Federation of Teachers (AFT), respectively. In the past six months, unionized teachers in cities across the country—Denver, St. Paul, Cincinnati, and Seattle, to name a few—have agreed to some sort of pay-for-performance

plan. Governor Gray Davis of California recently approved $50 million for one-time bonuses of up to $25,000 for teachers whose students show substantial test score improvement. Davis's plan, like other teacher pay-for-performance plans, attacks the notion that teachers should be engaged in deciding what's best for their students by shifting the focus from students' welfare to teachers' pocketbooks.

Paying teachers for student performance in not a new idea. History shows that most of the gains from such programs are destructive illusions that narrow the curriculum offered to students and encourage teachers and administrators to cheat— as we have recently seen with the high-stakes exams used in New York City public schools. Wilms and Chapleau (1999) describe pay-for-results schemes implemented in England, Canada, and the United States in the last two centuries and draw the following conclusions:

Few reforms that are forced on the schools (especially destructive ones like pay-for-results) will ever penetrate the classroom and positively change the teaching and learning processes. Teachers are every bit as adept at deflecting or sabotaging reforms of this kind today as they were at deceiving English school inspectors in the 1800s. Politically driven reforms like pay-for-performance are nothing more than reflections of public frustrations. And rather than helping to solve the root causes of failure, they paralyze us and deflect public attention from reforming the educational systems at their core. (p. 34)

Obviously, participants at the National Education Summit understand the centripetal position of teachers in education reform. If real reform is to be achieved, however, the root causes of problems faced by public schools must be addressed—social and economic inequalities. Standardized curriculum and high-stakes tests not only divert attention away from these inequalities but are used to justify and sustain them.

In the end, the summit is yet another portrait of power relations in neoliberal democracy. It represents our hierarchical society, in which citizens are made to be passive spectators, disconnected from one another and alienated from their own desires, learning, and work. The spectacle of standards, test scores, and summits obscures the role of parents, teachers, and students in decision making. The spectacle expresses what society can do, but in this expression what is permitted with regard to teaching and learning limits what is possible. Ultimately, the achievement of standards-based educational reform is the preservation of the unequal conditions of American existence.

Even as summiteers celebrate their successes, they face growing resistance to the mechanisms designed to allow a handful of private interests to control as much as possible of public educa-

tion and social life. In 1932, George S. Counts, in his speech "Dare the School Build a New Social Order?" made clear the central role of teachers not only in educational reform but in social change. Counts explicitly challenged teachers to develop a democratic, socialist society. While the summit is in the limelight, many teachers are working with parents, students, and other committed citizens to build a democratic society, one that challenges the impulses of greed, individualism, and intolerance that are embodied in much of what passes as educational reform today.

The bottom line is that the more members of local communities are allowed to decide on school curriculum and teaching methods, the more equitable and democratic the society will be. Standardized curriculum and high-stakes tests are attacks on democratic education. Organized parents, educators, students, and community people have an honest stake in democratic education and are responding to these attacks in good faith.

Notes

1. A different version of this article first appeared in March 2000 in *Z Magazine*, *12*(3), 45–48.

2. For an examination of the mythical crisis of U.S. schools see Berliner & Biddle (1995) and Rothstein (1998).

3. Public Agenda reports that results from their recent Reality Check survey show that overwhelming majorities of parents (83 percent), teachers (79 percent), employers (93 percent), and college

professors (90 percent) say having guidelines for what and how students are expected to learn helps improve academic performance.

References

Aratani, L. (2000, January 4). State may reward students with cash. *San Jose Mercury News* [On-line]. Available: http://www.sjmercury.com/local/education/docs/school010500.htm.

Berliner, D. C., & Biddle, B. J. (1995). *The manufactured crisis: Myths, fraud, and the attack on America's public schools.* Reading, MA: Addison-Wesley.

Gibson, R. (1999). *Who can answer the social crisis of the public schools?* [On-line]. Available: http://www.pipeline.com/~rgibson/DPSrouge.htm.

Johnson, J. (1999). *Standards and accountability: Where the public stands.* New York: Public Agenda.

Ohanian, S. (1999). *One size fits few: The folly of educational standards.* Portsmouth, NH: Heinemann.

Ross, E. W. (1999). Resisting test mania. *Z Magazine, 12*(9), 21–22.

Rothstein, R. (1998). *The way we were: The myths and realities of student achievement.* New York: Twentieth Century Fund Press.

Sacks, P. (2000). *Standardized minds: The high price of America's testing culture and what we can do to change it.* Cambridge, MA: Perseus Books. [The first chapter, "Meritocracy's crooked yardstick," is available on-line: http://www.fairtest.org/k12/psacks.html.]

Whitmire, R. (1999, December 16). Parents resist school standards: States back down after pressure builds against tougher student goals. *The Detroit News* [On-line]. Available: http://detnews.com/1999/schools/9912/16/12160179.html.

Wilms, W. W., & Chapleau, R. R. (1999, November 3). The illusion of paying teachers for student performance. *Education Week, 34*, 48. [On-line]. Available: http://www.edweek.org/ew/ewstory.cfm?slug=10wilms.h19.

PHILOSOPHICAL AND ANALYTICAL STANDARDS

Mordechai Gordon

What will happen if teachers become sufficiently courageous and emancipated to insist that education means the creation of a discriminating mind, a mind that prefers not to dupe itself or to be the dupe of others? Clearly they will have to cultivate the habit of suspended judgment; of skepticism; of desire for evidence; of appeal to observation rather than sentiment, discussion rather than bias, inquiry rather than conventional idealizations. When this happens, schools will be the dangerous outposts of a humane civilization. But they will also be supremely interesting places. For education and politics will then be one and the same thing because politics will have to be in fact what it now pretends to be, the intelligent management of social affairs (Dewey, 1986).

The "creation of a discriminating mind" is no less crucial today in America's schools than it was in 1922 when John Dewey first published the essay "Education as Politics" in the *New Republic*. Dewey was talking about the development of a "philosophical mindset," a mindset that embraces thinking as a continuous process of doubting, questioning, critically examining, and revising our beliefs. This chapter explores some of the fundamental facilities associated with a philosophical mindset and argues that schools in general and universities in particular should be committed to fostering it. Developing a philosophical mindset has to do with learning various philosophical skills such as interpreting texts, analyzing issues from multiple perspectives, deductive and inductive reasoning, connecting theory to practice, synthesizing and making distinctions, and providing a convincing argument to a problem. My contention is that given the complex nature of today's knowledge production systems, the decline of the influence of traditional moral and religious values, and the sparse and often shallow political debate going on in America, there is an urgent need to cultivate these philosophical skills. Let me begin by explicating the philosophical skills I have in mind.

Interpretation

Students in my graduate secondary education classroom management class constantly bring up instances of student misbehavior in their classrooms, ranging from coming late to class and not doing homework to threatening the teacher and physical violence. The focus is typically on the overt behavior of their students and the response is often frustration; my students say things like, "I cannot get my students to behave like normal students," or "some students don't belong in this school." It is as though many of my students suffer from the same problem that Michel Foucault attributes to many, if not most, historians who attempt to write history while knowingly obscuring their own point of view: "The final trait of effective history is its affirmation of knowledge as perspective. Historians take unusual pains to erase the elements in their work which reveal their grounding in a particular time and place, their preferences in a controversy—the unavoidable obstacles of their passions" (Foucault, 1984, p. 90).

Like the historians Foucault is talking about, my students often do not acknowledge their own perspectives, preferences, and passions concerning either the so-called problem students in their classes or teaching and learning in general. They unconsciously assume that their students' behavior is self-evident, that it does not need to be interpreted or explained, that it has no *meaning*. Yet, Foucault's and Nietzsche's emphasis on "knowledge as perspective" suggests that we are always viewing and analyzing historical events or students' behavior from a particular perspective that is grounded in a particular time and place.

The perspectival nature of knowledge further implies, not that historical events like wars are mere battles between two or more nations, but rather that wars are meaningful and make sense if we view them from particular vantage points and social historical contexts. Likewise, a student's violent behavior in school is not just an act of violence but is deeply significant if we analyze this act from the student's own perspective and context. Only by considering this perspective and trying to interpret the social, economic, and historical context of the student and the school do we have a chance of really comprehending the causes and significance of the violent behavior. The ontological assumption that I am making here is that human beings do not simply behave or respond to stimuli but are constantly engaged in the act of meaning making and making sense of the world.

Typically, there is more than one way to interpret and make sense of human phenomena such as students' violent behavior in the schools. The strict behaviorist, who focuses on our overt actions and attitudes, will attribute such behavior to the "lack of conformity to the school's norms" or to the fact that "some students have no respect for adult authority." A cognitive psychologist might account for the same actions by investigating whether or not the rules of appropriate conduct are fully understood and accepted by the violent students. Finally, a critical pedagogue would insist that the only way to make sense of this behavior is to view it in the context of the school culture as well as the broader social, political, economic, and moral culture of the community and the country as a whole. From this perspective, high school students' violent behavior in a disadvantaged urban neighborhood might be interpreted as acts of resistance to the inhumane and oppressive conditions of their school and community. The point that I wish to emphasize here is that since human phenomena and culture are highly complex and often ambiguous, it is crucial that students become skilled at interpretation as a way of clarifying and giving meaning to everything from poetry to violent behavior.

Moreover, interpreting a text, whether a book, a movie, or a student's behavior, will often lead us to a new way of viewing it and hence to a more complex and deeper understanding. However, some perspectives give us a dimmer or narrower rather than a clearer or more complex picture of that which we are trying to understand. For example, when reading and discussing texts in my classes, my students will frequently attempt to interpret them literally. Literal interpretations lead many of my students to conclude that the ideas they are learn-

ing (from Socrates to bell hooks) are impractical and therefore insignificant for them. Yet, when these same students are encouraged to consider the symbolic rather than the literal meaning of these theories, they often arrive at a new understanding of the ideas and are able to see how they can be applied in their own lives and work.

Such symbolic or metaphorical interpretations give us insight into texts that, like dreams, rarely make sense if we consider them literally. When I have shown the movie *Harold and Maude* in my class and asked students to talk about the approach to education that Maude represents, many of them have responded by referring to Maude as simply "a crazy old woman with no respect for the law." This literal perspective prevents these students from viewing Maude as a symbol of free spirit and active resistance to conformity to established norms. Once my students take this symbolic perspective, they are able to recognize that Maude's message has deep significance for them in the context of a system of education in which conformity to established norms, methods, and subject matter is the rule. In this way students not only gain a deeper understanding of the movie but are able to make connections between some of its insights and their own daily struggles in the public schools.

Analyzing Issues from Multiple Perspectives

When discussing with my college education students Paulo Freire's distinction between true and false generosity (Freire, 1993, p. 42), I often give the following example:

> *Let's pretend that when you leave Brooklyn College this evening and take the subway you encounter a beggar asking for some change so he can buy a hot meal. You reach into your pocket and pull out a five dollar bill and give it to the beggar with the intent of helping this hungry person get some food. Is this true or false generosity?*

Many students respond to this question by saying that this is a case of true generosity since the giver has a worthy intent of helping this hungry person buy a hot meal. Only upon further probing do such students realize that the issue is not so simple since neither the good intentions nor the five dollars in question will help this beggar get out of his dehumanized condition. Other students argue that this is a case of false generosity for precisely this reason, but they cannot identify the criteria by which one may distinguish true from false generosity.

This example is not intended as a critique of my students, but rather to illustrate the point that many, if not most, of the issues that we deal with in the curriculum, whether social, political, economic, aesthetic, or moral, are highly complex and cannot be simply evaluated from one vantage point. In this example, there are at least two perspectives that need to be taken into account. The first is what I call an "ethics of intent," the second, an "ethics of consequences." An "ethics

of intent," informed by various historical religious traditions such as Christianity, considers the intent of the doer as the most important factor in evaluating moral dilemmas. When assessing the moral worth of a particular action, such an approach tries to determine whether the deed was based on good/pure motives or evil/selfish motives. The problem with this approach is that one can never know for sure the motives and intentions of the human heart, as Immanuel Kant pointed out.

Moreover, even if the motives are evident, the actions of human beings, who can never be completely conditioned or controlled, always involve surprises and unexpected consequences. Think, for example, of the recent conflict in Kosovo and the NATO bombing of the Serb forces following their attempt to forcefully remove the ethnic Albanians from Kosovo. From the perspective of an "ethics of intent," one could probably argue that the NATO bombings were justified since they were aimed at stopping the removal of the Albanians from their home and the practices of ethnic cleansing. However, if one examines the NATO bombings in light of the consequences that they had for the ethnic Albanians, it becomes clear that these air raids greatly exacerbated the plight of the Albanians by speeding up their deportation from Kosovo, destroying their homes and infrastructure, and in some cases actually killing innocent civilians. This latter perspective is based on an "ethics of consequences," an ethics that considers the results of our actions as the primary criteria for evaluating their worth, regardless of the motives that may be driving these actions.

My intention is not to suggest that an "ethics of consequences" and an "ethics of intent" are mutually exclusive. Indeed, when our actions have positive results, the intention is usually good, too. Yet, these are two very different moral perspectives based on different assumptions, and they will often lead us to conflicting analyses and conclusions on the same issue. Further, as Freire suggests, an ethics of consequences is a much stronger position than an ethics of intent because it considers a moral dilemma from the position of the disadvantaged groups in society, a position that is often ignored or marginalized. Such a perspective is strong, according to Freire, because it is based on the values of social justice, critical citizenship, and democracy.

Yet, why is it so important that students in general and future teachers in particular become skilled at analyzing issues from multiple perspectives? To begin with, we are living in the midst of a technological revolution together with an explosion of information and new cultural forms that have a profound impact on the contemporary education curriculum. Here I am using the word "curriculum" in the broad sense to signify not only what the state board of education requires students to know but the various forms of cultural pedagogies and knowledge production systems that we are bombarded with.

As Douglas Kellner notes: "[C]ontemporary culture is marked by a proliferation of cultural machines that generate a panoply of print, sound, environmental, and diverse aesthetic artifacts within which we wander, trying to make our way through this forest of symbols. This requires the development of a new multimedia literacy that is able to scan, interact with, traverse, and organize new multimedia educational environments" (Kellner, 1998, p. 13). Kellner argues correctly that the new multimedia literacy that students require in order to interact and make sense of the myriad forms of cultural artifacts involves training in philosophy, ethics, and the humanities. Specifically, this means that our education system will have to "empower individuals so they can analyze and criticize the emerging technoculture, as well as participate in its cultural forums and sites" (Kellner, 1998, p. 13).

Moreover, the information, ideas, and values that students are exposed to in and out of school are typically complex rather than simple. For instance, every fall, millions of children in elementary schools across the United States are introduced to the subject and concept of Thanksgiving. Yet, as James Loewen (1996) has illustrated, there are numerous suppressions, distortions, and outright lies surrounding the history and meaning of this celebration. One of the main reasons for this sad truth is that the story of Thanksgiving has always been told from the perspective of the European colonists and therefore reflects only their ideological interests. The perspective of the Native Americans has been either marginalized or completely suppressed by most history textbooks and teachers.

This narrow and Eurocentric representation of Thanksgiving not only robs our students of a much more complex and less biased understanding of this important historical event but also misses a good chance to develop their critical thinking skills. The alternative to this feel-good history, according to Loewen, is not a feel-bad history but rather a more inclusive history that would allow students to "learn both the 'good' and the 'bad' sides of the Pilgrim tale. Conflict would then become part of the story, and students might discover that the knowledge they gain has implications for their lives today. Correctly taught, the issue of the era of the first Thanksgiving could help Americans grow more thoughtful and more tolerant, rather than more ethnocentric" (p. 97).

Finally, analyzing issues from multiple perspectives is more crucial today than ever given the fact that the United States is becoming a more diverse society, with many different ethnic groups who embody different cultures, values, and interests. And as John Dewey and many other progressive educators recognized, democracy is much more than a form of government; it is a society that encourages open interaction and dialogue among people from diverse races, genders, classes, and religions. Such interaction and dialogue is possible, I would ar-

gue, only if individuals and communities in this society acknowledge and respect the viewpoints of people who represent different backgrounds, values, and lifestyles. This means, for example, that heterosexuals in the United States need to be open to hearing the opinions and concerns of homosexuals on issues like same-sex marriage, even when the two groups disagree about the causes or virtues of a particular sexual orientation. In this view, democracy is at stake when only one perspective and ideology is valued above all others while other opinions and values are marginalized or censored. A flourishing democracy is one in which the citizens are able to make informed decisions and take action based on a comprehensive analysis of the issues at stake from multiple perspectives.

Deductive and Inductive Reasoning

In the opening passage of Plato's dialogue *Meno*, Menon asks Socrates the following questions: "Can virtue be taught? Or if not, does it come by practice? Or does it come neither by practice nor by teaching, but do people get it by nature, or in some other way?" Socrates responds by insisting that in order to answer these questions, one has to initially address a more fundamental question: "What is virtue?" His point is that if we want to discuss the qualities of something, we need first to arrive at a general definition of the thing we are talking about.

One way of interpreting this initial exchange between Socrates and Menon is to view it as a conflict or tension between two different ways of doing research: deductive versus inductive reasoning. By deductive reasoning, I mean a method of logical analysis that proceeds from general definitions of concepts or subjects to particular instances or examples that are subsumed under these definitions. Inductive reasoning, on the other hand, begins with a study of particular examples or phenomena and attempts to extrapolate from the results of this study a more general theory. In this section I will examine the import of both of these methods of doing research.

Deductive Reasoning

Socrates, who represents the deductive method of reasoning in the above example, makes one very important point: that in order to have a meaningful discussion about a complex and abstract notion like virtue, the participants of the debate need to clearly define the meaning of the terms they are using. Indeed, discussions often go nowhere and communication breaks down because each side is using the same words to signify very different things. Thus, defining the terms one is using is essential for the success of a debate insofar as it limits the possibility of confusions and keeps the debate focused. In my classroom discussions, I find myself constantly asking students to clarify the meaning of the terms they are using. Such probing is important not only in order to avoid

confusions but also because it forces students to stop and think about the meaning of the words they are using. Educationally speaking, this is a very important exercise in that it helps students clarify their ideas and gives them the chance to practice thinking coherently and critically.

In addition to clearly defining the terms one is using, deductive reasoning involves logical argumentation, that is, the ability to formulate a cogent and consistent argument with no internal contradictions. One of the most common fallacies involved with this aspect of deductive reasoning is the failure to distinguish between generalizations and universalizations. Specifically, this latter means that one is making a universal claim that, at best, has only general validity by ignoring all the exceptions to this claim. For example, I often hear students making statements like "If one tries hard enough in the United States, one always succeeds in the end." Aside from the ambiguity of the words "enough" and "succeed," this argument assumes that *everybody* who tries hard will eventually succeed, regardless of the overwhelming obstacles and hardships that some people face.

The main problem with this argument is that it ignores all those people in our society (including minorities, the poor, and the mentally challenged) who do not enjoy the same opportunities, rights, and privileges as the white middle and upper classes. Such universal statements typically lead one to artificially simplify a very complex and difficult issue such as the plight of the poor in the United States. Universal statements are also problematic in that they tend to undermine some of the basic tenets of democracy like diversity and protecting the rights of minorities and the disenfranchised. If everybody who tries hard enough eventually succeeds, then there is no reason for the government to intervene and help those people who are less fortunate and have historically been oppressed.

Inductive Reasoning

Unlike deductive reasoning, which proceeds from the general to the particular, inductive reasoning moves from particular phenomena to a general explanation of their nature and structure. Most scientific research, whether in the natural or the social sciences, employs some version of inductive reasoning by investigating a particular phenomenon (like the structure of atoms or teenage violence) in the hopes that this investigation will lead to the development of a more general theory. However, it is crucial to keep in mind that a theory is only one way of making sense of some aspect of reality, and as such it is never infallible or all-encompassing. Indeed, it is often the case that at any one time there are a number of competing theories that attempt to account for the same phenomenon.

What are some of the advantages that the process of inductive reasoning or theorizing give us? First is the idea that through inductive reasoning one is often able to overcome confusion or explain something that is obscure. Specifically, I am referring to the use of examples in order to help people understand a complex or abstract concept. Frequently, when I introduce an abstract concept in my classes (like "knowledge production"), many students will comprehend it much better when given a concrete example as opposed to a general definition. Giving an example to help people understand a complex notion is a way of thinking inductively because we are proceeding from a particular instance to the general definition of the notion it exemplifies.

The advantage of using concrete examples is that it greatly enhances our understanding of complex issues. Moreover, scientists and researchers are often hard-pressed to agree on a general definition of a phenomenon, such as the AIDS virus, that *must* be investigated since it poses a huge threat to humanity. Yet by studying particular cases of HIV and thinking inductively, these researchers are able not only to describe some of the features of this disease but also to invent powerful drugs that help to combat it.

Another advantage of theorizing is that it enhances our ability to engage in critical thinking—to reflect on and analyze the world. According to Terry Eagleton (1989), children are especially inclined to engage in theorizing. Eagleton argues that "Children make the best theorists, since they have not yet been educated into accepting our routine social practices as 'natural,' and so insist on posing to those practices the most embarrassingly general and fundamental questions, regarding them with a wondering estrangement which adults have long forgotten. Since they do not yet grasp our social practices as inevitable, they do not see why we might not do things differently." Children, in short, use theorizing to wonder about, make sense of, and critique the world around them. So they are much less likely than many adults to fall into the trap of thinking dogmatically and narrowly and taking things for granted.

While inductive reasoning opens up many great possibilities for us, this method of research may also lead people to think in overly simplistic terms. One of the most common mistakes made by researchers who use the inductive method is the attempt to isolate the "one cause" that presumably accounts for a very difficult and complex problem. Thus intelligence has been attributed to genetic endowment while adolescent violence has been explained away as a product of peer pressure. Such reductionistic theories assume that a single cause can provide an adequate explanation for the phenomenon being researched; such reasoning thereby exaggerates the importance of this cause while ignoring other relevant factors. Especially when dealing with human phenomena, it is almost always the case that there are many contributing factors, which are often interrelated, that account for these phenomena. In my classes, I emphasize the distinction between a cause and a contributing factor as a way of encouraging students to avoid thinking about complex problems in very simplistic, reductionistic terms.

Relating Theory to Practice

One of the most difficult challenges facing teachers, college professors, and scholars in general is the task of relating of theory with practice. However, as bell hooks points out, "it is evident that one of the many uses of theory in academic locations is in the production of an intellectual class hierarchy where the only work deemed truly theoretical is work that is highly abstract, jargonistic, difficult to read, and containing obscure references" (hooks, 1994, p. 64). Since such theories are inaccessible to a wide audience, they are often deemed useless and alienating by the very people they are designed to help. As such, they create a huge gap between theory and practice that serves to perpetuate class elitism. Like bell hooks, I believe that any theory that cannot be shared in everyday language cannot be used to educate the public.

Moreover, following educators like John Dewey, I believe that theory and practice are interrelated and that it is the teacher's responsibility to make their connections explicit. Throughout my college teaching experiences both in Israel and at Brooklyn College, I have discovered again and again that students frequently find it very difficult to make these connections on their own. Thus, in my courses, I not only give many examples that illustrate the relationships between theory and practice but I also require students to practice making such connections in virtually all the assignments they do. In this way, the students are constantly required to reflect on the connections between theory and practice with the hope that they come to realize that our philosophies shape the way we conduct our lives and that the experiences we have often help us revise and refine our assumptions, goals, and values.

To be sure, many of my students openly ask me to make these connections explicit and they constantly raise questions that indicate that they are trying to make sense of this issue. How else is it possible for students of education or medicine, for instance, to fully comprehend the things they are doing daily in the classroom or hospital? Dewey argues quite convincingly that if modern science has demonstrated anything, "it is that there is no such thing as genuine knowledge and fruitful understanding except as the offspring of *doing*. The analysis and arrangement of facts which is indispensable to the growth of knowledge and power of explanation and right classification cannot be obtained purely mentally—just inside the head. Men have to *do* something to the things when they wish to find out something; they have to alter conditions" (Dewey, 1966, p. 275). Thus, as Dewey asserts, it is only by experimenting with various techniques and practices that students are able to gain

genuine knowledge, knowledge that is tangible and comprehensible to them.

On the other hand, it is only through the power of theory that children as well as adults can make sense of many of the difficulties that they encounter in their lives and work. bell hooks makes this point very well: "Living in childhood without a sense of home, I found a place of sanctuary in 'theorizing,' in making sense out of what was happening. I found a place where I could imagine possible futures, a place where life could be lived differently. This 'lived' experience of critical thinking, of reflection and analysis, became a place where I worked at explaining the hurt and making it go away. Fundamentally, I learned from this experience that theory could be a healing place" (hooks, 1994, p. 61).

Drawing on hooks's insights, we can see that only by theorizing are children and adults able to interpret and make sense of the difficulties they encounter in their daily struggles. Theories provide us with a frame of reference and a language with which to name and critically analyze many of the problems we face daily. However, as hooks points out, theory is also a place of hope and healing. That is, theories provide us with a rich source of understanding not only of what *is* but also of how things could be different. Citizens who are struggling to make a difference need to become theorists who can imagine and create alternatives to many of the oppressive ideologies, practices, and "savage inequalities" that plague this society.

Synthesizing and Making Distinctions

One of the best insights regarding the significance of synthesizing comes from John Dewey, who strongly opposed the use of sharp distinctions like those between subject and object, the individual and the community, and freedom and authority. These distinctions, he believed, only serve to mystify an actual relationship in the lived world. Contrarily, he always insists on showing the interrelations between these "opposing" concepts in order to come to a better understanding of how we experience them. Regarding the distinction between authority and freedom, for instance, Dewey writes:

> The genuine problem is the *relation* between authority and freedom. And this problem is masked, and its solution begged, when the idea is introduced that the fields in which they respectively operate are separate. In effect, authority stands for stability of social organization by means of which direction and support are given to individuals; while individual freedom stands for the forces by which change is intentionally brought about. The issue that requires constant attention is the intimate and organic union of the two things: of authority and freedom, of stability and change. (Dewey, 1991, p. 131)

Dewey asserts that the problem of authority has traditionally been addressed by assuming that it is diametrically opposed to freedom. In his opinion, this way of resolving the issue can get us nowhere and even contributes to the problem since it posits a huge theoretical gulf between the two. The problem is rather to ascertain the relation between authority and freedom in experience in order to criticize it and suggest improvements. Dewey's point is that an adequate solution to the problem of authority has to begin by formulating the question differently: How is authority related to freedom?

Similarly, he thinks that rather than viewing the child and the curriculum as two opposing elements in the learning process, we need to expose the organic connections between the two. Thus, the shift of focus from the conflict between two concepts to the relation between them will often give us a new perspective from which to address the problem. When Dewey asks about the relationship between authority and freedom or between the child and the curriculum, he is not giving us a new answer to an old question but rather asking a very different and a much stronger question. Many advances in the natural and social sciences have come about in this very way: by reformulating an existing question and thereby redefining the terms of the problem.

No less important than the facility of integrating and showing the relationships between two concepts or phenomena is the ability to make distinctions and avoid confounding issues or concepts that should be kept separate. One distinction that is very important to maintain is the difference between relationship and identity. To suggest that two ideas or phenomena are related is very different than saying that they are the same. Thus, in a previous section of this essay I argued that theory and practice are closely connected. However, that does not mean that theory *is* practice. Theory refers to the assumptions, ideas, goals, and values that inform our practices as teachers, lawyers, or doctors, but it is not identical with what teachers, lawyers, or doctors actually do in their everyday jobs. Indeed, many times there is a certain gap between what we think and believe and how we actually act in our work.

An example of confounding issues is when a certain idea or concept is reduced to its function so that whatever fulfills the same function is regarded as the same. As Hannah Arendt states, "it is as though I had the right to call the heel of my shoe a hammer because I, like most women, use it to drive nails into the wall" (Arendt, 1977, p. 102). For instance, violence has commonly been equated with authority since both have at times fulfilled the same function—making people obey. In this case, the result is a distortion of both violence and authority and a blurring of the distinguishing lines between them. Historically speaking, authority, unlike violence, has precluded the external means of coercion, and when force has been used, authority itself has failed. This point becomes evident when we think of any number of local conflicts between a ruling oppressor and an oppressed people (e.g., Israel and the Palestinians, England

and the Irish Catholics). Typically in such conflicts, when the ruling power loses its authority over the oppressed minority, the former resorts to the use of force to maintain some control over the latter. Many political theorists and educators have recognized the importance of making this distinction between authority, on the one hand, and power, force, and violence, on the other. Such distinctions are important because they help us gain a clearer and more nuanced picture of a complex reality that defies any reductionistic, functional accounts.

Providing a Convincing Argument to a Problem

In order to get a good grasp of the meaning of "a convincing argument" it is helpful to compare it to the use of clichés. Throughout the seven years that I have been a college professor, I have found that students will often respond to a question I pose by using clichés and stock phrases. The problem with such use of clichés and hackneyed phrases is that it usually means that a person is not thinking critically and personally about the issue under discussion. When my college students use such language, I often find that they have not really reflected on the meaning of a given cliché before using it.

For example, when I ask my students about the meaning of "equality" as one of the principles of democracy, a common response is that "all humans are created equal." When I challenge them to explain in what sense human beings are, or should be, equal, many of them find it difficult to respond. My experience indicates that most students have not adequately reflected on the difference between universal equality as an ideal that is difficult to define, and legal, social, or political equality as a standard that democratic societies strive for.

Moreover, I find that clichés and phrases are frequently used by students in order to artificially simplify a complex problem. Such language prevents students from viewing a problem from several perspectives and hence from gaining a deeper understanding of the issue. To continue the previous example, most college students who are asked about the significance of equality in a democratic society are able to point to principles such as equal rights and equality of opportunity. However, many of these same students have not critically analyzed the various meanings of these principles. They have never really thought about whether equality of opportunity means that everyone should get the exact same opportunities, regardless of differences of race, gender, nationality, and so forth or whether it implies, on the other hand, that the government needs to intervene to give certain privileges to various sectors of society that historically have been discriminated against.

In short, my experience with college students indicates that while most of them are able to identify democratic principles such as equality, diversity, and freedom, they lack a deep understanding of what these principles de-

note and how they are related. I am suggesting not that this lack of understanding is a problem but merely that students use clichés and stock phrases to evade questions that should be addressed critically and thoroughly. Professors need to be mindful that when students use ready-made, common quotes, they usually do not have an adequate understanding of the issue.

Unlike the use of clichés and stock phrases, providing a convincing argument requires one to formulate a clear and coherent response to a problem that considers the issue from several perspectives. Initially, this means that the problem will have to be defined in a forceful or complex rather than a weak or simplistic way. Recall for a moment the exchange between Socrates and Menon about virtue. When Socrates insists that in order to answer Menon's questions about the qualities of virtue we must first address a more fundamental problem (namely, what *is* virtue?), he is essentially reformulating Menon's question in a stronger way. Generally speaking, Socrates is suggesting that in order to have a solid understanding of a problem, we must first articulate this problem in the most basic and precise terms.

The point is that to discuss the practical relevance of concepts such as virtue, democracy, or language, we must first have a clear sense of what exactly these concepts mean. For example, I would argue that in order to give an adequate response to the question about how to best teach English to new immigrants in the United

States, whether in bilingual education or in regular classes, one must first address the meaning of language. Hence, if language is just a means of communication, then it is clear that the best way to teach English to new immigrants in the United States would be in the kind of classes that provide them with the most effective and efficient methods of learning English. However, if language is first and foremost a way of expressing one's unique cultural identity, then the criteria for responding to this question change completely—from efficiency to freedom of expression, diversity, and social justice.

Providing a convincing argument to a problem also has to do with exposing the epistemological, political, moral, social, and economic assumptions and interests that support a certain view. In my classes I call this undertaking "the practice of making the implicit, explicit." The point that I try to get across to the students is that it is absolutely crucial for them to make explicit the underlying assumptions of various historical theories as well as of their own views and beliefs. Joe Kincheloe and Shirley Steinberg are correct when they write that "such an undertaking is not merely an attempt to, in the words of conservative critics, 'make students feel good at the expense of becoming educated.' On the contrary, it is a content based, discursively savvy, complex analytical educational process that requires a deep understanding of a wide variety of knowledge systems, the skills to cri-

tique them, and the cognitive facility to develop new insights to replace inadequate academic constructs" (Kincheloe & Steinberg, 1999, p. 242).

Students who are never encouraged to examine their basic assumptions all too often come to accept the theories and views they subscribe to as "natural," inevitable, and unchangeable. Such students will most likely find ways to adjust to the existing state of society and polity in America and become supporters of the status quo. They will only rarely gain those insights and critical abilities that will enable them to become active citizens and transforming agents.

Finally, providing a convincing argument to a problem involves the facility to follow one's argument through to its logical conclusion so that all its implications are clearly visible. Practically speaking, this means that teachers should expect their students not only to express their opinions on various issues but, more fundamentally, to support their views with substantial evidence. By "substantial evidence" I mean a justification that is thorough and can stand up to the test of reason and experience. If we neglect to do this we are shortchanging our students by robbing them of an opportunity to engage in genuine thinking and to gain excellent practice in becoming critical and active citizens.

Conclusion

The various philosophical and analytical skills described in this essay are neither mutually exclusive nor meant to be an exhaustive list of such skills. As I indicated earlier, there are close connections between interpretation and analyzing issues from multiple perspectives as well as between synthesizing and making distinctions and relating theory to practice. Also, one could certainly come up with additional facilities that would fall under the same rubric. Yet the philosophical and analytical skills I have outlined here offer teachers, students, and citizens a powerful arsenal with which to respond to many of the problems they face in this hi-tech, information-laden, multicultural society. These skills can take us far beyond the narrow and technical skills of the standards reform movement, which focus primarily on those abilities that merely enable students to consume information, pass standardized tests, and compete in the technological marketplace. Indeed, the skills I have described will prepare our students to become citizens who care deeply about politics and social issues and have the critical awareness needed to analyze complex problems and intervene constructively for the sake of a better world and a more democratic society.

References

Arendt, Hannah. (1977). What is authority? In *Between past and future*. New York: Penguin Books.

Dewey, John. (1966). *Democracy and education*. New York: The Free Press.

Dewey, John. (1986). Education as politics. In Jo Ann Boydston (Ed.), *John Dewey: Middle works* (Vol. 13). Carbondale: Southern Illinois University Press.

Dewey, John. (1991). Authority and social change. In Jo Ann Boydston (Ed.), *John Dewey: The later works* (Vol. 13). Carbondale: Southern Illinois University Press.

Eagleton, Terry. (1989). *The significance of theory*. Cambridge: Oxford University Press.

Foucault, Michel. (1984). Nietzsche, genealogy, history. In Paul Rabinow (Ed.), *The Foucault Reader.*. New York: Pantheon Books.

Freire, Paulo. (1993). *Pedagogy of the oppressed*. (Trans. by Myra Ramos Bergman). New York: Continuum.

hooks, bell. (1994). *Teaching to transgress: Education as the practice of freedom*. New York: Routledge.

Kellner, Douglas. (1998). Multiple literacies and critical pedagogy in a multicultural society. *Educational Theory*, *48*(1), 103–122.

Kincheloe, Joe L., and Steinberg, Shirley R. (1999). Politics, intelligence, and the classroom: Postformal teaching. In *Rethinking Intelligence: Confronting Psychological Assumptions about Teaching and Learning*. New York: Routledge.

Loewen, James. (1996). *Lies my teacher told me: Everything your American history textbook got wrong*. New York: Touchstone.

STANDARDS AND THE CURRICULUM

The Commodification of Knowledge and the End of Imagination

David Hursh

More and more teachers are encountering efforts to control their teaching by linking the curriculum to standardized, high-stakes tests that are then used to rank and judge students, teachers, and schools. States are developing subject area standards and then aligning the standards with statewide standardized tests. Increasingly, standardized test scores are being used by school districts to determine whether students should be promoted to the next grade or allowed to graduate from high school. Further, some states, such as Florida, are using test scores to rank schools and districts with the purpose of rewarding those teachers and schools with high scores and punishing those with low scores.

Consequently, given the public and fiscal pressure to produce high test scores, it should be no surprise that many teachers are being directed by district and school administrators to focus on raising test scores rather than on teaching for understanding. In the Rochester City School District in New York, high school teachers report that they are pressured to teach for the test. In addition, the district requires that teachers inform students which standard they are teaching during each lesson, and administrators enter the classroom unannounced to quiz students regarding the standard being taught. Elementary teachers are being directed to devote less time to teaching social studies, science, and the arts and more time to teaching the three Rs and preparing students for the statewide math and literacy tests. Teachers in Rochester and elsewhere report anecdotally that each year they devote a month or more to test preparation and administration. As part of the effort to improve schools, elementary schools are adopting "proven" programs, such as Success for All and America's Choice, in which teachers are provided with lesson scripts specifying what they and the students are to say.

How do we explain this shift from promoting teachers as thoughtful, intelligent practitioners who are partners in developing curriculum and methods to reducing teachers to mere technicians who implement curriculum, methods, and assessments designed by others? How do we explain the devaluing of subjects such as social studies and the standardization and simplification of the curriculum that remains? Why has the purpose of education shifted from developing knowledgeable, democratic citizens to developing productive workers? What is the rationale behind these efforts to standardize curriculum and teachers? Why do policies increasingly commodify knowledge and limit imagination?

In order to answer these questions, we need to understand how the government and corporations collaborate in reorganizing schools and the workplace in order to control teachers and other workers to promote economic growth and profit. Knowledge as an economic good—its commodification—and the standardization of teaching practices—the end of imagination—are part of an overall societal shift away from seeing people as creative producers of themselves, culture, and society to seeing people as producers and consumers of economic goods. These changes are also an outcome of the restoration of conservative politics, emphasizing a return to the supposed "common culture" of the "Western tradition," and the rise of neoliberal economics that empha-

sizes the right of the individual, and particularly the corporation as individual, to act free of constraint.

To make these factors more clear, I will situate these changes in teaching within the broader cultural, economic, and political context. From the late 1960s and continuing through most of the 1970s, workers were able to gain increasing control over their work and to win contracts paying higher wages. At the same time, citizens were able to gain concessions from the federal government that provided them with increasing rights to health care, a clean environment, and consumer and worker protection. In response to these gains, corporations and governments in the United States and in many other industrialized countries developed governmental and economic policies aimed at reducing the power of workers and personal rights and promoting economic growth and corporate profits.

Consequently, over the last three decades, we have witnessed a significant decline in the political power of teachers and other workers. This shift in economic and social policy has led directly to the realignment of education, and social studies in particular, to meet economic needs. The goal of education, and therefore the goal of teachers, has become promoting knowledge that contributes to individual and societal economic productivity and producing students who are compliant and productive. The curriculum is becoming standardized and is no longer valued for its role in developing political, ethical, and aesthetic citizens. Consequently, education is seen less as a way to critically assess the world and more as a way to improve economic productivity.

Standards, Assessment, and Accountability

Since the early 1990s national commissions and state departments of education have endeavored to produce curriculum standards. Wayne Ross criticizes the standards movement for misleading us with "a simple solution to the complex problem of what and how to teach and, as a result, divert[ing] us from attending to the conditions of schools and how they might be re-envisioned in more democratic ways" (Ross, 2000, p. 203).

Perhaps because of disputes over the national standards, there has been little effort to implement them. However, the lack of national and even clear state standards has not kept states such as New York and school districts such as Rochester from developing high-stakes tests that are used to hold accountable local school districts, schools, and teachers. In New York, teachers are affected both by the state regents' final exams that students are now required to pass in order to receive a diploma and by the high-stakes standardized tests in math, science, social studies, and language arts that occur throughout the student's educational career. Consequently, teachers from all subject areas are pressured to help prepare students to pass high-stakes tests in literacy and math, and the exams in those two ar-

eas become the focus of school for weeks at a time.

It is not, therefore, standards themselves that have transformed what and how teachers teach—after all, it is possible to have standards that emphasize questioning and creativity—but the increasing use of standardized tests and test scores to evaluate districts, schools, teachers, and students. Increasingly, teachers are evaluated only on how well their students perform on standardized tests, not on what and how their students are learning.

Given the difficulty of achieving agreement on standards in various subjects, how do we explain the persistence, particularly that of state departments of education, in developing standards and standardized tests and imposing them on teachers and students? In this chapter I will argue that the standards, assessment, and accountability movements are part of a larger global movement away from Keynesian economic policies and toward the currently dominant neoliberal economic policies. Neoliberal policies emphasize "the deregulation of the economy, trade liberalization, the dismantling of the public sector [such as education, health, and social welfare], and the predominance of the financial sector of the economy over production and commerce" (Vilas, 1996).

Current political and economic policies incorporate the ideas of neoliberalism—promoting knowledge in terms of its contribution to economic growth and discouraging imaginative thinking beyond the needs outlined by the state and its agencies. Such policies have a negative effect on our ability to see the world differently, consequently limiting education and citizenship. While the state and corporations present these policies as natural and inevitable, they are, in fact, historically contingent and therefore capable of being changed.

The link between the rise of neoliberal economic policies and the changing role of the state needs to be revealed and critiqued. Specifically, the neoliberal state, while claiming to limit the intrusion of the state into the life of the individual, in fact increasingly controls the individual in the interest of corporations through techniques of auditing, accounting, and management (Barry, Osborne & Rose, 1996, p. 14).

From Keynesian to Neoliberal Economics: The Rise and Fall of Personal Rights

The late 1960s and the 1970s are often portrayed as years in which radical antiwar protesters were pitted against a conservative, "Archie Bunker" working class. However, a more accurate portrayal of the period would depict not only an antiwar movement both at home and in Vietnam but also a labor movement engaged in disobedience, chaos, "counterplanning," malingering, and huge, militant wildcat labor strikes. It was in response to this crisis—a crisis of "excess" democracy and "excess" working-class power—and the vicissitudes of overproduction that the great right-wing backlash of the

last three decades was born (Parenti, 1999, pp. 108–109). From this economic and political crisis, corporations and the political Center and Right worked to roll back personal and labor rights and eventually supported state agencies, such as state departments of education and school districts, in imposing educational restrictions.

The rise of worker militancy was part of a larger movement by the disenfranchised and powerless to extend their rights (Parenti, 1999). African Americans fought for the right to vote; students, for free speech; and workers, for safer workplaces. Between 1964 and 1979, scores of laws were passed to protect workers, consumers, and the environment. The Environmental Protection Agency and the Occupational Safety and Health Administration were created. It was a time of increasing personal rights at the expense of corporate profits. As workers continued to gain wage concessions through labor activity and strikes, corporate after-tax profits declined from 10 percent in 1965 to 4.5 percent in 1974. "Throughout the rest of the Seventies," writes Christian Parenti, "inflation and unemployment persisted, labor unrest continued, and profits stagnated. Workers were claiming an unprecedented share of the wealth they produced. It was an unmitigated disaster for those who owned, and they would soon take terrible revenge" (Parenti, 1999, p. 118).

This revenge would be carried out by implementing two strategies. First, a recession would be initiated to deflate wage demands. Second, international trade policies would encourage corporations to set up factories and sell consumer goods in less developed countries while nations developed neoliberal economic policies that emphasize economic growth and property rights over social welfare and personal rights.

The first strategy, implementing a recession in order to deflate wage demands, was bluntly stated by Federal Reserve Board Chairman Paul Volcker, who in 1979 provided the following rationale for the recession: "The standard of living of the average American has to decline. I don't think you can escape that" (Parenti, 1999, p. 119). Similarly, Alan Budd, chief economic advisor to Margaret Thatcher, stated in 1992: "Rising unemployment was a very desirable way of reducing the strength of the working classes . . . what was engineered—in Marxist terms—was a crisis in capitalism which re-created a reserve army of labor, and has allowed the capitalists to make high profits ever since" (quoted in Parenti, 1999, p. 108).

The second strategy, that of promoting globalization and neoliberal economic policies and its implications for state and local education policies, will be the focus of the remainder of this chapter.

Deconstructing the Discourses of the Neoliberal State

Under neoliberal policies promoted by the International Monetary Fund and the World Bank, education is no longer promoted as a means of developing educated citizens but is viewed in terms of what it adds to the economy. The purpose of education has become developing the competitive individual who can compete in the marketplace (Peters, 1994, p. 66). As one economist affiliated with Argentina's Ministry of Economics stated: "What we try to measure is how well the training provided by each school fits the needs of production and the labor market" (Puiggros, 1999, p. 27).

The neoliberal state plays a complex role by transforming government from a site where different groups, such as corporations, workers, and the unemployed, bring pressure to bear in support of policies that reflect their own interests to a site where decisions are made based on what is good for economic growth. Further, while the neoliberal state claims to intrude less in the life of the individual, to "get government off people's backs," it in fact intervenes in individuals' lives through other governmental methods and tactics that are promoted, ironically, by those promoting less government.

The analysis of Andrew Barry, Thomas Osborne, and Nicholas Rose in their introduction to *Foucault and Political Reason: Liberalism, Neo-Liberalism, and Rationalities of Government* (1996) superbly describes the changing role and tactics of educational organizations, both governmental (i.e., state departments of education) and quasi-governmental (i.e., the National Board for Professional Teaching Standards). They write: "Paradoxically, neo-liberalism, alongside its critique of the deadening consequences of the 'intrusion of the state' into the life of the individual, has none the less provoked the invention and/or deployment of a whole array of organizational forms and technical methods in order to extend the field with which a certain kind of economic freedom might be practiced in the form of personal autonomy, enterprise and choice" (p. 10).

State departments of education increasingly intrude into the lives of teachers and teacher educators. They undertake their regulation through "technical methods such as accountings and auditing" (Barry, Osborne & Rose, 1996, p. 11). These technical means include standards, testing, and measuring tools that "tie techniques of conduct into specific relations with the concerns of government" and that "reconnect, in a productive way, studies of the exercise of power at the molecular level [in schools] with strategies to program power at a molecular level" (p. 13).

Further, as we saw above in examining recent developments in New York State, "Public authorities seek to employ forms of expertise in order to govern society at a distance, without recourse to any direct forms of repression or intervention. . . . Neo-liberalism, in these terms, involves less a retreat from governmental 'intervention' than a re-inscription of the techniques and forms of expertise required for the exercise of government" (p. 14).

Governmental and quasi-govern-mental organizations seek to govern not by specifying exactly what must be done but by presenting the requirements or standards as rational, unproblematic, and uncontentious and by providing a limited range of conditions under which they must be implemented. This makes it possible for the social actors, whether they be teachers or teacher educators, to have a false sense of choice and freedom. As Rose writes, the "formal political institutions" govern from a distance and "conceive of these actors as subjects of responsibility, autonomy, and choice, and seek to act upon them through shaping and utilizing their freedom" (Rose, 1996, pp. 53–54). Further, writes Rose, governments "are to be analyzed as practices for the 'formation and justification of idealized schemata for representing reality, analyzing it and rectifying it—a kind of intellectual machinery or apparatus for rendering reality thinkable in such a way that it is amenable to political programming" (Rose, 1996, p. 42).

The neoliberal state, through the use of standards, assessments, and accountability, aims to restrict educators to particular kinds of thinking—thinking that conceptualizes education in terms of producing individuals who are economically productive. At the same time, other kinds of rationality are excluded. Rose writes that these rationalities "deploy a certain *style of reasoning*: language here understood as itself a set of 'intellectual techniques' for rendering thinkable and practicable, and constituting domains that are amenable—or not amenable—to reformatory intervention" (Rose, 1996, p. 42).

Michel Foucault, in analyzing the state, wrote about the process of normalization and surveillance (Foucault, 1977, 1979). Thomas Popkewitz, in his book *Struggling for the Soul*, uses a Foucauldian approach to analyze how particular styles of reasoning become prevalent in the school. He particularly focuses on "how different pedagogical knowledges make (construct) the teacher who administers the child. . . . [T]he rules of 'reasoning' about teaching and childhood 'tell us' what to notice (and not to notice), what things belong together, and what things are not 'thinkable' within the rules and standards of the thinking applied (Popkewitz, 1998, p. 17).

These ways of thinking and knowing along with neoliberalism need to be critiqued and resisted. Pierre Bourdieu, in *Acts of Resistance: Against the Tyranny of the Market* (1998), encourages us to resist the logic of neoliberalism. "Everywhere we hear it said, all day long—and this is what gives the dominant discourse its strength—that there is nothing to put forward in opposition to the neo-liberal view, that it has succeeded in presenting itself as self-evident, that there is no alternative. If it is taken for granted in this way, this is a result of a whole labor of symbolic inculcation in which journalists and ordinary citizens participate passively and, above all, a certain number of intellectuals participate actively" (Bourdieu, 1998, p. 29).

The mantra of economic productivity and the market is so persistent as to

override any thought of other possibilities. In response, Bourdieu encourages academics to "analyze the production and circulation of the discourse" promoting the inevitability, the "naturalness" of global neoliberalism. Similarly Foucault, while not commenting specifically on neoliberalism, desired to examine the ways in which the present needs to be "*acted upon* by historical investigation, to be cut up and decomposed so that it can be seen as put together contingently out of heterogeneous elements each having their own conditions of possibility" with the "aim of destabilizing it" (Barry, Osborne & Rose, 1996, p. 5).

The attack on education by business is not new. Throughout the twentieth century, business leaders blamed schools for corporate inefficiencies and pressured educators to meet the needs of business. Beginning in the 1890s, businesses began blaming schools for the nation's economic problems (Kliebard, 1995). After World War II, the National Association of Manufacturers urged schools to "'indoctrinate students with the American way of life' and to teach that 'the American system of free enterprise has done more for human comforts than any other system'" (Fones-Wolf, 1994, p. 200). Since the publication of *A Nation at Risk* in 1983, schools have once again been the recipient of corporate blame for the state of the economy.

But the difference between then and now is the increasing hegemony of an all-encompassing discourse embedded within not only national but international policies. Such hegemonic discourses and policies make it difficult for teachers and others to resist "the tyranny of the market."

Possibilities for Resistance

Under the current neoliberal regime, education is valued for increasing the economic productivity of students as future workers and corporate profits. This shift represents "the triumph of the economy over politics and culture" (Kellner, 2000, p. 307).

However, as Bourdieu reminds us, writing as both a sociologist and a political activist: "knowledge must be deconstructed, . . . categories are contingent social derivations and instruments of (symbolic power)" and "the structures of discourse are politically charged social preconstructions" (Bourdieu & Wacquant, 1992, p. 47). The way in which the world is organized is not invariant but historically constituted and thus socially variable (p. 19). Therefore, it is crucial that we understand how neoliberalism changes the discourses about who we are and what we can think about. We need to examine the current social structures and to discourse about the role they play in the distribution of "material resources and in the forms of systems of classification, the mental and bodily schemata that function as symbolic templates for the practical activities—conduct, thoughts, feelings, and judgments—of social agents" (p. 7).

So far, the state's efforts to audit and control teachers have been largely uncontested. State policy making has been privatized (Blackmore, 2000, p. 140). Teachers are increasingly losing control over their work as test scores become supreme. As educators and citizens, we need to analyze and critique recent efforts to control teachers and students through standards and high-stakes standardized tests.

Acknowledgments

I would like to thank my doctoral students for their assistance on this paper, especially my doctoral assistant Camille Martina.

References

Barry, A., Osborne, T., and Rose, N. (1996). *Foucault and political reason: Liberalism, neo-liberalism, and rationalities of government*. Chicago: University of Chicago Press.

Blackmore, J. (2000). Globalization: A useful concept for feminists rethinking theory and strategies in education? In N. Burbules and C. A. Torres (Eds.), *Globalization and education: Critical perspectives*. New York: Routledge.

Bourdieu, P. (1998). *Acts of resistance: Against the tyranny of the market*. New York: The New Press.

Bourdieu, P., and Wacquant, L. (1992). *An invitation to reflexive sociology*. Chicago: University of Chicago.

Fones-Wolf, E. (1994). *Selling free enterprise: The business assault on labor and liberalism, 1945–1960*. Urbana: University of Illinois, 1994.

Foucault, M. (1979). *The history of sexuality*. London: Penguin.

Foucault. M. (1997). *Discipline and punish: The birth of the prison*. London: Penguin.

Kellner, D. (2000). Globalization and new

social movements: Lessons for critical theory and pedagogy. In N. Burbules and C. A. Torres (Eds.), *Globalization and education: Critical perspectives*. New York: Routledge.

Kliebard, H. (1995). The struggle for the American curriculum: 1893–1958 (2nd ed.). New York: Routledge.

Parenti, C. (1999). Atlas finally shrugged: Us against them in the me decade. *The Baffler, 13*, 108–120.

Peters, M. (1994). Individualism and community: Education and the politics of difference. *Discourse, 14*(2), 65–78.

Popkewitz, T. (1998*). Struggling for the soul: The politics of schooling and the construction of the teacher*. New York: Teachers College Press.

Puiggros, A. (1999). *Neoliberalism and education in Latin America*. Boulder, CO: Westview Press.

Rose, N. (1996). Governing "advanced" liberal democracies. In A. Barry, T. Osborne, and N. Rose (Eds.), *Foucault and political reason: Liberalism, neo-liberalism, and rationalities of government*. Chicago: University of Chicago Press.

Ross, E. W. (2000). Diverting democracy: The curriculum standards movement and social studies education. In D. Hursh and E. W. Ross (Eds.), *Democratic social studies: Social studies for social change*. New York: Falmer Press.

Vilas, C. (1996). Neoliberal social policy: Managing poverty (somehow). *NACLA Report on the America, 29*(2), 16–21.

EDUCATIONAL STANDARDS

For Whose Purposes? For Whose Children?

Patricia Hinchey

By way of introduction, let me offer a test and a metaphor. Please complete the following test item conscientiously before reading on.

Select the best answer to the following question:

> If a van carrying high school volunteers home to northeastern Pennsylvania leaves from an orphanage in Mexico City, the van will travel:
>   a. north and east
>   b. south
>   c. east
>   d. through Canada
>   e. all of the above

Does the answer seem self-evident? Or, does it at least seem clear that *d.*, and therefore *b.* and *e.*, can be eliminated? After all, what sense would it make to drive from Mexico all the way north to Canada if the final destination—Pennsylvania—is obviously well south of the Canadian border? And once those nonsensical answers are eliminated, does it seem obvious that the answer would therefore be *a. north and east* rather than *c. east*? Yes, of course, that's right: Pennsylvania is north and east of Mexico City and therefore those directions would have to be the best route and *a.* the best answer.

Such logic seems to make perfect sense, and it's a good bet that any test maker would identify *a.* as the correct answer. Still, no matter how logical a northeast route might seem, it was not the one actually taken in the real-world case of my son, who did indeed travel home to Pennsylvania from a service experience in Mexico City via Toronto, Canada. Huh? Say what? Were the Jesuit chaperones who drove the van stupid, as they might appear to a test maker who insisted that there was clearly only one best answer, and that it was *a*.? Couldn't the drivers see that the best route clearly could not include a visit to Canada, which would take them far north of Pennsylvania and force them to backtrack south?

Not at all. Although test makers conveniently ignore this reality, often there is no way to designate a best answer to a question without making an assumption about it. And, as assumptions vary, so will "best" answers. The assumption that a test maker might mistake for a self-evident truth—that the most desirable route would be the most efficient route—simply was not valid in the case of the Jesuit educators who led my son's trip to Mexico. Their assumption was not that the trip should be as efficient as possible, but that it should be as educative as possible. For them, the best route would serve several purposes in addition to returning the boys to their parents.

One purpose was accomplished before the group ever left school grounds. The boys would have to get along in close quarters for several weeks, so allowing them to plan a route through destinations they managed to agree upon, within some very generous boundaries, not only broadened their travel experience but also provided practice in the essential skill of negotiation. Moreover, a longer trip home allowed the boys more time to process their experience of living in a Mexican orphanage. What did they learn from being the outsiders in a foreign culture? What did they learn from living under conditions that seemed luxurious to the Mexican children but impoverished to them, in a

place where furniture, space, and privacy were minimal, where food was basic and rarely varied, and where work was physical and unending? What did they learn from seeing one of their own countless faded, name-brand T-shirts become a Mexican orphan's single most prized possession?

The assumption on this trip was that the more time the boys had together on the way home, the more opportunities they would have to reflect on, discuss, and learn from their experience. In contrast to the "logical" assumption that the best route is always the shortest route, the Jesuits' goal was for the trip home to allow enough time and opportunity for maximum learning. Therefore, no matter how patently silly it might first appear to traipse north to Canada and then south again, the best answer to the opening question for the Jesuits and their charges was genuinely *e. all of the above*. The world and its experiential richness rarely operate in the black/white, yes/no, right/wrong fashion that test makers so often assume.

The reality is that no one can reliably determine what makes most sense in any real-world context, what constitutes the best plan or answer in the face of any genuine dilemma, without questioning relevant assumptions and goals. Despite the insistence of many public figures that standards are obviously the best answer to the question "What should be done to improve education?", that assertion needs to be examined and defended in terms of its assumptions and goals before it merits widespread endorsement.

When officials call for standards and high-stakes testing based on standards as an "obvious" way to improve education, they are calling for a particular kind of standards—the version that Joe Kincheloe, Shirley Steinberg, and Danny Weil refer to as "technical standards" (see Weil, "Functionalism," this volume; Steinberg & Kincheloe, 1997, intro.). Technical standards incorporate one set of assumptions and one set of goals while entirely ignoring alternate assumptions and goals—those underlying the alternative version of standards that Kincheloe, Steinberg, and Weil refer to as "standards of complexity." An informed public must realize that before it is possible to judge any proposal that claims "*This* is obviously the best way to improve public education," it is necessary to ask—among other questions—"What assumptions are being made here about the goals of public education?"

The more that a test maker or politician or corporate executive insists that the answer to this question is obvious, the less we should trust the answer. There have always been a variety of competing purposes that might be embedded in public schools, and whatever we choose to do in schools will serve certain purposes and undermine others, whether any of those purposes are articulated or not. As surely as the "best" route home depends on the particular goal of the traveler, the merit of any call for standards depends upon whose goals are being served and whose goals are being sacrificed.

What Is "Public" about Public Schools?

Among common and decidedly implicit assumptions often made about public schools is this one: Public schools exist to serve American children. This key assumption is evident in rhetoric about "our kids" and what we owe them in schools: "*Our* kids"— who are presented as being the obvious responsibility of the entire community—deserve safety, challenge, good teachers, and so on. Of course, no one would argue against providing students with such things in schools, and because all of those things are good for kids, it seems self-evident that the purpose of schools is to promote the welfare of children. Nevertheless, that assumption is a fallacy.

In the history of the United States, public schools have never been benevolent and altruistic government institutions focused on the welfare of children. Instead, government supports public schools out of public tax monies in order to accomplish goals of the *state*. Although state purposes clearly underlie many educational initiatives, they go unnoticed because proposals are saturated with language that emphasizes the "obvious" goal of benefit to the child. It takes a very close look and a great deal of thought to penetrate the child-centered rhetoric and to uncover the real goals public education serves.

Joel Spring, expert in many facets of the philosophy and history of public education, describes three categories that are useful in sorting through the wide range of purposes common in public schools: *political*, *economic*, and *social* (2000, pp. 1–20). Spring suggests that *political goals* include those necessary to ensure the survival of democratic government in the United States. From this perspective, public schools are the means of identifying future political leaders and of educating the public for effective participation in democratic citizenship. Early on, leaders of the new United States had to struggle with the question of who would lead the country in years to come. No one believed the ignorant could effectively do so, but the belief that leaders needed to be well educated led to a fear that a ruling aristocracy might evolve if only the wealthy had access to education. As a result, even the earliest political leaders favored some form of public education to protect the country from the development of a wealthy and oppressive oligarchy. The idea that poor children as well as rich children need to be educated for possible political leadership, then, is one that was woven into the fabric of U.S. culture at its very founding, one that validates our cultural claim that any child can become president.

Of course, democracy also requires the participation of an informed citizenry, and so in addition to well-educated leaders, the country needs citizens who believe that democracy is the best of all possible governments and who have sufficient education to make informed and reasoned political decisions. Citizens must be able to read in order to be informed on issues.

They need to understand how government works in order to accept and play their own active role in it. They need to believe that democratic government is the most desirable government if the country is to remain politically stable and free from rebellious challenges. They need to believe that the country is firmly based on meritocracy, a fair system that gives all citizens equal opportunity to shape the future based on their abilities.

The public schools, then, were established largely to help ensure the survival of a democratic form of government in the United States, and today's schools continue to serve this political goal. Schools still cultivate loyalty to the existing system of government and its leaders, as they have from the inception of public schooling. For example, every February silhouettes of George Washington and Abraham Lincoln crop up in the windows of elementary schools nationwide, as dependably as crocuses pop up in the spring. Great leaders gave us a great country, children learn, and we need to remember that and to honor them and the government that is their legacy. Every morning, children pledge allegiance to the flag in a public ceremony affirming political loyalty. Much of what is done in schools, from voting for class president to writing essays on such topics as "The American I Most Admire," is intended to promote the patriotic mind-set that every government needs for its own survival.

Social goals, in Spring's characterization, involve efforts to shape and control young people in ways that will, theoretically, contribute to the good of society at large. Early on, for example, school attendance was made compulsory in an effort to reduce juvenile delinquency and crime, and today there is still a good bit of talk about "keeping kids off the streets" until they're at least sixteen, in the hope of keeping them out of trouble. More than one theorist has believed that schooling reduces the need for both current and future police enforcement because while keeping youth off the street, schools can concurrently inculcate values—respect for authority, say, or for hard work—that characterize a voluntarily hard working, taxpaying, deferential citizenry.

In recent decades, the expectation that schools will remedy social problems has steadily expanded. Schooling in itself is expected to lift students out of poverty, and this improvement is expected to have the domino effect of reducing unacceptable crime rates. In addition, the public has increasingly looked to schools to curb growing drug and alcohol abuse, and to educate safe drivers, and to curb premarital intercourse and pregnancies, and to prepare the young to balance checkbooks, maintain marriages, and responsibly parent children—and so on, and so on, and so on with, not unexpectedly, increasing controversy over *which* values and habits should be included on the list.

Currently, for example, there is heated public debate over what schools should say about homosexuality—if they are to say anything at all—as well as what they should or shouldn't say about AIDS, abortion, and contraception. Because schools can promote values among young people, they have long been recognized as potential tools of social regulation. In an increasingly diverse society, the classroom has become a prized means for shaping social climate and norms, for shaping the way citizens will live in the future—married or not, religious or not, bigoted or not. Because curriculum can have significant social impact (witness the countless parents who have been shamed into recycling by children exposed to environmental education), passionate public debate over what will and won't be taught in classrooms is sure to continue.

Finally, *economic goals* are those assuring the continued wealth and financial stability of the democracy. It's revealing to note, however, that many of the values that schools promote as being in the obvious best interests of society (like obedience and unquestioning respect for authority) also function to nurture the kind of worker that corporations might find most desirable. As public schools emerged in the late nineteenth century, for example, they were designed largely to educate future factory workers, and it is not hard to see how classroom routines acclimated students to a factory environment. Suffering the tedium of repetitious schoolwork prepared young people to tolerate the boredom of assembly lines. Learning to complete any task without question simply because an authority figure so ordered prepared them to meekly follow the orders of a supervisor. Being confined in large groups and uncomfortable conditions, lacking the freedom even to urinate at will, conditioned them to expect bosses to control their bodies as well as their minds in the workplace. In direct contrast, private schools—which have traditionally educated the wealthy children of factory *owners*—have prided themselves on offering active learning and small classes, an education preparing them for leadership rather than drudgery.

Over time, public schools have undergone changes that make it appear that they educate children more democratically, that they educate for much broader options than factory work. This democratization is thought to be embodied in the way schools now sort students into several categories. In this system, students are tracked into courses of study geared to the particular future the school determines most suitable for each child. A student deemed to be smart and hardworking (according to standardized tests, school performance, and teacher opinion) is offered rigorous coursework and schooled for college, while apparently less able students are offered coursework generally considered less challenging—generally vocational training. Those labeled least able are shuffled off to "remedial" courses, where they rarely remain long enough to graduate.

Schools and proponents of tracking believe that all of this sorting is reliable, truly based on merit and intrinsic ability. From this perspective, the school simply does the marketplace

the favor of identifying which young people might be suited for what kind of slot in the labor market and then providing appropriate education for students in each slot. A student from a low track who ended up in a minimal-wage job would, according to this perspective, have lacked the intrinsic talent to rise any higher. This is the "You can't make a silk purse out of a sow's ear" philosophy of education.

That job training is a primary responsibility of public schools is an idea trumpeted daily by politicians, business leaders, and assorted educators who insist that only a first-class, challenging education can keep the American workforce competitive. So loud and ubiquitous are such assertions, in fact, that underpinning nearly every public pronouncement and reform scheme is the implicit assumption that *the* most important job of public schools is to prepare the kind of workers that employers say they need. These days, businesses are very busy handing schools specifications for the kinds of workers they want, and many people simply accept the idea that schools should produce workers exactly according to those specifications. The claim is that if schools don't attend to this task, the GNP and the economic future of the country will be in danger. In some cases, economic peril is even more immediate. When schools don't teach young people what employers specify, executives begin suggesting to politicians that they might just have to take their businesses—and jobs—elsewhere (Morrison, 1996). For this reason, politicians, administrators, and parents alike tend to listen closely when business executives talk about curriculum.

Implicit Goals and Particular Agendas

Although many talk about education reform as if its goals were self-evident and immune to challenge, they are not. A major assumption embedded in public discourse about education is that any reform should strive to increase student performance on a variety of standardized tests, such as national competency exams and SATs. However, this tacit assumption goes unchallenged largely because psychometricians have spent decades persuading the public that numbers are always important and always trustworthy. Faith in good test scores as a reflection of quality has become so widespread that higher scores on any test have come to seem a self-evident good—like the assumption that any good route will be a short route.

The assumption that higher scores on some standardized test will indicate improved education underpins the technical standards movement, and it contains enormous implications for classroom practice. Essentially, by stressing a vast body of core content, technical standards promote still more of the same kinds of classroom practice we've had for decades: rote memorization of facts, facts, and more facts and the mechanical use of standard formulas to solve textbook problems. Both the assumption and the pedagogy implicit in the technical stan-

dards movement require thoughtful questioning. If technical standards are imposed on schools and the result is more of the same in classrooms, then whose agenda will public education serve? Which political, social, and economic goals will be advanced?

I would argue that the agenda and goals of the current standards movement, which are widely supported by politicians and business people as opposed to educators in the trenches, are those of political conservatives, of politicians protecting their own careers, and of business people interested in increasing their six- and seven-figure salaries and in paying larger and larger dividends to stockholders. Proponents of technical standards seem far less interested in educational reform than they are in protecting the existing power structure and their own, largely financial, interests. Ironically, the technical standards movement therefore supports an elite who function, and would continue to function, as the very oligarchy the founding fathers feared.

Consider, as a preliminary example, the need for schools to educate patriotic citizens. Which definition of patriotism should that be? The bumper sticker mind-set of "Love it or leave it" or an alternate conception that casts thoughtful dissent as both a patriot's right and responsibility? The first promotes blind obedience, a sheeplike mentality among followers, whereas the second promotes a critically questioning disposition, a habit of deciding for oneself the merit of an idea or plan and then taking a public stance, even if—perhaps especially if—that stance opposes majority opinion.

Is it genuinely in the best interests of the entire population for the norm to be "My country, right or wrong—but it's never wrong"? Do we want citizens ready and willing to sacrifice their children and spouses to any war politicians decide to wage? Or do we want citizens who ask hard questions about *why* such sacrifice is necessary; who exactly the sacrifice will benefit; how exactly they will benefit; and why politicians think the benefits are worth the wholesale death of young, and sometimes not so young, Americans? Will the country be better off if its people believe that any war must be a good war if leaders have decided to deploy troops? Does our national experience tell us that World War I, World War II, the Korean conflict, the Viet Nam conflict, and Operation Desert Storm must all have been equally justified on the simple grounds that leaders chose to send Americans to fight in them? Should citizens never ask questions and voice opinions about government actions? Should they be taught that it's unpatriotic to ask questions like "Who would make money on this war?" and "Whose sons and fathers and mothers and sisters are likely to die in this war?"

The answer to the question of which type of loyalty schools are expected to promote is rarely explicitly discussed, except perhaps in court cases brought by schools seeking to force students to participate in the ubiquitous flag pledging ritual. When it takes Supreme Court orders to de-termine and then remind schools that students are citizens guaranteed certain basic rights—including the right to follow their conscience in religious matters—then it's apparent that schools are currently devoted to producing mindless, unquestioned loyalty to government. Schools seeking court orders to force students to participate in loyalty pledges is just one example. Another is using textbooks that sanitize American history, universally depicting historical events as demonstrations of great American heroism and virtue.

Most, maybe even all, students have heard the slogans "Remember the Alamo!" and "Remember the Maine!" but have little understanding of the actual events behind them. This is true partly because classroom instruction stresses the memorization of factual tidbits instead of nurturing genuine understanding among students. It is also true, however, because history textbooks shape student perception by a careful selection of material. For example, a text might well mention a hardy and brave band at the Alamo defending that fort to the death, but it is sure to conveniently leave out any nasty questions about legitimate Spanish ownership of the territory in dispute. And although the Maine was not sunk by enemy fire after all, that incident is still cited as an example of American courage rather than as the convenient excuse for American aggression that it actually was.

Such textbooks mythologize people who died for the country while ignoring the historical truths about the causes of their deaths. They over-whelmingly tell the story of white men while ignoring or downplaying the contributions of women and the effects of white settlement on such groups as African Americans and Native Americans. This kind of selective history perpetuates the grand American narrative of a consistently glorious past, a narrative that is far more inspirational without factual clutter. What students are force-fed is an unquestioning loyalty to a country they are encouraged to perceive as having only a righteous and glorious history. Theft of Native American and Spanish territory and the wholesale killings of native peoples are inconvenient realities expunged from the national saga as it is currently replayed in schools, leaving a pervasive sense of Anglo-Saxon cultural superiority.

It is for this reason that the much more inclusive history/social studies standards drafted near the close of the twentieth century were widely reviled by conservatives—though they were widely embraced by the same people who embrace complexity. As an alternative to a definition of patriotism as blind loyalty and to the teaching of history as nationalistic propaganda, proponents of complexity argue for a patriotism that examines the various political and economic factors behind historical events and that includes a willingness to acknowledge past mistakes in order to learn from them. It calls for a definition of "an American" as something more inclusive than an aggressive white male.

For example, if students as future

voters are to genuinely understand why in the year 2000 several Native American tribes were pressing lawsuits against the United States government for reparation and the return of territory, they need to understand the shameful treachery of earlier politicians who strategized the theft of Native American land. They need to know about the government policy of starving tribes as a means of bringing them onto the reservations. And they need to understand that the contemporary poverty, drug abuse, and other social problems on tribal land can be readily linked to earlier duplicitous government actions. Lacking such knowledge, they will be ignorant voters and very probably angry bigots as well.

But instead of having learned such inconvenient facts, the vast majority of American students are barely aware that Native Americans even *exist* contemporaneously. While Navajo tribal lands include over 16 million acres and span multiple states and while other reservations exist all over the nation with their own leaders and political agendas, history books usually fail to mention this component of the American population at all—just as they fail to explain why there are Hmong people living in California (an explanation that would involve an inconvenient admission of more shameful behavior during the Viet Nam conflict) or why there has never been an African American president (an explanation that would involve acknowledging historical as well as current racism). To call attention to such affronts to genuine democracy would be to call for change in a power structure that is currently thoroughly entrenched. And obviously, that is not a goal the entrenched are willing to readily accept.

Any politician who calls for standards will, by default, be supporting one or the other of the opposing definitions of what it means for a school to educate a democratic citizenry, depending on what is to be taught and tested. Will tests ask nearly exclusively about white and male American war heroes, as they have for so many years, with romanticized versions of Betsy Ross, Sacajawea, or George Washington Carver thrown in as tokens of democratic representation? Or will they ask about a more factual, more inclusive, and less sanitized history so that students can understand the issues that accompany a truly multicultural democracy and, as adults, vote on them from an informed perspective? Will questions about the United States slaughter of Native American women and children at Sand Creek ever appear next to the battle it provoked, commonly referred to in American lore as Custer's Last Stand? Given the conservative uproar over and opposition to more inclusive curricula designed by the National Council of Teachers of Social Studies and constant conservative attempts to censor more representational literature in language arts classes, it seems certain that a core curriculum would be more of the "same old, same old," promoting the same old goals of established power.

As already noted, as the standards tests go, so will go the instruction. One of the reasons standards supporters argue so vehemently for standards and exams is that they expect the tests to drive instruction—and they will. If history tests focus on wars and military leaders, then wars and military leaders will continue to be the center of classroom instruction. So high have the stakes become already in standardized testing that teacher cheating has become an issue (Viadero, 2000). If teachers are willing to cheat to get the mandated results, if schools are willing to fire teachers whose students don't do well on whatever test comes down the pike, if states are constantly threatening takeovers of schools, then there is no question that the tests will promote the goals and definitions implicit in the questions asked. It's safe to count on the largely prosperous and prominent supporters of technical standards, who profit most from the status quo, to make sure that test questions *will* be about the domestic Betsy Ross rather than the rebellious Charlotte Perkins Gilman, about the Gettysburg Address rather than the 1969 Senate-issued report *Indian Education: A National Tragedy—A National Challenge.*

Yes, public schools serve the political purpose of supporting democratic government and a patriotic citizenry. But which definition of patriotism will students be exposed to? Love it or leave it? Or a definition that includes dissent as the constitutionally protected right of an informed citizenry? Yes, public schools serve social goals, seeking to improve social conditions. But whose definition of a good society will be imposed? That of the devout, who believe that beginning every day with prayer would go far in improving the behavior of young people? Or that of civil rights activists, who are more concerned with protecting personal freedom and who insist on the strict separation of church and state and on prayer as a private matter? And yes, schools do need to educate workers who are able to earn a living and who don't need to depend on the state for support. But what is a "good worker"? Is it one who follows orders without question, always with an eye on the corporate bottom line? Or is it one who has the intelligence and courage to blow the whistle when companies are sacrificing public health and safety to greed, as has happened in the tobacco industry?

There is, no doubt, some oversimplification in presenting such issues in terms of a dichotomy—technical standards vs. standards of complexity, and support for an existing elite vs. pursuit of social justice. However, juxtaposing the goals, assumptions, and practices implicit in the two oppositional standards proposals clarifies critical differences between them. Those who support standards of complexity have nothing to fear by speaking openly about their goals because they pursue ends that benefit the entire population: genuine democracy and social justice. On the other hand, there may be good reason why proponents of technical standards do not talk openly about their goals except in terms of

improving education and *raising test scores.* Exposed by thoughtful analysis, the goals of technical standards speak far less well of their supporters' agenda.

Implicit Goals of Technical Standards: Who Benefits?

Implicit Political Goals

The most obvious political concern of the technical standards movement is that of the politicians, who are far less concerned with the education of the populace, or with any other issue, than they are with getting themselves elected or reelected. Many politicians who have jumped on the current standards bandwagon have done so not because they sincerely believe that standards will genuinely improve education but because endorsing standards offers the appearance of caring about education without supporting any painful or costly alternative strategies or angering constituents.

Make no mistake, the technical standards movement is not about improving the education of young people. If improvement were the real goal, talk about implementing standards would have to include talk about funding reform. Educators like Jonathan Kozol have spent decades documenting educational problems that grow out of our current system of inequitable funding. Because as a country we rely primarily on real estate taxes to fund schools, all public schools are far from being equal. One school, for example, may have multiple computers in every classroom because it is blessed with wealthy homeowners and generous tax support. Meanwhile, in an adjacent district with low real estate values, another school cannot even provide its students with crayons or books. In one school district, there may be one highly qualified, full-time teacher for every twenty to twenty-four students, while in a nearby poorer district, a school may be unable to attract even one full-time teacher, qualified or not, for every thirty-five to forty students. Wealthy students may attend new, multibuilding campuses, while across the river poor students are crowded into abandoned roller skating rinks and into old gymnasiums. Every school's funding depends largely on its local tax base, and the poorest schools in the poorest areas are always the least supported and consequently have the least to offer their students in personnel, physical plant, support services, and supplies.

For all the rhetoric about good education not depending solely on money, there is a point at which the lack of money makes good education virtually impossible. How can children learn to read without books? How can they master math without pencil and paper? How can they become knowledgeable about history when the books they do have name Richard Nixon as the current president? How can children with asthma—so common in poor areas— concentrate on academics in windowless buildings where the air is choked with dust? Readers who have not seen

such conditions and who doubt they exist should either read Jonathan Kozol (1991, 1995) or start visiting the kinds of schools he documents. They do exist and they are a national disgrace. In recent years, state supreme courts have been acknowledging these unjust disparities and charging states to formulate more equitable funding systems. Nonetheless, politicians and the public at large continue to stubbornly refuse to acknowledge the problem. As history books sanitize history, standards proponents sanitize educational issues by ignoring these inconvenient facts because these educational truths will not help anyone get elected.

One reason for this is that a change to more equitable funding has proven to be a political nightmare. A New Jersey governor, James J. Florio, who implemented a more equitable school-funding plan soon found himself navigating highways flooded with cars sporting *Impeach Florio* bumper stickers. Florio, understandably if regrettably, jettisoned his own plan. Similar attempts have failed in other states. Charged by state courts with designing more equitable funding, state leaders have devised "equity" plans with no substance, hoping to appease voters with minimal changes and to appease courts with the appearance of reform. Courts, however, have not been fooled, and they have repeatedly rejected such sham plans in several states.

Because politicians know that helping to implement real funding reform might well end their political careers, politicians have rushed to embrace the current standards movement as a placebo. Supporting technical standards gives them fodder for speeches on their commitment to improving the schools without the political peril inherent in more substantive reform strategies. In short, insisting that states (1) implement standards and (2) punish students, teachers, and schools that don't measure up is an unrecognized form of political cowardice.

The teachers who have no books to teach reading and the students who have no pencils and paper for math will not suddenly be able to improve performance without those supplies. To punish them when they continue to fail to meet standards will allow politicians to proclaim their toughness and their insistence on quality, acting as though this empty rhetorical triumph can be equated with a good-faith reform effort. The technical standards movement, which insists that high-stakes testing will automatically bring quality, is a fraud designed to produce political capital.

Moreover, the type of standards being promoted, based on retention and regurgitation, supports the kind of schools that will continue to nurture obedience and docility rather than a critical, questioning disposition. And the theme of authoritarian control and obedience will bring with it the "Love it or leave it" notion of patriotism. Any system of rote memorization casts the teacher as an unquestionable authority and the student as a silent, obedient listener. Only the authority can know the right answer, and students must always defer to those who know better. Rather than learning how to formulate good judgment, students learn to doubt their own thinking, to routinely consider themselves naïve in the face of authority. This mental disposition lingers in citizens who are disposed to support any scheme government might propose, assuming that government experts know best what everyone should think about an issue.

Thus, technical standards cultivate dependence on authority. In direct contrast, standards of complexity stress critical thinking and autonomy. They encourage students to question any official representation of knowledge and to ask "Whose 'truth' is this? Who benefits from this version of the truth? Who is disadvantaged by it?" Proponents of complexity argue against tests involving right/wrong answers because they distort and over-simplify the world and undermine personal autonomy. A technical curriculum cheats students of the opportunity to learn to think for themselves and is much more likely to lead to a herd mentality than to the intelligence and independence required to ask hard questions. Every issue comes down to identifying who is "right" and every question is answered with: "If you're not with us, then you're against us"—a climate that inhibits honest discussion of difficult issues.

Nor are sanitized texts and reliance on authority the only elements of a standardized curriculum that promote mindless conformity and inhibit independent thinking. The imposition of standardized tests also curtails the possibility of independent and creative thinking. Because the test always looms around the corner, teachers are unlikely to explore avenues of curiosity with their students. "Is there another way to solve this kind of problem?" a student might ask. "It doesn't matter—you know one way, and that's enough for the test. We have to move on," a teacher might be forced to answer, given the overwhelming content and relentless clock-ticking that standards bring. "Can we go to the museum and *see* these paintings?" "No, there's no time. You know the titles and artists; that's enough for the test."

In this high-stakes environment, what is important in the classroom becomes whatever is important to those who have structured the tests and, through them, the classroom activity. The more challenging the curriculum (which is to say, the more inclusive the curriculum), the less space there is for teachers and students to bring in their own curiosity, interests, experiences, and concerns. There is room to focus only on the "facts" imposed upon them by politicians and business people outside the classroom. Far from strongholds of democratic activity, schools serving uncritical technical standards will remain mind-numbing factories shaping citizens in the habits of believing and doing what they are told without question. Students will learn to sacrifice their own curiosity and interests to the standardization imposed by one-size-fits-all, factual testing, designed by "experts" far removed from any classroom.

In addition to cultivating docility, technical standards also support the political agenda of the established elite by helping to maintain the myth of meritocracy. Of course, given the incredible disparity in resources, not all students will succeed. However, since poor students are those most likely to fail, this inequality is not a problem—from a political perspective. Someone has to work in fast food places, and someone has to sweep the streets. Someone has to take the blame for being lazy and stupid in order to provide some excuse for the dismal failures that poor schools will always have until funding inequities and other social injustices are resolved. But politically speaking, the continued failure of the poor is not an issue, especially since they are less likely to vote than the affluent and certainly will not be making large contributions to campaign funds. It's the middle class who must go to college and provide human capital for industry, and the more they're conditioned to do as they're told, the better.

What is important is only that schools continue to *appear* to offer all children an equal chance to succeed. If that appearance can be maintained, then the myth of American meritocracy can continue, along with the comfort of those who are well established in the current economy. Smug citizens living in upscale communities can reassure themselves not only that they've earned what they have but also that others can do the same if they just work hard enough in school, if they just apply themselves to the standards. If this false notion is perpetrated and maintained, the public discourse will not have to admit the absurdity of asking students to work harder at reading when they have no books or asking them to master technology when they have no computers.

The reality that the poor will very likely continue to fail actually makes it imperative for schools to continue nurturing the traditional definition of patriotism as uncritical acceptance of whatever government does. Were citizens taught to critically question current conditions, suddenly there might be significant challenges to the existing unjust and elitist structures now in place. This, of course, would be a threat to the status quo. So it is not surprising that mindless patriotism is promoted not only by sanitized history books and the installation of teacher as ultimate authority but also by several other essentially meaningless trappings common in public schools. Pledging allegiance to the flag and praising former presidents are easy routines to carry out, as is the establishment of a student government. None of these, however, provide meaningful lessons and experiences in genuinely democratic citizenship. Like the rhetoric of standards, the rhetoric and rituals of public schools regarding democratic education are surface gestures lacking substance.

For example, student government leaders are often elected on the same grounds as public officials: charisma, eloquence, looks, and promises. These qualities are enough, and the student body is not encouraged to check later performance against earlier promises,

as voters so rarely do in their communities. Nor does the student government have any real power; to learn this, student leaders need only try to effect substantive change in school policy. In fact, schools are among the most antidemocratic institutions imaginable. Students do not have freedom of speech or movement and precious little choice in any number of areas, ranging from where they may eat to when they may, and it is much easier and more comfortable for the powerful to praise democracy than to practice it.

To develop an active, critically questioning democratic citizenry would require very different standards, the kind promoted in these pages. Mass memorization would have to give way to diversity and creativity. What authorities think and the solutions to problems they provide would need to become far less important than the thoughts and solutions of students themselves. The most important thing would be not *the* answer to a problem, but the ability to depict how different solutions might be more or less appealing when examined from different perspectives, how different options offer greater or lesser advantages to various stakeholders.

For example, a current political and economic problem is the insistence of Native Americans that much of their land be returned to them. From a Native American perspective, this is a just solution because for decades tribes have been confined to the most arid and unproductive land in the country after the richest lands were seized from them. But the Black owners of a bed-and-breakfast property on land in dispute might see that solution as punishment for the crimes of others they have no connection to and never benefited from. From their perspective, such mandatory payment for crimes committed by others simply multiplies the original injustice. Both of these perspectives have merit; neither can be judged simply right or wrong. When we insist that students function in a limited world of yes/no and right/wrong answers, we give them no grounds for decisions except the rhetoric of authorities. Instead, we should be helping students learn to enjoy the hard thinking needed to untangle complex issues.

Of course, the votes of citizens who thoughtlessly follow the most persuasive speaker are easily won by politicians offering incredibly simplistic answers to complex problems—as in the case of those who promote technical standards as a reasonable cure for a problem largely caused by decades of political, economic, and social neglect of vast numbers of America's children. This is why the technical standards movement has such great political currency. Outside the educational community, few citizens are asking the hard question: "How is simply telling teachers and students that these tests *must* be passed going to magically make everything in schools better, especially in cases where the problem is lack of money rather than lack of will?" Schools have not educated people to ask such questions; they've

been too busy promoting respect for authority and political heroes.

So wishful thinking and blustery threats have seduced an uncritical public into thinking that technical standards are the answer. However, if they were the answer, if we could change outcomes simply by telling people they must do better or they'll be punished, we would long ago have remedied not only poor education but also car accidents, rude behavior, maybe even bad cooking. Simply wishing and threatening, however, is never going to make anything so.

Implicit Social Goals

As is evident from the above discussion, schools focusing on routine and memorization—a tradition reinforced by the technical standards movement—value and reward such personal characteristics as obedience and respect for authority. These characteristics are valued not only by school officials trying to ensure "coverage" of mandated curricula but also by parents, mainstream religious leaders, police forces, and the military, all for a variety of reasons of their own.

During the activist decade of the 1960s, when young people challenged the government and defied police, government, and military authorities, public schools and universities were harshly criticized for tolerating dissent among the young. Schools were too permissive, it was argued, and they needed to do more to keep students in line. Student activism demonstrated an uncomfortable social reality: an activist citizenry tends to be disruptive and challenging, an ever-present threat to those comfortably in power. Therefore, under the guise of pursuing a civilized and mannered society, schools reinforced the traditional rigorous control over students, teaching them to "go along" with teachers, and by implication all authorities, in order to "get along."

In the 1990s, a terrible spate of student violence gave conservative religious leaders an excuse to raise again the issue of school prayer, which the Supreme Court has now judged unconstitutional several times. It also gave parents and administrators an excuse to argue that schools need to be still more controlling of student bodies and minds, so that backpacks, the color black, and raincoats became marks of the student "outlaw." The fact that the violence was completely unexpected from the view of parents and authorities suggests that an explanation for such behavior must involve factors more complex than "There is no public prayer in schools" or "Schools don't monitor the clothing and belongings of students rigorously enough." Again, easy answers serving private agendas are substituted for thoughtful analysis that might look into messy social issues and difficult questions, like what kind of social climate might produce more students who value neither their own lives nor the lives of others?

It seems specious to argue that school prayer and stricter dress codes will cure student violence, but those actions fit the agenda of many conservative religious leaders and parents. The obvious benefit for these groups is that any measure that further conditions students to be controlled by authorities will make it easier for them as authority figures to exercise control in other areas. Beyond that benefit, however, such arguments also promote the cause of those religious citizens who would like to realize their goal of mandatory school prayer, and they also promise relief to those parents who would like nothing better than to delegate responsibility for taking a stance against purple hair and black T-shirts, transferring the contentious negotiation of teenage autonomy from the dinner table to the principal's office. Meanwhile, many school personnel, enculturated to believe that their job is to control students, cannot tolerate any student expression of individuality. They therefore welcome any opportunity to tighten school control over students and support any measure that increases control and decreases expressions of individuality. Technical standards fit that bill.

In addition to promoting conformity and submission as characteristics of good behavior, the standards movement also reinforces the idea that "winning" is a social imperative. Students learn competition as early as kindergarten and first grade, when good performance is rewarded with the "pay" of a gold star or another sticker and poor performance is punished by the lack of reward. The "winners" run home to their loved ones in happy excitement, with little thought to what their triumph costs the "losers." Shamed, the "losers" slouch home, offering their best efforts to their families, not with pride, but with apologies for not being "as good as" the others.

In this way children learn that they are not really created equal. By the age of five or six, some children begin learning in school that they just don't have whatever it takes to shine. Although we don't punish a five-year-old who wears size four or size eight clothing, we pretend that it is reasonable to expect all children to master exactly the same skills to exactly the same level in exactly the same order at exactly the same time. The mania for grading and assessing leads to confident proclamations about which children are "ahead" and which are "behind" in the race—and sadly, both they and their parents believe us.

Standardized testing will take such competitions and perceptions to new heights (or depths), as school officials bully students and teachers into pursuing higher and higher scores lest they lose funding, staff, and control. In the end, schools will have taught students that community life is a race, where everyone needs to run as hard as they can toward the same goals (set by others) and without a thought for those who fall behind. If they lose that race, they should either blame themselves for not trying hard enough or learn to accept that they don't have the right stuff to be successful.

In a society where unequal educational opportunity rigs the race against poor children, social stability and peace is more likely if winners and losers *both* perceive the race as fair. As in the hidden political agenda of technical standards, the social agenda values the appearance of fairness much more than actual fairness. Moreover, the notion of life as a race and material success as the reward of the "winner" prepares just the kind of person capitalist society needs: self-interested, competitive, and avaricious. Rather than improving life for those most in need, the technical standards movement will reinforce not only the status quo but also America's rampant "blame the victim" mentality. Its insistence on competition as a behavioral norm, rather than compassion and cooperation, will sustain the existing society that can calmly turn a blind eye to poor children who lack sufficient food and medical care as well as adequate educational opportunity.

Moreover, content standards offer those who support the status quo more leverage to force into and out of the curriculum any material they want for any element of their own agendas. Support for technical standards often appears in the rhetoric of the back-to-basics crowd, who argue, rightly, that too many children leave school without good reading, writing, and math skills and with little or no sense of history and geography. In the name of rigor, technical standards proponents argue that an appropriate remedy is to identify and test a "challenging" curriculum, and they boast, simplistically, that they have done just that—as if asking students to name the dates that Grover Cleveland served as president were the same as providing a quality education.

Interestingly, the more "challenging" the curriculum and test, the more support for existing divisions of races, ethnicities, and social classes we can predict. Does anyone expect that recognizing the massacre at Sand Creek, an example of genocide perpetrated by the U.S. military against Native Americans, is likely to appear on a "challenging" test when American schools have, for decades, presented history as the memorization of endless (white and male) names and battle dates? Wouldn't putting that item on a standardized test be likely to challenge many of the mainstream politicians calling for new curricula? Can any of these curricular experts name the date when the United States told the newly independent Puerto Rico that no, we weren't going to let it be independent after all? Can they name the forms of "Americanization" forced on Puerto Rican teachers and schools in the face of clamorous protest of professional educators and native students?

Perhaps the first thing worth noting here is that there's little merit to support the kinds of boasts people make about the goal of "expert" and "challenging" curricula. Venerating content standards as indicators of valuable rigor is downright silly because any subject expert can easily design a body of detailed factual content that would take more than twelve years to master. How long, for example, might it take to force children

to memorize the names of all of the world's large rivers, or even all the rivers in the United States—any of which a standards writer could decide is an element of "basic geographic literacy"? How long would it take to learn to pronounce and spell *Susquehanna* and *Monongahela?* The possibilities for prescribing facts are endless.

Standards designers in Pennsylvania, for example, went so far into academic esoterica as to claim that the term *virgule* is a "basic" and to boast that every child would have to learn its definition because it had been included in the state's standards. I am not making this up. How many readers of this text—holding how many degrees from how many institutions—have managed to thrive economically and socially without knowing that *virgule* is the technical name for a diagonal slash (as in and/or)? And how many of us use the virgule correctly, daily, without knowing its name? But from a standards perspective, the more obscure the content, the more "challenging" the test, and so the more serious the reform. Those of us unimpressed by elitist snobbery answer simply "Oh, *please*. Go try out for *Jeopardy*" because that's the only place where such trivia has a chance of doing anyone any good.

What are the social implications of elevating esoterica to the status of the academically essential? First, it will reinforce the country's existing, if everywhere denied, class system. Any attempt to name the specific things "everyone" should know makes it that much easier to sort people by class background. It is difficult to remember things we don't relate to, or things that have strong cultural definitions for us that are at odds with more academic definitions.

Imagine, for example, the possible difference in responses between poor Southern children and rich Northern children when asked something like "Is *poke* a noun or a verb?" Of course, multiple choice tests are not in the habit of allowing for cultural influence over answers and they themselves are steeped in mainstream culture, and so they would likely have no qualm about designating *verb* as the official right answer—because they said so, and student experience be damned. Never having eaten or picked poke greens themselves, test makers might simply assume that any student's alternate life experiences would be irrelevant.

As always, test makers pretend that the words in a test have only the meaning the test makers decide they have, that context and culture do not affect communication, and that linguistic experience has no influence on test results. These assumptions, absurd though they are, thus allow for the sorting of students into categories, both in school and in conversation, that correspond strikingly to socioeconomic status. ("Do you have a nanny?" "Oh, sure, and she eats more tin cans than any goat we ever had.")

Children from the middle class and upward who will be forced by parents to accept the need to learn any silliness set before them will, as always, toss this esoterica out in conversations with new people to signal they're in

the club of winners. As a would-be English teacher undergraduate, I asked my professors what justification I might give my students for having to read John Milton. I was told—and I know many readers will recognize this experience—"Tell them *Paradise Lost* might come up at a cocktail party sometime, and they won't want to look stupid." Twenty years later, my own well-bred masters students in English education at an Ivy League graduate school thought the cocktail party rationale a fine rationale indeed, and they were sometimes foolish enough to share it with some of the poorest children in New York City. Unfortunately, while I was busy arguing against such a severely limited, undemocratic, and stupid rationale for teaching English in a New York classroom, Pennsylvania policy makers were hiring folks who thought along these same lines to design their vaunted standards.

Poor children, meanwhile, who may have to struggle to master addition and subtraction without pencils and paper for practice, may well challenge a teacher who tries to shove useless factoids into their heads. Such children might themselves offer the best criticism of the technical standards movement with questions like "Well, how is knowin' that gonna help me keep the man at the store from cheatin' my gramma on her change?" or "How is knowin' that gonna help me take good care of my little brothers?" From a technical standards perspective, education is not about offering individual students skills and information to improve their lives; it is about keeping a national template of *the successful American* alive and well and about making sure that those who don't fit, who don't belong, are kept in their places.

The esoteric core curriculum approach has another appeal for conservatives: If the curriculum is stuffed full of the names of rivers and Latin terms, "frills" can be shoved out of schools without political messiness. The argument against teaching about constitutionally protected rights like abortion and free speech is a politically messy business, but few would challenge the assertion that "We have to see that our children learn the basics and that schools stop trying to teach everything under the sun. Schools have to stop trying to enforce social engineering and let parents handle their children's character education." It becomes easy for conservatives to argue against any topic they don't like, to lace up the mental and physical straight jackets that technical standards impose.

Once they are established as the arbiters of what is and what isn't "basic" and important enough to be included in a core curriculum, conservatives can easily sacrifice anything they want by arguing that children don't need it or by stuffing the curriculum so full of facts that there's no room for anything else. In such cases, it's interesting that the subjects sacrificed are generally ones that rich children will surely experience anyway and that poor children are highly unlikely to experience: art, music, dance, theater. Since the arts often lead the way in challenging existing social practices, it is best to exclude the poor from them, to shield them from such works as *Big River* (starring Huck Finn, independent poor teen extraordinaire) or *Sarafina* (dramatizing the political and racist murder of children in South Africa). Keeping the poor and even the middle class who lack real economic and social power away from such works helps promote a more peaceful society. It helps ensure that the disenfranchised don't start asking nasty questions about why American society follows its social leaders so uncritically, or why American universities and businesses continue commerce with countries steeped in human injustice.

The United States can afford to allow the rich, those who can spare seventy-five dollars for a theater ticket, to speculate on such issues because in general, their own financial interest can be counted on to stop them from going further than intellectual discussion. It's easy to decry exploitation, but pursuing justice at the cost of one's own pocketbook is another matter entirely, as politicians and power brokers well know. The reaction of the poor might be very different, however, because they have little to lose and much to gain by challenging existing practices. Therefore, exposing that segment of the population to art and its philosophical questioning is a much riskier business—one best avoided.

Besides, the language of art offers still one more tool for discriminating among classes. Anyone who can't respond to a question about the last play they've seen or the last classical concert they've attended is readily identified as a loser, and safely ignored. Nor can this truth be undone by the argument that many schools take their students, rich and poor alike, to the theater something like once a year. The very extraordinariness of the event for poor children signals to them that they are receiving a favor, a treat, and makes it clear that no one expects theater attendance to be routine for them. Further, the diminished art curricula at school will not be able to signal to them that the arts should be part of their everyday lives, to motivate them to learn about free exhibits and concerts and to take advantage of them.

Of course, the majority of society routinely generates its own art, since art is indeed a normal part of the human experience, but the established social arbiters name it "popular art" and dismiss it with a wave of their well-manicured hands. If an artistic work doesn't come from the few they've sanctified, then it can't truly be art. Anyone who genuinely believes that the arts community in the United States is untainted by ethnocentrism might consider why it took decades for anything written by women and minorities to appear in high school anthologies.

Ironically, while art and its challenges are being excluded from the experience of the lower classes, it is being co-opted by corporations. These days, more and more art is found in the offices of major corporations, which also plaster their names all over the concert and theater programs handed to their wealthy patrons. As business executives associate themselves with politicians to shape curricular content, they also associate themselves with the social elite in a community, those citizens most likely to serve on the boards of upper-class arts organizations and to be in the audience at events. If any art is deemed appropriate for more general public consumption, some corporation will let us know by sponsoring a free public exhibit or making a donation to a museum. Meanwhile, the social elite is joined by the corporate elite in the sponsorship and "appreciation" of cultural events. The lower classes, neither knowledgeable about scholarly art studies nor offered any signal that art should be of interest to them as well, stay outside an arena where serious social criticism often finds voice.

Implicit Economic Goals

Because it seems obvious that today's children will one day need to find jobs, businesses have been increasingly insinuating themselves into the education arena. In fact, one of the most distressing characteristics of the technical standards movement is its unexamined assumption that business is a natural partner of education. To critics, it seems obvious that what is in the best interests of corporations is not necessarily in the best interests of the children being educated. Increasingly, schools and politicians are allowing businesses to provide blueprints for the high school and college graduates they want to hire, and schools are rushing to fill the order for specified workers.

Why is no one stopping to ask what will happen if indeed all schools start to produce precisely the workers that businesses demand? Because we have already educated a docile and uncritical populace, for whom it seems self-evident that schools should enable students to find jobs when they graduate. But a more critical look at the assumption that schools should serve economic goals by producing a certain type of worker reveals other results that do *not* serve the best interests of either our students or our nation.

The most obvious result of a curricular focus on workforce training is that businesses would be blessed with a large, highly qualified pool of labor. Given laws of supply and demand, the logical consequence of this abundance would be extremely low wages. Multiple workers would be available to fill any existing job, and if one worker didn't accept an inadequate wage, another would.

This is precisely how schools and hospitals managed for decades to pay pittances to such professionals as teachers and nurses. "Teach girls to be teachers or nurses," schools were told, "and they'll find jobs." And that's what schools did, and some of the countless females so educated did accept wages at the level offered—because if they didn't, some other female would. Those professions are still trying to recover from decades of the devaluation of their profession allowed by an oversupply of well-educated labor.

Only when special training is not in abundance must businesses pay well for the work of the people they refer to as "human capital."

Another advantage is that businesses will be spared the effort and expense of training workers for their own needs—schools will do it for them. What's more, they will do it in neighborhoods where business taxes have concurrently been slashed. Businesses will not locate in areas where they are not given significant tax breaks, and such breaks commonly mean freedom from having to offer substantive support to local school districts. The benefits to business are clear, but what about the worker?

What about the worker who is laid off, said to have no currently useful skills? Such workers expect decent wages in return for years of hard work and loyalty to the company, but it's far cheaper to hire a newly trained high school or college graduate than to re-educate a worker with enough seniority to demand a decent wage. New hires can be paid entry-level salaries, which can be forced downward when there is a large skilled labor pool to draw on. For the new worker, the entry-level salary is a "take it or leave it" proposition, so the jobs are sure to be filled by someone. From the corporate perspective, there is no need to worry about the workers set adrift in midlife.

It is no accident that labor unions have never been a big part of the public school curriculum, nor is information about unions likely to appear in the new standards curricula. Businesses want to be involved in education because education can supply them with legions of cheap workers, allowing the highest possible executive salaries and largest returns to stockholders. It is a farce to listen to corporate executives talk piously about their concern for children while concurrently, behind closed doors, they are driving hard bargains with politicians to be sure corporate school taxes are minimal, if they pay any at all.

Moreover, it is in the best interests of business for schools to nurture competitiveness in students and to cultivate the myth of meritocracy. Business benefits from the idea that the "winner" is the one with the most—first the most stars, then the most points, then the most money—and that "losers" are people not worth our concern because after all, they "could" have won, too.

And if winning is *the* most important social value, then any means used to win, like poisoning the land and lungs of the nation, can be ignored because paying attention to them threatens the financial health of the company. Critical attention to such issues also threatens workers, for whom whistle blowing is seen only as a lose-lose proposition. Either whistle blowers will be fired by bosses angry over the truth telling, or the company will be in financial trouble and they'll lose their jobs anyway. Better to keep quiet.

Here the school-nurtured habit of accepting the actions of authorities, of docile obedience, comes in handy from a business perspective. "We know

best. Do as you're told. You don't need to think about what's important because we already know and did all the thinking that's necessary. You just do your job and let us do the rest."

Corporate executives and politicians, each for their own reasons, are in favor of technical standards, and between them they have created a climate where it is dangerous for anyone to oppose their liaison or their strategy. Alfie Cohen (1999) aptly describes the rhetorical dilemma created by politicians and power brokers and faced by standards opponents:

> Never underestimate the power of a catchy slogan and a false dichotomy. When a politician pronounces himself a supported of "law and order" or "a strong defense," you may protest that it's not that simple, but even as you start to explain why, you've already been dismissed as soft on crime or unwilling to defend Our Way of Life. ... Not only public officials but business groups and many journalists have played a role in reducing the available options to two: Either you're in favor of higher standards or you are presumably content with lower standards. Choose one. (pp. 88, 52)

The manufactured union between businesses and politicians in support of educational standards and the resulting dichotomy they've promoted provides both groups with a win-win situation. Politicians win votes because standards appear to be an easy fix for education. Businesses win by gaining a cost-free oversupply of workers trained to their specifications. Of course, both groups also have the added incentive of being able to denounce opponents as being against "better" education. Only kids lose—but their welfare is not and never has been the point of nonexperts who want to use the schools for their own ends.

Finally, among the corporate groups with an economic stake in technical standards is one worth mentioning individually: publishers of textbooks and exams. Textbooks are economically viable only when they can be sold in large numbers, and that can happen only when there is extensive agreement on what the content of a specific course and subject should be. If every teacher began using primary sources and individually selected materials, there would be an insufficient market for textbooks. But if curriculum is determined by technical standards and high-stakes testing, then the textbook company simply designs books that "cover" the test material.

Further, if there is going to be high-stakes testing, it is far easier and at least superficially more defensible for states to delegate test design to psychometricians and their ilk, the patrons of scan sheets. Standardized testing is already a gold mine for the educational publishing field, and more testing means more revenue for them. Certainly their economic interest lies with technical standards, with its emphasis on standardization and right/wrong answers. The profit factor certainly colors their claims to provide objectivity and reliability and to help

in the pursuit of educational interest—colors it, as a matter of fact, greedy green.

Answering the Critics of Complexity

I have offered a harsh picture of where the technical standards movement will take us: toward greater intellectual conformity, greater docility and deference to authority, a "love it or leave it" definition of patriotism, less security and lower wages for workers, greater profits at less expense for corporate officers and stockholders, and still clearer demarcation between the "haves" and the "have-nots." Critics of the call for a more critical and democratic version of school standards offer their own portrait of proponents of complexity: Softheaded and softhearted, unable to differentiate between the importance of a cultural artifact like a kachina and a cultural hero like John F. Kennedy, unable to discriminate between knowing something true and knowing nothing at all. We are relativists, they argue, guilty of devaluing everything by valuing nothing at all.

These are convenient criticisms, but totally unjustified. The point is not whether those of us arguing for critical standards believe that $2 + 1 + 1 = 4$, or whether we believe that children should be familiar with such math facts—clearly we do. But we also think it's important to know that the meaning of such "facts" changes as the context changes. In the case of this simple addition fact, for example, we note that those numbers can take on different meanings outside the world of academic concepts. In the context of today's families, for example, 2 + 1 + 1 can be said to equal 1, as when two grandparents move in with one widowed mom and one child, transforming the four people involved into *one* family who share expenses, responsibilities, lives, and love.

Everything hinges on context, on the meaning that someone is trying to make with words and numbers and historical narratives. Facts by themselves are meaningless. The Declaration of Independence was first signed in 1776. That's a fact. But what does it mean? Does it mean that 1776 is the year that colonists decided to fight for liberty and human dignity? Or does the meaning shift if we refine the factual description of the event, noting that 1776 marks the year when colonists decided to fight for the liberty and human dignity and riches of white, male landowners? In the world of fact-driven content, history trivia like dates, places, and the names of generals keeps students busy trying to pass tests; there's neither time nor inclination to nurture their understanding of historical events as the result of the complex interplay of a constellation of factors.

In contrast, rather than settling for memorized but sterile facts, the critical standards movement calls for standards that encourage students to look beyond facts themselves in an attempt to understand how and why multiple interpretations can be imposed upon

them. This means, for example, recognizing the existence of many populations in the United States, not just those with the most money or prestige. It means valuing understanding, rather than winning, as the proper goal of an education. It means sorting out the many factors that keep generations of the same families in poverty, giving up the easier, knee-jerk "blame the victim" response. It means, in short, developing a truly democratic and truly rigorous mind-set that places social justice alongside economic prosperity as a social goal for all Americans.

It is true that in this sort of system, all students would not learn the same content—the name of every river in the United States, for example. Instead, they might learn about a river near their homes, about how it influenced settlement and commerce, about how and why towns developed as they did in its vicinity, about battles it may have caused, about strategic benefits it brought during wartime. Instead of knowing the names of rivers and how to spell them, students would learn instead that water resources need to be understood if one is to understand the history and evolution of any area and its people.

Knowing names prepares students to take a multiple-choice test and little, if anything, else. In contrast, understanding the influence of one river in one place prepares students to ask and answer intelligent, complex questions—in an essay, for instance—about a geographical area they want or need to understand. The first sort of test confines students intellectually to the world of the school. The second type equips them for making sense of the world at large. Which is the more rigorous and desirable education, especially for a democratic citizenry?

Proponents of critical standards want to nurture students who become comfortable with complexity and adept at exploring multiple solutions to a problem, students who become immune to the empty promises of bombastic rhetoric. Of course students need to be skilled in math, language, and the functioning of democracy, and of course they need to be familiar with historical events and figures. They must have information— this is agreed. But the amount of information they have must be considered secondary to their understanding of information as a tool that can be used to benefit specific groups or individuals. They must understand that one set of facts may make a person seem heroic while a different set of facts casts the very same person as demonic. Today Joan of Arc is St. Joan. How is it, then, that she was burned at the stake as a witch? In an educational environment that stresses the need to deal with complexity, meaning making always takes precedence over coverage, and students must know not only what the facts are but *whose* version of reality they represent.

What type of citizen would come from schools pursuing standards of complexity? In contrast to the unquestioning citizens and workers produced by technical standards, these schools would nurture active citizens and critical workers. They would nurture citizens able to read and listen to political rhetoric thoughtfully, able to ask candidates hard questions like "How exactly do you plan to fulfill that campaign promise? How exactly do you plan to get such legislation in place, since both houses of your legislature have repeatedly killed similar bills every year for the last five years? What has changed that makes you think you can deliver on this promise?" Such citizens would have political memory and, as a result, they would consistently withdraw support for politicians who failed to deliver on campaign promises. They would ask not only about the benefits of a proposed government action but also about who exactly would receive those benefits as well as who might be hurt by the change, and to what extent.

Anyone who chooses to support educational standards needs to understand that different types of standards are being proposed, and that their support of one standards proposal over another translates to support for one kind of school over another, and one political, social, and economic agenda over another. Their support of one version of standards over another will also affect the type of citizen who lives next door, who votes in elections, who works for corporations. There is good reason to think carefully and choose well. The stakes are far too high to assume that all standard movements are created equal, or that what's

good for business and politics is good
for America.

References

Cohen, A. (1999, September 15). Confusing harder with better: Why the
"tougher standards" movement is undermining our schools. *Education Week*,
68(52).

Kozol, J. (1991). *Savage inequalities: Children in America's schools*. New York:
Crown.

Kozol, J. (1995). *Amazing grace: The lives
of children and the conscience of a nation*.
New York: Crown.

Morrison, R. (1996, June 5). An exercise
in government-approved truth [On-
line]. Available: http://www.edweek.
org.ew/1996/37morris.h15.

Spring, J. (2000). *American education* (9th
ed.). New York: McGraw Hill.

Steinberg, S., and J. Kincheloe. (Eds.).
(1997). *Kinderculture: Corporate constructions of childhood*. Boulder, CO:
Westview Press.

Viadero, D. (2000, May 3). High-stakes
tests lead debate at researchers' gathering. *Education Week*, *19*(34), 6.